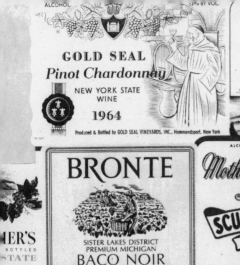

GOLD SEAL
Pinot Chardonnay
NEW YORK STATE
WINE
1964
Produced & Bottled by GOLD SEAL VINEYARDS, INC., Hammondsport, New York

1971
Mirassou
Monterey-Sa...
White B...
Produced and Bottled by
San Jose, Cor...
Alcohol 1...   By Volume

CALIFORNIA
BLACK MUSCAT
Jesuit Wines
PRODUCED AND BOTTLED BY
Novitiate of Los Gatos
LOS GATOS, CALIFORNIA
ALCOHOL 20%
BY VOLUME

ALCOHOL 14% BY VOLUME

BRONTE
Alcohol 12% By Volume

SISTER LAKES DISTRICT
PREMIUM MICHIGAN
BACO NOIR
MADE AND BOTTLED BY
Bronte Champagne & Wines Co., Inc.
AT THE BRONTE VINEYARDS, HARTFORD, MICHIGAN

Mother Vineyard
Southern
SCUPPERNONG
WINE
MADE FROM
NORTH CAROLINA SCUPPERNONG GRAPES
Produced and Bottled by
MOTHER VINEYARD WINE CO.
Petersburg, Virg...

MEIER'S
ISLE St GEORGE
OHIO STATE
HAUT
SAUTERNES
ALCOHOL 12% BY VOLUME
PRODUCED AND BOTTLED BY
Meier's Wine Cellars, Inc.
SILVERTON, OHIO, B.W.45
ONE OF THE WORLD FAMOUS
ISLE St. GEORGE VINEYARDS IN LAKE ERIE

KOSHER
FOR PASSOVER

MANISCHEWITZ
CONCORD GRAPE
SPECIALLY SWEETENED
ALCOHOL 12.5% BY VOLUM...
MADE AND BOTTLED BY
MANISCHEWITZ WINE CO., NEW YORK, N.Y. — B.W...
THE TRADITIONAL KOSHER WINE

GUILD · VINO DA
TAVOLA
RED
CALIFORNIA TABLE WINE
MADE AND BOTTLED BY GUILD WINE CO., LODI, CALIF., ALC. 12½% BY VOL

EXTRA QUALITY
PINOT
Canadian Champagne
Bright's

E·J
GALLO
HEARTY BURGUNDY
OF CALIFORNIA
We are often told by knowledgeable people that they are
delighted in having discovered a great wine in Hearty
Burgundy. Its rich, full-bodied flavor—from extremely
fine varietal grapes—will surprise you. Made and bottled
at the Gallo Vineyards in Modesto, Calif. Alc. 14% by vol.

Paul Masson.
California Brut Champagne

Beaulieu
Vineyard
BV
ESTATE BOTTLED
GEORGES DE LATOUR
PRIVATE RESERVE
NAPA VALLEY CABERNET SAUVIGNON
PRODUCED & BOTTLED BY BEAULIEU VINEYARD
AT RUTHERFORD, NAPA COUNTY, CALIFORNIA
ALCOHOL 12% BY VOLUME

Canepa
Select Estate Bottled
Lakes Region
Foch
ROBUST NEW HAMPSHIRE BURGUNDY

NATURAL FERMENTED
Produced by
Old Wine
Cellar
Bonded Winery No. 25
AMANA, IOWA
PIESTENGEL
Rhubarb Wine
Alcoholic Content 16-18% by Volume
Naturally fermented other than standard wine. Fermented
with excess sugar and water. This wine is carefully produced

FETZER
1970
ESTATE BOTTLED — MENDOCINO
DRY SAUVIGNON BLANC
PRODUCED AND BOTTLED BY
FETZER VINEYARDS
REDWOOD VALLEY CALIFORNIA
ALCOHOL 12% BY VOLUME

PRODUCED AND BOTTLED BY
Boordy Vineyard
CHILLED
SERVE THIS
Boordyblümchen
A Light White Table Wine Recalling
The Mushateller Of Austria And Germany
Alcoholic Contents
12% By Volume   1965
J. & P. Wagner, Props.
Riderwood, Maryland

Inglenook

MAISON FONDEE EN 1880
Hanns Wiederkehr
ARKANSAS
CHAMPAGNE
EXTRA DRY
NATURALLY FERMENTED IN THE BOTTLE

Stone Hill Wine Cellars
ESTABLISHED 1847
OLD MISSOURI
Sweet Catawba
GRAPE WINE
PRODUCED AND BOTTLED BY

NAPA VALLEY
CHARBONO
1968

LAKE ERIE ISLANDS

The Wines of America

Also by LEON D. ADAMS

The Wine Study Course
The Commonsense Book of Wine
The Commonsense Book of Drinking
Striped Bass Fishing in California and Oregon

LEON D. ADAMS

THE
WINES
OF
AMERICA

THIRD EDITION

Illustrated with Photographs and Maps

McGraw-Hill Book Company

New York   St. Louis   San Francisco   Toronto   Hamburg   Mexico

1 2 3 4 5 6 7 8 9 D O C D O C 8 7 6 5 4

ISBN 0-07-000319-X

LIBRARY OF CONGRESS CATALOGING IN PUBLICATION DATA

Adams, Leon David, 1905–
The wines of America.
Includes bibliographical references and index.
1. Wine and wine making—United States.
2. Wine and wine making—Canada.   3. Wine and wine making—Mexico.   I. Title.
TP557.A3   1984   641.2'22'097   84-3855

ISBN 0–07–000319-X

Book design and principal maps by Anita Walker Scott.

FOR TIMOTHY AND SUSAN

Contents

MAPS

Preface to the Third Edition

THE FAVORABLE RECEPTION given to this book's first two editions is gratifying to the author, but it also imposes a responsibility. As the one book that attempts to tell the whole story of wine in America, it needs to be kept up to date. Hence this third edition, which describes the explosive growth of winegrowing and wine consumption in America since the first and second editions appeared in 1973 and 1978.

More than 450 new wineries have begun production in thirty-two of the United States and in three Canadian provinces since the second edition was published. Forty-two of them are in states which had produced little or no wine from locally grown grapes in this century: Alabama, Arizona, Connecticut, Florida, Georgia, Idaho, Mississippi, Virginia, and Tennessee. There now are almost a thousand producing wineries in this country, and still more are being planned. Only as of press time is this book "complete."

One of the most dramatic developments is that the finest American wines have finally won recognition abroad and at home as equals to the Old World's classic best. Many American wines are being exported to Europe and are being featured on the wine lists of famous restaurants and hotels.

European vintners are discovering America. More than a dozen leading French, Swiss, German, and Spanish firms have begun planting their own vineyards and building wineries in the United States, most of them since the second edition of *The Wines of America* appeared.

Important new advances have been made in vinicultural research and wine technology. There are new grape varieties, new kinds of wine, and new kinds of wine containers. Women are playing an increasing part in the production of grapes and wine.

The most significant development is that while premium-priced wines have become more popular than at any time in this country's history, still greater gains have been made in the consumption of reasonably priced "house wines," both in restaurants and in American homes. I call them *everyday* wines because they are priced within the family budget for everyday use. Costlier vintages, priced like works of art (which many are), are bought for special occasions; I call them *Sunday* wines.

Since the first edition was published in 1973, twenty-three states have changed their laws to encourage the establishment of farm wineries. Legislators have come to realize how winegrowing contributes to their states' agricultural economy. Six states where the sale of table wines previously was restricted to liquor stores have lately permitted them to be sold in food stores, where they are convenient for people to buy with the other ingredients of meals.

U.S. consumption of wine from all sources has more than doubled, from 1.07 gallons per capita in 1968, when the wine revolution began, to 2.25 gallons in 1983. This is almost four times the .568 gallon record in 1914, the highest pre-Prohibition year. Table wine use has quadrupled since 1968, while consumption of apéritif and dessert wines has dropped and seems to be leveling off. Meanwhile, the consumption of distilled spirits has declined and was exceeded by wine in 1980 for the first time in this country's history. The trend away from strong drinks to table wine has potent cultural, social, and health significance. Wine has begun to civilize drinking in America.

LEON D. ADAMS

Sausalito, California
April 1984

1

America's Surprising Wines

I N THE QUANTITY of wine it produces annually, the United States ranks sixth among the winegrowing nations.* In the average quality of its wines, it ranks first.

The standard wines of America, available everywhere in thrifty jugs, are superior to any that householders in other lands get to drink with their daily meals. The best American wines, produced by those winegrowers who aim for highest quality and premium prices, have equaled most of the Old World's finest. The latter fact, repeatedly demonstrated in "blind" comparative tastings with the classic wines of Europe, is all the more surprising when it is remembered that Europe, with its two thousand years of experience, has thousands of vineyards whose vintages are sought after and treasured by connoisseurs, while the United States still has relatively few.

This country has two advantages over the Old World in winegrowing. One is in climates more hospitable to grapes—a subject about which a good deal follows, because climate is the key to the fascinating lore of wine. The other advantage is having started anew. The American wine industry, reborn when National Prohibition ended in 1933, chose the scientific approach to quality. Rejecting the traditions, cobwebbed cellars, and primitive methods that long hindered wine progress in Europe, it utilized the new research in viticulture and enology, in which the United States has led the world—research that has removed most of the guesswork from winemaking.

*Commercial wine production in the U.S. averages 435 million gallons yearly, compared to 2 billion gallons in Italy, 1.7 billion in France, 900 million in Spain, 820 million in the U.S.S.R., 620 million in Argentina, 250 million in Portugal, 200 million in Romania, 200 million in Yugoslavia, and 190 million in West Germany.

1

Exported now to many other countries, where they compete on even terms with the world-famous wines of France and Germany, American wines are still improving. As yet they have only approached the great quality they can achieve in the future. Already they are such a challenge to Old World wines that European vintners have begun imitating American wines. Nor is merely equaling European wines as great an achievement as it might seem because, as is well known in the wine trade, the wines under many famous French and German labels have changed greatly, not necessarily for the better, since the Second World War. Just as artists in other fields give their best performances for appreciative audiences, this country's winegrowers have continued improving their products for a wine-buying public that has shown it will appreciate and pay for them.

There is much to appreciate, not only in the fine wines of California and New York, but also in the vastly improved table wines of Washington, Connecticut, Idaho, Maryland, Michigan, Missouri, Oregon, Pennsylvania, Rhode Island, Texas, and Vir-

The Cabernet Sauvignon grape variety, the *cépage noble* of Bordeaux in France, also makes the finest red wines produced in the United States. (*The Wine Institute*)

ginia. Most of the latter states' wines as yet are seldom found outside their borders. Connoisseurs who live in Alabama, Colorado, Florida, Georgia, Illinois, Indiana, Kentucky, Massachusetts, Minnesota, Mississippi, New Hampshire, New Jersey, New Mexico, North and South Carolina, Tennessee, West Virginia, and Wisconsin can also find good wines at small vineyards in their own states, and thereby can promote the agricultural economy of their regions.

America produces good wines of every type made elsewhere on the globe. It also makes many types that are entirely its own. In fact, this country offers the widest spectrum of wine flavors that can be found anywhere in the world. This results principally from America's wide variety of climates. It is climate that principally determines which grape varieties can produce the best wine quality, and where. The right soil is essential, of course, but good soils for grape growing can be found almost anywhere, while ideal climatic conditions cannot. Each climatic district and each vineyard with its own microclimate will produce, from the same grape variety, a distinctly different wine. The Riesling grown in the warmer parts of the Napa Valley differs appreciably from Riesling grown on the cooler hillsides a few miles to the west, from Riesling grown at Piesport on the Moselle, and from Riesling grown in western Oregon or at Hammondsport, New York. And the Catawba grape makes a different wine when grown on Isle St. George in the middle of Lake Erie than from Catawba grown in the Ozark region of Missouri and Arkansas. Differences in the exposure of vines to sunlight, even in the same vineyard, influence wine flavors, too. (Yes, differences in soil account in part for differences in wines—especially between the wines of single vineyards—but European producers are wrong in claiming that soils are the chief reason the wines of their best vineyard districts are unique. Well-drained, warm soils capable of adequately nourishing the vines are essential for quality and yield. It is not true, as they would have us believe, that a special soil component climbs up through the vine, enters into the grape and its juice, and gives the wine a distinctive taste.)

America is one vast Vineland, so named by the Norse explorer Leif Ericson when he landed on Newfoundland *circa* A.D. 1000. Whether the berries he found growing wild there were really grapes as the saga says, or squashberries as some botanists now contend, Ericson was right. For in the expanse of North America between 50° north latitude in Canada and 20° north latitude in Central Mexico are the greatest natural grape-growing areas

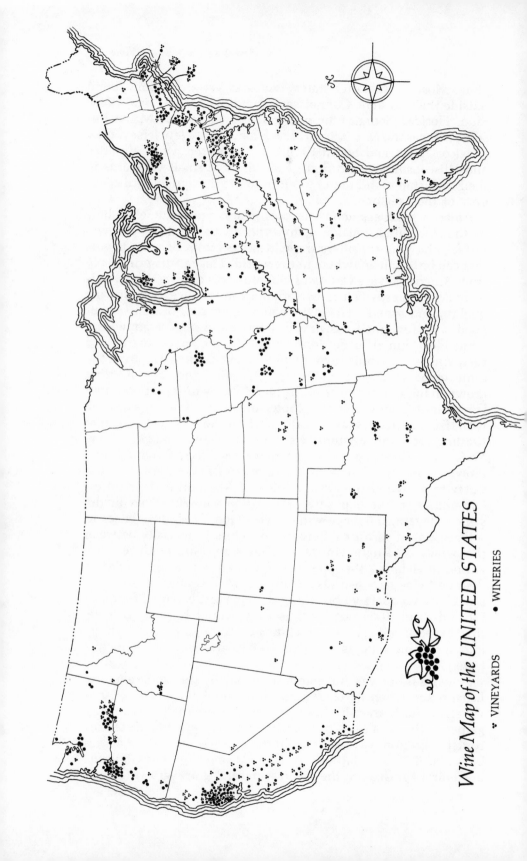

Wine Map of the UNITED STATES

᭹ VINEYARDS   • WINERIES

on earth. More species of the genus *Vitis,* the grapevine, grow wild here than in the rest of the world combined. The borders of the United States, which extend from 49° latitude in the State of Washington to 25° latitude in Texas and Florida, encompass vast regions superior, in terms of growing-season temperatures, to Germany's Rhineland at 50° latitude and to Champagne and Burgundy at 49° and 47° latitude in France. This country has hundreds of such areas, with enough total acreage to accommodate the Rhineland, Moselle, Champagne, Burgundy, and Bordeaux regions several times over.

In California's equable climate with its long rainless growing season and its mild winters, grape varieties transplanted from Europe thrive as well as, and often better than, in their Old World homelands. This is why California wines resemble those of Europe; they are made from the same grapes, the species called *Vitis vinifera.* Chardonnay, Chenin Blanc, Gewürztraminer, Sauvignon (Fumé) Blanc, Sémillon, Sylvaner, and Johannisberg Riesling are the favorite Vinifera whites; Cabernet Sauvignon, Carignane, Barbera, Petite Sirah, Pinot Noir, and Zinfandel are the most widely grown reds. In recent years Vinifera have also been increasingly grown in eastern Washington, in Oregon, and in Idaho, and the best wines from these three Pacific Northwest states already are beginning to challenge California's best.

When planted east of the Rockies, the delicate Vinifera vines require extra care and are grown to a limited extent, especially for prestigious, premium-priced wines. In the East and Midwest it is easiest to grow the hardier native American "slip-skin" grapes, the *Vitis labrusca,* which resist the rigorous eastern winters, false springs, and humid summers. Labrusca-type wines have, in varying degrees, the grapy or foxy flavor you taste in Concord grape juice, jelly, and jam. But fine white wines are made of the only slightly foxy Delaware, Dutchess, and Catawba, which are hybrids of Labrusca with Vinifera. These are exclusively eastern specialties, because Labrusca grapes fail to ripen properly in California. "Grape flavor" to most Americans means the foxy Labrusca taste. It comes chiefly from an ester, methyl anthranilate, which can also be synthesized in the laboratory. Labrusca wines, if fermented dry, are too harsh for the average palate, but millions of Americans like this flavor in sweet and semisweet wines. Some of the best eastern champagnes owe their appeal to the hint of Labrusca fragrance in their taste, delicately balanced by judicious blending with California or other nonfoxy wines.

In recent decades, as American consumers' tastes in wine have

Dozens of wine storage caves like this one were dug at Nauvoo, Illinois, by the Icarians, when they established vineyards there about 1850.

matured, Labrusca-type wines have lost some of their popularity, and Labrusca vineyards have begun to be replaced by still another group of hardy grape varieties, the French-American hybrids. These are crosses of wild midwestern American grapes with Vinifera, developed by grape breeders in France. Increasingly popular in eastern states are such hybrid white wines as Seyval Blanc, which some call "the Chardonnay of the East," Vidal Blanc, Rayon d'Or, Verdelet, Vignoles, and Villard Blanc. Best among the reds are Chambourcin, Chancellor, Léon Millot, Maréchal Foch, and Baco Noir.

Lowlands of the southeastern states, with their humid climates, are unsuitable for most bunch grapes, but are the natural home for still another grape species, the Muscadines, *Vitis rotundifolia*. Muscadines are more like cherries than grapes, and the best-known variety is the Scuppernong. At mountain or Piedmont elevations in these states, however, all four grape families—Vinifera, Labrusca, French hybrids, and Muscadines—are being grown successfully. In these southeastern highlands, the planting of Vinifera and hybrids has begun to increase in recent years.

Actually, grapes grow in all fifty states, and any grape can make wine. Grapes are now the principal fruit crop grown in America, having exceeded apples in volume since 1975. This country is estimated to have approximately 900,000 acres of vineyards, about one-fortieth of the total in the world. Commercial winegrowing is impractical, however, in areas with growing seasons of less than 120 days between the killing spring and autumn frosts. This rules out only Wyoming, much of Colorado and Montana, the northern portions of Maine, of Minnesota, of North Dakota, and of Wisconsin; and eastern Nevada, southeastern Oregon, and Alaska. Before 1900, wines were grown successfully in such unlikely-seeming states as Kansas, Iowa, Nebraska, and Oklahoma. These four states will soon resume growing wines again, when their legislators, departments of agriculture, and horticultural scientists awaken to the progress being made in winegrowing elsewhere.

California, with 739,000 acres of vineyards, more than five times the grape acreage of the other states combined, produces about 5 million tons of grapes annually and supplies about seven-tenths of the wine consumed in this country. New York, with 42,000 acres; Washington, with 26,000; Michigan, 12,000; Pennsylvania, 9000; Ohio, 3000; and other states with smaller vineyard acreages, produce altogether about a fourteenth of the wine consumed. The remainder, about a fourth of the total, consists of foreign wines, imported mainly from Italy, France, Spain, Portugal, and West Germany. California also supplies some other states' vintners each year with well over a million gallons of neutral bulk wines, wine spirits, and condensed juice (called grape concentrate) for blending with their own production.

The dominance of California prompts some people in other states to question whether wine can be grown profitably anywhere else, since California can produce the common types more cheaply; and before the wine revolution reached its height in the 1970s, California had a chronic grape surplus of a quarter-million tons per year. The best answer is the example of other states' thriving young farm wineries, many of whose wines are lighter and fresher than those of California. Again it is a matter of climate, for California does not grow the French-American hybrids, the Labrusca grapes, or the Muscadines. In fact, the Concord grape juice which my children drank at breakfast in our California home had to come from grapes grown in eastern Washington. Actually, the recurrent grape surpluses that have plagued California consisted of leftover raisin and table grapes—not of the fragile, shy-bearing fine wine-grape varieties that make the best wines.

Although table wine use in the United States has multiplied twelve times since the Second World War, this still is far from becoming a wine-drinking country. The obstacles that prevent regular wine use from becoming nationwide are outmoded state laws, relics of Prohibition, that hamper both the growing and the distribution of wine. In most states, a jungle of burdensome red-tape requirements and exorbitant license fees restrict the sale of wine. Although wine is now sold in all fifty states, more than half make it difficult to buy. Twenty-four states prevent the sale of table wines in groceries, restricting it to liquor outlets. This necessitates an inconvenient extra stop for the householder when he or she goes shopping for food, and furthermore, many liquor stores are not the kind of places where one is willing to be seen. One of the reasons per capita wine use in California is more than double that of the nation as a whole is that virtually all food stores in California sell wine. (When supermarkets in England began stocking wine during the 1960s, table wine consumption in that country jumped 15 percent in a single year.) At this writing, fifteen states still have many legally Dry localities—counties, cities, towns, and even precincts; and forty-three of the fifty states still have local or state blue laws forbidding the sale of any alcoholic beverage on Sundays. Twenty-six states impose taxes or markups on table wines at rates ranging from 50 cents to $2.25 per gallon. When added to the Federal tax, these result in pricing table wines as a luxury or as a sinful indulgence, instead of as an article of food. These are some of the reasons why the civilized custom of drinking wine with meals has not yet spread to such states as Arkansas, Iowa, Kentucky, Kansas, Mississippi, and Tennessee. Yearly wine consumption in these states still is less than seven pints per inhabitant, as compared to two and one-fourth gallons per year average for the nation. Oklahoma, Kansas, and Utah still prohibit their restaurants from serving their patrons so much as a glass of table wine with a meal. It is remarkable that in spite of the obstacles to wine-drinking that exist in most of this country, consumption of this beverage has increased as it has. The obstacles will be removed only when enough Americans and their legislators come to realize that wine belongs with food. For table wine is used principally at mealtimes; it is the only true mealtime beverage. This cannot be said of water, coffee, tea, soft drinks, beer, or of milk.

Another impediment to wine use, though a lesser one, is snobbery, which is defined as drinking the label, not the wine. The average American householder still seldom serves any wine and only thinks of doing so for some special occasion, such as the entertainment of important guests. Although more or less content in his or her daily life with a modest home and moderately priced automobile, he or she feels that if a wine is served it must impress the guests as a sign of affluence. For this purpose a reasonably priced wine will not do. Instead, the host or hostess buys an expensive wine the wine snobs recommend, and the rest of the time lives by bread alone.

Now comes the question most often asked about American wines: How do the individual types compare with their counterparts in Europe? The reply usually given evades the question by pointing out that wines, being farm products, are necessarily individuals, that no two natural wines can ever be identical in taste, and therefore that they should never be compared. This of course is nonsense; part of the fun in wines is in comparing them. What the inquirer wants to know is whether there are any basic differences in flavor or aroma between American wines and imports in general, that can be distinguished by taste. The answer is that there is no marked difference between American and European wines of the same types and ages when both are made of the identical grape varieties, grown in similar climates, aged in casks made of the same variety of oak, and when both are given the same treatment and care in the vineyard and winery. Even experienced tasters usually cannot tell the American and foreign samples apart. But note, please, that I have qualified my answer, and note in particular the reference to the same variety of oak. For if the grape varieties, the vineyard climates, and the care given the grapes and wines are identical, there still is one difference that even a neophyte taster can distinguish. It is the peculiar, complex bouquet of European wines that are aged in small wooden casks—a bouquet seldom found in barrel-aged American wines a decade ago. For more than a century, nobody ever guessed why this difference existed. In recent years, its cause has been learned. It results from the different species of oak trees that grow on the European and American continents, the kinds of oak from which wine barrels are made. The complex bouquet comes from the wood, not from the grapes. How this was discovered accidentally, through the stubbornness of an amateur California winegrower in the late 1950s, will be related in Chapter 13. Now that many American vintners have imported European oak casks and have aged some of their wines in them, woody bouquet is no longer an Old World exclusive.

This is not to say that America as yet has any wines closely resembling French sauternes or Italian chiantis, which are unique, but neither have France and Italy any wines like our Catawba, Magnolia, or Amador Zinfandel. Each country, because of differences in climate or in the grape varieties it alone grows, still has some wines that are exclusively its own. Nor does America yet offer any vintages to compete with $250-a-bottle Romanée Conti 1949 or with a Rheingau Trockenbeerenauslese 1969 at $175. American wines still generally lack the great bouquet from long bottle-aging that connoisseurs exclaim over, because too few years have yet elapsed since the wine revolution began, to provide many such venerable rarities; and the American system of collecting annual inventory taxes on producers' aging stocks has prevented the wineries from holding back their wines for many years after bottling. The consumer who wants really old American wines must buy them young and age them in his or her own cellar. On the other hand, among white wines, which require less age than reds, there are some California, Oregon, Washington, and New York Chardonnays for which true wine lovers are gladly paying higher prices per bottle in preference to well-known imports.

Nomenclature is another reason some American wines compete at a disadvantage with imports in the snob trade. For the bulk of this country's wine is sold as burgundy, chablis, champagne, rhine wine, port, and sherry—names which refer to old wine-growing districts in Europe. It is fashionable among Europe-minded connoisseurs to denounce all such wines as "imitations." Behind this charge is the French government, which for many years has tried to persuade all other wine countries to stop using wine-type names of French origin. Several nations, including Spain and Mexico, have yielded to this pressure officially, but the makers of Spanish champagnes, legally renamed *espumosos*, still also call them *xampan*. Spain, too, conducts a nomenclature campaign abroad, hoping to acquire a world monopoly on sherry (named by the British, who have trouble pronouncing Latin names, for the Andalusian sherry-producing district around Xéres or Jerez de la Frontera). Germany surrendered to the French on the wine-name issue long ago and calls its champagnes *Sekt* (derived from *sec*, the French word for "dry"); and Italian vintners call their sparkling wines *spumante*. Russia, however, goes on making vast quantities of its "shampanskoe," "portvein," "madera," and "koniak." The United States regulation defines fifteen* wine-type names of European geographic origin as "semigeneric" and requires them to be prominently qualified on labels with the true place of origin, as "American Burgundy," "Califor-

---

*Burgundy, claret, chablis, champagne, chianti, madeira, malaga, marsala, moselle, port, rhine wine, hock, sauterne, sherry, tokay.

nia Sherry," "Ohio Champagne," "Napa Valley Chablis," etc.
If the United States could be persuaded to give up the generic
names, France, in particular, would reap overnight a monopoly
on the vast markets which American vintners have built in this
country for champagne, burgundy, and chablis by spending
countless millions in advertising and promotion during the past
century. These names have been anchored in the American language for generations, along with French bread, Danish pastry,
English muffins, hamburger steak, Venetian blinds, and china-
ware. The generic names are the only ones the average wine
buyer understands. What else, the American vintners ask, could
you possibly call champagne?

A puzzling consequence of such labeling is that American vintners, being individuals, have never agreed on just what the semigeneric European names mean. Chablis is mostly white and burgundies are red (unless labeled white), but these wines can range
in taste all the way from bone-dry to semi-sweet, depending
upon which American winery makes them. I wonder how the
citizens of the small Burgundian town of Chablis, world-famed
solely for its dry white wine, must have felt when they first
learned in 1965 that Gallo of California had begun labeling one
of its two rosé wines as "pink chablis," and soon afterward
when the Italian Swiss Colony introduced a red wine labeled
"ruby chablis."

As a defense against the criticism of their generic wine-type
labels, American vintners are making increased use of grape-
variety names for their wines. They find this profitable, because
varietal names suggest rarity and quality, intangible elements
for which buyers are willing to pay extra. Burgundy brings a
higher price when it is labeled Pinot Noir, and chablis when
the label calls it Chardonnay. In consequence, as might be expected, the "varietal wine" list has grown considerably in recent
years. It once consisted mainly of Riesling, Cabernet, Zinfandel,
and muscatel from California, and Catawba and Scuppernong
from the East. But now, there are almost a hundred varietal
names on American wines, including three different "Rieslings,"
six different "Pinots," and numerous varietally labeled wines
of the French-American hybrid grapes. The result is delicious
confusion—partly because the average grape variety can be called
by any of several names—and especially in spelling and pronunciation. The latter is why many restaurants find it necessary to
print a number opposite each tongue-twisting item on their
wine lists. And now European vintners who ship wines to this

country have begun renaming their wines, too, for "varietal grapes"—the Old World's ultimate recognition of American success.

Varietally named wines are not necessarily better than those with generic labels. Some premium wineries that sell both "varietal" and "generic" wines produce burgundies that are among the best red-wine buys on the market. They must, because wines labeled "burgundy" and bearing their premium brands must be markedly better than lower-priced burgundies, many of which are very good.

Should wines that are labeled with the name of a grape variety consist entirely of that grape? For many years, when high-quality grapes were scarce, Federal regulations required the varietal content to be at least 51 percent of the grape named. But in 1983, with most vintners supporting the change, the minimum went up to 75 percent, and to 85 percent for wines labeled with names of small viticultural areas. (Wines named for the powerfully flavored Labrusca and Muscadine grapes were exempt from the new minimum, remaining at 51 percent.) Some consumer advocates insist that varietally labeled wines should contain 100 percent of the variety, but that would be a mistake. The best wines of the world are blended for balance and complexity, as when Cabernet Sauvignon is improved by blending with Merlot or Cabernet Franc.

Why aren't American wines named for the vineyard districts, as most European wines are? What seemed to be a step in that direction was an undertaking by the Federal government in 1980 to define the precise boundaries of American vineyard districts. Its purpose was to enable the government to prosecute those who might label spurious wines with the names of such increasingly famous viticultural areas as "Napa Valley" and "Finger Lakes." During the next few years, growers and wineries in almost a hundred localities across the continent petitioned the government to recognize their area names and boundaries; and the government obliged. Many of the newly approved names were soon added to the already cluttered labels of local wines. Any resemblance to the *appellation contrôlée* system of France, which specifies permitted grape varieties and limits wine yields, apparently ended there.

A third kind of American wine nomenclature, that usually conveys some generic, varietal, and district meaning, has emerged in recent years and deserves mention. It is the proprietary name, which identifies both the wine and the brand. Current examples include the Beaumont and Beauclair of Beaulieu Vineyard; the

Emerald Dry and Rhine Castle of Paul Masson; the Chateau La Salle of The Christian Brothers; and the Lake Country Red, White, and Pink from Taylor of New York. Perhaps such proprietary names, as their numbers grow in years to come, eventually will silence the critics and end the nomenclature wrangle. (All of the foregoing unravels only a few of the mysteries of American wine labeling. I attempt to solve the rest in Chapter 26, where vintage labels, "produced," "made," and "estate-bottled" are explained.)

In contrast to Europe, with its scores of thousands of small wineries, all of the American wines we are discussing come from only about a thousand bonded wineries. These range in size from the few dozen barrels in Winfield Tucker's and Donald Seibert's tiny South County Vineyard cellar at Slocum, Rhode Island, to the nearly 130-million-gallon Gallo Winery at Livingston, California, which is the largest in the world.

There were more than a thousand bonded wineries in this country as recently as the 1930s. The number soon shrank because large wineries, with the advantages of mechanization, automation, and efficient mass marketing, grew larger, while many smaller ones who could not afford these advantages went out of business.

But now we have hundreds of entirely new winegrowers, who have reversed this trend. Some have opened wineries and acquired vineyards because they saw the wine business expanding and becoming profitable for others. The majority, however, are primarily hobbyists—I call them the oenothusiasts—who are motivated less by hope of profits than by love of fine wines. After the Second World War, home winemaking became widely popular as a hobby in the United States, to such an extent that a new industry was created to supply the hobbyists with materials and equipment. Many of these hobbyists began to grow their own grapes, first planting vines in backyards, and in some cases buying additional land and establishing small vineyards. Then some of the oenothusiasts, finding their grape crops produced more wine than the 200 gallons per year the United States government permits a householder to make and possess tax-free, decided to bond their cellars and sell their wines. The result was that while many medium-sized commercial vintners, no longer able to compete with the giants, were closing their wineries, a greater number of nonprofessionals were opening new wineries to pursue their avocation. Fascinated by the romance and greatness of wine, many of these new small growers are striving to produce the world's finest bottles of wine.

In another industry, such a development might seem unimportant. But as later chapters will show, from Nicholas Longworth, a lawyer, to Philip Wagner, a journalist, avocational vintners have led the way to much of the progress of winegrowing in America. It is the new oenothusiasts who are now pioneering by planting vines and opening little wineries in new districts and in localities that supported wineries a century ago. It is they who are making winegrowing again a nationwide industry.

2

Four Centuries of History

MERICAN WINES have entered world competition as youngsters, for most of the present wine industry dates from the repeal of Prohibition in 1933, and most of its best vineyards were not planted until a full generation later. Yet, as Samuel Johnson said, "the present state of things is the consequence of the past," and the wines of today reflect in their flavors many long-forgotten events of the past four centuries.

Single dramatic episodes in American wine history have been portrayed in romantic pageants enacted at local vintage festivals and in several epic novels and motion pictures. But a complete story of winegrowing in this country would require volumes, because it would cover some four hundred years, at least forty-one states, and a thousand historic vineyards. Its cast of characters would include European despots, American Presidents, senators, and governors, Spanish padres, grape breeders, temperance crusaders, wine-minded journalists, college professors, and a whole procession of eminent vintners, both past and present.

Although winegrowing has influenced the economy and culture of many states, you are unlikely to find wine even mentioned in their histories, because the Prohibitionists erased it. Like the dictators who rewrite nations' histories to blot out other ideologies than their own, the fanatical forces responsible for Prohibition spent years of zealous effort obliterating all of the favorable references to wine they could find in printed texts, failing only to remove them from the Bible.* As a result, few Americans now associate winegrowing with such historic figures as Lord

*They did succeed, however, in getting references to "wine" changed to "cakes of raisins" in *The Short Bible* published by Scribner's in 1924.

Delaware, William Penn, Thomas Jefferson, the elder Nicholas Longworth, Padre Junípero Serra, General Vallejo, Captain John Sutter, or Leland Stanford. And scarcely anyone now living in Cincinnati, St. Louis, Pittsburgh, or Los Angeles realizes that these cities were winemaking centers a century ago. Even California, whose oldest industry is winegrowing, has begun only in recent years to designate its most famous old wineries as state historical landmarks because of their growing value as tourist attractions. The official textbook from which school children are taught California's history discusses virtually every product of the state's farms and factories, but until the 1970s it never once mentioned wine.

Each vineyard region in America has its own romantic story, the highlights of which I include in the later chapters devoted to the wines of the various states. Here I only touch on some of the major developments. Of particular interest are the stormy, tragic happenings during the Prohibition period and the striking changes which since Repeal have revolutionized winegrowing and wine-drinking throughout the nation. And because the events influencing wine in this country have occurred at widely separated places and times and might otherwise seem unconnected, I have also prepared a Brief Chronology of Wine in North America, which appears as Chapter 27.

• 2 •

The first American wines were made of wild grapes. Between 1562 and 1564, the first French Huguenots to reach North America made wine of the Scuppernong grapes they found growing near the present site of Jacksonville in Florida. Other early arrivals fermented the native grapes, too: the Jamestown colonists in Virginia in 1609 and the Mayflower Pilgrims at Plymouth to help celebrate the first Thanksgiving in 1623.

Then began more than three centuries of attempts to grow the fragile Old World wine grape, the Vinifera, in the East, all of them failing miserably. In 1619, Lord Delaware brought vines to Virginia from France and also French *vignerons* to tend them and to make the wine. The Virginia colonial assembly passed a law in 1623 requiring that every householder plant ten vines, and from 1651 to 1693 offered the colonists prizes for wine production, with no winners. In 1632, Governor John Winthrop of Massachusetts was granted Governor's Island in Boston Harbor on which to plant wine grapes. In 1643, Queen Christina of Sweden ordered John Printz, the governor of New Sweden, to encourage grape planting, and in 1662 Lord Baltimore tried unsuccessfully to grow them in Maryland. William Penn brought French and Spanish vines to plant near Philadelphia in 1683. Later plantings in Florida, Georgia, South Carolina, Rhode Island, and New York, and those of Jefferson at Monticello after 1773, also failed. The European vines took root and sometimes yielded small quantities of wine, but soon lost their leaves and died. The cold eastern winters were blamed, but what chiefly did the killing were plant diseases and insect pests, to which the wild vines that grow in these areas are immune. Had the colonists possessed the resistant varieties and modern chemical sprays which now enable Vinifera and its relatives to grow in many eastern states, wine in this country would have had a very different history. Indeed, if the early attempts to grow wine grapes had succeeded, America probably never would have come to Prohibition. Without good wine as a moderate daily beverage, the colonists and their descendants drank hard apple cider, then applejack and rum, and finally adopted whiskey as the national drink.

Wild grapes were still the principal source of American wines when in 1769,* six years before the American Revolution, Padre Serra is said to have brought Vinifera cuttings to California from Mexico when he founded Mission San Diego. If he actually planted them on his arrival, the date of the first California vintage could have been 1773. For the next sixty years, the only wine made in California was that fermented by the Franciscan friars at their chain of missions, mostly for the Mass, and for their own use on the table and as medicine.

• 3 •

The beginning of commercial winegrowing in this country dates from before the Revolution, when the first domesticated native wine grape was introduced in the East and came under regular cultivation. It was the red Alexander, later miscalled the Cape grape, a foxy Labrusca seedling (probably an accidental cross with Vinifera). James Alexander, the gardener to Thomas Penn, a son of William Penn, had found it growing near the Schuylkill River in the vicinity of Philadelphia, and planted it in Penn's garden. The hardy Alexander withstood the cold win-

*But the Mission grape, a Vinifera variety, was grown earlier for winemaking at the Franciscan missions in New Mexico; see Chapter 20. And the date when the grape was introduced to California is still a subject of dispute. The only verified date is 1779, when it was planted at Mission San Juan Capistrano.

ters and the vine pests that had killed the delicate European plants. Of the ten Alexander vines that grew in his Virginia garden, President Jefferson wrote prophetically in 1809 that

it will be well to push the culture of this grape without losing time and efforts in the search of foreign vines which it will take centuries to adapt to our soil and climate.

Jefferson's advice was heeded: The first extensive vineyards in Pennsylvania, Ohio, and Indiana were planted with the Alexander in the early 1800s. (To answer the perennial question of "which was first," Pennsylvania can claim this country's earliest commercial venture in winegrowing—at Spring Mill on the Susquehanna River northwest of Philadelphia, where the Pennsylvania Vine Company, formed in 1793, made wine in underground vaults from the Alexander grapes grown in its adjoining vineyard.) During the next half-century, scores of native varieties better than the Alexander were found or bred by nurserymen and grape breeders. The pink Catawba was introduced in 1823 by Major John Adlum of Washington, D.C.; the blue Isabella of South Carolina by William Prince of Flushing, New York, about 1816; the purple Concord in 1854 by Ephraim Wales Bull of Massachusetts; and the green Elvira by Jacob Rommel of Missouri in 1870, to mention only a few.

Planting of the domesticated native grapes spread through much of the East and Midwest, encouraged by the Federal and state governments. By 1840, winegrowing ventures had begun in Alabama, Missouri, Maryland, New York, and North Carolina, in addition to the states already named. Some, especially that of Nicholas Longworth at Cincinnati, prospered greatly. Others, such as those of the Kentucky Vineyard Society in that state, ended in failure. Ohio, the leading wine-producing state of the Union in the 1850s, was surpassed in the 1860s by Missouri. By 1880, when the Department of Agriculture published a special report on the progress of grape culture and wine production in the nation, winegrowing enterprises were also shown to be flourishing in Georgia, Illinois, Iowa, Kansas, Michigan, Mississippi, New Jersey, New Mexico, New York, Tennessee, Virginia, and West Virginia.

• 4 •

In the meantime, California had come into the picture. When the Franciscan missions were secularized in the 1830s, a few commercial vineyards were planted at Los Angeles. After the

Gold Rush of 1849, many of the newcomers turned from digging for precious metal to pressing liquid gold from grapes. News of their profits made from wine quickly spread, and an epidemic of vine fever swept the state. The California legislature, to stimulate the new industry, offered a four-year exemption from taxes for all new vineyards planted. Vines soon dotted hills and valleys through much of the 700-mile-long state.

California was boomed abroad as a new paradise discovered for the vine, a land of sunshine where grapes easily reached full ripeness every year. Experts came from France to investigate. In 1862, they reported in the French viticultural journal *Revue Viticole* that, indeed, California was one American region "capable of entering competition with the wines of Europe . . . in the distant future."

Better Vinifera grapes than the Mission variety, which Padre Serra had brought from Mexico, were imported early from France and Germany. By 1856, one California vintner was already shipping his wines to England, Germany, Russia, Australia, and China, and the state's wines soon began winning medals for quality at international exhibitions.

But the vine-planting boom in California soon created a surplus. In 1867, grapes were sold there for as little as $2 a ton and wine for 10 cents a gallon. Then, in 1869, the first transcontinental railroad was completed. It opened a quick route for wine

Oldest winery in California is this little adobe building at Mission San Gabriel, founded near Los Angeles in 1771. On its stone floor Indians trod the grapes which Franciscan padres fermented into wine for the Mass and for sale.

shipments to the cities of the East and Midwest. California, already producing more wine than any of the eastern states, invaded their markets across the continent.

• 5 •

The eastern markets in the late 1860s and 1870s were controlled by the Ohio, Missouri, and New York producers, and they bitterly opposed the imports from California. Vincent Carosso, in his scholarly history of *The California Wine Industry*, records that the eastern vintners accused the California shippers of selling their wines under counterfeit French and German labels (which was often true) and of putting California labels on eastern wines. Later, Carosso states, the easterners' tactics changed, and merchants in New York and Boston put California labels on the worst adulterated European and blended wines, while selling the best lots from California as European. Spoiled, doctored, and falsely labeled wines were widely sold. Eastern and western winegrowers joined forces to protect their markets from competition by low-priced European wines. In 1864, Congress granted them tariff protection against wine imports. The French tried to get the United States to negotiate reciprocal tariff reductions. Carosso tells how the New York and Ohio vintners helped the California Vinicultural Society to defeat the French efforts during the 1870s. (After the Second World War the United States, in order to help other American industries increase their exports to Europe, gradually traded away much of the import-tariff protection for American wines.)

A national pure-wine law was urgently needed, and that intensified the East-West struggle. California wanted such a law to prohibit the addition of sugar in winemaking. This the easterners opposed, because in vineyard regions with short, rainy growing seasons—such as Germany, northern France, and the eastern and midwestern states of this country—grapes often fail to develop enough sugar of their own to make wines with the necessary minimum alcoholic content, and also their juice is excessively tart. Such wines need to have sugar added during fermentation and to have their acidity lowered. But California, with its long, dry, sunny growing season, has more than enough sugar in its grapes and often not enough acidity; and since 1887 the state has prohibited any sweetening of its standard wine types except with fresh or condensed grape juice.

When the easterners protested that a Federal law against sugar in winemaking would put them out of business, a California vintner infuriated them with an invitation "to move their wineries to California's sunny clime, where pure wine can be made from the juice of grapes alone." The battle raged from the 1800s until the limited use of sugar was recognized by an act of Congress in 1894. Meanwhile, some of the eastern wineries had begun their present practice of buying neutral California wines in bulk to blend with their own and to soften their pronounced Labrusca and Scuppernong flavors. The East-West schism over sugar recurred following the repeal of Prohibition, but was healed after the Second World War, when both sides agreed on rules, since applied by the Federal government, on the use of sugar by the vintners outside California. The leading eastern vintners have always supported legal restrictions to prevent the few unscrupulous operators from using excessive quantities of sugar and water to stretch the number of gallons obtainable from each ton of grapes.

Before 1900, winegrowing was a full-grown, proud American industry. The brands of leading California, New York, Ohio, Missouri, and New Jersey wineries were competing with European vintages on many of the best restaurant wine lists. California wines in barrels were being exported regularly to England, Germany, Canada, Mexico, Central America, Australia, and the Orient, in direct competition with the wines of Europe. (It has been claimed but never substantiated that some went to France and returned to this country under French labels.) From the three dozen medals and four honorable mentions which American wines received at the Paris Exposition of 1900,* it is evident that their quality was excellent by international standards. I have tasted pre-Prohibition American wines that I would describe as great.

*The award winners were, from California: C. A. Baldwin, Cupertino; Ben Lomond Wine Co., Santa Cruz; Beringer Brothers, St. Helena; California Wine Association, San Francisco; California Winery, Sacramento; Chaix & Bernard, Oakville; Cuesta Francisco, no address given; Germain Wine Co., Los Angeles; Theodore Gier Co., Oakland; Grierson, Oldham & Co., San Francisco; Gundlach-Bundschu Wine Co., Sonoma; Secondo Guasti, Los Angeles; J. O'B. Gunn, Windsor; Charles Hammond, Upper Lake; Hastings Estate, Angwin; Richard Heney, Jr., Cupertino; Italian Swiss Agricultural Colony, Asti; W. S. Keyes, Liparita Vineyard, Angwin; Pierre Klein, Mountain View; Paul Masson, Saratoga; William Palmtag, Hollister; Repsold Company, Napa; Sierra Madre Vintage Co., Lamanda; Julius Paul Smith, Livermore; Southern California Wine Co., Los Angeles; Leland Stanford's Vineyard, Vina; To Kalon Wine Co., Oakville; H. J. Woolacutt, Los Angeles. From Florida: San Luis Vineyard, Tallahassee. From New Jersey: H. T. Dewey & Sons, Egg Harbor. From New York: Brotherhood Wine Co., Washingtonville; Empire State Wine Co., Penn Yan; Germania Wine Cellars, Hammondsport; Pleasant Valley Wine Co., Rheims; Urbana Wine Co., Urbana. From North Carolina: Garrett & Co., Weldon. From Ohio: Engels & Krudwig Wine Co. and M. Hommel, both of Sandusky. From Virginia: Monticello Wine Co., Charlottesville. From Washington, D.C.: Christian Zander.

• 6 •

But while the industry was reaching maturity during the nine-teenth century, the cancer which was to destroy it was already eating away at its vitals. Actually, it took the Drys a hundred years to terrorize and lobby Americans into accepting National Prohibition in 1920. Although the early temperance advocates aimed only at hard liquor and favored "light wine, beer, and happiness," even the first American Dry law, Indiana's 1816 prohibition against Sunday sale, made no exception for wine. As early as the 1830s, thousands of children were signing the pledge to abstain forever from all forms of alcohol, "the subtle poison of the devil." By the 1840s, the wineries' markets began drying up, as scores of towns and counties voted themselves Dry in New York, Michigan, Indiana, Georgia, Ohio, New Hampshire, and Iowa. But even while thousands of pulpits thun-dered that to drink anything alcoholic meant eternal damnation, the wine men could not believe that their business was threat-ened. For they, too, opposed the drinking of whiskey. Professor George Husmann, the pioneer of scientific winegrowing in Mis-souri, innocently predicted in 1866 that soon

wine, the most wholesome and purest of all stimulating drinks, will be within the reach of the common laborer and take the place of the noxious and poisonous liquors which are now the curse of so many of our laboring men and have blighted the happiness of so many homes.

Then whole states began going dry—Kansas in 1880, Iowa two years later, followed by Georgia, Oklahoma, Mississippi, North Carolina, Tennessee, West Virginia, and Virginia. Some of these states allowed the making of wine to continue for sale elsewhere, but this did not help their vintners. Barred from selling their wines locally, and unable to compete elsewhere with the wines from California, many of them closed their doors. The ruins of their great stone cellars still can be seen in many parts of the Bible Belt. Most of their vineyards were allowed to die.

The vintners in the "wet" states still could not see their ap-proaching doom, because occasional shortages of wine made their business seem good. What caused the shortages was the phyllox-era vine pest, which between 1860 and 1900 destroyed vast por-tions of the vineyards of Europe and California in the most destructive plant-disease epidemic of all time. And meanwhile the Drys were at work, busily brainwashing the nation against alcohol in any form. They demanded that mention of wine be removed from school and college texts, even including the Greek and Roman classics. At their insistence medicinal wines were dropped from the United States Pharmacopeia. They published books attempting to prove that the wine praised in the Bible was really unfermented grape juice. The Kansas State Horticultural Society printed the praises of fresh grapes as food, proclaiming that

to the glory of Kansas, 99½ percent of this luscious fruit which grows freely throughout the state, too good to be made a chief source of the degradation of the race, is used without fermentation.

By 1914, when the First World War broke out in Europe, thirty-three American states had gone Dry. Then, having instilled in the nation the mass guilt feeling about alcohol that now seems incredible to most people born since the 1930s, the Drys put over Wartime Prohibition in 1919, followed by the Eighteenth Amendment and the Volstead National Prohibition Act in 1920.

• 7 •

What happened next was totally unexpected. At first, the gloomy winegrowers began ripping out their vineyards, but soon they were wishing they hadn't, and instead began planting more vines. For the Drys had overlooked, or else failed to understand, an obscure provision of the Volstead Act—Section 29, which dealt with the home production of fruit juices. Originally placed in the law to placate the Virginia apple farmers, Section 29 permitted a householder to make "nonintoxicating cider and fruit juices exclusively for use in his home" to the extent of 200 gallons yearly. In 1920 began the peddling of "juice grapes"* to home winemakers and bootleggers from pushcarts in New York and from trucks in Boston and other cities. Suddenly, grape prices at the vineyards leaped from $10 a ton to the unheard-of figure of $100, and this started a feverish new rush of vine-planting across the nation. Soon more "nonintoxicating" wine was being made in America's basements each year than the commercial wineries had ever made before. Prohibition had brought the growers a bonanza.

The California grape growers, grown wealthy overnight, had only one gripe—a shortage of refrigerator cars—which they bitterly blamed on the railroads. Prosperity in the vineyard areas lasted exactly five years. Then, in 1925, the beleaguered railroads obliged by abruptly ending the car shortage. With plenty of

---

*To blot out memory of the Bacchic role of vineyards, the Department of Agriculture changed "wine grapes" in its statistical crop reports to the euphemism "juice grapes."

Wine tonics sold in most drugstores were a popular Prohibition-era tipple. (*Courtesy of Craig A. Kuhn*)

refrigerator cars, too much fruit was shipped, and when it rotted at the eastern terminals waiting for buyers who already had enough, the bottom dropped out of the grape market. From the collapse in 1925, except during the Second World War, California suffered from a chronic surplus of grapes until 1971.

More than a hundred wineries in California and New York and some dozens in New Jersey, Ohio, and Missouri survived the dry laws. Throughout Prohibition, they legally made sacramental wines and champagnes for the clergy, medicinal wines for sale by druggists on doctors' prescriptions, medicated wine tonics which required no prescription, salted wines for cooking (salted to make them undrinkable), and grape juice both fresh and condensed as a concentrate. Medicinal wine tonic became a popular tipple, because buyers soon learned its secret; when refrigerated, the horrible-tasting medicaments settled to the bottom of the bottle, leaving a drinkable wine. Of the sacramental wines, the greatest volume was sold through rabbis, because the Jewish faith requires the religious use of wine in the home. Anybody could call himself a rabbi and get a permit to buy wine legally, merely by presenting a list of his congregation. Millions of all faiths and of no faith became members of fake synagogues, some without their knowledge when the lists were copied from telephone directories. (My next-door neighbor in

San Francisco bought port and sherry at $4 a gallon from a
rabbi whose synagogue was a hall bedroom, which he called
"Congregation L'Chayim.")

· 8 ·

Some of the wineries profited richly from their sales of tonics
and sacramental wines, but after the grape market collapse, the
vineyardists remained in a desperate state of depression. California vineyard land that had jumped in price from $200 to $2500
an acre in 1923 sold for $250 an acre in 1926, when some farmers
offered their bankers deeds to their land to pay their debts. For
a time, the grape industry looked to grape concentrate for salva-
tion. Grape juice in kegs and also packages of pressed grapes
called "wine bricks" were being sold to some home winemakers.
With each keg or package came a yeast pill to start fermentation
and a printed warning not to use it "because if you do, this
will turn into wine, which would be illegal."

A "wine brick" (package of pressed grapes), sold during Prohibition to make
wine in American homes. With it came a yeast pill to start fermentation.
(*Brookside Museum*)

Captain Paul Garrett, of Virginia Dare fame, had a brilliant new idea. Why not sell concentrated grape juice in cans, together with complete winemaking and bottling "service" right in the buyer's home, and thus make wine available to everyone? And still more brilliant, why not let President Herbert Hoover's new farm relief program finance the scheme, since nobody needed relief more then the bankrupt grape industry? In 1929, Garrett led the largest surviving wineries of California into a giant combine with his New York wineries, called Fruit Industries, Inc. Mrs. Mabel Walker Willebrandt, the star of the attorney general's enforcement staff in Washington, D.C., was hired by the combine to avert any clashes with the Prohibition law. Fruit Industries got millions in loans from Hoover's Federal Farm Board to "salvage the grape surplus" by making it into grape concentrate. In 1931, the concentrate, called "Vine-Glo" (in a naming contest among grape growers, this name won over "Merri-Cal"), was advertised for sale throughout the nation. Full-page newspaper ads announced "Home delivery—guaranteed consumer satisfaction—Port, Virginia Dare, Muscatel, Tokay, Sauterne, Riesling, Claret, Burgundy—It's Legal!" Some of the wines expertly made from the Vine-Glo syrup were of surprisingly good quality. But when the Drys got a glimpse of the Vine-Glo ads and learned that "home delivery" meant winemaking service in the home, they were furious. They stormed Washington with protests. Soon the telephone rang at the Fruit Industries office in San Francisco. An official voice from Washington ordered: "Quit! Now, today, as of this minute!" The California Vineyardists Association pleaded for reversal, but to no avail. The Association denounced the Hoover administration for "betraying the grape industry," and Vine-Glo died on the vine.

In 1932, as the Dry era neared its close, a bill introduced in Congress brought new hope to the growers. It aimed to legalize light wine and beer without waiting for Repeal. Eleven percent by volume was proposed as the permissible alcoholic content for wine, and 3.2 percent alcohol by weight for beer, on the ground that beverages of these strengths would be "nonintoxicating." Hoping to speed the bill's passage—but without consulting the winegrowers—Senator William Gibbs McAdoo of California proposed a compromise: make 3.2 percent the figure for both wine and beer. To the wine people's disgust, the bill as thus amended was promptly passed. A few vintners actually diluted some wine to 3.2 percent and sold it—a watery, unappealing fluid which they scornfully christened "McAdoo wine."

• 9 •

The end of Prohibition on December 5, 1933, found the remnants of the wine industry mostly in ruins after thirteen Dry years. Almost the only fine, aged wines available were held by the few altar-wine producers for the Catholic clergy, who have always demanded quality in the wines they use to celebrate the Mass. Speculators, expecting quick profits, reopened many old cellars, some with casks moldy from long disuse. Wines hastily made in October and already half-spoiled flooded the country during that frenzied December. Their contents still fermenting, bottles blew up on thousands of store shelves and in windows, creating an odorous reputation for all products of the grape. In California, several million gallons of wine were condemned by the State Department of Public Health as unfit to drink and were either distilled into alcohol, turned into vinegar, or destroyed. Sound wines, too, spoiled after leaving the wineries, because restaurateurs and storekeepers, unaware that table and sparkling wines are perishable, stored the bottles standing up, allowing the corks to dry out and the wines to become acetic or oxidized.

Although the Eighteenth Amendment was dead, vast areas of the nation remained legally Dry under state and local Prohibition laws.* Dry-minded state legislatures imposed high taxes on wine, treating it as merely another form of liquor. In most of the states, exorbitant license fees and burdensome regulations prevented farmers from starting wineries to sell their grapes in the form of wine. Seventeen states established state or municipal monopoly liquor stores, the forbidding kinds of outlets which discourage householders from venturing inside to shop for wine. These stores usually offer only skimpy assortments, and consumers cannot order wines mailed to them from other states, because the postal laws still prohibit the shipment of any alcoholic beverage by parcel post.

• 10 •

A whole generation of maturing Americans, grown accustomed to bathtub gin and moonshine, were ignorant of wine, a foreign-

---

*State prohibition was not repealed by Kansas until 1948; Oklahoma remained Dry until 1959, and Mississippi until 1966. Even as recently as 1970, local Prohibition laws in 32 states still barred the sale of wine in 589 of the nation's 3078 counties and in hundreds more towns, school districts, and precincts representing 10 percent of the nation's area and 6 percent of the population.

seeming beverage which to them tasted sour—as many of the early shipments were. Most of the table wines made shortly after Repeal were poor in quality, and many were undrinkable. Some of their defects could have been corrected, but the main trouble was a lack of grapes suitable to make good dry table wines. Prohibition had left the nation with a vast acreage of vineyards growing the wrong grapes. During the "juice grape" boom of the 1920s, many California growers had grafted over their fine Riesling, Pinot, and Cabernet vines, whose tiny, thin-skinned grapes brought them only $50 a ton, to such coarse, thick-skinned varieties as the Alicante Bouschet, which brought $100 a ton at the vineyards because it shipped and sold well. (The Alicante also had red juice, and bootleggers could make 700 gallons of "dago red" from a single ton by adding sugar and water.) In the eastern states, too, the best native wine-grape varieties had been largely replaced by the hardy Concord, which is good for fresh grape juice but when fermented dry makes harsh, foxy-tasting table wines. The foreign-born, who had continued drinking wine with their meals throughout Prohibition, rejected the new commercial wines, preferring to go on buying grapes and making their own.

And to make matters worse, a flood of awesome books and articles, written by dilettantes strutting their knowledge, warned Americans that rigid rules must be observed in serving wines—only certain types with certain foods, in certain glasses, and at certain specific temperatures. Rather than risk committing social blunders, millions avoided serving wine in their homes at all. Except for sometimes sampling the cheap red wines served in Italian restaurants, and buying occasional bottles of sherry or port, most native-born buyers of alcoholic beverages stuck to beer and hard liquor.

As a result, there was little demand at Repeal for the dry, light (usually 12 percent) table wines, which are the principal wine types of the world because they are used mostly with food. One group of wines sold well—the dessert wines—port, sherry, tokay, and muscatel. At that time, these dessert wines were classed legally as "fortified" because they were strengthened with brandy to 20 percent alcoholic content. Because the Federal tax on wine is only a fraction of the tax on liquor, "fortified wine" was the cheapest intoxicant available, and much of it was drunk by the derelicts called "winos" on the skid rows of the nation. This situation created grave trouble for the wineries, as will be seen presently. Before Prohibition, table wines had outsold dessert wines in the United States by as much as three to one. But in 1935, the California wineries were shipping three gallons of dessert wines to one of table wines, and the wineries of Arkansas, Michigan, and Washington made the dessert or "fortified" types almost exclusively.

Such were the appalling legacies that Prohibition left in its wake. The once-proud American wine industry, which before 1900 had exported its wines around the world and won prizes at international competitions, was reborn in ruins. It was making the wrong kinds of wine from the wrong kinds of grapes for the wrong kind of consumers in a whiskey-drinking nation with guilt feelings about imbibing in general and a confused attitude toward wine in particular. Some of the vintners doubted that winegrowing would ever recover as a respected, economically sound industry. When a ruinous glut of the grape and wine markets developed after the 1935 vintage, many a grape grower, mourning the bonanza of the early "juice grape" shipping days, openly regretted the repeal of the Dry law.

• 11 •

Would the Federal government, which had destroyed the industry, help to restore it? Some members of President Franklin D. Roosevelt's administration thought it should. There was ample precedent for Federal assistance; the Department of Agriculture had encouraged winegrowing for more than a century, operating experimental vineyards and breeding wine grapes until Prohibition intervened. As late as 1880, the only Federal census statistics of state-by-state grape production were given in gallons of wine made, because the chief purpose of planting vineyards was to grow wine. This was always the case in other countries; nine-tenths of the world's grapes are grown for wine. Shipping of fresh grapes as a dessert fruit was unimportant until refrigerated freight cars were adapted for fruit shipments about 1887, and the raisin industry remained small until the 1890s.

Promptly at Repeal, Eleanor Roosevelt began serving American wines in the White House, restoring the custom that had prevailed until "Lemonade Lucy," the wife of President Rutherford B. Hayes, stopped it in 1877.

Dr. Rexford Guy Tugwell, a member of Roosevelt's famed "Brain Trust," made elaborate plans to restore winegrowing as a nationwide industry. Tugwell, who then was the assistant secretary of agriculture, even favored exempting wine and beer from taxation in order to hold down the consumption of hard liquor. In 1933 he sent the Agriculture Department's Dr. Charles

A. Magoon to Europe to collect the newest wine yeast cultures. At Tugwell's direction, two complete model wineries were built, one at the government's giant agricultural research center in Beltsville, Maryland, and the other at the Meridian, Mississippi, research station which served the southeastern states. Both wineries were fully equipped with crushers, presses, underground vats, and there was a brandy still at Beltsville.

But neither model winery ever crushed a grape. Congressman Clarence Cannon of Missouri, the perennial chairman of the House Appropriations Committee, was a lifelong Prohibitionist, and when word reached him of what Tugwell was doing, the project was doomed. "No Federal money shall go to any fermentation industry!" Cannon thundered, and he threatened to block the entire Department of Agriculture appropriation unless the wine work was suppressed forthwith. Cannon prevailed. The model wineries were stripped of their equipment, which was sold as government surplus.* During the next thirty years, "wine" was a word the Department's scientists feared to utter, and they would look around furtively before even mentioning "juice." It therefore deserves mention that when Representative Cannon died in May 1964, two Federal wine-quality research projects were promptly approved in Washington, D.C., and the work quickly got under way in the Agriculture Department's regional research laboratory at Albany, California, and at the Geneva Experiment Station in New York State.

• 12 •

A shortage of trained winemakers plagued the wineries at Repeal. Old-timers with better jobs elsewhere were reluctant to return to the cellars. Partially spoiled wines were doctored by chemists, who only made them worse. But back in 1880, by an act of the legislature, the University of California had established a special department to conduct wine research and to teach winemaking at its Berkeley campus. And fortunately, this fifty-three-year-old wine school was still intact. It had continued through Prohibition under the innocent title of "the fruit products laboratory," concocting nonalcoholic grape drinks and grape

*The Beltsville winery now houses a seed and nut laboratory and is called the West Building. How it came to be built is a legend still told and retold there. The winery at Meridian stood empty, its original purpose a whispered secret, until the station there was closed in 1965. On a visit several years ago to the Hallcrest Vineyard near Felton, California, I watched a shiny little crusher-stemmer receiving Cabernet Sauvignon grapes and learned that it came from the government's model winery at Beltsville, the winery that never crushed a grape.

jellies and teaching students the scientific processing of other fruits. Professors Frederic T. Bioletti and William Vere Cruess quickly switched their courses back to winemaking, and soon were graduating classes of enologists to man the wineries. The university launched new programs of wine research and grape breeding, took over the Federal government's neglected vineyard in Napa County, established an experimental winery and brandy distillery at its Davis campus, and developed intensive new instruction in vineyard and winery operation.

Except in New York, where Professor Ulysses Prentiss Hedrick and his colleagues resumed their wine-grape breeding work at the Geneva Station in 1934, the other grape states did little or nothing at Repeal to help their winegrowers or to improve their vineyards.

In Maryland, however, an amateur winemaker and newspaperman named Philip Wagner began about 1935 to plant a different kind of wine grape which was destined to change the taste of many American wines during the next few decades. Until then, virtually all of the wine grown outside of California had been made of native American grape varieties with their distinctive, usually foxy flavors. Wagner imported and planted the French hybrids, the nonfoxy crosses of Vinifera with indigenous American grapes, and proved that with the hardiness inherited from their native parents, they could thrive where the delicate Old World grapes had failed. These new grape varieties spread during the 1940s to vineyards in New York and Ohio; and by the 1970s, wines without the slightest trace of foxiness were being made from the hybrids in no less than twenty states. Wagner, the amateur, had spread the hybrids almost as far as the legendary Johnny Appleseed once spread the apple tree.

• 13 •

About this time, another journalist, wine writer Frank Musselman Schoonmaker, started still another trend that has influenced viniana profoundly in this country. Having entered the importing business in New York City following Repeal, Schoonmaker in 1939 added to his import line an assortment of the best California, Ohio, and New York State wines he could find, having them bottled by the wineries as Schoonmaker Selections. As an importer, he refused to call his American wines sauterne, rhine wine, chablis, or burgundy, the European type names they generally had borne before Prohibition. Instead Schoonmaker gave them varietal labels, naming each wine for the grape variety from which it was principally made. Varietal labels were not new, because wines called Cabernet, Riesling, Zinfandel, Catawba, Delaware, and Scuppernong had been on the market before the turn of the century. But Schoonmaker introduced additional grape names the wine-buying public had never heard of: Chardonnay, Pinot Blanc, Grey Riesling, Sémillon, Gamay, Pinot Noir, Grenache Rosé, Niagara, Elvira, Moore's Diamond. His wine selections were excellent; their strange names suggested rare quality and provided topics for conversation. These were extra values for which connoisseurs, until then the buyers of imports almost exclusively, were ready to pay. When other vintners saw Schoonmaker's American "varietals" begin to sell at premium prices in the best stores and restaurants, they lost little time in following suit. Varietal labels soon became the mark of the costliest American wines. Then, of course, more grape names began appearing on labels, and the "varietal" wine list grew during the next two decades to include Barbera, Chenin Blanc, Folle Blanche, Gewürztraminer, Green Hungarian, Petite Sirah, Pinot Saint George, Sylvaner, and dozens more.

An ironic twist developed when European vintners, recognizing a good thing, began in the 1960s to imitate the new American labels. Until then, only a few European wines—the Alsatian, some Italian, and the muscatels—had used any varietal names. But now, for the first time, there began appearing, on American store shelves, wines from France and Spain newly christened "Pinot Noir," "Chardonnay," and "Cabernet Sauvignon," mostly at low prices and of doubtful authenticity in most cases.

Frank Schoonmaker, the wine writer and importer who popularized the naming of American wines for the grape varieties from which they are made.

Amidst the chaos at Prohibition's end, a group of old-line California winegrowers organized the Wine Institute and set out to rehabilitate their industry. In 1934, they obtained reissuance of the state's minimum wine quality standards. They worked with the eastern producers toward national standards, which were issued by the Federal government two years later.

The Wine Institute's founders believed that by producing sound, inexpensive table wine and by educating the public to drink it daily with food, they could wean America from whiskey and gin and make this a wine-drinking country. Their models were France and Italy, whose yearly wine consumption has varied from twenty to thirty gallons per capita and consists almost entirely of table wine. This had always been the goal of such historic figures as Jefferson, Longworth, and Husmann, and of California's winegrowing senators, Leland Stanford and George Hearst.

In 1938, the Wine Institute persuaded the state's wineries to tax themselves for a nationwide educational campaign to spread the gospel of wine as the beverage of temperate, civilized dining. To administer the program, they created the Wine Advisory Board under supervision of the State Department of Agriculture. Advertisements, articles, booklets, and leaflets by the millions urged Americans to glamorize their dinners with wine and to use it in cooking.

Wine use grew. Consumption of commercial wine in the United States rose from 33 million gallons in 1934 to almost 90 million in 1940, nearly all of it American-grown. The 1940 volume amounted to eight-tenths of a gallon per capita, compared to a mere half gallon in the highest pre-Prohibition year. But while the advertisements preached the use of light table wine with food, more than two-thirds of the total consumed—almost all of the increase—was of the port-sherry-muscatel group, the 20 percent dessert or "fortified" wines. Table wine, on which the industry's future depended, was still its stepchild. Many of the growers became convinced that the Advisory Board's efforts to promote table wine were a waste of their money, that Americans could never be taught to drink wine with meals. If this country would ever consume as much table wine as dessert wine, they said, it would represent the millennium.

The misuse of dessert wine by the "winos" endangered the legal and social status of wine following Repeal. What made it worse was the word "fortified," invented by the British to describe sweet wines preserved by the 200-year-old process of adding brandy to arrest fermentation. Unfortunately, the American wine regulations in 1936 had copied those of England, and included this frightening nine-letter word as the legal designation for dessert wines. As a result, "fortified wine" began to be blamed for the miseries of the depraved alcoholics who drank it because it was cheap. Many people, to avoid associating themselves with "winos," even banned the 20 percent wines from their homes. Soon laws to tax "fortified wine" out of existence or to prohibit its sale entirely were proposed in several state legislatures. The legislators had no objection to port, sherry, tokay, or muscatel, overlooking the fact that they contained brandy, but they imagined that any wine called "fortified" must pack some mysterious power. In 1938, the vintners decided to get rid of the word, and they persuaded the government to ban it from all labels and advertisements. But the thought of dessert wine as "fortified" stuck in the public mind. In 1951, Treasury officials recommended to the House Ways and Means Committee that the Federal tax rates on wines be tripled on the ground that such wine was competing unfairly with high-taxed whiskey. A bill containing the new rates was promptly voted by the Committee. It was a body blow to the wine industry. At stake were the keys to its very existence: the historic tax advantage of wine over liquor and beer, the classification of wine as an article of food, and the treatment of winegrowing as an agricultural pursuit separate from the distilling and brewing industries. Alarm spread through the vineyard areas, and growers from all of the grape states besieged Washington with protests. Amendments to the tax bill in the Senate Finance Committee provided for smaller increases, resulting in rates of 17 cents per gallon on table wines and 67 cents on dessert wines. But to get the last mention of "fortified" erased from Federal regulations required an act of Congress, the wine law of 1954.

• 14 •

The gains in wine consumption were interrupted during the Second World War, because almost three-fourths of the raisin grapes previously used by the California wineries were diverted for use as food, and wine was in short supply. Also during the war, the whiskey distillers invaded the wine industry. What caused the invasion was the government's order converting liquor distilleries to the production of alcohol for war uses (an order which included the wineries' brandy stills). The distillers' only purpose in buying wineries was to provide their sales forces with something besides scarce liquor to sell during the war. But wine benefited from the distiller invasion, because the liquor firms supplied sorely needed capital for winery improvements, and they taught this country's winegrowers valuable lessons about packaging their products attractively. Only a dozen of the many hundreds of wine companies were actually acquired by the big whiskey firms; and when the war ended, most of the wineries were sold back to the growers.

At the conflict's end, wineries were rebuilt and re-equipped, and the planting of better grapes was accelerated. The number of wineries shrank, however, as many small growers gave up or were absorbed by the large firms. Of some 1300 bonded wineries operating in sixteen states in 1936, only 271 were left—but in twenty states—by 1960.

In 1946, the University of California released the first new varieties created in its grape-breeding program at Davis. Two of these, Ruby Cabernet and Emerald Riesling, made such good table wines that their planting since has spread throughout California and to several other countries. Meanwhile, too, Philip Wagner's French hybrid grapes had begun appearing in the New York and Ohio vineyards.

Winemaking, regarded for centuries as an art rather than a science, then began to benefit from modern research. Knowledge of the chemistry of grapes and wine advanced more in the decades following the Second World War than in the preceding two thousand years. The American vintners, in the process of rebuilding, with a new breed of technically trained winemakers, took advantage of the new knowledge, while most producers in the Old World were satisfied to continue making wine by rule of thumb as in the past. During the 1950s, the University of California at Davis became the world's leading center of viticultural and enological research. Winegrowers in other countries started sending their sons to Davis to be trained, and their governments invited experts of the Davis faculty to come and advise them on ways to improve their wines. The American Society of Enologists was founded in California in 1950. With its annual technical conferences and its quarterly *American Journal of Enology and Viticulture,* the Society attracted an international membership and became the leading organization of the winemaking profession in the world.

• 15 •

The quality of American wines improved after the war. Some of the wineries had replaced the coarse shipping-grape varieties in their vineyards with superior wine grapes. By 1956, the twenty-third year after Repeal, the California producers of premium wines felt they were ready to challenge the wines of Europe. They set up comparative tastings in cities across the country, pitting the best California vintages against their most famous Old World rivals. Bottles from France, Germany, Italy, Spain, Portugal, and California were bought at random from store shelves, the prices of the imports averaging double those of their native counterparts. Dealers and consumers were invited to come and taste the wines "blind," i.e., from numbered glasses; the bottle labels were hidden. Nearly 1500 tasters came to sixty-eight such tastings in three years. They sampled the wines and wrote their preferences on secret ballots. When the votes were counted, the results astonished even the Californians: California outscored Europe on champagnes, red table wines, and sherries, while the European white table wines, rosés, and ports were preferred over California's; and in the total point scores, California came out slightly ahead.

Only California wines could be thus compared directly with those from Europe, because both are made of the same Vinifera grape varieties. Eastern wines, being made of the foxy native grapes and as yet to a limited extent from French hybrids, could not. But California's monopoly of fine Vinifera wines was about to end. For while the "blind" tastings were going on, a new chapter in American wine history was opening near the town of Hammondsport in the Finger Lakes district of New York State. There, after three centuries during which repeated attempts to grow Vinifera grapes in the East had failed miserably, a Russian-born German emigré named Dr. Konstantin Frank had planted a vineyard of such Old World grapes as Riesling and Chardonnay, and his wines were thriving in the New York climate. In 1957, their first crop was made into wine, and with each successive vintage these vines have confounded the viticultural experts who had predicted they soon must die in the frigid winters.

• 16 •

By the mid-1950s, average yearly wine use in the United States had risen to 145 million gallons, and per capita consumption was approaching nine-tenths of a gallon. Of this total, California supplied 119 million gallons, twenty-two other states produced about 19 million, and 7 million were imports from Europe. New kinds of wine were beginning to court the beer-and-cola palates of Americans: the sweet, Concord-flavored kosher type; the soft red "vinos," successors to the old, astringent "dago red"; new semi-sweet versions of rosé; white and red table wines with slight carbonation; and the flood of 20 percent "special natural" flavored wines with such coined names as Thunderbird and Silver Satin. But two-thirds of the total still was high-alcohol dessert wine, the same proportion as before the war.

Despite the crazy quilt of different state laws, wine distribution improved. The leading California and New York premium producers began teaching restaurant, hotel, and club staffs, wherever the laws permitted, how to store table wines properly and how to sell them with meals. People who had never bought wine before sampled it in these establishments and began serving it to guests in their homes. But of all the developments during this decade, none did more to advance the use of wine in America than the vast improvement of the mass-produced, inexpensive California table wines, made possible by the enormous recent advances in grape-growing and winemaking technology. In the past most of these low-priced wines had been shipped across the country in tank cars to more than a thousand local bottlers, who sold them, not always in sound condition, under a multitude of local brands. But now, the largest California mass producers switched to bottling their own wines, and launched multimillion-dollar advertising campaigns on television to make their brands known. This, for the first time, brought reliably palatable, branded table wines in convenient jugs within the reach of millions of households at prices low enough for everyday use. By 1960, fewer than 200 local bottlers remained in business. These were mostly old-time vintners who had maintained the quality of the wines sold under their names.

• 17 •

The war had brought changes in popular tastes for food and drink. Millions of young Americans of both sexes, after military sojourns in the wine countries overseas, came home with a liking for continental cuisine and its liquid accompaniment, table wine. Postwar touring, spurred by bargain air fares, lured still more Americans to Europe, and they, too, returned with a new appreciation of wine. At home, people with new affluence and leisure took up gourmet cookery, and publishers noted the steady sales growth of books on wines and international cuisine. Wine tastings became popular as a new kind of social event in homes and at club and charity functions. Millions discovered wine as a symbol of status and culture. When college extension courses in wine appreciation were first offered for a fee, the classes were quickly oversubscribed by people thirsty for vinous knowledge.

Attitudes toward drinking were changing. As population shifted from rural areas to the cities, the old Bible Belt view of all imbibing as sinful began to fade. Dry counties in the "local option" states voted wet in increasing numbers, sending the WCTU forces down to ignominious defeat, and new movements were organized to repeal the remaining "blue laws" against the sale of liquor on Sundays. Women's magazines for half a century had refused to print advertisements for alcoholic beverages, but now solicited ads for wine and beer. Wives, who had always left liquor purchasing to their husbands as an exclusive prerogative of males, began buying the wine to serve with the family dinner.

• 18 •

What the grape growers a generation earlier had called "the millennium"—when the nation would drink as much table wine as dessert wine—came in 1968. Table wine, the industry's stepchild, had doubled in consumption volume, and champagnes, which are table wines with bubbles, had more than trebled in only ten years. Millions of Americans were adding dry table wines to their daily meals, while dessert wine consumption remained virtually unchanged. A few of the states with government-monopoly liquor stores began amending their laws to let table wines be sold in grocery stores. By 1972, total U.S. wine consumption had soared to nearly 340 million gallons, over a gallon and a half per capita, three times the rate before Prohibition, and these figures appeared certain to double again in ten more years. There were forecasts that wine use might reach three, five, even ten gallons per capita, that the country eventually could consume a billion gallons per year.

These developments set off the wine revolution, with reverberations across the continent and to wine countries around the world. Abruptly the whole national pattern of grape growing was reversed. To supply the better grapes required to make table wines, new vineyards were needed; California's surplus raisin and table grapes and the East's leftover Concords would no longer do. Several state legislatures, despite Prohibitionist opposition, voted appropriations for wine-grape research. A wave of vine-planting unparalleled in world history spread across the United States. Entirely new winegrowing districts were discovered and were planted with tens of thousands of acres in California and in eastern Washington. Winegrowing returned to the

Sacramento Valley and to the old Sierra foothill gold-mining regions; to Pennsylvania, Indiana, Virginia, and to the area around Hermann in Missouri; to the Willamette Valley of Oregon, and to the Ohio River Valley near Cincinnati, where Nicholas Longworth had made a famous Sparkling Catawba more than a century ago. Plantings of Philip Wagner's French-American hybrids and of Dr. Frank's unexpectedly successful Vinifera spread through the East and Midwest. Vintners in the old wine-growing districts switched their attention from dessert wines to table types and champagnes.

Developments during the 1970s and 1980s speeded at a dizzying pace. New wineries opened for business in California, Oregon, Washington, Maryland, Virginia, Texas, Missouri, Michigan, Indiana, Idaho, New York, and for the first time in recent memory, in New Hampshire, Rhode Island, Massachusetts, Georgia, Arizona, Oklahoma, Kentucky, Connecticut, the Carolinas, West Virginia, and Tennessee.

White table wines, made newly fresh and palatable by the technical advances in viniculture, became so popular, served cold as temperate substitutes for pre-meal cocktails, that the mid-1970s witnessed a revolutionary nationwide boom in white-wine consumption. Red and rosé wines also improved, but their main uses continued as accompaniments of food.

Ultramodern wineries were built, with research laboratories, mechanical grape harvesters, field crushers, centrifuges, temperature-controlled stainless-steel tanks, new European-oak casks, micropore filters, and computerized processing equipment. Growers and vintners learned for the first time to measure the pH of their grapes—the chemical symbol for hydrogen-ion concentration—that foretells the flavor-balance, color, aroma, and keeping quality of wine.

New American wine types appeared: *nouveau* reds, German-style "late-harvest" white wines of botrytized grapes, flavored "pop" wines, and "wine coolers" to compete with beer. In the early 1980s came a flood of "light" wines (low-calorie and low-alcohol, 7 to 10 percent instead of the usual 12), inspired by the popularity of light beers. New, too, were "soft wines," which also meant low in alcohol, but the "soft" wines tended to be sweet. Some wineries even made dealcoholized wines and offered them for sale in a few "test markets" to learn how many people might buy wine with all the alcohol removed.

Wine became Big Business in America during the 1970s. Investors scrambled to buy shares of winery owners' stock issues and to join tax-shelter partnerships in new vineyard ventures.

Unaware of winegrowing's past boom-and-bust history, they financed the planting of a half-million new acres of vineyards. Giant corporations in other fields, led by the returning whiskey distillers, snapped up control of family-owned wineries. The Coca-Cola Company of Atlanta invested in wine, buying Taylor and Great Western in New York in 1977, then added three wineries in California. French, Italian, Swiss, Spanish, German, and Canadian firms invaded the American wine industry, acquiring vineyards and building new wineries to make table wines and champagnes.

As wineries multiplied in numbers, they joined to publicize their individual districts and to attract visitors to their tasting rooms. Wine judgings, wine festivals, charity-benefit concerts, barrel tastings, wine auctions, and grape-stomping contests spread from California to the other winegrowing states.

During the early 1980s, the Federal government began determining the legal boundaries of nearly a hundred American viticultural areas, not only of such already famous districts as California's Napa Valley and the New York Finger Lakes region, but of new and old vineyard locations in nearly all of the winegrowing states. The names of the newly approved areas, like the appellations of European wine districts, began appearing on labels of premium American wines.

Connoisseurs who long had sneered at all American wines began to discover, from comparative tastings abroad and at home, that the best American vintages had equaled and surpassed many of Europe's classic wines. Viewing wine as an art form, they began paying such astronomical per-bottle prices for the rarest Chardonnays and Cabernets that many producers no longer could afford to drink their own wines.

Regular wine columns became features in hundreds of newspapers and magazines, augmented by a flood of new books about wine. Knowledge of wine became a requisite mark of culture like the appreciation of art, music, and literature. More than a million Americans enrolled in wine appreciation classes held on college campuses and at hotels, restaurants, and wineries.

Meanwhile, inexpensive table wines in jugs, in the new plastic "bag-in-box," and in kegs were increasingly stocked by restaurants, where servings by the glass or carafe became part of ordinary meals. Canned wines, tried and repeatedly rejected since the 1930s, reappeared in stores and were served on some airlines. There were experiments in packaging table wines in paper cartons like those used for the sale of milk.

Table wine consumption quadrupled in the fourteen years after 1969. It came as no surprise when, for the first time in history, annual wine consumption beginning in 1980 exceeded the consumption of distilled spirits.

But in half the nation, wine still was difficult for householders to buy, its purchase restricted by archaic state and local laws, barred in half the states from sale in groceries, where most people shop for all the ingredients of meals.

At the same time, the winegrowing countries of Europe, faced with vast wine surpluses, began flooding the American market with low-priced wines, partially subsidized by their governments. Imports from Europe, which had supplied only a twentieth of the U.S. market during the 1960s, had captured more than a fourth of the table wine market by 1983. As in California's grape-planting booms of the past, vineyards had been planted faster than the market could absorb the wine. Grape surpluses began to develop in the eastern and northwestern states as well. With U.S. wine consumption still growing steadily, the imports were blamed for the grape surpluses. In 1983 American winegrowers asked the Federal government to impose countervailing tariffs against the flood of subsidized wine imports. Their appeal was denied.

Also in 1983, Heublein, the Connecticut-based liquor firm, sold four of its California wineries to the Allied Grape Growers co-operative, retaining the only three that were yielding a profit. At the same time the giant Coca-Cola Company of Atlanta, after seven profitless years in the American wine business, decided to withdraw and sold its three California and two New York State wineries to one of its most aggressive competitors, the Seagram worldwide wine and liquor empire.

Meanwhile, in an entirely different direction, American winegrowing had become increasingly a romantic little business. Adventurous new pioneers had continued starting tiny new vineyards and building mini-wineries to produce handmade wines in localities where wine grew a century ago and in others where wine was never grown before.

Most important, because a nation's wines should be judged by the very best it produces, was the fact that American premium wines had far surpassed in quality most of those produced in the pre-Prohibition past. They were challenging, both at home and in export markets abroad, the finest wines produced in the rest of the world.

In the fifth decade since the rebirth of winegrowing in America, the nation was at last becoming the "Vineland" which Leif Ericson had named it a thousand years earlier. An entirely new chapter in the remarkable four-century history of wine in America had begun.

3

Scuppernong Country—The Original American Wine

I N THE SOUTHEASTERN STATES, and nowhere else in the world, there grows a grape so fragrant that the early navigators, approaching the coast in September, detected its rich scent long before they made landfall. It is the Scuppernong, from which southerners have made wine for almost four centuries to drink with their corn pone, fish muddle, and cake. This was the first, the original American wine.

The greenish-bronze Scuppernong and its many-hued relatives of the Muscadine or *Vitis rotundifolia* family are unlike any other grapes. They grow not in bunches but in clusters, each berry as large and rotund as a cherry or a marble. In the past they were seldom picked; instead, men walked beneath the vines, beating the canes with tobacco sticks, causing the ripe grapes to drop onto sheets or hammocks laid on the ground. Today they are picked by modern harvesting machines. As you drive through Scuppernong country, the dense, tangled mass you see behind a farmhouse is a single vine, as much a part of the scene as the tobacco barn. A single Scuppernong vine may cover a whole acre and produce, even without cultivation, a ton of fruit yielding five barrels of wine.

The juice of Scuppernong, if fermented dry, makes an amber, strong-tasting, intriguing though usually somewhat harsh wine. But when the wine is sweetened, as winemakers in Scuppernong country have always done, it becomes an exotic nectar reminiscent of fresh plums, with a musky aroma and taste entirely its own. The flavor of Scuppernong is so pronounced that if its wine is blended with Concord, the Scuppernong character will overwhelm and hide the foxy Labrusca taste. It was to such a blend of Scuppernong, Concord, and Catawba, with California wine added, that the late Captain Paul Garrett gave the name

Scuppernongs (Muscadines) are unlike any other grapes. They grow not in bunches but in clusters, each berry as large and rotund as a cherry or a marble. These grapes, bred by horticulturist Byard O. Fry at the University of Georgia Experiment Station near Griffin, are an inch in diameter.

Virginia Dare, and it was the best-selling wine in the United States during the two decades before Prohibition.

Scuppernong and its Muscadine relatives have long been the principal grapes grown on the humid Coastal Plain of the Carolinas, Florida, Georgia, and other southeastern states. Bunch grapes, the kinds that grow elsewhere, are attacked in the lowlands there by Pierce's Disease, an insect-borne bacterium to which Muscadines are resistant.

Bunch grapes grow at higher elevations of the Piedmont Plateau. In the uplands of North Carolina, for example, there were many vineyards and wineries making wine of Labrusca grapes before Prohibition. A number of them were clustered around Tryon in Polk County. In that community of estates and summer homes, I have seen a wine press and casks that were part of the pre-1900 Vollmer winery, still preserved at the Charles Briggs residence on Vineyard Road.

Ampelographies say that four of the most successful early American wine grapes originated in the Carolinas: the Catawba is named for the Catawba River in Buncombe County, North Carolina; South Carolina contributed the Isabella about 1816, the Lenoir in 1829, and the Herbemont, grown in the 1820s by Nicholas Herbemont of Columbia. Lenoir and Herbemont are resistant to Pierce's Disease.

Scuppernong Country

🍇 MUSCADINES   🍇 BUNCH GRAPES

• 2 •

A history-making revival of winegrowing has begun in seven
of the southeastern states, awakened by the wine revolution
to their vinous past. It is happening not only with Scuppernong
and its relatives, but with Vinifera and French hybrids in the
Piedmont, and in the lowlands with PD-resistant grape varieties
newly bred to make good table wines.

In the foothills of the Blue Ridge Mountains in northwestern
North Carolina is a fabulous 250-room four-acre French Renaissance palace as impressive as the chateau residences of European
royalty that attract visitors to the Loire Valley of France. The
palace is the famous Biltmore House, which crowns the 8000-
acre Biltmore Estate on US 25 off Interstate 40 at Asheville. It
was built before the end of the last century by the philanthropist
George Washington Vanderbilt.

When the wine revolution began exploding in the late 1960s,

it occurred to Vanderbilt's grandson, William A. Vanderbilt Cecil, that it would be fitting if Biltmore, like the Loire chateaux, could have a vineyard and grow its own wine, not of Muscadines but of Old World wine grapes. The elevation of Asheville and environs is between 2300 and 2600 feet, considered relatively safe from spring frosts; and at these elevations bunch grapes such as Concord and Catawba have long been grown in the Carolinas and in neighboring Georgia, Virginia, and Tennessee.

In the early 1970s, Cecil had Biltmore horticulturist Timothy Thielke plant a few acres of French hybrid vines in the Biltmore Gardens. The vines thrived, and an experimental winery was installed in a basement near the palace, with laboratory technician Martha Ward from New Hampshire University in charge. In 1979, when visiting connoisseurs had pronounced the wines good, Cecil had them put on sale, labeled "Biltmore Estate," at the postcard desk in the palace and in the Deerpark Restaurant, where they quickly sold out. He since has had Thielke plant seventy-five acres of such noble Vinifera varieties as Cabernet and Chardonnay in a new vineyard west of the French Broad River. Cecil has brought noted winemaster Philippe Jourdain to Asheville from southern France and has begun building a spectacular multimillion-dollar winery and tasting room to be

The Scuppernong "Mother Vine" on Roanoke Island, North Carolina, covers half an acre. Pictured with it is the late Raymond Hartsfield, who grew twenty-five acres of Scuppernongs in his vineyard at Holly Ridge, N.C.

completed by 1985 around the renovated old dairy barn at the
north end of the Biltmore Estate. Jourdain has made two vintages
of Vinifera wines, now called "Château Biltmore," and has begun
making champagne. The Biltmore vintage-dated Vinifera wines,
introduced in 1983, are bringing new prestige and glamor to
winegrowing in the South.

Hobbyist winegrowers who prefer Old World wine types to
Scuppernong have also been growing French hybrids and Vinifera in the Piedmont counties north of Winston-Salem and
Greensboro. In 1981, five such hobbyists bonded North Carolina's newest winery, the 1000-gallon Germanton Vineyards cellar,
in a converted dairy barn on Highway 8 in the Stokes County
village of Germanton. Each of the owners has his own vineyard:
retired farmer William McGee, brewery technologist Jerry Pe-
gram, psychology professor Scott Lawrence, retired executive
John Gillispie, and pediatrician Dr. Mallory Chambliss, who does
the chemical testing of the wines. Germanton Vineyard's first
vintage, blends of Foch, Chancellor, Seyval, and Baco Noir, was
sold out almost overnight.

• 3 •

If you wish to visit a modern Scuppernong vineyard, look
up former high school principal David Fussell, on the outskirts
of Rose Hill, North Carolina, off US 117. He is one of eleven
farmers who grow Muscadines in five southeastern counties.
They jointly own the first winery in Duplin County, the Duplin
Wine Cellars, built in 1976 and since doubled to 100,000 gallons
in size. Fussell and his brother Dan run the winery with technical
guidance from the State University's Dr. Dan Carroll. It is modern, with crushing equipment and tanks of stainless steel. They
make vintage-dated dry and sweet table wines named Carlos,
Noble, Scuppernong, and a pleasant semi-dry bottle-fermented
Scuppernong champagne. These can all be sampled in the winery
tasting room. The North Carolina legislature has passed special
legislation to permit this, because Duplin County is legally Dry.
In 1979 the Fussells also installed a pot still like those that during
Prohibition made "white lightning" moonshine in the nearby
hills. In the following year they made the first legal brandy in
North Carolina since the state went Dry in 1909. The brandy,
however, can only be bought in the state monopoly's liquor
stores.

Although Muscadines thrive in all of the southeastern states,
North Carolina claims Scuppernong as its own. The first account

of these grapes occurs in the logbook of Giovanni da Verrazano, the Florentine navigator who in 1524 explored the Cape Fear River Valley for France. He reported "many vines growing naturally there" and that "without all doubt they would yield excellent wines." Amadas and Barlow, sent by Sir Walter Raleigh to explore the Carolina coast from Roanoke Island in 1584, described a land "so full of grapes as the very beating and surge of the sea overflowed them . . . In all the world, the like abundance is not to be found."

Legend credits Raleigh with discovering the Scuppernong grape on Roanoke Island and introducing it elsewhere. This accounts for the fame of the so-called Mother vine, once called the Walter Raleigh vine, which is one of the tourist attractions at Manteo on the historic island near the site of Raleigh's Lost Colony. The vine has a trunk almost two feet thick, is said to be at least 300 years old, and still produces grapes. With a few neighboring vines, it supplied the Mother Vineyard Winery, which operated at Manteo until 1954.

In 1961, Richards Wine Cellars in Virginia, then the principal producer of Scuppernong wine under the Mother Vineyard brand, offered Carolina farmers five-year contracts to grow Muscadines at $200 a ton and also offered to provide them with vines to plant. A vineyard-planting boom started in North Carolina, where farmers' income from tobacco was beginning to decline.

Although Muscadine grapes can be eaten fresh or made into juice, jam, or jelly, the purpose of the plantings was to produce grapes for wine. In 1965, the North Carolina legislature, convinced that the state's winegrowing industry was about to be reborn, voted an appropriation for Muscadine grape and wine research. At the State University in Raleigh, Dr. William Nesbitt started breeding new Muscadine varieties especially suited for North Carolina climates, and Dr. Dan Carroll set up an experimental winery in the Food Science Department to develop new types of Muscadine table wine. James A. Graham, the state director of agriculture, predicted that "North Carolina Scuppernong will someday win a place among the distinctive wines of the world."

Grape acreage in the state jumped from less than 400 acres in 1966 to almost 3000 acres in the 1970s. New Muscadine varieties, self-fertile and more vigorous than Scuppernong, were introduced. They now come in all colors, jet black, red, freckled, and in pearl hues as well as in the traditional bronze. This presents a problem in wine labeling, for the Muscadines have such names as Mish, Hunt, Creek, Thomas, Higgins, Tarheel, Magnolia, Noble, and Carlos, while the only name northern consumers know for Muscadine is Scuppernong. The recent trend has been to call any wine Scuppernong when it is made predominantly from Muscadines.

• 4 •

The fabulous Captain Paul Garrett, who became a multimillionaire selling wine with the Scuppernong flavor, was a North Carolinian. He was the dean of American vintners when I knew him in the early 1930s, a tall, portly, forceful man with a deep voice and a soft southern accent. His title of "captain" was not military, but was bestowed by his employees, who also called him "the boss."

He was born in 1863, the second year of the Civil War, on the Edgecombe County farm of his father, country doctor Francis Marion Garrett. In 1865, his father and his wealthy uncle, Charles Garrett, purchased North Carolina's first commercial winery, the Médoc Vineyard, established in 1835 by Methodist preacher Sidney Weller near Enfield in neighboring Halifax County. Weller, a northerner, had made a fortune growing mulberries, had lost it in the silk business, then planted vines among his mulberry trees, and although an ardent Prohibitionist, had become wealthy again by making and selling wine.

At the age of fourteen, Paul Garrett quit military prep school and went to live with his uncle, who ran the winery, to learn the wine business. He worked in the vineyard, bought grapes from growers in neighboring counties, made the wine, loaded barrels on wagons, and taught Sunday school in the village of Ringwood. At twenty-one, when his uncle died, he became a salesman for the Garrett winery. He traveled through Arkansas, Tennessee, and Texas with a vial of Scuppernong wine in his pocket, inviting saloon-keepers to taste and to buy it for sale in competition with whiskey. In 1900, when he was thirty-seven, he contracted to sell the winery's entire output, but when his commissions mounted, the winery's new proprietor refused to deliver. Paul then established his own winery, first at Littleton, then at Chockoyotte, near Weldon, calling it Garrett & Company.

In the next nineteen years, Paul Garrett built a nationwide wine empire. He started by outbidding other wineries for Scuppernong grapes, buying all he could find. He began blending the juice with New York and California wines, but kept the Scuppernong flavor predominant. He called Scuppernong "the

Captain Paul Garrett, the North Carolinian whose Scuppernong-flavored "Virginia Dare" was the best-known American wine before and after National Prohibition.

finest wine in the world," but saw drawbacks in its name: Other vintners could use it on spurious wines; it was well known in the South, but the name meant nothing to northerners. Garrett also knew it was garbled from an Indian word, and he tried spelling it "Escapernong." He objected, too, to labeling American wines after European types as "sauternes" or "burgundy." Seeking a name that no one else could copy, he tried calling his white wine "Minnehaha" and his red "Pocahontas." Then he had a better idea: Because Scuppernong was the first American wine, he named it for the first child born of English parents in America—Virginia Dare—and Virginia Dare white and red became known to almost everybody in the nation.

By 1903 Garrett had five wineries in North Carolina, the largest one at Aberdeen, and vineyards on Dare Island and at Plymouth. But mounting Prohibitionist strength in the state threatened his wineries, so he established a larger plant at Norfolk in neighboring Virginia. When North Carolina went Dry in 1908, he had to rush the juice from his Aberdeen cellar to Norfolk before fermentation could set in and make it illegal. Nine years later, Virginia, too, had gone Dry, and Garrett moved permanently to New York State. By 1913, he had established vineyards and wineries at Penn Yan, Canandaigua, and Hammondsport in the Finger Lakes District and also the Mission Vineyard and Winery at Cucamonga in Southern California. When Wartime Prohibition began in 1919, he had seventeen plants processing grape juice or wine in North Carolina, Virginia, Ohio, Missouri, New York, and California, with a total capacity of 10 million gallons.

Garrett could have retired with his millions, but refusing to believe that Prohibition could last, he sought ways to hold his empire together until Repeal. He first sold dealcoholized Virginia Dare wine, which buyers spiked with alcohol, but its popularity soon waned. Then he lost a million dollars promoting a cola-flavored grape drink called Satenet, and another million on a venture in the flavoring extract business. He recouped with his Virginia Dare wine tonic, and then with grape concentrate for home winemaking. Then there was his ill-fated "Vine-Glo" venture, described in Chapter 2. Meanwhile he crusaded for modification of the Volstead Act to permit the sale of light wine, which he called "the antitoxin of alcoholism." If table wine could be sold as food, free of taxes like other farm products, he said, the winegrowing industry could furnish employment to 8 million Americans.

When Repeal arrived in 1933, Garrett was the only vintner ready again to sell his wine in every Wet state. Virginia Dare white and red were displayed in every wine store, and millions hummed the first* singing commercial ever broadcast for wine, "Say it again . . . Virginia Dare."

The enthusiastic Captain ranged through the South in the early 1930s, urging more planting of Scuppernong vineyards. He enlisted the help of Harry L. Hopkins and the Federal Rural Resettlement Administration. It was arranged that Scuppernong vines, five acres per family, would provide the chief cash crop for resettled farmers in Georgia and South Carolina, the cash crop second to tung oil trees in Florida, and the crop second to strawberries in Louisiana. In North Carolina, sufficient vines were propagated to set out 4000 acres. At Garrett's prompting, a grape growers' co-operative was organized to start a winery in Virginia.

But few new vineyards were planted. Dry Congressmen forbade Harry Hopkins to make grapes the basis for the economy of any Rural Resettlement projects. Besides, Garrett's campaign was forty years too early. Not enough markets were open for wine as yet; much of the nation and most of the South, in particular, were still legally Dry.

Scuppernong grapes continued to be scarce, and Virginia Dare gradually lost its unique flavor. As Garrett was compelled to rely more on his California vineyards for grapes, Virginia Dare became more and more a bland-tasting California wine.

In his sixty-second year as a vintner, still preaching "American

---

*But not the first advertisement ever sung for wine, because French champagne firms during the nineteenth century regularly paid performers in the music halls of England to sing such songs as "Champagne Charlie," which advertised Moët et Chandon, and "Clicquot, the Wine for Me."

wines for Americans," Captain Garrett fell ill of pneumonia in New York City, and on March 18, 1940, he died at the age of seventy-six. His family life had been tragic, three of his four sons dying as infants. When his fourth son, Charles, died in 1930 at the age of sixteen, the Captain built in his memory a great chapel on Bluff Point overlooking Keuka Lake in New York State, an architectural gem in the woods, which he deeded to the Rochester Diocese of the Episcopal Church. There the Captain and his wife are buried with their sons. Garrett's wine empire went out of existence, but his Scuppernong blend called Virginia Dare and his idea of building an American wine industry have survived.

• 5 •

The southern Bible Belt was described by the late Will Rogers as those states where citizens "stagger to the polls to vote dry." These are the last tottering strongholds of the professional Prohibitionists and their allies, the old moonshiners of the Blue Ridge and Great Smoky Mountains. As late as 1981, almost a third of the counties in the South still were legally Dry (more than a third in Alabama, Georgia, and Mississippi, more than half in Tennessee). Wine, where available, was burdened with exorbitant taxes or was variously restricted in sale. This, and the drinking customs—Coca-Cola in the morning, as traditional as the Englishman's afternoon tea, and corn liquor with branch water as the beverage of hospitality—help to explain why little table wine theretofore was drunk in the South. It is changing gradually now, however, because with the influx of industries, thousands of families have moved in from northern states where the use of dry table wines is becoming customary. Per capita wine consumption in the South has more than doubled in ten years, and more Dry counties are voting Wet. Winegrowing is reviving in those southern states where the political strength of the Drys is waning, but it lags in states where they are still strong.

South Carolina, although legally Wet, is a case in point. It had two thousand acres of vineyards and led the southern states in grape growing until North Carolina experienced its Muscadine-planting boom. But much of South Carolina's grape crop is shipped fresh or as juice to wineries in New York and Georgia, and the state's promotional literature makes no mention of wine.

Among the scrub pines in the Sand Hills country near Patrick in Chesterfield County is the largest single vineyard in the South,

300 acres neatly planted with Muscadine and Labrusca grape varieties and with berries for blackberry wine. Adjoining the vineyard is the oldest winery in South Carolina, Tenner Brothers. It is an unprepossessing concrete structure, recently increased in capacity to 2 million gallons by a battery of outdoor wine tanks of stainless steel, and is not open to visitors; it is absentee-owned. Sal, Al, and Lukie Tenner, former Charleston tire dealers, entered the wine and restaurant business at Charlotte, North Carolina, in 1935, then established the winery at Patrick in 1953 when South Carolina granted them a preferential tax on wine made from South Carolina grapes and berries. The tax on their wine was 45 cents a gallon compared to $1.08 on wines from outside the state. Several years later the Tenner Brothers had financial difficulties, and in 1966 they sold out to Mack Sands's companies, which operate the Richards winery in Virginia, the Canandaigua winery in New York State, and the Bisceglia winery in California.

South Carolina has two younger wineries. At Woodruff in Spartanburg County, Richard Leizear in 1976 organized a group of grape growers to convert his grape-juice plant into the half-million-gallon Oakview Plantations winery and made a wide variety of grape and fruit wines, but it did not prosper and was sold to new owners, who renamed it the Foxwood Wine Cellars. Its main current products are Muscadine, Labrusca, apple, and peach wines.

Two miles north of Lake City, off Highway 378 in Florence County, wine buff dentist Dr. James Truluck planted twenty acres of vines in 1972 and began making table wines in his home. Seven years later, he had built a three-story 35,000-gallon winery with an underground aging cellar, modeled after those the doctor admired while he was with the Air Force Dental Corps in southern France. Now he has added an attractive tasting room, and Truluck white, rosé, and red wines are being sold in Lake City, Charleston, and in two other southern states. At first he grew only French-American hybrid grapes, but soon began adding Vinifera varieties. In 1982 he sold his first Cabernet Sauvignon and White Riesling and started making bottle-fermented champagne of a Munson grape named Ellen Scott. The Truluck Vineyard, expanded to 120 acres, is managed by the doctor's sons Jay and Bowen.

In 1980 South Carolina, to encourage the planting of wine grapes, passed a farm winery law that reduced the state excise tax from 59 cents a gallon to 5 cents on locally grown wines. A South Carolina Grape Festival is celebrated each August at York, sponsored by the York County Grape Growers Association and the York Junior Chamber of Commerce. The festival features grape judging, a grape stomping, a beauty pageant, a queen contest, and a parade. For the first nine years the program contained nothing about wine, but since 1974 the growers' wives have been distributing their recipes for homemade wine to the celebrants. Concord was the county's main grape variety when the festival was founded, but because of its low sugar content, many of the vineyards have been replanted lately with Muscadines. York County grape growers own two mechanical harvesters, which work especially well in Scuppernong vineyards. The growers once also talked of building a winery, but when Virginia vintner Mack Sands increased the price he had been paying them for Scuppernongs, the winery proposal died.

The South Carolina Agricultural Experiment Station at Clemson University has an experimental vineyard, but the university has no wine research program. Horticulture Professor Harold J. Sefick, who bred grapes at Clemson for twenty years, happened to have a hobby interest in winemaking. Of necessity, he conducted his wine experiments at home.

Although the Drys have kept South Carolina's winegrowing history a secret, they have neglected to change the state map. It still shows the town of Bordeaux (originally New Bordeaux), named for the most famous wine city of France. New Bordeaux was founded by French Huguenot emigrés, who in 1764 were granted 30,000 acres by the British government to found a grape and wine industry along the upper Savannah River.

Old-time residents of Abbeville, in the South Carolina Piedmont, still remember Dr. Joseph Togno's Montevino vineyard and winery; the physician's rock house, built in 1859, is a landmark of the town. The city of Aiken, near the Savannah River nuclear plant, was famous in the 1860s for a claret made there by Benson and Merrier's Winery from Isabella grapes. The Aiken Vinegrowing Society published in 1858 an essay on winegrowing in the South in which the author, A. de Caradeuc, advised farmers to grow grapes in addition to their cotton, sugar, and rice:

A few leisure days in the winter, of which there are so many, and a few hours in the grassy season, devoted to one or two acres of his hitherto poorest and most worthless land, will insure him a handsome income, and a pleasant beverage more wholesale and agreeable than Peach Mobby or Persimmon Beer, and more conducive to his and his children's morale than Whiskey, that bane of our country, which it will finally drive out of use.

• 6 •

The wine revolution has also reached Georgia, with four wineries starting to produce Vinifera wines in the Peach State's northeastern hill country in 1983.

In the village of North High Shoals off Highway 53 in Oconee County, University of Georgia engineer Bill Rosser and his wife Barbara bonded a 10,000-gallon modern cellar and tasting room on their four-year-old, thirteen-acre Apalachee Vineyard and crushed their first commercial vintage of Riesling, Carmine, and Cabernet Franc. Rosser and a dozen other growers of Old World wine grapes have organized the Georgia Grape Growers Association and in 1983 obtained passage of the state's first farm winery law. It allows the winegrowers to sell wines on their premises and at as many as five additional retail outlets which they can establish elsewhere in the state. Georgia-grown table wines are taxed 40 cents a gallon by the state, compared to $1.50 per gallon collected on such wines grown elsewhere.

In the same year, on Interstate 85 at Braselton in Jackson County, ground was broken to start construction of Château Elan, planned as a half-million-gallon winery with 250 acres of six Vinifera varieties already being planted along the Interstate, all part of a future convention center, hotel, and restaurant complex. Château Elan (a French word that suggests enthusiasm) is a $5 million investment by Georgian and European businessmen headed by Donald Panoz, who owns pharmaceutical firms in Georgia and Ireland. President of the winery is former California winemaker Edmund Friedrich. Born and trained in viniculture in the Moselle Valley of Germany, Friedrich made wine in Arkansas and at two large California wineries before he quit the San Martin Winery in 1982 to start Château Elan.

The third new Georgia winery, Habersham Vineyards, was opened a year later in Baldwin, near Gainesville, by Atlanta investor Tom Slick and his wife Lindy. Their thirty-acre mostly Vinifera vineyard is three miles north of Clarkesville. The Slicks also use Vinifera grown by Gay Dellinger at her Split Rail Vineyard near Cartersville. Fourth to open was Chattanooga (Tenn.) internist Maurice Rawlings' 5000-gallon Georgia Wines cellar near Chickamauga.

There already were two Georgia wineries. Three years before the farm winery law was passed, vegetable grower Thomas Bunn and his wife Bernelle had begun making tomato wine on their Happy B Farm at Forsyth, southeast of Atlanta, but found they couldn't sell it because the old Georgia law prohibited sale at the winery. The legislature changed that in 1979, and the Bunns since have been selling their tomato wine and have added wines of apples, peaches, and Scuppernong.

The other Georgia winery is the 2-million-gallon Monarch Wine Company plant on Sawtell Avenue in Atlanta, but its principal product is peach wine. It was built in 1936, when Georgia repealed its Prohibition Law and Governor Eugene Talmadge was seeking a way to dispose of the state's peach surplus. He got the legislature to set lower taxes on wine made of Georgia-grown fruit than on out-of-state wines. Monarch's owners also operate a fruit distillery at Roberta in Crawford County.

General James E. Oglethorpe, the founder of Georgia in 1733, required the first settlers to plant grapes for wine and mulberries for silk, for shipment to England. Although Oglethorpe prohibited drinking in the colony, there is evidence that wine was made during the General's time. The first commercial winegrower probably was Thomas McCall, whose vineyard was planted in Laurens County on the Oconee River before 1823. The *Southern Cultivator* in December 1858 referred to Charles Axt of Crawfordsville in Taliaferro County as "one of the most successful vintners of the South." By 1880, when the U.S. Department of Agriculture made its study of grape and wine production, Georgia was the sixth largest winegrowing state in the nation, producing 903,244 gallons from 2991 acres of vineyards, almost double the gallonage made in New York State in that year. The leading Georgia winegrowing counties were Bibb, Chatham, Fulton, Houston, Pulaski, and Randolph. Wild Scuppernong was the chief grape used, but the red bunch grape called Norton was reported making the best Georgia wine. In the 1890s the Georgia Vineyard Company at Tallapoosa in Haralson County was making 50,000 gallons of wine and juice annually, and forty families in a Hungarian settlement nearby were making wines that sold at fancy prices in New York. All this ended, however, when the state went Dry in 1907.

In contrast to Georgia's Piedmont counties, where the four new wineries are growing Vinifera grapes, the lowland counties of the state grow only Scuppernong and other Muscadines. There are prolific Scuppernong vineyards in Sumter County, the home of former President and ex-peanut farmer Jimmy Carter at Plains. A large Muscadine vineyard also thrives among the lakes at the famous Callaway Gardens near Pine Mountain in Harris County. The crop there is used to make Muscadine preserves, jelly, and sauce, which are featured in the Gardens' country gift and food stores. There is also a delectable Muscadine ice cream.

Georgia, unlike South Carolina, encourages viticultural research. New Muscadine varieties have been developed at the Horticultural Research Station at Experiment, south of Atlanta. Its Fry grape, named for retired Georgia grape breeder Byard O. Fry, is almost as large as a golf ball. Planting of Muscadines by Georgia farmers has quintupled since 1965 from 200 to more than 1000 acres. Easy to cultivate and to harvest mechanically, they yield almost ten tons to the acre. Most of the Muscadines are grown to make wine, but not for Georgians to drink. Much of the crop is shipped to New York State to be made into Scuppernong wine for consumption in the North.

• 7 •

Even more dramatic, from the historical standpoint, is the revival of winegrowing in Florida, where four wineries have started since 1979 and more are being planned.

When the British admiral, Sir John Hawkins, relieved the starving French Huguenots at Fort Caroline in Florida in 1565, he found they had "twenty hogshead of wine made from the native grapes." Since the grapes almost certainly were Muscadines, that Florida Scuppernong, made four centuries ago, was the original American wine.

In Florida, as in the other colonies, there were early attempts to grow Vinifera wine grapes brought from Europe, with the same disappointing results. After the Civil War, immigrants to Florida from the North brought their favorite Labrusca grapes, such as Concord, Niagara, Worden, and Ives. Extensive plantings were made around Orlando, and by 1894 there were 500 acres in Orange County alone, but by 1900 most of the vineyards had died. Then came the Prohibition-era wine-grape boom of the 1920s. Nearly 5000 acres of new vineyards were planted in Lake, Orange, and Putnam counties, this time mainly of the Munson hybrid varieties that were growing in Texas. Several years later, most of those vines, too, had succumbed to "the grape decline"—Pierce's Disease. After each of these debacles, there remained only the wild native Muscadines.

A half century after the last unsuccessful attempt to grow grapes for wine in Florida, farm leaders noted that commercial-size Muscadine vineyards were springing up in several counties of the state. The grapes were being sold at "U-pick" prices to home winemakers and to householders as fresh dessert fruit. This attracted the attention of citrus growers, many of whom, plagued by periodic crop-destroying freezes, were looking about for some other fruit to grow.

In 1979, the Florida legislature decided to try once again to develop a wine industry in the Sunshine State. As vineyardist Tom Hughes put it to the 200-member Florida Grape Growers Association, "It is time to bring winegrowing back to its original home." At the behest of the grape growers, the legislature voted to free locally grown wine entirely from the exorbitant $1.75-per-gallon Florida wine tax, which in 1983 was raised to $2.25 per gallon, highest in the nation. This offered any wine grown in Florida a substantial selling-price advantage over wine brought from elsewhere to be sold in the state.

As soon as the legislature had acted, the state universities at Gainesville and Tallahassee were embarked on programs of wine-growing research. Almost all of the grapes growing in the Florida "U-pick" vineyards were Muscadines, and this was also true in the vineyards of the four farm wineries which started during the next four years. This presented a wine-palatability problem. People who grew up where Muscadine grapes ripen, breathing their intense fragrance, love wines with the Muscadine taste, but it is not always acceptable to wine consumers who were reared anywhere else. (Perhaps, suggests Florida scientist Joseph Marcy, it takes repeated exposure to products with intense flavors before we develop a liking for them, as with limburger cheese.)

But also being planted in Florida were new disease-resistant bunch-grape varieties that can be used to make wines free of the overpowering Muscadine taste. From one such grape named Stover, Dr. Robert Bates at the university's food science laboratory at Gainesville has made white wines that taste surprisingly like California and Old World types. Meteorologist Dan Mills, at Esmond and Malinda Grosz's vineyard near Ocala, experimented with their newly planted Stover grapes and made a nearly perfect Old World-style champagne. The Stover, some think, may be the grape with which to make blended wines that can dilute the powerful Muscadine flavor yet retain a hint of its fragrance.

There already was a citrus winery at Tampa, named Fruit Wines of Florida, before the 1979 state wine law was passed. The four new ones started since have increased the number in the state to five. Fruit Wines' owner, Joseph Midulla, dislikes the Muscadine taste. He since has planted a sixty-acre vineyard, including the Stover, along Hays Road off Route 52 in Pasco

County, twenty miles north of Tampa. His Fresno State University-trained enologist Mary Studt has made a white Stover wine so good that Midulla named the wine for the grape's originator at the Leesburg Research Center, retired Professor Loren H. Stover—"Laurens Blanc." Midulla also named a new non-Muscadine red wine for Stover's successor, Dr. John Mortensen—"Jean de Noir."

Veteran hobbyist winemaker Foster Burgess and his wife Rebecca operate Florida's first farm winery, built in 1980. It is the 10,000-gallon Alaqua Vineyard cellar on their nine-acre Muscadine vineyard on Highway 20 ten miles north of Freeport, near the Eglin Air Force Base and Choctawhatchee Bay. Their best-selling wine, a sweet white called Welder for that grape, has scarcely any of the Muscadine taste, but in their semi-dry and sweet red wines called Noble, that fragrance is pronounced.

Burgess's daughter Jeanne had left two years earlier for Mississippi State University, the nearest school that specializes in wine, to earn a postgraduate enology degree. She returned to manage and make wine at the new 10,000-gallon Florida Heritage Winery and its attractive tasting room, which were built in 1981 by Tampa internist Dr. Robert C. Price, Jr. and his wife Inge. It is a mile northwest of Anthony, off US 301 in Marion County. Jeanne's first wines, equal to the best Muscadines, were the 1981 dry Welder white and her red Carlos dry and semi-dry.

In 1983, Jeanne left there to manage the new 50,000-gallon Lafayette Vineyard and Winery, a two-story French Provincial cellar and tasting room on US 90 off Interstate 10, seven miles east of the state capitol in Tallahassee. It is on a seventy-acre vineyard of Muscadines, Stover, French hybrids, Vinifera, and Florida H 18-37 (a non-Muscadine not yet named), planted that spring for attorney Gary Ketchum and accountant C. Gary Cox.

California orthopedic surgeon Terrell Bounds and his wife Beverly have planned a winery to be built by 1985 on Interstate 10 at De Funiak Springs in Walton County. It will use the grapes from their nearby forty-acre Chautauqua Indian Hill Vineyard, planted in 1980 with Muscadines.

Another new Florida winery named Wines of St. Augustine opened in 1983 opposite Ybor Square in the city of Tampa. It is headed by veteran enologist Edward Gogel, who has made every conceivable type of wine in Illinois, New York State, North Carolina, and California. He plans to produce Florida Muscadine, Stover, and a Florida orange champagne. In 1984, home winemakers David Brightbill and Mike Hunter were preparing to build a "Black Creek Farm Winery" on the Miccosukee Land

Co-operative near Tallahassee, which would increase to six the number of wineries in the state.

• 8 •

Alabama, the very heart of Dixie, has a commercial winery, the first to open in the Cotton State during this century. It is Jim and Marianne Eddins's 60,000-gallon Perdido Vineyard mission-style cellar on their fifty-acre all-Muscadine vineyard at the Rabun-Perdido exit from Interstate 65 in Baldwin County, fifty miles northeast of Mobile. Alabama-born civil engineer Jim Eddins and his biologist wife began planting their vineyard in 1972. They sold grapes to "U-pick" home winemakers and some to a Florida vintner (until he died). The Eddinses wanted to build a winery, but in Alabama at that time only licensed wholesalers and retailers and state monopoly stores were allowed to sell wine. They appealed to the legislature, and a farm winery law was passed in June 1979. The Eddinses rushed to get their winery built in time to crush their harvest in September, but only to watch Hurricane Frederic strip the grapes off their vines. To make the 1979 vintage, they had to buy Muscadines from Arkansas.

Alabamans like the Perdido wines that they taste at the winery, especially the almost-dry white Magnolia, the semi-dry White Muscadine, and the Noble dry red. In 1981, Jim began blending Magnolia and Noble to make a rosé. He thought of naming it for the nearby stretch of Gulf coast that people call "the Redneck Riviera," but Marianne demurred. A woman visitor, newly returned from Europe, suggested, "Why not say it in French?" When the label was printed, Perdido Vineyard overnight became famous nationally and abroad because "Rosé Cou Rouge" on their label translates to "Redneck Rosé."

What few Alabamans know is that their state has a winegrowing history dating back to the early nineteenth century. After Napoleon's defeat at Waterloo in 1813, remnants of his scattered army emigrated to a Vine and Wine Colony near the present community of Demopolis on the Tombigbee and Black Warrior rivers. The colonists brought and planted vines from Bordeaux, but all the vines died, and most of the settlers eventually returned to France. Another winegrowing colony, of members from northern European countries, settled in 1880 in northern Alabama, opened several wineries, and founded a town they named Fruithurst, which maps still show on Highway 78. Four vineyards and wineries continued operating at Fruithurst until the early

1900s, when the new Prohibition laws were drying up the markets for wine, and the colony declined.

Vinifera and French hybrid wine grapes grow well in the mountain areas of northern Alabama. The Eddinses plan to buy grapes from the new vineyards springing up there, and to begin making some Old World wine types in addition to their Muscadine kinds.

• 9 •

Mississippi had vineyards and wineries a century ago, and since repealing its Prohibition law in 1966—the last state to do so—it again has become a winegrowing state.

The *Southern Cultivator,* in March 1875, described the Scuppernong wine made by J. M. Taylor of Rienzi, Alcorn County, Mississippi, as "nonpareil, a great gift of the gods to the Sunny South." Dr. Dunbar Rowland's *History of Mississippi* records that wines from twenty Mississippi counties were exhibited in 1885 at the World International and Cotton Exposition in New Orleans. There were thirty-one wineries in Holly Springs, Enterprise, Forest, Meridian, Waynesboro, Carthage, Oxford, and Pontotoc until the state went Dry in 1908.

It therefore was not surprising that with Mississippians drinking a million gallons per year of wine from elsewhere, the state legislature in 1976 passed a law to revive winegrowing, reducing the enormous $1800 winery license fee to $10 and cutting the state per gallon wine tax from 35 cents to 5 cents for Mississippi wine.

A year later, Ottis Rushing and his agronomist son Sam opened the new Winery Rushing on Old Drew Road three miles east of Merigold and made the first wine produced legally in the Magnolia State in eighty years. The law allowed them to use grapes from other states until their thirty-acre Muscadine vineyard could begin to bear grapes. By the 1980s their vines were bearing, Sam had expanded the winery to 25,000 gallons, and his wife Diane, besides running their tasting room, was selling seven Rushing wines in all the wet counties of the state.

The second Mississippi winery, opened the year after the Rushings', is at the Thousand Oaks Vineyard on Highway 82 west of Starkville. Bob Burgin manages the vineyard and winery while his wife Peggy runs cellar tours, holds tastings, and does all the wine marketing. Although their main wines are of Muscadines, they have four types made of French hybrids, which grow on half of their twenty-five acres.

On Frost Bridge Road off Highway 510 in Matherville, Wayne County, is the 50,000-gallon Almarla Vineyard winery, bonded in 1979. Dr. Alex Mathers, the former director of scientific services for the Federal bureau in Washington that supervises the nation's wine industry, first experimented in growing French-American hybrids, but when the hybrid vines began to die, he planted thirty-five acres of Muscadines. He makes ten red and white wines and is proudest of his dry chablis and burgundy, although all of his best sellers are sweet. (Almarla stands for Alex, his wife Margaret, and their daughter Lala.)

Mississippi's fourth winegrower is veterinarian Scott Galbraith, who opened his 10,000-gallon Old South Winery in 1979 on Concord Street in Natchez, around the corner from his home. His thirteen-acre Muscadine vineyard is at Meadville, several miles away.

Mississippi State University at Starkville has the leading winemaking school in the South. Dr. Louis N. Wise, the MSU vice president, launched a wine research project in 1975 when a state survey confirmed that Mississippi could grow grapes profitably. A Swiss-type chalet on a hill overlooking the campus became the handsomest enology laboratory in the nation. In charge is microbiologist Boris Stojanovic, whose parents were winegrowers in Yugoslavia. His assistant is appropriately named Richard P. Vine, the former New York State winemaker who co-authored with Walter S. Taylor the *Home Winemakers Handbook*, published in 1968. In 1981, Vine published *Commercial Winemaking*, a textbook of his own.

• 10 •

Tennessee, too, was once a winegrowing state. A Catawba wine from the Willowbeck Vineyard, near Wartrace in New Bedford County, won first prize at the 1857 State Fair in Nashville and at the 1875 Louisville National Fair in competition with wines from northern states. The Chattanooga *Times* in 1880 reported there were "150 acres around Chattanooga within a radius of five miles entirely devoted to grape culture" and that "nearly every cultivated field between Rossville and the railroad tunnel has a vineyard of some size."

A preliminary step was taken in 1977 to revive winegrowing in the Volunteer State. The Tennessee legislature passed a Grape and Wine Law setting a $50 annual license fee for wineries and reducing the state's exorbitant $1.18 per gallon wine tax to 5 cents on wine from products of Tennessee farms. Four small

Tennessee wineries have opened since 1980 and the building of several more is expected when the state corrects flaws in the 1977 law. The flaws, inserted in the law by the liquor lobby, restricted wine sale at wineries and prohibited winegrowers from selling at wholesale. The retail sale restriction was partly corrected in 1983.

First of the new Tennessee wineries to open for business was retired Air Force Sergeant Major Fay Wheeler's Highland Manor Winery, a 1000-gallon cellar in the basement of his home on Highway 127 three miles south of Jamestown in otherwise Dry Fentress County. He has seven acres of Vinifera, French hybrid, and Labrusca vines, planted since the early 1970s. His wife Kathy has turned her dining room into their tasting room. Their first vintage of Cabernet Sauvignon in 1980 quickly sold out.

In the same year, ceramic engineer Terry Tiegs of the Oak Ridge Laboratory bonded the 2000-gallon Tiegs Vineyard winery in the basement of his home on Jackson Bend Road off Highway 95 three miles south of Lenoir City. Tiegs's Cedar Cellars Red and White were made of the mélange of bunch-grape varieties on his young three-acre vineyard. A year later, Everett and Miriam Brock bonded a 10,000-gallon cellar among the tourist shops on Brookside Village Highway in Gatlinburg and named it the Smoky Mountain Winery because it is near the entrance to Great Smoky Mountains National Park. Michael Mancuso, the former owner of the Villa Medeo winery in Indiana, made the Smoky Mountain wines. Tennessee's fourth winery, on Madison Avenue in Memphis, is named Laurel Hill for owner Raymond Skinner's young twelve-acre Vinifera and hybrid vineyard in Lawrence County.

What progress has been made thus far in reviving the state's wine industry results from the work of the Tennessee Viticultural and Oenological Society, organized by hobbyist winegrowers throughout the state in 1973. One of the leaders is retired Judge William O. Beach, who grows grapes near his home at Clarksville and makes wines and champagnes that have won prizes in competitions at Nashville and Atlanta. When the remaining flaws in the state law are corrected, Judge Beach intends to open a winery on his Beachhaven Vineyard.

Tennessee has many different climates between the mountains on the east and the Mississippi River on the west. There are many small vineyards of bunch grapes on the central plateau, where there are traces of pre-Prohibition wineries, and of Scuppernongs at lower elevations. Grape growing is of special interest as a way to supplement the declining income of Tennessee tobacco growers.

If the progress in reviving viniculture continues in the seven states covered in this chapter, the flavor spectrum of good American wines is likely to include many from the southeastern states.

4

The Middle Atlantic States

WINE TOURING in eastern America can be both a fascinating and a puzzling experience. Why is it, you may wonder, that Virginia, with centuries of winegrowing experience, has become dotted with new winegrowing estates during the past few years, yet the entire state is producing less wine than it did two decades ago? How does one explain that Pennsylvania, with more than 9000 acres planted to grapes, had not even one producing winery until 1963, but now has more than thirty? What enabled little New Jersey, with only several hundred acres of vines, to make as much as 800,000 gallons a year until the 1970s, when it dwindled to a fraction of that quantity? And how did it happen that vines from a seven-acre vineyard in Maryland revolutionized the planting of wine grapes in hundreds of localities in the United States and Canada? To unravel these paradoxes, one needs to know some of the wine history of these states, their Wet-Dry politics, and the widely different taste preferences for wine that are emerging in America.

• 2 •

Virginia, as we have seen, was the first of the colonies to cultivate grapes for wine. The attempts to grow Vinifera, which began in 1619 under Lord Delaware, continued in Virginia for almost two centuries. Some of the vineyards succeeded in producing quantities of wine before plant diseases and insect pests killed the European vines. About 1716, historian Robert Beverley won a wager of 700 guineas from his neighbors by producing 700 gallons in a single vintage from his three-acre vineyard at Beverley Park in King and Queen County. But Beverley appar-

64

ently made the wine from native wild grapes, which he cultivated together with his few French vines. The only Virginia wines of any note in the eighteenth century were the red and white Rapidan, made by a colony of Germans who settled on the Rapidan River in Spotsylvania County after 1770. George Washington planted a garden vineyard at Mount Vernon, but there is no record of his having made any wine, although he made cider and distilled considerable quantities of applejack. In 1773, Dr. Filippo Mazzei of Tuscany brought Italian winegrowers with ten thousand European vine cuttings in a chartered ship to establish winegrowing in Virginia. Most of Mazzei's cuttings were planted at Monticello, the estate of Thomas Jefferson, in what is now Albemarle County. For thirty years Jefferson continued trying to grow Vinifera, even importing some of his vines directly from Château d'Yquem, and he is said once to have even imported some French soil. An advocate of wine as a temperate beverage, he hoped to establish winegrowing as an American industry, and while minister to France from 1785 to 1789, he made his own scientific studies of viticulture and winemaking. Jefferson finally admitted his failure with Vinifera when he recommended in 1809 that native vines, such as the Alexander, be planted instead.

In 1835, Dr. Daniel N. Norton of Richmond produced a domesticated nonfoxy native blue grape that made Virginia claret wine famous during the latter half of the nineteenth century. The Norton was virtually a Virginia monopoly, because this grape variety is difficult to ripen in regions north of the Potomac. Following the Civil War, winegrowing based on the Norton and other native grapes spread through the Piedmont and Blue Ridge regions. The Virginia Winegrowers Association had branches in Albemarle, Norfolk, Warren, and Fairfax, the leading grape-growing counties. The Monticello Wine Company at Charlottesville became so noted for its Norton Claret, which won a gold medal at Vienna in 1873 and a silver medal at Paris in 1878, that the city was called "the capital of the Virginia wine belt." The company's Delaware, Catawba, Hock, Norton Port, Virginia Sherry, and grape brandy, as well as the Claret, were sold throughout the East.

Virginia's wine production totaled 232,479 gallons by 1880, making it the eleventh largest wine-producing state in the Union. But during the next few decades, cities, counties, and whole states were going Dry. Competition from California wine was increasing. The markets for Virginia wines began to shrink. Grape prices declined, growers neglected their vineyards, and the vines soon died. When Virginia passed its state prohibition law in 1914, few vineyards of any size remained in the state.

A move to revive the Virginia wine industry was started by Captain Paul Garrett when National Prohibition ended in 1933. Garrett praised "the noble Virginia Claret," and Professor Ulysses P. Hedrick, the great New York viticulturist, described the Norton as "the best red wine grape grown in the Eastern States . . . best when grown in the soil and climate of central Virginia." A few of the old wineries reopened, and in 1934 the Monticello Grape Growers Co-operative Association was formed at Charlottesville with Bernard Peyton Chamberlain, an amateur winegrower and author of a wine book, as its president. Extensive plantings of grapes in the Piedmont counties were planned, but they never materialized; only a few thousand gallons of claret were made by the Association. Again, some new vineyards were planted after the Second World War, but lacking a market for their grapes, they were soon abandoned. When Professor George D. Oberle, who had organized the new wine-grape testing program at New York's Geneva Experiment Station, joined the Virginia Polytechnic Institute College of Agriculture at Blacksburg in 1948, he found nine wineries still bonded to operate in the state. But three were just then going out of business, and most of the others seemed likely to follow.

To historic Petersburg in Virginia after Repeal came Mordecai E. (Mack) Sands, retracing the footsteps of Captain Paul Garrett. Sands had decided to produce sweet Scuppernong wines in Virginia, as Garrett did, from grapes grown in the southeastern states. After he opened Richard's Wine Cellar on Pocahontas Street in Petersburg in 1951, the winery grew to more than 2 million gallons. Also like Garrett, Sands and his son Marvin persuaded farmers throughout the South to plant thousands of acres with Scuppernongs. But why make Scuppernong wine in Virginia when the grapes are grown in states farther south? The Sandses never explained, but it may be remembered that Garrett, too, established a winery in Virginia to avoid the hazards of Prohibition elections in the then Dry-dominated South.

Born in Brooklyn in 1898, Mack Sands entered the wine business in 1932 as a partner of Joey Applebaum in Geffen Industries, a small Long Island City winery which turned out millions of gallons during the early years following Repeal. Many of today's Federal wine regulations are said to have been aimed at reducing Geffen Industries' copious output from relatively few tons of fresh grapes. After Applebaum retired wealthy in 1945, Sands established a winery at Canandaigua, New York, where Garrett had had one of his many plants. Then, leaving his son Marvin in charge at Canandaigua, Mack Sands moved to Virginia to open the Richard's winery, which he named for his infant grandson. In 1956, the Sandses bought the Mother Vineyard Winery at Manteo, North Carolina, moved it to Petersburg, and adopted the Mother Vineyard name for their Scuppernong wine. Later they added the Tenner Brothers vineyard and winery at Patrick, South Carolina. Now, with their wineries in three eastern states and the Bisceglia winery in California, acquired in 1976, the Sandses have become the biggest vintners in the East. Their sweet pink Labrusca-flavored (20 percent) Richard's Wild Irish Rose, made at Canandaigua, is the largest-selling wine of its kind.

But for Mack Sands to become the successor to Garrett, one thing remained: to recover the Virginia Dare name. Following the Captain's death in 1940, Garrett & Company had moved to Cucamonga in California, then twice had been merged with California wineries. Ownership of the Virginia Dare brand meanwhile had passed to the Guild Wine Company of Lodi, California. The Sandses finally contracted with the Guild Company for a franchise to use the name. In 1967, Virginia Dare wines came back on the market. But only the white Virginia Dare has the Scuppernong flavor. The Sandses use the same Virginia Dare brand name on a "complete line" of generic, Labrusca, and blackberry wine types, all bottled at Canandaigua. (Richard's Wine Cellars no longer make Scuppernong. It is now made at the Sandses' winery in South Carolina.)

The three other large Virginia wineries made mainly fruit and berry wines, but Laird & Company's Virginia Wine Cellar at North Garden, which traces its founding back to 1780, also makes a "Sly Fox" brand of Labrusca grape wine.

• 3 •

The most rapid spread of winegrowing in the East has occurred in Virginia. Plantings of wine grapes have exploded from fewer than fifty acres in 1973 to almost a thousand acres in a single decade. The first plantings were of French-American hybrid varieties, but before long two-thirds were of the best Vinifera types. Twenty-three estate wineries, including two owned by Italian and German firms, opened in the Old Dominion during the short space of seven years. More vineyardists were getting ready to open wineries, and French and Swiss interests were exploring Virginia microclimates with the same idea.

What caused this dramatic growth? Grape growers knew that Virginia winters are milder than the extremes that can damage vines in states farther north. Virginia's legislature, aware of the gains in national wine consumption and of the state's nineteenth-century importance in winegrowing, passed a law in 1980 to encourage the starting of wineries on farms. Landowners in the rolling hills of Virginia's Piedmont saw wine grapes as a profitable new farm crop that could save their estates from the wave of urbanization approaching from Washington, an hour's drive away.

The first new Virginia winery to offer its estate-bottled wines for sale was airline pilot Charles Raney's Farfelu Vineyard cellar, opened in 1976 in a converted barn on his French hybrid vineyard off Route 647 in Rappahannock County near Flint. (Farfelu, he explains, is French slang for "unusual, far out.") Second, by a month, was Archie M. and Josephine Smith's Meredyth Vineyard winery, built around their one-time stable five miles from Middleburg on Route 628. Their son, Dr. Archie III, and his wife Suzelle returned from his philosophy-instructor job at Oxford University in England to help his parents run Meredyth Vineyard and its tasting room. Investment banker Albert Weed opened the third new winery on La Abra (The Cove) Farm in the Blue Ridge foothills of Nelson County, three miles northeast of Lovingston.

An ambitious winegrowing project in Virginia also began in 1976 on County Road 777 in Orange County near Barboursville. Zonin, Italy's largest privately owned wine company, started planting what Gianni Zonin said would be a 250-acre all-Vinifera vineyard. By 1980 the first twenty acres were producing, and Zonin's 20,000-gallon Barboursville winery was turning out Cabernet Sauvignon, White Riesling, and Chardonnay.

Elizabeth Furness meanwhile was honored by Governor John Dalton for producing Virginia's first Vinifera wine sold outside the state. It was the 1977 Chardonnay grown on her twenty-six-acre Piedmont Vineyard on Route 626 halfway between The Plains and Middleburg.

In the same year Zonin began, New Jersey utility executive James Randel and his wife Emma began planting French hybrids on her great-grandfather's estate off Route 686 two miles north of Edinburg in the Blue Ridge foothills of Shenandoah County. Their Shenandoah Vineyards winery has made Seyval Blanc, Chancellor, and Chambourcin equal to other wines of these grapes grown in the East. All Virginians during the early 1980s backed the new winegrowers of Shenandoah Valley in their fight to preserve that appellation on wine labels. There was bitter disappointment when the Federal government in 1982 granted the vineyardists of California's Shenandoah Valley in Amador County the same right to use the appellation, qualified with the name of the state.

In 1979, Dr. Gerhard W. R. Guth, a wealthy Hamburg, Germany physician, brought viticulturist Joachim Hollerith to Virginia from the famous Geisenheim Institute to begin planting Riesling and Chardonnay on the doctor's 2000-acre dairy farm on County Route 611 southeast of Culpeper. A winery named Rapidan Vineyards was built there in 1981, and its first three vintages have received wide acclaim.

In 1980, Professor of English and published poet Tom O'Grady of Hampton-Sydney College in Prince Edward County and his wife Bronwyn began selling Vinifera and hybrid wines from their six-acre Rose Bower Vineyard and tiny winery on Route 686 six miles west of the college. At Carter's Bridge on Route 20 south of Charlottesville, Pan American pilot Michael Bowles and his stewardess wife Lynn made their commercial debut in 1981 with their Montdomaine Cellars Chardonnay. By 1982, Jerusalem-born geologist Dirgham Salahi and his wife Corinne were expanding their 5000-gallon Oasis Vineyard winery to 75,000 gallons to accommodate the harvest from their thirty-acre vineyard near Hume. Other Virginia estate wineries included Karl Hereford's MJC Vineyards at Blacksburg, Robert Viehman's The Vineyard at Winchester, retired Navy Captain Josh Sherman's Chermont winery on County Road 626 near Esmont, Robert and Phoebe Harper's all-Vinifera Naked Mountain Vineyard on the southwest slope of that mountain near Markham, Joseph Geraci's Tri-Mountain cellar at Middletown, John Marquis's Blenheim Vineyards winery at Charlottesville, Arthur and Ercelle Rogers' Château Naturel Vineyard at Rocky Mount, and William Morrissette's small cellar at Woolwine, a locality to which the government granted the exclusive viticultural-area appellation Rocky Knob.

Latest to be bonded, in 1983, was Felicia (Mrs. John) Rogan's 10,000-gallon Oakencroft Farm winery on the seven-acre Vinifera and hybrid vineyard near her husband's Boar's Head Inn at Charlottesville. Mrs. Rogan led in founding the Jeffersonian Wine Grape Growers Society and its annual Albemarle Harvest Wine Festival, which has been held at the Inn since 1981. The Society has asked the government to approve "Monticello" as the viticultural area label for Charlottesville wines.

In the first French investment in winegrowing in the East,

forty acres of Vinifera vines were planted in 1983 on Route 612 south of Culpeper for Vavin, a group headed by Norman Martin of Culpeper and Jean Leduc of Paris. Construction of their 100,000-gallon Prince Michel Winery and planting of fifty more acres began in 1984.

Five miles west of Charlottesville, on County Road 677 near Ivy, the Seagram Wine Company has planted a ten-acre experimental vineyard of Vinifera varieties.

The Norton grape, which first made Virginia wines famous, apparently has not yet been used by any of the new Virginia wineries.

Enough comparative tastings with vintages grown elsewhere have thus far been held to prove that Virginia is producing world-class wines.

Virginia's very first champagne can be tasted at the Ingleside Plantation winery in Oak Park, Westmoreland County, off Route 636. How the champagne came to be made is a remarkable tale. Belgian-born Jacques Recht retired in 1980 as professor of enology at Brussels University because he and his wife Liliane had decided to sail their thirty-six-foot catamaran across the Atlantic to America's Great Lakes. During the ocean crossing, they happened to read James Michener's *Chesapeake,* so they sailed into the Bay and up the Potomac instead. By coincidence they met nurseryman Carl Flemer, who with his son Douglas was building the Ingleside winery and needed a winemaker. Recht took the job for a few weeks. He made a champagne of the hybrid grape Rayon d'Or, then decided to stay and make another of Chardonnay; and at this writing he was still there.

• 4 •

West Virginia once had a wine industry, and like its eastern neighbor, is becoming a winegrowing state again. Wine was made in the Kanawha River Valley near Charleston as early as 1826, when Nicholas Longworth was beginning to plant Catawba grapes for wine along the Ohio River south of Cincinnati. In that year, the Charleston *Western Courier* told of a dinner in the city at which toasts were drunk in a local wine "of excellent quality." One of the sights around Charleston is the newly restored Friend Brothers winery on Dutch Hollow Road in the city of Dunbar. Vaulted stone cellars are built into a hillside on which hundreds of acres of vines flourished before the Civil War. Labor shortage forced the winery to close in 1864. There still were vineyards and traces of old wineries when the Mountain State went Dry in 1919. At the repeal of Prohibition in 1933, West Virginia was one of the seventeen states that adopted the state monopoly liquor-store system, which attracts campaign contributions to governors from liquor firms that want the state stores to stock their brands.

During the late 1970s, as winegrowing began to revive in neighboring states, a farm winery bill was introduced in the West Virginia legislature and promptly was vetoed by Governor John D. ("Jay") Rockefeller IV. The bill was reintroduced in each of the next two annual legislative sessions and each time was vetoed again. But the third time, in 1981, a state grape growers' association had been organized. The legislature overrode the governor's veto while farm district legislators and vineyardists sang a song composed for the occasion, "Bye Bye Jaybird."

Charleston dentist Wilson Ward, confident the bill would pass eventually, had already started a winery, his 5000-gallon Fisher Ridge cellar on his young seven-acre hybrid and Vinifera vineyard near Liberty, twenty-five miles northeast of the capital. His "Fisher Ridge White" blend became the first West Virginia wine legally sold in this century.

In the same year the law became effective, Dr. Charles Whitehill, professor of music at Potomac State College at Keyser in eastern West Virginia, crushed the 1981 vintage at the tiny West-Whitehill Winery on Keyston Road. The winery is on the three-acre vineyard owned by the professor's partner, lawyer Stephen West, who lives across the nearby Pennsylvania border.

As this was being written, former navy supply officer Robert Pliska and his wife Ruth were bonding West Virginia's third winery, which they had built three years before on their twelve-acre vineyard of French hybrids off US 220, a mile northwest of Purgitsville.

Another bill repeatedly vetoed by Governor Rockefeller during the 1970s was also passed by the legislature over his veto. It allowed the sale of table wine in groceries for the first time since Repeal. When wines went on sale in foodstores in late 1981, West Virginia's rate of wine use, until then the lowest in the nation, jumped from two quarts per capita to seven quarts in a single year.

• 5 •

In Maryland, the seventeenth-century attempts to grow Old World wine grapes differed little from those in Virginia. Lord Baltimore, who is credited in many books with planting a 300-

acre vineyard on St. Mary's River in 1662, did establish "The Vineyard" land grant, but no vines were ever planted there. Recent research by Dr. John R. McGrew in Maryland discloses that Lord Baltimore's vines were brought from Europe but that they died before they reached the site. All of the early Maryland wines were made from wild grapes, says Dr. McGrew, until about 1756, when Colonel Benjamin Tasker, Jr., planted two acres with the Alexander grape at his estate, Belair (now a Levittown), in Prince George's County, and made his first "burgundy" three years later.

Winegrowing evidently then became popular, for the state legislature in 1828 incorporated a Maryland Society for Promoting the Culture of the Vine, empowering it to establish vineyards and to produce wine "for the purpose of introducing into the State of Maryland, and into our country generally, the extensive cultivation of the vine."

A Maryland resident of this period, Major John Adlum, gave America the Catawba grape. Adlum, a soldier of the Revolution, a judge, and a surveyor, settled after the war on Pierce's Mill Road, near Georgetown, and for many years experimented in winegrowing and other horticultural research. His estate of 200 acres, which he named "The Vineyard," is now a part of Rock Creek Park in Washington, D.C. In 1823, Adlum wrote *A Memoir on the Cultivation of the Vine in America and the Best Mode of Making Wine,* the first book on winegrowing to be published in this country. In it he relates his unsuccessful attempts to grow foreign vines and his subsequent success in making acceptable wines from indigenous grapes.

Adlum found the Catawba growing beside an inn operated by a Mrs. Scholl at Clarksburg in Montgomery County, Maryland. Mrs. Scholl's father appears to have acquired the grape directly from North Carolina, where it is said to have been found growing wild in 1802. One version credits a Senator Davy with bringing the vines to his friends in Maryland as gifts for their gardens. Adlum took cuttings from Mrs. Scholl's vines and planted them in his vineyard. The wine he made from their grapes was better than any he had made before. He first named the wine "Tokay" and sent samples to all the members of Congress. He also sent Thomas Jefferson a sample with one of his red wines. A letter from Jefferson to Adlum on April 11, 1823, reads:

I received the two bottles of wine you were so kind as to send me. The first, called Tokay, is a truly fine wine, of high flavor, and, as you assure me, there was not a drop of brandy in it; I may say it is a wine of good body of its own. The second bottle, a red wine, I tried when I had good judges at the table. We agreed it was a wine one might always drink with satisfaction, but of no particular excellence.

Adlum renamed the grape Catawba, which is evidence that he was aware of its origin on that river in North Carolina. He supplied cuttings to Nicholas Longworth, who planted them at Cincinnati and made the grape and its wine world-famous. A quarter-century later Adlum wrote that "its equal has not yet been found." Adlum said, in a letter to Longworth, that: "In bringing this grape into public notice, I have rendered my country a greater service than I would have done, had I paid off the National Debt."

• 6 •

Because in the mid-1930s a home winemaker in Baltimore disliked the Labrusca flavor of a wine he made from native grapes, the course of winegrowing in much of North America has been altered significantly during the past few decades. Failing to grow in Maryland the Vinifera grapes he preferred, this amateur introduced to this country the French-American hybrid varieties that are now planted extensively for winemaking in most states east of the Rockies and in Canada.

The amateur was Philip Marshall Wagner, an editorial writer for the Baltimore *Evening Sun*. Born in 1904 at New Haven, he grew up in Ann Arbor, Michigan, where his father was a professor of Romance languages at the University of Michigan. His parents drank wine with their meals at home, and Philip developed the taste of a connoisseur. When he joined the *Sun* in 1930, the eleventh year of Prohibition, his liking for wine led him to make it at home in partnership with a next-door neighbor. Finding it easier to make bad wine than good, he began reading French viniculture texts. Soon he had written a text in English, *American Wines and How to Make Them*, as a service to fellow amateurs.

Wagner had begun by buying grapes from California to make his wine, but when Prohibition was ending in 1933, his favorite varieties, Zinfandel and Carignane, were not being shipped to the East; the reopened wineries were using them in California. He then made a vintage out of the eastern Delaware grape, but being accustomed only to Vinifera wines, he had no liking for its Labrusca taste. Wondering what else he could use to make his wine, he happened to read about the hybrid wines that were

Philip and Jocelyn Wagner at their Boordy Vineyard nursery in Riderwood, a suburb of Baltimore. (*Courtesy of Hudson Cattell*)

being grown in France. He ordered a supply from Bordeaux, found others already in some American collections, and planted at Baltimore all he could get. By 1936, Wagner had made some wines from the hybrids that convinced him it was possible to grow, east of the Rocky Mountains, "wines that taste like wine."

He began writing articles and revised his book to tell others about the French hybrids. Then, people came asking to buy vines from him, and he soon found himself in the nursery business.

More vines planted meant more grapes harvested from his vineyard—more than enough grapes to make the 200 gallons per year the government permits a householder to produce free of tax. So the Wagners, Philip and his wife Jocelyn, built a winery. Then, when the winery, bonded in 1945, was full, the quantity of wine was more than they could drink, and the excess had to be sold. The Wagners made their first sales to Baltimore restaurants, Wagner delivering the wines himself on the way to the *Sun* office each morning. When he was too busy, Jocelyn made the deliveries; and both Wagners came to know the tradesmen's entrances of most hotels, restaurants, and clubs in Baltimore.

It was not long before connoisseurs in New York and Washington learned that entirely new kinds of American wines were being made in Maryland. More orders for wine than the Wagners could fill came from stores and hotels throughout the East. Making only 8000 gallons per year, they could have sold twenty times as much, but they decided not to try, and turned over their wine sales to a Washington wholesale house.

"Boordy Vineyard, J. & P. Wagner, Props." consisted of a little wood-and-stucco, French-type winery and seven hillside acres beside the Wagners' colonial farmhouse in Riderwood, one of Baltimore's more exclusive northern suburbs. What does "Boordy" mean? "Nothing," replied the Wagners, "except a small Maryland vineyard and its delightful products."

Wagner retired from the *Sun* to care for the vineyard and to update his books, rewriting his forty-year-old classic with a new title, *Grapes into Wine*. In 1981, the Wagners closed the Boordy winery and sold its name and equipment, but kept the Boordy Nursery to continue supplying their hybrids to growers in every state except Hawaii. The colonial farmhouse beside the nursery is still their home.

• 7 •

After thirty-five Boordy vintages made by the Wagners beginning in 1945, the thirty-sixth, the 1980 vintage, was crushed at the Boordy winery's capacious new home, the Robert Deford farm on Long Green Pike in Hydes, another Baltimore suburb ten miles northeast of Riderwood. To get ready for the vintage, young Robert Deford III had spent the preceding year studying enology in the University of California wine school at Davis. Rob's father, mother, sister Sally and her husband are his partners. Deford Sr. had produced grapes for the Wagners for many years, and his two-acre vineyard at Hydes is being expanded to twenty acres. Besides the well-known Boordy dry white and dry red, the Defords have added the first varietally labeled Boordy wine, the 1980 Seyval Blanc.

• 8 •

A Johns Hopkins University savant started what is now Maryland's oldest winery, the Montbray Wine Cellars, in 1966. It is near Westminster in Silver Run Valley, a quiet, idyllic depression in the undulating hills ten miles north of Westminster, only two miles from the Pennsylvania border. Dr. G. Hamilton Mowbray, a researcher in psychology, discovered the fascination of wine while studying for his doctorate at Cambridge University in England. Returning to Maryland to do research in the sensory processes at the University, he began growing hybrids in collaboration with Dr. Singleton. A visit to Dr. Frank in New York

State in 1958 inspired him to plant Chardonnay, Riesling, Pinot Noir, and Muscat Ottonel. They survived a series of winter freezes and thrived so well that he sold his home, because there was not enough land, bought a hundred-acre tract at Silver Run, and moved his vines there. His 7000-gallon winery (named for a Norman ancestor) is in an old German-style barn, which he has insulated, and on which he has painted a Pennsylvania Dutch hex sign to keep away hailstorms and floods. ("It works," says Mowbray; "we've had neither.")

Montbray is a family operation. Dr. Mowbray is the wine-maker, but his wife Phyllis does the labeling, keeps the books, and helps in the vineyard, and son Paul comes from New York to help with the vintage. Two nights a week Dr. Mowbray teaches classes in winemaking and wine appreciation at the university and community colleges. He serves in a consulting capacity to several other wineries in the East. Montbray wines, all aged in oak, are distinctive and flavorful. His perfectly dry 1980 Seyve Villard was a rare achievement, flawlessly delicious with all the lovely taste of lusciously ripe grapes. A record October freeze in 1974 enabled him to make America's first ice wine.*

Maryland now has a total of ten wineries, and that number may soon increase. On a hillside facing Church Hill Road in Frederick County, pharmacist W. Bret Byrd and his schoolteacher wife Sharon began in 1972 the planting of their present twenty-five acres of Vinifera and French hybrid vines. They built a concrete-block winery into the hill and began selling Chardonnay labeled "Byrd Vineyards" and hybrid wines labeled "Church Hill Manor," the name of their estate. They since have doubled their winery's capacity to 20,000 gallons. In eastern Frederick County, energy research analyst John (Jack) Aellen, his wife Lucille, and their six children in 1973 began planting two acres of French hybrids on their Berrywine Plantation Livestock Farm. Four years later they bonded part of their barn and made their first wine from Maryland, Virginia, and Pennsylvania grapes. Aellen decided on winegrowing because he says grapes are a good crop for a blind man. (He was virtually blinded by a chemical explosion in 1957, but he can distinguish between light and dark.) The Aellens' winery is six miles northwest of Mount Airy on Glisans Mill Road. Near Downsville in Washington County, rocket propulsion engineer Robert Ziem and his wife Ruth

---

*The American counterpart of Germany's rare *Eisweins*. In occasional years of early autumn frosts, some of the grapes still unpicked in Rhineland vineyards develop unusually high natural sugar content, become partially frozen, and when pressed, yield rare fragrant sweet nectars.

bonded a 5000-gallon winery in 1977 on their five acres of hybrid and Labrusca vines off Spielmann Road. Their wines include Delaware, Dutchess, Seyval Blanc, Chambourcin, Chancellor, and Maréchal Foch.

The first two viticultural-area appellations in Maryland, Catoctin and Linganore, were established by the Federal government in 1983. In the same year, members of the lively Maryland Grape Growers Association, organized in 1981, started four Maryland wineries. President Albert Copp and Michael de Simone combined their crops to open a winery on Copp's Woodhall Vineyard in Baltimore County near Sparks. On Hoffman Mill Road two miles from Hampstead in Carroll County, De Witt Truitt and his wife Michele, both lawyers, started the 2000-gallon White Marsh Cellars on their eighteen-acre vineyard of Chardonnay, Riesling, and Seyval. Outside of Mount Airy, Fred and Carol Wilson were bonding the Liberty Tavern winery on their three-acre Elk Run Vinifera vineyard. At Brooksville in Montgomery County, the 7000-gallon former Provenza winery was leased by Roger and Judy Wolf, Jerry and Ann Milne, and UC Davis–trained enologist Bob Lyon to combine the crops of Wolf Hill and Burkittsville Vineyards into the first Catoctin Vineyards wines. Members of the association are convinced that Lord Baltimore's three-centuries-ago vision of vast expanses of Maryland vineyards growing fine wines is about to come true.

• 9 •

New Jersey, despite its small size, was the ninth state in the Union in volume of wine production during the 1960s. A decade later, however, the owners closed down the two big cellars across from New York City that had been making hundreds of thousands of gallons of wine per year from grapes brought from other states.

In the 1980s, the Garden State is witnessing a rebirth of its more than a century of winegrowing tradition. The oldest and the newest of the state's eleven wineries are aiming to bring back the era when wines grown in New Jersey vineyards were among the finest in the East.

Oldest is the House of Renault, with its 130-acre vineyard and newly improved half-million-gallon winery on Bremen Avenue in Egg Harbor City, a southern New Jersey town that got its name from the nests of sea birds found by early fishermen along the nearby inlets from the sea. Louis Nicholas Renault came to the United States from France before the Civil War to represent the ancient champagne house of the Duke of Montebello at Rheims. Deciding to settle and make champagne in this country, he studied locations in both East and West, and was most impressed with the vineyards already thriving around Egg Harbor in Atlantic County. In 1864, he bought land for the present Renault vineyard, and by 1870 had introduced his New Jersey Champagne. Renault and the neighboring wineries such as Hiram Dewey & Sons won prizes for their wines at the Centennial Exposition at Philadelphia in 1876, and Egg Harbor soon became known as "the wine city." During the 1880s leading citizens and officials of Philadelphia came each year to the wine-tasting receptions held for them by the Egg Harbor vintners.

Louis Renault died in 1913 at the age of ninety-one and was succeeded by his son Felix. In 1919, John D'Agostino bought the company and operated it under a government permit through the fourteen years of Prohibition. His chief product was Renault Wine Tonic, which had an alcoholic content of 22 percent and was sold in virtually every drugstore in the nation. After Repeal, he acquired two old California wineries, Montebello at St. Helena and St. George at Fresno, and brought their wines in tank cars to Egg Harbor City for blending and bottling. His Charmat-process champagnes, mostly blends of California with New Jersey Labrusca wine, were sold nationwide. They were advertised by giant images of Renault bottles, which for many years lined highway roadsides in Massachusetts, Florida, and California.

The early Egg Harbor winegrowers grew a grape named Noah, which originated at Nauvoo in Illinois but thrived best in the sandy, chalky soils of southern New Jersey. The Noah imparted a characteristic dry, tart, faintly foxy flavor to white wines that no other eastern district could match. When the phylloxera aphid was devastating the vineyards of Europe in the 1870s, Noah vines were imported from America and planted extensively in France, and Noah is one of the few American grape varieties still grown there to make wine. In 1972, the Renault winery did something it probably should have done a century earlier: It introduced a semi-dry wine advertised as "new, dry and different," labeled "New Jersey State Noah White Varietal Dinner Wine."

The Renault winery passed through the hands of two more owners after the death of John D'Agostino in 1948. When I visited there in the 1960s and mid-1970s, there were evident signs of neglect. A renaissance of Renault began in 1976, when the estate was purchased by Joseph P. Milza, publisher of the Toms River *Daily Observer*. Milza added French hybrids to the vineyards, and has had viticulturist Ronald Reed plant a block of Johannisberg Riesling grapes, while a new winemaker, New York–trained William Bacon, has made improvements in the winery's table wines and Charmat-process champagnes. Renault receives visitors for winery tours seven days a week at the rate of 100,000 per year. One of the attractions on the tour is the museum of wineglass art masterpieces collected throughout Europe by Maria D'Agostino, the sister of the winery's second owner. Renault hospitality director Barbara Muller arranges luncheons and dinners for connoisseur groups.

Also being improved is the old Gross Highland cellar, which German immigrant winemaker John Gross founded in 1934 on Jim Leeds Road in Absecon, north of Atlantic City. In 1982, the winery's name was changed to Bernard d'Arcy Wine Cellars for Gross's grandson "Skip" D'Arcy, who has been running it since his father died in 1963. D'Arcy has begun replanting his mainly Labrusca vineyard with Vinifera and French hybrid and has employed a new winemaster, UC Davis–trained Nathan Stackhouse, to improve the Charmat-champagnes and table wines. Stackhouse's next project is to produce a bottle-fermented fiftieth-anniversary D'Arcy champagne by 1984. Like Renault, D'Arcy Cellars offers daily tastings both at Absecon and at its new retail outlet in Manasquan.

The chief developments in the rebirth of New Jersey wine-growing were directly related: the passage of a state farm winery law in 1981 and the founding of four estate wineries in north-central New Jersey to produce vintage-dated premium wines from New Jersey–grown grapes.

Veterinarian Dan Vernon, a home winemaker since boyhood, and his wife Lynn began planting seventeen acres of French hybrids and Vinifera in 1979 on their rocky hillside farm facing Burrell Road west of Route 517 near Oldwick. With computer scientist Jack Schaller as their viticulturist and enologist, they converted their horse hospital into the 9000-gallon Tewksbury (named for the township) Wine Cellars. Their specialties are Seyval Blanc, Cayuga White, Gewürztraminer, Chardonnay, and an everyday blend named Tewksbury Red.

The Hunterdon County Grape Growers Association, which includes the Vernons and fifty of their neighbors, persuaded the legislature to pass the farm winery law, which cut the license fee for small wineries from $400 to $50 and the state excise tax from 30 cents to 10 cents per gallon on wine made wholly from New Jersey–grown grapes.

Soon the Vernons' grape-grower neighbors were applying for farm winery licenses. Psychologist James R. Williams and his wife Jonetta, with eight acres mainly of hybrids, opened the Del Vista Vineyard winery on Everittstown Road near Frenchtown, on the Delaware River. Dr. Williams convinced the Federal government to approve "Central Delaware Valley" as the name of their viticultural area; it extends across the river into Pennsylvania. Dr. Michael Fisher, the head chemist of Merck Sharp & Dohme pharmaceuticals and president of the Hunterdon Association, bonded the Amwell Valley Vineyard winery on his several acres of hybrids along Route 514 south of Ringoes. Business consultant Don Fennelly and his wife Betty, who has taught cooking schools, have bought equipment for the Fennelly Farm Vineyards winery on Woodglen Road in Glen Gardner. Their daughter Tess Donadeo, a graduate chemist, is their enologist.

There are five more New Jersey wineries. The Jacob Lee family began making old-fashioned Labrusca wines in 1938 from the grapes they grow across Route 130 at Bordentown. A year earlier, the Tomasello family bonded their winery on White Horse Pike at Hammonton to resume making table wine and champagne of the grapes on their seventy-acre vineyard that dates from 1888. Matthew Antuzzi opened his winery in 1974 on the Bridgeboro–Moorestown Road at Delran, not far from Philadelphia. Of the same vintage is Savo Balic's winery on Route 40 north of May's Landing. The youngest of the old-fashioned New Jersey wineries is Frank and Dorothy Polito's cellar at Vincentown, which has a founding date of 1978.

• 10 •

In Cumberland County, New Jersey, there is a town named Vineland—but for its vineyards, not for its wines. It was founded as a bone-Dry community in the early 1860s by a real estate developer named Charles K. Landis. To Vineland there came in 1868 a man who fanatically hated wine, a dentist named Thomas B. Welch. It was here that Welch started the fresh grape-juice industry, which led to the planting of Concord grapes across the United States—and a century later to the development of the kosher type of wine.

Dr. Welch, the Communion steward of his Methodist church, happened to read of Louis Pasteur's studies of the fermentation of wine, published in France in 1866. This suggested to Welch a way to improve the decoction of raisins steeped in water which Prohibitionist ministers of the time used for Communion in place of wine. Experimenting in his kitchen at Vineland, he succeeded in sterilizing the sweet juice of New Jersey grapes, and by 1870

Dr. Thomas Bramwell Welch, the wine-hating New Jersey dentist who founded the grape-juice industry, which led to the planting of Concord grapes across North America and a century later to the development of the kosher type of American wine. (*Welch Foods, Inc.*)

had begun a small business with his son Charles, also a dentist, selling "Dr. Welch's Unfermented Wine" for church use. Later, when sales of the product spread from churches to drug stores and groceries, the name was changed to "Dr. Welch's Grape Juice."

In the 1880s and 1890s, grape rot attacked many New Jersey vineyards, and the Welch Company, needing more grapes, moved in 1896 to a new vineyard area at Watkins Glen in the Finger Lakes District of New York. A year later, the Doctors Welch built a processing plant at Westfield in the Chautauqua Grape Belt. During the next half-century, a chain of Welch plants, which are now owned by the National Grape Co-operative (also called Welch Foods), spread to Pennsylvania, Michigan, Arkansas, and to the State of Washington.

What the wine-hating Doctors Welch never knew, because they died in 1903 and 1926, was that a half-century after the father's death the Welch Grape Juice Company would start making a fermented Welch wine.

• 11 •

Pennsylvania, where commercial winegrowing began, now ranks fifth in the nation in grape production (after California, New York, Washington, and Michigan), harvesting 55,000 tons yearly from more than 9000 acres of vineyards. But until now, only a small fraction of this tonnage has been produced for wine. Most of the grapes have been Concords, grown for grape juice. Since the repeal of Prohibition, Pennsylvania has supplied some of its grapes to wineries in neighboring states, but until 1963 produced no wine of its own.

Now, because a Pennsylvania law pushed through by farmers fifteen years ago encourages winegrowing, scores of small vineyards have been planted in almost all parts of the state. There now are thirty-one Pennsylvania wineries, and more are being planned.

The Keystone State has a strange wine history. William Penn attempted to establish a Pennsylvania wine industry, bringing French and Spanish vines to Philadelphia in 1683. "The consequence," he predicted, "will be as good as any European countries of the same latitude do yield." Penn's attempt to start a vineyard failed, but the Penn Colony's interpreter, Conrad Weiser, succeeded. Weiser's vineyard, near Womelsdorf in the Tulpehocken Valley, where his home is now a state park, regularly supplied Riesling vines to the governor of Virginia, according to his diaries.

As mentioned earlier, it was near Philadelphia that the first domesticated native wine grape was discovered by James Alexander before the Revolution.

In 1793, a Frenchman, Pierre Legaux, founded the Pennsylvania Vine Company to cultivate European grapes and produce wine at Spring Mill, on the north bank of the Schuylkill near the present Philadelphia suburb of Conshohocken. The Alexander was the only grape that survived. Legaux claimed it was one of the Vinifera varieties he had imported from the Cape of Good Hope, and he named it the Cape of Constantia. Others called it the Cape, Black Madeira, Schuylkill Muscadell, and eventually the Alexander. From the Spring Mill Vineyard, the Alexander spread throughout Pennsylvania, and to Ohio, Virginia, Kentucky, and Indiana during the early part of the nineteenth century. Legaux's company did not prosper, however. Its vineyard and winery were abandoned several years before his death in 1827.

Meanwhile, Thomas Eichelberger from Germany planted Alexander grapes about 1818 between York and the Susquehanna River, and York became the center of early viniculture in Pennsylvania. There also were vineyards along the Schuylkill from Reading to the Germantown section of Philadelphia, where in 1830 Edward H. Bonsall had a winery and a vineyard of Alexander, Isabella, and Catawba.

But the Pittsburgh area, west of the Alleghenies, soon outdistanced the eastern part of the state in wine production. Grape planting began there as early as 1793, when Colonel George Morgan, a friend of Benjamin Franklin, started a vineyard at

Morganza, Washington County. It was "Father" George Rapp, the leader of the communistic theocracy known as the Harmonie Society, who made the Pittsburgh district known for its wines. Rapp, the son of a grape grower of Württenberg, came to Pennsylvania in 1803, seeking land on which to settle his followers. He bought 5000 acres on Connoquenessing Creek in Butler County, brought 200 families of Rappists in three shiploads from Germany in 1804, and built the town of Harmony. The colonists planted ten acres of Old World grapevines and also produced silk, but because the vines died, they abandoned the place in 1814 and established New Harmony in the Wabash Valley of Indiana.

In 1824, the Harmonists returned to the Pittsburgh area, and on 3000 acres along the Ohio River, eighteen miles north of the city, they built another town and named it Economy. Here they again planted vineyards, apparently of native grapes, and established several industries, including a winery and a distillery. Economy became famous for its wines, woolens, and other products. The colony declined after Rapp's death in 1847, but its industries, including winegrowing, continued for more than fifty years.

Evidently more vineyards were planted in the vicinity, because in the Patent Office report for 1855, Victor Scriba of Pittsburgh described forty to fifty acres of vines, principally of Catawba, growing on hillsides facing the Allegheny, Monongahela, and Ohio Rivers. He wrote that "the wine made from the Catawba, as well as from the Isabella grapes, is good and praiseworthy, and sells from one to two dollars a gallon."

In 1880, when the special census of United States wine production was made, Allegheny County led the state in wine production with 45,000 gallons, compared to a total of 13,000 gallons made in Adams, Bucks, Cumberland, Lancaster, and Northumberland counties in southeastern Pennsylvania.

Winemaking around Pittsburgh continued at least until 1900. The *American Wine Press and Mineral Water News*, in its issue for November of that year, refers to the Claret, Riesling, and Catawba wine still being produced by the Economy Wine Vaults.

But one of "Father" Rapp's teachings, in addition to sobriety and simple living, was celibacy; and by 1905 few of the Harmonists remained, victims of their own virtue; and the Society was dissolved. In 1912, Economy was renamed Ambridge. Two city blocks of the old Economy buildings have been preserved by the state at Ambridge, including dwellings, shops, a granary, Rapp's thirty-five-room Great House, and the Music Hall, in the cellar of which are the colony's wine storage vaults. Wine is still made in the Economy vaults, but not for sale. Daniel Reibel, in charge of the cellar, picks a bushel of grapes each autumn from the arbor beside the building. He invites a few young visitors to wash their feet and to tread on the fruit, and then ferments another vintage of Economy wine.

A third Pennsylvania vineyard district was established in the middle of the last century in Erie County, along the shore of Lake Erie. At North East, a town strangely named because it is in the far northwestern corner of the state, the South Shore Wine Company began making wine in 1863 from Isabella and Catawba grapes. The winery building, with its cavernous cellars, still stands and houses the South Shore Inn restaurant. Thirty years later, Concord grapes had replaced wine varieties in the district because Americans were learning to drink bottled grape juice, which had been introduced to the public by Dr. Charles Welch at the 1893 Chicago World's Fair. In 1900 the Welch Company established at North East the world's biggest grape-juice plant. Although a few Erie County wineries continued operating until Prohibition in 1920, Concord grapes have been the county's chief farm crop ever since.

· 12 ·

When Prohibition was repealed in 1933, scores of wineries reopened in New York, New Jersey, and Ohio, but not in Pennsylvania. For the Keystone State had adopted the monopoly state store system that was purposely designed to discourage the purchase of liquor or wine. Pennsylvania's Liquor Control Board is the biggest of the seventeen state monopolies; it operates more than 700 liquor stores. Although beset during its half-century of existence by public criticism and moves to close its outlets in favor of privately owned stores, the PLCB has survived.

Nobody but an amateur would have wanted to start a winery under this system, for wine could only be sold in the state monopoly stores. But there was one such amateur. Philadelphia businessman Melvin Gordon, while vacationing in Europe in the mid-1950s, had been charmed with the idea of growing fine wines. On his return home he bought a farm at Birchrunville, west of Valley Forge, added a tractor, barrels, a grape crusher, and a hand-bottling machine, and planted a few acres of French hybrid vines he got from Philip Wagner at Baltimore. Gordon's vines produced well, and in 1963 he bonded the tiny Conestoga Vineyard winery, the first to be opened in Pennsylvania in this century. When his 1964 vintage was ready, he offered it to the Liquor Control Board. I tasted his wines from the barrels, and they were good, but Gordon couldn't serve me any at lunch. In order to drink his own wine, he would have had to buy it at a state store. A year later, when the state stores began selling Gordon's wines, word got around that wines were actually being grown in Pennsylvania, and dozens of the best Pennsylvania restaurants added Conestoga vintages to their wine lists. Gordon sold Conestoga several years later, and its subsequent owners abandoned Birchrunville for pastures richer in wine-buying tourist traffic.

• 13 •

Meanwhile, other amateur winemakers far north in Erie County had a better idea. One was Douglas P. Moorhead, who while stationed with the army in Germany in 1957 had visited vineyards on the Rhine and tasted wines of the White (Johannisberg) Riesling grape. A graduate in pomology from Pennsylvania State University and the son of an Erie County Concord grower, Moorhead resolved that when he returned to America, he would plant the true Riesling in the vineyard at Moorheadville, which is named for his family. He obtained vines of Riesling and other Vinifera from Dr. Frank and also French hybrids from Philip Wagner. He began making wines in the family cellar and discussed them with other amateur winemakers who often bought grapes from his father. In 1960 Moorhead and a partner, William Konnerth, organized the Erie County Wine Club, which soon had a waiting list of other home winemakers wanting to join. Because winemaking equipment for amateurs was difficult to buy, the two young men made joint purchases for the club. This soon became a business, which they named Presque Isle Wine Cellars to express their hope of someday starting a winery. The firm now furnishes thousands of home winemakers throughout the country with grapes, juice, winemaking equipment, and supplies, including a booklet on winemaking by Konnerth that is one of the best available.

Moorhead's Vinifera and hybrid plantings thrived. He became convinced that Erie County, with its 194-day growing season, has the best climate for high-quality white wines and champagnes in the East, equaled only by the Lake Erie Islands. Neighboring growers became interested and made trial plantings of both groups of wine grapes. A committee of growers was formed in 1967 to consider starting wineries in the county. State Secretary of Agriculture Leland H. Bull became interested and allocated state funds to Pennsylvania State University's experiment station at North East for a study of wine-grape growing. The growers' committee found that for wineries to operate profitably, the Pennsylvania law would have to be changed, that farmer wineries should be permitted to sell their wines to the public and to restaurants without going through the monopoly Control Board. In 1967, a bill was introduced in the legislature, seeking to permit Pennsylvania winegrowers to sell at their winery premises table wines of their own production from Pennsylvania grapes. The Liquor Board opposed the bill, insisting that only its state monopoly stores should be allowed to sell wine. Its powerful opposition kept the measure dormant for a year. But on the last day of the next legislative session, in August 1968, the farmers succeeded in bringing the bill to a vote. It passed both houses, 171 to 13 and 36 to 9.

Within weeks of their victory, Erie County grape growers began building wineries to crush the 1969 vintage. North East became a mecca for wine lovers and tourists. On a five-mile stretch off US 20 and Route 5, four wineries now offer cellar tours and tastings daily (including Sundays; they are exempt from the state's blue laws). Passage of the "limited winery" law allows them to sell their table wines to consumers and restaurants and to the monopoly store system as well. First to open in 1969 was the Moorheads' 10,000-gallon Presque Isle winery at Moorheadville, three miles west of North East. It produces excellent French hybrid and Vinifera wines, including Vignoles, Vidal, Seyval, Aligoté, Chardonnay, Gamay Beaujolais, and one of the best Cabernet Sauvignons I have found in the East. At Presque Isle you now are welcomed by Doug's wife and partner Marlene; Konnerth has retired.

Three miles east on Route 5 is the 175,000-gallon Penn-Shore winery, owned by a group of growers headed by George Luke, Blair McCord, and George Sceiford. Its tasting room offers a dozen wines ranging from pink and white Catawba to champagne and sparkling burgundy made by UC Davis–trained enologist Steven Reeder. On Route 5 beyond the state university's field research station is the Spanish-style winery of 50,000 gallons, opened in 1974 by Joseph Mazza and his son Robert. Farther east, on US 20 near the New York State border, is the 10,000-gallon Heritage winery of the Bostwick family, who have 300 acres of Labrusca varieties which supplied the former grapejuice plant in Erie. Penn State University has been doing wine research and teaching since the winery law passed in 1968.

Excitement about the state's new wine industry started a wave of vineyard planting in southeastern Pennsylvania, where wine-growing had begun almost two centuries before. By 1983, a dozen producing vineyards and wineries were offering cellar tours and tasting in six counties west and north of Philadelphia. Among the best known for prize-winning Vinifera and French hybrid wines is the Naylor Wine Cellars, off Route 24 two miles north of Stewartstown. Richard and Audrey Naylor have built a new 50,000-gallon winery and tasting room to replace the former potato cellar where they began making wine in 1978. They then enlarged their vineyard to seventeen acres.

The next winery north of Naylor is John and Timothy Crouch's Allegro Vineyards cellar of 2000 gallons on Sechrist Road, two miles south of Route 74 near Brogue. Its name reflects their former occupation; John played the oboe and Tim the violin in chamber-music orchestras around Washington, D.C. They bought a neglected fifteen-acre vineyard in 1978 and two years later were turning out half a dozen hybrid and Vinifera wines, including a Cabernet Sauvignon–Merlot blend that won a prize in an eastern competition.

A few miles farther north, on Drytown Road three miles south of Rawlinsville, is Tom and Lucinda Hampton's charming little Tucquan Vineyard winery, where they make estate-bottled French hybrid and Labrusca wines. Tom, a millwright, and Lucinda, a part-time rural letter carrier, began making wine in their barn in 1974, and four years later built their 3000-gallon winery and tasting room. Since opening the winery, they have doubled the size of their vineyard to ten acres.

Third oldest Pennsylvania producer, after Presque Isle and Penn-Shore, is Suzanne Dickel's 40,000-gallon Lancaster County Winery, which she bought in 1979 from the neophyte wine-grower who had started it seven years before. Directional signs to the winery guide you the eight miles south from Lancaster, the heart of the Pennsylvania Dutch Country. Vineyards there are tended mainly by Amish men and women, who still wear Old World costumes and drive little horse-drawn black buggies. The Amish continue making wine in their homes as they did in Germany. But the more numerous Mennonites in Dutch Country disapprove of the wineries. The Mennonites, like the Amish, made wine in the Old Country but became stern teetotalers after they settled here.

Also in Dutch Country is the Nissley Vineyards winery on Route 1 north of Bainbridge, near the Susquehanna River. Retired Lancaster bridge builder J. Richard Nissley and his son

John began planting vines on their cattle farm in 1972 and four years later converted a century-old stone farm building into one of Pennsylvania's most attractive and largest (40,000 gallons) wineries.

In 1971 Joseph and Antoinette Lembo closed the restaurant on Valley Street in downtown Lewiston, which they had operated for thirty years. Six years later they turned the building into a winery to crush the French hybrid grapes they had planted on a seven-acre farm outside of town.

Farther west, beyond Gettysburg, is Ronald Cooper's Adams County Winery, a mile northwest of Orrtanna on Peach Tree Road. Cooper, born in England, where he became a home winemaker, planted his three-acre vineyard mostly with Vinifera varieties. He thinks Gewürztraminer may prove the best grape for this part of Pennsylvania. His other interest is in building pipe organs, and he intends to provide organ concerts at the winery from time to time.

The 6000-gallon Kolln Vineyards winery on Route 550 in Bellefonte, six miles from Pennsylvania State University, is operated by Martha and John Kolln, who both teach at the university, she in English and he in engineering, while their eldest son Timothy cares for their four-acre vineyard.

In Bucks County, ex-newspaper advertising manager Jerry Forest and his wife Kathy became modern winegrowing pioneers when they planted their ten-acre vineyard of French hybrids and opened their Buckingham Valley Winery off Durham Road in 1966, two years before the legislature passed the winery law. Jerry is the winemaker and Kathy tends the vines, which she covers with tobacco netting in autumn to protect them from the grape-stealing birds. A short distance north, on US 202 in the village of Soleburg, is the Bucks County winery and wine museum, which realized a long-held dream of Arthur Gerold, a former New York theatrical costumer and wine buff. Housed in a converted antique barn since 1973, the museum displays color transparencies of Pennsylvania grapes, a collection of seventeenth-century wineglasses, and mannequins attired in early American costumes.

Reviving winegrowing in the area north of Pittsburgh, mechanic Paul Lapic, his wife Josephine, and his brother Walter planted a five-acre vineyard at New Brighton in Beaver County and bonded the 5000-gallon Lapic Winery in 1977. "La Pic" was the brand they chose for their seven table wines.

In 1982, the Pennsylvania law was changed to allow each of the state's more than thirty wineries to open as many as three retail tasting-room outlets in cities. Among the first to take advantage of this were food technologists Arthur and Martin Keen, the new owners of the Conestoga Vineyards winery, which they had moved into the former Queen Dairy in downtown Lancaster. Their first tasting rooms are in Fogelsville, Intercourse, and Lancaster. The wines bottled in the former dairy are labeled "Conestoga Vineyards Estate Bottled" because the Keens, who own a four-acre vineyard at Landisville, had applied earlier to the Federal government to establish "Lancaster Valley" as a viticultural area, and the petition was granted in 1982.

New Pennsylvania wineries bonded in the 1980s include the Chadds Ford cellar on US 1 near Brandywine Battlefield State Park, established by former New York State winemaker Eric Miller and his wife Lee, a writer; the Conneaut Cellars at Conneaut Lake, started by school district executive Alan Wolf and his wife Phyllis; Anne and Stephen Bahn's tiny winery and three-acre vineyard on Goram Road near Brogue; Peter Capozzi's 5000-gallon Blue Ridge Winery and five-year-old vineyard on Pine Road at Carlisle in Cumberland County; gynecologist Dr. Tom Mebane's 10,000-gallon Nittany Valley Vineyard cellar in State College; Eugene Cromer's Quarry Hill winery at Shippensburg in Franklin County; the Calvaresi Winery in Reading; Thomas Broccardi's little Neri's Winery and three-acre vineyard on Bridgetown Pike near Langhorne in Bucks County; and the Franklin Hill Vineyard winery opened by vocational teacher Charles Flatt and his wife Elaine, a nursery-school teacher, on their thirteen-acre vineyard at Bangor in the foothills of the Pocono Mountains.

5

Ohio, Once the Premier Wine State

HE RISE AND DECLINE of Ohio wines could supply compelling material for a historical novel, because the Ohio wine star has risen not once, but twice, each time only to fall; and now it is rising again. Scores of new vineyards and twenty-three new wineries producing new kinds of wine have sprung up since 1970, including six near Cincinnati, where the state's wine industry began more than a century and a half ago.

This could also make an epic movie, with such characters as wine millionaire Nicholas Longworth, poet and connoisseur Henry Wadsworth Longfellow, and Ohio's colorful winegrowers of today. And if filmed in such settings as the storied Ohio River, the ancient wine caves beneath Cincinnati and Sundusky, and the vine-clad islands of Lake Erie, the plot could weave war, intrigue, politics, and Prohibition-era gunplay without veering a grape's-width from actual history.

• 2 •

Nicholas Longworth,* the five-foot-one "crazy Jerseyman," came to Cincinnati from Newark in 1803 at the age of twenty-one with little more than the clothes on his back. It was the year Ohio became a state. He studied law for six months, established a lucrative practice, invested in land in the mushrooming town, and became the wealthiest man in Ohio. Winegrowing then was just beginning along the riverbanks at Cincinnati. It became Longworth's hobby. He also saw that drunkenness de-

---

*The great-grandfather of the Nicholas Longworth who was Speaker of the House during the Coolidge administrations, and who was the son-in-law of President Theodore Roosevelt.

creased in direct proportion to the use of light table wines, and he decided that by producing such wines he could woo Americans away from hard liquor.

In 1823, Longworth planted a vineyard on Bald Hill, overlooking the Ohio River in the part of Cincinnati known as Tusculum. The site is now the city's Frederick H. Alms Memorial Park, in which some of the old vine roots still grow. He imported thousands of vines from Europe, but they died, so he made his first wine from the native Alexander and Isabella. Then he heard of a "wonder grape," the Catawba, grown by Major John Adlum of Georgetown, and in 1825 he obtained Catawba cuttings from Adlum. Three years later, when Longworth tasted the first Catawba wine pressed from his grapes, he quit his law practice and gave his full attention to winegrowing. By 1842 he was cultivating 1200 acres of vineyards at Tusculum, in the Delhi Hills, and on the present site of Eden Park, and began making America's first champagne.

Longworth's white Catawba wine and his champagne, which he called Sparkling Catawba, were sold throughout the East and even in faraway California. They were so successful that California winegrowers began planting Catawba grapes and attempted to copy the sensational Ohio wines. Longworth once accused New York hotels of substituting French champagnes for his, which he sold them at the then fancy price of $12 a case. His fame reached England. A writer for the *Illustrated London News* in 1858 described the still Catawba as "a finer wine of the hock species and flavour than any hock that comes from the Rhine," and declared that "the Sparkling Catawba, of the pure, unadulterated juice of the odoriferous Catawba grape, transcends the Champagne of France."

But a more lasting tribute was the "Ode to Catawba Wine" by Longfellow, which begins:

> Very good in its way
> Is the Verzenay,
> Or the Sillery soft and creamy;
> But Catawba wine
> Has a taste more divine,
> More dulcet, delicious, and dreamy.

Some say the gift of a few bottles from Longworth inspired Longfellow to write the poem at his Cambridge home in 1854. But it is evident to anyone who reads all eleven stanzas that the bard had actually visited Cincinnati and had learned from Longworth about the many American grape varieties named in

Nicholas Longworth, "the crazy Jerseyman," who founded the Ohio champagne industry, planting his first vineyard in 1823 and making the first American champagne in 1842. (*Public Library of Cincinnati and Hamilton Co.*)

One of Nicholas Longworth's Catawba vineyards on the Ohio River near Cincinnati, circa 1850. (*Public Library of Cincinnati and Hamilton Co.*)

the "Ode," including the grape that "grows by the Beautiful River."

• 3 •

Ohio was the premier wine state by 1859, producing nearly 570,000 gallons yearly, more than a third of the national total, twice as much as California. Cincinnati was "the queen of the West"; the Ohio was "the Rhine of America." There were 3000 acres of vineyards along the river between Cincinnati and Ripley, forty miles upstream, and a large acreage under vines across the river in Kentucky.

But just as Cincinnati's wine star reached its zenith, a plague began to spread through its vineyards. The violet-hued skins of the Catawba grapes were turning black, and many of the berries were found to be hollow shells. A cobwebby growth wilted the leaves and stems, and the vines began to die. Black rot and oïdium (powdery mildew) wrought this destruction at a time when modern preventive sprays were still unknown.

Longworth had half a million bottles in the caves beneath

his two Cincinnati "wine houses" in 1860, but was running short of grapes to produce more wine. His dream fading, the little man in his latter years grew absent-minded; he carried numerous papers in his hat and a memorandum sheet pinned to his coat sleeve. When he died in 1863, two years after the outbreak of the Civil War, his business was divided among his heirs, and it was abandoned a few years later, for most of the vineyards were dead. Not less than 10,000 acres of vines in southwestern Ohio were obliterated by the "vine sickness" during the late 1850s and 1860s, and only a few were replaced. Cincinnati wines were virtually a thing of the past.

• 4 •

In the meantime another part of Ohio, two hundred miles north of Cincinnati, was achieving prominence as a winegrowing

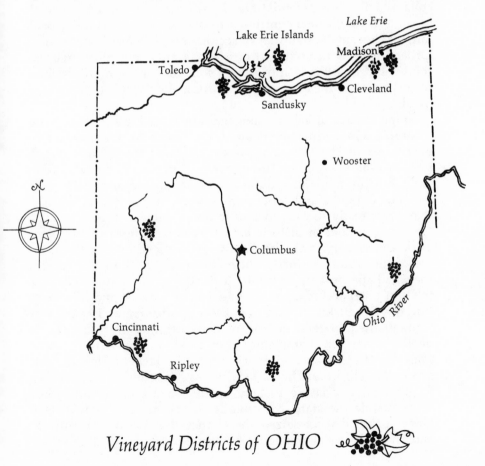

Vineyard Districts of OHIO

district. Grape planting had begun as early as 1836 along the shore of Lake Erie and on the islands that extend toward the Canadian border. Here the lake-tempered breezes kept the vines free of disease. In the decade after 1860, at least 7000 acres of vineyards were planted in northern Ohio, from Toledo to beyond Cleveland, some by growers who migrated from Cincinnati. In 1870, a half-million-gallon winery on Middle Bass Island claimed to be the largest in the nation, and the Lenk winery at Toledo turned out 400,000 gallons in that year. By 1900 several of the Sandusky wineries had won medals for their wines at judgings in this country and in Paris and Rome. The comeback of Ohio wines was complete.

• 5 •

Then, in 1920, came Prohibition, and the Ohio wine industry collapsed for the second time. During the Dry years, several of the state's vintners continued to operate by government permit, making small quantities of sacramental and medicinal wines. Others made wines without official sanction, and when Federal food and drug officers approached some of the Lake Erie Islands to inspect the vines for spray residues, they were driven away by shotgun blasts.

Grape acreage along the lake again increased during the 1920s to supply home winemakers and bootleggers. At this time, however, most of the Ohio vineyards switched from wine grapes to Concords because of the expanding market for fresh grape juice. But the wineries around Sandusky maintained their vineyards of Catawba and other wine grapes, and at Repeal in 1933 they were ready to cash in on the boom demand they expected for wines. Richer in historic background than most of the New York wineries, with the best grape-growing climate in the East, and with wines distinctly different from those of California, they had the best opportunity to install their brands again on the best hotel and restaurant wine lists of the East and Midwest. But the Sandusky vintners let the opportunity at Repeal slip through their fingers. Instead of concentrating on selling their quality wines and champagnes, they tried to compete for volume sales with the low-priced wines shipped to local bottlers in tank cars from California. The Ohio wineries even tried unsuccessfully to get their legislature to levy a dollar-a-gallon tax on wines from outside the state. Meanwhile the vintners of New York's Finger Lakes district seized the chance that Ohio had muffed, and Finger Lakes champagnes became the chief sparkling wines sold in the United States. In 1937, there were 161 wineries in Ohio. By 1967, there were 25 left, only 15 making wine from Ohio grapes.

• 6 •

While those more than a hundred wineries, mostly in northern Ohio, were closing their doors between the 1940s and 1960s, a southern Ohio grape grower's son named Henry Sonneman had purchased Bavarian immigrant John C. Meier's grape-juice plant near Cincinnati and was making his sparkling "Meier's Unfermented Catawba Grape Juice," in a champagne bottle, a popular store item in most of the United States and Canada.

Having begun at Repeal making wine as a sideline, Sonneman soon renamed his plant "Meier's Wine Cellars," but then found he needed more grapes than he could buy in southern Ohio. In 1941, he bought a vineyard on an island in Lake Erie called Isle St. George. He enlarged the vineyard to cover half of the island and brought the grapes to Cincinnati to be made into wine. During the next two decades, Sonneman expanded his Meier's Cellars to 2 million gallons, making it one of the biggest wineries between New York State and the Rockies. By then he was shipping two dozen table wines, ports, sherries, and bulk-process Ohio champagnes, as well as his Catawba grape juice, to forty states and two foreign countries.

Sonneman died in 1974. Two years later, Robert C. Gottesman's Paramount Distillers of Cleveland bought Meier's Wine Cellars and most of Isle St. George, and in the next two years Gottesman purchased three century-old northern Ohio wineries.

When I revisited Meier's Wine Cellars in 1982, I found few outward changes there since Sonneman's time. The winery was still attracting visitors at the rate of thousands per year. They were touring the cavernous cellars, sampling Meier's wines in the *Weinstube,* or lunching in the winery's restaurant. But there was a new production manager, Edward (Ted) Moulton from New Jersey, also experienced in winemaking in New York and Pennsylvania. Moulton was shuttling between Cincinnati and Gottesman's three northern wineries, welding them into a single chain.

• 7 •

For today's wine tourist, no other district in America offers historic vineyards and colorful wineries in settings as uniquely spectacular as those that still operate along the shore and on the "Wine Islands" of Lake Erie.

From Sandusky eastward to the Pennsylvania border, a ten-mile-wide strip of land facing the lake is dotted with vineyards, some of which are now threatened by urbanization. West of Cleveland, which has some large bonded cellars, are three producing wineries. On Detroit Road in the Cleveland suburb of Westlake is the 170,000-gallon Dover Vineyard winery, established in 1934 by eighteen grape growers of Cuyahoga and Lorain counties. Zoltan Wolovits, a winemaker who came here from Hungary following the 1956 revolution, owns it now. The winery is under the same roof as the Dover Chalet restaurant, and diners there are sometimes privileged to watch how the wines are made. On Webber Road in adjoining Avon Lake, Allan Klingshirn and his wife Barbara run the ten-acre Labrusca vineyard that Allan's father started in 1935. Nearby on Walker Road, Alex Christ tends his father's twenty-three acres and continues making Concord and Niagara jug wines; his father has retired.

East of Cleveland, in Geauga, Lake, and Ashtabula counties, is the main Concord area of Ohio. Most of the Concords are now harvested mechanically. The three old roadside wineries between Wickliffe and Geneva have not changed, except that the Willoughby winery has been moved to adjoining Willowick.

• 8 •

A new generation of oenothusiasts brought the wine revolution and seven new wineries to this northeastern Ohio Concord grape district between 1969 and the early 1980s.

The first was industrial engineer Arnulf Esterer, a home winemaker who had happened to read about Konstantin Frank, the pioneer grower of Vinifera at Hammondsport, New York. Esterer went to Hammondsport, worked two vintages without pay for Dr. Frank, and learned the latter's secrets of growing Vinifera in the East. In 1969, Esterer began planting Chardonnay and Johannisberg (White) Riesling on ten acres beside Interstate 90 six miles from the Lake Erie shore, ten miles west of Conneaut in Ohio. His wife Kate became Conneaut's rural mail carrier, besides caring for their four children. They named the vineyard Markko for the Finnish ex-policeman who sold them the land. The Markko Vineyard and the beginning of its winery were four years old when I happened by in 1973 and sampled its 1972 Riesling from the cask. I was amazed; its fresh Riesling fragrance was closer to a young Moselle than any dry American

Riesling I had tasted yet. My notes made that afternoon read: "Is it an accident? Can he duplicate this wine?" Esterer's later Riesling vintages did approach the 1972. His Chardonnays and Cabernet Sauvignon, introduced in later years, could also hold up their heads against most comparable California and European wines. When I last visited Markko Vineyard in 1982, Kate still was the rural mail carrier, but the children were helping in the vineyard and winery.

It was on that same day in 1973 that I met in the neighborhood another home winemaker named Willett Worthy. A North Madison investment banker, Worthy had just finished planting nine acres of Chardonnay, Gamay Beaujolais, Pinot Noir, and French hybrids on Route 528 six miles south of Madison. Now he has thirty-two acres, has built his 25,000-gallon Grand River winery, and is devoted full time to his winegrowing career. He buries some of his delicate vines, such as his Vinifera, in winter, and uncovers them in spring. His principal wines, when I last stopped by, included Chardonnay, Sauvignon Blanc, Merlot, Gewürztraminer, Vignoles, and other leading French hybrid types, and a white-wine blend he has named for his daughter Adrienne.

When Worthy was first starting, his entire crop went to the Cedar Hill Wine Company, which had started in 1981. This 7000-gallon winery is jammed incredibly into the basement of Dr. Thomas Wykoff's tiny Au Provence French provincial restaurant in the Cleveland Heights section of Cleveland. Dr. Wykoff, who heads the Ear-Nose-Throat Department of St. Luke's Hospital, began home winemaking and French cooking in 1970 when he returned to Cleveland from an assistant professorship at a medical school in New Orleans. To combine these new interests, he converted a former beauty shop into a ten-table restaurant, first installing modern winemaking equipment in the basement. He makes a dozen excellent wines including Pinot Noir, Chambourcin, several blends of his own, and a *méthode champenoise* champagne. They are only for sale in the restaurant, where a liberal supply is also used in the kitchen. The name of the doctor's wines is "Chateau Lagniappe," a New Orleans expression for "a little bit extra."

Also in the early 1970s, Anthony P. Debevc of Madison, Ohio, earned his pomology degree at Ohio State University and persuaded his father, Tony J. Debevc, to add ten acres of French hybrid grapes to the thirty acres of Concords grandfather Antone from Slovenia had planted before Prohibition in the Grand River Valley near Madison. With lumber from an old barn, the father and son built a two-story chalet beside the vineyard on Doty

Road and named it Chalet Debonné. Wines are for sale in the tasting room upstairs with cheese, crackers, sausage, and home-made bread. The winery has been expanded to 70,000 gallons, an experimental planting of Vinifera has been added to the vine-yard, and Anthony is thinking of adding a champagne.

East of Worthy's vineyard, on Route 307 toward Geneva, is the chalet-type Ferrante Wine Farm cellar, opened in 1981. Far-ther west, on Gore Road off US 20 in Conneaut, is County Tax Assessor Alfred Bucci's 2000-gallon winery in his home. He added an "a" to the name, thinking "Buccia Vineyards" would be easy for wine buyers to remember. To his three acres of Seyval Blanc, Aurore, and Baco, he has added some Vinifera vines. During the same year two more wineries opened in the area. Noted ophthalmologist Dr. Hiram Hardesty bonded the Hilltop Winery overlooking his two-acre partly Vinifera vine-yard on Circle Road near West Farmington. Dana Daughters started the Daughters Wine Cellar on his small vineyard on North Ridge Road near Geneva. In 1982, Lakewood industrial engineer Nicholas Holian built the future Fox Run Vineyards winery adjoining the inactive Cohodas winery on County Line Road, and began replanting its vineyard, which once covered forty acres.

• 9 •

Sandusky, which succeeded Cincinnati as the wine capital of Ohio, is a venerable lakefront city with strange diagonal thor-oughfares. When Longworth's vineyards at Cincinnati died, the Catawba found its adopted home here, as local maps with such landmarks as Catawba Point, Catawba Island, and Catawba Road testify. Sandusky, situated midway between Cleveland and To-ledo, is now the center of a miles-long strip of summer resorts and beaches that is billed, with the neighboring islands, as "Lake Erie Vacationland." Near the city's straggling waterfront stand several century-old wineries, some of whose wine caves are tun-neled beneath the streets. The Engels & Krudwig cellar on East Water Street, founded in 1863 and once famed for its Diedes-heimer and Laubenheimer wines, is still bonded because old wines remain in some of the casks. But in recent years builder Edward Feick and his wife Anita have converted the upper por-tion of the building into a series of retail shops. Nearby is the John G. Dorn winery, which began in 1872 with Longworth's original casks but closed in 1957. On Clinton Street stood the great cellar of Michel Hommel, whose 1889 champagne won him medals at the Paris Exposition of 1900, but it was closed in 1967 and soon afterward was destroyed by fire.

There are two wineries in the Venice section of Sandusky, four miles west of town. One is the 10,000-gallon cellar William Steuk left, when he died in 1975, beside the four acres of vines that remain of his grandfather's vineyard, which dates from 1855. Winemaker Tim Parker, a former medical student who works for Steuk's heirs, turns out four Steuk champagnes and a half dozen Labrusca table wines. A dry red, named Black Pearl for a native grape bred by Kaspar Schraidt at Put-in-Bay, won a prize in the first Ohio wine-quality competition in 1980. Its powerfully foxy taste had been mellowed by several years' aging in oak.

On nearby Bardshar Road are the forty-acre Mantey vineyard and the Mantey winery, one of the three century-old cellars that Robert Gottesman bought after acquiring the Meier's Wine Cellars near Cincinnati in 1976. The Mantey winery was built in 1880 to make wine for the German immigrant families around Sandusky. It was closed during Prohibition and was reopened after Repeal by brothers Norman and Paul Mantey, grandsons of the founder. The Mantey wines, when I first visited there in the 1960s, were Catawba, Concord, sauterne, port, sherry, and the like, sold in screw-capped bottles. When dry mealtime wines began to be popular in the mid-1970s, the Manteys replaced some of their native vines with French hybrid varieties and started selling Baco Noir, Baco Rosé, and Seyval Blanc in traditional bottles with straight corks. When Gottesman took over the Mantey winery in the late 1970s, he replaced its pre-Prohibition wooden casks with stainless-steel tanks and soon had quadrupled the winery's size. He made it his main production facility for his northern Ohio grapes. A tasting room was opened there to sell all of the Mantey and Meier's Wine Cellars wines.

Five miles north of Sandusky, on the peninsula called Catawba Island, is the ivy-covered limestone Mon Ami champagne cellar of four levels, two of them underground, built about 1872. It is another of the historic northern Ohio wineries that Gottesman bought. Mon Ami's products are bottle-fermented champagnes, produced with pre-Prohibition-era riddling racks and disgorging equipment, which the new owner plans to modernize. Upstairs is the Mon Ami Restaurant, refurbished since 1980 with bas-relief plaster murals of vineyards. Tours of the winery and tastings with cheese are offered for a small charge. With its picturesque vaulted cellars, the Mon Ami winery is a showplace for the Sandusky area wine industry.

• 10 •

Jutting above the surface of Lake Erie, between Sandusky and the Canadian boundary that bisects the lake, is the cluster of little, oddly shaped islands that long grew Ohio's best wines. The Lake Erie Islands are a viticultural curiosity: Being warmed in late autumn by the surrounding waters, they enjoy the longest grape-growing season in the northeastern United States. The island grapes are harvested as much as six weeks after the vintage ends on the mainland. In the winter, the lake freezes over, so solidly that automobiles can cross to the islands, and even this benefits the vineyards, because the cold air in spring delays the buds from opening until the danger of spring frosts has passed. From Sandusky and nearby Port Clinton, ferryboats serve the islets, except when the lake freezes over, and they carry most of the grape harvest to the mainland.

Few places in the world have transportation systems like the islands' air service. Hopping from island to island and to Port Clinton daily through the year are six-passenger planes small enough to use the island airstrips. Flipping between islets only one to eleven miles apart, they carry the islanders' children to and from high school on the mainland, and they also deliver groceries, coal, and island wines. For four decades the planes used were relics of the early age of aviation, the 1928-vintage Ford tri-motors famed as the "Tin Geese." A government edict no longer allows the relics to be used in the air-ferry service, but rides in them are still offered to tourists at Port Clinton.

Kelley's Island, the largest on the United States side of the lake, was planted with grapes by 1845, and the first winery north of Cincinnati was built there six years later. By 1880 vineyards on the island covered 750 acres and supported five wineries. Because Kelley's is the closest of the group to the mainland, summer cottages, camps, and beach clubs have supplanted all but two of the vineyards. In the early 1980s, Kirt and Toby Zettler planted three acres of Chardonnay and Riesling on the southeastern corner of Kelley's Island. They planned to build a Kelley's Island Winery on the site of the Beatty cellar, which operated from 1865 to about 1900.

South Bass Island, now more often called Put-in-Bay, is the most famous because of its role in the War of 1812 and the lofty Peace Monument that stands at the entrance to its bay. It was from here that Commodore Oliver Hazard Perry sailed to meet the British fleet on September 12, 1813, and here he put in after the battle to send his memorable dispatch of victory:

"We have met the enemy and they are ours—two ships, two brigs, one schooner, and one sloop." In earlier days, when paddle-wheel steamers brought vacationists from Cleveland and Toledo, there were palatial hotels on this island. A streetcar line once ran from the steamer dock to the sprawling Victory Hotel, since destroyed by a great fire.

There still are vineyards on both sides of quaint Put-in-Bay Village, but with tourism now the principal industry, only one winery, the Heineman Cellar, remains active. Norman Heineman, born on the island, and his son Louis till the thirty-five-acre vineyard that Norman's father Gustav planted after coming here in 1883 from the winegrowing region of Baden in Germany. In 1897, a year after the winery was built, workmen digging a well on the property stumbled into a huge cave of green crystal stalactites. The Heinemans charge tourists a fee to visit the cave, and a tour of the 50,000-gallon winery is included. They make eleven kinds of table wine, including a dry white Catawba, a Seyval and a Vidal Blanc, a sweet red Concord, and a blend of Catawba and Concord that they call "Sweet Belle." The wines are sold by the glass or bottle, and some of the visitors like them well enough to order shipments made by the case to their homes on the mainland.

From South Bass it is only a rowboat ride to pistol-shaped, three-mile-long Middle Bass Island and its chief landmark, the Lonz Winery, a frowning medieval-style castle on the lakeshore.

Jutting above the surface of Lake Erie is the cluster of little vine-covered islands that grow Ohio's best wines. This is Isle St. George, which was granted Federal viticultural-area recognition in 1982. (*Courtesy of Meier's Wine Cellars*)

This is the third historic northern Ohio winery that Edward Gottesman acquired. To the yachting fraternity of the entire Great Lakes region, the Lonz winery with its nearby harbor became a haven for bacchanalian festivity after the repeal of Prohibition. Island-born George Lonz, a bubbling, droll, Falstaffian host, sold his Isle de Fleurs Champagne by the bottle, rented guests the glasses in which to drink it, and often played the violin to entertain them. The forty-five-acre vineyard adjoining the winery dates from 1862, when it was planted by Andrew Wehrle from Alsace. He also built the original winery, but it was replaced twice following disastrous fires. It was Lonz who in 1942 built its turrets and battlements, once aptly described as "a mason's caprice." Lonz died in 1969 and the winery was closed three years later. Gottesman reopened it in 1982, and the first cuvées were laid down to revive the production of bottle-fermented Lonz Isle de Fleurs champagne.

From the Lonz castle it is an easy walk to the remaining winery on Middle Bass. It is owned by the Bretz family. Leslie Bretz, born there on Christmas Day in 1893, inherited the tiny cellar from his grandfather, Joseph Miller from Baden, who built it in 1865. The Bretz wines, Delaware, Concord, Catawba, and champagne, are sold entirely to tourists on the island.

Isle St. George in 1982 was the first island granted "viticultural area" recognition by the Federal government. Navigation charts, however, identify it as North Bass; the islands smaller than Kel-

George Lonz built this castle-like winery in 1942 on Middle Bass Island in Lake Erie to make his Isle de Fleurs Ohio champagnes.

ley's were all named for the fishing along their shores. The soil is cultivated for vineyards to a depth of only two inches, but the limestone underneath is crisscrossed by fissures and caves through which the water circulates and to which the roots of the vines readily penetrate. Sometimes the limestone must be blasted with dynamite in order to plant more vines. Isle St. George is only a mile long and covers 700-odd acres. Its highest point is scarcely fourteen feet above the lake level. Some of the fifteen families who live on the island are descendants of the winegrowers who planted the first grapes in 1844. There is a one-room grammar school, but the older children fly daily to and from Port Clinton High School, occasionally staying over- night on the mainland when their aerial schoolbus is grounded by fog or storm. There are no stores on the island, but a telephone call via the interisland cable can bring an air taxi in less time than you can get a taxi in your city. Television reception is of the best, and there is year-round fishing, because when the lake freezes over, its surface becomes dotted with wooden shanties, outfitted with stoves inside, for anglers who come from far and near to fish through holes in the ice. Dale Burris, who manages the vineyard, was born on the mainland, but has lived on the isle all his life except when he served in Viet Nam. (He won the heavyweight boxing championship of the Army in 1966.)

The largest planting of Vinifera grapes in Ohio began on Isle St. George in 1977. By 1982, when I last was there, there were sixty-seven acres of Chardonnay, Johannisberg Riesling, Ge- würztraminer, Pinot Noir, and Cabernet Sauvignon. The Riesling vines appeared the healthiest; the second most vigorous-looking were the Cabernets. The rest of the 298 acres were Catawba, Delaware, Concord, and the French hybrids Baco and Chelois. (The 1981 Isle St. George Johannisberg Riesling which I tasted at the Meier's Cellars near Cincinnati was a very good wine. A 1981 "Ohio Gewürztraminer" was even better, but the label didn't specify just where the grapes were grown.)

• 11 •

The revival of winegrowing in southern Ohio, where Long- worth's vineyards once flourished, was sparked by Henry Sonne- man in the early 1960s. At his urging, state viticulturists planted demonstration vineyards of wine grapes in several counties along the Ohio River. Wistar Marting, who had one of the test plant- ings at his farm on Creek Road near Clarksville, opened the 5000-gallon Tarula winery in 1965. Marting died a few years later. High school teachers Chris and Greg Hayward were running the three-acre vineyard and making the Tarula French hybrid wines when I last was there.

In 1969, Kenneth and James Schuchter planted twenty acres of hybrids and Labrusca types at their truck farm on US 22, two miles west of Morrow in Warren County. A year later they opened the Valley Vineyards winery and soon were doubling it in size. They began holding three-day wine festivals each September at Morrow, attended by thousands. During the 1970s the Schuchters built a new and modern 80,000-gallon winery and enlarged their vineyard to forty-five acres. Visitors there are offered a tray of twelve wines for tasting at 10 cents each. They say that a charge for wine tasting is required by the Ohio law.

On Bethel–New Hope Road west of Neal's Corner, Charles and Alice McIntosh began adding French hybrids to their vineyard of Labrusca varieties, and in 1972 built a hospitality room where they serve their wines with Wisconsin cheese. On the Ohio River shore three miles west of Manchester, veteran home winemaker Kenneth Moyer planted ten acres of French hybrid grapes in 1970. He and his wife Mary converted a former dance hall into a winery and restaurant where they serve meals with bottle-fermented Moyer champagne and table wines. The champagne sold so well that in 1980 Moyer opened another winery at New Braunfels, Texas, made champagne there of California grapes, and kept running his Ohio winery besides.

Computer analyst and wine hobbyist Norman E. Greene of Lebanon and his wife Marion began planting a mostly French hybrid vineyard of twenty acres in 1974 on Route 48 south of Ridgeville. Three years later, in a yellow one-time tobacco barn near their vineyard, they opened the 8000-gallon Colonial Vineyards winery. Combining his profession with his avocation, Greene made Colonial Vineyards the first computer-equipped farm winery in the state. When the computer told him that his Seyval Blanc was one of his slower selling wines, he changed its name to "chablis," and its sales immediately doubled.

In 1973, family physician Dr. Louis Jindra of Jackson and his wine hobbyist son Louis began planting twenty acres of French hybrids on Camba Road, five miles south of the town. Seven years later, with their vines in full bearing and having equipped a 5000-gallon Louis Jindra winery with temperature-controlled fermentation equipment, they began selling vintage-dated Seyval Blanc, Vidal Blanc, Baco Noir, and Maréchal Foch Chelois.

Two years after the Jindras started their vineyard, home winemaker Ralph Wise, a quality-control engineer whose great-grandfather owned the Kramer Wine Gardens at Dayton, Ohio, in pre-Prohibition times, began planting three acres of vines on Newkirk Lane three miles north of Lowden in southern Ohio. His wife Laura and their five children helped him turn a pre-1820 log barn into the 4000-gallon Brushcreek Vineyards winery, which they intend to enlarge to 10,000 gallons as soon as they win enough customers for their French hybrid and Labrusca wines.

In western Ohio, mechanical engineer Homer K. Monroe built the 3000-gallon Vinterra Vineyard winery in 1976 on the fifteen acres of French hybrids he had planted along Stoker Road two miles northeast of Houston (pronounced the New York way, not the Texas way). His wife Phyllis Jean, a former teacher of literature, presides over their charming tasting room. The Monroes make one of Ohio's best Baco Noirs. Five miles north, on Route 47 east of Route 66, is the equally small, partly underground Marlo Winery, named for Margaret and Milo Strozensky. He is both a sales engineer and the pastor of the Jackson Center Lutheran Church, which uses Marlo wine for Communion services. Margaret, the executive secretary at a local hospital, runs a gift shop at their winery. Their three acres of vines include French hybrids and Labrusca varieties.

The families of business consultant Ed Stefanko and electronic engineer John Feltz are partners in the twenty-acre mostly French hybrid vineyard and attractive 15,000-gallon Heritage Winery, which opened in 1978 on Wheelock Road south of Nashville. Stefanko was getting ready to introduce a Heritage bottle-fermented champagne. The Heritage owners and the Strozenskys have persuaded the Federal government to recognize their locality, "Loramie Creek," as a viticultural area. (Other appellations established in Ohio are "Grand River Valley," "Ohio River Valley," "Lake Erie," and "Isle St. George.")

On Route 55, a half mile west of Interstate 75 near Troy, is the 70,000-gallon Stillwater Winery, the handsomest and one of the most modern (1981) in Ohio, built partially underground and surrounded by landscaping. Its hospitality room, adorned by the works of local artists and homemade wreaths of grapevine prunings, is the most attractive in the Midwest and a fitting place to taste the Stillwater table wines and bottle-fermented champagnes. Its twenty-four-acre mostly French hybrid vineyard is five miles west at the Harry Jones II estate on the Stillwater River, which explains the winery's name. Overhead sprinklers protect the vines from damage by the locality's periodic frosts.

Harry Jones III is Stillwater's president, James R. Pour is the secretary and winemaker; the viticulturist is part-owner Dave Polson, and Ohio champagne maker Al Boffo is the consultant on sparkling wines.

Also new since 1977 are some wineries I haven't yet visited, such as the Wyandotte Cellars at Gahanna, Stone Quarry Vineyards near Waterford, Breitenbach Cellars at Dover in southeastern Ohio, and the Granville Vineyard near the town of that name. Ohio wineries totaled forty at this writing, and still more were preparing to start.

At press time, the state's newest winery was being prepared for bonding by Marion physician Dr. Thomas Quilter and his wife Mary on their four-acre Shamrock Vineyard, which is on Rengert Road three miles northeast of Waldo. The Quilters, long-time home winemakers, began planting the vineyard at their weekend retreat with French hybrids in 1971, and sold most of the grapes to other hobbyist enologists. Since then the Quilters have been building a model 2000-gallon winery of their own.

• 12 •

In 1981, the Ohio legislature adopted a tax-supported program to advance the state's vinicultural industry. It reduced the 26-cents-per-gallon state wine tax to 2 cents on the products of Ohio wineries smaller than 500,000 gallons and appropriated 3 cents per gallon of wine tax revenue to finance a long-range program of grape research and promotion of Ohio wines.

Ohio's move added it to the seventeen other states that already were criticized for taxing their home-grown wines less than those brought from other states or from abroad. In defense of the new law, the Ohioans replied that by taking this action more than a century after Nicholas Longworth's death, they had embarked on a long-overdue effort to realize his dream of creating an American Rhineland in Ohio.

6

New York, Champion of the East

NEW YORK has led the eastern states in volume of wine production since the repeal of Prohibition. The Empire State, with seventy-six wineries, produces about 32 million gallons of wine per year and is thereby second to California, which makes about twelve times as much. Of the 32 million gallons, about one-tenth, or well over 3 million, is champagne—about one-sixth as much of this bubbly wine as California makes.

Vineyard acreage in the state declined during the 1970s from 43,000 to 42,000 acres, but there were dramatic improvements in the quality of New York State wines. They were caused by the planting of 5000 acres of French hybrid and Vinifera winegrape varieties. These displaced some of the foxy-tasting Labrusca varieties, such as the Concords grown to make fresh grape juice. Concords still dominate the vineyards of New York. There also was some increased planting of Dutchess, Delaware, Elvira, and Catawba, the Labrusca varieties that make the least foxy-tasting wines.

By the early 1980s, some New York State wines, especially the whites, were challenging and outscoring California and European wines in comparative tastings, and were winning connoisseur praise as world-class wines.

New York has four principal vineyard districts, each with distinctive wines and colorful wineries that are covered in the two following chapters; and now a fifth district, which is described in this chapter, has lately been planted with Vinifera vines.

Best known, because of its scenic attractions and numerous wineries, is the Finger Lakes district in the west-central part of the state. But more important, because it has half of the state's total vineyard acreage, is the Chautauqua district, in the far west-

ern corner, bordering Lake Erie. Third in importance is Niagara
County, which extends eastward from Niagara Falls. The fourth
district is the Hudson Valley, only an hour or two from Manhattan. The fifth, which is both old and new, is the eastern end
of Long Island.

More than a million gallons of California bulk wine are
shipped each year to large New York wineries for blending purposes, in addition to California neutral brandy used in producing
New York State dessert wines. Less than half of the state's
175,000-ton average annual grape crop is used by New York
wineries. The rest is used in fresh Concord grape juice, jelly,
or jam, or is eaten fresh. A partial explanation is found in the
peculiar history of winegrowing in New York. Prohibitionist
influence during the past century accounts for the predominance
of the Concord grape and for New York's strange beverage-con-
trol laws, which long discouraged the establishment of additional
wineries and actually discouraged the purchase of wine.

• 2 •

New York was one of the first states to cultivate grapes, but
was one of the last in the East to develop a wine industry. Vineyards were planted on Manhattan Island more than three hundred years ago, when Peter Stuyvesant was governor of New
Netherland between 1647 and 1664. Stuyvesant sternly regulated
the sale of liquor, but he favored the use of wine. He even
authored an ordinance requiring that sailors on the high seas
be provided with a daily ration of wine to protect their health.
His successor, the first English governor of New York, Richard
Nicolls, granted a monopoly to one Paulus Richards to plant a
vineyard on Long Island. The French Protestants who settled
in Ulster County on the Hudson after 1667 tried unsuccessfully
to grow European grapes, but they then cultivated wild grapes
to make wine for use in their homes. The healthy crops from
their vines so impressed Governor Nicolls' successor that he expressed the belief, in a letter to the Lords of Trade in London,
that the New York colony alone could produce enough wine
to supply all the dominions of the Crown. In 1737, Robert Prince
established the Linnaean Gardens at Flushing on Long Island,
and from there the Isabella wine grape of South Carolina was
introduced throughout the East after 1816. Vines grew in New
York City as late as 1846, when the horticulturist, Alden Spooner,
published a book on winemaking. Spooner described the wine
he made at his own vineyard in Brooklyn, and mentioned other

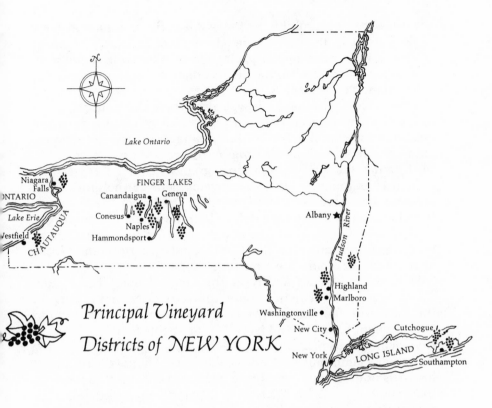

Principal Vineyard

Districts of NEW YORK

vineyards thriving there, on Manhattan, and at Southampton and New Utrecht on Long Island.

In 1818, a Baptist deacon, Elijah Fay, planted the first vineyard in what is now the Chautauqua Grape Belt along Lake Erie in western New York State and eastern Pennsylvania. Near the present village of Brocton in Chautauqua County, he set out wild vines which he had brought from New England. Because the wild grapes were harsh and excessively foxy, he replaced them in 1824 with Isabella and Catawba, and in 1830 Deacon Fay made ten gallons of wine. But it was not until 1859, when wineries were already operating along the lakeshore in Ohio, that the first of several "wine houses" around Brocton was built by the Deacon's son, Joseph Fay.

But the temperance movement, born in 1808 at Moreau in Saratoga County, was beginning to spread. By 1835 the state temperance society was advocating total abstinence from alcoholic beverages in any form. From New York State the temperance movement evolved into the nationwide crusade that brought about National Prohibition in 1920. In 1845, the Drys got a law passed prohibiting the public sale of liquor in New York State, but it was repealed two years later. They scored again in 1855, obtaining the passage of another state prohibition law, but it was declared unconstitutional.

Chautauqua County, where the Fays lived, was one of the centers of the Dry crusade. It was also where the Concord grape variety was introduced—not for winemaking, because dry wine made from Concord is harsh—but as a table grape. The temperance crusaders, with psalm-singing fervor, exhorted farmers of the Chautauqua district to produce grapes, not wine. It was Dry influence, as much as the later development of the grape-juice industry by the ardent Prohibitionist Dr. Welch, that caused the Chautauqua–Erie Grape Belt to become a fresh-grape district instead of a wine center. Although wine-grape varieties have lately been introduced in this three-county district, nine-tenths of the vines here still are Concords.

Winemaking began tardily in the Finger Lakes district, too. The Finger Lakes wineries credit the start of their industry to the Reverend William Bostwick, an Episcopal minister, who in 1829 brought Catawba and Isabella vine shoots from the Hudson River Valley and planted them in the rectory garden of his new church at Hammondsport on Keuka Lake. He gave cuttings to his parishioners, and soon there were vines in most gardens in the neighborhood. In 1850, at South Pulteney, four miles up the lake from Hammondsport, Andrew Reisinger, a vinedresser from Germany, planted a vineyard in which he introduced pruning and cultivation, operations unheard of before in the region. But it was not until 1860 that the commercial production of wine began in the area, with the building of the Pleasant Valley Winery near Hammondsport. This was concurrent with the death of the Cincinnati wine industry, then three decades old, from the vine disease that killed Nicholas Longworth's vineyards along the Ohio River. The Pleasant Valley Winery began by hiring champagne makers from Cincinnati. Other wineries began springing up around Hammondsport, and this created interest in wine-grape growing here at a time when the Concord variety was taking over in the Chautauqua region. Today, although the Finger Lakes district still produces only a third of the state's total grape crop, almost half of its vineyards are planted to wine varieties.

The oldest wine district in New York State is the Hudson River Valley. The first commercial winery there opened in 1839, two decades before those at Brocton and Hammondsport.

In the Niagara district, grape growing began about 1840, but as in the Finger Lakes region, there is no record of wine being made commercially there before 1860.

The foregoing explains why, in the extensive report on wine production in the United States which E. M. Erskine, secretary of the British Legation in Washington, prepared for his government in 1859, New York State's infant wine industry was not even mentioned. Erskine gave enthusiastic descriptions of wine-growing in Ohio, Missouri, Indiana, Illinois, Pennsylvania, Kentucky, Tennessee, Arkansas, the Carolinas, and California. His omission of New York could scarcely have been inadvertent.

The Finger Lakes wine industry expanded rapidly after the Civil War and this soon became the chief wine-producing region of New York State. An influx of German and Swiss immigrants, many of them from wine districts, helped to improve vineyard practices. As wineries were built along the lakes, their wines began winning medals for quality in Paris, Vienna, and Brussels, and the vintners proclaimed their district "the Rhine and Epernay of America." In 1882, the Geneva Experiment Station was founded, and it began a program of grape breeding and vineyard improvement. New York wines grew steadily better, and by the turn of the century such New York brands as Great Western were listed by restaurants and hotels across the country. I have in my files a copy of the menu of a banquet held at the Waldorf-Astoria Hotel by the American Winegrowers Association in February 1916. Of three dozen wines on the list for this dinner, eleven were from the Finger Lakes and Hudson Valley districts of New York, fifteen were from California, three from New Jersey, and one from Ohio.

When Wartime Prohibition began in 1919, most of the New York wineries were forced to close. Yet the ruin wrought in the industry was less complete than in California. Several of the New York vintners managed to survive the Dry years by switching to the production of grape juice. Most of it was sold in kegs with labels that said: "Caution—Do not add yeast or admit air or the contents will ferment." This, of course, is what the buyers proceeded to do.

With their Labrusca-flavored grapes, New York vintners also developed superior bottled grape juices, jams, and jellies—products which California, because it grows the relatively bland Vinifera grape varieties, was never able to match. A few of the New York wineries also obtained government permits to continue making wine and champagne for sacramental, tonic, and cooking uses. When Captain Paul Garrett in 1929 organized Fruit Industries, the giant grape-concentrate combine headquartered in California, Garrett's own Finger Lakes and Brooklyn wineries were the only ones in New York State to join. The chief Finger Lakes vintners, having remained independent with their own production and sales organizations, were thus better prepared to resume full-scale wine production and sale, when Prohibition ended in 1933, than were most of their California competitors.

• 3 •

In the latter years of the Dry era, when early repeal of the Prohibition Amendment was anticipated, public officials in most of the states set to work writing laws and regulations intended to control the sale of liquor within their borders as soon as it would become legal. Each state devised a different system that reflected the attitude of its legislators toward drinking. In New York, Prohibitionist influence was still strong, and it was strongest in the upstate counties that controlled the legislature at Albany. In consequence, the New York law that was written and became effective in 1933 was aimed at restricting the production and consumption of liquor—and it lumped wine with hard liquor. It discouraged the establishment of wineries by setting exorbitant annual license and filing fees. Farmers, who would have opened small wineries to sell their grapes in fermented form to their neighbors, could not afford to pay the fees. (The minimum New York winery license was $635, plus other fees and bond requirements making the total cost more than $1000 per year. Included was $250 for the privilege of sale at the winery, without which few small winegrowers can exist.)

Worse, the law restricted to liquor stores the sale of wine for home consumption, while it allowed food stores to sell beer. The State Liquor Authority at first issued some 1700 liquor-store licenses to serve all of New York's sixty-two counties. These licenses promptly skyrocketed in value, to such a point that one retailer in New York City sold the key to his store for $60,000 more than the value of his stock. Then the store owners, to protect their monopoly on the sale of wine and liquor by the package, organized strong associations and established a well-financed lobby in Albany. For four decades, this lobby defeated every bill introduced in the legislature to let food stores sell wine. Liquor stores in the state numbered about 5000, but housewives were reluctant to shop in liquor stores for the main ingredients of family meals. And to make the stores especially uninviting, a provision of the law prohibited them from stocking anything except sealed packages of liquor and wine—not even soda, lemon juice, cigarettes, or nuts, let alone such household merchandise as wine glassware. The buying of wine for its principal use—that of a daily mealtime beverage, the natural accompaniment of food—was thus discouraged by the New York law, as effectively as it was discouraged by the state monopoly stores in Pennsylvania and other monopoly states.

• 4 •

New wineries began opening in New York State in the mid-1970s. It was caused by a sharp drop in New York wineries' buying of local grapes to produce New York State wines. Some of the big wineries, finding their customers preferred wines with less Labrusca flavor than in the past, were increasing their purchases of bulk California wines for use in their blends. For decades before the 1970s, the farmers had prospered by selling most of their grapes to the big wineries and the rest to the grape-juice plants. But before the 1975 harvest, the wineries notified the growers they would buy only a fraction of that year's grape crop.

Suddenly faced by a grape glut, the farmers left hundreds of tons of that year's grapes to rot on the vines. A deepening gloom spread through the vineyards. It turned to anger in 1976, when the state's biggest winery came out with three new New York–California blends advertised as "New Taylor wines from the State of Californewyork."

The angry farmers began to notice how the grape growers in neighboring Pennsylvania were starting new wineries on their farms to sell their wines at retail, a practice the New York law restricted to 5 percent of the quantity the winery produced. A few New York growers sought to start their own wineries, but found they could not pay the excessive license fees. They demanded that the state come to their aid. Legislators were sympathetic, but little happened until some of the farmers threatened to back the recurring bills at Albany to permit the sale of wine in grocery stores.

In 1976, in a hitherto unprecedented action, Governor Hugh Carey announced a state-sponsored program to promote the sale of New York wines in stores and restaurants. He proclaimed November of that year as "New York State Wine Month" and held an elaborate tasting in the Four Seasons restaurant at which most of the wines wholly produced from grapes grown in the state were displayed. The governor also sponsored a bill in the legislature to reduce the minimum license fee for small farmer wineries to $125 per year. It was passed by the legislature, and in a publicized ceremony was signed into law.

Immediately scores of farmers banded together to build wineries. Within a year, twelve new cellars were opened for business. Until the farm winery bill became law, New York State had just twelve wineries producing wine primarily from grapes grown on their own vineyards. By 1983, the new farm wineries numbered forty-seven, increasing the state total from thirty-nine wineries to seventy-six. Most of the farm wineries aim to produce "château" wines the way small winegrowing estates do in California and in Bordeaux. New York's local grape growers' revolution changed the face of viniculture in the Empire State.

But the revolution was not yet over. The farmers next pushed new bills in the legislature to allow the farm wineries to hold tastings, to stay open on Sundays, to offer their wines freely for sale at the cellars, and to open branch outlets in the cities. Each new bill was promptly passed and signed into law. When they were allowed to stay open on Sundays, the wineries' sales immediately soared.

Meanwhile, the perennial bill to permit the sale of wine in food stores was reintroduced and as in the past was fought tooth and nail by the liquor lobby. This time it was amended to specify that for the first five years the groceries could sell only wines grown in New York State; but although backed by the grape growers, it was defeated, too. When a food-store wine bill eventually passes in New York, it will be followed by the other eastern states that have restricted wine sales to liquor stores since the repeal of Prohibition, including Pennsylvania, Rhode Island, Connecticut, New Jersey, and Massachusetts.

· 5 ·

The Empire State's fifth winegrowing district is the breadbasket of New York City, the still largely rural eastern half of Long Island between Patchogue and the Sound. If the several new Long Island farm wineries being built or planned during the 1980s make wines as fine as the Hargrave Vineyard's 1975 first vintage of Cabernet Sauvignon, Pinot Noir, Sauvignon Blanc, and Chardonnay, this district is the future Pauillac and Côte d'Or of New York.

Long Island's climate, moderated by the surrounding waters, is New York's best for noble Vinifera grapes. It has a 210-day growing season, forty-five days longer than in the Finger Lakes. There is historical evidence that "Moses the Frenchman" Fournier had extensive vineyards there as early as 1640, more than three centuries ago. Why present-century winegrowers planted no wine grapes on the Island before 1973, when Alex and Louisa Hargrave started their vineyard, was a viticultural mystery until agricultural experts recently supplied the answer: In the Island's moist climate, it only became possible to control vine pests late in this century, when modern sprays came into use.

It was Louisa, born on the Island, who persuaded six-feet-seven Alexander, who was thinking of becoming a winegrower, that this might be a good place to start. They bought a sixty-six-acre former potato farm on Alvah's Lane, off Route 48 at Cutchogue on the Island's North Fork, and two years later, with their vines growing well, they air-conditioned an old potato cellar and equipped it as their winery with stainless steel and new oak casks.

In 1979, when the Hargraves' wines were selling well on the New York City fine-wine market and the vineyard was being enlarged to fifty-five acres, a rush to plant more Vinifera on the Island began. Former air traffic controller Ken Conrad and Manhattan advertising executive Lyle Greenfield started ten- and twenty-acre vineyards on the Island's South Fork. In 1983, as partners, they built the 15,000-gallon partially underground Bridgehampton Winery a mile north of town on the Bridgehampton–Sag Harbor Turnpike. Also ready for the 1983 vintage was the Island's third winery, a former potato barn at Peconic on Route 25, equipped by former restaurant owners Patricia and Peter Lenz, who have thirty acres of grapes and plan to make the first Long Island champagne. West of the Lenz's winery, on another thirty-acre vineyard, was the future Peconic Bay Vineyards winery of air controllers Ray Blum and Bill Littell. At East Hampton on the South Fork, Massachusetts winemaker David Tower leased an idle school building as his future Hampton Vineyards winery.

Some were predicting that another decade would find Long Island potato fields displaced by a dozen wineries and by 10,000 acres of Vinifera vines.

7

The Finger Lakes Wineries

Five large Finger Lakes district wineries—
Pleasant Valley, Taylor, Gold Seal, Widmer's, and Canandaigua Industries—have long produced three-fourths of the wine made in New York State. Taylor, which also owns Pleasant Valley, is the third largest producer of bottle-fermented champagnes in the world, next to Henkell in Germany and Moët et Chandon in France. This chapter describes these principal Finger Lakes wineries and their new farm winery neighbors.

• 2 •

The Finger Lakes—Canandaigua, Keuka, Seneca, Cayuga, Owasco, Skaneateles, and half a dozen others—are so long, narrow, and parallel in their north–south direction that the Indians thought them the imprint of the hands of the Great Spirit. Scooped out by glacial action ages ago, these deep blue lakes make the eleven counties of the district a spectacularly scenic vacationland. Among its chief attractions are the picturesque vineyards and wineries, most of which offer cellar tours and tasting hospitality to visitors.

As in other vineyard regions that border bodies of water, the Finger Lakes temper the extremes of temperature along their shores and thereby protect the grapevines from the killing frosts of spring and fall. The snowy winters, however, average several degrees colder than in Germany and France. Winter temperatures sometimes drop to eighteen or twenty degrees below zero (compared to nine degrees below, the lowest temperature recorded at Geisenheim in Germany's Rheingau during the first half of this century), and protracted freezes in some years have damaged the Finger Lakes vines.

116

The gas-operated "bird-banger" fires a shotgun-like blast every 45 to 60 seconds to frighten birds away from the ripening grapes in this Finger Lakes vineyard. (*Taylor Wine Company*)

Mechanical harvesting machines, which appeared in the region for the first time in 1968, have now supplanted most of the human vintagers. Each machine harvests an acre an hour and does the work of forty pairs of human hands.

Grapes can be grown on the rocky, steep, and rolling hillsides near any of the lakes, but at present the vineyards are concentrated along Canandaigua, Keuka, Seneca, and Cayuga in Steuben, Yates, Schuyler, Seneca, and Ontario counties. Keuka, known as "The Crooked Lake" because of its irregular Y shape, has vines along its hillsides all the way from Hammondsport at its southern end to Branchport and Penn Yan at the northwestern and northeastern tips. Between the two forks of Keuka, lofty Bluff Point with its Captain Paul Garrett chapel extends twelve miles into the lake and is gracefully draped with vines. In early days excursion steamers plied the larger lakes, and once, during

Vineyards border Keuka, "The Crooked Lake," near Hammondsport, N.Y. (*Taylor Wine Company*)

a rate war between rival steamship companies, vacationists could travel seventeen miles on Keuka from Hammondsport to Penn Yan for a 10-cent fare. Now highways border the shores, and the lakes serve for such sports as boating, swimming, and fishing, but not for skating, for the lakes seldom freeze over.

• 3 •

In the quiet, pleasant town of Hammondsport, the birthplace of pioneer aviator Glenn Curtiss, winemaking is the principal industry. Each October, the local churches hold a public Sunday service overlooking Keuka Lake to bless the grape harvest.

Driving southwest from the town, the first big cellar you see is the oldest in the district, the Pleasant Valley winery, home of Great Western wines and champagnes. It is named for the narrow valley through which the inlet to Keuka Lake flows. Above a tree-shaded archway that leads into the original underground wine vault is a stone plate carved with the names of Charles Davenport Champlin and his farmer neighbors, who founded the company in 1860. Today the cool vault, walled with hand-cut native stone, serves as a unique tasting room for the thousands of visitors who annually tour the 6-million-gallon winery and sample its products. Here the first New York

Oldest of the Finger Lakes wineries is the Pleasant Valley Wine Company, founded in 1860. It produces "Great Western" wines and champagnes. (*Taylor Wine Company*)

The cellar crew at New York State's Pleasant Valley winery in 1884. (*Taylor Wine Company*)

State champagne was made when the Civil War ended in 1865. Joseph Masson, trained in France and hired by Champlin from the M. Werk champagne cellars in Cincinnati, made it and called it Sparkling Catawba, as Nicholas Longworth did. Two years later the wine was entered in the Paris Exposition, and though the fruity Labrusca taste was strange to the European judges, they gave it an honorable mention award. Joseph Masson was joined at Hammondsport by his brother Jules, who had been superintendent of the Longworth Wine House at Cincinnati until the grape sickness obliterated the vineyards there. In 1870, the Masson brothers served a new sparkling blend of Delaware and Catawba to a meeting of the Pleasant Valley Grape Growers Association. Presiding at the meeting was famed horticulturist Colonel Marshall Wilder of Boston, who on tasting the wine exclaimed, "Truly, this will be the great champagne of the West!" By West, Wilder explained, he meant our entire continent, the New World. His remark gave Great Western champagne its name, strange though it seems for a product of New York State.

In 1873 at the Vienna Exposition, Great Western became the first American champagne to win a gold medal in Europe, and it later gathered additional prizes at Brussels, Philadelphia, and Paris. For half a century before Prohibition, this champagne "from Rheims, New York" was the leading sparkling wine made in this country. Rheims was the name of a post office in the winery; and though the office was closed long ago, the old address still appeared on the company's letterhead until 1970. Rheims is also the name of the winery's station on the eight-mile-long, single-track Bath & Hammondsport Railroad, built by the company's owners in 1872 to haul their wine and brandy to market. The B. & H., still operating profitably today, is famous for its nickname, "The Champagne Trail," and also for its slogan, "Not as long as the others but just as wide."

When Prohibition came, Pleasant Valley was one of the few wineries to keep open because it held a Federal permit to make wines for sacramental use. This permit, however, did not include the winery's principal product, champagne, because officials of the Prohibition Bureau insisted that champagne was not a wine. Pleasant Valley's chief owners, Malburn and Charles Champlin, grandsons of the founder, filed suit against the government. Rather than fight the suit, the bureau granted them special permission to sell champagne to the clergy. For two years the Champlins enjoyed a rich monopoly as the only winery privileged to supply bubbly to servants of the Lord. But then other vintners made a fuss, and the government again yielded, permitting competitors' sacramental wines to sparkle, too. Pleasant Valley's business then dwindled, but the company still managed to survive, by selling grape juice to home winemakers, until Repeal. When Charles Champlin died in 1950, Pleasant Valley stock was sold to eastern financiers.

For many years past, the owners of the neighboring Taylor Winery had had their eyes on Great Western, and in 1961 the Taylor family saw a chance to buy its stock. They acquired a controlling interest and made the production and sale of Great Western wines a division of Taylor.

The late Greyton Taylor and his son Walter (of whom more presently) took charge of the Pleasant Valley winery and began adding "varietals" to its list of "generic" table wines. The first three "varietals" were Delaware and Diamond, named for white Labrusca grape varieties, and Isabella, which makes a Labrusca rosé. In 1964, Pleasant Valley made history by introducing the first Finger Lakes wines made entirely of the new French-American hybrid grapes. The company then began changing its generically named table wines to "varietals" named for the increasing proportions of the French grapes in their blends. "Aurora" was added to the label of Great Western sauterne, and the burgundy became also "Baco Noir." In addition to these, Great Western has introduced a series of new wines since Dominic Carisetti, trained at UC Davis, became the senior winemaker. In 1980 and 1981 he made estate-bottled Great Western ice wines (see page 76) of Catawba and the French hybrid Vidal Blanc. The newest

Great Western vintage-dated wines are of the New York State hybrid Cayuga White and the white French hybrid Verdelet.

• 4 •

Walk a scant hundred yards from the Great Western cellars and you reach the Taylor winery. By acquiring the Pleasant Valley Wine Company in 1961, Taylor became legally, as well as in fact, New York's "Bonded Winery No. 1." With its capacity of 24 million gallons, Taylor is now the largest American winery outside of California. When I first visited Hammondsport in the late 1930s, Taylor consisted of just four buildings, the main one a four-story mansard-roofed structure with vaults cut back into the stone hillside. This quaint pre-Prohibition edifice now serves as a visitor reception center and office building. It is flanked by a complex of three dozen new above-ground processing and aging cellars and warehouses covering some fifty acres. The traditional method of clarifying bottle-fermented champagnes has been mechanized by introduction of the transfer process, in which the champagnes are filtered instead of being disgorged by hand.

Taylor dates from 1880, when Walter Taylor, a master cooper, came to Hammondsport with his bride to make barrels for the thriving wineries. The young couple settled on a seven-acre vineyard, and two years later bought a seventy-acre farm on Bully Hill, north of town. Taylor planted half of it to Ives and Delaware, the grapes then most in demand for red and white wines. He had worked with his father, George Taylor, before his marriage, and he now brought his father and mother to the farm. Three sons, Fred, Clarence, and Greyton, and two daughters, Flora and Lucy, were born to Walter and Addie Taylor between 1883 and 1903. All five grew up in the business and helped it grow. Salesmen selling Taylor wine in bottles and barrels covered territories in several states before the First World War. In 1919, when Wartime Prohibition began, most of the Hammondsport wineries closed their doors, but the Taylors went into the grape-juice business instead. The four-story mansard-roofed Columbia Winery, built in 1886, was for sale, and the Taylors bought it and moved there from Bully Hill. When the Taylors saw the end of Prohibition was near, they began modernizing the winery. At Repeal, their wines were among the first on the market, and they began their climb to leadership in the East. On taking over the Pleasant Valley winery, the Taylor Wine Company "went public," the first major American winery to put its stock on the open market. Until the Taylors died—Fred in 1968, Greyton two years later, and Clarence in 1976—the management of Taylor was a family clan.

"Uncomplicated wines," port, sherry, sauterne, rhine, burgundy, claret, rosé, champagnes, and vermouth long were the mainstays of the Taylor line. The once-strong Labrusca flavors became less pronounced as the new plantings of French hybrid grapes increased. The champagnes have only a hint of Labrusca fragrance. There now are four Taylor wines with proprietary names: Lake Country Red, White, Pink, and Gold. All are blends with French-American grapes, but have enough Labrusca character to make them distinctly different from California wines. In 1981, "soft" versions of the Lake Country wines were added, with 8 percent alcoholic content instead of the standard 12.

In 1977, with the Taylors gone, both the Taylor and Pleasant Valley wineries were purchased by the Coca-Cola Company of Atlanta, Georgia, in an exchange of stock valued at $93 million. In the next few months, Coca-Cola bought two California wineries—Sterling in the Napa Valley and the Monterey Vineyard cellar—and after building a new Taylor California Cellars winery in 1982, became the third largest producer and marketer of wine in the United States (after Gallo and Heublein) and intended soon to become Number One. This was of historic Bacchic interest because Coca-Cola thereby had come full circle. Few realize that in 1885, before Coca-Cola became the American temperance drink, it was "French Wine Coca," a patent nerve tonic based on wine, sold in Atlanta drugstores.

Then in 1983, after six profitless years in the wine business, Coca-Cola suddenly sold all of its wine properties, including Taylor and Great Western, to the worldwide Seagram Wine Company. This raised a question, not yet answered at this writing, of future planning of New York wine production by Seagram, which already owned the competing Gold Seal winery, a property it had acquired in 1979.

• 5 •

On Greyton Taylor Memorial Drive, a mile and a half north of Hammondsport, are the 96,000-gallon Bully Hill winery, the Greyton Taylor Wine Museum, and the Winemaker's Shop. These are the works of Walter Stephen Taylor, the grandson of the Taylor Winery's founder and once his late father's assistant at the Pleasant Valley winery.

Fired by his uncles in 1970 for publicly attacking the Taylor companies, Walter installed his own winery in his grandfather's horse barn and converted the original wooden winery into the museum dedicated to his father. The chief museum exhibits are relics of the more than fifty wineries that once operated around the Finger Lakes—vineyard implements, coopers' tools, presses, bottles, and old advertisements of wine. One of the prizes is an ancient brandy still, a reminder that the pre-Prohibition wineries here also made and sold brandy. The Winemaker's Shop next door sells grape juice, winemaking equipment, and supplies to amateur enologists. Walter is the co-author, with one-time Pleasant Valley winemaker Richard P. Vine, of the *Home Winemaker's Handbook,* and he illustrated the book himself.

The Bully Hill winery turns out estate-bottled table wines named for the French hybrids, plus "varietals" of the native Delaware, Diamond, and Ives, and blends of hybrids and Labrusca types called Bully Hill red, white, and rosé. Added in 1976 was a bottle-fermented brut champagne produced from Seyval Blanc.

To sell his wines, six-foot-three, mustachioed Walter Taylor flies and hitchhikes across the country, wearing blue jeans and hiking boots and carrying a back-pack, guitar, harmonica, and a box of grapevines. He often distributes vines to his fellow passengers when he travels by air. Walter's zany sales methods obviously work, because Bully Hill wines are sold in forty states. In 1983, when New York State reduced its distillers' license from $21,000 to $100, he announced he would begin distilling brandy from Concord grapes.

• 6 •

Four miles up West Lake Road (Route 54A) from Hammondsport is venerable Gold Seal, the most imposing stone winery in the East. Founded in 1865 as the Urbana Wine Company, it is the second oldest in the district and looks its age, with its many stories under nineteenth-century gabled roofs crowned by lines of dormer windows and a pair of steeples. Only the highway and a narrow line of trees separate the winery from the waters of Keuka Lake, where steamers docked in early days to bring supplies and to load champagne. This is the home of nationally distributed Gold Seal, Henri Marchant, and Charles Fournier wines and champagnes.

In the spring of 1865, as General Lee was surrendering at Appomattox Courthouse, a group of Hammondsport merchants and Urbana Township farmers, following the example of Charles

Champlin and his neighbors at Pleasant Valley, organized the Urbana Company to build the winery and to make champagne. Their product was first called "Imperial," but in 1887 it was renamed "Gold Seal." The firm prospered for half a century before Prohibition. During the thirteen-year Dry era, when it was headed by Corning newspaper publisher and former Congressman Edwin Stewart Underhill* and his son, it made sacramental and medicinal wines as the Gold Seal Products Company. At Repeal in 1933, the firm name was changed back to Urbana. In 1957, during a two-year association with Louis Benoist of Almadén in California, the company became Gold Seal Vineyards, Inc. In 1979 control was purchased by the House of Seagram, which owns Paul Masson Vineyards and dozens of other vineyard properties around the world.

In its more than a century of operation, wine production at Gold Seal Vineyards has been headed by men of French heritage. The first was Charles Le Breton, hired from the Roederer champagne cellars of Rheims. Jules Crance, from Moët et Chandon at Epernay, served from 1921 to 1923. In 1934, President Underhill of Urbana asked Charles Fournier, the chief winemaker of Veuve Clicquot Ponsardin at Rheims, to recommend someone who could restore Gold Seal to its pre-Prohibition greatness. Fournier took the job himself, came to Hammondsport as Urbana production manager, brought his own champagne yeast from Veuve Clicquot, and became an American citizen.

Educated at the University of Paris and at French and Swiss wine schools, Fournier had seen the planting of the improved French hybrid grapes spread in those countries. In 1936, while Philip Wagner was getting started with hybrids in Maryland, Fournier introduced to Hammondsport the hybrid varieties since known as Rosette and Ravat Blanc. He introduced his own champagne blend, Charles Fournier Brut, to the American market in 1943, and it scored an immediate success. In 1950, for the first time in the history of the California State Fair at Sacramento, eastern and foreign wines were invited to be judged in open competition with those produced in California. Charles Fournier New York State Champagne Brut was awarded the only gold medal—an event so discomfiting to the California vintners that no out-of-state wines were invited to their state fair again.

In 1953 Fournier hired Dr. Konstantin Frank to start a nursery of Vinifera grapes at Urbana. The story of Dr. Frank and of

*Of the same Underhill family whose members pioneered commercial grape growing in the Hudson Valley. All were descendants of Captain John Underhill, who came from England in the seventeenth century.

his association with Fournier is told in the following section, but it should be pointed out here that the first Vinifera wines produced commercially in the East came from Fournier at Gold Seal. I was one of those present at the winter 1961 dinner of the San Francisco Wine and Food Society, in historic Jack's Restaurant, when Gold Seal New York State 1959 Chardonnay and Johannisberg Riesling were served for the first time in the West. To the several California vintners in attendance that memorable night, it was a shock to realize that their long-acknowledged monopoly on the production of fine Vinifera wines in North America might at last be at an end.

Tall, lean, bespectacled Charles Fournier, in appearance and speech resembling a foreign diplomat more than a vintner, retired in 1967 at the age of sixty-five but continued as the honorary lifetime president of Gold Seal until his death in 1983. Since Fournier's retirement, Gold Seal production has been headed by another French-trained enologist, technical director Guy Devaux from the Societé Marne et Champagne of Epernay.

Their French heritage did not cause Fournier and Devaux to undervalue the "real grape" flavor of the principal New York State grapes. Since 1972 Gold Seal has been producing a sweet, slightly bubbly red wine labeled "Labrusca" for that family of native grapes. It became so popular, despite some confusion with the Lambrusco wines from Italy, that Gold Seal later added a sweet "Labrusca white."

The best-selling table wine, of the seemingly endless list Gold Seal makes, is Catawba Pink, a medium-sweet Labrusca-flavored rosé. But the company's best—now made by Fresno State University–trained enologist James Gifford—are the Fournier Brut and Henri Marchant transfer-process champagnes, the Fournier Chablis Nature, and the vintage-dated, estate-bottled Chardonnays and late-harvest Rieslings grown on the company's Valois vineyard on the east side of Seneca Lake.

• 7 •

On Middle Road, a short drive from the Gold Seal Vineyards brings you to the small winery, the Vinifera vineyard, and the one-story red-brick house of Dr. Konstantin Frank. A sturdy, proud, assertive man, he is the Russian-born German scientist who, after countless others had failed for three centuries, has shown dramatically that the Old World grape, the Vinifera, can be grown in eastern America. He is also the most controversial figure in the eastern wine industry, because he publicly condemns the French-American hybrid grapes which others have planted in preference to Vinifera.

Konstantin Frank was born in the Ukraine on July 4, 1899, the fourth of ten children of a farmer whose crops included grapes. He fought in the White Russian army, studied agriculture at the polytechnic institute of Odessa, organized collective farms in the southern Ukraine for the Communists, then completed his studies, taught viticulture and enology, and did grape research at the local agricultural institute. During the German occupation, he became the institute's director. When the Second World War ended, he went to Austria and Bavaria and managed farm properties for the American occupation forces.

In 1951, at the age of fifty-two, Dr. Frank emigrated with his wife and three children to America, arriving in New York with forty dollars, unable to speak English. He got a job washing dishes at an Automat restaurant and saved enough to buy a one-way ticket to the nearest grape research station—the New York State Experiment Station at Geneva. There he described his Russian experience and applied for work on grapes. But instead, he says bitterly, "they let me hoe blueberries," and for two years he did only menial work.

Seeing the Finger Lakes growers planting the new French hybrids, he inquired why Vinifera were not being planted instead. The winters are too cold here, he was told; the delicate European varieties were likely to die when the ground froze. Having grown Vinifera himself in Russia—"where the temperature goes to forty below, where we had to bury the entire vine in winter, where when we spit, it froze before it hit the ground"—Dr. Frank vehemently disagreed. He argued that the Old World grapes planted in the East during past centuries could not have died from cold, that rather they were killed by diseases and pests; and these, he pointed out, modern science now had ways to control.

Dr. Konstantin Frank, the Russian-born German scientist who proved that the Old World's Vinifera grapes can be grown in eastern North America, and who opposes the French-American hybrids. (*Donald J. Flanagan, Buffalo, N.Y.*)

His argument came to the attention of Charles Fournier. Gold Seal's then-president, too, had known frigid winters in Europe, and had seen Chardonnay and Pinot Noir thriving at Rheims and Epernay, seven degrees of latitude farther north than Hammondsport, after winters when temperatures in the French Champagne district fell below zero. Fournier realized that the emigré scientist might be right, and in 1953 hired him as a consultant for Gold Seal Vineyards.

Dr. Frank told Fournier what his research in Russia had shown: What were needed in climates where the ground froze in winter were hardy roots onto which the Vinifera vines could be grafted—roots that would ripen the wood of the vine before the first winter freeze. To search for such roots, the two men set out on a tour of the Northeast countryside. In the garden of a convent in Québec, they found Pinot vines growing and were told that they yielded wine, in that stern climate, in one year out of three. From the monk in charge of the garden, they obtained some of his roots. Back at Gold Seal, they began grafting—to the Canadian roots and some of their local ones—Riesling, Chardonnay, Gewürztraminer, and Cabernet Sauvignon vines they obtained from the University of California vineyard at Davis.

During the next five years, thousands of experimental grafts were made and planted. In February 1957 came the critical test: Temperatures on the lake slopes plummeted to twenty-five degrees below zero. Some of the hardiest Labrusca vines, Dutchess and Isabella in particular, were frozen and bore no grapes that year. On some of the Concord, Delaware, and Catawba vines, a tenth to a third of the buds were killed. But on the first Riesling and Chardonnay vines that had been grafted on hardy roots, fewer than a tenth of the buds showed any damage. And when vintage time came in the fall of that year, these vines at Gold Seal produced ripe grapes at a rate that promised crops of three to four tons per acre. Fournier needed no further convincing, but began planting the noble Vinifera vines as fast as he could get enough rootstocks on which to graft them.

Dr. Frank, triumphant, bought a tract of land nearby and started planting a vineyard of his own. When the first commercial New York State Vinifera wines, made at Gold Seal, were introduced in 1961, Dr. Frank proclaimed it "the second discovery of America," his own contribution to the nation of which he had become a citizen. He built his own winery, named it Vinifera Wine Cellars, and put his own wines on the market in 1965. He since has increased the winery's capacity to 60,000 gallons and his vineyard to seventy-eight acres, and has imported from Russia and Germany cold-resistant strains of additional Vinifera grape varieties. A son-in-law, Walter Volz, now manages the vineyard, and Dr. Frank's son, Willibald, markets the wines.

Virtually everyone who has tasted the Vinifera wines of Hammondsport has praised them. Dr. Frank's Trockenbeerenauslese 1961 was served in the White House and in the executive mansion at Albany. When first introduced, it was priced in stores at $45 a bottle and outsold equivalent German wines that cost a third less. Some of his Chardonnays that I have tasted at the winery have had the full character of French white burgundies, and one of his four-year-old Pinot Noirs had the nose of a ten-year-old wine.

But none of the Finger Lakes wineries except Gold Seal has been willing to plant any acreage of Vinifera. Dr. Frank blames the Geneva Experiment Station, which has pronounced the Vinifera varieties "marginal," less hardy than the French hybrids, too risky to be cultivated by anyone except an expert, and not recommended for large-scale commercial planting in New York State.

This enrages Dr. Frank, who incidentally enjoys a fight. He insists that the Vinifera require no more care than the hybrids and claims that they ripen better at Hammondsport than in Germany or France. "The Genevans say the growers must be experts to grow these grapes here," he fumes. "The poor Italian and Russian peasants with their shovels can do it, but the American farmer with his push-button tools cannot. It is unbelievable that the hybrids, prohibited everywhere except in France and the United States, not good enough for poor Italian or even poor Russian peasants, can be called good enough for the Americans, the most prosperous people in the world."

Answering Dr. Frank's attacks, the Geneva Station still recommends the hybrids, but concedes in its publications that his Riesling wines are "comparable to those of Germany," that his Chardonnay and Pinot Noir "stand with the finest French burgundies," and that "there is undoubtedly a place for a certain percentage of these superb connoisseurs' wines."

Charles Fournier, the man in the middle of the controversy, avoided taking either side. When Fournier told me that Gold Seal would continue to grow Vinifera, he explained: "It is still a young experiment. We feel safer with the hybrids, but we love the Vinifera wines." Fournier believed the future of Vinifera in the East would depend on the wine-buying public; that if we are willing to pay the prices for fine eastern wines that we pay for prestige European labels, the eastern vintners will find it profitable to plant the *cépages nobles* and to produce superlative wines of their types.

• 8 •

Returning on Middle Road toward Hammondsport from Dr. Frank's winery, you can visit the 20,000-gallon Heron Hill Vineyards winery, opened in 1977, one of the first following the passage of the New York farm winery law. It is built on two levels into the side of Bully Hill. Peter Johnstone, a former copywriter for a New York City advertising agency, came here in 1970 and planted the third Vinifera vineyard on Keuka Lake, twenty acres of White Riesling and Chardonnay. His vines have suffered so much damage in subzero winters that he has begun burying them each fall and uncovering them in spring. "Vinifera are very useful in winning awards," says Johnstone, discussing the prizes Heron Hill has won in three successive state fair competitions. But much of the wine Heron Hill sells is made of the Seyval Blanc and Ravat Blanc hybrids that his partner, John Ingle, grows at Canandaigua Lake.

A mile south of Hammondsport, on the road to Pleasant Valley, is the 15,000-gallon De May Wine Cellars, which also started in 1977. French winemaker Serge de May brought his winemaking equipment with him from Vouvray in France. His wife and three children work in the winery.

Atop a hill overlooking Bluff Point opposite Keuka Lake State Park is the nineteen-room Greek revival mansion called Chateau Esperanza, built in 1838 by a wealthy landowner as his family home. During this century it has served variously as an art gallery, and for church services, and as a county home. In 1979 the chateau became a winery, and its wines, labeled with the names of the growers of the grapes, won prizes at the New York State Fair. Four years later, winemaker John Lebeck and his wife Sherri had left the chateau. Their successor was the former Bully Hill winery cellar master, Dana Keeler.

Nearby, on Italy Hill Road, which extends west from Branchport, is the Finger Lakes Wine Cellar on seventy-five acres of French hybrid and Labrusca vines. Arthur and Joyce Hunt, the owners, are the sixth generation of descendants of Adam Hunt, who came to Yates County in the early 1800s and purchased part of what then was the town of Jerusalem. The winery was opened in 1981 in a renovated barn. Visitors are invited to tour the vineyard on a haywagon before tasting the Hunts' Aurora, Cayuga White, Delaware, Dutchess, Niagara, and Seyval.

If you continue north from Branchport, Route 54A will take you to Penn Yan, where a warehouse on Liberty Street once was Captain Paul Garrett's Penn Yan wine cellar. (Yes, Penn Yan sounds like an Indian name, but it stands for Pennsylvanians and Yankees, the earliest settlers of this area.)

On Highway 54, which skirts the east side of Keuka Lake, is the 140,000-gallon, metal-roofed Villa d'Ingianni Winery, opened in 1973 by Dr. Vincent d'Ingianni, who came here from New Orleans twelve years before. The winery is owned now by James and Carole Kilgore, who have vineyards on Bluff Point.

Opposite the south end of Bluff Point, on Dutch Street, is the McGregor Vineyard Winery, built in 1980 by Eastman Kodak research scientist Robert H. McGregor on the eighteen-acre Vinifera vineyard he began planting nine years before. His wines, including Riesling, Chardonnay, Gewürztraminer, and Pinot Noir, are among the finest grown in the Finger Lakes district.

On Bath Road in Dundee, Father Thomas Lee Hayes was planning in 1983 to open a winery, to be named "The Parson's Cellar," adjoining the American Youth Hostel. He is the only Episcopal priest to have operated an American winery, the High Tor Vineyard cellar in the Hudson Valley, where he was briefly in charge for an interim owner in 1971.

· 9 ·

At the head of Seneca Lake are the city of Geneva and Cornell University's big State Agricultural Experiment Station, where a program of grape and wine research has been under way since 1962. For thirty years after the end of Prohibition, the influence of Drys in Albany still prevented any official mention of the word "wine." When Prohibition began in 1920, the great horti-culturist Dr. Ulysses Prentiss Hedrick saved the Geneva Station's wine grapes for himself and had his chauffeur take them home and make them into wine for him. Hedrick, whose chief interest was winegrowing, wrote two books of advice to home winegrowers without the university's blessing. He was also the first—long before Dr. Frank—to prove that it is possible to grow Vinifera in the East. "We know now how to control the infections and fungi that attack them," he wrote in 1945 in his *Grapes and Wines from Home Vineyards*. Hedrick, however, found it necessary to cover his Vinifera vines with earth before each winter to keep them from freezing.

At Repeal in 1933, the late Professor John Einset, born in Norway, revived the wine-grape breeding program at Geneva. Forty years later it yielded the station's first nonfoxy wine grape, named Cayuga White. It was followed in 1982 by Horizon, a white blending grape.

Although New York State has no separate college department of viticulture and enology such as that at the University of California, the Pomology Department at Cornell was renamed "Pomology and Viticulture" in 1974. Besides undergraduate courses in viticultural subjects and food fermentation taught at Cornell, there is advanced instruction at Geneva, where graduate and postdoctoral students work on wine projects. Experimental wines made at Geneva now number several hundred per year. Annual workshops are held there for professional enologists, with extra sessions at intervals for farm wineries and amateurs. Two Californians are now members of the Geneva faculty, viticulture professor Dr. Robert Pool, and food science professor Terry Acree. Advances in research at Geneva helped lead to the formation in 1976 of an eastern section of the American Society of Enologists, headed by the Taylor winery's research director, Andrew Rice. It was not until 1982 that an associate professor of enology was appointed at Cornell. He is Dr. Thomas H. B. Cottrell, a onetime Cornell student who helped found the Cuvaison winery in California in 1974.

A faculty group of Cornell amateur winemakers, who called themselves the Ithaca Oenological Union, helped Dr. Frank in 1967 to organize the American Wine Society, which had its headquarters at the home of Emeritus Professor of Chemistry Albert W. Laubengayer until it was moved in 1973 to Michigan, then nine years later back to New York State.

• 10 •

A revival of winegrowing is in progress along the shores of Seneca and Cayuga lakes, southeast of Geneva. Some say these areas have the best climates for wine grapes, including Vinifera, in all of the Finger Lakes region.

The first winery to start between the lakes in more than half a century was built in 1976. It is the Wagner Vineyards' 100,000-gallon octagonal cellar on the east shore of Seneca, on Route 414 southwest of Lodi. Navy veteran Stanley Wagner and his sons and daughter have made this an estate winery, producing only vintage-dated wines grown on their own 120-acre vineyard, a fifth of which grows such Vinifera as Johannisberg Riesling and Chardonnay. Their UC Davis–trained winemaker, Christopher Johnson, began producing champagne in 1980, starting with a sparkling rosé. Other Wagner wines are Aurora, Seyval, Delaware, De Chaunac, and Rougeon. In 1983 the Wagners added an open-air restaurant beside the winery, overlooking Seneca Lake.

South of Wagner, on the same road, is the 20,000-gallon Poplar Ridge Vineyards winery, built in 1981 on a twenty-acre vineyard by David Bagley, who was Wagner's first winemaker. One of the best Poplar Ridge wines in its first vintage was its Cayuga White. Poplar Ridge adjoins the Gold Seal winery's Valois vineyard, where it grows its best Vinifera grapes.

In the village of Hector, two miles south of Valois, there is an example of the rapid change taking place in the Finger Lakes grape industry: the modern, two-story, 37,000-gallon Wickham Vineyards winery and tasting room, built in 1981 on a hilltop facing the town. For eighty years, five generations of Wickhams grew Concords on their 165 acres for the big Taylor winery and for a nearby grape-juice plant. They added ten acres of French hybrid wine varieties in more recent years. In 1980, the present three generations of Wickhams, realizing that this district's future is in producing table wines, assigned twenty-five-year-old Will Wickham V to build a winery. Will V hired a Fresno State University–trained winemaker, Bill Lamberton, and the winery was built in time to make five wines in 1981. Three were whites—one of which, Cayuga White, won a gold medal at the state fair—plus a red and a rosé. Will's wife Bernice and the rest of the Wickhams all are helping to sell the wines. Next on their program, they say, will be a Wickham champagne.

The 1981 vintage was also the first for landscaper Ed Grow's Rolling Vineyards Farm Winery, on his sixty acres of vines south of Hector. Since 1979 he had replanted half of the vineyard, which dates from the 1880s, with wine-grape varieties, and had been equipping a modern winery in his one-time barn.

· 11 ·

In earlier days, ferryboats from Valois crossed Seneca Lake, but now, to visit the wineries on the west shore, you must drive around the lake through either Geneva or Watkins Glen.

On Route 14, nine miles north of Watkins Glen at Dundee,

is the 45,000-gallon Glenora Wine Cellar and tasting room. It was built in 1977, a year after passage of the farm winery law, by Springledge Farms owner Eastman Beers, his son-in-law Gene Pierce, and two fellow growers, who cultivate a total of 500 acres of hybrids and Labrusca varieties around Dundee, as well as some Vinifera near Hector on the east side of the lake. Glenora wines, made by UC Davis–trained John Williams and his successor, Mike Elliott, from the same school, have been the most consistent Finger Lakes medal winners in eastern wine competitions. The winery's specialties are Seyval Blanc, Ravat Blanc, Cayuga White, Johannisberg Riesling, and Chardonnay. In 1982 it began producing a *méthode champenoise* Glenora champagne of Chardonnay, to be released in 1985.

Continue north from Glenora until you pass Stone Jug Road, and a moment farther you can find, to your left, the Hermann J. Wiemer Vineyard winery. Born at Bernkastel on the Mosel, trained at the Geisenheim Institute and in three German wine districts, Hermann came to New York State in 1968 to be the winemaker at the Bully Hill winery. He then started his own nursery business and experimented for eight years on techniques of growing Vinifera in the Finger Lakes climate until, with thirty acres of his own vineyard producing, he began building his own 25,000-gallon winery in 1979. The first Riesling Wiemer offered for sale was one of the best I have tasted in the East, and his Chardonnay, aged in European oak, was almost as fine. His late-harvest Riesling 1982 has drawn rave reviews from connoisseurs. Wiemer has also begun making a *méthode champenoise* sparkling wine, to be introduced in 1985. It will be the first Johannisberg Riesling champagne produced in the East.

Just south of the village of Himrod, Hall Road takes off from Route 14 toward Seneca Lake. About a mile toward the lake, bordering a vineyard, is a group of nineteenth-century buildings. Count their chimneys and you will see how Walter Pedersen's Four Chimneys Farm Winery gets its name. A former barn is the winery, a few thousand gallons' total capacity, mostly in plastic drums. Pedersen, who once taught cultural subjects at a school in Maryland, came here with his wife and seven children in 1975. He became acquainted with neighboring grape growers, and by 1980 he was making ten kinds of wine. The labels say they are made "from organically grown grapes," which means, he says, grown without sprays, herbicides, or artificial fertilizers. He says he sprays his vines with herbs and seaweed. The wines have such names as Rose of Sharon, Kingdom Red, and Eye of the Bee. The latter's label says it consists of "organically grown

Concord grapes with honey added." Most of Pedersen's grapes are Labruscas, but he has also planted some Gewürztraminer. I found his almost-dry Catawba and his late-harvest Dutchess quite palatable wines. He also has some of his Concord juice canned for sale in health-food stores.

• 12 •

On Route 89, which skirts the west shore of Cayuga Lake, is the tiny Lakeshore Winery, where Seneca County Extension Agent William H. Brown and his wife Doris crushed their first commercial vintage of Johannisberg Riesling in 1982. Their address is the village of Romulus, but to find their Lakeshore Winery, look for the mill wheel on the front lawn. The Browns, veteran home winemakers, began planting their all-Vinifera vineyard of Riesling, Chardonnay, Gewürztraminer, and Cabernet Sauvignon in 1978.

South of the Browns, where County Road 128 intersects Route 89, is the winery bonded by New York State Wine Grape Growers President Douglas Knapp on his family's Knapp Farms, in time to crush the 1983 harvest and to lay down his first cuvée of champagne.

Cayuga Lake Road, near Ovid, takes off east toward the lake. There is the Plane's Cayuga Vineyard winery, bonded in 1980 by Dr. Robert Plane, the president of Clarkson University, and his wife, Mary Moore Plane, a former administrator of Cornell University. They first began planting their forty-five acres of Vinifera, hybrids, and Dutchess in 1972.

There is appealing material for light opera in the story of the Lucas Family Vineyard winery, south of the Planes. To find it, take County Road 150 east from Route 89 toward the hamlet of Interlaken. It is on your left just before you reach Route 96. Bill Lucas works seven-day weeks as a tugboat captain, towing oil barges on the Hudson River and along the Atlantic coast. In alternate weeks he works with his wife Ruth and their three children in their nine-acre vineyard and 6000-gallon winery, a former cow barn. They produce five vintage-dated Lucas Family wines and two others, called Tugboat White and Tugboat Red. The Lucases bought their farm and moved here from the Bronx in 1974. They took extension courses in viticulture and hired Poplar Ridge Vineyard's David Bagley as their winemaking consultant. When the Lucases' 1980 vintage was ready for bottling, Ruth turned her kitchen into a wine shop and tasting room. A fitting climax to their story is that the 1980 Lucas Family Cayuga

White and De Chaunac won medals at the New York State Fair.

On East Covert Road, which extends between Routes 89 and 96 near Interlaken, are the ten-acre Americana vineyard and attractive 2500-gallon winery that Ithaca College Professor James R. Treble and his wife Mary Anne opened in 1981. Professor Treble provides chemistry service to other Finger Lakes farm wineries in his spare time.

A mile and a half south of the Trebles, on the lake side of Route 89 opposite Trumansburg, is the Frontenac Point Vineyard of agricultural marketing expert James Doolittle and his wife Carol, who is the editor of the American Wine Society's *Journal*. Doolittle earned his degree in viticulture at Cornell in 1975 and three years later began planting their eighteen-acre vineyard, half with French hybrids and half with Riesling, Chardonnay, and Pinot Noir. They bonded their home winery in 1982 in time to bottle their first wine, a pleasing blend of Maréchal Foch and Chelois, followed by a Chelois Rosé and a delectable late harvest Chardonnay.

• 13 •

Naples, at the south end of Canandaigua Lake in Ontario County, has been the home of Widmer's wines since their first vintage in 1888. Widmer's Wine Cellars, with its capacity of 3 million gallons, is the only winery in Naples Valley and is its chief industry and tourist attraction.

Yankees of English and Scottish origin were the first settlers in this valley. Presumably it was they who named it incongruously for Naples in Italy, for surely the German and German-Swiss immigrants who arrived in the mid-nineteenth century would have named it the Rhine Valley, which it more nearly resembles, and from which many of them came. Most local histories credit the founding of the Naples grape industry to the German vinedresser, Andrew Reisinger, who came here from the Hammondsport district in 1852, although Edward A. McKay, an attorney of Naples village, had planted a vineyard of Isabella grapes four years before. It was also a German, Hiram Maxfield, the leading banker of Naples, who built the first winery here in 1861.

Maxfield's wines and champagne were already well established when in 1882 John Jacob Widmer came to Naples with his family from the Swiss village of Scherz. Jacob wanted to go into the wine business, but there already were several wineries around

The Widmer Winery's "cellar on the roof," in which sherry ages outdoors in oak barrels for four years at Naples, N.Y.

Naples, and banker-vintner Maxfield, to discourage more competition, refused to lend Widmer any money. Jacob succeeded, however, in getting a thousand-dollar loan from the rival Granby bank. He bought and cleared a tract of land, and planted grapes on its western slope to get the morning sun. By day, Jacob and his wife Lisette toiled in the vineyard, and by night they built their home with a stone-walled basement, in which they made their first wine. By 1910 their business had grown to such a point that they could afford to send their youngest son, Will, to the Royal Wine School of Germany at Geisenheim. There Will was trained in Old World viniculture and wine lore, which the company and its products still reflect today.

During Prohibition, the rival Maxfield Cellars closed down, but the Widmers kept going by making grape juice, nonalcoholic wine jellies, and wine sauce. At Repeal in 1933, Widmer's and Maxfield's both resumed making wine, but Widmer's was already far ahead. Then President Will Widmer bought out and absorbed the competitor whose founder, half a century earlier, had refused John Jacob Widmer a loan.

While at the Geisenheim wine school, Will Widmer had learned that when Riesling grapes are left late on the vines in autumn, they grow sweeter and richer, and that sometimes a beneficent mold grows on them, causing them to shrivel and to develop an unusual flavor and aroma. He also learned that wines made from such grapes bring premium prices when labeled "Spätlese" (late picking), still higher prices when labeled "Auslese" (selected picking), and astronomical prices when labeled "Trockenbeerenauslese" (dried-berry-selection). The kindly mold is *Botrytis cinerea,* called *Edelfäule* in Germany and *pourriture noble* in France. In the fall of 1939, Widmer went walking through his vineyard after the harvest. On some of the leftover white grapes he saw a gray mold developing, and he decided it must be the *Edelfäule.* He picked all the graying berries he could find, fermented their juice, and ended up with eleven gallons of Spätlese wine. The grape variety wasn't the true Riesling, the noble member of the Vinifera family, but the Labrusca variety known as Missouri Riesling, planted by his father many years before. Dr. Ulysses Hedrick's books state that the Missouri Riesling was bred about 1860 by Nicholas Grein of Hermann, Missouri, by crossing Taylor, a local *Vitis riparia* seedling, with a Labrusca variety. But to Will Widmer, the wine tasted like Riesling, and "Widmer's New York State Riesling" is what he called it, and what its label continued to say—in some years with "Spätlese" or "Auslese" added—until Will Widmer died in 1968. Widmer always insisted that Hedrick's books were wrong, that Missouri Riesling must have been at least a relative of the true White Riesling, or that at least its Labrusca parent must have had some Vinifera blood.

The samples of Widmer Riesling Spätlese that I tasted in those years indeed resembled good semi-dry German Rhine wines, and to my surprise, because I have tasted other wines of Missouri Rieslings, the Widmer versions had no noticeable Labrusca taste.

When in 1939 author-importer Frank Schoonmaker was looking for American "varietal" wines to sell with his line of imports, his nationwide tasting tour took him to Naples. He found Widmer's, like the other eastern wineries, selling most of its wines as sauterne, burgundy, rhine, port, and sherry, but Will Widmer also had some unblended wines of Elvira and Delaware. Beginning in 1941, Schoonmaker introduced the eastern wine-buying public to Canandaigua Lake Elvira and Delaware, and with them an assortment of "varietal" wines made from Widmer's other grapes: Niagara, Salem, Dutchess, Vergennes, Moore's Diamond, and Isabella. Widmer's thus became the first New York State winery to specialize in "varietal" wines. During the next three decades Niagara became the best seller among the company's long list of wines. The samples of Widmer's Lake Niagara I have tasted have shown me why. To my taste it has been the ideal blend of the grapy Labrusca flavor in a tart, medium-sweet white wine.

Widmer's was different in several additional ways. One was its use of vintage labeling, which the other Finger Lakes wineries avoided because they preferred to blend together wines of different years. I once tasted at the winery an eleven-year-old Wid-merheimer which was remarkably fresh for a white table wine of that age and which, though made of native grapes, had no perceptible Labrusca taste. This was also true of an eleven-year-old port, which, I was amazed to learn, was made entirely of Concord grapes. Eastern winemakers claim the foxiness disap-pears from Labrusca wines if they are stored for several years in small casks.

Widmer's chief trademark is its "cellar on the roof." The first thing you notice as you drive up the valley toward the winery is the main cellar roof covered with barrels—some twelve thou-sand of them in tiers four deep—enough to cover several acres. In these barrels, exposed to summer heat and winter snow, the sherries are aged for four years before blending in a solera-like system. I have seen sherries aged outdoors this way in Ohio, California, Mexico, and South America (in Uruguay, it is done in glass jugs), but never in the vast quantity exposed at Widmer.

Ownership of Widmer's changed hands three times between 1961 and 1983. Rochester financiers, the first new owners, sold it to the R. T. French Company, that city's producer of mustard and spices, who in 1970 planted a vineyard in California to pro-duce Vinifera wines for Widmer's, but soon gave up that venture. The present owners are five Widmer's executives, including UC Davis–trained winemaker Dan Robinson. They made Widmer's one of the state's leaders in producing Charmat-process cham-pagnes, then joined the California trend to "light" or low-calorie wines. Their first entry, Lake Niagara light white, was soon joined

Tying vines to trellis wires in the Widmer Vineyard at Naples, N.Y.

by America's first "light" champagne. Both of the Widmer's "lights" were 7.2 percent in alcoholic strength.

• 14 •

In the city of Canandaigua, at the opposite end of the lake from Naples, is the second largest Finger Lakes winery, Canandaigua Industries. Its sprawling 12-million-gallon plant offers no visitor tours, nor is it surrounded by vineyards. It is the New York winery of Marvin and Mack Sands, who also own Richard's Cellars in Virginia, Tenner Brothers vineyard and winery in South Carolina, and the Bisceglia Bros. winery in the San Joaquin Valley of California.

Back in 1954, Marvin Sands was operating Canandaigua as a bulk wine plant when he and his sales manager, the late Robert Meenan, had a bright thought. It occurred to them that pink wines might gain new popularity in this country if their French name—*vin rosé,* which Americans have difficulty pronouncing— were changed to simply "rose." This gave them the idea for what since has become one of the largest selling wines in the nation—their Richard's Wild Irish Rose. Pink, sweet, Labrusca-flavored and made in both 12 and 20 percent versions, it was named for Marvin's infant son Richard, who thirty years later was made the executive vice president of the firm. Canandaigua makes many other wines, including "J. Roget" charmat champagnes, an almond-flavored sparkler called Almande, and a musky dessert wine named Canada Muscat for that New York grape. An assortment of blended table types is sold under Captain Paul Garrett's Virginia Dare label, the rights to which the Sands bought in the 1960s. Their Virginia Dare white has a little of the Scuppernong flavor that once made the brand name famous. Canandaigua even adds a touch of the fragrant Scuppernong to some of its other wines, including its Wild Irish Rose. Canandaigua's wines can be sampled at the company's tasting room, which was built in 1979 adjoining the fifty-acre Sonnenberg Gardens, the city's chief tourist attraction, on Route 21.

• 15 •

Another Finger Lakes winery that is interesting to visit is the O-Neh-Da or Eagle Crest vineyard, hidden among the hills beside Hemlock Lake in Livingston County. The post office address is Conesus, but the winery is reached by a roundabout route through Livonia Center or Hemlock, the nearest villages.

For more than a century this old-fashioned cellar, with its two underground levels, has supplied O-Neh-Da altar wines to the clergy throughout the East. Now visitors are invited daily to tour the winery and taste both its commercial and altar wines. The former are named for such grapes as Cayuga White, Ravat, and Chancellor.

O-Neh-Da, the Seneca Indian word for Hemlock, was founded in 1872 by Bishop Bernard McQuaid, the first Catholic bishop of Rochester, who said, "We can retire to the peaceful slopes of Hemlock Lake and in the cultivation of the grapes help priests to say Mass with wine that is wine." It was owned by the Society of the Divine Word, a missionary order whose lovely grottoes beside St. Michael's Seminary can be visited on the way there. Descendants of the Cribari wine family of California bought the property from the Society in 1968 and are among the present owners, and they still specialize in making altar wines.

Twenty miles north of Conesus, on Turk Hill Road in the outskirts of Fairport, is the model Casa Larga farm winery. Andrew Colaruotolo built Casa Larga for his family in 1978 on their thirteen-acre mostly Vinifera vineyard, which he had begun planting four years earlier. His wife, son, and two daughters run the 11,000-gallon winery and tasting room, while the father enjoys caring for the vines, much as he did as a young boy in his parents' vineyard in the Frascati wine district of Italy. The vintage-dated Casa Larga wines, produced entirely from the family's own grapes and ranging from Chardonnay, Riesling, and Aurora to Cabernet Sauvignon, De Chaunac, and Pinot Noir, have been consistent award winners in eastern quality competitions.

8

Chautauqua, Niagara, and the Hudson Valley

T HE Chautauqua–Erie Grape Belt, the sixty-mile-long stretch of New York's Lake Erie shore which the fanatical Prohibitionists, Doctors Thomas and Charles Welch, made famous as "the grape juice capital of the world," has also become a wine district. There now are seven wineries in the Grape Belt, four of them opened since the farm winery law was passed in 1976.

For generations, most of the grapes grown here were Concords for fresh use and for juice, but since the increases in table-wine consumption during the 1970s, many vineyards here have been partially replanted with French hybrid and Vinifera grapes. Wineries in other New York districts depend on the Chautauqua district to furnish a large part of their wine-grape supply.

This is the district which the late Professor Ulysses Hedrick called, because of its climate, "the second most important viticultural section of eastern America, next to the Finger Lakes." In grape production, however, it is first, because its 23,000 acres of vines, of which one-ninth are now wine-grape varieties, produce more than half of the state's total annual harvest. Almost 100 of the new mechanical harvesting machines now operate here, picking more than four-fifths of the grape crop.

The Grape Belt is narrow, extending inland from Lake Erie only three to sixteen miles, because grapes grow only in those sections where lake breezes protect the vines from spring and fall frosts. In New York State, the Belt extends from Erie County southwestward to the Pennsylvania border. The Chautauqua County shore section, one of the most productive, is now threatened by urbanization, which worries the Chautauqua farmers because they have nowhere else to go.

• 2 •

It was near Brocton in Chautauqua County that Baptist Deacon Elijah Fay founded the grape industry of western New York and northwestern Pennsylvania, when he planted his vineyard of wild grapes in 1818. At Brocton the first winery in the area was built in 1859 by Deacon Fay's son Joseph, with two partners, Garrett Ryckman and Rufus Haywood. Additional wineries soon started up nearby: the Wine House of Thomas Quigley in 1862, the South Shore Wine Company across the Pennsylvania line a year later, the Empire Vineyards winery of Ralph D. Fuller in 1867, and the Jonas Martin cellar, on the foundation of which St. Patrick's Church in Brocton now stands.

Brocton is also where the bearded mystic, Thomas Lake Harris, built a winery in 1867 to make his "Brotherhood" wines, which he claimed were "infused with the divine aura, potentialized in the joy spirit." The strange story of Harris centers around his utopian "Brotherhood of the New Life" and his semi-communistic colonies in three states. Relics of his Brocton colony, which he named "The Use," can still be seen near the lakeshore. Harris's great house on West Lake Road is now the residence of businessman Douglas Hayes. The ground floor of the winery, on Peerless Street, serves a family as a garage and chicken coop, but the underground cellar is still intact. Mrs. Prudence Work, editor of the Brocton *Beacon*, has found the ruins of at least six more nineteenth-century wineries between Brocton and nearby Portland.

While the Chautauqua Belt wineries thrived during the 1870s, using Delaware, Catawba, and Isabella grapes, Ephraim Bull's new Concord grape variety was introduced to the district. With the Concord, a table-grape industry began to develop. At the same time, the Dry crusade, which had begun in the eastern part of the state, was spreading westward. It found its strongest footholds in two Chautauqua County villages, Jamestown and Fredonia. At Fredonia, in 1873, Mrs. Esther McNeil organized the first unit of the Woman's Christian Temperance Union. Her WCTU ladies, denouncing the local wineries for the sin of allowing grapes to ferment, exhorted all God-fearing farmers to plant the Concord in place of the Delaware and Catawba, because the Concord was tolerated as a fresh eating grape, while the Delaware and Catawba were grown only to make wine.

During the 1880s, table grapes sold well in the eastern cities, and Concord planting reached boom proportions. Chautauqua County merchants, doctors, and lawyers, everyone who could shake loose a down payment, bought farms and set out more Concord vineyards. Two factories were built just to make the baskets in which the grapes were shipped for sale. Concord production swelled to such a point during the 1890s that much of the crop remained unsold. The bottom then dropped out of the market, and many who had invested their last dollars were ruined.

In 1897, attracted by the surplus of cheap Concords, there came to Chautauqua County the ardent Dry dentists, the Doctors Welch, who had started the grape-juice industry. Only a year earlier they had moved their juice-pressing operation from Vineland, New Jersey, to Watkins Glen in the Finger Lakes district. The Watkins Glen operation was successful, but they chose a new site at Westfield, eight miles southwest of Brocton, and built there the world's first large grape-juice plant. The Welches were then launching the first advertising campaign for their product; renamed only seven years earlier, it was now "grape juice" instead of "unfermented wine." Dr. Charles Welch gave up his dental practice when he moved to Westfield, and became its most prominent citizen. Old residents still remember him for his shock of white hair, his flowing artist-style ties, the autos in which he raced between the plant and the vineyards, and the high-toned restaurant he opened at the Welch plant, where Concord grape juice was always served, but never any wine or liquor. It became a tradition in the county that Dr. Welch personally would start each grape-picking season by issuing a ten-minute blast of the Westfield plant's steam whistle. By 1913, when Secretary of State William Jennings Bryan shocked the diplomatic world by serving Welch's Grape Juice instead of wine to the British ambassador at a state dinner in Washington, an entire Welch Block had been constructed in Westfield.

Wartime Prohibition forced the local wineries to close, but the vineyardists still prospered, selling their surplus grapes to home winemakers and bootleggers in the cities. Local boosters then established an annual grape festival at Brocton. Notable for the absence of any mention of Bacchus, it celebrated instead the memory of Deacon Fay and praised only the fresh Concord grape and its pasteurized juice. By the end of the 1920s, the fact that the county had once produced wine was almost forgotten.

At Repeal, in 1933, two small wineries were opened in the district. One was at Fredonia. The other, at Brocton, was primarily a grape-juice plant that began making wine as a sideline. Its proprietor was the financial wizard, Jacob Merrill (Jack)

Kaplan, once known as "the Boston molasses king." In 1945, Kaplan bought control of the Welch Grape Juice Company from a Tennessee banking syndicate, which had acquired it after the death of Dr. Charles Welch in 1926. And at the Brocton plant in 1950, Kaplan put the Welch Company into the wine business—a development at which the Doctors Welch, father and son, must have revolved many times in their graves. This was when the new kosher wine type, in which extra sweetening makes the Concord flavor pleasant to taste in a wine, was setting sensational sales records in every state where wine was sold. Wineries across the country were buying Concord grapes or juice and rushing into production with their own versions of the sweet kosher wine. Kaplan's idea was that by giving his version the Welch name, which signified the Concord flavor to millions, he could outsell the kosher leaders, Manischewitz and Mogen David. But his "Welch's Refreshment Wine" failed to sell, perhaps because its label didn't say it was kosher. And in 1959 the Welch Company, which Kaplan meanwhile had sold to the National Grape Co-operative Association, abruptly discontinued making wine.

• 3 •

In 1960, a young agricultural expert named Fred Johnson came home to Westfield, his birthplace, after a ten-year stay in South America. He surveyed the seventy-year-old Concord vineyard his father had left him, studied the trends in local agriculture, and concluded that the long-range future of the Chautauqua Grape Belt lay not in producing more Welch's Grape Juice nor in supplying the kosher wineries, but in growing distinctive dry table wines.

He began ripping out his Concord vines and replanting most of his 125 acres with wine grapes—French hybrids, Delaware, and Ives. In what had been the farm's cold storage house for apples, he installed casks and a crusher, and in 1961 he started the Frederick S. Johnson Vineyards Winery, the first to open in the area in twenty-eight years, and began making the Chautauqua district's first estate-bottled wines.

Johnson, a torpedo-bomber pilot in the Pacific during the Second World War, was not a stranger to winemaking. As a boy, he had helped his father make wine at home from Delaware and Catawba grapes, and at Cornell he had been trained in horticulture and chemistry. After the war, as a specialist in tropical agriculture, he had worked on pineapples for Dole in Hawaii, then had set up Nelson Rockefeller's plantations in Venezuela and Ecuador. Exposed during his travels to the wines of many countries, he was amazed that Chautauqua had not become an important wine district long ago.

His 75,000-gallon winery uses only part of his grapes; the rest are sold fresh. His "Johnson Estate" labels, which he designed himself, picture his vineyard and the 150-year-old brick house in which he was born. His wines, which have won a consumer following in New York and some neighboring states, include Seyval Blanc, Chancellor Noir, Delaware, dry white, rosé, dry red, and vin rouge. But his best thus far is a wine Johnson had never intended to make. In 1975, he had promised to sell his crop of Delaware grapes to another winery. The buyer decided he could not use them, and the grapes remained unpicked for several weeks. They became infected with botrytis, "the noble mold," and young winemaker William Gulvin made them into a late-harvest wine. Johnson and his wife Cecily named the wine Liebestropfchen (little lovedrops). It created a sensation at tastings, winning a silver medal at the eastern wine judging in 1977. Johnson, however, sees the Chautauqua district's future in such wines as his white French hybrids, which contain enough Delaware to give them fragrance without a recognizable Labrusca taste. Vineyard and winery tours and tastings are offered visitors from June through August at the Johnson winery on West Main Road.

There is a winery on Bourne Street in Westfield that doesn't offer tastings or tours. It is the 6-million-gallon Wine Group winery, which makes Mogen David kosher Concord and a dozen other "MD" wines. Mogen David, the world's biggest maker of Concord wines, moved from Chicago to Westfield in 1967 to be closer to its main supply of grapes. After the move to Westfield, Mogen David was purchased by the Coca-Cola Bottling Company of New York, which in 1981 sold Mogen David and the 30-million-gallon Franzia Winery in California to the Wine Group—which accounts for the present name.

• 4 •

Fourteen miles from Westfield, on the other side of Brocton, is Fredonia, which orator Chauncey Depew once called "the most beautiful village in New York State." In Depew's time, guidebooks listed as Fredonia's chief landmark the drinking-water fountain erected in memory of WCTU pioneer Esther McNeil. The fountain still gushes forth the drink of temperance in Lafayette Park in the center of town, but guidebooks nowadays ignore the lady, and instead list as tourist attractions the five Chautauqua Belt farm wineries and their tasting rooms. The closest is the Chadwick Bay winery on Route 60 in Fredonia at its intersection with Lakeview Road. (Nearby Dunkirk's early name was Chadwick Bay.) Grape growers George Borzilleri, Jr., and Rick Mazza opened the 32,000-gallon cellar in 1981 and offered thirteen 1980 vintage wines, the best of which was a Chambourcin.

On Cliffstar Avenue in Dunkirk is the Fredonia Products winery, which Leo Star's Manischewitz kosher wine built from a few small tanks in the year of Repeal to its present capacity of 4 million gallons. In 1964, the firm, which had long bought local Concords, began planting 500 acres of wine grapes—Delawares, Catawbas, and French hybrids—in mostly virgin land west of Fredonia. A galaxy of Leo Star's nephews now produce an assortment of Concord and other fruit wines, but their principal product is fresh grape juice, which they ship in giant refrigerated tank trucks to Brooklyn to be made into Manischewitz wine.

Also in Dunkirk, on South Roberts Road off US 20, is the 32,000-gallon Woodbury Vineyards winery and tasting room, opened in 1979. It features estate-bottled, vintage-dated Chardonnay, Riesling, Gewürztraminer, Pinot Gris, Pinot Noir, various wines of French hybrid and Labrusca grapes, and blends called Glacier Ridge white, red, and rosé. Added in 1980 was the first champagne produced in the Chautauqua Grape Belt, a Chardonnay Champagne Brut. The Woodburys began planting Vinifera in 1966 on the farm their great-grandfather had bought in 1908. In the early 1970s, I tasted a homemade sample of their Chardonnay and was amazed; it was equal to a true chablis. It would be interesting to know whether its quality should be credited to their vineyard's microclimate or to the soil of its site, a glacial gravelly ridge, or to both. Former chemistry teacher Gary Woodbury heads the family's winery venture, helped by Page Woodbury, his sister-in-law.

On King Road off Route 39, between Fredonia and Forestville, is the 40,000-gallon Merritt Estate winery, which in 1977 was the first to open in the Chautauqua Belt under the farm winery law passed the year before. The cool cellar, equipped for modern production and aging, provides a home for the wine grapes grown on the 100 acres of Triple M Farms, named for the noted horticulturist James M. Merritt and his sons William and James, the latter of whom heads the winery. Its principal wines are Aurora, Seyval Blanc, Maréchal Foch, Niagara, and rosé, but there are two sweet table wines, Sheridan white and red, named for that neighboring town.

Twelve miles west of Westfield, on East Main Road (US 20) in Ripley, is the Grape Belt's newest winery, named Schloss Doepken. When John Simon Watso and his wife Roxanne were about to open their 10,000-gallon winery in 1980, they decided against calling it Watso and settled instead on Doepken, which is Roxanne's maiden name. Watso, a chemist with a full-time job in Connecticut, bought their sixty-acre Concord vineyard in 1972 and devoted eight years to replanting twelve of the acres with Riesling, Gewürztraminer, and Chardonnay. He converted an ancient barn into the winery, installed stainless-steel tanks and oak barrels (the latter for aging), and added a tasting room. Schloss Doepken wines, besides Chardonnay and Riesling, have such names as Schloss Blanc, Chautauquabloomchen, Ripley Red, and Roxanne Rouge.

• 5 •

Dry influence in the Grape Belt is not yet dead. A history of the county's grape industry, published serially in a county newspaper, scrupulously avoided any mention of wine. The Chautauqua County Historical Museum in Westfield still contains no mementos of the early-day wineries. And wine is still illegal at Chautauqua, the famous century-old summer center of religion, education, music, and recreation on Chautauqua Lake. This not surprising, for Chautauqua is where the WCTU really began. There, in 1873, Mrs. McNeil's fanatical followers laid the detailed plans for the national organization that was formed at Cleveland a year later, the plans that ultimately brought about National Prohibition. To this day, the owners of homes at Chautauqua hold their property on a condition, fortunately not enforced, that if any "intoxicating liquor" is ever used on their premises, their land, houses, and all the contents are automatically forfeited to the Chautauqua Institution.

But by the 1970s and 1980s, the local view of wine had changed to a considerable degree. When, for example, Silver Creek holds its annual Festival of Grapes in that Grape Belt town in September, the printed program contains advertisements from the farm wineries and from local dealers in wine; and a home-winemaking contest is now one of the main festival events, ranking in public interest with the baking contest, the festival ball, the crowning of the queen, and the parade.

• 6 •

New York's third most important winegrowing district is Niagara County, with some 2800 acres of vineyards. At this writing Niagara County had only one winery, but with a third of the vineyard acreage planted to wine grapes, increased production of Niagara County wines may be expected in the future.

Viticulturally as well as geologically, the Niagara district is unique. It consists of the Niagara Peninsula, only twenty-five to thirty miles in width, that separates Lake Erie from Lake Ontario. Through the peninsula flows the Niagara River, rushing over the Falls and down its deep gorge, spilling the waters of Lakes Erie, Superior, Michigan, and Huron into Lake Ontario. The inland seas on both sides of the peninsula moderate its climate, making the plains that face Lake Ontario a land of peach and cherry orchards and vineyards. On the Canadian side of the river, which is the international border, almost the entire grape and wine industry of eastern Canada is situated, with twelve times the vineyard acreage on the New York side. There are spots where the Canadian and New York vineyards, separated by the river, are less than two miles apart.

The winter climate is milder, with fewer days recording below-zero temperatures, than in most of the other grape districts of New York. An eighteen-year study by the Geneva Experiment Station, published in 1968, showed that Lewiston, Westfield, and Long Island are best suited for the cold-tender grape varieties such as Vinifera (of which Niagara has several acres), which make the finest wines.

Winegrowing in Niagara County began before the Civil War. County Historian Clarence O. Lewis has found records showing that a winery operated at Lockport during the 1860s and that it had vineyards on both sides of the town. It was at Lockport, in 1868, that the Niagara grape variety, sometimes called the white Concord, was created by crossing Concord with a vine called Cassady. A Niagara-growing boom followed and lasted until the 1890s, when too many grapes were produced, the market collapsed, and many vineyards were uprooted.

A single winery operated at Lewiston from 1933 to 1970, specializing in champagnes offered to the honeymooners and millions of other visitors who come from everywhere to gaze at the awesome Falls. It was Château Gay, opened at Repeal by the Canadian firm which owned the Château Gai winery near the Canadian city of Niagara Falls. It prospered until it was moved to an ornate new building in 1966. Four years later it went bankrupt and closed, then was reopened by new investors, and closed again in 1973.

In 1979, Paul Lops, Jr., who once operated Château Gay, started an entirely new winery, which he named Niagara Wine Cellars, on Ridge Road (Route 104) in Cambria, eighteen miles east of the Falls. When I was last there, Lops was making some very acceptable Riesling, Chardonnay, Vidal Blanc, Chancellor, and Foch, plus a pleasant wine of Siegfried Riesling. Lockport attorney Richard N. Lein, a talented amateur winegrower, introduced the Siegfried Riesling, a winter-hardy German variety, to his Fairmount Farms.

• 7 •

The Hudson River Valley, with sixteen wineries and some 1200 acres of vineyards, is the oldest winegrowing district in the United States. Wine has been made continuously in this historic valley for at least three centuries, since French Protestant refugees settled at New Paltz in Ulster County in 1677. When their plantings of European vines failed, the Frenchmen made wine of the native wild grapes until such domesticated varieties as the Isabella became available early in the nineteenth century.

The first large commercial vineyard in the valley was planted with the Isabella about 1827 on Croton Point, the peninsula that is now Westchester County's Croton Point Park, on the east shore of the Hudson thirty-five miles north of New York City. No marker or plaque exists to tell the thousands who now enjoy picnicking at the park that this was once their state's most famous vineyard. Campers who take shelter in the great cavern hollowed out of the hillside are unaware that it originally served as the aging vault for Croton Point wines.

Dr. Richard T. Underhill, the bachelor physician who planted vines there, was so enthusiastic about grape culture that he abandoned his medical practice in the city to give the vineyard his full time. He was also the first American advocate of the Grape Cure, the diet of fresh grapes then popular in Europe, where it was believed to prevent dyspepsia, liver ailments, and a long list of other diseases. Dr. Underhill first sold his grapes fresh, but later established a winery on the peninsula. His Croton Point wines were offered in New York City during the 1860s as "the pure product of the grape, neither drugged, liquored, nor watered, recommended by leading physicians in all cases where a stimulant of a bracing character is required." Members of the Underhill family were prominent in the New York wine industry for several more decades.

• 8 •

The oldest active winery in the United States is at Washingtonville, several miles from the river in Orange County. It is the Brotherhood Corporation winery, established in 1839. Its ancient caves, which resemble those beneath old wineries in Europe, are the largest wine storage tunnels I have found in North America. They are well worth visiting, though some of the capacious vaults are empty, and the great vineyards which once covered this part of the valley are no more. The last vines were uprooted in 1960 to enlarge the winery's parking lot, where a dollar charge is made for parking in the afternoons.

Situated only fifty-one miles from New York City, the Brotherhood winery now specializes in selling its wines at retail to visitors, of whom more than 300,000 come each year for free tours of its caves and to sample the wines (also free) from paper cups. Two dozen hosts deliver impressive one-hour lectures on the romance and the making of wine and on its uses in cooking. Merry evening parties are held in the cellars for the Brotherhood of Wine Tasters, loyal customers who sometimes use profes-

Oldest active winery in the United States is the Brotherhood Corporation, established in 1839 at Washingtonville in the Hudson River Valley. It kept open through Prohibition, producing sacramental wines.

sional-type scorecards to rate the Brotherhood wines. I found their quality adequate, typical products of the Delaware, Catawba, and other Labrusca grapes the company buys in the Hudson Valley, Chautauqua, and Niagara districts. Of the twenty types the company sells, the best were the brut champagne, the sparkling burgundy, and the sauterne, in which the Labrusca taste was least pronounced.

I went to Washingtonville expecting to unravel there the early history of Brotherhood wines and their connection with the fabulous Thomas Lake Harris, whose utopian Brotherhood of the New Life gave the wines their name. My research in California had shown that Harris's religious, semi-communistic Brotherhood had first made wine in the Hudson Valley before it moved to Brocton, then to the Fountain Grove Vineyard in Santa Rosa, California. I therefore assumed that it was at the Brotherhood winery that Harris's winemaking began. Imagine my disappointment when Columbia-trained Francis Llado Farrell, who had owned the Brotherhood winery since 1948, told me he had never heard of such a person as Thomas Lake Harris, nor of his Brotherhood religious cult, either!

Since that visit, the mystery has been cleared up by further research, by studying the numerous books that have been written about the fantastic career of Harris, and by Farrell's wife Eloise, who has investigated the local historical sources.

The founder of this Brotherhood winery was not the English-born Harris, but Jean Jaques from France, who settled at Washingtonville in 1816. Jaques, a shoemaker, was the first to plant grapes in Orange County, soon after Dr. Underhill started his vineyard at Croton Point. In 1838, Jaques sent his first grapes to market and received for them only 13 cents a pound, so he decided in the following year to make his crop into wine. He sold some to the First Presbyterian Church, of which he was an elder. For many years thereafter, Jaques had a prospering trade in sacramental wines, which kept the Brotherhood winery open during Prohibition. It still enjoys a lucrative clerical trade.

Harris's Brotherhood of the New Life first made wine during the 1860s, not at Washingtonville, but at his third colony, which was at Amenia in the Hudson Valley. (His first two colonies were at Mountain Cove, West Virginia, and at Wassaic, New York.) Winegrowing was the Amenia colony's industry. It kept the disciples busy while angels dictated the sermons and celestial poems that Harris claimed came to him when he was in a trance. He preached that his wines had divine and miraculous powers, "the finer electro-vinous spirit of the collective body of the grape," and that therefore they brought joy without alcoholic intoxication.

There were bizarre occult and sexual practices in his colonies, including "celibate marriage," Harris dictating where wives and husbands were to sleep, usually apart. Harris was the patriarch, wielding absolute power and holding the devout members' personal fortunes. His disciples included many wealthy people, including Laurence Oliphant, the renowned British author and former Member of Parliament, and Lady Maria Oliphant, his mother. It was with Lady Oliphant's jewels that Harris purchased the larger tract at Brocton, to which the colony moved from Amenia in 1867. Eight years later Harris abandoned his heaven at Brocton to found his new one at the Fountain Grove Vineyard in California; the colony at Brocton fell apart soon after he left. Harris ruled at Fountain Grove until 1892, when, embroiled in lawsuits and scandals about free love, he suddenly left Fountain Grove in the charge of his samurai Japanese secretary, Baron Kanaye Nagasawa, and sailed for England. He lived there for a time, and died in New York in 1906.

Meanwhile, Brotherhood wines and Brotherhood Grand Monarque Champagne were being sold throughout the United States and even in Europe and Africa. The Brotherhood Wine Company had its own five-story building at Washington and Spring streets in New York City and boasted of vineyards at Washingtonville and at Hammondsport in the Finger Lakes.

But how could Harris, in trouble with his disciples at Amenia, at Brocton, then in California, have possibly built this vast wine business, and what was its connection with his Brotherhood of the New Life?

The answer, it turns out, was a pair of enterprising New York wine merchants—Jesse and Edward R. Emerson, father and son. During the 1870s, the Emersons bought the wine from Harris's Brotherhood colony at Brocton, and also bought some wine from Jaques, blended them together, and sold the blend, with Harris's blessing, under his Brotherhood name. Then in 1885, Harris having left for California, and John Jaques and two of his sons having died, the surviving Jaques son, Charles, sold the Washingtonville winery to the Emersons. They promptly changed its name from Blooming Grove, which Jaques had called it, to Brotherhood.

· 9 ·

There are no million-gallon wineries in the Hudson Valley such as those in the Finger Lakes and Chautauqua districts, but there are more small estate wineries here than anywhere else in New York State, because of the valley's proximity to New York City. Eight of them have bonded their cellars since the farm winery law was passed in 1976.

Near New City, twenty-eight miles up the Hudson from Manhattan, is the High Tor Vineyard, which for a quarter of a century was the most famous small winegrowing estate in eastern America. It is the subject of a delightful book, *The Vintage Years,* in which playwright Everett Crosby related his trials and successes in planting his dream vineyard on that craggy mountain and eventually winning connoisseur acceptance of his French hybrid wines. Crosby sold High Tor in 1971 to a restaurateur who kept it alive for five years and then closed it down. In 1981, New York economist Christopher Wells bought the property and resumed making High Tor wines, but mainly from hybrid grapes he brought from the Chautauqua Belt.

One of the most charming wine estates in the East is the seventy-two-acre Benmarl Vineyard and its 50,000-gallon winery, perched on a hill above US 9W, overlooking the Hudson at Marlboro in Ulster County. From his five-year stay in Europe following the Second World War, when he became a member of Burgundy's Confrérie du Tastevin, noted illustrator Mark Miller wanted to become a winegrower. He found the site in 1956, the original vineyard where in 1867 Andrew J. Caywood developed the Dutchess grape, one of the best of the white Labrusca varieties. Miller found some of the ancient vines still growing on the property and the crumbling ruin of a century-old winery nearby. Records of the town of Marlboro dating from the 1700s are decorated with its symbol, a bunch of grapes. Miller named the estate Benmarl; *ben* is early Gaelic for hill, *marl* describes its slaty soil. He planted a dozen acres with French hybrid vines and a half-acre with Chardonnay. Before building his winery, he organized fellow wine lovers into a unique kind of co-operative. Members of the Benmarl Societé des Vignerons bought vinerights of two vines each, which entitled each *vigneron* to the Droit du Seigneur, an invitation to help with the harvest, and the right to a dozen bottles of personally labeled wine. Miller's wife Dene designed the rustic winery buildings where the Societé members gather each year. They buy four-fifths of the output of Benmarl wines, which have such names as Cuvée de Vigneron, Marlboro Village Red, Seyval Blanc, and Chardonnay. Miller also now produces a champagne of the French hybrids Seyval and Verdelet, but in deference to the French he refuses to call it champagne; its label reads "sparkling wine."

On Western Avenue, in the center of Marlboro, is a 100,000-

gallon winery and tasting room with three different names. It is the Marlboro Champagne Cellars, the name under which it started in 1944. Since 1976 it has also become the Great River Winery, which is the brand of vintage-dated table wines it makes of hybrid grapes grown in New York State. Four years later it was bought by Windsor Vineyards, the subsidiary of California's Sonoma (Rodney Strong) Vineyards that sells you wines under your own "personalized" label. The thrice-named winery's most interesting wine is an appealingly palatable dry red called Great River Vincent Noir for that Canadian-bred hybrid grape.

On a winding country road, southeast of Marlboro, is New York stockbroker Allan Mackinnon's 1500-gallon Cottage Vineyards winery. A prior owner planted the eight-acre vineyard with Vinifera vines that produced disappointingly skimpy crops. Mackinnon bought the vineyard in 1979, made one vintage of Riesling, then began replanting with red and white French hybrid vines. He meanwhile led his neighbors in petitioning the Federal government to recognize the Hudson Valley region as a distinct viticultural area, a petition that was granted in 1982.

Just north of Marlboro, beside an eleven-acre vineyard on the west side of US 9W, is the 32,000-gallon Cagnasso Winery. After twenty-five years of winemaking in northern Italy, his birthplace, next in Mexico, and then at the giant Gallo Winery in California, Joseph Cagnasso came to Marlboro in 1977 to open this winery of his own. He makes a dozen different table wines, mostly of French hybrids, in his stainless-steel tanks and oaken casks, invites his customers to taste them all, and sells his entire output at the winery in bottles or jugs. His helper is technical librarian June Ramey, who first met Cagnasso when she was the Gallo Winery librarian.

At Milton, six miles north of Cagnasso, is the Herzog family's Royal Kedem kosher winery. It entertains thousands of visitors each year in its tasting room, which is downhill from the winery in the old New York Central railroad station on the Hudson shore.

Another winery and tasting room, named West Park Vineyards, was opened in 1983 on a four-year-old six-acre vineyard of Riesling, Sauvignon Blanc, and Chardonnay in the village of West Park. It is a partnership of Kevin Zraly, the famous cellarmaster of New York City's Windows on the World restaurant, and New York businessman Lou Fiore.

• 10 •

On a lofty bluff overlooking the Hudson near Highland on US 9W, there is a 200-acre Italian winegrowing estate, so nearly perfect in its setting of vines on rolling hills that it might have been transplanted in one piece from the hills of Tuscany. In the middle of the vineyard, clustered around the manor house and garden, are stone winery buildings and the homes of families of vineyard workers, some of whom have lived here all their lives. This is the Hudson Valley Wine Company, established by Alexander Bolognesi from Bologna after he retired from a Wall Street banking career in 1907. It still produces the same estate-bottled Labrusca wines and champagnes that the Bolognesi family did, though it has been owned since 1972 by former importer Herb Feinberg, one of the three brothers who formerly operated Monsieur Henri Wines. When I first visited the estate, Bolognesi's widow, Valentina, maintained a firm rule against visitors to the winery. The new owner, however, saw it as a perfect Hudson Valley tourist attraction. He established winery tours and tastings, a Saturday evening champagne film festival by reservation, and a restaurant in the manor house for group luncheons and dinners. There is a charge for parking, but the tour and tasting are more than worth it.

• 11 •

Across the Hudson north of Poughkeepsie, three hobbyist winegrowers have started the first wineries to operate in Dutchess County since Thomas Lake Harris's Brotherhood of the New Life abandoned its vineyard colony at Amenia more than a century ago. Novelist William Wetmore has built a 15,000-gallon winery on his fifteen-acre Cascade Mountain Vineyard of French hybrids six miles north of Amenia, at the intersection of Flint Hill and Cascade Mountain roads. The winery, built in 1977, was an outgrowth of a high school studies project thought up by Wetmore and his wife Margaret for their son Charles. Their vintage wines are estate-bottled Harvest Red, white, and rosé, a full-bodied Reserved Red, and one the Wetmores call Le Hamburger Red to poke fun at American wines with fancy French names.

A few miles west of the Wetmores, on Schultzville Road two miles from Clinton Corners, New York book designer Ben Feder and his wife Kathy installed a 10,000-gallon winery in the ancient barn on their fifteen-acre Clinton Vineyard in 1977. Their estate-bottled Seyval Blanc has won listings in many New York City restaurants. In 1980 they also introduced a *méthode champenoise* sparkling wine they call Seyval Naturel.

Ten miles farther north, near Millerton, Manhattan heart surgeon George Green and his artist wife Sheila bonded in 1975 what may be this country's smallest commercial winery—300 gallons—in the cellar of their country home on Silver Mountain Road. They tried growing various French hybrids in their two-acre vineyard and found the Maréchal Foch grew best and made the best red wine. The judges at the Wineries Unlimited eastern wine competition apparently agreed, awarding the Greens' Northeast Vineyard Foch two gold medals, a silver, and a "best of class" award since 1979.

On McNeill Road, northeast of the village of Mount Ross in Columbia County, horticulturist-author (*Gardening under Glass*) Jerome A. Eaton and his artist wife Shirley built a model 3000-gallon winery in 1981 on their five-acre vineyard, planted five years before. After trying various wine grapes to learn which do best in their microclimate, the Eatons chose Seyval, and began bottling their first Seyval Blanc vintage in 1983.

Westchester County, too, again has a winery, which may remind local wine-history buffs of Dr. Underhill's Croton Point vineyard that supplied New York City with its "pure product of the grape" more than a century ago. At Hardscrabble and Delancy roads in North Salem, which is near the Connecticut border, Manhattan psychiatrist George Naumberg and his wife Michelle bonded their 7500-gallon North Salem Vineyard cellar in 1979 on the dairy farm they had bought fifteen years before. After experimenting with dozens of different varieties of grapes, which they sold mostly as juice to home winemakers, they settled on Seyval and bottled their first vintage in 1981. "Freud took three months off every summer," says Dr. Naumberg, explaining how he can practice psychiatry and yet spend September and October at the vineyard every year.

• 12 •

Three farm wineries have opened since 1978 on vineyards in the foothills of the Shawangunk Mountains on the west side of the Hudson Valley.

A sign on Route 52 at Pine Bush points to Richard and Valerie Eldridge's 5000-gallon Brimstone Hill cellar on the four-acre vineyard they began planting in 1969 beside their home on Brimstone Road.

On Hardenburgh Road near Pine Bush, John R. Baldwin, the market research manager of Hoffmann La Roche pharmaceuticals, and his wife Patricia bonded a 1000-gallon cellar in 1982 on their nine-acre Baldwin Vineyard of French hybrids, which they say they soon will double in size.

Four miles farther west, in Walker Valley, is the very attractive estate winery opened in 1978 by Gary Dross, chairman of the physical education department of Orange County Community College. He had begun planting his twelve acres of French hybrids and Vinifera six years earlier beside his parents' home. His first Walker Valley Vineyard wines were estate-bottled 1980 Riesling, 1981 Seyval, and 1980 Autumn Red. He plans next to enlarge his vineyard to fifteen acres and to begin building an underground aging cellar.

It is too early to predict whether the Hudson Valley can someday regain the importance it enjoyed as New York State's leading wine district two centuries ago. But sixteen wineries, six of them new since 1976, are at least a promising start.

9

The Vine Grows in New England

I N THEIR BOOK on *American Wines,* published in 1941, Frank Schoonmaker and Tom Marvel speculated that if the American colonies had undertaken from the start to cultivate the hardy native grapes instead of attempting in vain to grow the delicate Old World varieties, a winegrowing industry would have developed in the stern climates of the New England states as it did elsewhere in the East. They went on to declare that if given the right conditions, such a development eventually would be "inevitable."

The "inevitable" is coming to pass, but not with the hardy native grapes. It is happening with the delicate Old World grapes, which modern advances in viticulture have now made it possible to grow in these climates. Moreover, oenothusiasts are finding that some parts of New England are as climatically suited for grape growing as some of the present viticultural areas of other eastern states. Commercial winegrowing in New England dates only from 1968, but it already is past the pioneering stage. Thirteen New England wineries were producing commercial wines in 1983, five in Connecticut, five in Rhode Island, two in Massachusetts, and one in New Hampshire. Three more wineries were preparing to open in Connecticut during 1984.

• 2 •

The history of winegrowing in New England goes back two centuries but has been obscured by time and by Dry attitudes in American agriculture, which focused attention on fresh grapes rather than on wine. That grapes grow abundantly, both wild and under cultivation, in this part of America is shown by the names given in colonial times to such places as Martha's Vineyard,* the twenty-mile-long island off the Massachusetts coast, and to the island town called Vineyard Haven. Nantucket Island, too, was once noted for its grapes.

The great seal of the State of Connecticut is a picture of three grapevines bearing fruit, symbolizing one of the agricultural activities of the early settlers. During the seventeenth century, a large planting of European vines was made at the mouth of the Piscataqua River near the present site of Portsmouth in New Hampshire, and presumably it failed. But an early Massachusetts vineyard, the one planted by Governor John Winthrop on Governor's Island in Boston Harbor (which is now part of Logan International Airport), apparently produced grapes for a time. The payment Governor Winthrop undertook to make for the island in 1632—a hogshead of wine per year—was actually made by him and his heirs in the form of wine (sometimes of apples), until Adam Winthrop made a cash settlement in 1683.

Grape growing in Massachusetts during the nineteenth century is described by Alden Spooner in 1846. "Great quantities of grapes are raised in and about Boston," Spooner wrote, "but we do not know of any large vineyards for wine. Men of wealth raise foreign varieties in hot houses, and the finest grapes I have ever seen were at horticultural exhibitions in that city."

New England's principal contribution to American viticulture was the Concord grape, named for the historic town in Massachusetts whence it came—the principal grape now grown in the eastern, midwestern, and northwestern states. Its originator, Ephraim Wales Bull, became interested in grape growing as a boy, when his father had a vineyard at Bullville in the Hudson River Valley of New York. As a young man, employed as a goldbeater in Boston, Bull raised grapes in his garden on Fayette Street in that city, and on a larger scale when he moved in 1836 to Concord, where he also made his own wine. There, in 1843, trying to find a hardier dark grape than the Isabella, he sowed the seeds of numerous whole grapes that he picked from the local wild Labrusca vines. Among the seedlings that sprouted, in 1849, one of the hardiest and most prolific yielded the purple, foxy-flavored grape he named the Concord. Bull propagated the vine from cuttings, and in 1854 he offered the Concord to nurseries at $5 per vine. But the nurserymen propagated the vine themselves, and Bull earned little from the countless millions of its

---

*Historians have found no trace of any Martha for whom the island might have been named. Current opinion is that the name is a corruption of Martin, referring to a friend of either the discoverer, Bartholomew Gosnold, or of the first proprietor, Thomas Mayhew.

progeny that were planted throughout the nation. He became embittered and died a poor man in Concord's Home for the Aged in 1859. Bull's tombstone records his resentment against commercial nurseries in these words: "He sowed, but others reaped." One of the historic shrines at Concord is Bull's Grapevine Cottage on Lexington Road, next door to The Wayside, which once was the home of his friend, Nathaniel Hawthorne. Visitors are told that a massive grapevine beside the cottage, still bearing abundant crops each season, is Bull's original Concord vine.

I have found only one record of commercial winegrowing in New England during the nineteenth century, a letter published in the *American Wine Press and Mineral News* for August 1900. The writer, one Albert Bernard of Meriden, Connecticut, described Meriden as a wine-producing locality at that time. In particular, he mentioned a Coe Farm southwest of Meriden as having cultivated Concord and Worden grapes for wine between 1894 and 1897 and as having produced "a superior claret" that was sold in Hartford and in New York City.

• 3 •

The present winegrowing revolution in Connecticut dates from the legislature's enactment of a farm winery law in 1978. It reduced the minimum winery license fee from $1600 to $160 per year for wineries producing up to 75,000 gallons of wine made at least half from Connecticut-grown grapes, and also enabled them to hold tastings and sell their wines as farmers in most other winegrowing states do. This set off the planting of Vinifera and French hybrid vineyards throughout the Nutmeg State, including some on its declining tobacco fields.

On Chestnut Hill Road, a mile from the center of Litchfield in western Connecticut, is the 16,000-gallon Haight Vineyard winery, opened in a converted century-old barn in the same year the farm winery law passed. Textile manufacturer and gentleman farmer Sherman P. Haight, Jr., had begun planting his fifteen-acre vineyard three years before. To supplement the crop from his young vines, he brought grapes from New York State to help make his 1978 vintage. His winemaker is Edward Shorn Mills, who had worked for five years with Hermann Wiemer at the Bully Hill winery in New York State. Haight's daughter Katie is the laboratory technician and also runs the tasting room. By 1983 the Haight vineyard was being doubled in size and was starting to make champagne. Its table wines, some of which have won medals in New York competitions, include Chardonnay, Riesling, and blends of French hybrids called Covertside red and white.

The second Connecticut winery to be licensed is retired chef Peter Kerensky's St. Hilary Vineyard cellar, also in a converted barn, on Webster Road at North Grosvenordale in the northern part of the state. Kerensky, the former executive chef at Brown University, was the first to ask the legislature to adopt a farm winery law. He had been raising grapes as a hobby for twenty years. Kerensky grows only Labrusca grapes on his seven acres; he disdains the idea of raising Vinifera. "Everybody makes Chardonnay," he says. St. Hilary wines—three whites, three reds, and three fruit wines—are sold only at the winery. Kerensky's wife Mary, who named the winery for her great-grandmother Hilary, runs the tasting room.

Motorists on Routes 101 and 169 south of Pomfret in the northeast corner of Connecticut can scarcely help but notice at that intersection a twelve-sided (dodecagon) structure, cylindrical at one end, surrounded by vines and landscaping on a knoll. It is the 25,000-gallon Hamlet Hill Vineyard winery, built in 1980, the first in Connecticut to be designed especially for wine production and sale. The upper story is an attractive tasting room, in which you push a button to hear a recorded voice that guides you on a tour of the modern winery below. The voice is that of Pomfret wire and cable manufacturer August W. Loos, who with his wife Joan owns the winery; she designed the tasting room. Loos began planting grapes in 1975 on fifteen acres below his spectacular castle-like home on Hamlet Hill, northwest of Pomfret. His labels picture the home, named Elsinore for the castle in Shakespeare's *Hamlet*. The vineyard was developed by William Sitts III, a pomology graduate from the University of Georgia who worked for four years at the Woodbury Farms in the Chautauqua district of New York. The winemaker and new viticulturist is former philosophy professor Dr. Howard Bursen, who, like Haight's winemaker Hills, once worked with Wiemer at Bully Hill. Hamlet Hill wines are vintage-dated Seyval Blanc, Red Castle, White Reel, and Drumlin Rosé. Due in 1985 is a *méthode champenoise* sparkling wine. A "Brunonian Reserve" Seyval was produced especially in 1980 for Loos's alma mater, Brown University.

On Taugwonk Road off Route 184, three miles north of Stonington in northeastern Connecticut, is the 3500-gallon Stonecrop Vineyard winery, opened in 1980 by Pfizer fermentation chemist Thomas B. Young and his wife Charlotte. (Stonecrop is an herb that grows in the locality.) The Youngs began planting their

eight-acre vineyard with Vidal, Seyval, Rayon d'Or, and Maréchal Foch in 1977, but made their first vintage of purchased
grapes. Stonecrop estate-bottled 1980 Foch won the best-of-cate-
gory award in a New England wine competition.

Also on Taugwonk Road, a quarter-mile south of the Youngs,
is the Clarke Vineyard, on which a 10,000-gallon winery was
to be built in time to crush its first vintage in 1983. The owner,
Tom Clarke, is a marketer of building materials. He and his
wife Barbara grew Vinifera grapes in Connecticut and in the
Hudson Valley before they acquired their present land. They
have planted ten acres of Chardonnay, Riesling, Pinot Noir, Vidal, Seyval, and Foch.

Two miles farther north, on a hilltop facing Chester Main
Road in North Stonington, still another future winery was being
equipped during 1983 in a three-story former dairy barn. It is
on the twenty-one-acre Crosswoods Vineyard of New York corporate lawyer Hugh Connell and his wife Susan. They began
planting Vinifera vines there in 1981.

Overlooking Lake Waramaug in Warren, off Route 45 north
of New Preston, is the 10,000-gallon Hopkins Vineyard Winery,
opened in 1982 by dairy farmers William and Judith Hopkins
on the fifteen-acre vineyard of French hybrids they began planting four years before. Hopkins Vineyard Barn Red, Waramaug
White, and Sachem's Picnic Wine are among the offerings to
visitors for tasting in the farm's two-century-old former dairy
barn.

Twenty miles south, on Albert's Hill Road off Route 84 in
Newtown, is still another future Connecticut winery. It is on
Colorado computer expert Bruce McLaughlin's vineyard, where
ten acres of French hybrid and Vinifera vines were planted beginning in 1978.

• 4 •

The revival of winegrowing in New England began in New
Hampshire. In 1958, pharmacist John J. Canepa and his wife
Lucille moved from New York to Laconia in the Granite State
because John was offered a job in the Laconia Clinic. They made
their new home in a cottage on Governor's Island in nearby
Lake Winnipesaukee, where they had spent several summer vacations.

On walks on the island during that autumn, they noticed how
the wild grapevines, pruned only by winter gales, climbed sixty
feet high in the pine trees. Picking some of the wild grapes,

they found them sweet; and the Canepas' dream of becoming winegrowers was born. John had known wine since childhood, when his Italian-born father crushed grapes each autumn in the family garage and served the fermented juice, diluted with water, to his children. As a pharmacist, John knew chemistry and had learned some wine technology from a part-time job, analyzing wine samples for an importer, he had held during his senior year at Columbia University. The Canepas thought it would be fun to try, in a region where grapes grew wild, to grow them under cultivation for wine.

They began buying wine books, devoured their contents, and learned that wine can be grown where there is enough sunshine to ripen the grapes. The Canepas bought 800 vines of American and French hybrid varieties that might ripen in New Hampshire and survive the Laconia winters, which dip to fifteen and twenty degrees below zero. In the spring of 1965, John planted all 800 of the vines on three test sites, Lucille helping to dig the holes. Some of the vines produced grapes. Neighbors began planting vines. Newspapers photographed the Canepas' vineyard. The Grape Growers Association of New Hampshire was organized with Canepa as chairman. Word of what was happening reached New York City, and a wine merchant there wrote to the Canepas, offering to sell any wine they might produce.

At that time there were no vineyards worthy of the name in any of the New England States. There began a pilgrimage to Laconia of professional experts from the Geneva, New York, research station, and from wineries in the Finger Lakes, who wanted to see for themselves the improbable sight of wine grapes growing in New Hampshire.

In 1968, the Canepas bought a farm near Belmont. John quit his job at the clinic and built a modern winery, the White Mountain Vineyards of New Hampshire, on Durrell Mountain Road, just off Route 107. In 1970, Canepa estate-bottled Maréchal Foch, New Hampshire Burgundy, and Lakes Region Dry White Dinner Wine went on sale in the state monopoly liquor stores and a dozen restaurants. The winery was enlarged to 85,000 gallons and the vineyard to fifteen acres. John added blends with California wines, and apple and strawberry wines, which he shipped to stores in neighboring states. The winery became a tourist attraction. A bill passed by the legislature in 1971 allowed direct sale of wine at the winery to visitors. At least fifty farmers supplied grapes to the Canepas, including a few who planted vines in Maine and Vermont.

In December of 1982, when Canepa was seventy-three, Miami

real estate developer John Vereen and his wife Florence bought the White Mountain Vineyards from the Canepas, built a log cabin tasting room above the winery, and began a campaign to make their wines, renamed "Mont Blanc" and "Winnepesaukee," symbols of hospitality in the Granite State. Vereen retained enology professor Thomas Cottrell from the New York Geneva Station as a consultant to train Vereen's sister-in-law Peggy Dubois as a winemaker. But John Canepa did not retire. He continued visiting the winery daily as an unpaid consultant, enjoying the results of his dream. Lucille, too, still visits the winery and serves special visitors her seedless Concord grape muffins, except when she is away singing at weddings or funerals. White Mountain is still the only winery in the Granite State.

• 5 •

The first winegrowing estate to start production in Massachusetts in this century is on the island named Martha's Vineyard in the Atlantic Ocean, ten miles off the southern tip of Cape Cod. Electronics engineer George Mathiesen and his wife Catherine, home winemakers from California who had built a summer home on the island, decided in 1971 to try growing grapes because they found the island climate, moderated by the ocean, is relatively mild. They planted three acres with Vinifera vines obtained from Dr. Konstantin Frank, built a 4000-gallon winery, and by 1974 were selling Chicama Vineyard Massachusetts White Riesling and Chardonnay to stores on the island and on Nantucket, the island to the east. Chicama (pronounced Chikay-ma) is named for the Indian path that reaches it from Stoney Hill Road.

To help the Mathiesens, the Massachusetts legislature in 1977 enacted a farm winery law that reduced the minimum winery license from $4500 to $22 per year. Their vineyard since has been enlarged to thirty-five acres and the winery to 20,000 gallons. Two of the Mathiesens' six children have completed their college training and now work full time with their parents. Michael is the vineyard manager and has planted twelve acres of his own. Lynn learned champagne making by working at the Hanns Kornell and Domaine Chandon cellars in California, and she now makes two Chicama Vineyards champagnes—Sea Mist White and Blanc de Noir. The Mathiesens bring Zinfandel and Chenin Blanc grapes from California to supplement their own, but they are proudest of the wines from their own vineyards, such as Pinot Noir, Merlot, Gewürztraminer, Pinot Gris, and Cabernet Sauvignon.

Winegrowing has also spread to the Massachusetts mainland since the 20,000-gallon Commonwealth winery opened on Court Street in historic Plymouth in 1978. When the winery offered Massachusetts farmers contracts to buy any wine grapes they might grow, several vineyards were planted, most with French hybrids and a few with Vinifera, in the area between Dartmouth and Westport on the Bay State's southern coast, and a few on the southern coast of Cape Cod. The Commonwealth winery was established by David Tower, a Boston native who was trained in enology at the UC Davis wine school and who had also worked for two years at wineries in Germany. The first Commonwealth wines were made of grapes Tower purchased from New York State, Pennsylvania, and California, but he said he planned eventually to feature wines grown in Massachusetts and someday to produce a New England champagne. The Commonwealth winery doubled its capacity in its first five years, and moved to new, larger quarters on Lothrop Street in Plymouth in 1983.

• 6 •

Rhode Island, the smallest and most densely populated of the fifty states, has one of the mildest climates in the East. The Ocean State had vineyards and wineries until Prohibition, and since the enactment of a state farm winery law in 1977, it has five wineries again. Although it is not an island, it benefits from the influence of Narragansett Bay and of the rivers that flow into Rhode Island Sound. With young vineyards already producing in New Hampshire, on Martha's Vineyard, and on Long Island, it was not surprising that three wineries were bonded on vineyards in different parts of Rhode Island beginning in 1974.

The state's first home-grown wines, labeled estate-bottled Rhode Island Red and America's Cup White, reached the market in 1977, from Jim and Lolly Mitchell's just-completed 15,000-gallon Sakonnet Vineyard winery. Sakonnet Vineyard is located on West Main Road, north of Little Compton, in Newport County. Mitchell, a chemical engineer who had worked in thirty-three countries before he became a winegrower, says that temperatures at Little Compton rarely fall below zero and that the average is within two degrees of the minimum at Bordeaux.

By 1983, six years after its first wines reached the market, the Sakonnet Vineyard had been expanded to forty acres and its winery to 40,000 gallons. Its wines included Riesling, Chardonnay, Seyval, Chancellor, Foch, Spinnaker White, Compass Rosé, and Chillable Red. Sakonnet also produced a Sparkling Vidal, Rhode Island's first champagne, in 1982.

Rhode Island Winery Number One, because it was the first to be bonded in the state, is in the former dairy barn of H. Winfield Tucker's turf and potato farm on Indian Corner Road, near the tiny post office of Slocum in Washington County, on the west side of Narragansett Bay. It is called South County Vineyards, a partnership of Tucker with Connecticut investment analyst Don Seibert. They planted two acres of Vinifera vines, which failed to produce satisfactory crops. Their only wines, at this writing, are made of grapes grown in New York State.

The third of the Rhode Island wineries is an all-Vinifera winegrowing estate on six-mile-long Prudence Island near the middle of Narragansett Bay. It is reached by a ferry from Bristol that runs twice a day. Former Connecticut bakery owner and business consultant William Bacon, his island-born wife Natalie, and their sons Nathaniel and William moved in 1973 from the mainland to begin growing wine on Natalie's ancestral estate. Their first Chardonnay was sold to island visitors three years later and to stores and restaurants on the mainland in the following year. It since has been winning awards in eastern wine quality competitions. Nathaniel cares for the vineyard, while William, the younger son, is the winemaker and also teaches five student grades in the island's one-room school. The Bacons made their first wine in a converted milkshed, but in 1981 they built a 4500-gallon partially underground winery in a space blasted into the side of a hill. Their vineyard, now expanded from three to twenty acres, produces Riesling, Gewürztraminer, Pinot Noir, Merlot, and Cabernet Sauvignon in addition to the award-winning Chardonnay.

Rhode Island's fourth winery is the 1500-gallon Diamond Hill Vineyard cellar, bonded in 1979 by Warwick jewelry wire manufacturers Andrew and Peter Berntson and their wives, Jean and Clara, on their five acres along Diamond Hill Road in Cumberland, in the northwestern corner of the state. The fifth is Providence lawyer Philip di Sano's 1000-gallon winery, located on his acre of young French hybrids near the intersection of Stony Lane and New Road near Exeter in Washington County.

Meanwhile, the New England winegrowers have argued with the Federal government about establishing viticultural-area appellations that can be used on labels of their wines. At this writing, the government was considering two separate appellations, one for "Martha's Vineyard," which might include Chappaquiddick and Nantucket Islands, and another, "Southeastern New England," to include the islands and parts of Rhode Island, Massachusetts, and Connecticut.

Although winegrowing in the New England region is still young, enough has already happened to bear out the prophecy of a Boston *Globe* editor, who in 1967 headlined a story of the vineyards then being planted: "Soon, Yankee Wine!"

10

Wines of Some Mid-Continent States

At hermann, missouri, in 1866, the year after the Civil War, Professor George Husmann penned his first book, *The Native Grape and the Manufacture of American Wines.*

"The nation is affected with grape fever," he wrote. "I firmly believe that this continent is destined to be the greatest wine-producing country in the world. America will be, from the Atlantic to the Pacific, one smiling and happy Wineland, where each laborer shall sit under his own vine, and none will be too poor to enjoy the purest and most wholesome of all stimulants, good, cheap, native wine."

In that year Missouri surpassed Ohio as the second largest winegrowing state of the Union, and the grape-planting fever was spreading through such neighboring states as Iowa, Kansas, and Illinois.

But local prohibition laws and vine diseases were also spreading while Husmann wrote his book. Too many grapes were being planted for the wineries to absorb, and the prices paid for grapes declined. Vineyards became neglected, were attacked by plant pests, and were abandoned to die. Husmann, professor of horticulture at the University of Missouri, abandoned his home state in 1881 to become a winemaker in California's Napa Valley. He had discovered in a single visit during that summer how ideal the conditions were for winegrowing there.

National Prohibition in 1920 closed all of the mid-continent wineries except two monasteries which continued producing altar wines. A few dozen commercial wineries reopened in 1933, but much of the area was still legally Dry, and there was little demand for any wine except the cheapest dessert types. Eighteen states between the Appalachians and the Rockies (not counting

Michigan) have produced less than 3 percent of American wine
since Repeal.

Yet all of these states are natural grape-growing country; Labrusca-type grapes flourish in tens of thousands of midwestern
gardens, and more vine species grow wild here than anywhere
else on earth. Most of the wine produced in the world today
comes from vineyards grafted to, or crossed by hybridizing with,
native midwestern vines.

• 2 •

More than a century since Husmann wrote his book, millions
of Americans, including midwesterners, have begun buying table
wines, and now there is grape fever in the Show Me State again.

Vineyard Districts of MISSOURI

A state-backed effort has been under way since 1978 to regain Missouri's onetime greatness among the winegrowing states by coordinating vinicultural research with improved winegrowing techniques. New vineyards have been planted and old ones expanded in a dozen Missouri counties. Sixteen wineries with their own vineyards have been established within the past eight years, giving the state a total of twenty-six.

Professor Husmann's hometown, the picture-book Missouri River hamlet of Hermann, is one of the places where it is happening. For the first time in half a century, wine is flowing from the huge, turreted Stone Hill Winery, which Michael Poeschel from Germany began building in 1847 on the hilltop at the south edge of town. It once held more than a million gallons and was the second largest in the nation. Its wines, such as Hermannsberger, Starkenberger, and Black Pearl, won eight gold medals at world's fairs between 1873 and 1904. When Prohibition closed the winery, Ottmar Stark ordered all of its vineyards destroyed, virtually ruining the economy of the town. The great Stone Hill cellars then were used to cultivate mushrooms, producing sixty-five tons each year.

In 1965, farmer James Held, whose ancestors came to Hermann 128 years earlier, saw that table wines were becoming popular in Missouri. He arranged to move into the second floor of the old winery with his wife Betty Ann and their four children. The Helds installed antique casks and his grandfather's wooden roller-crusher in one of the underground vaults and made a thousand gallons of Catawba wine. Their first wine sold so well that they since have cleared the mushroom beds out of the other seven vaults and now turn out 60,000 gallons per year of Missouri Riesling, Catawba, Niagara, Norton Seedling, Concord, Chelois, and a very pleasant dry, nonfoxy Catawba champagne. The Helds have quadrupled to fifty-five acres their vineyard of Norton, Catawba, and French hybrid vines on the bluffs above the Missouri River. Their son Jonathan and daughter Patricia, sent to study at Fresno State University in California, have returned with enology degrees. Stone Hill offers wine tastings and tours of its cellars, and has opened its own restaurant and wine museum.

Wine has been part of the flavor of Hermann since grapes were first planted there by Jacob Fugger in 1843. Many of its citizens, including the Helds, rear their children by "the Hermann formula: the first year wine, the second year wine and sauerkraut." The revival of Hermann's days of wine and glory is now celebrated on the third weekend of each May with German bands, folk dancing, knackwurst, and a house tour of "Little Germany." In autumn the Helds hold a three-week Oktoberfest at the winery.

When I last visited Hermann in 1982, a second winery had opened on East First Street in the center of town. Banker James Dierberg had renovated the three-story Krupp brewery and its caves, built in 1847, and turned it into the modern Hermannhof Winery, with a tasting room. He had also planted a sixty-acre vineyard of French hybrids in the Gasconade Hills. The principal Hermannhof wine is a blend named White Lady of Starkenburg, named for a town across the river. Dierberg has also begun making champagne.

• 3 •

A Missouri winery almost as old as Stone Hill at Hermann was reopened in 1968 at Augusta, a town of German heritage on the Missouri River Bluffs thirty miles west of St. Louis. The proprietor is former accountant Lucian Dressel, who as a young man became enamored of wine during his travels in Europe. On completing his studies at Harvard and Columbia, he recognized the trend to wine-drinking in America and decided to become a winegrower. Touring with his wife Eva, he found the place at Augusta where there were eleven wineries before Prohibition, and six of their crumbling skeletons remained. Another old brick cellar with underground storage vaults was in better condition; it had been converted into an apartment house and was for sale. The Dressels bought it and discovered that this was originally the Mount Pleasant Vineyard of Friedrich Münch, a famous Lutheran minister and grape breeder, who wrote *School for American Grape Culture*. Münch built the winery in 1881, and his prize-winning wines were known from coast to coast.

Dressel replanted two dozen acres of the original vineyard with French hybrid and Labrusca types and named his first wines "Emigré" red, white, and rosé. He since has planted and made wines of three grape varieties grown long ago by Münch. One is a nonfoxy cross made by the late Texas grape breeder Thomas Volney Munson between the Herbemont of South Carolina and the Mississippi Valley post-oak wild grape; Munson named the cross for Münch. Dressel's Münch is somewhat like Italy's light Valpolicella but has a powerful bouquet of its own. Second was Norton or Cynthiana, which Münch spelled Cynthianna, a spelling Dressel has retained. Third was Missouri Riesling, the Labrusca-type grape bred at Hermann about 1860. Some of Dressel's Missouri Rieslings are not detectably foxy, and some vintages have had the aroma of botrytis, the noble mold. In 1981 he introduced a brut and an extra-dry champagne. Dressel predicts that while New York State thus far has been better known for its white wines than for its reds, the Missouri River area soon will become recognized as producing the fullest-bodied American red wines.

When in 1980 the Federal government made known that it was preparing to establish American viticultural areas, a petition by Dressel and his neighbors to have the Augusta area so recognized was the first one in the entire nation to be approved. (A petition to establish the Hermann area, too, as a viticultural area was approved in 1983.)

• 4 •

There are four more wineries along the Missouri River besides the three already mentioned, and two more preparing to start. Harold and Larry Kruger have been making old-fashioned Labrusca wines since 1977 in an earth-covered concrete structure off Highway 41, two miles north of Arrow Rock. On Road D north of Portland, fifteen miles west of Hermann, are the fifteen-acre Green Valley Vineyard and its modern 20,000-gallon winery, established in 1973 by retired chemical engineer Nicholas Lamb, his sons, and his wife Margarette, whom you can meet in their tasting room. The Lambs' vintage-dated French hybrid wines regularly win medals in the annual quality competitions at the Missouri State Fair. On Road B off Route 100 near Berger are the seven-acre vineyard and 2000-gallon winery of Ozark Airlines pilot James Bias and his wife Norma. Since buying a small Catawba vineyard in 1980, they have been planting French hybrids, and have also begun making mead. At the intersection of Stone Church Road and Highway E, seven miles west of New Haven, are the five-acre, 5000-gallon Edelweiss Vineyard and Winery, established by Günther Heeb and his wife Janet in time to make their first wine in 1982. Heeb was born and was trained in winegrowing in the Rheinhessen district of Germany. Seven miles east of New Haven, on Road B off Route 100 near Berger, is the Sunny Slope Vineyard, where Ozark Airlines pilot John Eckert and his wife Sandra are preparing to build a winery and begin producing wines by 1984. On Augusta Bottom Road, across the river from Washington, genetics professor Paul Levine of Washington University Medical School at St. Louis is beginning to build his Osage Ridge Winery and rustic tasting room into a hillside below his vineyard. On the same road, toward Augusta, is an 8000-gallon winery named Montelle (little mountain) Vineyards. Former St. Louis journalist Clayton Byers and his wife Nissel have made wine since 1970 from the numerous hybrid grape varieties they have planted on their land and on a neighbor's farm. Their son Brian, who once worked at the Tarula Vineyard in Ohio, has joined Montelle Vineyards as their director of operations. Anthony Kooyumjian, another Ozark Airlines pilot, and his wife Martha have reopened the winery at Wepprich's Wine Gardens in St. Charles, where winemaking was begun by Emil Wepprich's grandfather in 1859. The Kooyumjians, who have a young three-acre hybrid vineyard on the river bluffs south of St. Charles, have renamed the old Wepprich cellars The Winery of the Little Hill.

• 5 •

Wine grapes have been planted again in the part of Missouri's Ozark Plateau known as Big Prairie, where the principal grapes grown until now were Concords for the Welch co-operative's grape-juice plant at Springdale, Arkansas.

The first modern winery and the first to make champagne in this region was built in 1970 at St. James, where the Ozark grape festival is held each September. James Hofherr and his wife Patricia chose the Big Prairie section as the place for their venture because most of Missouri's 2000 acres of vineyards were there. Their 56,000-gallon winery and its rustic tasting and sales room are on the access road beside Interstate Highway 44, a mile from their fifty-acre vineyard on Springfield Road. Signs in the winery invite visitors to take a self-guided cellar tour. Hofherr holds a degree in microbiology from the University of Texas. He had five years' experience with the Bardenheier winery at St. Louis before coming to St. James and also had made champagne for a year at the Post Winery in Altus, Arkansas. The Hofherrs' table wines range from Catawba and Niagara to such popular hybrid types as Aurore, Chelois, and Baco Noir. To my taste, their best have been their Villard Blanc of that white hybrid and their flavorful dry red of the rare Neva Munson grape. They also make mead and various wines of other fruits than grapes. The Hofherrs have sent their son John to study viticulture and enology at Fresno State University in California, where he graduated in 1983.

Signs on Highway U, four miles east of St. James, will guide you to Heinrichshaus, a 2000-gallon winery bonded in 1978 by engineer Heinrich Grohe and his wife Lois, an art teacher, on their ten-acre French hybrid vineyard. When Grohe came to St. Louis from his native Germany in the 1950s, he rejected Missouri wines and began making his own, which led to planting his own vineyard, too. Heinrichshaus wines are hybrid blends named Prairie Blanc, Vidal Blanc, De Chaunac, and Vidal.

A third new winery in the Big Prairie region opened in 1982. It is the Ferrigno Vineyard and Winery on Highway B, four miles north of St. James. The winemaker is Dr. Richard A. Ferrigno, who teaches sociology part time at the University of Missouri in nearby Rolla. He has planted French hybrids in a twenty-five-acre vineyard which originally grew only Concords. His wife Susan receives visitors to their 7000-gallon winery, attractively converted from a former dairy barn. By prearrangement Susan also provides luncheons for groups. The Ferrignos are proudest of their Vidal Blanc and their red wine of Chelois.

• 6 •

On Interstate 44, east of St. James, is the village of Rosati, named by Italian immigrants at the turn of the century for their bishop, who built the first Catholic cathedral west of the Mississippi. At the edge of the village is the 75,000-gallon Rosati Winery, popular with tourists who stop to taste wines and Catawba grape juice in its wine garden.

Growers who had planted Concords for sale to Welch built the winery during the Depression years of the late 1930s to provide a home for surplus grapes the co-op could not buy. When the Second World War broke out, Welch bought the place to use as a grape depot. German war prisoners were quartered in the winery and made preserves for the military until the war ended. Damaged by fire in 1969, it was bought and rebuilt by veteran horticulturist Robert Ashby and his wife Sally. Ashby had once taught agriculture at the state university in St. James. Henry, their horticulturist son, cares for their seventy-acre vineyard. Son-in-law Ronald Moreland, their winemaker and general manager, makes a very pleasant dry champagne. Ronald's wife Liz presides in the wine garden and tasting room.

• 7 •

On the Meramec River near Steelville, a few miles southeast of St. James, is Dr. Axel Norman Arneson's Peaceful Bend Vineyard. His winery, a two-story wooden structure with a Dutch barn–style roof, is built into a hillside.

Dr. Arneson, professor of clinical obstetrics and gynecology at Washington University School of Medicine, first learned about winemaking by helping his father ferment grapes for their home use in Texas during Prohibition. His travels in later years through Europe so stimulated his interest in viticulture that in 1951 he purchased some French hybrid vines from Philip Wagner and planted them on his Missouri farm. When his Peaceful Bend winery was bonded in 1972, the doctor made three wines, each a blend of several hybrids. The red was named Meramec for the river, the white was called Courtois, the name of the township, and the rosé was named for the Crawford County village of Huzzah. The name of the winery, which is on Highway M, comes from the deep bend the river makes at the Arneson farm. The doctor is fascinated with the history of Missouri viniculture and is writing a book that traces Professor George Husmann's career.

Twenty-five miles west of Steelville, on Road W which takes off from US 63 near Vida, is the 5000-gallon Carver Wine Cellar, opened in 1979 by research physicist Laurence Carver of the university branch at Rolla and his wife Mary. It is located on the six-acre, predominantly Vinifera, vineyard they had begun planting two years before. The Carvers, transplanted from California, prefer wines of Vinifera, which are difficult to grow here. The list of Carver wines includes hybrids: Seyval as well as Chardonnay and Riesling among the whites, Baco Noir, Chancellor, and Villard Noir as well as Cabernet Sauvignon among their reds.

On Road CC, off US 63 seven miles north of Licking, about twenty miles south of the Carvers, is the 6000-gallon winery of St. Louis chiropractor Val Reis and his wife Joy. They began planting their eight-acre hybrid and Labrusca vineyard in 1972 and opened the winery in 1978. Their featured wines are hybrid "varietals," Vidal, Villard and Seyval whites, and Léon Millot red.

• 8 •

Winegrowing has also returned to western Missouri, where there were many wineries a century ago. The town of Independence, with Shaffer's Winery and Lohse's Native Wine Garden, was known for its wine long before Missourians came to know

Harry Truman. A history of Newton County records that in 1867 Hermann Jaeger of Neosho advised French viticulturists to graft their phylloxera-devastated vineyards onto wild Ozark vine roots. He shipped them seventeen carloads of rootings and later was awarded the Cross of the French Legion of Honor.

The first winery to open in the Kansas City area since the repeal of Prohibition is a concrete and plastic cave and tasting room at the Midi Vineyard on Road F in Jackson County, four miles northeast of Lone Jack. It began when structural engineer Dutton Biggs read about Philip Wagner's vines and planted a half-acre of them in 1970 to make wine in his home. Three years later, Biggs met University of Missouri philosophy professor George Gale and his wife Carol of Kansas City. They persuaded Biggs to become their partner in establishing the present ten-acre Midi Vineyard and 7000-gallon winery. The best wine I have tasted there was a red of the hybrid Léon Millot.

Since Biggs and the Gales started the Midi Vineyard winery, three more have opened in western Missouri. In 1976, a group of farmers headed by Catawba grower Hershel Gray opened the 5000-gallon Ozark Mountain Cellars in Gray's concrete milk barn near Chestnut Ridge, thirteen miles south of Ozark; they have quadrupled its capacity since. In 1980, farmer Ed Smith and engineer Richard Phillips started the 2000-gallon Bristle Ridge winery in Montserrat, off US 50 near Knob Noster State Park. Ozark and Bristle Ridge make both French hybrid and Labrusca wines.

At the corner of Rock and Spring Streets in the town of Weston, northwest of Kansas City, is the only winery, complete with tasting room, that I have ever found housed in a former church. It is the Weston Vineyards winery of University of Missouri mathematics professor Elbert Pirtle and his wife Patricia. Dr. Pirtle began making wine in 1979 in a corner of the century-old one-time Royal Brewery. He grows French hybrid grapes on thirteen acres near Camden Point, east of town. Two years later, the Pirtles moved the winery across the street into the handsome one-story brick building that was erected in 1867 as the German Evangelical Lutheran Church. The church building also provides space for Patricia Pirtle's gift shop.

• 9 •

Missouri's chief early center of wine and champagne production was at St. Louis, where the Mississippi and Missouri rivers meet. There Professor Husmann established *The Grape Culturist,* one of the first American periodicals on viticulture, and wrote two books after the one quoted from at the beginning of this chapter. Like Jaeger at Neosho, Husmann shipped millions of phylloxera-resistant Missouri vines to reestablish the dying vineyards of Europe. In his time there were vineyards and wineries in forty-eight Missouri counties.

A stone-arched maze four levels below an entire block on Cass Avenue in St. Louis was once the home of the Missouri Wine Company, established in 1832. It was purchased in 1859 by Chicago connoisseur and political leader Isaac Cook, who won such fame for his Cook's Imperial champagne that its name is still used on a California sparkling wine. Cook's Champagne Cellar was reopened after Prohibition by the American Wine Company, headed by Alsace-born Adolf Heck, Sr. Heck, the father of the Heck brothers who later owned the Korbel vineyard in California, was uncomfortably short of capital until a little-known Swiss firm invested in Cook's stock in 1939. Five years later, during the Second World War, government investigators tracing Nazi investments in this country discovered that the secret owner of the Missouri winery was Hitler's foreign minister, ex-champagne salesman Joachim von Ribbentrop. The American Wine Company was seized by the government and was sold several times until it became part of the Schenley liquor empire in 1946, the same year von Ribbentrop was hanged for his war crimes. Cook's champagne continued to be made as Heck Senior made it—from California wine with eastern Catawba in the blend—after 1954 no longer in St. Louis, but at the Guild winery in Lodi, California.

• 10 •

Missouri's biggest winery is the 950,000-gallon Bardenheier's Wine Cellar on Skinker Parkway in St. Louis. Owned for 110 years by four generations of Bardenheiers, it was bought in 1983 by former chemistry professor E. Dean Jarboe's Future Coatings, Inc., of St. Louis, which supplies American wineries with epoxy linings for large steel wine storage tanks.

Although primarily a blender and bottler of California wine for sale in thirty midwestern states, Bardenheier's in 1970 had become a Missouri winegrower, planting fifty acres of French hybrids on the big Lost River Ranch of Ott Coelln at Koshkonong on US Highway 63 near Thayer in south-central Missouri. This is the area, six miles from the Arkansas border, where Michael Brand, the founder of nearby Brandsville, began producing

Ozark Maid wines in 1887. The Bardenheiers named their Missouri-grown wines, all reds, Chateau Thayer Chelois, Maréchal Foch, and Baco Noir. Jarboe, the new owner of Bardenheier's, had owned a small experimental vineyard of Vinifera and hybrids since 1981 at Gerald, south of Hermann, but in 1984 he began adding forty acres of Vinifera to the vineyard at Koshkonong. His new plantings are mostly the newly popular German crosses of White Riesling.

• 11 •

Larger than any of the other winegrowing projects under way in Missouri are two entirely new ones beginning in the southernmost corners of the state. In 1982, the first twenty acres of Dr. J. Frank England's Bois d'Arc Vineyards were planted along Highway AA two miles east of Washburn, in southwestern Barry County. More acres were being added in 1983, and construction of the initially 20,000-gallon Winery of the Seven Vineyards was to begin in 1985. Dr. England, a microbiologist who owns 1700 acres in Barry County, says bois d'arc means "wood of the Osage bow," although people elsewhere translate it as "hedge apple" or as "Osage orange."

In the southeasternmost corner of Missouri near Sikeston in Scott County, the pilot 5000-gallon Moore-Dupont Winery was bonded in 1982 at surgeon Jean-René Dupont's twenty-acre hybrid and Vinifera vineyard on Highway 91, west of Bell City. The Moore-Dupont project includes both Dr. Dupont's property and the 140-acre vineyard of grape grower J. Handy Moore, who also grows some Vinifera varieties. The pilot winery will be enlarged sufficiently to use both Moore's and Dr. Dupont's grapes.

• 12 •

The current effort to regain Missouri's onetime greatness among the winegrowing states began in 1978, when a task force of agricultural and business leaders was appointed by the governor. It was inspired and headed by St. Louis retailer David C. Kay, who heads the "905" stores that operate throughout Missouri. This led to the appointment of a Missouri Wine Advisory Board, headed by Kay, and to the undertaking of a coordinated vinicultural research program at the University of Missouri, which was financed in 1983 by adding 4 cents to the state's 30-cent-per-gallon wine tax, the proceeds to support research and promotion of Missouri wines. The research program had been launched in 1980 when Bruce Zoecklein, the enology instructor at Fresno State University, was brought from California to become the Missouri state enologist. Two years later, a state extension viticulturist, Cornell-trained Larry Lockshin, was brought from New York State.

Zoecklein says Missouri hybrid wines are already equal to any now grown east of the Rocky Mountains. He believes that areas in southern Missouri can also produce Vinifera wines like those of California and Europe. He adds that Missouri already grows two all-American grape varieties, Norton and Cynthiana, that make dry red wines equal in flavor, bouquet, and in mellowness with age, that can compete in quality with any other red wines in the world. Within the coming decade, he predicts, aged samples of these two red wines will win recognition for Missouri as one of this country's fine-winegrowing states. To which David Kay adds: "With our University's first four years of research already producing impressive results, and with more than a dozen modern new vineyards and wineries started since our program began, Missouri viniculture has made more progress since 1978 than in the almost half a century since the end of Prohibition."

• 13 •

Winegrowing has also revived in Indiana, where there were vineyards and wineries more than a century ago. Eight wineries now operate in the Hoosier State, all of them opened since the legislature adopted a farm winery law in 1971.

When Pennsylvania enacted its 1968 law permitting small wineries, Professor William Oliver, teaching law at the University of Indiana in Bloomington, saw a way to turn his winemaking hobby into a business. He wrote a virtual copy of the Pennsylvania law and got it passed by the Indiana lawmakers, many of whom were his former students. In 1972 he opened his Oliver Winery on Highway 37, seven miles north of the university campus. The Oliver Winery prospered, making table wines from the professor's hybrid grapes and mead from Indiana honey. He has enlarged his vineyard to forty acres and his winery to 35,000 gallons. In the tasting room, where his wife Mary presides, visitors can buy wine by the glass, bottle, or case between eleven and six daily. Cheese, bread, and sausage are also for sale and can be enjoyed in the winery's picnic grounds.

Twelve miles east of Oliver's winery and two miles west of Route 45 at Trevlac is the Possum Trot Vineyards winery, on Possum Trot Road. Retired Navy Commander Ben Sparks and his wife Leora opened the winery in 1978 after installing the latest in winemaking equipment in their century-old barn. It holds 3000 gallons, which accommodates the crop from their five acres of hybrid vines. They make two wines, a white blend of Vidal and Vignoles and a red of Maréchal Foch. Sparks heads the Indiana Winegrowers Guild, which holds an annual grape and wine symposium in conjunction with the Purdue University Extension Service.

In the far northwestern corner of Indiana, a mile from the Michigan border, is the Banholzer Wine Cellar, three miles east of Hesston on County Road 1000 North. Carl and Janet Banholzer sold their interest in Michigan's Tabor Hill Vineyard in 1971 and established the vineyard and 35,000-gallon winery in the following year. Most of their French hybrid wines have proprietary names, such as La Fleur for white and Kaisertahl for red. In seasons following especially mild winters, they harvest enough grapes from their Vinifera vines to make Chardonnay and Cabernet Sauvignon.

New vineyards have also sprung up along Indiana's Ohio River shore. At Cape Sandy, south of Leavenworth, John J. Easley planted twenty acres of hybrids with some Vinifera in 1970. His winery, named Easley Enterprises, is in an old creamery building on North College Avenue in Indianapolis. His first wines, Cape Sandy Baco Noir and De Chaunac, were introduced in 1977. In the old river town of Madison, nuclear engineer Scott Conboy and his wife Elsa are replanting the ten-acre vineyard of hybrids Michael Mancuso left when he closed the Villa Medeo winery in 1981 and moved to Tennessee. Scotella Vineyard will be the winery's new name. On North Dearborn Road at New Alsace is the twenty-acre, mostly Vinifera vineyard planted in 1972 by Dr. Donald A. Shumrick, chairman of otolaryngology at the University of Cincinnati Medical Center. The doctor and his wife Nora are building the Château Pomije (her Bohemian family name) Winery near Cincinnati in Ohio to use their Indiana grapes.

• 14 •

The earliest record of winegrowing in Indiana was at Vevay, Switzerland County, in 1804, twelve years before Indiana became a state. Eight years earlier, Jean Jacques Dufour had left his father's vineyard at Vevey (the French spelling) in Switzerland with an ambitious plan to found a Swiss winegrowing colony in America. He organized the Kentucky Vineyard Society in 1798 and planted European and Alexander vines along the Kentucky River, twenty-five miles south of Lexington. His Kentucky vineyards were damaged by frost and plant pests and were abandoned by 1809. Dufour meanwhile bought the present site of Vevay and named it for his Swiss home. Here he planted the grape variety which Pierre Legaux of Philadelphia had falsely named "the Cape grape," really a chance Labrusca hybrid, the Alexander. Legaux's mistake turned out to be Dufour's good fortune, for the hardy Alexander flourished at Vevay, where any European grape would have perished. At Vevay, Dufour wrote one of the first American books about winegrowing, *The American Vine Dresser's Guide.* It was published in 1826, a few months before he died. With his death, winegrowing at Vevay went into a gradual decline. Thomas Jefferson and Secretary of State Henry Clay approved of Vevay wine, and Clay once had a dozen bottles sent to him, to be served to some distinguished visitors. When he opened the bottles he found all twelve filled with whiskey, substituted by his son James, who must have liked the wine.

When Nicholas Longworth introduced the Catawba to Ohio in the 1820s, the Indiana winegrowers began switching their plantings to that "wonder grape." By 1880 Indiana was producing 100,000 gallons of wine yearly and selling much of it in Cincinnati. But by then the rot which had killed Longworth's vines had spread to such Indiana centers as Vevay. Grape production elsewhere in the Hoosier State reached an all-time high in 1911, when its crop totaled 11,000 tons. It declined during and after Prohibition, until by 1954 only 900 tons were produced.

• 15 •

An intermediate chapter after Vevay in Indiana's wine history had begun in 1814 in the far southwestern corner of the state, when "Father" George Rapp abandoned his utopian winegrowing colony at Harmony near Pittsburgh. He resettled some 400 of his celibate Rappists on a tract along the Wabash River and named it Harmonie. Rapp found winegrowing there "somewhat better here than in Pennsylvania, yet not so good by far as in the old country." As recorded earlier, the Harmonie Society abandoned Indiana and moved back to Pennsylvania in 1825. Another utopian named Robert Owen then bought the land and renamed it New Harmony. Since restored by the state for its historical importance, New Harmony now helps attract visitors to the Golden Raintree Winery, which is fifteen miles to the east on the St. Wendel–Blairsville Road.

Named for the Oriental tree that rains golden blossoms each June on the streets of St. Wendel, the 50,000-gallon Golden Raintree Winery was founded in 1975 by a group of southern Indiana businessmen and farmers to revive grape growing in the area. As their winemaker they hired Murli Dharmadkari, a Hindu who earned his Ph.D. in viticulture and enology at Ohio State University and who also had worked in a winery at Circleville in Ohio. Dr. Murli says southern Indiana, with its 200-day growing season, is a good place to grow grapes, and he proves it by the prizes that are regularly awarded Golden Raintree hybrid and Labrusca wines in eastern quality competitions. He makes sixteen different wines with such names as Chablis, Criterion, Harmonie, Santi, and Directors Choice, which are sold at the winery and in Indiana, Illinois, and Kentucky stores. The winery, the most modern in Indiana, is built into the side of a hill. An underground tunnel connects it to a Swiss chalet tasting room, to which a restaurant has been added.

The newest in Indiana is the 40,000-gallon Huber Orchard Winery, off St. Johns Road and US 150 in Starlight, twelve miles across the border from Louisville, Kentucky. Kentuckians drive the twelve miles to buy the Huber Orchard hybrid, Labrusca, apple, and strawberry wines. When Carl and Gerald Huber first turned their dairy barn into a winery in 1978, they bought grapes from other growers, but in 1983 they began planting eight acres of hybrid vines of their own. They were encouraged to make the new investment by the marked improvement in their business since the Indiana legislature amended the law in 1982 to allow its farm wineries to stay open on Sundays.

During the early 1980s, when winegrowers in other states were petitioning the Federal government to establish viticulture-area appellations with which to label their estate-bottled wines, Milan, Indiana, grape grower and former TV reporter John Garrett proposed "Ohio River Valley" as an area name. The government granted his petition in 1983, including the parts of Indiana, Ohio, West Virginia, and Kentucky which border the Ohio River, in this, the largest American viticultural area thus far given a regional name. Garrett and his wife Dorothy promptly began building the 9,000-gallon Villa Milan winery, to begin using their ten acres of French hybrid grapes by 1985.

· 16 ·

When you explore southern Indiana, you also should stop at Saint Meinrad Archabbey and Theological Seminary on Route 545, south of I-64. Besides its famous old buildings, stained-glass windows, and its art collection, the Archabbey also has the oldest winery in the state. Wine has been made there since the monastery was established in 1854. The first wines were made of wild grapes, but ten acres of Concords were added around the turn of the century. About 5000 gallons are made in the monastery basement each year, not for sale but for the Mass and to accompany the monks' evening meal. The Concord wine needed sweetening to be palatable, and it was not popular with the 160 resident priests and brothers, so Brother David Petri was sent to Konstantin Frank's New York State vineyard to work for a year, where he learned to make drier wine, and to bring back and plant some of Dr. Frank's Vinifera vines. During the 1976–1977 winter, the Vinifera vines were killed by minus-twenty-two-degrees temperatures, while the Concords survived. Brother David since has begun planting French hybrids, which make very acceptable dry wines.

• 17 •

Kentucky's climate is as favorable for winegrowing as Indiana's, at least in terms of weather. The evidence is in the 1880 Federal census of winegrowing, which showed 138,173 gallons of wine produced in Logan, Boyle, Washington, and twenty-seven other Kentucky counties, compared to 99,566 gallons in Indiana that year. But the political climate of the Blue Grass State was especially unfavorable when two farm wineries started in Kentucky during the 1970s. Two-thirds of the state's 120 counties had laws prohibiting any sale of wine or liquor, and there were other legal problems besides.

F. Carlton Colcord, a Kentuckian who had traveled in Europe, planted twenty acres of hybrid vines in 1970 on his farm, four miles west of Paris in Bourbon County (for which Kentucky whiskey is named), because he thought winegrowing could improve the depressed economy of the state's Appalachian region. Before he started his winery, he asked the legislature to reduce the state's minimum license fee of $1500 per year, far too much for any small winery to pay. The legislature cut the fee to $250, but it prohibited Colcord from selling wine to stores or restaurants and from selling to any consumer more than a quart of any type of wine per year. Colcord's winery opened in 1976 in the one-time distillery town of Paris. His wines were of better than average midwestern quality, but their sales, thus restricted, were so disappointing that by 1982 he had put up his winery for sale.

In the same year that Colcord's winery opened, electrical engineer Paul Laine and his wife Jane started the 50,000-gallon Laine

Vineyards winery beside their fifty-four acres of hybrids off Route 51, west of Fulton in southeastern Kentucky. Like Colcord, the Laines found the restrictions on their sales made their investment a losing proposition.

In 1981, a group of Kentuckians led by philosophy professor Robert Miller of Eastern Kentucky University met at Lexington and revived the Kentucky Vineyard Society, which Jean Jacques Dufour had founded in 1798 to finance the grape-growing colony he was starting along the Kentucky River. The Society persuaded the legislature to amend the law, removing the restriction on wineries' sales to retailers and raising the limit on their sales to consumers from a quart to a twelve-bottle case.

When I last checked, the Laines were thinking of reopening their winery. "It may take a few more years," says Professor Miller, "but Kentucky will become an important winegrowing state again."

• 18 •

Illinois has three wineries, and if the state legislature passes a farm winery bill, first proposed in 1981, it is likely soon to have more.

Grapes have been grown commercially for more than a century in many parts of the Prairie State. The 1880 census showed Illinois producing 142,359 gallons of wine in 1859 and 10 million pounds of grapes as late as 1919, the year before Prohibition began.

On the Mississippi River, at the far western edge of the state, is a winery that has grown its own grapes since pre–Civil War times. Few people in Chicago or Springfield know it exists. Fred Baxter's Gem City Vineland vineyard and winery at Nauvoo produces seven Labrusca-type wines, ranging from Niagara and Concord to red, white, rosé, burgundy, and sauterne. The cellars and the 120-acre vineyard date from 1857, eight years after Baxter's English great-grandfather came to Nauvoo with Etienne Cabet's French communistic Icarian sect (about which more will follow). Members of the Baxter family invite you to take a self-guided tour of the winery and its century-old casks. Until 1977, the Illinois beverage law would not let them sell you their wine or even offer you a taste. When it was modified in 1976 to allow a winery to sell part of its production at retail, the Baxters promptly built a tasting room, where visitors now can sample the wines with Nauvoo blue cheese. But there still are other unreasonable requirements in the law, which is why there are not many vineyards and wineries in Illinois.

Nauvoo is especially worth visiting for its strange history, its restored homes of the original Mormons, the caves of its old wineries, and for the annual symbolic Wedding of Wine and Cheese, an ancient French ceremony that is part of the Nauvoo Grape Festival on the weekend before Labor Day. In the wedding pageant, written by the Benedictine Sisters of St. Mary's Academy in Nauvoo, the "bride" places the wine on a barrel which symbolizes the altar; the "groom" places the cheese beside it, and the magistrate encircles both articles with a wooden barrel hoop, which symbolizes the wedding ring.

Nauvoo was founded by the first Mormons, led by their founder, Prophet Joseph Smith. They fled here from western Missouri in 1836 and drained malarial swamps to build their temple and the city, "Nauvoo the Beautiful," which then was ten times the size of Chicago. Political quarrels with non-Mormons led to riots, and in 1844 a raging mob in Carthage shot and killed Joseph Smith and his brother Hyrum; two years later the temple was burned to the ground. To escape further persecution, the Mormons in 1846 abandoned Nauvoo, leaving it a virtual ghost town, and began their epic wagon journey into Utah, led by Brigham Young. To Nauvoo five years later came Cabet and his Icarians, who moved into the empty Mormon homes. The Icarian brand of communism failed to work, and Cabet abandoned his utopia, leaving behind many of his flock while others went to California. Meanwhile, winegrowing became the leading industry of Nauvoo, John Tanner from Berne in Switzerland having planted the first vineyard in 1847.

The winery that Alois Rheinberger from Lichtenstein founded in 1850 now serves as Nauvoo's Historical Museum. Memorabilia on display show that Rheinberger's wines became famous and were known as late as the nineties in such faraway places as St. Paul and New York. In the museum cellar you can see his press and his other winemaking implements, and the huge stone he used as a weight on his press is on the lawn nearby. An acre of Rheinberger's vineyard still bears grapes in the Nauvoo State Park. The extent of pre-Prohibition winemaking at Nauvoo can be estimated by counting the dozens of vaulted wine caves that honeycomb the hills along the river shore.

When Prohibition emptied the Nauvoo wineries, it was found that the wine caves had just the proper temperature and degree of moisture for the culture of blue cheese. This was the birth of Nauvoo's cheese industry, now celebrated by the Wedding of Wine and Cheese.

• 19 •

Forty miles southwest of Chicago, on Pauling Road near the town of Monee, an ancient Illinois Central railroad station stands beside a vineyard of French hybrids interspersed with Delaware and Catawba vines. Beneath the quaint old station is an 18,000-gallon wine cellar that produces bottle-fermented champagne. This is the Thompson Vineyard and Winery, owned by Dr. John E. Thompson, a nutritionist and former instructor in physiology at the Illinois Institute of Technology, who also owns the adjoining Thompson Farms. Dr. Thompson has operated the vineyard and winery as a hobby since he bought it from Bern Ramey and the late Joseph Allen in 1970. Ramey, a champagne maker from Ohio's Lake Erie Islands, a graduate of the University of California–Davis wine school, was then a lecturer and writer on wines in Chicago. He planted the vineyard in 1963 because he wanted to prove that wine as fine as any can be grown in Illinois. But inspecting the vineyard one morning in the spring of 1968, Ramey discovered strange streaks on the leaves of the vines. The lead edges resembled the teeth of a saw—unmistakable symptoms of injury by the weed-killer known as 2,4-D used on adjoining cornfields. Ramey & Allen Champagne was already on the market and winning connoisseur favor in Illinois, but soon half of the vines were stunted back to year-old size. Part of the vineyard was ploughed under and the winery was closed. "It cost us a quarter of a million dollars to learn that grapes cannot be grown in corn country," Ramey says. Neighboring farmers since have promised Dr. Thompson to spray no more with 2,4-D. His brut white and pink champagnes, named respectively for Père Marquette and Père Hennequin, the Jesuit priests who explored the Midwest, can be bought at the winery when the doctor is there. Ramey now lives in California, where he has published a book entitled *The Great Wine Grapes*.

• 20 •

In the Chicago suburb of Roselle, at the intersection of Irving Park and Roselle roads, is the 10,000-gallon Lynfred Winery, opened by former restaurateurs Fred and Lynn Koehler in 1975. The winery is in the basement of a onetime residence; the tasting room is upstairs. The Koehlers make better-than-average table wines from California and Michigan grapes. A small patch of grapevines decorates their visitors' parking area.

Ready to open a fourth Illinois winery, as soon as the farm winery bill passes, are chiropractor and expert home winemaker Wilfred Enders and his wife Linda, who have a ten-acre vineyard of hybrids and Vinifera beside their home, three miles east of Port Byron in the northwestern corner of the state. They have designed their label and named their future winery the Terra Vineyard and Wine Cellar. While waiting for the legislature to act, Dr. Enders delivers his grape crops to three wineries in Iowa and Wisconsin, and at one of those in Iowa, he has made some excellent wines and champagnes. The Enderses and other vine-yardists in five neighboring states have organized the Upper Mississippi Valley Grape Growers Association and have been holding annual technical seminars on midwestern winegrowing since 1981.

• 21 •

The 2,4-D weed-killer has also damaged Baxter's vines at Nauvoo, but it has done far more damage in the century-old winegrowing districts of Iowa and Kansas.

Yes, you read correctly: Kansas, the home of Carry Nation, had a well-established wine industry until the state was voted Dry in 1880. The fanatical Prohibitionists expunged its history from the state archives, but the evidence remains in the shells of venerable Kansas wineries, underground cellars walled with stone, which you still can see along the rivers in the eastern part of the state. One of the oldest, three miles northwest of Wathena, was built in 1872 by Emanuel Madinger, who compared the vineyards along the west bank of the Missouri to those of his native Württemberg in the Rhineland. The 1880 Federal census shows that 226,249 gallons of wine were produced in that year by vineyards in Doniphan, Labette, Wyandotte, Leavenworth, and thirty-eight other Kansas counties. When the state went Dry, Concords replaced wine grapes in Kansas. This pleased the Dry-dominated State Horticultural Society, which in a 1901 publication referred to grapes as "a fruit too good to be made into a chief source of the degradation of the race."

• 22 •

Although the Drys are powerful in Kansas, one of the three states where (as in Oklahoma and Utah) you still cannot buy a glass of wine with your meal in a restaurant, wine consumption in the Sunflower State has doubled in the past decade to three quarts per capita. Home winemaking is also popular, and many new wine-grape vineyards have been planted in Butler, Chautauqua, Reno, and Sedgwick counties. Some Kansas grapes have been sold to wineries in Missouri. Experiments in growing French hybrids are being conducted at Wichita by research horticulturist Dr. Thomas J. Schuneman for Kansas State University. He says the threat of 2,4-D, which killed the vineyards that made Kansas wines a century ago, has been reduced with the use of low-volatile, amine forms of herbicide.

One Kansas home winemaker, pediatrician Dr. Robert Rizza, planted three acres of hybrids and Labrusca varieties beside his home south of Halstead in 1978, and the vines did so well that he wanted to start a winery. But the doctor learned that a state winery license would cost $25,000 per year and he still would not be allowed to sell his wine to neighbors. He appealed to legislators, and in 1983 Kansas passed a farm winery law that permits sale at the winery. The license fee is still exorbitant, $1100, but Dr. Rizza has planted seven more acres and intends to start a winery by 1986, when the new vines should mature. He hopes that, by then, the license fee may be reduced.

• 23 •

As for Iowa, with 2,4-D killing more vines each year and with a politically entrenched state liquor monopoly uninterested in agriculture, little is left of the state's once-important wine-growing industry except scattered vineyards around Council Bluffs and near Keokuk, and the ten quaint little wineries of the Amana Colonies.

The Amanas and their wines are something out of another world. The colonies are seven Old World villages on the banks of the Iowa River, ten miles north of Interstate 80 and eighteen miles southwest of Cedar Rapids. An eighteenth-century German communistic and religious sect called The Community of True Inspiration came here in 1854 from Ebenezer, New York, purchased 25,000 acres of virgin prairie, and built a utopia named Amana, a biblical word meaning "remain true." Three more colonies, Middle, West, and South Amana, were built two miles apart, an hour's travel by ox team. Higher and Upper South Amana were added in between, and the small town of Homestead was purchased outright.

Communism survived here for almost three generations. Everything was owned by the Amana Society; the members worked without pay in the mills, shops, and fields and had their meals together in communal kitchens. But in 1932 the Depression threatened them with bankruptcy, and communism was forsaken for capitalism. The colonists became stockholders of a corporation which paid them wages, and capitalism worked: One of the colonies' several industries, Amana Refrigeration, has become the biggest maker of home freezers in the world.

Most of the tiny Amana wineries make piestengel and grape wines in the basements of the owners' homes. Piestengel is rhubarb wine; the word means pie stalk in German. It comes dry and sweet, white and pink, and usually doesn't taste of rhubarb; it has a flavor of its own. During the 1970s, some of the wineries added dandelion and cherry wines to their assortment, and in some years a few make wines of wild grapes. Nine-tenths of Amana wine is sold to tourists, who taste and buy it in the cellars and drink it in the local restaurants. The tourists are happy to pay $8 a gallon for the Amana products—more than double the price of many standard wines—because, in the rest of Iowa, wine to take home can only be bought in the state monopoly liquor stores. A special section of the Iowa law, adopted when Prohibition was repealed, allows the native wineries to sell their

In the Amana Colonies of Iowa, the principal product is piestengel, a rhubarb wine. Linda and Leslie Ackerman make piestengel in the basement of their tiny winery at South Amana.

homemade wines to anyone; but only a few are sold in the monopoly's stores. The Amana wineries are so popular with visitors that they have doubled in number; there were only five in 1972. Most Amana wines are labeled "other than standard wine" because to reach their usual 16 percent alcoholic content, more sugar must be added than Federal wine regulations allow.

In the old days, each Amana colony had its communal winery, which provided each family with a daily allowance of wine. Workers in the fields received an extra portion at three each afternoon. "Our village winery was under our church," the late Friedrich Ackerman, who owned the South Amana Winery, told me when I first visited the Colonies. "But our elders ordered all the barrels emptied when Prohibition became the law in 1920, and the wine ran in the ditches for hours." His grandson Leslie runs the winery now.

The vineyards were abandoned during the 1920s, and when the wineries reopened at Repeal, they got their grapes from a vineyard near Fort Madison on the Mississippi. Then the Fort Madison vineyard was ruined by 2,4-D, and most of the grapes since have come from Council Bluffs or from Fred Baxter's vineyard, across the river at Nauvoo. A new Amana vineyard was planted in the 1960s by Ramon Goerler, a Navy veteran and a graduate of the University of Iowa, who with his wife Betty owns the Old Wine Cellar and Colony Wineries; but the deadly weed-killer from nearby cornfields killed his vines, too.

An eleventh Iowa winery at McGregor on the Mississippi makes wine from California, Missouri, and Illinois grapes as well as from apples, apricots, and cherries from other states. Cedar Rapids wine buffs Robert and Joyce Lawlor, intending to start a winery at McGregor, first sent their daughter Christine to California to learn how to make wine. When she returned in 1974 with her enology degree from Fresno State University, the 8000-gallon Christina Wine Cellar was opened on A Street in McGregor. Four years later, a second Christina Cellar, three times as large, was opened on Vine Street in La Crosse, Wisconsin.

In 1880, when the national census of winegrowing was taken, Iowa produced 334,970 gallons of wine, thirteen times as much as the 26,000 gallons the state produces today. Some of the best-known Iowa wines came from the hundred-acre White Elk Vineyard of Hiram Barney near Keokuk. An 1879 article in *The American Wine and Grape Grower* said that Barney's wines "have some reputation in the East but are better known in the West and South." White Elk wines bore varietal labels such as Catawba,

Ives, Norton's Virginia, Delaware, and Clinton, and were described as "the pure juice of the grapes whose names they bear."

Nebraska, across the Missouri River from Council Bluffs, also had many wineries in the 1880s, principally around Omaha, Plattsmouth, and Nebraska City in Cass, Nemaha, and Sarby counties. The vineyard of Julius Pitts, who had a winery near Plattsmouth, was still producing grapes in the 1970s, but at this writing there were no wineries in the Cornhusker State.

• 24 •

"Wisconsin is no place to grow grapes," I was told in 1973 by Dr. Malcolm Dana, chairman of that state university's department of horticulture. Yes, he said, there were seven wineries in Wisconsin, but they mostly made cherry wines, although one had also made a wine of wild grapes. Then Dr. Dana told me about a young electrical engineer and home winemaker, employed part time at the university, who was interested in growing grapes at Prairie du Sac, twenty miles away. His name was Robert Wollersheim.

Wollersheim, when I reached him by telephone, told me a surprising story. He had just bought a nineteenth-century stone winery with hillside caves and traces of a vineyard that had once been owned by the Hungarian immigrant "Count" Agoston Haraszthy, who later made winegrowing history in California.

The Haraszthy story was familiar; he had settled in Wisconsin about 1840, founded a town he named Haraszthy, which later became Sauk City; had raised livestock, started a sawmill and hopyard, had run a Mississippi steamboat and the first ferry across the Wisconsin River; had planted European grapevines, most of which froze during the first winter; and had left for California when word came of the discovery of gold there in 1848. Title records of Wollersheim's property showed that Haraszthy had owned it in 1847. The later dates in the records don't contradict the story. Carved in stone with a bunch of grapes on Wollersheim's seventeen-room house adjoining the winery was the date "1858," and the native-limestone winery bore the date of 1867.

Some years after that telephone conversation, I visited the Wollersheim Winery, which is on Highway 188 across the river from Prairie du Sac and Sauk City. Bob Wollersheim, his pretty wife Jo Ann, and Bob's parents had already harvested crops from the fourteen acres of French hybrids they had planted since 1973 on the south-facing hillside that a former owner named

Peter Kehl had called "the Kehl Weinberg." Bob had equipped the vaulted cellar with stainless-steel tanks, century-old casks from an Ohio winery, and new European- and American-oak barrels. His estate-bottled Seyval Blanc and Aurora wines, on sale in the tasting room upstairs, were as well made, fruity, and pleasing as any comparable wines grown in the East. There were a half dozen other wines, made of Riesling and hybrid grapes Wollersheim had bought from Pennsylvania, and a wine he makes of Door County cherries. Jo Ann was conducting a bevy of visitors on the tour of the vineyard, winery, and the reopened hillside tunnels. She later sold them sausage, cheese, home-wine-making supplies, foreign wines, wine books, and local art in the tasting room. The Wollersheim children were helping, Steve in the cellar, Julie and Eve elsewhere. The winery, now listed in the National Register of Historic Places, attracts 30,000 visitors per year.

Bob still teaches engineering half time at the University. What does he think of growing wine grapes in the corn and dairy country of Wisconsin, where the winters are severe? Bob replies that Peter Kehl from the Rhineland, who bought the place from Haraszthy, grew Riesling as well as native grapes of the Labrusca family, but that Kehl's vineyard was killed by the record winter freeze of 1899 and was never replanted. Wollersheim's best yields have come from the hybrids Seyval, Maréchal Foch, and Léon Millot. He also has planted two acres of Riesling, but covers

Ruins of long-forgotten nineteenth-century wineries dot many states across America. This cave, across the river from Sauk City, Wisconsin, may have been dug by "Count" Haraszthy before he moved to California in 1848.

Agoston Haraszthy, the colorful Hungarian "Count" who founded Sauk City in Wisconsin, then emigrated to Sonoma, where he became "the father of modern California viticulture." (*The Wine Institute Library*)

those vines with earth from fall until spring. "We have a longer growing season, up to 170 days, than many winegrowing districts of the East," Bob says. "Wine grapes can grow as well here as in the Finger Lakes district of New York." Other farmers have bought vines from the Wollersheim vineyard and have started vineyards along the Mississippi River shore.

Another Wisconsin vineyard, 150 miles northwest of Wollersheim's, has attracted newspaper headlines by developing "grapes with fur coats." It grows grapes that are said to survive thirty-five-degrees-below-zero temperatures without burying the vines in winter, the practice long followed in the colder winegrowing districts of Europe and North America. Hobbyist grape breeder Elmer Swenson, on two acres of his former dairy farm east of Osceola, has bred crosses between commercial grape varieties and wild Riparia vines that without winter covering produce grapes each year. Swenson and his partner, Minnesota science teacher Bill Smith, thus far have patented the winter-hardy St. Croix and Swenson Red varieties and Kay Gray for white. All three grapes have produced palatable table wines. An even finer white wine has been made of an as-yet-unnamed Swenson cross numbered N 2–22. If the experience of the first growers of these varieties continues to hold true, Swenson's crosses may make possible the development of a profitable winegrowing industry in the northern tier of states.

• 25 •

Minnesota, where the winter-hardiness of grapes is a first concern, has joined the list of winegrowing states.

In a former creamery at Maple Lake, thirty-five miles northwest of Minneapolis, hobbyist grape grower David Macgregor bonded his Lake Sylvia Vineyard winery in 1976. His first 700-gallon vintage was made of grapes Macgregor had bred himself, blended with Swenson Red and with French hybrids. It was the first commercial wine grown in Minnesota since the turn of the century, when a winery at Stillwater had made wine of grapes grown there. Macgregor, a businessman's son, has been growing grapes and making wine since he was sixteen years old. He studied horticulture at the University of Minnesota, met Elmer Swenson there, and started his own grape-breeding project on his five-acre vineyard beside Lake Sylvia, which is near Maple Lake. He has written a monograph on viticulture in Minnesota, published by the state grape growers' association.

In 1977, the North Star State's second commercial winery opened for business in a brand-new Minnesota log cabin on the Alexis Bailly Vineyard near the town of Hastings, fifteen miles southeast of Minneapolis. Lawyer David Bailly named his ten-acre vineyard and 5000-gallon winery for his great-great-great-grandfather, who founded Hastings in 1854. David Bailly planted his vineyard on Kirby Avenue in 1973 with French hybrids and a few vines of Swenson Red. His wines, a white of Seyval and reds of Maréchal Foch and Léon Millot, reached the market in 1978. His best have been the Léon Millot, which has deep color and full body and flavor, and a *nouveau* version of his Foch. Bailly also makes a mead of Minnesota honey, an apple wine, and a grape-and-apple blend. Besides his own grapes, he uses some of Swenson's and the crops of other Minnesota vineyards, including engineer Gerald Eisert's six acres near Red Wing, and insurance representative Richard Williams's five acres near Cambridge.

Macgregor's monograph says grapevines in Minnesota should be buried each fall under straw or other mulch and covered with earth. A grape named Beta, bred about 1870 by Minnesota farmer Louis Suelter, survives without cover in winters as cold as forty below zero, as the wild Riparia vines also do. Wine of Beta is unpleasantly foxy-tasting and harsh. What the northern states need is a grape as hardy as Beta that will also make appealingly palatable wine.

• 26 •

Oklahoma has many productive vineyards and many favorable microclimates for winegrowing, but as in some other midwestern states, its unfavorable political climate has defeated attempts since the 1970s to establish an Oklahoma winegrowing industry.

One attempt was a project in 1970 by the Oklahoma Office of Economic Opportunity to settle 300 welfare families, each to grow grapes on a twelve-acre vineyard, at Caney in the southern part of the state. The first ten such families settled at Caney in 1972, but then there was a change in the state administration, and the project was suddenly abandoned.

Fifty acres of hybrid and Vinifera vines at Caney are still producing healthy crops each year. Some of the grapes are bought on a "U-Pick" basis by home winemakers, and the rest are sold to a winery in Texas.

Wayne Pool and his wife Susan moved from California to the vineyard at Caney in 1979, bought winemaking equipment, and obtained Federal licenses to start the Arrowhead Vineyards winery. Then they were told by state officials that the Oklahoma law would prohibit them from selling wine on the premises.

Another Oklahoma winery, the 20,000-gallon cellar opened by Pete Schwarz at Okarche in 1970, uses no Oklahoma grapes, but buys Concords from Tontitown in Arkansas. He has a permit to sell his product at the winery, which state officials told Pool would be unconstitutional, and says he will continue unless the state orders him to stop.

Professor Herman Hinrichs of Oklahoma State University told me a decade ago that grapes are a dependable crop in the Sooner State. He believed there is a commercial future for Oklahoma wines. Apparently he had not studied the political climate of the state.

A winery that operated at Oklahoma City in the 1890s has been designated as a national historic site. Former Mayor George Shirk found records at the state historical society showing that one Edward Fairchild had come to the city about the time of the 1889 land run and soon had begun making wine. Shirk looked up the land records, paced off Fairchild's site, and found the winery half buried in mud.

· 27 ·

When I tell my friends in the East and West that good table wines and champagnes are now being made in Arkansas, they are amazed and some are openly skeptical, because few Americans, even former Arkansans, have ever associated Arkansas with the gentle art of appreciating wines. Yet it is true that in this part of the changing South, new vineyards of wine-grape varieties have been spreading through the Ozark backwoods, and that the state's eight wineries are now concentrating on the produc-

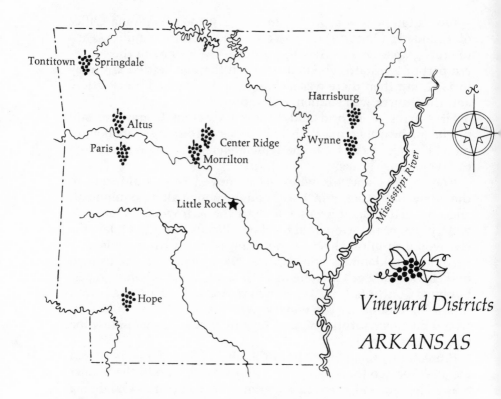

Vineyard Districts

ARKANSAS

tion of table wines for mealtime use. Two of them have made Arkansas champagnes.

Most of this is taking place around a little town called Altus on the Ozark plateau in the northwestern part of the state. Near the outskirts of Altus, a narrow road that winds up St. Mary's Mountain through the woods has been named Champagne Drive. About a mile up the road, in a wide clearing at the summit, stands a wine cellar that resembles a Swiss chalet. Nearby are clusters of wine tanks of fiberglass and stainless steel. These are the Wiederkehr Wine Cellars, which with its capacity of 1,500,000 gallons is the largest and most modern winery in the Southwest. Adjoining is a two-story Alpine inn with a tasting room, gift shop, and a Swiss Wein Keller Restaurant which serves such dishes as quiche Lorraine and poulet rôti au vin blanc.

Here, in August of each year, the Altus Grape Festival is celebrated with pageantry, music, vineyard workers wearing lederhosen, pretty girls in bright Swiss peasant frocks, and with a King Bacchus crowning the festival queen. At the edge of the clearing the Wiederkehr vineyards begin. Rows of grapevines stretch across the sandy plateau that slopes toward the wide

Arkansas River Valley—some 500 acres planted to French hybrids, Delaware, Campbell's Early, Cynthiana, and a hundred acres of Johannisberg Riesling, Chardonnay, Gewürztraminer, Cabernet Sauvignon, and other Vinifera vines.

The settlers of Arkansas made wine more than a century ago from the Scuppernong and other Muscadine grapes that grow wild through most of the state, but the frontiersmen generally preferred moonshine whiskey to wine. Between 1879 and 1900, Swiss, German, and Italian immigrants settled in the Ozark plateau country and began cultivating American bunch grapes. They made wine for their own use, then opened small wineries to make it for sale. Prohibition closed the wineries and brought to Arkansas scouts of the Welch Company, looking for new lands to grow more Concords for Welch grape juice and jelly. In 1923, a Welch plant was built at Springdale and a boom in Concord planting ensued. Vineyard acreage in Arkansas expanded to 9000 acres by 1925, almost four times the 2400 acres there now.

During the Depression, Arkansas faced a grape surplus, so at the repeal of Prohibition in 1933 the state legislature voted to revive the wineries. This was done by taxing wines from outside the state 75 cents a gallon and letting Arkansas wines pay only a 5-cent tax. More than a hundred wineries sprang up in Arkansas, but the chief product they turned out was 20 percent "sneaky pete," made from surplus Concords as a cheap intoxicant. This brought a reaction; many Arkansas counties voted themselves dry, closing the wineries. By 1957, only sixteen were left.

Though by then most of the grapes grown were Concords, the Swiss and German growers whose families had settled at Altus about 1880 still grew the native wine grapes. One of these was Herman Wiederkehr, who made table wines, the kinds his father, Johann Andreas Wiederkehr fron Weinfeld in Switzerland, had always served at home. Herman and Mary Wiederkehr worried that Franklin County might vote Dry at any time and close their little winery. Seeing no future in wine, they sent their five sons to colleges to study for other professions. But their youngest son, Alcuin, coming home on his vacations from Notre Dame and the University of Arkansas Law School, kept saying he wanted to be a winegrower. When a new Arkansas law was passed to let a winery continue operating even if its county went Dry, Alcuin quit law school and went to the University of California at Davis to study viticulture and enology, joining his older brother Leo there. Alcuin had a chance to go to

Europe as an exchange student. He requested France, and was sent to Bordeaux. He worked in the vineyards, helped in the vintage, and came home filled with new ideas. He began planting the French hybrid grapes he had seen being used to make French wines, and added an experimental plot of Vinifera vines from Dr. Konstantin Frank. During the next fifteen years the two brothers enlarged the Wiederkehr vineyards and built the family winery to twenty times its original size.

Most of the Wiederkehr wines and champagnes have resembled the principal wines of the northeastern states, but the White (Johannisberg) Riesling, which I have tasted on several occasions, could have passed for a fine German or California wine. The assortment at the winery includes such specialties as Edelweiss, Vin Blanc Sec, and two different rosés. A dry cocktail sherry of Villard Blanc has been good, and a Muscat table wine called "Arkansas Mountain Moscato di Tanta Maria" was outstanding. On my first visit to the winery several years ago, I tasted from the cask a dry Cynthiana that had sufficient tannin and body to develop bouquet with age. I told the Wiederkehrs such a wine, if given bottle-age, could win recognition beyond Arkansas as the state's most distinctive wine. Alcuin Wiederkehr didn't agree; the last Cynthiana I tasted at Wiederkehr's was sweet.

The first Wine Festival at the Wiederkehr Wine Cellars in Arkansas, 1966.

He hoped someday to compete against European and California wines with Arkansas Rieslings and Chardonnays.

• 28 •

At the bottom of St. Mary's Mountain, with a Swiss chalet front like Wiederkehr's, is the 500,000-gallon Post Winery. The Wiederkehrs and the Posts, who are cousins, turn out the lion's share of the million gallons now produced in Arkansas, and both now sell some of their wines in neighboring states.

Five-foot-five Mathew J. Post, the former mayor of Altus, insists that his winery is a year older than the Wiederkehrs' because his great-grandfather, Jacob Post from Bavaria, founded it in 1880. Like his uphill neighbors, Post welcomes visitors, inviting them to tour his attractive cellar and to taste his assortment of wines, which include a really admirable dry champagne, a reasonably dry burgundy, a medium-sweet Cynthiana, white and red Muscadine wines, various Labrusca table wine types, port, and sherry. Matt Post and his wife Betty have twelve children, ten of whom help at various jobs in the vineyard and winery, including Matt Junior, who is now the winemaker, and Joe, who became the cellar tour guide at the age of eleven. With the rising demand for dry and semi-dry table wines, the Posts have added twenty-five acres of French hybrids to their 120 acres of vines, and also some of the new North Carolina varieties of Muscadine grapes, which are recommended by horticulturist Dr. Justin Morris of the University of Arkansas.

Adjoining Mathew Post's winery is the smaller Mount Bethel Cellar, operated by his brother Eugene. The younger Post has been making table wines since a law was passed in 1965 to allow restaurants to sell Arkansas wine with meals.

At Paris, south of Altus, Robert and Betty Kay Cowie, who came from Ohio and opened their small winery in 1967, make a dozen kinds of wine from Cynthiana, Muscadine, French hybrid, and Labrusca grapes they buy. When their dry Cynthiana won a silver medal in the eastern wine competition in New York State, they decided to begin planting a vineyard of their own. The wineries at Center Ridge and Harrisburg make both table and dessert types. In 1983, a new winery called Mt. Kessler Cellars opened on Dixon Street in Fayetteville. Frank Sharp, who owns the Ozark Mountain Smokehouse there, thought it was time to begin making his own wine to sell with his smoked sausages and cheeses.

• 29 •

A winegrowing revolution has exploded in Texas since 1974, when a feasibility study financed by businessmen through Texas A&M University showed that most parts of the Lone Star State could grow grapes of some kind. From thirty acres then growing around a single century-old winery at Del Rio on the Rio Grande, acreage planted to wine grapes across the state multiplied tenfold by 1983, and the number of wineries increased to sixteen. Influential Texans, accustomed to thinking big, envisioned millions more acres being planted with vines, adding wine to the impressive list of products for which Texas is a major source. They were convinced that within another decade Texas would stand behind California as the nation's second winegrowing state.

The largest development is west of the Pecos River in far western Texas, where in 1975, the year after the feasibility study, the oil-rich University of Texas began planting experimental vineyards on its oil lands. When the vineyards were producing well, the university invited negotiations with commercial vintners, one of whom might lease the land, build a winery, and pay the university a percentage of its sales. In 1983 a Texan and French-owned consortium named Gill Richter Cordier signed such a thirty-year lease and began building a 1.5-million-gallon winery on the university's vineyard, which by then totaled a thousand acres, in time to crush its first vintage in 1984. The winery is ten miles west of Bakersfield on Interstate 10. Gill Richter Cordier is headed by Austin businessman Richardson B. Gill, a partner in the Llano Estacado Winery at Lubbock. Cordier, the Bordeaux wine and spirits firm that owns seven châteaux, will produce the firm's wine. The Richter Company, which has a nursery at Montpellier, will manage the vineyard.

Most impressive is the unexpectedly high quality of the wines made of the university's grapes by research scientist Dr. Charles O. McKinney at an experimental winery in Midland since 1981. Although summer heat at the vineyards equals that of California's sizzling Central Valley, the grapes were picked fully ripe as early as July. Dr. McKinney's samples that I tasted had the fresh taste and balance of wines from California's coastal valleys.

French, Swiss, and German interests also were planting Vinifera vineyards on grazing land at Valentine, a hundred miles west of Bakersfield. They offered to sell vineyards to families who would migrate from Europe to become winegrowers in Texas and neighboring New Mexico.

There are factors that limit vine productivity in many parts of Texas, such as frequent hailstorms, the presence of cotton root rot, and saline groundwater in some localities. Hailstorms are a problem in the high plains section around Lubbock, which has produced the most Texas wine until now. Hailstones as large as baseballs have been known to level whole vineyard sections and to kill horses and cows.

The Llano Estacado Winery, on Farm Road 1585 three miles south of Lubbock, was established in 1976 by three faculty members of Texas Tech University, chemistry professors Clinton McPherson and Roy Mitchell, and horticulturist Robert Reed. Llano Estacado is Spanish for the high plains or Staked Plain region, named, legend says, for the wooden stakes Francisco Vasquez Coronado drove in the giant buffalo grass to guide him back from his exploring trip to New Mexico in 1542. The winery has been enlarged to 40,000 gallons and its vineyards to 220 acres, and a tasting room was added in 1982. Dr. McPherson's son Kim, trained in the University of California wine school at Davis, is the winemaker. He is preparing to start making champagne.

A second Lubbock district winery named Pheasant Ridge was opened in 1982 by Charles Robert (Bobby) Cox III and his wife Jennifer at Bobby's father's twenty-seven-acre Vinifera vineyard, on Farm Road 1729 two miles east of New Deal. Winemaker Bobby is also the assistant to Dr. William Lipe at the Texas Agricultural Research and Extension Center in Lubbock.

Since 1979, four winegrowing estates have begun production in the area called the Hill Country, which extends northwest from San Antonio and Austin for about eighty miles. The 1974 feasibility study recommended that only French hybrid grapes be planted in this area, but the Hill Country vineyards have produced good crops from Vinifera vines grown on their own roots.

Largest of the three is Austin lawyer Hugo Edwin Auler's and his wife Susan's modern 33,000-gallon winery on their thirty-acre Fall Creek Vineyard, which is named for the nearby hundred-foot falls. The handsome cellar is on Road 2241 near Tow (pronounced like cow), near Lake Buchanan. The best wines I tasted there were the 1979 Sauvignon Blanc and the 1980 Villard Blanc. On Highway 16 near Eckert, north of Fredericksburg, is the equally modern 30,000-gallon winery of former Austin food broker Robert Oberhellman on his nineteen-acre all-Vinifera vineyard, planted since 1976. His wines, introduced for sale in 1983, included excellent Chardonnay, Cabernet Sauvignon, and Pinot Noir. Smallest of the Hill Country wineries is the 6000-

gallon cellar opened in 1982 on the twenty-acre Cypress Valley Vineyard, planted by University of Texas engineering professor Dale Bettis since 1977. It is on Shovel Mountain Road two miles north of Cypress Mill. The viticulturist is the professor's wife Penny, who earned her horticulture degree at Texas A&M University in 1978 and her Master of Science degree four years later at Fresno State University in California. There also are two Hill Country bonded wineries that have no vineyards: the 18,000-gallon Guadalupe Valley cellar at New Braunfels, which began bottling California wine in 1975 but now buys some Texas grapes, and the nearby champagne cellar opened in 1980 by Ohio winegrower Kenneth Moyer, who uses California wine.

There are three vineyard estates in the West Cross Timbers district, west of Fort Worth. Oldest and best known is Arlington osteopath Bobby Smith's Buena Vida Vineyards winery, a 50,000-gallon stucco structure opened in 1978 on the doctor's twelve-acre mostly hybrid vineyard, planted four years earlier off Route 199, four miles south of Springtown. The doctor's son Steven is the winemaker. The principal Buena Vida wine, of which Steven says he can't produce enough to meet the demand, is Texas Gold Premium Red, an almost-dry blend of hybrids in which Maréchal Foch predominates. The Buena Vida wine I have liked best was its 1981 Chambourcin. Steven plans to introduce a *méthode champenoise* sparkling wine by 1985.

The Sanchez Creek Vineyard and winery at Weatherford on the Brazos River has new owners. Professor Ron Wetherington, chairman of the anthropology department of Southern Methodist University at Dallas, and his wife Judith bought the place in 1983 from retired newspaper publisher Lyndol Hart, who bonded the 10,000-gallon winery three years earlier on the eight-acre hybrid and Cabernet vineyard he had begun planting in 1975. Judith Wetherington's father, Joseph Swift, is the new vineyard manager; Dr. Wetherington is the weekend winemaker.

Facing a vine-covered hilltop off Road 3325 near Aledo, eighteen miles west of Fort Worth, are two handsome log houses. One is the residence of Fort Worth orthopedic surgeon Henry C. McDonald and his wife Jane Marie. The other is their model 10,000-gallon Château Montgolfier winery, named for the Montgolfier brothers, in whose balloon the first flight of man was achieved in France in 1783. Downhill from the log houses is a field where on calm mornings and evenings, when the doctor isn't too busy in the young vineyard or in the winery, he inflates his balloon to soar over the neighboring farms and streams. Château Montgolfier's first vintage was crushed in 1982, supplemented by grapes from the western high plains.

All three "West Cross Timbers" wineries are situated in legally Dry Parker County. Dr. Bobby Smith has opened a Buena Vida Visitor Center on Route 199 in neighboring legally Wet Tarrant County, where Steven and his wife take turns presiding over the tasting room.

In far western Texas, there are mountainsides where high-altitude climates are as cool as in the premium coastal valleys of California. Aiming to grow the very best Lone Star State wines, onetime Texas "oil princess" Gretchen Glasscock in 1977 planted fifty-five acres of Vinifera vines a mile high on the southeastern slope of Blue Mountain, seven miles south of Fort Davis.

With the wine revolution exploding elsewhere in Texas, what has happened at the century-old 5000-gallon Val Verde Winery at Del Rio, across the Rio Grande bridge from Ciudad Acuña in Mexico? Tom Qualia, whose grandfather Frank from Milan opened the adobe winery in 1883, has begun to modernize, replacing his old-fashioned wooden casks with stainless-steel tanks, installing a new press and refrigeration equipment, and sealing the often-oxidized Felipe del Rio wines with corks instead of screwcaps. Tom is also experimenting with new grape varieties to learn whether they can replace the Herbemont and Lenoir or Black Spanish grapes, which his grandfather and father Louis believed were the only ones that could survive in the hot, moist climate in that part of the Rio Grande Valley.

There also are new grape plantings in the El Paso Valley, where Franciscan priests at Ysleta Mission produced wine for the Mass as early as 1662. That was a century before the first wine grapes were introduced to California. Dozens of wineries flourished on vineyards around El Paso until early in this century, and others operated around Montague and Fredericksburg, until competition from California and the approach of Prohibition caused their sales to decline.

• 30 •

There is a five-acre vineyard at Denison on the Red River in north-central Texas that exists for a reason unlike any other in the world. The T. V. Munson Memorial Vineyard was planted in 1975 beside Denison Airport, on the Grayson County College west campus, as a monument to America's most famous grape breeder, Dr. Thomas Volney Munson. Munson and Hermann

Jaeger of Missouri were awarded the French Legion of Honor Cross of Mérite Agricole in 1888 for saving the vineyards of France. Like his friend Jaeger, Munson shipped carloads of American phylloxera-resistant vine roots to France during the 1870s. Onto those roots the Old World wine grapes were grafted, thus saving them from the phylloxera scourge.

Dr. Munson's greater achievement was the breeding of native American grapes that were resistant to midwestern weather and plant pests. He had developed more than 300 new grape varieties when he died at the age of seventy in 1913. But the Prohibition movement was spreading, wineries were closing, vineyards were being uprooted, and most of Munson's collection was lost. The only commercial wines named for Munson's wine grapes now are Missouri vintner James Hoffher's Neva Munson, his neighbor Lucian Dressel's Münch, and Brights winery of Canada's President Port.

In recent years, grape enthusiast Wallace E. Dancy of Arkansas has enlisted students of the vine in many states in a movement to restore the Munson collection. The W. B. Munson Foundation of Denison has financed the Memorial Vineyard, to which a museum and library were being added in 1983. At Grayson College, Professor of Agriculture Roy Renfro, in charge of the Munson Vineyard, has started teaching a viticulture course. At this writing, 115 of Munson's varieties have been located, some as far away as Japan, and 65 have already been planted in the vineyard at Denison. While the collection is being reassembled, the Munson grapes are being tested for their wine quality and for their ability to grow in various parts of Texas and the Midwest.

Some of the Munson varieties are being grown for wine by a group of vineyardists in northeastern Texas. In 1984 they built the Lone Star state's newest winery, the 40,000-gallon Texas vineyards cellar, at Ivanhoe, forty miles east of Denison.

11

Wines of Michigan

ALTHOUGH MICHIGAN ranks fourth among the states in grape growing and sixth in wine production, few of our connoisseur writers ever write anything about Michigan wines. Yet I have tasted many Michigan wines and found them all clean and sound, and more than a few lately that I have rated as excellent. The fruit belt of Michigan is as capable, climatically speaking, of producing fine wines as most of the other viticultural districts east of the Rockies, including even the justly famous Finger Lakes region of New York. But until very lately, few of the Michigan wineries tried to produce anything fine, for reasons only their history and their peculiar state law can explain. Now, with newly planted Old World wine-grape varieties, with new modern wineries and modernization of some of the old, they are trying, and the quality image of their wines has improved.

The best way to know Michigan wines is to visit the wineries, which numbered fifteen at last count, eight of them new since 1974. They are hospitable, offering tasting and tours from spring through fall daily including Sunday afternoons. There is a four-day Wine & Harvest Festival at Paw Paw in mid-September, when you can sniff the grape fragrance as you approach the town. Some of the individual wineries also hold festivals of their own.

• 2 •

Michigan's western counties, behind the towering sand dunes on the Lake Michigan shore, are one of the great fruit-producing sections of the earth. The deep lake waters, which rarely freeze over, yield warmth for the vineyards and orchards in winter,

205

and cool winds from the lake in spring usually retard the buds from opening until the danger of killing frosts has passed. This beneficent climatic influence enables fruit to grow all the way from the Indiana border north to Grand Traverse Bay, a stretch of some two hundred miles.

In four southwestern counties—Van Buren, Berrien, Cass, and Allegan—more than 15,000 acres are planted to grapes, mostly picked by the new mechanical harvesting machines since 1968. All but a few hundred acres here are Concords, because four-fifths of the state's grape crop is used for juice and jelly or is sold fresh for table use. The other fifth goes into wine.

At the far northern end of the fruit belt, the lake-bordered peninsula that is Leelanau County and the Old Mission Peninsula to the east have climates that are less hospitable to Concords and more hospitable to wine grapes. Until now cherries have been the principal fruit crop on these two peninsulas, which extend north of Traverse City, the sour-cherry capital of America. Vineyards of French hybrid and Vinifera wine grapes have been newly planted among the cherry orchards, and five of the newer Michigan wineries are here.

Michigan's new interest in winegrowing has also inspired some planting of vines in the eastern half of the state, between Saginaw Bay and Lake Erie. Two new wineries there are making wines of French hybrids, while a third makes wines of fruits other than grapes.

What has caused the recent increase in Michigan winegrowing is that wine consumption in the state has grown more than a third in this decade. The planting of new vineyards has brought a warning from Horticulture Professor Gordon S. Howell of the state university against creating grape surpluses, of which this state has had its share in the past.

• 3 •

The wineries of Michigan, including the oldest, are still comparatively young. There were no famous wineries with castlelike cellars in the state before Prohibition, such as those in Ohio, Missouri, and New York. But the growing of fruit, including grapes, began in southern Michigan in the mid-nineteenth century. By 1880, when the national winegrowing census was taken, there were 2,266 acres of vineyards in the state, and Michigan wine production in that year was 62,361 gallons valued at $75,617. At that time more wine was made in southeastern Michigan, along the Lake Erie shore, than on the Lake Michigan side.

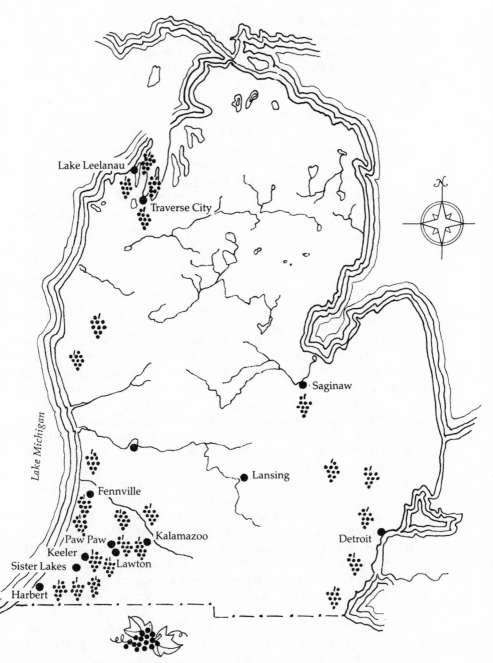

Lake Leelanau

Traverse City

Saginaw

Lake Michigan

Lansing

Fennville

Kalamazoo

Detroit

Paw Paw

Keeler

Lawton

Sister Lakes

Harbert

Vineyard Districts of
MICHIGAN

Philip Wagner, who grew up at Ann Arbor, recalls that before Prohibition there were many small wineries operated by German farmers in Monroe and Muskegon counties.

What started the massive vineyard plantings in southwestern Michigan was the grape-juice boom. When the Welch Grape Juice Company, with its newly built plant at Westfield, New York, began about 1900 to buy Concords from neighboring states, the planting of Concords began in Van Buren and Berrien counties.

The original Michigan wineries were closed by Wartime Prohibition in 1919, but the grape boom continued, for in that year Welch established its own grape-juice plant at Lawton, near Paw Paw. Then a huge demand developed throughout the nation for grapes for bootleg and homemade wine, an opportunity in which the Michigan vineyards shared.

Still another outlet opened for Michigan grapes during the 1920s: Four new wineries sprang up in the Canadian town of Windsor, across the river from Detroit. Much of their "exported" wine, consigned to distant countries, traveled only as far as the Michigan and Ohio shores.

Next came the Great Depression, and with it Repeal in 1933—and the market for grapes collapsed. The price of Michigan Concords fell to as low as $10 a ton. Fifteen wineries began operating in the Detroit area, including two that were moved, complete with crushers and casks, across the river from Canada. Soon there was a surplus of wine as well as of grapes, because Michigan wines, made of the foxy Concord, could not compete with those coming from other states and from abroad. One of the Canadian vintners from Windsor proposed a remedy: Reserve the Michigan wine market for Michigan wines. This accounts for one peculiarity of the Michigan wine law, which taxes wines from outside the state at 51 cents per gallon but Michigan wines at 4 cents, provided they are made at least 75 percent of Michigan-grown grapes for which the winery has paid the grower at least $100 a ton (originally $55 a ton in 1937). The remaining 25 percent of the grapes can come from outside the state, and arrives principally in tank cars from California. The second peculiarity of the law classified as hard liquor all wines above 16 percent in alcoholic strength. This created in Michigan a new class of wine previously unknown in America—16 percent "light" ports and sherries. The sale of standard ports and sherries, which range from 17 to 20 percent, alcohol was restricted to stores operated by the state liquor monopoly, while the "light" versions were sold in licensed, privately owned stores along with the 12 percent table and sparkling wines. California, New York, and Ohio wineries were thereby compelled to begin making 16 percent "light" dessert wines in order to compete with the Michigan wineries.* This continued until 1982, when the state legislature removed wine from the monopoly liquor stores and allowed licensed stores to sell standard dessert wines. Sales of the "light" ports and sherries soon declined.

For two decades, prospering with their protective state tax and preferential distribution of their "light" dessert wine types, the Michigan wineries made no attempt to compete with out-of-state table wines. But after the Second World War, Michigan consumers developed a liking for dry table wines, and the Michigan producers saw their sales beginning to shrink. From the four-fifths share of the Michigan wine market they had enjoyed before the war, their share dropped by 1981 to less than a fifth. The Michigan wineries had begun making good table wines and champagnes, but too late. Their sales were so poor that the state administration in 1982 financed a publicity campaign with the slogan: "Say Yes to Michigan Wines."

• 4 •

The first Michigan producer to begin improving the quality of its table wines was Bronte, whose million-gallon winery is on its vineyard five miles south of Hartford on the road to Keeler in Van Buren County. Bronte's Italian-trained winemaker, Angelo Spinazze, was responsible for planting the company's first fifty acres of French hybrids beginning in 1933. Seven-tenths of Bronte's 150 acres consisted of the hybrids by 1983. Bronte's Baco Dinner Wine, introduced in 1962, was the first Michigan commercial wine to be labeled with the name of a French hybrid grape. I remember tasting at the winery in the early 1970s a dry red, proudly labeled "Sister Lakes Premium Baco Noir," that was superior to most of the burgundies then made in the East. When I recently revisited the winery, Spinazze was featuring such table wines as Vidal Blanc, Aurora, and Maréchal Foch.

Bronte was started in May 1933, six months before Repeal, by retired dentist Theodore Wozniak in the old Columbia brewery building on Riopelle Street in Detroit. Its first product was 3.2 percent wine, which had just been legalized together with 3.2 beer. To make this curious potion, full-strength wine was

---

*But this also taught California vintners a valuable lesson; see the discussion of minimum alcohol content standards on pages 238 and 239.

The Warner Vineyard winery at Paw Paw is the largest in Michigan.

diluted to 3.2 percent alcoholic content with water and a fluid extract of the South American beverage herb called *maté*, which tastes somewhat like tea. "Bronte," the name of the extract, was chosen as the company's name. At Repeal, Dr. Wozniak made wine out of Concord grapes that were trucked to Detroit from the fruit belt. In 1943, he bought the farm in the Sister Lakes District near Keeler and built the present winery there. Bronte was the first winery in Michigan to make Charmat-process champagne (in 1946) and claims to have been the first in the world (in 1964) to bottle the sparkling wine called "Cold Duck" (a claim which others share).

• 5 •

Biggest vintner in the state is Warner Vineyards, which has 3 million gallons' capacity in its winery on Kalamazoo Street in Paw Paw and in its fermenting cellar at nearby Lawton. A farmer and banker, the late John Turner, founded the firm, originally named Michigan Wineries, in 1938. His son-in-law and his grandson, James K. and James J. Warner, and members of the Turner family own 250 acres of vineyards and buy grapes from four hundred other growers. Besides still wines, the company makes champagnes, still and carbonated grape juices, grape concentrate, and grape essence (the methyl anthranilate ester extracted from Concord grapes, which is used to impart the pungent Labrusca flavor to grape drinks). Notable in the assortment now available for tasting in Warner's "Ye Olde Wine Haus" tasting room are bottle- and bulk-fermented champagnes, ports and sherries, Chelois, De Chaunac rosé, Maréchal Foch, estate-bottled Seyval Blanc and Aurora Blanc, a sweet wine named Liebestrauben, and a new Vintners Trio of red, white, and rosé table wines.

• 6 •

Two more wineries in Paw Paw offer tours and tasting. Next door to Warner on Kalamazoo Street is the million-gallon St. Julian cellar, with a handsome tasting room built since a fire destroyed part of the building in 1971. Mariano Meconi started this winery in 1921 at Windsor, Ontario, as the Italian Wine Company, moved it at Repeal to Detroit, and five years later brought most of its equipment to Paw Paw. It is named for the patron saint of his birthplace, the village of Falaria near Rome. Meconi's grandson, David Braganini, and winemaker Charles Catherman run the winery now. In 1981, St. Julian opened a second winery in Frankenmuth, southeast of Saginaw, using grapes from Neil Arnold's ten-acre vineyard of French hybrids in Tuscola County. The best St. Julian wines in recent years have been its bottle-fermented champagne and its 1981 Vidal Blanc and Vignoles Reserve. The latter two varieties, increasingly grown in Michigan, are becoming competitors to Seyval as the best hybrid grapes to make fine white wines.

The half-million-gallon Frontenac winery on West Michigan Avenue in Paw Paw makes forty different wines and offers them all for tasting, along with a delicious hot spiced wine, in its attractive retail store. Most of the Frontenac table wines have had the Labrusca flavor of Concord and the other native grapes principally grown around Paw Paw.

The southernmost winery in western Michigan is the Lakeside or Molly Pitcher cellar at Harbert, a quarter mile from Lake Michigan. It attracts crowds of tourists because it is on the busy Red Arrow Highway just off I-94. Food faddist William Lett Ruttledge from Ireland started the Molly Pitcher winery in 1934 to make port wine, then found he couldn't sell it, and switched to making Concord wine because it is the only kind California doesn't produce. Lawnmower manufacturer Cecil Pond bought the winery from Ruttledge in 1975 and made both French hybrid wines and the Concord kinds that tourists seem to like. In 1982 the winery acquired a new president, Leonard Olson, who

Leonard Olson found botrytis, the "noble mold," growing on his Vidal Blanc grapes in Michigan in November 1975.

planned to introduce a new "Leonard Olson Family" line of premium wines.

• 7 •

When the Tabor Hill Vineyard and Wine Cellar, near Baroda in Berrien County, opened for business in July 1972, it was the first new winery to start in Michigan in a quarter of a century. Three additional "firsts" distinguish the establishment: It was the first in Michigan devoted exclusively to growing premium-quality wines; the first to grow such noble Vinifera grapes as White Riesling and Chardonnay; and the first (1974) to have its wines served in the White House. President Ford served Tabor Hill Baco Noir and its hybrid white, called Trebbiano, at a state dinner for the chancellor of Austria. The winery also made history when its then-winemaker Leonard Olson produced Michigan's first late-harvest botrytized Riesling and Vidal Blanc. Olson left in 1981 after selling the winery to Whirlpool scion David Upton. The new winemaker is former chemistry teacher Richard Moersch. In charge of the twenty-acre vineyard is Michigan State University–trained horticulturist G. Michael Merchant. A restaurant was opened at the winery in 1982.

To find Tabor Hill, take the Bridgman exit from I-94 and head east seven miles, keeping a lookout for the series of signs that lead you to the winery. The building above the vineyard that looks like a ski chalet is the restaurant and tasting room.

• 8 •

The Welsch family's Fenn Valley Vineyard, three miles southeast of Fennville in Allegan County, is Michigan's closest approach to a European winegrowing estate. The romance of wine attracted Chicago lumberman William Welsch and his son Douglas, a biology teacher, to Fenn Valley in 1974. Both were home winemakers. They built homes for their families there and began planting the first forty of their present seventy acres of hybrid and Vinifera vines. A year later they built a château-like winery into the adjoining hillside. Theirs is a family undertaking. Douglas, with degrees in biology and chemistry, is the winemaker. His wife Lynn, sister Diana, and father and mother all help in the business. The 100,000-gallon winery is a model of completeness, with a tasting room, a home-winemaking supply shop, and balconies from which visitors can watch how the wines are made. Most of the wines, regular medal winners at the annual Michigan State Fair judgings, are estate-bottled from the vineyards surrounding the winery.

When California wineries introduced "light" (less than 10 percent in alcoholic strength) wines with multimillion-dollar advertising campaigns in the early 1980s, an ironic comment by Doug Welsch expressed a reason some consumers may come to prefer midwestern and eastern wines: "We're often asked if we can make a 'light' wine. Yes we do, but we don't label it as such. The naturally cool climate here in West Michigan enables grapes to ripen fully without unduly high sugar content. Many of our wines are in the 8½ to 9 percent alcohol range—*naturally* light."

In 1981, the Welsches' petition to establish Fennville as a viticultural area was approved by the Federal government, making this the first in Michigan to be so recognized. (Second to be approved was the Leelanau Peninsula in 1982, and parts of five southwestern Michigan counties were designated as a "Lake Michigan Shore" viticultural area in 1983.)

• 9 •

From the Welschs' vineyard at Fennville it is 200 miles due north to Traverse City and 6 miles farther on Highway 37 to the Château Grand Travers vineyard and winery. This is a third of the way along Old Mission Peninsula, the spectacular narrow finger of land that extends eighteen miles to the middle of Grand Traverse Bay.

To this spot chunky millionaire entrepreneur and ex-college gymnast Edward O'Keefe, of the Canadian brewing family, brought viticulturists from Germany in 1975 to plant the chateau's forty-acre vineyard of White Riesling and Chardonnay, facing the western arm of the bay. By 1979 a model 50,000-gallon winery was built adjoining the vineyard, and Geisenheim-trained enologist Roland Pfleger was producing a dozen excellent

Bernard Rink's Boskydel winery and vineyard at Lake Leelanau, Michigan.

vintage-dated estate-grown Vinifera wines, ranging from Chardonnay and Scheurebe to Gamay Beaujolais and Merlot, as well as an assortment of cherry and apple wines.

O'Keefe was not the first to start winegrowing in this northern Michigan area. Bernard Rink, the librarian of Northwest Michigan College at Traverse City, and Michigan State University chemistry professor emeritus Robert Herbst had pioneered the growing of French hybrid wine grapes on the nearby Leelanau County peninsula for more than a decade, in Rink's case since 1965. Bernie Rink bonded his own 8000-gallon Boskydel Vineyard winery on his twenty-acre vineyard in 1976 and offered his first half-dozen hybrid wines—the best of which were a white Vignoles and a red De Chaunac—for sale. Rink's winery, a cave in the hillside facing Lake Leelanau, is sixteen miles north of Traverse City on County Road 641. The town of Lake Leelanau is three miles farther north. Rink is able to keep his full-time job as a librarian because, he explains, "I have an indulgent wife and five sons," who help him in the vineyard and winery.

With Lake Michigan on the west and Grand Traverse Bay on the east, the Leelanäu and Old Mission peninsulas have the climate-moderating lake influence on both their sides. "If we can find enough good microclimates for wine grapes here," says Bernie Rink, "the Leelanau Peninsula can become the Napa Valley of Michigan."

As though to support Rink's prediction, orchardist Charles Kalchik in 1975 began planting thirty acres of French hybrids and Vinifera on his nearby Hilltop Farms. Construction of the 80,000-gallon Leelanau Wine Cellars with the latest stainless-steel equipment was begun a year later at Omena, twenty-five miles north of Traverse City on Highway 22, and a Leelanau tasting room was opened five miles south of Traverse City on US 31 and M-37. Judith Jensen, the first feminine viticulturist in Michigan, heads an all-girl crew she calls "the Grapettes" in caring for the Leelanau vineyards. Cellarmaster John Haw and Winemaker Ed Dyne turn out both grape and cherry wines and have begun making bottle-fermented champagnes.

The Leelanau wine rush was on. In 1978 Lawrence Mawby, whose parents run Mawby's Farm Market in the peninsula town of Suttons Bay, bonded the L. Mawby Vineyards Winery on the ground floor of his hilltop home. With 2500 gallons capacity, it is Michigan's smallest winery, but Larry plans to expand when he plants more vines than his present nine acres. His first two wines, red and white blends of hybrids, are already winning praise from connoisseurs.

Two years later, the fourth Leelanau Peninsula winery opened on Road 22 between Leland and Glen Arbor. Bruce and Debbie Simpson named it the Good Harbor Vineyards because it is only an eighth-mile from the shore of Good Harbor Bay. The 9000-gallon cellar is next door to the Manitou Farm Market, owned by Bruce's parents. He began making wine while attending Michigan State University's classes in horticulture and then spent a year at UC Davis studying viticulture and enology. The fifteen-acre vineyard of hybrids will be expanded to forty acres, he says.

The newest Michigan winery is the 10,000-gallon Seven Lakes Vineyard cellar on Tinsman Road, two miles from Fenton and across from Seven Lakes State Park, south of Flint. Retired Detroit envelope manufacturer and wine buff Harry Guest, his wife Marion, and their winemaker son Chris began planting their fifteen acres of hybrids in 1978 and crushed their first vintage of Chancellor and De Chaunac Rosé in 1982, soon to be followed by such whites as Seyval, Vidal, and Vignoles.

One of Michigan's newest vineyards is the acre of Maréchal Foch planted in 1979 by the nuns of the Sisters of Mercy home in the central Michigan city of Alma to produce altar wine for the Mass. "We feel that growing our own altar wine is appropriate to our apostolic work," explains Sister Margaret Mary Turner, "because in Scripture there are so many references to the vine."

• 10 •

The one Michigan contribution to *viniana* that has brought international imitation is Cold Duck, the bubbly pink wine that exploded from Detroit during the 1960s to become part of festive drinking halfway around the world. Its story is as bizarre as its name.

In Germany early in this century—authorities disagree on just when—partygoers who saved the contents of open wine bottles by pouring them together after a celebration called the mixtures *kalte ende* (cold end), a German phrase for leftovers. Because *ende* sounds like *Ente* (duck in German), the term for leftover wine became *kalte Ente;* it was a German pun. Kalte Ente became the name of a popular drink in Germany. It is usually made there of white wine and *Schaumwein* (champagne), flavored with a spiral of lemon rind and sugar, and is served either in a punch bowl or by the glass.

Back in the 1930s, Detroit restaurateur Harold Borgman, on a wine-buying trip in Germany, tasted Kalte Ente, and on returning home introduced it as a bar drink in his restaurant, the Pontchartrain Wine Cellars. He made it by mixing a New York State champagne and a California burgundy. It was Borgman who translated the name into English—the duck you don't eat, but drink. It became locally famous.

Two Detroit vintners, both Pontchartrain patrons, claim to have originated the idea of putting Cold Duck into bottles. Bob Wozniak, whose father headed the Bronte winery, says he first thought of it in 1963. But, at the same time, Detroit importer William O'Connor gave the Mandia winery of Clintondale, New York, an order to make and bottle the mixture for him.

The name and taste of the concoction tickled the celebration bone of Americans. Within months, vintners in other states followed with their own versions, inevitably with duck wings on the labels. The Internal Revenue Service officially recognized the product as a blend of champagne and sparkling burgundy, requiring that the label specify bulk process if the champagne is made that way.

Because the first Cold Ducks were made of eastern Labrusca grapes, the big California wineries found it necessary to import vast quantities of Concord juice from the State of Washington to make their versions taste the same. Other California producers found their Cold Ducks sold as well or better without Labrusca grapes, so long as the wines were made new, fresh, foamy, and sweet.

Cold Duck had only begun to fly. In 1970 its production spread to Canada and Mexico, then to faraway Australia, and finally reached Europe. French vintners began shipping French Cold Duck to this country, followed by Cold Ducks from Italy and from Germany. The bubbly pink drink was also introduced in

France, its name translated there to *Canard Froid Froid.* In America, the brewing industry responded with a Malt Duck, while vintners created a Cold Hawk, a Blueberry Duck, a Strawberry Duck, and a carbonated mixture of white wine and cranberry juice called Cold Turkey.

Now I hear that bottled Cold Duck may not have originated in Michigan after all, that German vintners have been selling white Kalte Ente in bottles since before the Korean war, and that they have a red version called Turkenblut. There is also a story that attributes the original *kalte Ente* pun to the famous German diplomat, Franz von Papen, at a dinner given by Kaiser Wilhelm II.

But perhaps this is merely history, for vintners now report that Cold Duck sales in the United States have slumped ominously since the 1970s. One of my champagne producer friends, who never got around to producing a Cold Duck of his own, gleefully predicted it may become a dead duck erelong.

12

California—Paradise for the Vine

MUCH OF what has been written since Repeal about California wines stresses the industry's colorful history, such as the fact that the Spanish mission fathers brought wine grapes here from Mexico two centuries ago, as though that were the reason this state has nine-tenths of this country's vineyard acres and produces four-fifths of American wine.

The real reason, seldom mentioned and therefore not understood, was best expressed almost a century ago by Professor George Husmann, explaining why he abandoned his post as professor of horticulture at the University of Missouri to become a winegrower in California:

A visit to this shore, in the summer of 1881, convinced me that this was the true home of the grape, and that California . . . was destined to be the vine land of the world . . . We have the finest climate in the world and can always make a good product even in the most unfavorable seasons. We can raise grapes and make wine cheaper than any other nation or climate. We have the world for a market. We can satisfy every taste.

Husmann, of course, did not dwell on the spring frost disasters that strike California vineyard districts at least once in each decade, nor on the constant hazards of vine diseases, pests, sunburn, or water shortages, which keep vineyardists from enjoying a carefree life in California or anywhere else.

Yet it is true that it is easier to raise Vinifera grapes in the fabulous climates of California than in any other part of the globe. The Old World grape varieties will grow and ripen anywhere there is water and good soil in the Golden State, except at frigid mountain elevations and on the foggiest portions of

218

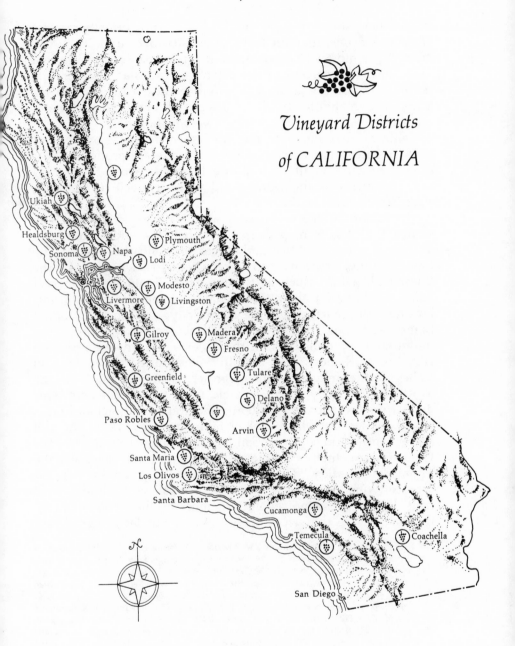

Vineyard Districts

of CALIFORNIA

Ukiah

Healdsburg
Sonoma Napa Plymouth
Livermore Lodi
Modesto
Livingston
Gilroy Madera
Fresno
Greenfield Tulare
Delano
Paso Robles
Arvin
Santa Maria
Los Olivos
Santa Barbara
Cucamonga
Temecula Coachella
San Diego

the northern seacoast. California's long, warm, normally rainless growing seasons, its mild winters, and its low humidity which discourages most vine pests make it a paradise for the Vinifera vine. Only one percent of the earth's surface has weather that resembles—but for growing Vinifera grapes scarcely equals— that of the great viticultural districts of California. Their climates are the secret envy of the winegrowers of Europe.

California has not only one, but so wide an assortment of such climates, that within its borders there are produced, year after year, wines of all the traditional types grown in the leading wine countries of the world—and with no need to add cane sugar to the juice of the grape.

The ranges of these climates, which are evident when you glance at the state map, help to explain the wide differences you find in the qualities and prices of California wines. The light-yielding, delicate, costly grape varieties which make the finest table wines (such as Riesling, the Pinots, and Cabernet Sauvignon) develop their highest flavors when grown in the valleys near the coast, where the sunny days are cooled by ocean breezes and fogs. The University of California classes these premium table wine districts, in the order of the coolness of their climates, as Regions I, II, and III.* The northern San Joaquin Valley, farther inland, is much warmer in summer and is classed as Region IV; vineyards there yield more tons to the acre. This district produces many excellent wine grapes and includes Lodi, where the famous Flame Tokay table grape grows. In the still hotter central and southern San Joaquin Valley—Region V—the vineyards are chiefly of table and raisin varieties, especially the Thompson Seedless. They yield tremendous crops, which are used for wine and brandy as well as for sale as fresh and dried fruit. Before the wine revolution, most of the wines made in Region V were the sweet dessert types, but large acreages of

*In 1938, Professors Albert Winkler and Maynard Amerine classified the climates of California vineyard districts into five regions by their average daily temperatures during the growing season (April through October) and compared them to the wine districts of Europe. They measured "degree-days," the number of days when temperatures exceed 50° F. For example, when the temperature for a day averaged 70°, it was expressed as "20 degree-days." Region I means 2500 degree-days or less and includes Geisenheim (1709) and Trier (1730) in Germany, Beaune (2400) in the French Burgundy region, and Sonoma (2360) and Oakville (2300) in the coolest parts of the Sonoma and Napa Valleys. Region II means 2500 to 3000 degree-days and includes Bordeaux (2519), the Italian Piedmont region (2980), and most parts of the Napa and Sonoma Valleys. Region III means 3000 to 3500 degree-days and includes the Livermore Valley in California and Tuscany in Italy. Region IV, 3500 to 4000 degree-days, covers central Spain, areas from Lodi to Ceres in the northern part of the San Joaquin Valley, Davis in Yolo County, and Cucamonga in Southern California. Over 4000 degree-days is Region V and includes the central and southern San Joaquin Valley and the Sacramento Valley.

wine grapes have been planted there since the late 1960s, and table wine greatly exceeds dessert wine in the valley's production now. The Cucamonga district, east of Los Angeles, has a Region IV climate and produces mainly inexpensive wine grapes for all types of wine, while the coastal valleys of Southern California are as cool as the coastal districts farther north. Finally, there is the Coachella Valley near the Salton Sea, in the southeastern corner of the state, where, in almost furnacelike heat, great irrigated vineyards supply ripe grapes for fresh table use as early as May and June, to bring high prices in the eastern markets.

In sunny California, grapes develop higher sugar content than in the sun-starved northern wine districts of Europe, but their acidity (tartness) is usually not as high. This is why, in "blind" tastings—the popular social game in which you try to distinguish one wine from another by smell and taste—the easiest way to tell California wines and champagnes from those of Europe is to mark those with higher acidity as European; the California samples are likely to be softer, less tart.

Even the cooler California districts may be too warm and sunny for some of the Old World wine-grape varieties, such as Germany's White (Johannisberg) Riesling and Burgundy's Pinot Noir. Though the Riesling and Pinot Noir ripen early, with high sugar contents, and make consistently fine wines in California, their wines differ appreciably from those that grow in their Old World homelands, where these grapes barely ripen by the end of the season. Perhaps California's climate is too ideal. Wines, like people, seem to be more interesting, to have greater depth and complexity of character, if they have to struggle to reach maturity.

Another characteristic of California weather—low humidity— prevents in the warmest districts the growth of the "noble mold" (*Botrytis cinerea*) that grows on ripe grapes in Europe and gives unique flavors to French sauternes and to Germany's rare Trockenbeerenauslese wines.

These few differences between the finest European and California table wines are easy to recognize in "blind" sampling. But if the wines you are tasting are red bordeaux or white burgundy types, and the California and French samples are both made of the same grape varieties, grown in the best climates (and have been stored in the same kind of oak barrels), they will be much more difficult to tell apart. For the grapes that make these latter two wine types develop ideal acidity in balance with their sugar content in the California coastal valleys and make some of the best wines in the world.

Vintage scene in California *circa* 1877. Drawn by P. Frenzeny from an illustration in Harper's Weekly.

Still another difference between California and European table wines—which you are unlikely to detect by taste—is in alcoholic strength, which is also the result of climate. Because it is the grape sugar that fermentation turns into alcohol, California table wines are usually one to three points higher than their European counterparts in percentage of alcohol by volume. Riesling in Germany, for example, seldom makes wines stronger than 8 or 9 percent; in California its wines readily reach 11 and 12. Perhaps grape-growing locations will yet be found in the Golden State with climates in which this grape will ripen at the levels at which it is harvested in the vineyards of the Moselle and Rheingau.

What European growers envy most about California weather is that the grapes ripen sufficiently every year to make sound wine without chaptalization—the addition of sugar to their juice, the practice that is common elsewhere in North America and in the famous winelands of Europe (see Chapter 26). This is why it is often said (and as often challenged) that "every year is a vintage year in California." Of course, the truth of this statement depends on what is meant by "a vintage year."

In the European fine-wine districts, which are subject to cold and rainy weather during their growing seasons, grapes ripen fully in the occasional years when they receive sufficient sunshine; in their normal years it is necessary to add sugar to the grapes. The purpose of vintage labels on European wines therefore is to enable buyers to choose the wines of the "vintage" (good) years—to avoid buying the mediocre or the bad. In sunny California, no such purpose is served by vintage labels. Here, about once in a decade, abnormally early autumn rains result in lower-than-normal grape sugars; but even then, the sugar levels are sufficient to make sound wines. The three worst-weather autumn seasons in California vintners' recent memory, 1948, 1957, and 1972, would have been considered "vintage years" in Europe, for in each of those seasons lovely natural wines were made.

Wines from individual California vineyards do vary in flavor and quality from year to year, as the weather and the grapes inevitably vary. Thus, a vintage date on a California label is of some interest to connoisseurs besides telling them how old the wine is. But here again, the point is that sound wines are produced every year from the juice of the grape alone. By European standards, the claim that "every year is a vintage year in California" is therefore literally true.

• 2 •

Some of the highlights of California's wine history were reviewed in Chapter 2, and the colorful stories of individual California districts and winegrowers are contained in the regional chapters that follow. But the overall story of California wines before, during, and since Prohibition is only now becoming clear.

While wines were made first at the Franciscan missions, the chain of church settlements established from San Diego to Sonoma between 1769 and 1823, the wines the padres made could not have been very good. The inferior Vinifera grape they introduced—the Mission variety, also called the Criolla—had been grown for two centuries in Mexico before it was brought north by the great Franciscan friar, Junípero Serra. The Mission grape impeded the development of fine wine for almost a century until better Vinifera varieties were introduced.*

The well-annotated histories of early California wines by Herbert B. Leggett, Irving McKee, and Vincent Carosso tell the fantastic story of Agoston Haraszthy, the Hungarian "count" or "colonel" (he was neither), and credit him with bringing the

---

*Although it is of the Vinifera species, no counterpart of the Mission grape has ever been found in Europe. Ampelographers say it probably grew from a seed brought from Spain via Mexico by the *conquistadores*.

better Vinifera varieties from Europe to California between 1851 and 1862. But Haraszthy was not the first to do this, nor was he the first to introduce the Zinfandel grape to America. As Chapter 25, on "varietal grapes," will show, the Zinfandel was already here when Haraszthy left Hungary for the United States.

Because the Prohibitionists labored for years in California, as elsewhere, to erase the history of wine in America, its role in building the economy of the Golden State—more important than the mining of gold—is seldom if ever mentioned in the school books. Grapes, mostly used by wineries, are California's most important fruit crop. Many people who now bear the names of great pioneer California families—in agriculture, government, banking, publishing, education, and industry—may not know that their forebears were prominent winegrowers, who contributed to the character of the state's wines of today.

Vineyards were flourishing and wine was being made at nearly all of the twenty-one Spanish missions by the second decade of the nineteenth century. The chief exception was Mission Dolores at foggy, chilly San Francisco, where the padres used grapes they obtained from Missions Santa Clara and San José.

When commercial viniculture began at Los Angeles in the 1830s, at the time the Mexican government secularized the missions and caused most of them to be abandoned, there were 100,000 vines on the site of the present City of the Angels. An early writer, Alexander Forbes, was already telling America and Europe that California offered "a wide and promising field for the cultivation of the grape in all varieties."

The first commercial winegrower of note in California, Jean Louis Vignes (appropriately named; *vigne* is French for vine), was so successful at his El Aliso Vineyard in Los Angeles that in 1834 he sent to France for eight of his relatives to join him, for he believed that this land was destined to rival "la belle France" in both the quantity and quality of its wines, including champagnes. It was Vignes, not Haraszthy, who was the first to bring European wine-grape cuttings to California, having them sent in the early 1830s to Boston and then brought around Cape Horn to Los Angeles.

How swiftly winegrowing spread through the state is evident from the fact that, before the discovery of gold on the American River in 1848, there already were vineyards as far north as Santa Clara, Alameda, Contra Costa, Sacramento, Yolo, Sonoma, and Napa Counties. The Gold Rush brought the first wine boom in the 1850s; many of the newcomers found winemaking a surer road to riches than the trail to the mines. When the California legislature in 1859 exempted new vineyards from taxation, grape-planting fever reached epidemic proportions. By 1863 there were 12 million vines in the state, most of them planted in the preceding half-dozen years.

Glowing descriptions of California's marvelous winegrowing climate were published abroad before the Civil War. The French viticultural journal, *Revue Viticole,* reported in a series of articles between 1859 and 1862 what French viticultural experts found in a survey of the state: that California has a climate that makes it capable someday of "becoming a serious competitor" to France in the production of fine wine. This may help to explain why France, to this day, still maintains trade barriers that impede commercial shipments of California wine, although it imports wine in vast quantities from almost everywhere else.

• 3 •

Leggett brings out another characteristic of the California industry: its periodic wine-price declines, its recurring cycles of boom and bust. The first bust was recorded in 1858 and 1859 at Los Angeles, where wine was so plentiful and some of it so poorly made that the value of vineyard land suddenly dropped by half, and wine was difficult to sell at 50 cents a gallon. "But the bubble wasn't broken," Leggett comments, "it had merely shrunk temporarily."

Much of the early-day California wine was obviously bad, and a great deal of it was sold under counterfeit European labels. However, the wine that Vignes and his nephews made was good enough by 1860 to be sold under their own name in New York; and a San Francisco firm of vintners, Kohler & Frohling, was regularly shipping its bulk wines to England, Germany, Russia, Japan, China, and South America as early as 1856. Some improvement in the quality of California wines was evidenced during the 1860s and 70s. This is generally credited to the spectacular "Count" Haraszthy, to his expedition to Europe in 1861 for vine cuttings, and to his voluminous writings about viniculture. Later chapters will show, however, that there were many other viniculturists, principally from Europe and more experienced than the "Count," who imported their own foreign vines and who were making good wines from superior grapes before he made any from his.

The second wine-market bust came in 1876. Although the world economic depression of the 1870s had begun three years earlier, grape planting in California had continued without a letup, from 30 million vines in 1873 to 43 million by 1876. When the break came, grape prices plunged to $2 a ton, wine to 10 cents a gallon, and brandy to 37 cents. Barnyard animals were turned into the vineyards to dispose of the grapes. Many vineyardists uprooted their vines and planted fruit trees instead. But those winegrowers who survived the crash planted better grape varieties and improved the quality of their wines. With the help of late spring frosts in 1879, which reduced that year's grape crop by a third, the industry prospered again by 1880.

During the early 1880s, the devastation of European vineyards by the phylloxera vine louse was at its height, and the resulting shortage of French wines helped the California growers to sell theirs at a profit. What they did not know—and had failed to realize even when the destructive vine pest was positively identified on vines at Sonoma in 1873—was that the plague was killing their own vineyards at the same time.

• 4 •

It was the phylloxera—when it spread statewide and threatened to destroy the entire California industry—that influenced the legislature, by the act of 1880, to establish a State Board of Viticultural Commissioners, and also a department for viticultural research and instruction in the University of California. Although there was bitter rivalry between the Commissioners and the University, which led to the abolition of the Viticultural Commission in 1894,* the spread of phylloxera was finally checked. It was controlled by the same means as in France— by grafting the Old World vines onto phylloxera-resistant native American roots. The roots which saved the California vineyards came principally from Missouri, but were actually imported from France. Californians first tried to use the roots of the local wild vine, Vitis californica, then learned the French were having success with the midwestern roots and began ordering theirs from France.

Two men are credited with eventually stopping the havoc wrought by phylloxera in the state. One was Professor Husmann, the erstwhile Missourian. The other was Eugene Woldemar Hilgard, professor and later dean of agriculture at the University of California. Born at Belleville, Illinois, where his German-born father grew grapes, Hilgard experimented with viticulture in Mississippi and Michigan before coming to California in 1875.

---

*A Board of Viticultural Commissioners was established again by the legislature in 1913, and it continued until Prohibition.

When frost threatens vines in spring, sprinklers in this California vineyard turn on automatically. Ice forms as temperature drops, releasing heat that keeps the buds from freezing. Sprinkling continues until danger is past.

Working first on the phylloxera problem, he planted a vineyard on the Berkeley campus, where the Life Sciences Building now stands, and had a wine cellar near old South Hall. (The University vineyard was bitterly protested by the Livermore winegrowers, who feared the wind might carry the phylloxera pest over the Berkeley hills to them.)

Hilgard made important contributions to wine improvement in the state. At a time when some of the small vintners were still having their grapes trodden by Chinese coolies and Indians, he called for the building of large, modern wineries that could be operated scientifically. He advocated the slow fermentation of wines at controlled low temperatures. He was the first to point out the sole defect in California's climate, that when grapes are left on the vines until their sugar content is at its peak, their acidity drops too low—thus challenging the European idea, in which the California growers believed, that every additional day of sunshine is so much gain to the quality of wine. He urged that the grapes be harvested early, when their acid is in balance with their sugar, because "what is true in the cloudy climate of Europe is not necessarily true in California." He also opposed overcropping (letting vines bear too heavy crops), which lowers the quality of the grapes and wines. These are lessons that many California growers have only lately begun to learn.

Abhorring drunkenness, and himself a user of light red wines with his meals, Hilgard also advocated that the alcoholic content of California table wines should be kept low. In this he was opposed by Charles Wetmore of the Cresta Blanca Vineyard, the executive officer of the Viticultural Commission, who favored fermenting them to 15 percent strength. Hilgard's assistant and successor, Professor Frederic T. Bioletti, was the first to divide California into viticultural districts by their climates—the coastal counties for table wines and the interior valleys for dessert types.

• 5 •

The prosperity of the winegrowers lasted until 1886, when a bumper grape crop, the result of still more plantings, brought on the third California wine bust. This time bulk-wine prices sank to 6 and 8 cents a gallon. In 1889, Publisher William Randolph Hearst, whose father, Senator George Hearst, owned a vineyard in Sonoma County, published in his San Francisco *Examiner* a call for "all patriotic citizens to do all in their power to assist in placing the business of winemaking, which is of such vast importance to the state, on the best and firmest basis."

Most of the published replies to Hearst urged the planting of fewer grapes, the drying of more raisins, and the distilling of more brandy—remedies for overproduction that were still being attempted seven decades later. But Professor Hilgard's reply to Hearst was that the best remedy would be expert winemaking and longer aging to improve the quality of the wines.

Quality did improve. Although the bulk wines that went begging may not have been very good, there were in California, by 1890, at least a hundred great winegrowing estates owned by some of the wealthiest families of the state, who produced fine wines for pride rather than for profit alone, and who won medals for them in international competitions. Glimpses of the glamour and wealth of these nineteenth-century winegrowers can be had in Frona Eunice Wait's *Wines and Vines of California,* published at San Francisco in 1889, with its descriptions of such opulent estates as Captain Gustav Niebaum's Inglenook Vineyard at Rutherford, "Lucky" Baldwin's Santa Anita Ranch, Senator Hearst's Madrone Vineyard near Agua Caliente, Tiburcio Parrott's "Miravalle" in the Napa Valley, and the Warm Springs Vineyard of Josiah Stanford, brother of the governor and senator, who had his own great vineyard at Vina in the Sacramento Valley.

It is not generally realized that many of these pre-Prohibition wines were great. During the 1920s and 30s, I tasted numerous California wines of the 1914, 1915, and 1916 vintages. The long-lived Cabernets and Zinfandels, in particular, and also some of the dessert wines, were superb. I have a few of these venerable bottles in my cellar, given to me by heirs to the collections of departed connoisseurs, and I have found an occasional one still good after half a century.

· 6 ·

The third depression in the California wine industry lasted from 1886 to the mid-90s. In 1892, when Zinfandel grapes were selling at San Francisco for $10 a ton and Missions, if they could find buyers, at half that price, a brilliant British accountant named Percy T. Morgan had arrived in that city with two dollars in his pocket. He registered at the Palace Hotel and soon enlisted some prosperous clients, including the old vintner firm of S. Lachman & Company. Within two years, the persuasive Morgan convinced his client and six other big wine firms to form the California Wine Association. The CWA grew to giant size, operating as many as sixty-four California wineries. Another such group, the Winemakers Corporation, was formed at about the same time. The CWA and the Corporation stabilized prices by bringing grape and bulk-wine supplies under their control. Meanwhile, the grape crop was being reduced by the continuing ravages of phylloxera, and still further by the severe spring frost of 1896, which helped to bring the third wine bust to an end.

The San Francisco earthquake and fire of 1906 destroyed 15 million gallons of the CWA's inventory and gutted all but one of its several cellars in the city. Morgan then built, on the shore of San Francisco Bay near Richmond, what was at that time the largest winery in the world, which he named Winehaven. From Winehaven, with its own pier for ocean vessels, the CWA shipped California wines, in bottles under its "Calwa" label and in barrels under its "Big Tree" brand, to most countries of the world.

By 1911 an oversupply of grapes broke the wine market for the fourth time, and Morgan retired to his mansion in the Los Altos Hills. Most of Winehaven's vast wine stores eventually were shipped to Britain and Germany, which could not pay for them during the Great Depression of the early 1930s; also, an entire cargo was lost in a North Sea shipwreck. Winehaven was not finally emptied of its wine until 1937. The huge, fortresslike red brick structure and its small city of workmen's homes still stand as a monument to Percy Morgan; they are now part of a naval fuel depot.

• 7 •

The tragic developments in California at the start of Prohibition were briefly reviewed in Chapter 2: the initial uprooting of vineyards, the short-lived boom in planting "juice grapes," the unfortunate grafting-over from delicate fine-wine grapes to coarse varieties that shipped well, and the grape market bust in 1925 when too many grapes were shipped east. In 1927, halfway through the Prohibition period, California vineyards covered 635,000 acres, an all-time high and much of it surplus, almost the acreage the state has today.* The California Vineyardists Association, formed the year before, employed a "czar" for the industry, who promised to find new uses for the grape surplus. Herbert Hoover, then Secretary of Commerce, had picked a railroad expert, Donald D. Conn, for the job. Conn's ideas for new products, such as grape candy, grape salad, grape pie, and raisinade, failed to sell any fruit. And fresh California grape juice, made from the bland-tasting Vinifera varieties, could not compete with the more flavorful Concord juice from other states.

A law proposed at that time to prohibit further planting of vines was ruled unconstitutional. Farmers then were offered five dollars per acre to uproot their vines, but only a few of them did. This was when Captain Paul Garrett formed Fruit Industries, with Donald Conn as its head, to salvage the grape surplus by selling it as concentrate for home winemaking—only to have its "Vine-Glo" advertisements suppressed by the Hoover Administration in 1931 under pressure from the Drys. In 1930, the Federal Farm Board and California banks lent nearly $25 million to convert surplus grapes into raisins and grape concentrate, and to limit shipments of fresh grapes to eastern markets. Almost half a million tons were thus diverted from the marketing channels in that year. This staved off bankruptcy for the grape growers, and the short crop of 1931 kept them in business until the wineries, anticipating Repeal, bought and crushed extra quantities of grapes in 1932 and 1933.

The California vintners flooded the nation with wine at Repeal in December of 1933, then found they had far too much left.

*Vineyards in the 1920s produced fewer tons per acre than now. Yields have increased enormously in recent years. The 1927 crop from 635,000 acres totaled 2.2 million tons, compared to almost 4 million tons produced from only 536,000 bearing acres in 1975.

Almost overnight, more than seven hundred wineries had been bonded in the state, many of them by bootleggers to whom the government granted amnesty, conditioned on their payment of Federal taxes on their stocks. Much of their wine had soured and was later condemned by the State Department of Public Health. The California industry remained in a depressed condition as severe as that during the latter Prohibition years. There was so little demand for table wine that of some 800 wineries in the state in 1934, only 212 were left by 1938.

At the end of the Dry era, wine in California was sold principally in bulk, as was still the custom in the European wine countries at that time. The bulk wines were sold in "barrel houses." The typical "barrel house" was a liquor store with a rack holding from six to a dozen barrels with spigots, from which buyers who weren't too fastidious about vinegar and flies could fill their own gallon jugs or demijohns for a few dimes per gallon. Chain food stores refused to stock any wines at all until the "barrel houses" were outlawed, in 1945.

Most California wines were shipped in tank cars to bottlers in other states, and, when inexpertly handled before bottling, were less than palatable when sold. The nation's connoisseurs failed to appreciate the few—bottled in California by the handful of premium-quality producers who had survived Prohibition—that were fine.

• 8 •

During the first five post-Repeal years, overly bountiful sunshine presented the California vineyardists with three bumper grape crops and two of moderate size, far more than the struggling wineries, the raisin packers, and the fresh-grape shippers could absorb. Each spring the growers prayed that frost might come to reduce the yield (naturally, of their neighbors' vineyards, not their own), but their prayers were in vain. The curse of Prohibition was replaced by the curse of plenty, which was more to be feared than frost.

In the fifth Repeal year, the situation was so desperate, with a record grape crop of 2,531,000 tons, half of it surplus, that an "artificial frost"—the Grape Prorate of 1938—was voted under a California farm law. That emergency measure required every vineyardist to convert 45 percent of his harvested grape crop into brandy and to hold it off the market for at least two years.

The grape growers in the coast counties bitterly opposed the Prorate. They maintained that the surplus existed in the hot

San Joaquin Valley, not in the cool districts near the coast. Their leaders in the Wine Institute backed an opposite kind of plan, the Wine Advisory Board consumer-education program.✻ Voted in the same year as the Prorate, the wine-education program was unpopular with some of the larger wineries, several of whom fought for several years in the courts to avoid paying the assessment that supported the Board. They could not believe that wine would ever become popular in the whiskey-, beer-, and cola-drinking United States. Renewals of the Board program were almost defeated twice, but each time the old table-wine producers, who believed that Americans someday would learn to drink table wine with meals, produced enough votes to keep it alive.

The 1938 Prorate was a success as an emergency surplus-control measure. Half a million tons of that season's grapes were converted into brandy under the Prorate—and this later turned out to have been fortunate in another way, as we shall see. But the coast counties winegrowers meanwhile pushed a bill through the legislature specifying that no such program could ever apply to their grapes again.

The year following the Prorate brought still another disastrously heavy crop. The resulting 1939 wine glut forced twenty large San Joaquin Valley wineries into a conglomerate called "Central California Wineries Inc." Intended to keep surplus bulk wine off the market and thereby to bolster grape and wine prices, the CCW merger nearly got the wine industry and cooperating bankers indicted under the Federal antitrust laws. The refusal by the grand jury at San Francisco to vote that indictment was one of the few defeats in the legal career of a certain bright young lawyer in the antitrust division. He was Joseph Alioto, who three decades later became the mayor of the city.

Then came the Second World War, which suddenly cut off the supplies of European wines and diverted raising grapes for food. This temporarily ended the surplus. The war years were a period of wine shortages, high prices, and frenzied prosperity for the growers and vintners. But when the conflict ended, the

---

*The Wine Institute was incorporated in 1934 as the successor to the Grape Growers League (1931) and the Wine Producers Association (1933). The Marketing Order for Wine, assented to by two-thirds of the California wineries in 1938, created the Wine Advisory Board as an instrumentality of the State Department of Agriculture. The Marketing Order, renewable every three years, levied assessments—of 1 cent and 1½ cents on each gallon of California table and dessert wines shipped to market—which supported the Board's program. The Board contracted with the Wine Institute to perform most of the educational and market-expansion work until the Marketing Order was terminated in 1975. A grower-vintner movement to revive the Marketing Order began in 1984.

grape surplus was back to haunt them—and the wine market crashed in 1947.

Artificial frosts in new forms were tried again. A state marketing order for wine processors kept some of the surplus wine off the market between 1949 and 1952 by limiting the quantity which each winery was allowed to sell in bulk during specified periods. At the same time, a "marketing order for grape stabilization" was adopted to raise millions for the purchase and diversion of surplus grapes from normal marketing channels. Nature, however, obliged with natural frosts that reduced the 1949 and 1950 crops, and the stabilization funds were given back to the wineries. Again, in 1961, a new artificial frost was voted, this time under Federal auspices. It diverted almost 40 million gallons of surplus Central Valley dessert wine into industrial alcohol, and functioned for two years, but was defeated by another grower vote in 1963. Attempts during the next several years to hatch new surplus-control plans met with failure.

• 9 •

Of what did the surplus consist? Not of wine grapes; California had been woefully short of wine grapes since Repeal. It consisted of the heavy crops of raisin- and table-grape varieties grown in the hot San Joaquin Valley—grapes which could also be used to make low-priced dessert wines and brandy. The chief raisin variety, the Thompson Seedless, was widely planted by the valley vineyardists after Repeal because it had three outlets. It could be sold in July as a fresh table grape, or laid on trays between the vine rows in August to be sun-dried as a raisin, or if market prices for table grapes and raisins proved unattractive during the summer, the Thompson crop could be left on the vines until October and sold to the wineries. Table grapes such as the Flame Tokay, Malaga, and Emperor were widely planted, too, because they had two outlets: Whatever part of their crops the growers could not sell to be eaten fresh did not need to go to waste; the leftover grapes were delivered to the wineries for crushing.

Thus the valley wineries became victims of the viticultural calendar, serving as the salvage receptacle for the leftover three-way Thompsons and two-way table grapes. Some grower-owned wineries in the valley existed solely to salvage the table-grape culls. Better grapes, needed to make better wines, remained scarce. Growers in the valley saw no reason to plant wine-grape varieties, which have only one use—to make wine.

The planting of three-way Thompsons and two-way table

America's only wine tanker, the SS *Angelo Petri*, carried full cargoes of bulk wines from Stockton, California, through the Golden Gate and the Panama Canal to East Coast ports from 1957 to 1971. (*Bethlehem Steel Corporation*)

grapes, easy to grow and dispose of, doubled in the San Joaquin Valley after the Second World War. By the mid-1960s the acreage of Thompson vines in the valley amounted to almost half of the grape acreage in the state, and the valley's table-grape acreage represented almost a sixth. California's annual grape harvest was averaging more than 3 million tons, and less than a fifth of it consisted of wine grapes. The valley's wine industry was dominated by leaders of the raisin and table-grape industries, some of whom owned wineries but who seldom drank any wine themselves; they regarded it as a drink for skid row. It was they who dictated the artificial frost programs, which treated wine as a by-product of grapes. They argued that grape growing is a single industry of three segments—fresh, dried, and crushed—and that the wineries, coming last, must salvage the vast surplus tonnage in order to prevent waste. This made economic sense of a sort, and economists, bankers, and government agencies readily agreed. The fact they ignored was that the salvage outlet was using half of the valley's grape crop.

• 10 •

Prosperity had come to the coast-counties' vineyards by the mid-1960s because Americans since the war had been learning to drink table wines, especially those with the varietal names of coast-counties grapes. Soon there was a shortage of such premium wine grapes as the Rieslings, the Pinots, and Cabernet.

At the same time, urban sprawl was gobbling up old vineyards in the districts close to San Francisco Bay. The California climate that favors vines also attracts people, and the best vineyard land is also the best for housing tracts, the worst destroyers of vines. The state's population had jumped from 6 million at Repeal in 1933 to 15 million by 1960 and rose to 20 million in 1970, a rate of growth that could mean 38 million or even 40 million by the year 2000. To save the coast-counties vineyards, a state law in the 1960s provided for the creation of agricultural preserves—known as "green belts"—in which land is taxed on its value for farming, not at the higher rates charged for homes. The agricultural-preserve law came too late to save some of the vineyards. Fortunately, however, a few of the coast vintners found new climatically favored lands in sparsely settled areas outside the path of population growth and moved their vineyards there—a dramatic development described in the chapters on those areas.

• 11 •

But also since the Second World War, California vintners, including those in the San Joaquin Valley, had gotten around to doing some of the things that Professor Hilgard had advised seven decades earlier. They were modernizing their wineries, outfitting them with refrigeration and new equipment of the latest scientific designs. The new generation of enologists, taught in the University of California's wine school at Davis and at the new Department of Viticulture and Enology at Fresno State University, brought scientific new cellar treatments to the ancient art of making wine.

In addition to dessert wines—their chief product—the valley wineries had always produced some dry and semi-sweet table wines, but those had averaged poor in quality and had been used primarily for blending with coast-counties wines. Gradually, the valley table wines began to improve, and became at least reliably palatable and sound. In the 1960s, the valley vintners finally learned to make acceptable table wines out of their raisin- and table-grape varieties. They achieved this by adopting early harvesting and low-temperature fermentation, which Hilgard had advocated in vain. For such grapes as Flame Tokay, Thompson Seedless, and Emperor are, after all, members of the

Vinifera (wine-bearing) family, and their juices when expertly handled can be made into clean, though bland-flavored table wines and even into champagnes, at remarkably low cost. (This helps to explain some of the extremely low-priced, yet quite palatable California table and sparkling wines found on the market in recent years; there is Tokay or Thompson juice in many of the whites and even in some of the rosés and reds.)

• 12 •

A different vineyard product—brandy—emerged after the Second World War to provide a home for some of the San Joaquin Valley grapes. In a way never expected, it turned out that the bitterly fought 1938 Prorate had been a boon, after all. By forcing the production and aging of vast quantities of brandy in that year, the Prorate had launched the California brandy industry on its way. During the war, emigré experts trained in brandy-blending in Europe had surveyed and tasted the aging Prorate stocks. From the best of them, these experts had blended a new type of beverage brandy, lighter than the cognacs and armagnacs of France and different in bouquet. At the war's end, new-type distilleries were designed to make this distinctive brandy. So popular did it become that brandy consumption in the United States quadrupled between the war and 1970; three-fourths was this new California type. These European experts made still another notable discovery: that the Thompson Seedless, if harvested when its sugar-acid ratio is in balance, is an excellent basic grape for brandy. By 1969, an eighth of the valley grape harvest—320,000 tons, mostly of surplus Thompsons—was distilled to make 16 million wine gallons of the new type of brandy that Americans have shown they prefer.

• 13 •

Then came another remarkable development—the introduction of "pop" wines. When in 1955 the government first authorized "special natural wines" to contain natural pure flavors without paying an extra excise tax, San Joaquin Valley wineries introduced a wide assortment of new flavored wines with exotic coined names. The first of these were mostly of 20 percent alcoholic content, and they sold well, but they mainly succeeded in reducing the wineries' sales of their sherries, ports, tokays, and muscatels. Three years later, the Congress voted to allow

"still" wines to contain carbon dioxide gas up to seven pounds*
pressure per square inch—enough to produce a slight "pop"
when the bottle is opened—also without paying any additional
tax. It then occurred to the makers of flavored wines that there
might be some Americans who would like low-alcohol wines
with flavors of other fruits besides grapes, also carbonated with
seven pounds of "pop." When these slightly fizzy grape, apple,
pear, strawberry, and tropical fruit types, mostly 8 to 10 percent
in alcoholic content, hit the market in the late 1960s and early
1970s, they scored an overnight success. Their production reduced the Thompson surplus that had depressed the Central
Valley's vineyard industry for two decades, for there is no better
grape than the bland-tasting Thompson to blend with exotic
fruit flavors. By 1971 the "pops" accounted for almost one-tenth
of all the wine consumed in the United States. They attracted
new consumers, particularly the young, serving as a bridge between the sweet taste of bubbly soda-pop and the different tastes
of traditional dry or medium-dry mealtime wines. But many
of the new consumers soon crossed that temporary bridge; by
1976 sales of the "pops" began a steep decline. Six years later,
their market had slumped by 40 percent from the peak it had
reached in 1971.

• 14 •

When the consumption of table wines first outstripped dessert
wines in 1968 and set off the wine revolution, it caught both
the California grape growers and the vintners by surprise. In
1849 the cry was "gold"; now the cry was "wine grapes." The
planting rush started in the north coast counties, but quickly
spread to the central and southern coast districts, which share
the climates classed as Regions I, II, and III. It soon became
evident that the narrow coastal valleys could not produce enough
grapes for the expected future wine demand, that the hot interior
valley thenceforth must supply most of the table wines. Soon
much of the San Joaquin's agriculture was in ferment, shifting
from table grapes, raisins, cotton, peaches, and oranges to grow
"varietal" grapes for table wines instead.

In 1971 came news from the University: Dr. Harold Olmo
had bred for hot climates a dozen new red-grape hybrids which,
when planted in the warm valley, had made experimental wines

*Increased to fourteen pounds by an act of Congress in 1975.

described by some tasters as equal to most coast-counties Cabernet Sauvignons. The new vines had yielded eleven tons per acre at Fresno, almost double what the true Cabernet produces in cooler climates. Wines made from these grapes at Fresno State University had traces of Cabernet character and were superior to most reds previously grown in the valley. The first of these grapes, a cross of Cabernet with Grenache and Carignane called Carnelian, was introduced for general planting in 1973. An even better red-wine grape named Centurion came in 1975, followed by Carmine, an improvement over Cabernet for Regions I to III. In 1981 came a spicy new white-wine grape named Symphony.

Equally important for the Central Valley were new experiments in hot-climate winegrowing. University scientists showed that by retraining vines on trellises to let the leaves shade the grapes from the scorching valley sun, ripening of the fruit could be slowed, the sugar content increased without lowering the acidity, and the flavor thereby enhanced, enabling the valley to grow appealingly palatable table wines.

Other advances in California, though of a different kind, were amendments in 1971 and 1979 to the state wine standards that had been effective since Repeal. The first change allowed California sherries to be bottled at 17 percent alcoholic strength and port types at 18 percent, greatly improving the flavors of these dessert-wine types, which until then had been required to be at least 19½ percent. California sherries improved still further when the submerged-culture *flor* process, invented in Canada, (see page 499), came into general use.

The 1979 amendment repealed the minimum standards of 10 percent strength for white wines and 10½ percent for reds, set

This wind machine protects vines from frost damage in the Napa Valley. Propellers mix freezing air near the ground with warmer air above. (*John Gorman, San Francisco* Examiner)

forty years earlier, when most California wines were being shipped east in tank cars, to reduce the spoilage of table wines. By lowering the state standard to the Federal minimum of 7 percent, this amendment made possible the nationwide introduction during the 1980s of "light" and "soft" California wines.

In the coast counties, the growing national popularity of fine table wines spurred the replanting of old vineyards with the noblest wine-grape varieties, the building of the first new estate wineries, and the modernization of some of the old. By the mid-1970s, these wine estates were releasing some superlative wines, the best of which were Chardonnays and Cabernet Sauvignons. Europe-minded American connoisseurs, accustomed to admiring the great wines of France, acknowledged that these wines were fine, but it never occurred to the connoisseurs that they were tasting the finest of these types in the world.

A tasting held in Paris in May of 1976 had a historic impact on the quality reputation of California wines. Nine French judges, tasting "blind," scored two 1973 wines made in the Napa Valley, a Chardonnay and a Cabernet Sauvignon, as finer, respectively, than four of the greatest French white burgundies and four classified great growths of red Bordeaux. When the scores became known, and when parallel results came from a series of further tastings by more French judges scoring different California wines (plus one Oregon Pinot Noir), forty years of connoisseur sneering at American wines began turning to effulgent praise.

• 15 •

New kinds of California table wines appeared during the 1970s. Because of the white-wine boom, hundreds of growers grafted white-wine grape varieties to their red-grape vines, but an oversupply of reds remained. From the white juice of their red grapes, many wineries introduced "blanc" and rosé versions of Zinfandel, Cabernet Sauvignon, and Pinot Noir. Also new were weeks-old *nouveau* or *primeur* red types to compete with the Beaujolais *primeur* wines coming each winter from France. Botrytized "late harvest" California whites matched for the first time the semi-sweet German *spätlese* types with the exotic aromas and flavors created by the Edelfäule or "noble mold." Some of the state's vineyards introduced unfiltered and unfined red wines that purported to deliver extra flavor but required decanting before they could be served.

Increasing numbers of California wineries adopted vintage-

year labeling, which they had avoided since Repeal, having preferred to keep the tastes of their wines uniform from year to
year by blending their new wines with their old.

Back-labels appeared on California bottles describing the acid
and sweetness levels of the grapes, the dates, length and temperature of fermentation, and the various kinds of oak casks in which
the wines had been aged. Labels of some reds even named the
future year when the contents of a bottle should mature with
optimum flavor and bouquet and be ready to drink. No wines
from other countries had ever flooded buyers with such technical
details. Many wineries began labeling wines with the names
of the individual vineyards in which the grapes had been grown.
Names of local vineyard districts, such as those that enhance
the market values of French wines under the *appellation contrôlée*
system, started appearing on most estate-bottled California
wines. The number of these districts multiplied when, in the
early 1980s, the government began approving the boundaries
of more than three dozen California viticultural areas, most of
which the wine-buying public had never heard of before.

Still lacking in the Golden State, however, were enough wines
with sufficient age to compete directly with the rare treasures
in great cellars of the world—wines with great bouquet and
taste from many years spent mellowing in cask and bottle. This
lack was partly corrected by an action of the California legislature
in 1970. The amended law permits a vintner's inventory of wines
and brandies to be taxed by county assessors only once, in the
month of March following the vintage, and to be aged for as
many more years as the vintner might choose, without paying
this tax again. Several California wineries during the 1980s began
setting aside Cabernets to be aged at least four years before
release. But only a few vintners had yet seen the opportunity
to age their sherries for whole decades in oak, as is done in
Spain by the *solera* system of blending young wines with the
very old.

• 16 •

When the explosive national gains in table-wine shipments
began in the late 1960s, out-of-state investors suddenly became
interested in winegrowing, which they had long ignored as an
unstable business. Multimillion-dollar companies, visioning table wine as an American growth industry in its earliest stages,
sought to buy out old family-owned California wineries. With

only two exceptions (Beaulieu and Beringer), the families refused to sell.

National Distillers, which had owned three California wineries during the Second World War but had sold them after the conflict, returned to winegrowing in 1967, buying the Almadén Vineyards and pouring millions into their expansion. Two years later, Heublein, the Connecticut company which two decades earlier had introduced Americans to vodka, bought control of the Petri–United Vintners group of farmer-owned wineries and also purchased Beaulieu, one of the top-rated Napa Valley producers. Heublein thereby took second place to Gallo, which had become the world's largest winery when it outranked the Petri–United Vintners group in size the year before.

A decade later came giant Coca-Cola of Atlanta with its three California wineries, aiming to overtake Gallo in sales with its Taylor California Cellars wines. In 1983, the worldwide Seagram Wine Company entered the war for California wine sales leadership, taking over marketing for its Paul Masson wineries, control of which it had owned since 1942, and buying Coca-Cola's three wineries and their brands. Meanwhile, Heublein sold four of its wineries to the Allied Grape Growers co-op in 1983, and Heublein dropped to fifth place among California wineries in size. Seagram became second to Gallo, followed by Guild, by Allied's ISC Wines, by Heublein, and by Almadén.

A stream of foreign investors in California winegrowing had begun when Moët-Hennessey of France built its Domaine Chandon champagnery and planted vineyards in the Napa Valley in 1974. Then came investors from Germany, who bought the Franciscan and Buena Vista wineries in the mid-1970s, followed by the Swiss firm that acquired Cuvaison of Calistoga in 1979. During the early 1980s, eight more French companies bought California vineyards and planned wineries, most of them to make champagne. By 1983, four Spanish winemakers had bought land to be planted with vineyards for wineries they would build in the Golden State.

Meanwhile, hundreds of smaller investors—physicians, lawyers, engineers, computer scientists, airline pilots, film and TV luminaries—established small winegrowing estates or reopened old, cobwebbed cellars with vineyards in the California coast counties. The number of California wineries more than doubled within twelve years, from 240 in 1970 to more than 550 by 1983.

• 17 •

More than a quarter-million acres of new vineyards were planted in California between 1969 and 1983. Meanwhile, old-line vineyardists, who remembered the industry's past boom-and-bust history, were issuing stern warnings against the grape-planting and winery-building spree. Recalling that Americans had never been wine drinkers, they foresaw the danger of creating a grape and wine surplus again.

In the early 1970s, a sharp drop in grape prices made it evident that warnings were sound, that too many vineyards had been planted too soon. More than a few speculators in vineyards lost their entire investments, and financing agencies found themselves owning vineyards they had never intended to buy. The surplus turned out to be a lucky mistake, for in the drought years of 1976 and 1977 the extra grapes averted what would have been a severe shortage of California wine in those years.

While national wine consumption grew by 20 percent during the 1970s, the area of vineyards in California increased 40 percent—from 500,000 acres in 1970 to 738,000 acres in 1982. Meanwhile, wines from Europe, which had supplied only a twentieth of the U.S. market during the 1960s, had captured more than a fourth of the table wine market by 1983. There again was an oversupply of California grapes. In 1982 it was conservatively estimated that as much as 280,000 tons, two-thirds of it consisting of wine-grape varieties, went unharvested, left hanging on the vines.

• 18 •

The California vineyard and wine scene visible to the tourist is also changing markedly each year. The new mechanical harvesting machines, given their first trials here in 1968, are now picking two-thirds of the wine and raisin grapes. (Winegrowers in Europe have adopted the grape-picking robots, too.) Winemakers say mechanical harvesting, because it is speedy, results in better wines, because hand-picking in the vineyards is slow and can be done only by day. The robots can harvest by night, picking the grapes when they are cool and fresh, and precisely when they reach ideal ripeness. Some mechanical harvesters have crushers mounted on the machines, the juice protected by sulfur dioxide and by a blanket of carbon dioxide until it reaches the winery.

Vineyards, too, have changed in appearance. In many of them you see what look like cables running along inside the vine

Flexible arms shake grapes off the vines onto a conveyor belt as this mechanical harvester straddles a vineyard row in California. (*Upright, Inc.*)

rows. They are part of the drip-irrigation method, invented by the Israelis after the Second World War to bring water to crops in the Negev Desert. A valve at each vine feeds water to the vine root a drop at a time. Old-fashioned vine-training, in which each vine resembled a stunted tree, has been replaced by miles of trellises. Many vines are trained on cordons, which make it possible to do some of the pruning by machine.

Subterranean wine cellars, usually damp and moldy, became passé years ago, when vintners learned to build insulated, spotlessly clean cellars above the ground. Stainless-steel tanks have replaced most of the old redwood and concrete vats for the fermenting and storage of wine. Now you see some wineries with no roofs at all: batteries of steel tanks that stand exposed to the sun while temperature-controlled water circulates inside their shells and keeps the wine as cool as though it were underground.

Though grape growing and winemaking will become increasingly mechanized and automated in years to come, in California and other states vineyards will always be beautiful, and there will be increasing use of picturesque small oak casks for the aging of wine. The romance of the vineyards and cellars is part of the flavors of their wines.

Old-fashioned redwood tanks in a Lodi, California, winery.

Many modern wineries use centrifuges instead of filters to remove yeast cells and other solids from their newly fermented wines. (*The Wine Institute*)

• 19 •

To the visitor who would explore the California wine country, the puzzle is where to begin, for more than 12,000 vineyards and more than 550 wineries dot the countryside in forty-one of the state's forty-eight counties. The vineyards cover more than a thousand square miles.

But a tour is well worth undertaking, and it can start almost anywhere, for more than 150 of the wineries welcome visitors to taste their wines, and twice as many can be visited by appointment made in advance. Some also provide space for picnics and for outdoor charity-benefit summer concerts and plays. In fact, wine-touring, with tasting, has become one of California's chief visitor attractions, vying with redwood forests, Spanish missions, and Disneyland for the tourist trade.

There are wineries of every description: charming ivy-clad castles; grape-processing plants with steel storage tanks that resemble oil-refinery-tank farms; family-sized vineyards that specialize in shipping wines by the case to their individual customers' homes; estates of gentleman farmers who grow wine only as an avocation; church-owned cellars alongside monasteries; and also, scores of tasting rooms, which, though related to wineries, operate mainly at city and highway locations to sell their wines to the public.

Though representative California wines are now available in all of the fifty states and increasing numbers of foreign countries,

Temperature-controlled stainless-steel tanks. A freezing solution flows between the inner and outer shell of each tank. The winemaker is Michael Robbins, at his Spring Mountain Vineyards winery.

the only way to get acquainted with the full assortment is to go where the wines are produced, because the variety is far too great to be stocked in even the largest stores.

Californians themselves drink almost a third of the wine produced in their state. Not only because they are Californians; seven out of ten of them were born somewhere else and discovered wine after they arrived. The main reason for California's high wine consumption, four and a half gallons per capita per year including imports, is that the state's laws recognize wine as food and allow it to be sold freely in all kinds of stores and at the lowest state excise tax rates in the nation—1 cent per gallon on table wine, 2 cents on dessert types, 30 cents on champagnes.

If you wish to cover all of the California wine districts, to meet the vintners in person and sample their products at the cellars, the trip will take at least a month. Since almost 5 million tourists each year now visit the wineries, which haven't enough of their finest and oldest wines to serve the crowds, you should plan your tour with enough time to search for the best.

13

Sonoma, Mendocino, and Lake

HEADING TOWARD the north coast wine country from San Francisco, you cross the Golden Gate Bridge and drive through suburban Marin County. Since the Second World War, housing tracts have replaced the scores of Marin vineyards that flourished before Prohibition, but lately a few new ones have been planted apart from the path of urban growth, and four wineries have opened in the county since 1975. The one to see (but be sure to telephone ahead) is the Pacheco Ranch Winery on its ten-acre, mostly Cabernet vineyard, north of San Rafael and across Highway 101 from Hamilton Air Force Base. The family of Herbert Rowland, a great-grandson of pioneer farmer Ignacio Pacheco, bonded the 10,000-gallon winery in 1979. From its grapes before the winery opened, and from those grown on Richard Duncan's Quail Hill Vineyard in northern San Rafael, the Cuvaison winery in Napa County made the first post-Repeal Marin Cabernet Sauvignon, in 1973. When it went on sale at $10 a bottle, it quickly sold out.

Researcher Terry Leighton and port-wine maker Russell Woodbury operate small wineries in two Marin industrial areas. San Francisco art gallery owner Sean Thackrey in 1982 bonded a 4000-gallon winery at his home in the Marin beach community of Bolinas.

At Ignacio in northern Marin, you turn inland on the Black Point Cutoff, cross the Petaluma River into southern Sonoma County, then follow Highways 121 and 12 into Sonoma Valley, which Jack London named the Valley of the Moon. At your left on 121, as you pass Meadowlark Lane, the big Spanish sparkling wine producer Freixenet is preparing to build its three-level Sonoma Champagne Caves winery and has begun planting a hundred acres of Chardonnay and Pinot Noir.

This lower part of the valley, cooled by fogs from San Pablo Bay five miles to the south, is Region I in the classification of wine districts by climate (page 220). A few miles farther, as the valley narrows between the Sonoma and Mayacamas ridges of the Coast Range, it becomes Region II, and farther on, Region III.

Highway 12 leads to the picturesque Spanish pueblo of Sonoma and to the restored Mission San Francisco Solano de Sonoma (founded 1823), the northernmost of the Franciscan mission chain, and to the valley's sixteen wineries, of which Buena Vista, Sebastiani, and Hanzell are the best known.

Sonoma Mission is where winegrowing north of San Francisco began. When the Mission was abandoned by order of the Mexican government in 1834, the provincial *comandante,* General Mariano Guadalupe Vallejo, took over its vineyard, planted more vines on his own extensive lands, and became Sonoma's first commercial winegrower. At his home, Lachryma Montis, northwest of the town plaza, you can see the awards his vintage 1857 Sonoma Red and Sonoma White wines received at the 1858 California State Fair. Vallejo's example soon was followed by his brother-in-law, Jacob Leese, and by many others, including Jacob Gundlach, an experienced winemaker from Germany.

In 1856 came the spectacular "Count" Agoston Haraszthy, attracted by the success of the Sonoma winegrowers. Haraszthy, a political exile from Hungary, was a promotional genius of many interests, among which was a passion for raising grapes. He had tried and failed to grow them in Wisconsin, where he founded the town of Haraszthy (now Sauk City) before migrating to California in 1848. He imported European vines to San Diego, where he speculated in farming and was elected sheriff. Settling later in San Francisco, he planted European vines near Mission Dolores, where they failed to ripen because of the summer fogs. He then moved them to a location near the Crystal Springs Lakes in adjoining San Mateo County, where they failed again.

On his 1856 visit to Sonoma, Haraszthy found the vines were thriving, and promptly bought the vineyard originally established by General Vallejo's brother, Salvador. The "Count" transplanted his vines again, this time to Sonoma. He built a palatial Pompeian villa on a knoll, surrounded it with formal gardens and fountains, and named it Buena Vista. He wrote pamphlets extolling California's winegrowing climate and sold cuttings of his imported vines to farmers throughout the state. In 1861, he got himself appointed by Governor John G. Downey to visit Europe to study winegrowing and to import more grape varieties. From this trip he brought back 100,000 vines of some 300 varieties (for which the state failed to pay him) and material for his book, *Grape Culture, Wines, and Wine Making*. For these exploits he became known as the father of modern California viticulture.

Two years after his return from Europe, with financial backing from San Francisco banker William Ralston, Haraszthy organized the Buena Vista Vinicultural Society. Two sandstone wineries were built at Buena Vista, with tunnels extending into the hillside. The "Count" became General Vallejo's rival in the state fair wine competitions, but Vallejo had employed French winemaker Victor Faure, and usually won more medals than Haraszthy. The rivalry was friendly; Haraszthy's sons, Arpad and Attila, had married two of the general's daughters.

Haraszthy had sent Arpad to France to learn champagne making in the cellars at Epernay, but Arpad's attempts to make champagne at Sonoma were failures. And financially, so was the Buena Vista Society, even when its champagne was finally perfected by a French expert; the San Francisco *Alta California* described it as "the largest winegrowing estate in the world, and also the most unprofitable." At length, banker Ralston refused to supply any more capital. Haraszthy was accused of extravagance and was deposed as head of the society in 1866. In disgust, the "Count" left for Nicaragua and a new adventure, to establish a sugar cane plantation and make rum for the export trade. In 1869, he disappeared. On his plantation was a stream infested with alligators. It is believed that he tried to cross it on a tree limb, and fell.

During the 1870s, the phylloxera vine louse invaded Buena Vista and neighboring vineyards. By then, Arpad Haraszthy had moved to San Francisco and become a wine merchant, later acquiring the Orleans Vineyard in Yolo County.

The aging tunnels of Buena Vista collapsed during the earthquake of 1906. The vineyards were virtually gone, and the wineries had been closed. During Prohibition the Haraszthy story was forgotten.

• 2 •

At an auction held in Sacramento in 1941, San Francisco newsman Frank Bartholomew bought a 435-acre tract of Sonoma land that he had never seen, intending to build a country home. Inspecting his purchase, he found on the property two abandoned stone buildings that might once have been wineries. Nobody in the neighborhood could tell him what they were. Thinking that I might know their history, Bart asked me to come to Sonoma and look them over. When I told him the strange Haraszthy story and that he had bought Buena Vista, he was amazed.

Journalist Bartholomew perceived what such a story might be worth in prestige if, as a winery owner, he could bring back Buena Vista wines. That, in the following decade, is what he and his wife Antonia did. They reopened the tunnels, replanted the vineyard, employed experts to produce premium new Buena Vista wines, and by retelling the dramatic Haraszthy story, made them nationally known. They succeeded where Haraszthy had failed; they made Buena Vista pay. In 1967 they sold the old buildings, the majestic eucalyptus grove in which they stand, and the name to a Los Angeles liquor distributor. A new 700-acre vineyard was planted and a modern half-million-gallon winery was built facing Ramal Road in the Carneros district, six miles south of Sonoma. At old Buena Vista, the original press house was transformed into a tasting room and the second old cellar became storage for aging wines. In 1979 Buena Vista was sold again, this time to A. Racke's wine and spirits firm of Bingen-am-Rhein in Germany, one of whose sons, Marcus Moller-Racke, is now Buena Vista's president. Its wines, made by Sonoma-born, Davis-trained winemakers Don Harrison and his successor, Jill Davis, have continued to be among California's best. The newest, a spicy blend of Gewürztraminer and Riesling named Spiceling by the German owners, was introduced in 1982.

When Bartholomew sold Buena Vista, he retained most of the original vineyard. In 1973, at the age of seventy-five, he opened his own Hacienda Wine Cellars in a onetime hospital beside his vineyard home. Four years later A. Crawford Cooley, who has a vineyard in northern Sonoma County, became a co-owner of Hacienda, and the winery was doubled to 86,000 gallons. Its wines, made by Davis-trained Steven MacRostie, have been regular medal winners in quality competitions.

Buena Vista and Hacienda, both with tasting rooms and picnic grounds, are only a few hundred yards apart, but Buena Vista is reached by Old Winery Road, while to get to the Hacienda Cellars you take Castle Road and then Vineyard Lane.

• 3 •

The revival of Sonoma's wine industry is celebrated during the last weekend of September by its annual vintage festival, with pageants, nostalgic costume parades, and the ceremonial blessing of the grapes. These events are held around such landmarks as the Mission, the other historic structures around the plaza, and the Bear Flag Monument, where in 1846 California was proclaimed a republic free of Mexican rule.

Among the more conspicuous Sonoma landmarks are those named Sebastiani for the founder of the town's principal winery. These include the Sebastiani Theater, Sebastiani Apartments, Sebastiani Dance Hall, and the Sebastiani Bus Depot. In fact, the late Samuele Sebastiani is said to have once offered the city fathers a fabulous sum if they would rename Sonoma for him.

His grandson Sam, who now runs the 6-million-gallon Sebastiani Winery at Spain and Fourth streets, tells how Samuele arrived in Sonoma in 1896 from Tuscany, saved enough money while making cobblestones for San Francisco streets to buy the old Milani winery in 1904, outlasted Prohibition by making sacramental and tonic wines, and became Sonoma's leading citizen, building some of its streets and giving it a parochial school.

Since taking over at the death of his father August in 1980, Sam has focused the winery on its estate-bottled Sonoma wines, such as Chardonnay, Eye of the Swan Pinot Noir Blanc, and Proprietors Reserve Cabernet Sauvignon and Zinfandel. Sebastiani is one of the few wineries that have Cabernets for sale that are five to fourteen years of age. But it also sells America's youngest red. In 1972, it introduced America's first *vin nouveau,* a six-week-old Gamay Beaujolais, and put it on the market in mid-November, the same time the equally young Beaujolais *primeurs* arrived from France. Generically named wines, such as chablis and burgundy, reach the market after year-end under the August Sebastiani Country Wines label, introduced in 1982 and featured in the winery's tasting room. In the latter year came a Sebastiani brut *méthode champenoise* sparkling wine, riddled and disgorged at another company's winery while Sebastiani prepared to build a champagne cellar of its own.

Although its wines are sold in all fifty states and in several foreign countries, Sebastiani is still a family operation. August's widow Sylvia is chairman of the board, and her cookbook, *Mangiamo* (Let's Eat), has been sold at the winery since 1970 at the rate of five thousand copies per year. The vice presidents are Sam's California legislator brother Don, and Dick Cuneo, their brother-in-law. Their latest contribution to Sonoma is a wine and cooking school, opened upstairs from the Sebastiani Theater in 1984.

• 4 •

Southern Sonoma Valley has two more wineries, one new and the other old.

On Gehricke Road, uphill from Sebastiani, building contractor Peter Haywood and his wife Anita began making wine in 1980 of the first crops from the eighty acres of premium grape varieties they and a predecessor had begun planting four years before. This is where Major Jacob Snyder, a contemporary of Haraszthy, made a wine that won the "Best White" award in a judging at San Francisco in 1864. The new owners, having begun winning medals for their Riesling, plan to double their Haywood Winery to 50,000 gallons and to open a tasting room.

In the Vineburg district, two miles southeast of Sonoma, best reached via the Lovall Valley and Thornsberry roads, is the historic Gundlach-Bundschu Rhinefarm and its 100,000-gallon winery, reopened in 1973 to produce again the wines, once famous under its Bacchus brand, that winegrower Jacob Gundlach from Bavaria and architect Emil Dresel from Geisenheim made after founding the Rhinefarm in 1858. In that year Gundlach returned to Germany and brought back the first Riesling vines to be planted in Sonoma County. With the addition of his son-in-law Charles Bundschu, the firm became Gundlach-Bundschu in 1895 and built great wine vaults in San Francisco, which were destroyed in the earthquake and fire of 1906. Sixty-seven years later, Gundlach's great-grandson Towle Bundschu was still cultivating the 120-acre Rhinefarm, selling the grapes, when his son Jim, trained in farming, and son-in-law John Merritt, a dairy chemist, rebuilt the winery around three of its original stone walls. Their first wines were a white named Kleinberger, a Sylvaner-Riesling blend called Sonoma Riesling, and Zinfandel. The Rhinefarm, since enlarged to 300 acres, grows the only Kleinberger grapes (known as Elbling in Germany) produced commercially in the United States. The winery's tasting room is open to visitors on weekends.

• 5 •

On a private road up a hillside just north of Sonoma, there is a tiny jewel of a winery, a millionaire's plaything that is unique in the world of wine. On thirty acres of beautifully terraced vines stands a partial copy of the Clos de Vougeot château in Burgundy, with a miniature model winery inside. The vineyard is called Hanzell (Zell for the late financier and ambassador to Italy, James D. Zellerbach, who had it planted in 1952, and Han for Hana, his wife). A procession of subsequent owners has preserved the Hanzell name but not the price of its Chardonnay and Pinot Noir, which connoisseurs have bid up to $15 and $20 a bottle from the $6 for which Zellerbach sold them, precisely what he found they cost him to produce. The small output is snapped up each year by buyers who prize Hanzell wines as superb rarities, which they are.

What Zellerbach never knew, as he died in 1963, was that one of his expensive whims would lead to the solution of a century-old winemaking mystery and would cause scores of America's leading vintners to make an important change in the flavor of their wines.

While living in Europe during the 1940s, Zellerbach had developed a liking for the Montrachet and Romanée Conti wines of Burgundy's Côte d'Or. He conceived the idea of attempting to grow identical wines on his 200-acre Sonoma estate. While home on a visit, he invited the viticultural experts of the University of California to tell him how this might be achieved.

He followed every costly, specific detail of their advice, except one. Instead of American white oak barrels, then customarily used to age wines in this country, he insisted on ordering from France the wooden-hooped oak barrels, called *pièces*, that he had seen in the cellars of Burgundy; he liked their primitive look.

When the first Hanzell wine, the 1956 Chardonnay, was ready, he had his winemaker, Ralph Bradford Webb, send him a quantity in Rome. Zellerbach submitted it to European experts to taste. They identified it as a white burgundy, but couldn't decide from which Côte d'Or vineyard it came.

California vintners tasted Hanzell wines and recognized their French flavor. It was the elusive flavor certain French wines possess, often described as their "complexity." American researchers had tried for years to explain it, attributing it to peculiarities of French climate or soil. Now its source was known: the barrels Zellerbach had bought in France. California wineries began buying similar barrels from coopers in Beaune and Bordeaux. Their wines, too, acquired that elusive "complex" taste.

But why should French barrels make a difference? Aren't all oak barrels the same? The explanation was found in forestry libraries: Different species of oak trees grow on the European and American continents. European oaks, usually referred to by French coopers as Limousin, Nevers, Troncais, or Yugoslavian according to the localities where they grow, have a varietal vanilla-like fragrance markedly different from that of American white oaks* —a fragrance that the wood imparts to the wine. Now that wineries here have filled whole cellars with European barrels, some have decided they prefer American oak after all. A little Limousin or Nevers oak flavor in a Chardonnay or Pinot Noir is desirable, they say, but too much hides the aroma of the grape and can even ruin a fine wine. "It gives me splinters in my esophagus," said one of my connoisseur friends recently, describing a Chardonnay that had spent too much time in European oak.

Since 1975, Hanzell has been owned by young Australian-born Countess Barbara de Brye (née Smith), who was educated in England, studying archaeology at Cambridge, and is so devoted to winegrowing that she once planted an English vineyard. With her husband Jacques, a Parisian banker, she often comes to stay at her Sonoma estate and to visit their California friends. The countess likes clarets as well as burgundies, so winemaster Robert Sessions has planted five acres of Cabernet Sauvignon and of the five blending grapes used in Bordeaux on the ridge above the original vineyard. This will increase the number of Hanzell wines to three.

• 6 •

There were more than a hundred wineries in Sonoma Valley during the last century. Their wines rivaled those of Napa Valley, the neighbor to the east. Among the most celebrated vineyards were Captain J. H. Drummond's Dunfillan Vineyard north of Sonoma, the nearby Madrone Vineyard of United States Senator George Hearst,† Charles Kunde's Wildwood Vineyard near Kenwood, and Kohler & Frohling's Tokay Vineyard at Glen Ellen, which is now part of the Jack London State Park.

During Prohibition, the southern Sonoma Valley became a summer playground for sporting types from San Francisco because it is close to the city. Great vineyards were chopped into

---

*Native American white oaks, from which most barrels for wine and liquor aging are made, are chiefly of the species *Quercus alba, Q. lyrata, Q. prinus,* and *Q. bicolor.* The main oak species grown in Europe for wine or brandy barrels are *Q. robur* and *Q. sessilis.* Suppliers of cooperage say these species do not grow in this country, except perhaps in some northeastern states.

†The multimillionaire mine owner and newspaper publisher, the father of William Randolph Hearst. The senator bought the Madrone Vineyard in 1885, planted it with the finest Bordeaux varieties, and was proud to serve his own wines and brandy to his guests in the national capital. After his death in 1891, his widow, Phoebe Apperson Hearst, sold the winery to the California Wine Association.

small holdings, while the vineyard estates of wealthy San Franciscans in the Napa Valley remained more or less intact. After Repeal, the several wineries that reopened in Sonoma Valley sold jug wines to passersby or in bulk to the bigger wineries.

Now, since the table-wine boom of the late 1960s, winegrowing in the Valley of the Moon has come back to life. Besides the new plantings by the Bundschus and Sebastianis, Arthur and Fred Kunde have enlarged and replanted their grandfather's Wildwood Vineyard, which again stretches far into the eastern hills. A mile and a half up Moon Mountain Road from Highway 12 is the seventy-acre Carmenet Vineyard, planted since 1975, on which a winery with three immense new underground tunnels was built in 1983 for a group of investors headed by Richard Graff. "Carmenet" is a French collective term for the wine-grape varieties grown in Bordeaux.

A left turn on Madrone Road from Highway 12 takes you to Harry Parducci's quarter-million-gallon Valley of the Moon winery, which dates from 1940. Its 200 acres include part of Senator Hearst's onetime Madrone Vineyard.

If you wish to visit Kistler Vineyards, whose wines have brought high prices in twenty-five states since 1980, take a right turn on Nuns Canyon Road, then jog left up Nelligan Canyon Road for three steep curvy miles. The cellar is partly underground, carved out of a hill. In 1979 Stephen Kistler, after two years' study at Fresno State University and UC Davis and three years' experience at a Santa Clara County winery, began with his brother John the clearing of thirty acres of forest and the planting of premium grape varieties. In the same year, their associate, former chemistry professor Mark Bixler, made their first wine of purchased Sonoma and Napa Valley grapes. At 1700 feet elevation and without irrigation, their vines were slow in maturing; their first estate-bottled wines were due in 1985. Also in the eastern hills is the Adler Fels winery, two miles up Los Alamos Road. Its name is German for "eagle rock," a nearby eagle-beaked peak.

A left turn from Highway 12 on Dunbar Road leads to the Grand Cru winery, named by two young wine-buff engineers who in 1971 bought the eighty-five-year-old Lemoine bulk winery and spent the next ten years rebuilding the concrete tanks into storage cellars and making good wines they sold in a new chalet-style tasting room. Former Oroweat bakery executive Walter Dreyer and his wife Bettina, a gourmet cook, bought Grand Cru in 1980 and doubled its size to 150,000 gallons.

Two miles farther on Highway 12, on your right, is the Kenwood Winery, built in 1905 by Julius Pagani to make bulk wine, but purchased in 1970 by young John Sheela and Martin and Michael Lee to make premium table wines. They replanted the twenty-acre pre-Prohibition mixed-variety vineyard with vines of noble lineage, installed stainless-steel tanks and new oak barrels in the cellar, and converted the front into a tasting area, which is open daily except on holidays. Research chemist Dr. Robert Kozlowski is the part-time head winemaker.

Another mile north brings you to grape-grower Joseph T. Martin's modern 50,000-gallon St. Francis Winery and its tasting room, on your left. It was built in 1979 beside the ninety-acre vineyard Martin planted eight years before. For its first four years, he made wines for some of the still newer Napa and Sonoma wineries while their own cellars were being built. The St. Francis wines are estate-bottled Chardonnay, Riesling, Gewürztraminer, Pinot Noir, and Merlot.

Across the highway, beside the road that climbs Adobe Canyon to Sugarloaf State Park, is Chateau St. Jean,* which since its founding in 1974 has become one of California's most spectacular and famous winegrowing estates. Three wealthy San Joaquin Valley grape growers visualized and financed this version of what should constitute a modern Sonoma Valley chateau: a French Mediterranean-style mansion, formal gardens, picnic grounds and a hiking trail for guests, vineyards climbing a mountain, a winery modeled after Château Lafite, and the other essential— high-quality, high-priced wines and champagnes.

Another essential is the dedicated young winemaster, Santa Rosa–born Richard Arrowood, trained at two state colleges and in three older Sonoma County wineries (Korbel, Italian Swiss Colony, and Sonoma Vineyards). Big, cherub-faced Dick Arrowood received his dream assignment when he made the first Chateau St. Jean wines in leased space at the Sonoma Vineyards winery. Planting of the chateau's 124-acre vineyard began in the following year, but the winery wasn't even partially complete until 1977.

Arrowood amazed the wine trade by introducing seven different Chardonnays of the same vintage, eight different Rieslings varying in flavor, and four different reds of Cabernet and Zinfandel—all from different vineyards, some of which were identified on the labels. His creations are frequent medal winners at regional and state competitions.

*Note there is no circumflex accent over the "a" in "Chateau." This also may remind you to pronounce "Jean" the American, not the French way. No saint is involved; the winery is named for Mrs. Jean Merzoian, one of the investors' wives.

One of his botrytized 1975 Rieslings had the initials "TBA" on its label, signifying that had it been made in Germany it would have qualified in the proportion of botrytized grapes to be called a Trockenbeerenauslese wine. It was priced at $40 a bottle. But in 1978 the Washington bureau that approves wine labels notified Arrowood that "TBA" could no longer be allowed on an American wine label. The German government had complained to the bureau that the initials could be construed as meaning it was a German wine.

Chateau St. Jean's wines can be sampled daily in the mansion, which was built about 1920 by Duluth lumber and mining magnate Ezra Goff as his California home. Only there can you buy the chateau's best bargains, its press wines, labeled Vin Blanc and Cabernet Rouge. You also can take a self-guided tour of the winery.

The first St. Jean champagne, a four-year-old experimental blanc de blancs, was introduced in 1977, but since 1980 the company's sparkling wines have been made with ultramodern equipment in a former cannery at Graton, seventeen miles west of the chateau. The champagne master is Davis-trained Edgar ("Pete") Downs.

• 7 •

Winegrowing has also revived in the hills above Glen Ellen, Jack London's home, on the western side of Sonoma Valley, where such famous pre-Prohibition vintners as Kohler & Frohling and Joshua Chauvet established their vineyards and wineries more than a century ago.

To Glen Ellen in 1980 came the Benziger family, who own a century-old New York liquor importing house, and bought Wegnerville, a onetime country resort adjoining Jack London State Park. They replanted the thirty-acre vineyard, where Julius Wegner began growing Zinfandel in 1865, expanded the winery he had dug into the hill, and within two years were selling vintage-labeled Glen Ellen Winery wines made of purchased Sonoma County grapes. Thirteen members of the Benziger family settled in Wegnerville, which in Jack London's time included a hotel, a rooming house, a dancehall, and a church. Five sons of Bruno Benziger work in the vineyard, winery, and tasting room, bossed by Michael, eldest of the five. Their father helps them sell the wines. When the vineyard matures and bears full crops, estate-bottled Sauvignon Blanc and Cabernet will be the Benzigers' principal wines, they say.

Facing Enterprise Road on the slope of Sonoma Mountain, northwest of Glen Ellen, is the Coturri Vineyard, where Harry Coturri and his winemaker son Tony have made "natural" wines since 1979 from the grapes grown by Tony's brother Phil, who writes poetry and manages vineyards for neighboring growers.

Across a fence from the Coturris, but facing Sonoma Mountain Road, are former symphony violist Patrick Campbell's thirty-acre Laurel Glen Vineyard and the modern winery he built in 1980, near the house he occupies with his wife and their three small daughters. Campbell has petitioned the Federal government to recognize Sonoma Mountain as a viticultural area, different climatically from the rest of the Sonoma Valley appellation which the government established in 1982.

Atop a hill on the east side of nearby Warm Springs Road is comedian Tommy Smothers's vineyard estate. Tommy planted his twenty-five-acre vineyard in 1978 to supply grapes for the wines his brother Dick had begun making at Dick's home near Santa Cruz. Because Dick's Vine Hill vineyard needs replanting, Smothers wines henceforth will be made in Sonoma County, says Tommy, either in a new winery or in space rented in some other vintner's cellar.

Bennett Valley, reached by Bennett Valley Road from near the Smothers estate, had many wineries before Prohibition, and has one again. In 1977, Davis-trained Meredith (Merry) Edwards was hired to make wine from the grapes on Sandra McIver's forty-acre Matanzas Creek Vineyard at the base of Bennett Peak, five miles from Santa Rosa. Stainless-steel crushing equipment and tanks were set up on a concrete pad outside a former dairy barn, which Merry filled with oak barrels. The 15,000-gallon winery since has turned out some of Sonoma County's best Chardonnays, Cabernets, and Pinot Noirs. Merry is one of the first three woman winemakers to manage California wineries during the 1970s. The others are Mary Ann Graf and Mary Ann's successor at Simi Vineyard, Zelma Long.

High in the Mayacamas Mountains, eight miles northeast of Santa Rosa, are the vineyard and winery of former Detroit engineer Fred Fisher, grandson of the Charles Fisher who, in the days of horsedrawn carriages, created the Fisher Body, which later became the classic shape of General Motors automobiles. Having become fascinated with wine lore during his army service in Germany, in 1973 Fisher bought a pre-Prohibition vineyard off St. Helena Spring Mountain Road, moved there with his bride Juelle, replanted the vineyard, and built a 30,000-gallon winery of douglas fir and redwood timbered and milled on the site. Fisher Vineyards Chardonnay and Cabernet have been sought after by connoisseurs since their first vintage in 1979, and their winery has won an architectural award.

• 8 •

Sonoma County had only twenty wineries when I wrote the first edition of this book in 1973. The second edition, five years later, described fifty-five. At this writing, I count 112, most of which I have visited, but this chapter can describe fewer than half of them. Eighty-eight of the 112 and most of the county's 29,000 acres of vineyards are north of Santa Rosa, the bustling county seat. Most of the wineries have tasting rooms that are open daily; some also offer picnic facilities.

Some of the greatest California wines before and after Prohibition came from the Fountain Grove Vineyard, which stood on a hillside four miles north of Santa Rosa. It was to Fountain Grove that the mystical prophet, Thomas Lake Harris, moved his Brotherhood of the New Life in 1875 from Brocton, New York. Among the disciples who came with Harris to his new California heaven were the Missouri viticulturist, Dr. John W. Hyde, and the Japanese nobleman, Baron Kanaye Nagasawa. While the Fountain Grove Press poured forth Harris's pamphlets, sermons, and hymns, Dr. Hyde and his pupil, Baron Nagasawa, planted 400 acres with Pinot Noir, Cabernet, and Zinfandel. By the early 1880s Harris was shipping Fountain Grove wines, "potentialized with the electro-vinous spirit of joy," across the United States and as far as his old headquarters in England. Involved in new scandals about free-love practices at his utopia, Harris departed suddenly for England in 1892. Nagasawa was left in charge and became Fountain Grove's owner when Harris died in 1906. The baron was noted as a wine judge and for his knowledge of viticulture, acquired from Dr. Hyde and their mutual friend, Luther Burbank, the Santa Rosa botanical wizard. Nagasawa maintained the vineyard and was preparing to reopen the winery at the repeal of Prohibition, when he died. His estate hired an incompetent winemaker, and the first post-Repeal Fountain Grove wines were moldy and sour. Then mining magnate Errol MacBoyle bought the estate, partly to acquire the baron's collection of samurai swords and Japanese art, and partly to impress his millionaire friends with his own private brand of champagne. MacBoyle hired two winemakers, emigrés from Germany, Kurt Opper and his cousin, Hanns Kornell. During the 1940s Opper restored Fountain Grove to greatness. His 1945

Johannisberg Riesling and his Pinot Noir were the best made that year in the state. But after MacBoyle's death in 1949, his widow Glendolyn remarried and let the vineyard fall into neglect. Opper then quit to join the Paul Masson Vineyard at Saratoga, and in 1951 Fountain Grove was closed for good.

• 9 •

From an old cottage at the country crossroads called Trenton, ten miles northwest of Santa Rosa, come two red wines prized by California connoisseurs, Swan Vineyard Zinfandel and Pinot Noir. Joe Swan, the son of a teetotaler North Dakota schoolteacher, first became interested in wine by reading about it in novels, and made his first vintage at the age of fifteen. When he grew up and became an airline pilot, he continued making wine at home as a hobby, and once planted a Chardonnay vineyard at 5000 feet elevation in eastern Tulare County, just to see what kind of wine that mountain climate could produce. Winemaking fitted into flying, which was mostly on Western Airlines' San Francisco–Los Angeles run. He took short courses in winemaking at the UC Davis wine school, and in 1969 bonded a 2000-gallon cellar in his house. His Zinfandel made that year, of grapes fermented extralong on the skins and clarified without filtering, was the first to win him fame. His 1972 Pinot Noir, which he fermented with some of the stems as they do in Burgundy, was one of the few I had tasted in California that had the Côte d'Or cachet; I have tasted several others since. Swan retired from flying in 1974 but did not enlarge his winery. Winegrowing for him is still a hobby and he believes that small winegrowers should stay small. The ten-acre Swan vineyard, where his wife June and daughter Sandy help pick the grapes, contains Pinot Noir, Chardonnay, and a patch of Cabernet Sauvignon; he buys his Zinfandels.

Two miles southwest, on Graton Road toward Occidental, the Torres winegrowing family of Spain in 1983 purchased a fifty-acre former apple orchard and planned within two years to build a Torres California winery there. Besides their original winery at Vilafranca del Penedes in Catalonia, the Torres family has another winery in Chile.

On Olivet Road, near Guerneville Road northwest of Santa Rosa is the 50,000-gallon De Loach Vineyard winery. Onetime San Francisco fireman Cecil de Loach and his wife Christine, both with degrees in anthropology, settled with their two young sons on the old vineyard here in 1969 and sold the grapes from its Zinfandel vines to the co-op winery at Windsor. Six years later they built their own winery, which their sons now help them to run. De Loach estate-bottled wines went on sale in their tasting room and in restaurants and stores. De Loach has become the president of the co-op and still sends it half of his grapes.

About three miles west of De Loach, on Laguna Road, is the 2-million-gallon Martini & Prati Winery, a group of old wooden and concrete cellars, one of which dates from 1881. Elmo Martini and Edward Prati, descendants of old Sonoma winegrowing families, make mainly bulk table wines for other California wineries. When the Fountain Grove winery closed, they bought its famous label and used it to introduce their own bottled wines, which are sold in their tasting room.

Farther west, on Guerneville Road at the Vine Hill intersection, young Thomas Dehlinger and his father, Berkeley radiologist Dr. Klaus Dehlinger, planted fourteen acres of premium wine grapes and built the 14,000-gallon Dehlinger Winery in 1975. Tom, a UC Davis graduate, had been one of Bradford Webb's successors as the winemaker at Hanzell Vineyard. He lives with his wife and children in the octagonal house uphill from the winery.

At the end of Ross Station Road, off the Gravenstein Highway (Route 116) south of Forestville, is the 130-acre Iron Horse Vineyard, planted by Sonoma Vineyards of Windsor along Green Valley Creek during the grape rush of the early 1970s. (The name refers to a onetime miniature railroad on the property.) The winery's second label is "Tin Pony." In 1975 the vineyard was bought by Sonoma Vineyards' former cellarmaster Forrest Tancer in partnership with international lawyer Barry Sterling and his wife Audrey, who rebuilt the century-old home on the property into one of Sonoma County's most glamorous chateaux. They built a 55,000-gallon winery, produced estate-bottled wines and champagnes, and petitioned the Federal government to establish Green Valley of Sonoma as a viticultural area, distinguished from Green Valley in Solano County, which the government had approved in 1982.

A mile south of Forestville is the 20,000-gallon former Russian River Vineyard winery, modeled after a hop kiln, with a twenty-five-acre vineyard planted in 1964. Michael Topolos, who teaches a course in wine appreciation at Sonoma State University, took it over three years later and renamed it Topolos at Russian River. Besides assorted table wines, he makes an apple wine.

On hilly Martinelli Road, which climbs northward from Route

116 west of Forestville, is Domaine Laurier, a 30,000-gallon winery bonded in 1978 by Barbara and Jacob Shilo on their thirty-acre vineyard. Barbara, an artist, designed the labels of their estate-bottled wines, which are made by Davis-trained winemaker Stephen Test with the guidance of consultant Mary Ann Graf.

Perched in the hills past Cazadero and only three miles from the Pacific is the well-named Sea Ridge Winery and its eight-acre vineyard of Pinot Noir and Chardonnay. Wine lovers Tim Schmidt and Dan Wickham, marine biologists employed at the Bodega Bay Marine Laboratory, decided that the windy coastal hills of Sonoma County might be the place to grow Burgundian grapes. They began planting vines in 1979 and opened their 10,000-gallon winery a year later, meanwhile buying grapes from other vineyards until theirs would mature.

• 10 •

On the left bank of the Russian River, two miles east of Guerneville and just past the woodsy summer resort colony of Rio Nido, are the Korbel vineyards and champagne cellars with their quaint Norman tower, which once housed a brandy still.

The winery dates from 1886, when the Korbel brothers, natives of Bohemia, gave up lumbering along the Russian River because they had cut down most of the trees. They planted vines where there had been a grove of redwoods, and built the cellar with bricks they baked in a homemade kiln. They made only still wines and brandy until 1896, when they were joined by an expert winemaker named Franz Hazek from Prague. Hazek brought choice vine cuttings from Europe and made a dry sparkling wine called "Grand Pacific" to compete with Arpad Haraszthy's "Eclipse" and the champagne of Paul Masson. The Korbels renamed the wine Korbel Sec and followed it with a sparkling burgundy named Korbel Rouge. Hazek's successor was another Czech named Jan Hanuska, who so jealously guarded his secret *cuvées* that nobody was allowed to enter the winery in his absence, not even the Korbels.

Korbel is now owned by the Heck family, whose progenitor Adolf, from Strasbourg, reopened the Cook's Imperial champagne vaults for the American Wine Company in St. Louis at the repeal of Prohibition. He sent his eldest son, Adolf L. Heck, to the Geisenheim Institute in Germany to learn winemaking, and made him Cook's champagne master when he returned. When the U.S. government seized the American Wine Company in 1944 because of its secret ownership by Hitler's foreign minister, Joachim von Ribbentrop, the younger Heck moved to the Sweet Valley winery at Sandusky, and for six years made Ohio champagne.

In 1951, Adolf Heck came to California to become president of the Italian Swiss Colony, and his late brother Paul managed the Colony's winery at Asti. Then came the opportunity the Heck brothers had been waiting for: Anton (Tony) Korbel, less interested in champagne than in judging dog shows, was offering the vineyards and winery for sale. The brothers bought it, and Adolf, with his champagne-making experience in Germany, Missouri, and Ohio, became the president and winemaker of Korbel.

The Hecks since have replanted and enlarged the vineyards to 600 acres. They added a brandy that is distilled for them in the San Joaquin Valley. A complex of new wine cellars and brandy-blending plant were built in one of the older vineyards. The original brandy warehouse was converted into a wine shop, with a Gay Nineties-style tasting room adjoining. It replaced the tasting room in the old railroad depot which Tony Korbel had bought for $5 from the Northwestern Pacific in 1935. Adolf's son Gary grew up and became the company's president. New champagnes were added: Korbel Natural, which is almost bone-dry; Korbel Brut, which is almost dry; Extra Dry, sweeter but not as sweet as the Sec; and a sparkling Korbel Rosé, which is semi-dry. In the 1980s came Blanc de Noirs, made entirely from Pinot Noir, and a Blanc de Blancs, made entirely from Chardonnay.

A machine was invented at Korbel in the 1970s that riddles (shakes) thousands of champagne bottles at once to send the sediment, formed by fermentation, down into the bottle necks; it is fascinating to watch. Another machine, invented in France, disgorges the bottles (removes the sediment) automatically. This enables Korbel to advertise that its champagnes are "fermented in *this* bottle," a slap at bottle-fermenting competitors who use the modern transfer method of disgorging.

Korbel has reduced its production of table wines since 1974. The five it now makes are sold only at the winery and in a few Northern California cities.

• 11 •

On the Trenton-Healdsburg Road, just north of River Road, is the Mark West Vineyards winery, which Pan American pilot Bob Ellis and his wife Joan began converting from a dairy in

1976. Joan is the winemaker while Bob, between transpacific flights, cares for the vineyard, which borders Mark West Creek. In 1982, they added a tasting room and a schedule of summer plays. Their estate-bottled wines are Chardonnay, Riesling, Gewürztraminer, and Pinot Blanc, followed in 1984 by their first *méthode champenoise* sparkling wine, a 1981 Blanc de Noirs.

Slusser Road, east of Trenton, extends north past the county airport to the ultra-modern Sonoma Cutrer winery, built in 1981 and not yet open to visitors, and to the largest of its five all-Chardonnay vineyards that total 800 acres. This is a long-range project, begun in 1973 by onetime fighter pilot and Harvard MBA Brice Jones, for a group of investors interested only in producing proprietor-grown Chardonnays and champagnes. The first of three Chardonnays was introduced in 1983. A year before, winemaster William Bonetti had laid down the first *cuvée* of Sonoma Cutrer champagne, to be released in 1987.

In the village of Windsor, eight miles north of Santa Rosa, the 750,000-gallon Sonoma County Co-op Winery ages its members' bulk wines before they are shipped in tank trucks to the Gallo Winery at Modesto. The building is a relic of the past, the last of the statewide chain of wineries established by Kohler & Frohling, the greatest of early California wine firms, founded in 1853 at Los Angeles by Charles Kohler and John Frohling, musicians from Germany. In 1894, Kohler & Frohling was absorbed by the California Wine Association, which operated the cellar until Prohibition. The co-op was organized in 1935 to provide a home for its members' grape crops.

· 12 ·

The main tourist attraction around Windsor is the complex of two adjoining wineries among the vineyards facing Old Redwood Highway south of Healdsburg. The building on your left is the 300,000-gallon Piper Sonoma champagne cellar, built in time to release its 1980 vintage in 1982. The building on your right, shaped like a cross, is the Sonoma Vineyards or Rodney Strong winery, which is eleven times as large. In the Piper Sonoma tasting room you can compare its Sonoma County Brut sparkling wine with another of the same vintage named Blanc de Noirs, which spent an additional year in contact with its yeast before it was disgorged. There now is also a third champagne, with unique character of its own, named Tête de Cuvée, that has been aged thirty months on the yeast.

A short walk from Piper Sonoma, in the Sonoma Vineyards

Red wine ages in barrels, then in bottles, in Sonoma Vineyards winery.

tasting room, you can sample the dozen table wines that winery makes from the grapes grown on the 1200 acres of vines it controls. The best come from its Alexander's Crown, River West, River East, Le Baron, and Chalk Hill vineyard estates. Sonoma Vineyards also makes the still wines from which Piper Sonoma makes its champagnes.

Sonoma Vineyards had its beginnings in 1980, when Rodney Duane Strong disbanded his Rod Strong Dance Quartet, at the age of thirty-three, after performing on Broadway and at the Lido in Paris. He "didn't want to be an old dancer." He began bottling bulk wine under the name of Tiburon Vintners in a century-old railroadmen's boarding house on the waterfront of Tiburon, across the bay from San Francisco. Four years later, he introduced the mail-order sale of wine with "personalized labels," such as "Bottled Expressly for Tom and Mary Jones." This proved a sensational salesmaker, so Rod and his red-haired dancing partner and wife, Charlotte, leased the old Monte Carlo winery near the Co-op at Windsor, and named it Windsor Vineyards. When the table-wine boom was reaching its peak in 1970, the Strongs built the cruciform Sonoma Vineyards winery, keeping the Windsor name for their mail-order wines. The firm then went public, selling enough stock to plant thousands more acres of vineyards. But the 1974 "grape bust," caused by overplanting, caught the Strongs overextended, and Renfield Importers of New York became a part owner of Sonoma Vineyards. In 1980 Piper-Heidsieck, the two-century-old French champagne firm, began a joint venture with Renfield and Sonoma Vineyards to build the Piper-Sonoma cellar, which was finished in the following year.

On a tour of the Piper Sonoma cellar, you can see the latest advances, developed in France, in the *méthode champenoise*. No longer does a *remueur* or riddler shake and turn each upside-down bottle daily for weeks to bring the sandlike sediment, caused by refermentation, down into the bottle neck. Instead, at Piper Sonoma, bins containing hundreds of bottles are shaken on a computer-controlled machine called a *gyropalette*. Nor is there any more hand labor in the disgorging and refilling of the bottles with *dosage*. These, too, are done by machines, virtually without the bottles touching human hands.

• 13 •

North of Sonoma Vineyards, Limerick Lane leads east across the freeway to the 12,000-gallon Sotoyome Winery, built in 1974 by former University of California history instructor William Chaikin and printer John Stampfli, who learned enology at UC Davis. The name refers to the Sotoyome land grant, named for the Indian tribe that once inhabited this part of the Russian River Valley.

At the end of Grant Avenue, two miles southeast of Healdsburg, is the Cambiaso Winery, which Giovanni and Maria Cambiaso built on their hillside vineyard in 1934. Their son Joseph and daughters Rita and Theresa took it over in the 1940s and began replacing the Carignane vines with Cabernet Sauvignon. In 1972 they sold out to the Likitprakong family, distillers in Thailand, who quadrupled the capacity to 600,000 gallons with stainless-steel tanks. The enologist is Fresno State–trained Robert Fredson, a fourth-generation member of the Sonoma family that for almost a century has operated the Fredson bulk winery on Dry Creek Road. The Cambiaso wines, available at the tasting room, range from white to red in bottles, magnums, and four-liter jugs.

America's first college-trained woman head winemaker, Mary Ann Graf, served at the Simi Winery near Healdsburg. She won her enology degree at UC Davis in 1965.

Between the Old Redwood Highway and the Russian River on the west are the 200-acre Foppiano Vineyard and million-gallon winery, which the descendants of John Foppiano from Genoa have owned since 1896. Louis Joseph Foppiano, the founder's grandson, switched during the 1960s from shipping bulk burgundy and chablis in tank cars to eastern bottlers to begin supplying "varietal" wines to other California wineries. The fourth generation of Foppianos, now in charge, have re-planted parts of the vineyard with additional noble grape variet-ies, and have built an attractive tasting room in the farmhouse where their father Louis was born. Their wines, under the Foppi-ano and Riverside Farm brands, have begun winning medals at the expertly judged Sonoma County Harvest Fair.

From the Foppiano winery it is a quarter-mile north to Healds-burg, the wine capital of Sonoma County. Healdsburg has cele-brated that fact since 1972 with its annual Russian River Wine Festival. On the festival day, a Sunday in mid-May, three dozen wineries set up tables in the town plaza and offer samples to those who buy tickets. The ticket buyers later go on from the plaza to the nearby wineries' tasting rooms, where the sampling is free. In 1976, *Wine West* publisher Mildred Howie organized the wineries as the "Russian River Wine Road" to co-sponsor the festival and issue maps showing their locations in the thirty-mile stretch between Guerneville and Cloverdale.

Nine wineries were operating within the Healdsburg city limits when I last made a count, but the number has changed from year to year. Largest is the million-gallon, century-old, onetime Scatena bulk winery on Grove Street, owned since 1940 by the Seghesio family, whose 300-acre vineyard is south of Cloverdale. In 1982 the Seghesios began bottling their own table wines, which include the only California chianti made of the classic Tuscan grape mixture of Sangiovese, Canaiolo, Malvasia, and Trebbiano. Second largest is the 450,000-gallon Clos du Bois cellar on Fitch Street, with its newly opened tasting room. Some

Clos du Bois wines are named for its vineyards (which total 1000 acres), such as Marlstone, Briarcrest, and River Oaks. On Plaza Street, in the center of town, is the aging and bottling cellar of former Foreign Service officer William Wheeler, whose vineyard and winery are on West Dry Creek Road, five miles away. Newest in town is the J. W. Morris winery, which was moved from Concord to Grant Avenue in Healdsburg in 1983 to make wine from Kenneth Toth's Black Mountain Vineyard grapes in Alexander Valley. On West North Street is the 12,000-gallon Toyon Vineyards winery, but winemaker Donald Holm says he plans soon to move the cellar to his vineyard on Highway 128. Also new is the Alderbrook Vineyard on Magnolia Lane.

On Healdsburg Avenue, a half-mile north of town, is the venerable stone million-gallon Simi Winery with its landscaped gardens, picnic area, and tasting room. It dates from 1876, when San Francisco wine dealers Giuseppe and Pietro Simi named it Montepulciano for the town in central Italy where they were born. Oilman and grape grower Russell Green bought it in 1970 from the late Isabelle Simi Haigh, renamed it Simi, and resold it four years later to a Scottish beer and whiskey firm. Since 1980 it has been a property of France's biggest wine and spirits company, Moët-Hennessy, which already owned the Domaine Chandon champagnery in the Napa Valley. In 1982, after making medal-winning wines from purchased grapes for eight years, Simi planted a hundred acres of vineyard land in the Alexander Valley, in order to begin calling its wines estate-bottled when the vineyards mature.

• 14 •

Beside the Highway 101 freeway, just north of the Windsor offramp, is the 50,000-gallon Landmark Vineyards winery, reached through an avenue of giant cypress trees. The winery was built in 1974, when winemaker William Mabry III was graduated from the UC Davis wine school. His father, a retired Air Force colonel, had embarked in winegrowing two years before, planting a hundred acres of premium grapes, some at his Sonoma home and some in the Alexander Valley. The Landmark specialties, Chardonnay, Cabernet, and Zinfandel, can be bought at the winery, but appointments are required for tasting and cellar tours.

Brooks Road, just east of the Landmark winery, winds three miles uphill to the 250-acre Balverne Vineyard, named for a village in Scotland by the group of California investors, headed by William Bird, who began planting this impressive estate in

1973. Construction of its 200,000-gallon winery began in 1979 under the supervision of UC Davis–trained winemaker Doug Nalle. One of its first wines in 1981 was a "varietal" of the rare Scheurebe grape, of which Balverne has twelve producing acres. It is a Sylvaner-Riesling cross named for its hybridizer in Germany, Dr. George Scheu. Another Balverne wine is Healdsburger, a Scheurebe-Riesling blend. Its first red wine, an oak-and-bottle-aged 1980 Zinfandel, was introduced in 1983, followed a year later by the 1981 Chardonnay. Originally part of the Sotoyome land grant which encompassed Windsor and Healdsburg, the 700-acre estate was owned early in the century by onetime Italian Swiss Colony winemaker Giulio Perelli-Minetti and later by M. L. Jacobs, inventor of the forklift. Bird says Balverne will feature estate-bottled wines with the Chalk Hill appellation, which the Federal government established in 1983.

On the west side of Chalk Hill Road, east of Balverne, are two more winegrowing estates, also planted since the early 1970s. A mile south of Spurgeon Road is San Francisco lawyers Frederick and Donna Furth's 200-acre Donna Maria Vineyard and its 65,000-gallon winery, built in 1980. The name came with the land and was kept because Mrs. Furth's name is Donna and his mother's name is Maria. "Chalk Hill Winery" is their second label. The Donna Maria wines thus far are Chardonnay, Sauvignon Blanc, Cabernet Sauvignon, and a limited quantity of a late-harvest, botrytized Sémillon.

Three miles north of Donna Maria are the 69-acre, mostly-Cabernet vineyard and the 200,000-gallon peach-colored winery built in 1980 by San Francisco businessman Stephen Zellerbach, a nephew of the ambassador who founded the Hanzell Vineyard. This Zellerbach prefers Bordeaux-style red wines, and his first estate-bottled releases in 1983 were Cabernet Sauvignon and Merlot. The appellation on the Zellerbach labels is Alexander Valley, the southern boundary of which includes the Zellerbach Vineyard. Vice president of the winery is his wife, the former Cecile "Cici" Nervo, whose family once owned the pre-Prohibition Nervo winery near Geyserville. The winemaker is UC Davis–trained John Jaffray.

• 15 •

When in 1959 Russell Green planted his first fifty acres of vines in the Alexander Valley, there was only one winery in that ten-mile-long valley, east of Asti and Healdsburg between the Russian River and Highway 128. Several wineries had operated in the area in the late 1880s and early 1900s, but most of the vineyards had been replaced during Prohibition by prune orchards and livestock farms. Since the wine revolution, most of the valley has become carpeted with vineyards, and by 1983 the number of wineries had increased to nine.

In 1973, the Demostene family, who had owned the inactive pre-Prohibition Soda Rock bulk winery, converted a prune dehydrator into the 100,000-gallon Sausal Winery, named for a nearby creek, equipped it with stainless-steel tanks, and began making vintage-dated Zinfandel.

While the Demostenes were starting their Sausal Winery, Harry (Hank) Wetzel III was still a year from winning his degree in enology at UC Davis. His father, Harry Jr., was superintending construction of their 65,000-gallon Alexander Valley Vineyards winery, which was finished in time for the 1975 crush. Two years later, the Wetzels released the first estate-bottled wines from their 120 acres of vineyards, planted since 1963. When Hank's sister Katie finished her studies in agricultural economics at Davis, she took charge of marketing the wines, which include Chardonnay, Chenin Blanc, Gewürztraminer, Riesling, Cabernet, and Pinot Noir. There is daily tasting, and visitors can see, uphill from the winery, the family graveyard of Cyrus Alexander, the Rocky Mountains trapper who came here in 1841 to manage the Sotoyome land grant, and for whom the valley is named.

Across the road and north of the Wetzels is the Johnson brothers' Rancho Sotoyome winery, also opened in 1975. Tom, Jay, and county supervisor Will Johnson salvaged equipment from older wineries to begin bottling wine in their rebuilt barn. Tom, a veteran home winemaker, had worked for two years learning to make wine on a commercial scale. They also bought a huge theater pipe organ from a church near Sacramento to adorn their tasting room, where there are monthly concerts by guest artists.

A quarter-mile southeast of the Wetzels is the partly underground Field Stone Winery, built in 1977 by Wallace Johnson, the former mayor of Berkeley and pioneer maker of grape-harvesting machines. All you can see of the 30,000-gallon winery is its front stone wall, in which there is an arched redwood door. All the rest, the stainless-steel fermenting and oak aging casks, the centrifuge and the bottling, are hidden inside a sylvan knoll that borders the 140 acres of vineyards. When Johnson died in 1979, his son-in-law, the Rev. Dr. John C. Staten, came from the Bay Area with his wife Katrina and became the first

Presbyterian minister to manage a winery. (He still teaches courses part time at the Presbyterian Theological Seminary at San Anselmo.) Microbiologist Jim Thomson is the winemaker. Field Stone is best known for its Cabernet Sauvignon, Riesling, and Gewürztraminer.

The newest winery in Alexander Valley is the Hafner family's modern reconstruction of the legendary winery, built in 1893, for which Red Winery Road is named. When University of California public affairs officer Richard Hafner and his wife Mary decided to build a winery on their hundred-acre vineyard, they copied its design from an old photograph of the original barn-red winery that once stood at the intersection with Pine Flat Road. When it was finished in 1982, their son Parke and his wife Sarah, both recent graduates of UC Davis, moved into the upper floor of the winery in time to make that season's vintage of Hafner wines.

From Alexander Valley Road, three miles north of Healdsburg, a two-lane private road winds uphill through oak groves to a champagne-yellow château with a red tile roof and red-shuttered windows edged in cut stone. The exterior suggests a Bordeaux château, though neither France nor any other winegrowing country has a winery quite like this. Inside are batteries of shiny temperature-controlled stainless-steel fermenting tanks, rows of upright American and European-oak casks, and thousands of oak barrels, bungs at their sides, standing seven tiers high.

This and the 270-acre vineyard (Cabernet Sauvignon, Merlot, Chardonnay) stretching north from Alexander Valley Road to Lytton Station Road comprise the Jordan Winery and Vineyard, which crushed its first 100,000-gallon vintage in 1976. The winery was built to hold a half-million gallons because four vintages would age here in oak and bottle to full maturity before the 1976 vintage of Jordan Cabernet Sauvignon would be released in 1980.

Thomas Nicholas Jordan, Jr., Illinois-born Denver geologist, athletic, dark-haired, amiable, and cigar-smoking, a friend of the Rothschilds, a director of the Banque National de Paris, world-traveled owner of the Filon Exploration Company, has long been an admirer of Bordeaux clarets. In 1970 he had decided to buy a château in Bordeaux when on one of his occasional visits to San Francisco he was discussing Bordeaux vintages with a waiter at Ernie's Restaurant. The waiter asked whether he had tasted any California Cabernets. Jordan had not.

"When I had my first taste of a twelve-year-old private reserve

Beaulieu Cabernet," says Jordan, "I realized I wouldn't have to cross the ocean to visit my château if I could build one in California; so that's what I did."

Jordan tasted more California Cabernets with bottle-age before he made up his mind. He consulted André Tchelistcheff, who had made the great Beaulieu wine, and assigned Davis-trained J. Michael Rowan to plant his vineyard where there had been orchards of prunes. Tall, charming, blue-eyed Sally Jordan, a former English teacher, discussed with architect Robert Arrigoni and designer Richard Keith how a winery exterior could express the quality of a fine California Cabernet. The design they chose includes apartment suites at the north end of the winery to house distinguished visiting buyers of wine, and a kitchen where French chefs prepare memorable luncheons and dinners. A quarter-mile to the north, they have built their French country-style home.

The decision to release no Cabernet until it had been aged for four years was Jordan's because, he said, "All this will be for nothing unless we grow a great wine." This also applied to their first white, an estate-bottled Chardonnay released in 1981. The Jordan Winery can be visited by appointment.

When I last visited the Alexander Valley, I found the century-old Soda Rock bulk winery active again. Transylvania-born Charles Tomka, Charles Jr., and their wives were making wine there and selling "Charlie's Country Wines" in an improvised tasting room.

• 16 •

Westside Road takes you west under the freeway from Mill Street in Healdsburg and turns south to six wineries along the west bank of the Russian River. On your right, a mile from the freeway, is the 76,000-gallon Mill Creek Vineyards winery, a family operation of Charles and Vera Kreck with their sons and daughters-in-law. On their seventy-acre vineyard they equipped a former cattle barn with stainless-steel tanks and oak barrels in time to produce their first estate-bottled "varietal" wines in 1975. During their second vintage, because of the white-wine boom, they tried to make a white wine of their Cabernet grapes, but the white juice picked up a reddish instead of a golden tinge, yet wasn't pink enough to be sold as a rosé. Wine writer Jerry Mead happened by, tasted the wine, and at his suggestion they named it Cabernet Blush.

Next south, at number 2201, are four buildings high on a hillside, three of them geodesic domes, that are the 24,000-gallon Hultgren & Samperton Winery. Each is at a different level so that the wine flows by gravity from the production dome to the conventional-style barrel-aging building, to the laboratory and bottling in the downhill domes. Winemaker Ed Samperton had a decade's experience in Burgundy, then made prize-winning wines for two northern Sonoma wineries before this one was built in 1978. His partner, J. Leonard Hultgren, is a New York advertising executive.

A mile farther, on your right, is the 6000-gallon Belvedere winery, built on a fourteen-acre vineyard in 1981 by Peter Friedman, the former advertising executive who created the first personalized labels for Rodney Strong's Tiburon Vintners. Friedman's new partner is investment banker William Hambrecht. They label their wines with the names of such well-known northern Sonoma vineyardists as Robert Young of Alexander Valley and Healdsburg dentist Roger Bacigalupi, whose grapes they buy.

Around a curve on your left is a three-towered stone hop kiln. It is a state historical monument to Sonoma County's one-time hopgrowing industry, which died after the Second World War when American brewers cut down the hoppy bitterness of their beers. Its two lower floors house physician-conservationist Dr. Loyal Martin Griffin's 35,000-gallon Hop Kiln Winery, which he bonded in 1975 because his friends wanted to buy some of the homemade wines he had produced there since buying the surrounding seventy-acre vineyard seventeen years before. Hop Kiln estate-bottled "varietals" such as Zinfandel are frequent medal-winners at the Harvest Fair, but better known are his "A Thousand Flowers," a Riesling-Colombard blend, and "Marty Griffin's Big Red," made from four unidentified black varieties that have grown since the 1880s in a corner of the vineyard. In 1979 Dr. Griffin began making a champagne that he named "Verveux Méthode Champenoise."

Another mile south and uphill from the "River Bend Ranch" sign on your right is a onetime hop kiln that has lost its drying tower. This has been former newspaperman Davis Bynum's winery since he moved in 1973 from his first one, started in the rear of a store near Berkeley eight years before. His wines are mostly "varietals," but he is also famous for a young red he once named "Bynum's Barefoot Burgundy" as a spoof on big wineries' fluffy advertisements.

• 17 •

Ten miles of vineyards line the Dry Creek Valley between Healdsburg, where the creek joins the Russian River, to Lake Sonoma, created by the building of Warm Springs Dam. If you enter the valley on Dry Creek Road from northern Healdsburg, the first structure on your left is the 300,000-gallon Fredson bulk winery, which dates from 1890, on the Fredson family's seventy-acre vineyard.

A mile farther on your right you will see a mass of shiny stainless-steel tanks without any sign to indicate who the owners are. They comprise the Gallo Sonoma winery, which began as the Frei Brothers' wooden cellar in 1880, and which has been enlarged to 6.4 million gallons since its purchase in 1976 by Gallo of Modesto from the heirs of Walter and Louis Frei. Here Gallo ferments some of the grapes of Sonoma Co-op members and those from the thousand acres of premium varieties the Gallos have planted since the late 1970s along Frei Road, northeast of Graton, where the Freis once had their apple orchards. From here came the first and widely praised "Wine Cellars of Ernest and Julio Gallo" Cabernet Sauvignon, which was introduced in 1982. Aged in oak at Modesto, the Cabernet bore no vintage date, although it could have because it was made entirely of the 1978 crop. When a second batch of the Cabernet appeared a year later with a "Vintage 1978" label, it was the first Gallo wine ever to show the year it was produced. The words "estate-bottled" may also be added to the labels of future vintages if Gallo begins aging and bottling some of its wines here, as its Sonoma neighbors expect. This, however, awaits Federal approval of a "Northern Sonoma" appellation, which was proposed by Gallo and other growers in 1982.

Across and north from the Frei driveway, Lambert Bridge Road passes the small vineyard and 6000-gallon winery of German-born enological consultant Robert Stemmler, and at your left is the 100,000-gallon Dry Creek Vineyard winery. A visit to France in 1970 inspired David Stare, a civil-engineering graduate from the Massachusetts Institute of Technology, with the idea of someday owning a Médoc-style winegrowing estate. He came to California after a disappointing try at growing French hybrid grapes in Maryland, took graduate courses in viticulture at UC Davis, bought this Dry Creek Valley site, and planted fifty acres of premium grapes on the former prune orchard. In 1972 he began building his chateau, bought grapes for his first few vintages, and within three years was producing medal-winning wines. Dry Creek Vineyard welcomes visitors. There is space for tasting in the winery entrance, where you can buy Stare's premium wines and also some inexpensive blends under his Idlewood brand.

Across the creek and a short distance south on West Dry Creek Road is the 40,000-gallon winery built in 1976 by Gerard Barnes Lambert, a scion of the St. Louis pharmaceutical firm. He designed the cellar especially to produce estate-bottled Cabernet and Chardonnay from the eighty-acre vineyard he planted seven years before. To avoid confusion about which was here first, he named the winery Lambert Bridge instead of for himself. Lambert and his wife Margaret have a home across the road.

Near the valley's southern end is the 20,000-gallon Bellerose Vineyard winery, opened in 1979 by former music professor Charles Richard and his wife Nancy, on the site where in 1887 Captain Everett Wise built a stone cellar with two-foot-thick walls. They replanted fifty acres of the old vineyard with classic Bordeaux grape varieties and by 1982 were selling vintage-dated Cabernet and rosé.

More wineries can be reached from the northern half of West Dry Creek Road. On your left, past Lambert Bridge, is the 10,000-gallon Rafanelli winery in a onetime storage barn. Americo Rafanelli, who once produced only bulk wine, now makes estate-bottled Cabernet and Gamay from his twenty-five acres of grapes.

If you turn left on Wine Creek Road you can see, beside the large oak trees on your right, the site of Domaine Michel, the mission-style winery being built for Tom Jordan's Swiss banker friend from Geneva, Jean-Jacques Michel. Jordan's viticulturist Michael Rowan planted the fifty-acre vineyard in 1980 for Michel with Cabernet, Merlot, Cabernet Franc, and Chardonnay. The Jordan winery was to make the 1983 vintage, but Rowan planned to have Domaine Michel crush its own grapes by 1984.

A few miles farther north is the Preston Vineyards winery. Young Stanford business school graduate Louis Preston spent a year studying viticulture and enology before he and his wife Susan began making wine in a former prune dehydrator beside his family's old Zinfandel vineyard in 1975. He planted forty more acres of grapes, and by 1982 Preston estate-bottled wines were selling so well that a new 30,000-gallon cellar was built, with three cupolas on its roof.

Beyond the Preston winery, West Dry Creek Road approaches a dead end. High on a hillside at your left is the 5,000-gallon Duxoup Wine Works. "The first thing we'd ever built was our house here, and that work was duck soup," explain winemakers Andy and Deborah Cutter, "so that's the name we chose." Equally improbable is Deborah's career. After rearing four children, she studied fermentation science at UC Davis and in England, worked in a brewery, held winemaker jobs in two Sonoma County wineries, and now works part time for another in Napa Valley. Andy sells Duxoup Syrah and Gamay to restaurants and stores.

• 18 •

Off ramps of Freeway 101 north from Healdsburg past Geyserville lead to a dozen more wineries, both new and old. The Lytton Springs exit takes you west to an old fifty-acre Zinfandel and Petite Sirah vineyard at the intersection of Chiquita Lane. Some of the best Zinfandels sold in the early 1970s by the Ridge Vineyard of Cupertino were made of grapes from this Lytton Springs Vineyard. Then a group headed by Dee Sindt, editor of *Wine World* magazine, bought the vineyard and built the Lytton Springs winery across the road. Mississippi-born winemaker Bura Walters has made each vintage there since 1977.

The Independence Lane exit, farther north, leads west and uphill to the architecturally appealing 3.3 million-gallon Souverain Cellar, which was designed to resemble a hop kiln, and to its Souverain Restaurant and tasting room, from which you get an excellent view of the Alexander Valley to the east. In summer, the fountain in front of the winery becomes a stage, and the courtyard serves as an outdoor theater for dramatic and musical events.

This is the third winery to be named Souverain since 1970. J. Leland Stewart first gave the name to a winery east of St. Helena that has now become Burgess Cellars. A group of Napa Valley vineyard owners, who bought that winery from Stewart and sold it to Tom Burgess, built two entirely new Souverain wineries, naming this one "Souverain of Alexander Valley" and another, in the Napa Valley, "Souverain of Rutherford." While this Souverain winery was being built during 1972, the Pillsbury flour-milling firm of Minneapolis ventured into the wine business, guided by the late Frank Schoonmaker, and bought both of the new Souverain wineries. Three years later, Pillsbury had lost millions on its wine venture and offered the two Souverains for sale. Owners of St. Helena's Freemark Abbey cellar bought "Souverain of Rutherford" and renamed it the Rutherford Hill Winery. This "Souverain of Alexander Valley" was purchased in 1976 by North Coast Cellars, a group of some 200 grape growers who have 10,000 acres of vineyards in Sonoma, Napa, and Mendocino counties. The winery makes many wines for independent growers and merchants and bottles them under dozens of different brands, but makes a score of "varietals" under its own name that are sold throughout the nation and abroad.

Across the freeway from Souverain, Independence Lane leads to the 200-acre Trentadue Vineyard and 200,000-gallon Trentadue Winery. Leo and Evelyn Trentadue grew grapes in the Santa Clara Valley before they came to Sonoma County and built their winery and tasting room in 1969. Their labels display the number "32," which is *trentadue* in Italian.

Back on Freeway 101, a short drive north takes you to the Canyon Road exit, where you go west and take a right turn on Chianti Road to the 2.5-million-gallon Geyser Peak Winery, on the hill to your left. It doesn't look its size; a pipeline under the freeway connects it with the forest of tanks on the other side. The original wood and fieldstone structure dates from 1880, when one August Quitzow built it as both a winery and a brandy distillery. There were several later owners, including Dante and William Bagnani, who made Four Monks vinegar here after the repeal of Prohibition, and the Schlitz (later Stroh) Brewing Company, which bought Geyser Peak in 1972 and transformed it into a chateau-like showplace with stained-glass windows, a flagstone terrace, a fountain guarded by high black-iron gates, and a visitor center hosting summer brown-bag operas.

During the Schlitz and Stroh breweries' ownership, Geyser Peak pioneered bag-in-box wines in 1975 under its Summit brand, and also experimented with six-packs of canned wines. Since its purchase in 1982 by the banking and grape-growing Henry Trione family of Santa Rosa, Geyser Peak has featured estate-bottled vintage wines, some under the Trione name, from the 1100 acres of Sonoma vineyards that the family owns. There also are Brut and Blanc de Noirs *méthode champenoise* sparkling wines and a pair of "soft" (8.5 percent) wines, Riesling and Chenin Blanc. John McClelland, who formerly headed Almadén Vineyards, became the president of Geyser Peak in 1983. Armand Bussone, who came to Geyser Peak from Almadén in the 1970s, makes all the wines. Henry Trione and his sons, Mark and Victor, are teammates on the Geyser Peak Polo Team.

On Canyon Road, a mile west of the freeway, is the 640,000-gallon Pedroncelli Brothers' Winery. John and James Pedroncelli took over their father's hillside vineyard and small wooden bulk-wine cellar in 1955, when John completed a short course in enology at UC Davis. In the following year, the brothers bottled three of their wines and entered them in the state fair. To their surprise, all three won medals, silvers for their burgundy and rosé, and bronze for their Zinfandel. This attracted the notice of San Francisco wine merchant and importer Henry Vandervoort, Bordeaux-born, who was looking for a new supply of bulk wines good enough to bottle for his restaurant customers under their private labels. The Pedroncelli wines bottled by Vandervoort sold so well that the brothers began bottling some under their own name. When Vandervoort saw them making their rosé entirely of Zinfandel, he suggested they give it a varietal name. In 1958 it became California's first Zinfandel Rosé to win commercial fame. The brothers doubled their father's sixty acres with such classic varieties as Cabernet Sauvignon and Pinot Noir. They added an extra cellar for aging wines in oak casks and a tasting room, and have continued winning awards at the Pomona Fair.

Chianti Road, paralleling the freeway, leads to two more wineries. The first, built in 1902, is on the 350-acre Seghesio Vineyard, which once was part of the Italian Swiss Colony. This is where Eugene and Edward Seghesio age the wines they make in their Healdsburg cellar. Their office is the transplanted onetime Chianti railroad station.

Next is the 100,000-gallon Lyeth Vineyard winery, a steepled two-story French provincial chateau with guest suites around a landscaped courtyard, built in 1982. The owners, headed by former Santa Barbara air racer and restaurateur Munro L. "Chip" Lyeth (pronounced Leeth), planned to introduce the first wines from their hundred-acre vineyard in 1984, a classic Cabernet blend and a white of Sauvignon Blanc and Sémillon, both simply named "Lyeth."

• 19 •

At the village of Asti, across the freeway, a resurrection is occurring at the 10-million-gallon Italian Swiss Colony winery, which was shut down in 1982 as it approached its centenary, which would be in 1987. A new owner, the ISC Wines subsidiary of Allied Grape Growers, is reopening the winery and the huge Swiss chalet tasting room that had welcomed tourists for half a century, when the Heublein liquor conglomerate abruptly closed the whole place down.

ISC Wines is reviving the Italian Swiss Colony name, remembered by millions from its "little old winemaker" TV commercials of the 1960s and 1970s. Heublein had shrunk the name to "Colony" after buying the winery from United Vintners in 1968. ISC Wines has also brought back winemaker Edmund A. Rossi, Jr., a son and grandson of the Rossis who made Italian Swiss wines famous before and after Prohibition. He had worked during the preceding decade at the Heublein winery in the San Joaquin Valley.

Untouched by the successive ownership changes is the famous little "church shaped like a wine barrel" built in 1907, because it stands on adjoining land donated by the archbishop of San Francisco.

The Colony's early history was that of a philanthropic farming venture, started by San Francisco grocer-turned-banker Andrea Sbarboro in 1880 to settle penniless Italian and Swiss immigrant farmers on land where they could support themselves by growing grapes. Each worker would be given board, room, and wine for his daily use and would be paid monthly wages of $35, but $5 would be deducted each month for the purchase of stock in the Colony, which would make him an independent vineyard owner in twenty-five years. Vines were planted, and the place was named Asti for the resemblance of the hills to those around Asti and Canelli in the Italian Piedmont. The colonists, however, refused to allow the deduction from their wages; they preferred dollars in hand to independence in the future. Sbarboro accepted defeat, and the Colony became a private vineyard venture. A winery was built in 1887, but the first vintage turned to vinegar. Sbarboro then persuaded one of the Colony's supporters, San Francisco druggist Pietro C. Rossi, to take charge. A graduate in pharmacy of the University of Turin, Rossi knew the principles of winemaking, and under him the Colony prospered for two decades. Before the turn of the century, Asti wines were winning medals for excellence in Europe and America, and were being shipped in barrels to Europe, South America, China, and Japan. The Colony acquired more vineyards and wineries at nearby Fulton and Sebastopol, at Clayton in Contra Costa County, and at Madera, Kingsburg, and Lemoore in the San Joaquin Valley.

During a price war in 1897, Rossi kept surplus Sonoma wine off the market by building at Asti what was then the world's biggest underground wine tank. Made of concrete, it held 300,000 gallons. Its completion before the vintage was celebrated with dancing inside the tank to the music of a military band. The tank was still in use in 1982.

Sbarboro and Rossi erected elegant villas for their families and entertained famous personages from around the world.

When Rossi's twin sons, Edmund and Robert, finished their studies at the University of California, the family celebrated with a trip through Europe. While in France, Pietro Rossi met champagne maker Charles Jadeau of Saumur and persuaded him to come to Asti. Two years later, Jadeau's Golden State Extra Dry Champagne won the grand prix at the Turin international exposition.

Tipo Chianti red and white, bottled in raffia-covered Italian *fiaschi*, were the Colony's most popular wines, but the Italian government objected to an American wine being called chianti. In 1910 the Colony renamed the wines "Tipo Red" and "Tipo White," not to please Italy, but to stop other wineries from calling their wines "Tipo." This four-letter word in Italian means "type" or "imitation," but in one of the quirks of wine nomenclature, it became the American name for any wine in a chianti flask. The original Tipo Red was a tannic, long-lived wine unlike Italian chiantis, which are softened by blending white grapes with red. The 1914 Tipo, which was served at a Wine and Food Society banquet in the San Francisco Stock Exchange Club in 1936, was one of the best pre-Prohibition California wines.

Pietro Rossi was killed in a horse-and-buggy accident in 1911. Two years later, the Italian Swiss Colony was taken over by the California Wine Association. In 1920 came the next disaster, Prohibition. Sbarboro had fought the Drys to the last. His solution for intemperance was to encourage the drinking of wine instead of hard liquor. Chronic drunkards, he said, should be jailed for thirty days and given dry wine with their meals, and if not cured should be given the same treatment for sixty days more. His disparagement of liquor so annoyed some whiskey distillers that they attempted a boycott of the Colony's wines.

During Prohibition, Edmund and Robert Rossi with vineyard superintendent Enrico Prati bought back the Colony from the CWA and supplied grapes, juice, and concentrate to home winemakers until Repeal. The Rossi twins foresaw the failure of Prohibition, and it was they who in 1931 led the old-time California winegrowers in forming the Grape Growers League, which became the Wine Institute three years later.

During the years before the Second World War, the Italian Swiss Colony under the Rossis became the third largest wine company in the nation, with its La Paloma Winery near Fresno using the surplus grapes of Joseph di Giorgio's vast vineyards in the San Joaquin Valley. When the whiskey distillers invaded the wine industry during the war, National Distillers bought the Colony and added another winery, Shewan-Jones at Lodi.

Thence came the French-sounding name, Lejon, for the Colony's brandy and champagnes; Lejon was a contraction of the name of Lee Jones, the kindly, crusty former revenue inspector who founded Shewan-Jones.

When the Rossi brothers retired, Edmund became the manager of the Wine Advisory Board and guided its national program of wine education until 1960. And the brothers' sons, working for Heublein during the 1970s, were still concerned with Italian Swiss wines; Edmund Jr. supervised the making of the excellent Colony Classic wines after the mid-1970s, and Robert Jr. was in charge of Heublein wine production.

During the 1970s, the huge winery at Asti mainly aged and bottled Heublein brandies and made mostly the Colony and Inglenook Navalle "varietal" table wines. It briefly again made red Tipo, which had regained some of its old-time flavor. At the rising cost of labor, the hand-wrapped Tipo bottle cost more than the wine inside.

Most ISC wines are now being produced at its three wineries in the San Joaquin Valley, but at Asti it is expected in the future to produce premium estate-bottled, vintage-dated "varietal" table wines from grapes grown in northern Sonoma and Mendocino counties.

The story of the Colony's purchase by Louis Petri, then by Heublein—which was merged in 1982 with R. J. Reynolds (tobacco)—and of the events that created the new ISC Wines firm in 1983, will be told in Chapter 19.

· 20 ·

From Asti, Washington School Road winds east across the Russian River to River Road, where there are two more wineries. A quarter-mile south of the School Road intersection is comic Pat Paulsen's thirty-five-acre vineyard and the modern 55,000-gallon winery that he and his wife Betty Jane bonded in 1980. Pat's favorite wine is their Muscat Canelli, but they also produce estate-bottled Sauvignon Blanc and Cabernet. Their winemaker is T. James Meves, who also makes wine for his relatives, the Rowland family, at their Pacheco Ranch Winery in Marin County.

Two miles north, facing River Road on your left, are the fifty-acre vineyard and 100,000-gallon Cordtz Brothers winery, which former journalist and history professor William Cordtz and his family bonded in 1979. This once was the David Hall winery, founded in 1905. Here, during the 1950s, the late vineyardist

Hollis Black produced the first estate-bottled premium "varietal" wines to come from a small northern Sonoma County winery after Repeal.

From an interchange on Freeway 101 north of Asti and six miles south of Cloverdale, Dutcher Creek Road points south toward the Dry Creek Valley. At your left, past the turn, you may see the Diamond Oaks Vineyard tasting room, which was to be built in 1984 beside the winery which the Alfonso Rege family founded in 1939 to make bulk wine for San Francisco restaurants. South San Francisco realtor Dinesh Maniar, born in Bombay, and his wife Judith, who own 400 acres of vineyards in Sonoma and Napa counties, bought the old winery from an interim owner in 1982 and enlarged it to 200,000 gallons to make their Diamond Oaks and Thomas Knight premium wines.

At your right, two miles south, is San Francisco customs broker Arthur J. Fritz's new, completely underground 60,000-gallon Fritz Cellars. The two-level winery, designed and built by manager Christopher Stone, was opened in time to release its 1980 Chardonnay and 1981 Fumé Blanc. If passing traffic here seems sparse, note that by 1985 a million visitors per year are expected to visit a new recreational attraction nearby—Lake Sonoma, created by the lately completed Warm Springs Dam.

Hiatt Road, a mile north of Dutcher Creek Road, leads west to San Francisco psychiatrist Douglass Cartwright's 4000-gallon Jade Mountain Winery and vineyard. The place is named for the mass of unpolished jade Dr. Cartwright once dreamed of finding, but never found, on Mount Alice nearby. The gate to the winery is kept locked except when the doctor, his psychologist wife Lillian, and their four children are there.

Downhill from the Cartwrights, a sign facing Hiatt Road from an eight-acre patch of Chardonnay vines reads "Icaria Vineyard." This sign, and the name of Icaria Creek on the map of Sonoma County, are the sole visible reminders that a communistic colony of French winegrowers operating five wineries flourished along this road from the 1880s until the early years of Prohibition. The Icarians who settled in Sonoma County were remnants of the utopian communistic sect that Etienne Cabet led in 1849 from France to Nauvoo, Illinois. There (as related in an earlier chapter) they planted vineyards and continued producing wine long after Cabet abandoned the Nauvoo Icarian colony in 1856. San Franciscans Russell and Catherine Clark named their vineyard for the Icarians to preserve this long-forgotten chapter of Sonoma wine history.

A mile beyond the Dutcher Creek interchange, the freeway

ends and you enter Cloverdale, a wine town that celebrates an annual citrus fair. A mile farther, Cherry Creek Road leads a block west, to where the late Emil Bandiera opened a small winery in 1937 to make red wine that he sold by the barrel and in jugs. His son and grandson ran it until 1980, when a group of coast-counties vineyard-owning investors headed by Adolph Mueller II bought and rebuilt it to hold 300,000 gallons and named it the California Wine Company. They make and bottle wines under such labels as Bandiera, Arroyo Sonoma, Sage Creek, Potter Valley, and John H. Merritt. The latter is the winemaker and manager, the brother-in-law and former partner of the Gundlach-Bundschu winery's Jim Bundschu.

• 21 •

Three miles beyond Cloverdale, still following the Russian River, you enter Mendocino, northernmost of the important coastal wine counties. For more than a century, Mendocino, like northern Sonoma, produced mainly bulk wines, but since the 1960s, premium wine-grape planting has increased its vineyards to almost 11,000 acres and made it one of the fine-wine districts of the state. There were only six wineries in the county when I prepared the first edition of this book in 1973. They now number twenty-six.

One of the newest is the 5,000-gallon Mountain House Winery, which former Chicago antitrust lawyer Ronald Lipp installed in 1980, in the garage beside an old farmhouse at the intersection of Highway 128 and Mountain House Road, five miles north of Cloverdale. A vacation spent working at a Napa winery, and enology courses he took at UC Davis, convinced Lipp that winemaking would be more satisfying than his lawyering career.

On the west side of Highway 101, a mile south of Hopland, is an old hop kiln with a "Wine Tasting" sign outside. This is Jim and Mary Milone's 20,000-gallon Milano Winery, so named, he explains, "because Milano is easier to spell and pronounce than Milone." If you approached Hopland on Mountain House Road, you might have noticed Jim's father's Sanel Valley Vineyard of Chenin Blanc, Petite Sirah, Cabernet Sauvignon, Carignane, and Zinfandel, which supplies the grapes to make Milano wines.

Take Route 175 four miles east from Hopland to see Mendocino County's most spectacular winery. It is the 240,000-gallon McDowell Vineyards Cellars, said to be the first solar-heated and cooled winery in the world. Built in 1979, by former mechanical engineer and military flier Richard Keehn and his wife Karen on their meticulously groomed 360-acre vineyard, it is open to visitors by appointment, Thursdays to Sundays. There are exhibits and frequent concerts and art shows. The second-floor balconied tasting room is adorned by five kinds of sculptured Mendocino woods. Their ten estate-bottled wines, made in the ultramodern cellars by UC Davis graduate George Bursick, have already begun winning medals. The winery name on their labels is also their viticultural-area appellation, the sixth approved by the government in 1982. The microclimate of the valley, settled by gold-seeker Paxton McDowell in the mid-1850s, is classed as Region II.

In downtown Hopland there are two tasting rooms, both for the same winery. The large one at the left, the onetime Hopland High School gymnasium, was bought by the Fetzer winery (whose story is told later) in 1976 as a "Mendocino Wine Country" exhibit and souvenir shop. A block farther on the right is the Bel Arbres tasting room, representing a second brand of Fetzer wine.

Three miles north of Hopland, the venerable white farmhouse you see on your left was opened in 1983 as a tasting room for the as yet unfinished Baccala or Fawn's Glen Vineyard winery, which is a hundred yards farther north. Newport Beach insurance expert William Baccala was building a 20,000-gallon, partly underground winery, expandable to five times that size, on the 140 acres of vineyard he had begun planting in 1976 on former grazing land.

Two miles farther north, McNab Road extends east two miles through vineyards to not one, but two separate wineries owned by members of the same family. One is the Tyland Vineyards 30,000-gallon rustic redwood cellar and tasting room, built in 1979 by Holland-born, former Martinez contractor Dick Tijsseling (pronounced Tyse-ling) and his wife Judy, who own thirty acres of vineyard, planted in 1972. A hundred yards away is the concrete-walled Tijsseling Family Vineyards winery, three times as large and also with a tasting room. Dick built it in 1981 for his parents, Herman and Alida Tijsseling, who own 200 acres of vines. Their winemaker, University of Belgrade–trained Miles Karakasevic, makes bottle-fermented champagnes, introduced in 1983.

• 22 •

From US 101, which soon becomes a freeway, take Route 253 west for a winding thirty-mile mountain drive via Boonville, Philo, and Route 128 to Mendocino's newest winegrowing district, the Anderson Valley. In its Region I climate, twelve miles from the ocean, are seven young wineries and an eighth about to be built for Champagne Roederer of France.

Three miles past Philo is the 25,000-gallon Navarro River Vineyards winery, opened on a thirty-five-acre vineyard in 1975 by former stereo systems marketer Edward Bennett and his partner, Deborah Cahn. Besides making five fine "varietal" wines, Bennett sells bottled fresh Gewürztraminer grape juice. He began bottling it in 1978 because his son was allergic to milk, and soon was getting orders for it from points as distant as the Virgin Islands. Because Gewürztraminer juice is spicy as well as sweet, it may become California's first successful competitor to the Labrusca grape juices of the East. Juices of most other Vinifera grapes are relatively bland in taste.

On the hilltop across the road to your left, and also with a tasting room, is the 75,000-gallon Edmeades winery, opened on a 35-acre vineyard by Deron Edmeades in 1972.

A half mile farther on your right, a narrow country lane winds southwest across two rickety bridges to the Lazy Creek Vineyard. Veteran Swiss-born and trained chef and banquet manager Johann Kobler and his wife Theresa began planting its twenty acres when they bought the land in 1973. Three years later, they bonded their 5000-gallon winery, which you may visit if you telephone ahead.

Across and west from the Koblers' entrance road are the twenty-five-acre Husch Vineyard with its 25,000-gallon winery and tasting room, which were the first to start in Anderson Valley when Tony and Gretchen Husch bonded the cellar in 1971. Eight years later, it was bought by Davis-trained winemaker and Ukiah Valley grape grower Hugo Oswald III. He has continued winning awards for the estate-bottled Husch Vineyard wines.

On both sides of the road, past the Husch Vineyard, are the sixty acres of Pinot Noir and Chardonnay that were being planted in 1983 for Champagne Roederer of Rheims, the third French champagne producer (after Moët-Hennessy and Piper Heidsieck) to invest in making champagne from California grapes. Its winery was to be built across the road from Husch in time to make the 1986 vintage. The site is part of the 584 acres that Roederer bought in 1982.

A quarter mile farther you will find Holmes Ranch Road climbing into the eastern hills. Uphill on your left, at number 1200, is the seven-acre Pepperwood Springs Vineyard and the 10,000-gallon winery that Larry and Nicki Parsons, who have a food business in Contra Costa County, bonded in 1981 to make their first vintage of Chardonnay. Larry says he has been blind from birth but had years of winemaking experience before the Parsons moved here with their two children in 1980. He is an expert mechanic, repairs their tractor, and moves around the vineyard without any help.

On Guntley Road, the next to the north, Davis-trained Milla Handley and her realtor husband, Rex McClellan, have bonded the thousand-gallon Handley Cellars beside their home. She uses grapes from her father's vineyard in Dry Creek Valley.

Graphic artist Allan Green's eight-acre Greenwood Ridge Vineyard winery, on a hilltop six miles from the Pacific, is said to be the westernmost in the United States, which seems likely when you notice how the map of California bulges westward at that point. More interesting than his location is his Riesling, the first (1980) vintage of which won gold and silver medals at the Orange and Los Angeles counties' competitions in the following year. His Cabernet, a blend with Merlot, was released in 1983. To visit his 6000-gallon winery, take Greenwood Road northwest from Highway 128 past Hendy Woods State Park and watch for the "Greenwood Vineyard" and "Allan Green" signs.

• 23 •

On State Street, north of Ukiah, is the ultramodern 2.5-million-gallon Cresta Blanca Winery, which was one-eighth that size when the Mendocino Growers Co-op built it in 1946. It is now owned by the Guild Wineries of Lodi, which in 1971 bought the Cresta Blanca name from Schenley Distillers, when the original Cresta Blanca winery near Livermore was closed. Displayed in the tasting room are fourteen table wines this winery makes of Mendocino and other coast-counties grapes. Also for sale here are all of the Cresta Blanca champagnes, dessert wines, and brandy that Guild makes in other parts of the state.

North of Cresta Blanca, on State Street adjoining the freeway where Highway 20 takes off north of Calpella, is the winery the Weibel family of Alameda County built here in 1972 to process the grapes from their 400 acres of Mendocino County vineyards. The wines made here go to the Weibel winery at Mission San Jose for finishing and bottling. Beside the winery is a tasting room, shaped like an upturned champagne glass, in which the dozens of Weibel wines and champagnes are displayed.

West of the freeway, three miles north of Ukiah, is the 1.5-

million-gallon Parducci Wine Cellars, the oldest and best-known winery in the county, with its Mediterranean-style tasting room and picnic grounds. Adolph Parducci opened the original winery at the repeal of Prohibition, selling most of his wine to the road-side trade and shipping the rest in tank trucks to vintners in the San Joaquin Valley. In 1964, his sons, John and George, entered the State Fair competition with a fresh, fruity dry wine of French Colombard, a grape name that had not appeared on a California label before. It won a silver medal, and mail orders for Parducci wines began coming from Bay Area gourmets. When the sons took over the business, they planted premium varieties in the family vineyard, added more acreage in the Talmage district, and embarked on a long-range fine-wine production plan. In 1973, majority ownership of the Parducci winery was bought by the Teachers Management Institute, with a membership of several thousand California schoolteachers. The new owners kept the Parducci brothers in charge of producing and marketing the wines.

Across the Russian River, on East Side Road, is the 10,000-gallon Whaler Vineyard winery, so named by Russ and Ann Nyborg because they sailed the Pacific whaling grounds on yachts and ocean tugboats before settling here with their three children in 1973, to plant their twenty-four-acre vineyard. They began building the winery eight years later, when their grapes were fully mature.

Four miles farther east is the 19,000-gallon Hidden Cellar, bonded in 1981 by grape buyer Dennis Patton and former forester Joe Rawitzer, and well named because it is at the bottom of a thickly wooded canyon, reached only by unpaved Mill Creek Road.

In a secluded western arm of nearby Redwood Valley, reached by Uva Drive and Bel Arbres Road, is the Fetzer Vineyards winery, which operates those two Hopland tasting rooms. Its capacity is 1.3 million gallons, six times the size of the winery the late Bernard Fetzer built in 1968. Kathleen, his widow, is proud that ten of their eleven offspring are running the business. John, the eldest, is president; Robert and Joe care for the 600 acres of surrounding vineyards; Jim manages the bottling room; daughters Mary Rodrigue and Patti handle the sales, Diane makes their champagne, Dan is the artist, Richard runs the trucks, and Teresa Oster has managed both of the tasting rooms. Some of the Fetzer wines bear the names of other growers who supply the Fetzers with additional grapes. One such grower is John

Scharffenberger, who also makes his own champagne and Eagle-point table wines in a cellar on Talmage Highway.

The Fetzers' head winemaker is Paul Dolan, who with his wife Lynne runs the 5000-gallon Dolan Vineyard winery on Inez Way, a mile to the north. They built it as a weekend project to carry on Paul's family tradition; he is a grandson of the late Edmund Rossi, Sr.

On Tomki Road, two miles north of the Dolans, is the thirty-acre "organic" Frey Vineyard, owned by physicians Paul and Marguerite Frey. After selling their grapes to wineries for thirteen years, they bonded the 4000-gallon Frey Vineyard winery in 1980, helped by five of their twelve children, and began selling seven vintage-dated "varietal" wines, two of them estate-bottled, the rest from purchased grapes. Son Jonathan is the winemaker; Matthew built the homemade stainless-steel tanks. Dr. Paul, born in New York, was a Lutheran preacher before he earned his medical degree at Indiana University, then was a government doctor to the Navajo Indians before practicing psychiatry at the Mendocino State Hospital. When it closed in 1972, he retired. Dr. Marguerite still practices medicine in Mendocino County.

Potter Valley, thirteen miles northeast of Ukiah, has several hundred acres of vineyards, many of them planted during the 1970s, and was recognized as a distinct viticultural area by the Federal government in 1983. Its first winery is the Braren & Pauli cellar, 6000 gallons of stainless-steel tanks and oak barrels bonded in 1979 in a former dairy barn on Hawn Creek Road, a mile west of the town. Geologist Larry Braren of Petaluma is the winemaker. Farmer Bill Pauli has thirty-five acres of young vines near the winery.

• 24 •

Lake County, reached by Highway 20 from Calpella, has begun to awaken to its glamorous winegrowing past. Its vineyard acreage has multiplied tenfold, from fewer than 300 acres in 1965 to more than 3000 by 1983. Four wineries have opened in the county during the past six years. Vintners in other counties are labeling some of their best wines to show that they are made of Lake County grapes.

Before Prohibition, Lake County had thirty-three wineries and 1000 acres of vines. Among its most famous winegrowers were California's first chief justice, Serranus Clinton Hastings, who owned the Carsonia Vineyard and Champagne Cellars at Upper Lake; Colonel Charles Mifflin Hammond, whose Ma Tel Vineyard at Nice on Clear Lake produced wines that won awards at the Paris Exposition in 1900; and the English actress Lillie Langtry, whose Guenoc Vineyard south of Middletown has lately been revived.

From where Highway 20 meets Route 29 at Upper Lake, a ten-mile drive past Lakeport will take you to Mathews Road and the handsome new 150,000-gallon Château du Lac or Kendall-Jackson winery, opened in 1981 by Burlingame attorney Jess Jackson and his wife, the former Jane Kendall, on the ninety-five-acre vineyard they began planting with premium wine grapes seven years before. Their winemaker is UC Davis–trained Jed Steele, who came from the Edmeades Vineyard in 1982.

Two miles farther south, on the east side of Route 29, is the 200,000-gallon Konocti Winery and tasting room, built in 1979 by Lake County Vintners, a group of two dozen neighboring grape growers whose vineyards now total 500 acres. In 1983, plans to triple the winery's size were announced, with Ukiah vintners John and George Parducci as equal partners with the growers' group. Since California-born winemaker William Pease came here from the Colcord Winery in Kentucky, his Konocti wines have won two dozen medals in quality competitions.

Another seventeen miles brings you to the 10,000-gallon Lower Lake Winery on your right, a mile past the town of Lower Lake. When it opened in 1977, it was the county's first new winery to start since the Prohibition era. Alhambra orthopedic surgeon Dr. Harry Stuermer and his wife Marjorie financed the redwood building, its stainless-steel tanks and oak barrels, for their winemaker son Daniel, his wife Betty, Dan's sister Harriet, and her husband, Tom Scavone.

Twenty-five more miles take you past Middletown, and on Butts Canyon Road to the 100,000-gallon Guenoc Winery, on a hilltop to your left. If you phone ahead for an appointment, you can visit there and learn the romantic story of the celebrated beauty Lillie Langtry, who bought Guenoc Ranch in 1888, brought a vigneron from Bordeaux, and sold wine with her portrait on every bottle until she sold the place in 1906. Since 1963, the ranch has been owned by the Magoon family of Hawaii, who have replanted the vineyard, restored Lillie's home, and built the winery in 1981. In that year, Guenoc Winery, with its 270-acre vineyard on the 23,000-acre Guenoc Ranch, became the first American winery with a federally approved viticultural-area appellation of its own. (The next Lake County appellation may be "Clear Lake," for the vineyards surrounding the lake.)

Humboldt County, north of Mendocino and Lake, thus far has only a few acres of grapes, but has four wineries of a few thousand gallons each in and around Eureka, the county seat. Dr. J. Roy Wittwer's cellar, and mathematics teacher Robert Kirkpatrick's cellars, are in the city; oceanography instructor Robert Hodgson's is at Fieldbrook, and Dean Williams's is at McKinleyville. Hodgson and Williams have an acre or two of vines each, but most wines made in Humboldt County thus far have been made of Napa County grapes.

Professor Albert Winkler, the UC Davis viticulturist, searching for potential new premium grape districts, has found climates favorable for winegrowing in eastern Humboldt, around Alderport and Blocksburg. Dr. Winkler suggests that "a real adventurer might find it interesting" to plant vines on some of the slopes near the Hoopa Indian Reservation around Weitchpec, the steelhead fishermen's paradise on the upper Klamath River.

Someday the north coast wine district may stretch northward beyond Mendocino and Lake for another hundred miles.

14

Napa, the Winiest County

NAPA COUNTY, separated from Sonoma on the west by a spur of the Mayacamas mountain range, is the winiest county in the United States. It has more than 130 bonded wine cellars and 28,000 acres of vineyards, almost as many acres as Sonoma, which is twice Napa's size.

The Napa Valley, where most of the county's vineyards and wineries are, is only five miles wide and twenty-five miles long. Outside the town centers, the valley is an almost unbroken expanse of grapevines, a scene that is idyllic and unique.

Visitors come here from all over the world. Highway 29, which traverses the valley's west side, is known as The Wine Road, and it merits the name. On one twelve-mile stretch there are forty-three wineries, almost four per mile. The largest and some of the smaller ones welcome the public to tour their cellars and taste their wines. Tourists' cars on the road are bumper-to-bumper on most weekends. The visitors listen to the lectures the winery guides give, sip the samples offered afterward, and make purchases of the wines they like best. Some of the guests make a day of it, moving from one winery to the next and the next, until the tasting rooms close at four or five in the afternoon. The majority of the wineries receive visitors by appointment only. Some winery owners say they may someday begin to charge for parking or tasting, or even begin closing on weekends, in order to reduce the size of the crowds.

Meanwhile, the fame of Napa wines is spreading, in gourmet publications, in travel magazines, in the new wine books, on select wine lists, and on television dramas such as *Falcon Crest*. But, except for the motorized crowds and the modern media, this is really a repetition of their history, for Napa wines first became famous almost a century ago.

• 2 •

The Napa River, Napa County, and Napa city are named for the Napa Indians, one of the so-called Digger tribes who once lived there. "Napa" is said to mean "plenty" or "homeland," but some early records say it was originally the Indians' word for fish, which abounded then in the streams and supplemented their diet of roots, seeds, grasshoppers, and worms.

Some five thousand Indians inhabited the county before white settlers came from Sonoma during the 1830s. Forty years later, smallpox and bloody wars with the newcomers had reduced the Indians' numbers to scarcely a score. The wholesale slaughter of the Indians is commemorated in the grisly name that was given in 1839 to the Ranch Carne Humana land grant south of Calistoga: *Carne humana* is Spanish for "human flesh."

From Sonoma, the first settlers brought the Mission grape to Napa. In 1836, George Calvert Yount, the North Carolinian trapper and explorer, built his fortified log blockhouse two miles north of present-day Yountville and two years later planted Mission vines he brought from the Sonoma vineyard of General Mariano Vallejo. Yount's first vintage could have been in 1841. There is additional evidence that wine was being made at several locations in Napa County during the 1840s, but the earliest records available show Yount producing 200 gallons annually by 1844. Planting of the better imported grape varieties was begun about 1852 by William and Simpson Thompson on their Suscol land grant south of Napa city. In 1859, Samuel Brannan, the ex-Mormon millionaire of San Francisco, purchased three square miles at Calistoga and began planting choice cuttings he had collected on a tour through Europe.

Robert Louis Stevenson, honeymooning in the valley and writing his *Silverado Squatters* in 1880, described the Napa vintners' search for the best vineyard sites: "One corner of land after another is tried with one kind of grape after another," he wrote. "This is a failure; that is better; a third best. So, bit by bit, they grope about for their Clos Vougeot and Lafite . . . and the wine is bottled poetry."

By the late 1800s, there were 4000 acres of vines and 142 wineries in Napa County. In Napa city, the rivershore was lined with wineries, such as the Uncle Sam and Napa Valley cellars, from which wine was barged to San Francisco, much of it for shipment around Cape Horn to Atlantic ports. Connoisseurs in New York and San Francisco were already serving wines from the To Kalon Vineyard of Hamilton Crabb near Oakville, from the Inglenook Vineyard of Captain Niebaum at Rutherford, and from the vineyards of Charles Krug and Jacob Schram at St. Helena and Calistoga, to mention a few.

Napa vineyards covered 18,000 acres in 1891. Since then, like a magic green carpet, they have shrunk dramatically and spread repeatedly in response to alternating plagues and booms.

The phylloxera plague, which had begun a decade earlier, devastated all but 3000 acres before 1900, but during the following decade nearly half of the dead vineyards were replanted with vines grafted on resistant roots.

Napa again had almost 10,000 acres in 1920, when an even worse plague—Prohibition—struck. It did not destroy the vineyards, but economics compelled the growers to graft over their Cabernet, Pinot, and Riesling vines to the tough-skinned varieties that were preferred by the buyers of grapes shipped east for homemade and bootleg wines. Repeal in 1933 was a disappointment to the Napa winegrowers, too, because it brought little demand for their dry table wines. There still were only 11,500 acres of vines in the county by 1965.

Then the wine boom began, and vines began to spread throughout the valley again. As vintners raised their offers for "varietal" grapes, growers grafted back the vineyards from shipping varieties to the noble Cabernets, Rieslings, and Pinots. The growers started buying sprinkler systems and wind machines to guard their vines from frostbite on chilly spring nights. You see more of these huge fans in the Napa Valley than in any other vineyard district in the world. When disastrous frosts hit the coast counties in late April of 1970, the wind machines throbbed and smudge pots burned all night—much to the annoyance of those valley residents who do not grow grapes—and saved half of the crop. The least loss, incidentally, was in those vineyards protected by sprinklers, which kept the vines coated with a protective film of ice.

As the planting fever spread, scores of Napa prune orchards were ripped out and replaced with wine grapes. New vineyards also sprang up in the mountains west and east of the valley, on slopes that had been bare of vines since the phylloxera epidemic eighty years before. Twenty-one pre-Prohibition Napa wineries were refurbished and reopened for business, and eighty-one entirely new wineries were built in the county between 1979 and 1983. At least six more were in the planning stage. Three Napa wineries were bought by the giant Heublein conglomerate and three by European beverage companies, but most of the old established wineries turned down multimillion-dollar offers to sell.

Vineyard plantings in Napa County more than doubled after the late 1960s and may soon exceed 30,000 acres. But not by much, for that is all the space left in the county with the soil, drainage, and climatic conditions considered suitable for the commercial cultivation of wine grapes.

A bitter struggle has raged for over a decade to protect this open space from urban sprawl, which already has wiped out many fine vineyards in the other counties neighboring San Francisco Bay. When in 1968 the Napa Board of Supervisors blocked the subdividers' bulldozers by enacting a minimum twenty-acre agricultural reserve zoning law,* the land-development interests challenged the law in the courts; and in 1979 the minimum was doubled to forty acres. The Supervisors also compelled the state highway division to reroute a projected new freeway that would have cut a six-lane swath through the valley's main vineyard areas. While these battles dragged on, alarmed conservationists came up with an idea to save the vineyards if all other measures failed. They hoped to persuade the Federal government to designate the Bay Area grape-growing districts as a National Vineyard, like the National Parks.

• 3 •

Napa, like Sonoma and Mendocino, has many climatically different winegrowing districts. A striking example is the Carneros ("sheep" in Spanish) district, the first you reach when driving east from Sonoma on Highway 12–121. Enter the Napa Valley at its lower end, where the vineyards are close to San Pablo Bay. Because the Carneros is cooled in summer by winds and fogs from the salty bay, it is called the burgundy district of Napa County; its climate is rated as low Region I. Such burgundian grape varieties as Chardonnay and Pinot Noir seem to develop higher flavors here—at least one more point of acidity in balance with their sugar content when ripe—than when grown farther up the valley. Vintners whose main vineyards are in those warmer areas have acquired lands in this district to grow these two grape varieties in particular. On the other hand, Cabernet Sauvignon, a Bordeaux variety, fails to ripen fully in some of the Carneros vineyards except in unusually warm years, al-

---

*Under this Napa County law, no house may now be erected in the main vineyard areas on any parcel of land smaller than forty acres. Another measure that is helping to protect the vineyards is the state's 1965 Land Conservation Act. Under the state law, landowners who pledge to use their property only for agriculture for at least ten years can have it taxed on its value for farmland instead of at its higher value for business or for subdivisions. This is called "greenbelting the land."

though when it does reach full ripeness here, it makes a superlative wine.

There now are four producing wineries in the Carneros, and soon there will be a fifth, but before Prohibition there were many more. One was the stone castle that can be seen from the highway, in the spectacular Winery Lake Vineyard to the left, with its lake and modernistic sculptures. This once was the Talcoa Vineyard, where viticulture professor George Husmann in 1883 wrote his third book to explain why he had abandoned the University of Missouri to become a winemaker here in California: " . . . the true home of the grape . . . destined to be the vine land of the world." The present castle was built as a winery in 1885 by Michael Debret and Pierre Priet, winegrowers who emigrated to Napa from France. Since 1960 it has been the baronial residence of art collector Rene di Rosa, who has replanted the 225-acre vineyard with premium grape varieties. Wineries and home winemakers who buy di Rosa's grapes are proud to print "Winery Lake Vineyard" on the labels of their wines.

The intersection of Duhig Road with Highway 121 marks where the Swiss owners of the Cuvaison Winery near Calistoga began planting a 350-acre new Carneros vineyard in 1980 and where they plan to build an entirely new Cuvaison winery when the vineyard matures. At your left, a few hundred yards along the highway, is the 50,000-gallon Mont St. John winery and tasting room, built in 1978 by veteran wineman Louis Bartolucci to use the grapes from his son Andrea's young Madonna Vineyard, on the west side of Duhig Road.

From the "Madonna" sign at Las Amigas Road, a left turn will bring you to the two-story, 35,000-gallon Acacia Winery, built in 1982 on its fifty-acre Chardonnay and Pinot Noir vineyard that was planted four years earlier for a group of forty-nine California investors, some of them wine-buff physicians.

A right turn from Las Amigas onto Buchli Station Road leads to the 700,000-gallon Bouchaine Vineyards winery, built in 1980 around the shell of the onetime Garetto Winery for a group of eastern states investors organized by Dupont executive David Pollak, of Delaware. Bouchaine is Pollak's ancestral name. Among the investors are newsletter publisher Austin Kiplinger and Garret Copeland, a Dupont heir. Winemaker Jerry Luper, a partner, custom-crushes and bottles wine here for a half dozen other wineries while making the first Bouchaine Chardonnay and Pinot Noir for release in 1984. Thirty acres of its own vineyard were planted in 1982.

On the east side of nearby Cuttings Wharf Road are two buildings with red tile roofs, the brandy distillery built in 1983 by R and S Vineyards, a joint venture of Schramsberg Vineyard with Remy-Martin Cognac of France. Its eight onion-shaped pot stills (alembics) are the first in Napa County. The distillery borders the Carneros vineyard, which was owned before Prohibition by Judge John Stanly, whose La Loma winery faced neighboring Stanly Lane.

On Dealy Lane, which extends north from Highway 121 and Old Sonoma Road, is the 100,000-gallon Carneros Creek Winery, built since 1973 by self-taught young winemaker Francis V. Mahoney in partnership with San Franciscans Balfour and Anita Gibson of Connoisseur Imports. Their thirty-acre vineyard grows only Pinot Noir, but the winery also specializes in making Amador and Yolo counties Zinfandels.

In 1982, winegrowers in this area convinced the Federal government to establish "Los Carneros" as a viticultural area including parts of both Napa and Sonoma counties, the county name to appear on each label in addition to the Carneros name.

• 4 •

Different climates are found in the uplands of Napa County, where temperatures vary with the altitude and with the angle of exposure of each slope to the sun. The upland growers will tell you that certain grape varieties, Riesling in particular, develop higher aromas and more delicate balance in their vineyards than when grown on the valley floor. Before you continue up the valley, a side trip to explore this aspect will be worth your while.

Redwood Road, at the north end of Napa city, takes off in a northwesterly direction through a thickly wooded canyon into the hills. In a six-mile drive of many turns, you climb a thousand feet and reach an undulating mountain meadow that is carpeted with 150 acres of vines. Side by side in this vineyard stand the imposing mission-style monastery of the Christian Brothers, an ivy-clad stone winery, and a modest brick office building that faces the road.

The monastery is the Novitiate of Mont La Salle, where young men are trained to join this worldwide Catholic teaching order,* founded in France in 1680 by Saint Jean Baptiste de la Salle. In this vineyard grow the grapes for the Brothers' estate-bottled

---

*Officially, Fratres Scholarum Christianarum (the initials F.S.C. follow the members' names) or Brothers of the Christian Schools.

This vineyard on Mount Veeder in Napa County dates from 1864. It was replanted by Theodore Gier, who built the adjoining winery in 1903. The Christian Brothers bought it and built their Mont La Salle Novitiate beside the winery in 1930.

wines, Napa Fumé, Pineau de la Loire, and red Pinot Saint-George. The old winery is one of five the Brothers own; it is where they long bottled and aged their table wines. The brick building is the corporate headquarters of their Mont La Salle Vineyards, which, the Brothers want you to know, is a taxpaying concern like any other commercial vintner. Though the Brothers are educators, not priests, they take similar vows and wear much the same clerical garb, including black ankle-length robes. Members who live at the Napa monastery supervise the vineyards and wineries. The cellarmaster and vice president is courtly Brother Timothy, whose picture you see in the magazine ads. Brother Tim was graduated from the Brothers' high school in Los Angeles as Anthony Diener, then taught chemistry before coming to Mont La Salle in 1936.

Remembering that winemaking monks in the monasteries of Europe advanced the art and science of the vintager through the Middle Ages, it is of historical interest that The Christian Brothers of California are now the largest church-owned producer of wine in the world. They also are now the largest producers of Napa grapes and wines, and also of California brandy and premium-priced California dessert wines.

They began making wine in 1882 at their original novitiate

Brother Timothy (Anthony Diener), the chemistry teacher who became cellarmaster of The Christian Brothers wineries of 1936.

in Martinez, first for their table and altar use, then for sale. The city of Martinez began growing up around the novitiate, so they decided to move, and in 1930 bought the Napa upland site. The vineyard here was originally planted by one H. Hudemann about 1864, later was owned by Rudolf Jordan of the pre-Prohibition wine firm of A. Repsold, then was purchased and replanted by Oakland vintner Theodore Gier, who built the stone cellar in 1903.

When the Brothers began making wine here in 1932, the name on their labels was Mont La Salle, which is still used on their altar wines. In 1937, the name on their commercial labels was changed to "The Christian Brothers"—which many buyers still mistake as meaning some brothers named Christian. Including their altar wines, which are sold only to the clergy, they make some fifty different products, ranging from burgundy and brandy through nearly the entire list of generic and "varietal" table, dessert, and sparkling wine types. Many of them are distinctive, especially the Château La Salle, a sweet but noncloying light table wine made principally of the Muscat Canelli or Frontignan grape; it is the best-known wine of its type in the world. For almost a century, the Brothers refused to label their wines with vintage dates, preferring to blend different vintages to keep each type uniform in taste. As consumer demand grew in the mid-1970s, they began labeling special blends with lot numbers in which you could read the vintage years the blends contained. In 1977, the Brothers unbent further and introduced their first-ever vintage-dated wine, a special lot of 1976 Gewürztraminer.

Since their blended brandy made its debut in 1940, the Brothers have added more vineyards in the Napa Valley, making a total of 1300 acres in the county and 200 more in the San Joaquin Valley. They also added four more wineries, two of them at St. Helena and one each at Reedley and Fresno. By 1983 their wines were known throughout the nation and were being exported commercially to forty-five countries around the world. They now have an additional brandy, named "XO Rare Reserve," which resembles French cognac because it contains 50 percent potstill brandy aged in wood for eight years.

Millions have tasted the Brothers' wines at their Greystone cellar, which is seventeen miles north of Napa on Highway 29. Many others remember the Wine Museum the Brothers maintained in San Francisco from 1974 until 1983. Jointly maintained by then-distributor Alfred Fromm, it acquainted visitors to the Bay City with the noble cultural history of wine.

• 5 •

From Mont La Salle, if you have telephoned ahead for appointments, a tortuous drive up Mount Veeder Road to wineries on the slopes of that 2600-foot extinct volcano is well worthwhile. Two winding miles beyond the Brothers' monastery, a dirt road leads left to the Pickle Canyon Vineyards of John Wright and Moët-Hennessy, of whom more will be told. A short way farther are the 20,000-gallon Mount Veeder Winery and twenty-acre vineyard that Henry and Lisille Matheson of Coral Gables, Florida, bought in 1983 from lawyer Michael Bernstein and his wife Arlene, who decided to retire after running the winery for a decade. They met the Mathesons through a "for sale" advertisement in the *Wall Street Journal*.

A little farther on your right, a sign marks the entrance to South Africa-born, former journalist Elaine Wellesley's ten-acre Quail Ridge vineyard of Chardonnay. She makes her wine in the century-old onetime Hedgeside Distillery on Atlas Peak Road, north of Napa city.

Still farther, Lokoya Road takes you west to the spectacular Mayacamas Vineyard, one of the highest in Napa County, and its forty-five acres of terraced vines. At this elevation, far above the valley fogs, the grapes ripen with high acidity a week earlier than on the valley floor. In an average winter the vineyard is blanketed with snow. In late summer, when the ripening grapes become juicy and sweet, birds become a major threat. Then large areas of the mountain vineyards are covered with nets, particularly along the borders, where the feathered robbers first attack. In the volcano's crater stands a three-story cellar of native stone, built by John Henry Fischer from Stuttgart in 1889. This is the kind of place that lures amateurs who dream of owning a winery and growing great wines. In 1941, just such amateurs, British-born chemist J.F.M. (Jack) Taylor and his American wife Mary purchased Mayacamas, replanted the abandoned vineyard, reopened the old winery, and sold stock to their first customers at $10 a share. After three decades, they sold Mayacamas to young San Francisco investment banker Robert Travers, his wife Elinor, and six limited partners. The Traverses, living in the old still house beside the winery, make vintage-dated "varietals"— Cabernet, Chardonnay, and Zinfandel. In some years they also have made a late-harvest 17 percent Zinfandel essence from Amador County grapes.

Also on Lokoya Road, but impossible to reach unless you have a Jeep, is Lore Olds's 6000-gallon Sky Vineyards winery on his twenty-acre all-Zinfandel vineyard. Lore is the assistant winemaker at the Mayacamas winery.

A mile farther, the number "4035" marks the entrance to the ninety-acre vineyard and 40,000-gallon winery of Chicago-born onetime Navy underwater demolition expert Hamilton Vose III, who came here in 1970, cleared part of the forest to plant ninety acres of Chardonnay, Cabernet, and Zinfandel, and finished building his winery by 1977. Besides his estate-bottled Chardonnay and Cabernet, he makes a white wine of Zinfandel that he has named "Zinblanca."

• 6 •

Returning to the Wine Road near Napa and heading up the valley, you can experience the change in climate as you drive. It may be noticeably cool until you reach Oakville, because the lower valley's weather is Region I. From Oakville to St. Helena, it becomes warmer, averaging Region II. When you approach Calistoga, summer days are still warmer, and that part of the valley is classed as Region III.

After leaving Napa, you will see a large expanse of vineyards at your right, extending north from Oak Knoll Avenue, and a venerable, orange-colored, three-story winery in a grove of oaks near the highway. This is the Trefethen Vineyard, which has a checkered past. Napa bankers James and George Goodman built the winery in 1886 and named the place Eshcol for the brook in Biblical Canaan, where the Israelites sent by Moses found the enormous grape cluster described in Numbers 13:17– 24. Eshcol wines won medals and achieved considerable fame. Farmer Clark Fawver bought Eshcol in 1904 but made only bulk wine; Fawver drank nothing except an occasional beer. He closed the winery during Prohibition and reopened it at Repeal. After his death, it served as a storage cellar for the Beringer winery until connoisseur-industrialist Eugene Trefethen bought it in

1968. Trefethen's son John, a onetime Navy diver, modernized the winery and the 600-acre vineyard. In 1976 John and his bride Janet introduced the first estate-grown Trefethen Vineyard wines, followed by nonvintage blends called Eshcol White and Eshcol Red. Three years later, an international jury, comparing California Chardonnays to French white burgundies in a blind tasting at Beaune, in France, startled the French by giving the highest score to Trefethen Chardonnay 1976. The Trefethens use only about half of the grapes they grow. The rest are mechanically harvested by night for Domaine Chandon champagne.

Across the freeway, paved roads extend west from Solano Avenue to three wineries built since the late 1970s. The first is former Lockheed engineer Bruce Newlan's 10,000-gallon Alatera or Newlan cellar, bonded in 1977 near his vineyard, planted eight years before. On the north side of Hoffman Lane is retired airline pilot Gerald Hazen's Château Chèvre, named for the goat's-milk dairy farm where he made his first wine in 1979. Across the lane is the 35,000-gallon Lakespring Winery, built on a seven-acre vineyard in 1980 for the three food-producing and exporting Battat brothers of San Francisco. Frank Battat is a veteran home winemaker of excellent Cabernet.

At Yountville village, three miles north of the Trefethens, the big brick Groezinger winery and distillery has been transformed into a tourist shopping complex named "Vintage 1870." That was the year when Gottlieb Groezinger from Württemberg began building the structure and planting his great vineyard nearby. The Groezinger cellar stood idle through Prohibition and until the wine shortage during the Second World War, when for a few seasons wine was made there again. Now the old buildings contain restaurants, a theater, and dozens of shops, including one where most of the wines grown in Napa County are for sale.

· 7 ·

Across the freeway from Yountville, beside the old state Veterans' Home, is Moët-Hennessy's Domaine Chandon, a glamorous showplace of vaulted stone champagne cellars and tunnels, complete with a French restaurant featuring *haute cuisine* and a museum of antique implements used in France to produce champagne, opened in 1977. Visitor tours begin in the museum, then show the bottling, the secondary fermentation, the aging *en tirage*, the riddling, and the disgorging by the traditional *méthode champenoise*. The tours end in a salon where the champagnes can be purchased by the bottle or by the glass.

Moët-Hennessy, the giant French champagne, brandy, and Dior perfume firm, made history in 1973 when it became the first important French firm to enter the American winegrowing industry, acquiring 900 acres of Napa County vineyard land through its California subsidiary, Domaine Chandon. Chandon president John Wright purchased 600 acres in the Carneros district, 100 at Yountville, 200 on Mount Veeder, and 10 acres on that mountain for a vineyard of his own. For the first *cuvées,* grapes were purchased from several Napa vineyards and were vinified at the Trefethen winery. Edmond Maudière, the chef de caves of Moët et Chandon at Epernay, shuttled between France and Napa five times each year to make the blends. Introduced in late 1976, they were labeled "sparkling wine"—not "champagne," which, the French insist, comes only from 55,000 delimited acres between Epernay and Rheims. The first Chandon Napa Valley Brut was crisp, almost bone-dry, slightly more tart and thereby more French-tasting than most California champagnes. Maudière used mainly Pinot Noir and Chardonnay wines with a tenth of Pinot Blanc and Ugni Blanc in the blend. The second wine, Blanc de Noirs (100%), was an equally brut but slightly fruitier pink champagne, actually salmon color, the shade the French call *oeil de perdrix* (partridge's eye). Then came a sweet apéritif named Panache, an unfermented juice of Pinot Noir with added brandy, similar to the Ratafia de Champagne and Pineau des Charentes sold in those regions of France.

Moët-Hennessy's first California wine, however, was not a champagne, but a tart still Chardonnay press-wine labeled "Fred's Friends," made at Trefethen two years before Domaine Chandon was built. It was named, with Gallic jocularity, during a visit to Napa by Moët-Hennessy president Count Frédéric Chandon de Briailles from Epernay, and became so popular that it was followed by a "Fred's Friends" Pinot Noir Blanc. Both are available at the winery as long as each vintage lasts. Later Chandon products are Reserve Napa Valley Brut and Chandon Nature champagnes. California is not the only place outside France where Moët-Hennessy produces sparkling wines. Subsidiaries make "Graf Chandon Sekt" at Wiesbaden in Germany, "M. Chandon Champaña" in Argentina, and a similar product at Garibaldi in Brazil.

• 8 •

On your left just north of Domaine Chandon, where a small sign reads "Napanook Vineyard," is where another French investor plans to build a winery, as yet unnamed, by the mid-1980s.

Bordeaux vintner Christian Moueix, the director of Château Petrus in the Pomerol section of Bordeaux, is associated in that project with Robin Lail and Marcia Smith, the daughters of one-time Inglenook Vineyard proprietor John Daniel, Jr.

There are still more wineries on both sides of the highway. A gravel road extends east from Washington Street in Yountville to personnel specialist Bradley Terrill's 20,000-gallon Hopper Creek Winery, built in 1981 on his six-acre creekside vineyard. Beyond Yountville, the small winery with its geodesic dome at your left is Napa Cellars, the first to open with a tasting room on this stretch of Highway 29 when the winery was bonded in 1975. Six partners, who bought all the grapes they used, sold it to European investors in 1984. Visible ahead on your right as you pass Yount Mill Road is a new stone winery perched on a knoll. This is the 80,000-gallon Robert Pepi (pronounced peppy) Winery, built in 1981 by retired South San Francisco fur-dresser Robert A. Pepi on his fifty-acre vineyard, planted eleven years before. His son Robert manages the winery, which specializes in Sauvignon Blanc, Sémillon, and Chardonnay.

Beyond the vineyards at your left you can see a three-story, turreted stone winery atop one of the western hills. Built in 1885 by a wealthy New Yorker, Captain John Benson, it produced wines he labeled with a picture of a little girl sleeping in a hammock and the legend "Without a Care." For a half-century after the onset of Prohibition, the great building stood empty and neglected until 1979, when Oklahoma wine-buff nurseryman H. Gilliland Nickel came to Napa Valley looking for a winery site, and bought the vacant ghost. Exploring the structure, he found above the topmost window on its western facade this legend carved in stone: *Far Niente*— Italian for "do nothing"—and chose Far Niente as his winery's name. Nickel equipped a temporary cellar in Sausalito in 1980 and made two vintages of Napa Valley Chardonnay there. Meanwhile, 100 acres were replanted in the vineyard beside Far Niente, which in 1868 had been part of Hamilton Crabb's famous To Kalon. Three years later, Far Niente was completely refurbished and re-equipped. The surroundings were beautifully landscaped, and venerable Far Niente had become one of the nation's loveliest wine estates. Nickel moved his household into the upper story and made his first estate-bottled Cabernet, to be released in 1985.

A mile left on Oakville Grade, where the road becomes steep, is the 100,000-gallon Vichon Winery, which buys all its grapes. Partner-winemaker Dr. George Vierra, trained in chemical engineering at Oregon State University, served at two other Napa wineries before building this one in 1982. The name Vichon comes from *VI*erra and partners Bru*CH*er and Wats*ON*. A dozen other partners are restaurant and hotelmen whose establishments sell Vichon wines. Only three varieties are made here: Chardonnay, Cabernet, and a Semillon-Sauvignon blend called Chevrier, one of the synonyms of Sémillon.

In Oakville village, there is a stucco-fronted winery on the right that dates from 1886. Originally it was the Nouveau Médoc Vineyard cellar of Brun & Chaix, who were refugees from the troubles in France following the Franco-Prussian war. Jean Adolph Brun knew winemaking, and his partner, Jean Chaix, was experienced in growing grapes. They bought a vineyard and built a stone winery during the 1870s on Howell Mountain east of St. Helena, but then, to be close to the railroad, built this second cellar on the flat at Oakville. By 1889 their vineyards covered 115 acres; their Nouveau Médoc sweetish red wine was the favorite in New Orleans, and their whites were popular in California and the East. But Brun died young, and in 1916 Chaix and his widow sold the property. The buyer was the California Wine Association, which in turn sold to the Covick Company, makers of sacramental wines during Prohibition. In 1940, the cellar was sold at auction to the Napa Wine Company of Louis Stralla. He sold it six years later for $250,000 to the Cella Vineyards of Fresno. Now Heublein crushes and ferments the grapes there for the estate-bottled and coast-counties "vintage" Inglenook table wines. Next door is another cellar, named the Madonna winery when it was built in 1892. It was used after Repeal to make wine and brandy by the Bartolucci Brothers, who owned extensive vineyards nearby, and in 1969 became the winery of Oakville Vineyards, owned by a group of connoisseurs headed by Wilfred E. van Loben Sels, which became defunct in 1977. Then the winery was bought to increase the Napa Valley–produced portion of Inglenook wines.

· 9 ·

On your left, a short distance past Oakville, is the mission-style Robert Mondavi Winery, which has multiplied in size to 1.8 million gallons since 1966, when Robert, at the age of fifty-four, left his family's Charles Krug Winery, of which he was part owner, and began building this one for himself and his children. With its handsome bell tower, wide lawns, and three tasting and dining rooms, this winery annually attracts almost 300,000 visitors, who tour the cellars in groups and buy a fourteenth of its output. Thousands more attend the benefit concerts, cooking demonstrations, and art shows, with tastings at the intermissions, that are scheduled here throughout the year.

Bouncy, enthusiastic Robert travels three continents, surveying winemaking methods and exploring possible joint ventures, including his much-publicized one with Baron Philippe de Rothschild of Bordeaux. The first joint-venture wines, named "Opus One," 1979 and 1980 blends of Cabernet Sauvignon with Cabernet Franc or Merlot, were introduced in 1984 with a suggested retail price of $50 per bottle.

Most per ton grape prices in Napa Valley are influenced by a formula devised by Robert in 1977 in relation to the retail per bottle prices of his eight "varietal" wines. The formula doesn't relate to the much higher prices of his "reserve" wines. Mondavi buys a portion of his grape supply and cultivates some 1000 acres of his own. His elder son Michael now manages the business. In charge of winemaking is the younger UC Davis-trained son Tim, who since 1973 has been making an as-yet-unnamed and unreleased Mondavi champagne. Daughter Marcia handles the winery's east coast sales.

There is a second Robert Mondavi Winery in the Lodi district, fifty miles east of Napa, that makes and sells far more wine, and at lower prices, than this one at Oakville does. In 1979 Robert bought the 6-million-gallon former Cherokee growers' co-op bulk winery, re-equipped and named it the "Robert Mondavi Winery Woodbridge." There he produces and bottles Robert Mondavi vintage-dated white, red, and rosé in bottle, half-bottle, and magnum sizes. Except for the "RM" insignia at the top of the Woodbridge label, the wines from the two Mondavi wineries look much alike.

· 10 ·

Just past and across from Mondavi are four much smaller estate wineries in a row. Only the farthest has a tasting room. First is the 18,000-gallon Johnson Turnbull cellar, built in 1979 on the 21-acre vineyard that San Francisco attorney Reverdy Johnson and his wife Martha with their architect partner William Turnbull planted four years before. Next is Napa television dealers Richard and Sharon Evensen's winery, on their same-sized vineyard, built in the same year. The Evensens produced their first estate-bottled Gewürztraminer in 1979, with the help of their daughter and two sons. Across the next driveway are the two winery buildings of Jack and Dolores Cakebread, which hold a total of 50,000 gallons. They began making wine as a hobby in 1973 while replanting the old twenty-acre vineyard where their newer winery now stands, while Jack continued operating his Oakland garage. Their son Bruce enrolled at UC Davis to earn his enology degree and became the Cakebread winemaker in 1977. Among the redwood trees beyond the Cakebreads is the James Allen Family's 20,000-gallon Sequoia Grove Winery and tasting room, attractively equipped in a century-old onetime barn. Language teacher Allen bought the twenty-acre vineyard in 1978 and four years later released the first estate-bottled Sequoia Grove Chardonnay. Jim's wife Barbara and brother Stephen work with him in the vineyard and winery, with the help of their four children and the mother of the Allen brothers, Olive Ann. In 1982 the Allen brothers and a dozen partners began planting an additional 110 acres of Chardonnay and Pinot Noir in the Carneros district, opposite Winery Lake.

As you approach the hamlet of Rutherford, Niebaum Lane winds a mile left through vineyards and "private road" signs and past a century-old Victorian mansion to an equally antique, onetime carriage house, newly crammed with oak barrels and stainless-steel tanks. This is movie entrepreneur Francis Ford Coppola's 40,000-gallon Niebaum-Coppola Estate Winery, bonded in time to produce a 1978 vintage Cabernet Sauvignon–Cabernet Franc blend, released in 1984, that Coppola says "will be ready to drink in 2001." Coppola has replanted 100 acres of the original Inglenook Vineyard, retaining ten acres of older vines. The mansion, the carriage house, and the nearby Inglenook winery, now owned by Heublein Wines, are what remain of Finnish sea captain Gustav Niebaum's estate, which before and after Prohibition grew some of the finest American wines. Coppola, a collector of rare Bordeaux and burgundies, bought the estate from an interim owner in 1975. Visitors to the adjoining old Inglenook winery sometimes see helicopters overhead, bearing Coppola and Hollywood film crews from San Francisco to shoot new Coppola epics in Napa Valley locales.

• 11 •

When Captain Gustav Ferdinand Niebaum (originally Nybom) had made his fortune in the Alaska fur-sealing trade, he wanted to build a ship. But his wife did not share his love of the sea, so he adopted winegrowing as a hobby instead. In 1897 he bought a young vineyard named Inglenook from one W. C. Watson and retained the name, which suggests a pleasant nook by a fireside. Niebaum replanted the place with vines he imported from the best wine districts of Europe. He then built the three-story Gothic winery of stone, now covered with ivy, that serves as the Inglenook visitor center and tasting room. It was finished in 1887, when the captain was forty-five.

Niebaum's aim was to grow wines as fine as any in the world, regardless of expense or financial gain. He often said that the only wines on which he ever made a profit were those he gave to his friends. A perfectionist, he wore white cotton gloves when he inspected his cellars, and woe betide the employees if his gloves became soiled. His sample room was a gustatory chapel with tinted Dutch glass windows and antiquities worthy of a European museum. He also made brandy, but becoming offended one day by the manner in which a revenue agent inspected his distillery, the captain ordered it to be torn down the following morning.

Frona Eunice Wait, writing in 1889, described Inglenook as the California equivalent of Schloss Johannisberg in Germany or of Châteaux Lafite and d'Yquem in France. In that year Niebaum achieved his goal, when Inglenook wines won quality awards at the Paris Exposition. They continued to do so until his death in 1908, at the age of sixty-six. Twelve years later came Prohibition, and the winery was closed.

At Repeal in 1933, Niebaum's widow Suzanne entrusted the reopening of Inglenook to Carl Bundschu, of the great pre-Prohibition wine firm of Gundlach & Bundschu. Six years later, Mrs. Niebaum's grandnephew, John Daniel, Jr., took charge. Captain Niebaum had never allowed the Inglenook brand to appear on any bottles except his best. Bundschu and Daniel were enjoined by Mrs. Niebaum to conduct the business the same way. They seldom made any profit for Inglenook, but they restored it to the eminence it had reached in the captain's day.

In 1939, the San Francisco Wine & Food Society held a dinner in tribute to Inglenook, at the Palace Hotel. Among the wines served were four relics supplied by Daniel from the family cellar: Inglenook Sauterne 1907, Riesling 1910, Pinot Noir 1892, and Napa Valley Red 1884. Those ancient vintages, though frail and varying from bottle to bottle, gave us proof of the great longevity of Napa Valley wines. The Pinot Noir, which had been recorked in 1912, was exquisitely delicate, rich in bouquet, magnificent. That evening we also drank up the last few bottles of Niebaum's brandy, *circa* 1885. It was that dinner which caused me to choose the Cabernet of Inglenook to start my own cellar collection of Napa Valley reds, which includes every vintage bottled from 1938 to 1964. Two years are missing, because the entire '45 and

'47 vintages of Cabernet were sold in bulk; John Daniel didn't consider them fine enough to bear the Inglenook name. The Cabernets of the early 1940s required ten to eleven years of aging in wood and glass to develop great bouquet, and some of them have retained it for over forty years. Early Inglenook vintages have brought hundreds of dollars per case at the annual Heublein auctions in recent years.

Daniel was one of the first premium vintners to adopt (in 1940) varietal instead of generic labels for most of his table wines. The exception was his rosé, first made in 1935, which he named Navalle for the creek that curves through the Niebaum (now Coppola) estate. Under Daniel, Inglenook carried on the Niebaum tradition for twenty-five years. It therefore was a shock to the lovers of its wines and of antiquity to learn in 1964 that the winery had been sold to giant United Vintners (now part of the Heublein–R. J. Reynolds conglomerate)—even though Daniel stayed on. He continued to live in the great Niebaum house, which Coppola now owns. He retained and enlarged the family vineyards and continued as a member of the Inglenook tasting panel until his death, in 1970. Why did he sell the winery? He never gave his friends a reason, but Daniel, unlike the Rothschilds of Europe, had no sons to carry on.

Most of the estate-bottled Inglenook "varietals" are still being made, as well as the "cask selection" vintages of Cabernet Sauvignon, but no wine has been made at Inglenook since the crushing and fermentation were moved to Oakville. Huge barrel-aging and bottling cellars have been built, the former unhappily placed directly in front of the old winery, partly obscuring its classic

Georges de Latour, the founder of Beaulieu Vineyard. (*San Francisco* Examiner)

facade. The "estate" represented by the "estate-bottled" label has been enlarged to include 1500 more Napa Valley acres owned by members of the Allied Grape Growers co-op. Six generic and "varietal" coast-counties "district wines" are made at Oakville and bottled at Inglenook under an "Inglenook Vintage" label that is priced at about half that for the estate-bottled line. Eight still lower-priced "Inglenook Navalle" generics and "varietals" that can come from anywhere in California are made, bottled, jugged, and packed in plastic bags at Heublein's gigantic plant at Madera in the San Joaquin Valley.

* 12 *

In 1883, while Captain Niebaum was building the great Inglenook winery, a stocky little twenty-six-year-old Frenchman, Georges de Latour from Périgord, arrived in San Francisco to seek his fortune. During a try at gold-mining in the Sierra foothills, he lost what little money he had. Then, because his family in France had made wine and he had learned chemistry at the Ecole Centrale in Paris, he took himself to the north coast wine country. He traveled by horse and wagon among the wineries, buying the sediment and crust (argols) from their wine tanks to make cream of tartar, which he sold to be made into baking powder. For sixteen years he built up his cream of tartar business at Healdsburg in Sonoma County, but meanwhile planned to become a winegrower. In 1899, when Inglenook wines were already famed at home and abroad, de Latour bought an orchard and wheatfield immediately north of Inglenook. His wife Fernande named it Beaulieu, "beautiful place." He went to France, brought back vines of the best French varieties to plant on his land, and opened his first small winery. Several years later he acquired additional vineyards at Oakville and on the east side of the valley along the Silverado Trail. In 1923 he bought the Seneca Ewer winery across the road from his home vineyard, enlarged its stone cellar, and made it the main Beaulieu winery.

When Inglenook, its owner long dead, was closed down at the beginning of Prohibition, de Latour kept Beaulieu open, for he held the approbation of San Francisco Archbishop Patrick Riordan as a supplier of altar wines, which were legal, to the Catholic church. He prospered during the Dry years, building a nationwide business in altar wines, which Beaulieu still enjoyed until 1978. At Repeal he was one of the few vintners ready to supply fine, fully aged California wines to the connoisseur trade. In the wine judging at the Golden Gate International Exposition in 1939, his Beaulieu burgundy (which he made of Cabernet Sauvignon grapes) was chosen above a hundred other entries to receive the grand prize for red wines.

At the home vineyard, de Latour and his wife—a stately, gracious *grande dame*—added wings to their rambling country house, planted formal gardens studded with fountains and statuary, and made Beaulieu the most famous estate in the Napa Valley. They dispensed hospitality to San Francisco high society and entertained such illustrious personages as President Herbert Hoover and Sir Winston Churchill, and visiting nobility. They made annual visits to France, which was how it happened that their daughter, Hélène, was married in 1924 to the Marquis Galcerand de Pins, himself a winegrower at his ancestral estate, the Château de Montbrun in Gascony.

Georges de Latour was said to be the colorful central character of the best-selling novel of 1942, *The Cup and the Sword,* which fifteen years later became the film *This Earth Is Mine.* I can confirm this because, after his death in 1940, I furnished the background material to the author, Alice Tisdale Hobart; and she rewarded me by making me a recognizable character (Galen Ritter, the ex-newspaperman) in the book. The French winegrower and hero of the story, Jean-Philippe Rambeau, portrayed in the movie by Claude Rains, bore only a basic resemblance to de Latour because Mrs. Hobart took pains to alter his picture sufficiently—by giving him wineries in both the San Joaquin and Napa valleys—to avoid the possibility of a lawsuit. I was disappointed by the novel, however, for the author put all of her dramatic writing into her fictional scenes and none into the single episode that was true—the climax to de Latour's career—the greatest funeral held in San Francisco in that decade, at which four archbishops presided.

De Latour was a great judge of wine and also of winemakers. When his enologist, Professor Leon Bonnet, retired in 1937, de Latour and the Marquis de Pins traveled to France to find a successor. At the Institut National Agronomique in Paris, they asked Professor Paul Marsais to recommend a man. Marsais had a Russian assistant, a research enologist named André Tchelistcheff, who he thought might be right for the job. Tchelistcheff was hired and arrived at Rutherford in time for the 1938 vintage.

In bringing Tchelistcheff to California, de Latour did as much for the state's wines in general—and later for the wines of Washington State—as for the wines of Beaulieu. Tchelistcheff was born in Moscow in 1901, the son of a law professor, and was educated in Czechoslovakia after serving in the czarist and White

André Tchelistcheff, "the winemaker's winemaker," was born in Russia, educated in Czechoslovakia, and trained in France before coming to California in 1938 at the age of 37.

Russian armies. This intense little man was thirty-seven when he left France. He brought to California the latest findings of French enological and viticultural research. When he first tasted Napa wines, he decided that Cabernet Sauvignon grown in this climate was destined to become one of the great wines of the world. He persuaded de Latour to build a separate cellar to age Beaulieu Cabernet in oak barrels for at least two years. When the Cabernet from the new cellar was bottle-ripe, he matured it for another two years in glass. Released the year after the founder's death, it was named "Georges de Latour Private Reserve." It was the 1936 vintage, and was priced at $1.50. (At this writing, the ten-year-old Private Reserve brings $30 a bottle in the few stores that have any in stock. The five-year-old can be bought at the Beaulieu tasting room in Rutherford for $18, but there is a limit of two bottles per buyer. BV Private Reserve Cabernet has become the single most praised and most sought-after American wine.)

For years Tchelistcheff urged the Beaulieu owners to concentrate on producing only Cabernet or at most two other fine wines—to discontinue selling their dozens of different types. "With thirty wines to take care of," he argued, "I am producing little starlets when I should produce only great stars." But like other medium-sized American wineries which tried to sell their brands nationally, Beaulieu had to continue offering "a complete line."

Besides managing the BV vineyards and winery, Tchelistcheff for fifteen years maintained his own enological laboratory in St. Helena. He tutored several young enologists at other wineries who since have made some of the best post-Repeal California wines. One of those he trained was his son Dimitri, who later produced some of the best wines in northern Mexico and then helped pioneer modern winegrowing on the island of Maui in Hawaii. André himself has guided the Washington State wine industry in its first concerted effort to produce premium Old World–type table wines. Since retiring from BV in 1973, he has been consultant for a dozen wineries in California as well as in Washington, besides guiding many of his small winegrower friends in their quest for enological greatness. At the 1970 meeting of the American Society of Enologists, the nation's wine industry joined to pay him tribute as "the winemaker's winemaker," presenting him with the annual A.S.E. merit award.

In 1969 the admirers of Napa wines, still perturbed over the sale of Inglenook five years earlier, got another shock when Beaulieu and four of its five vineyards were sold to the Heublein conglomerate. "It's a terrible wrench," said the Marquise de Pins, who had succeeded her mother as Beaulieu president, "but circumstances force changes; it's more practical for a big organization to operate in these times." However, the de Pins and their daughter, Dagmar Sullivan, kept the Beaulieu estate, which is de Latour's original Cabernet vineyard and the source of the grapes for BV Private Reserve. Dagmar and Walter Sullivan are selling the grapes to Heublein, but a small winery stands on the old vineyard, and there is a de Latour grandson, Walter Sullivan III, who someday may be interested in following his ancestor's steps.

Despite the change in ownership, Tchelistcheff, now in his eighties, still keeps a loving eye on Beaulieu vineyards and wines. His standards are maintained there by his son Dimitri, who since 1970 has been BV's technical director, working with Davis-trained enologist Thomas Selfridge and Chairman Legh Knowles, whose voice on BV radio commercials has been familiar to millions since 1975.

Although Inglenook and Beaulieu both are now Heublein–R. J. Reynolds companies, they are managed by separate Heublein divisions. BV still sells both generic and "varietal" table wines, and five dessert wines purchased in the San Joaquin Valley and aged at Rutherford, and since 1955 has offered two champagnes, one of them now called "Champagne de Chardonnay." Its best buys, in my opinion, are the second-grade Cabernet and the Burgundy, priced about a third as much as the Private Reserve. A still better buy is a five-year-old claret, sold in 1983 for $10 a magnum in stores. BV also produces an excellent chablis, a Grenache Rosé, sweet and dry Sauvignon Blancs, Gamay Beaujolais, and one dessert wine of its own, Muscat Frontignan, from this choicest of Muscat grapes, which de Latour had planted in his vineyard on the Silverado Trail. Added since 1976 are a Cabernet-Merlot blend named Beau Tour, a Pinot Noir named Beau Velours, and since 1980, an estate-bottled four-year-old Los Carneros Pinot Noir and a white of the Burgundian grape named Melon, which most California winegrowers call Pinot Blanc.

Beaulieu, with a visitor center built in 1974, including a theater where a film on winegrowing is shown, is one of the attractive tasting stops on the Wine Road.

• 13 •

Across the Wine Road, north of Beaulieu, is the stucco-fronted 50,000-gallon Grgich Hills Cellar of Croatia-born winemaker Miljenko (Mike) Grgich and Austin Hills, of San Francisco's Hills Brothers coffee dynasty. Grgich is famous as the producer of the California Chardonnay Château Montelena 1973, which triumphed over four leading white burgundies of France in the internationally publicized blind tasting by French experts in Paris in 1976. The building of this winery in 1977 realized a dream Grgich had cherished since emigrating from Yugoslavia nineteen years before. A winemaker since boyhood, when he trod grapes in his father's winery, he holds degrees in viniculture from Zagreb University and worked in five Napa wineries before leaving Château Montelena to achieve his goal, a winery of his own. His 1973 Chardonnay was a blend from three vineyards, two in Napa Valley and one in the Alexander Valley of Sonoma County. He now chooses the best grapes from Hills's vineyards but buys grapes elsewhere, too.

A right turn on Galleron Road takes you to the twenty-acre Sullivan Vineyard. Southern California graphic designer and home winemaker James O. Sullivan began planting the vineyard with Cabernet in 1972, and six years later began building a 14,000-gallon winery when he moved with his wife Jo Ann and their five children to their new home here.

On your right, with entrance on Galleron Road, is the redwood-fronted 900,000-gallon Franciscan Vineyards winery and its attractive tasting room, from which visitors can take a self-guided cellar tour. It is noted for its award-winning, estate-bottled Chardonnays and champagne and for its excellent nonvintage "Cask 321" burgundy and chablis. Built in 1971, Franciscan had a succession of owners until 1979, when it was purchased by the Peter Eckes Company, West Germany's leading producer of fruit juices and brandy. Its vineyards now total 500 acres, half on its Oakville ranch and half in the Alexander Valley. President of Franciscan is Davis-trained winemaker Thomas Ferrell, who first earned fame by producing the Inglenook Vineyard's "cask selection" vintages of Cabernet, Pinot Noir, and Pinot St. George. The production manager is Leonard Berg, also Davis-trained, a son and nephew of noted enologists. In 1975, Franciscan was the first winery to make a commercial wine of Carnelian, the light red University of California grape variety that Professor Olmo developed by crossing Cabernet, Carignane, and Grenache.

Across the Wine Road in a eucalyptus grove is Bernard and Evelyn Skoda's 80,000-gallon red-tile-roofed Rutherford Vintners cellar and tasting room, built in 1977. French-born Skoda has worked in wineries since his youth in Alsace. A Second World War veteran of the French and American armies, he spent fifteen years helping manage the nearby Louis Martini winery until he could build his own. The Skodas have two vineyards, of Riesling at the winery and of Cabernet a half mile south. Helping in the winery are their son Louis and daughter Jacqueline.

A quarter-mile farther on your left is Whitehall Lane, and at its intersection with Highway 29 is the 20,000-gallon winery named for the lane when it was built in 1979. Partner Arthur Finkelstein, an architect, is the winemaker, helped by his brother and partner, Napa plastic surgeon Dr. Alan Steen. With their wives, Charlene and Bunnie, and four children, they live on the adjoining twenty-six-acre vineyard.

Right turns on Zinfandel Lane and on Wheeler Way take you to a 60,000-gallon winery on the 80-acre vineyard that was planted in 1971 by Roy Raymond and sons, the year after Raymond quit as manager of the Beringer winery at its purchase by Nestlé of Switzerland. Roy's wife Mary Jane is a granddaughter of Jacob Beringer. The first estate-bottled Raymond Vineyard wine, the botrytized 1975 White Riesling, won a gold medal at the Los Angeles Fair in 1977, the year it was released for sale. Raymond Chardonnay, Chenin Blanc, Zinfandel, and Cabernet have continued winning medals each year since. Roy Jr. is also the viticulturist for the Guenoc Vineyard and winery

Louis Michael Martini, who said he made his famous Moscato Amabile by accident. (*San Francisco* Examiner)

in Lake County, and his brother Walter is the winemaker at both wineries.

West Zinfandel Lane leads to the Flora Springs winery, the handsome century-old structure that faces you from the base of a hill. It was built in the early 1880s by James and William Rennie from Scotland, who made wine there for a time and then moved to the Barton winery at Fresno. In 1979, retired Bechtel Corporation president Jerome Komes, his wife Flora, his son John, and daughter Julie Garvey and her husband Patrick had 60,000 gallons of stainless-steel and oak casks installed in the venerable cellar. They named it Flora Springs for the elder Mrs. Komes, and produced their first vintage of Cabernet from its hundred-acre vineyard in the following year. The senior Komeses live in the attractive home to the south, which was also a winery when it was built by Charles Brockhoff from Germany in 1885.

More wineries line both sides of the Wine Road as you approach St. Helena. At White Lane, on your right, is the white stucco V. Sattui cellar and cheese shop, built in 1975. It offers tasting and sells sausages, pâtés, cheeses, and breads that you can enjoy in its adjoining picnic ground. Daryl Sattui and his blonde Finnish wife Mirja named it for the winery his great-grandfather Vittorio operated on Bryant Street, in San Francisco's Mission district, from 1894 until 1920, when it was closed by National Prohibition. Daryl makes "natural, unfined, and unfiltered" red wines, mostly of grapes trucked down from Amador County.

A little farther on your right, a sign invites you to the Heitz Cellar tasting room, which fronts on a Grignolino vineyard. It is worth a stop, but be sure to save time for a later visit (but phone ahead) to the Heitz family's winery and vineyard, two miles to the east.

On your left is the big Napa Valley Co-operative Winery, which makes wine out of Napa grapes for Gallo and sends it all, except what the grower members drink themselves, in tank trucks to Modesto. The Co-op cellar is two wineries in one, for it was built around a much older stone winery that once belonged to Oakland vintner Theodore Gier.

Next door to the Co-op is the Sutter Home winery, a fixture in this Napa location since 1906, but its products are not Napa wines. What it mainly produces are full-bodied, flavorful Zinfandels from grapes trucked down from the Sierra foothills of Amador County, 100 miles to the east. It also makes a white wine of Zinfandel and a light sweet Muscat table wine, which can be sampled in the tasting room. The winery name goes back to 1890, when John Sutter, a cousin of Captain Sutter of Sutter's Fort fame, founded a winery on Howell Mountain. It was moved to St. Helena in 1906 and after Prohibition made bulk wine. Sutter Home has been owned by the Trinchero family since 1947, and having no vineyard then, Louis (Bob) Trinchero began buying Zinfandel grapes from an old Amador vineyard west of Plymouth. So popular has the Zinfandel become that the Trincheros have expanded the winery to 700,000 gallons.

Beside the Sutter home is wine-book collector Jim Prager's 6000-gallon Port Works winery, where he lives with his wife Imogene and their seven children and makes vintage-dated ports and Cabernet table wine.

• 14 •

Across the road from Sutter Home is a 3-million-gallon, ivy-clad winery with a tasting room and a modest sign facing the highway that says "Louis M. Martini Winery." The name is also the brand on the three dozen Martini wines, respected wherever California wines are sold, although the winery has been run by his son, his grandson and two granddaughters since its colorful founder died in 1974, at the age of eighty-seven.

Louis Michael Martini was born in 1887 in the seaport of Pietra Ligure on the Italian Riviera, the son of a shoemaker. At thirteen, he came to San Francisco to help his father Agostino fish in the bay, make and sell wine and shellfish, but at nineteen he was sent back to Italy to study winemaking because a vintage of his father's wine had spoiled. Later he made wine at a vineyard his father rented near Pleasanton in Alameda County, then in successive seasons at the Bradford Winery in Thornton and the Guasti Vineyard near Cucamonga. Early in the Prohibition era, as a partner in the former Italian Swiss Colony winery at Kingsburg in Fresno County, he made a grape concentrate called "Forbidden Fruit," a name which appealed to the nation's home winemakers. At Repeal he switched to making bulk wine and shipped it in tank cars to eastern wineries. Meanwhile he built this winery at St. Helena and quietly amassed a hoard of fine table wines, which he aged in the nearby Rennie (now Flora Springs) winery. In 1937, he had bought the 300-acre Mount Pisgah Vineyard on the Sonoma County side of the Mayacamas range, and renamed it Monte Rosso for its red volcanic soil. In 1940, he sold the Kingsburg winery, moved his family to St. Helena, and put his whole stock of aged wines on the market at once.

One of the wines he introduced in 1940 was his Moscato Amabile. It is still sold, but only at the winery, where you are told it is so delicate it must be kept under refrigeration until served. When I first asked Louis how he made it, he said it was an accident. At Kingsburg, in 1928, he found several barrels of Muscat of Alexandria juice that had lain in a corner all winter because his fermenting tanks were full. In spring, when the juice was tasted, Martini expected it to be spoiled, but instead it sparkled like champagne. He couldn't remember what else had been put in those barrels, but years later admitted he had added some yeast. Moscato Amabile has yet to be duplicated in this country. However, Cyril Ray describes in his *Wines of Italy* a semi-sparkling 8 percent Muscat wine called Moscatello, made in Liguria and favored there for family picnics.

Louis Michael's son Louis Peter meanwhile had studied winemaking at the University of California at Berkeley and Davis, and joined the winery after four years in the Air Force during the Second World War. Louis Peter lives with his wife Elizabeth on the old Edge Hill Vineyard, founded in 1870 by the pioneer Indian fighter, General Erasmus D. Keyes. Their home has two-foot-thick walls, for it was once the Edge Hill winery.

In 1977, Davis-trained grandson Michael Robert became the winemaker. Granddaughter Carolyn Martini Cox became the winery manager, and her sister Patricia the comptroller in 1982. Grandson Peter has made a Martini winery film.

The Martinis have kept adding vineyards, buying a part of the Carneros property on Stanly Lane in 1942, 200 acres on the Russian River below Healdsburg in 1962, more Carneros acreage two years later, and in 1970 replanted the 100-acre Oak

Glen Vineyard in Chiles Valley, where ninety-one years earlier Professor George Husmann from Missouri had written his final book, *Grape Culture and Wine-Making in California.* By 1983, the Martinis were planting their sixth and seventh vineyards, one in Pope Valley and one in Lake County west of Highway 29 near Lower Lake, bringing their total to 1000 acres. They have produced a vintage chart of all their "varietals" since 1959, with annual recommendations of how many years each can be expected to continue improving with age.

You still can buy nonvintage, ready-to-drink Martini "mountain" red, white, and rosé at everyday prices in bottle and magnum sizes. The vintage-dated "varietals" cost more, and still more is charged for some of the "special selection," "vineyard selection," and "private reserve" whites and reds that are sold only at the winery. Martini pale dry sherry is the best of its type in California, a blend of wines as old as fifteen years with younger, submerged-culture *flor* sherries. Martini still is the only winery that makes a "varietal" wine of Folle Blanche, a white grape grown on the Monte Rosso vineyard. I once congratulated old Louis Michael on having planted Folle Blanche, a grape the university doesn't recommend for California, but which makes a lovely dry, crisp wine resembling chablis. "I didn't plant it," he replied; "it was growing there when I bought the vineyard."

After labeling all their wines "California" for many years because they prefer to blend their Sonoma and Napa County wines, the Martinis lately have begun observing the new trends toward district appellations and vineyard designations, with such labels as "Monte Rosso Vineyard," "Sonoma Valley," and "North Coast." "But the most important thing on a label is the brand name, the name of the winery," Louis Peter says. That he is right is evidenced by the fabulous offers constantly received and rejected from big distillers and conglomerates who would like to buy the Martini name.

• 15 •

Next door to Martini is the impressive South St. Helena Cellar of The Christian Brothers. Built in 1965 to store bottled wines, it has been enlarged as the beginning of a winery complex more immense than anything the valley has ever seen. New crushers and presses have been installed, and the Brothers now make their Napa table wines and eventually may bottle them here.

The old town of St. Helena has three bonded wineries within the city limits and also a considerable acreage of vineyards, which unfortunately are not protected by the county zoning law. Although most of the city's 5000 residents are concerned in some way with winegrowing, there are many who oppose the drinking of wine. They are the Seventh Day Adventists, whose big St. Helena Hospital frowns down on the vineyards from the hill east of town; they also oppose the consumption of tea, coffee, and meat.

The St. Helena Library, which you reach by turning right on Adams Street to Library Lane, contains the only public wine library in the United States. It is supported by the Napa Valley Wine Library Association, which at this writing anyone may join for $15 a year, and which conducts periodic wine tastings and wine appreciation courses, the latter taught by the local winemakers.

A left turn to the west end of Adams Street takes you to floriculturists Harmon and Mary Brown's 8000-gallon Spottswoode winery on their forty-acre vineyard, some of which dates from the 1880s. Their winery, in the cellar of the 1882 vintage Victorian home, was bonded in 1983.

Five miles west of St. Helena, on a private road beyond the onetime White Sulphur Springs resort, noted winemaker Philip Togni and urban planner Michael Marston have reopened the Lyncrest winery, which operated briefly about 1972. From the grapes on a fifty-acre pre-Prohibition vineyard there, Togni produced the 1982 vintages of Marston Vineyard Cabernet, Zinfandel, Grenache, and Petite Sirah.

· 16 ·

From St. Helena, a half-hour climb of Spring Mountain Road affords glimpses of some once-famous mountain vineyards, replanted during the 1970s in response to the new demand for fine table wines.

The steepled century-old stone mansion hidden in the trees at your left, where the hill becomes increasingly steep, was once Tiburcio Parrott's Miravalle, named for its view of the valley. In 1981, it became familiar to millions of television watchers as *Falcon Crest,* because every episode of that drama pictured its facade, implying that the fictional saga of a Napa winegrowing family took place here. Beside the venerable mansion is the handsome Spring Mountain Vineyards winery that Michael Robbins built in 1976 to match its design. (Falcon Crest Chardonnay and Pinot Noir 1980 went on the market during 1982.)

Tiburcio Parrott, the wealthy illegitimate son of a San Fran-

The Château Chevalier winery, built in 1891 on Spring Mountain in Napa County, was abandoned during Prohibition and reopened eighty years later during the wine revolution. (*Jay Golick*)

cisco banker, was a friend of the Beringer Brothers and had the mansion built in 1885 to resemble the Beringers' Rhine House. A gentleman farmer, Parrott grew here a claret he called Margaux, which, the late Almond R. Morrow told me, was the greatest California wine produced before Prohibition. It was produced until Parrott died in 1894, at the age of fifty-four.

Robbins, an Annapolis graduate engineer and property manager from Iowa, had operated a Spring Mountain Vineyards winery since 1968 in another Victorian mansion on the Wine Road, when he bought Miravalle in 1974 and had Parrott's mansion restored. He has replanted twenty-five acres of the original Miravalle vineyard, but the first wines made for him here were from vineyards Robbins owned near Yountville. The new winery includes a ninety-foot-long wine-aging tunnel dug by Chinese laborers in Parrott's time.

A half-mile farther, a narrow private road through forests of oaks and redwoods leads to the great La Perla Vineyard, which is one of the most spectacular in the world. Literally miles of valleys and hills, rising to 1500 feet elevation, are contoured or terraced and carpeted with vines, most of them replanted during the past decade. Charles Lemme from Germany built the stone La Perla winery in the 1870s. His successor was Claus Schilling of the San Francisco family of dealers in wine, spice, coffee, and tea. Now La Perla is owned by realtor-vineyardist

Jerome Draper, whose son Jerome Jr. hopes someday to rebuild and reopen the winery.

A mile beyond the La Perla entrance, also on a private road, is Château Chevalier. With its Victorian exterior, twin steeples and stained-glass windows, this is one of the loveliest old stone cellars in the United States. Gregory Bissonette, once a jet-fighter pilot, was a San Francisco stockbroker when he began making wine at home and took some enology short courses at UC Davis. In 1969 he bought the abandoned chateau that wine merchant George Chevalier had built in 1891. Bissonette quit his job and moved with his wife Kathy and their six children into the top two floors of the winery. He cleared the steep hillside of trees and brush and replanted sixty acres with Cabernet and Chardonnay, doing most of the back-breaking work himself. He purchased grapes to make his first wines in 1972, calling them "Mountainside Vineyards," reserving "Château Chevalier" for wines of his own grapes. In 1976, the first estate-grown wines were released, a deep-colored, deep-flavored 1974 Cabernet and a 1975 Chardonnay. In 1983, after fourteen years of a successful winegrowing venture, the Bissonettes sold the chateau to John T. Nickel of Oklahoma, the brother of Far Niente proprietor Gilliland Nickel. In 1984, John and his wife Sandra were preparing to take up their residence at Château Chevalier.

On Langtry Lane, above the La Perla Vineyard, Fritz Maytag of the Newton, Iowa, family owns the hundred-acre York Creek Vineyard, which once was part of La Perla. But Maytag, who is busy running the Anchor Steam Beer Brewery in San Francisco, sells his choice grapes to premium-producing wineries, makes wine at home for his own use, and, although he has no plan to enter the wine business, says, "I may have a winery someday."

Two miles farther, at the end of Langtry Lane, is an Alpine chalet–style winery named Cain Cellars, built in 1982 beside a seventy-acre mountain vineyard that electrical engineer Jerry Cain and his wife Joyce began planting on a former cattle ranch, two years before.

Uphill from Langtry Lane, a gravel road winds a mile northward to the Robert Keenan vineyard. The stone winery, built by Peter Conradi in 1904, had lain idle since 1937. Keenan, the owner of a San Francisco insurance firm, bought and remodeled the cellar, replanted the surrounding vineyard with forty-seven acres of Cabernet Sauvignon and Chardonnay, and with former Chappellet Vineyard winemaker Joseph Cafaro in charge, made wine there again beginning in 1977.

Still higher on the mountain, at almost 2000 feet elevation,

Fred Aves and his son Russell have built the handsome stone Yverdon winery, which has quatrefoil stained-glass windows, Tudor arches, and the first hillside tunnels dug in Napa County during this century. Aves, a Los Angeles manufacturer of auto supplies, began making wine in his bathtub in 1962, then sold his factory because he was bored and wanted to become a wine-grower. Father and son cut and laid every stone of the winery by hand and assembled their casks and barrels from staves imported from Italy. Yverdon is the name of the village in Switzerland where Aves's grandparents were winegrowers.

At the mountain crest an unpaved road at the right leads to old vine stumps and tunnels that are traces of pre-Prohibition wineries, their names long forgotten. Present-day pioneers have replanted vines in patches of brush and forest and opened two small wineries. One is Sonoma dentist, Dr. Peter Minor, who had begun planting his eight-acre Ritchie Creek Vineyard when he dug his 4000-gallon winery into the hill in 1974, to make his first Cabernet Sauvignon. The road branches right from Minor's place to the forty-acre Smith-Madrone Vineyard and 15,000-gallon winery of schoolteachers Stuart and Charles Smith. They built the winery in time for their first crush in 1977. Awards and praise since have greeted each estate-bottled vintage of their Riesling, Chardonnay, Cabernet, and Pinot Noir.

Also on Spring Mountain, but reached by continuing two miles up Madrona and a private road from St. Helena, is the steeply terraced, hundred-acre Newton Vineyard and its partly underground 50,000-gallon winery. When it was built in 1979, it was called the Richard Forman winery, but then was given the name of his partners, Peter Newton and his Chinese wife, clinical psychologist Dr. Su Hua Newton. Its first three vintages were made of purchased grapes, but the first estate-bottled Newton wines, classic blends of Cabernet Sauvignon, Franc, and Merlot, and of Sauvignon Blanc with Sémillon, were due in 1984. Eleven years earlier, former London journalist Newton was the principal founder of the Sterling Winery, where Forman was the wine-maker, and which was sold to Coca-Cola of Atlanta in 1977.

• 17 •

Just beyond the business district of St. Helena is the Beringer winery, with its picturesque Rhine House, gardens, and maze of wine-aging tunnels dug a thousand feet into the limestone hillside almost a century ago—a tourist attraction that brings hordes of visitors throughout the year. The title of "oldest Napa winegrower" belongs to this winery because it has never closed since it was built in 1876, and has made wine in every vintage since 1879, including the Prohibition years, when it made sacramental wines.

Jacob and Frederick Beringer came to the United States from Mainz on the Rhine, where Jacob began his winemaking career. From 1872 to 1878, Jacob worked at the nearby Charles Krug winery while the Beringer cellars and vineyards were being established. Frederick then joined him and built the Rhine House, the elegant seventeen-room mansion which stands beside the winery. Its counterpart was built by their uphill neighbor, Tiburcio Parrott, who also grew grapes for the Beringers on his Miravalle estate. After the Beringer brothers died, Jacob's descendants bought the shares held by the widow and children of "Uncle Fritz," who sold the Rhine House and moved away. Jacob's son, Charles Tiburcio Beringer, let the quality of the wines decline, but was succeeded by his nephew Otto, who improved them and bought back the Rhine House from absentee owners, transforming it into a colorful visitor center and tasting hall.

In 1970, President Gerard Gogniat of Nestlé, the multinational Swiss maker of chocolate, Nescafé, and other food products, decided to enter the fast-growing wine business in the United States. He bought Beringer and its vineyards in the Napa and Knights valleys. A new 2.25-million-gallon winery was built across the Wine Road, while the old winery and its tunnels became exclusively an oak cellar for the aging of wines. More land was acquired and planted throughout the valley, increasing Beringer vineyards to 2800 acres. Myron Nightingale, the famed creator of Cresta Blanca Premier Sémillon, became Beringer winemaster in 1970, and a decade later, with his wife Alice, again made an induced-botrytis Sémillon, which was named for them in 1983. Beringer table wines made from purchased grapes are sold under the winery's original Los Hermanos name in magnums, and in the company's patented airline package containing a single bottle and a glass.

The Beringer winery is also the headquarters for the Nestlé-related international importing firm, Wine World, which markets the Crosse & Blackwell line of French, German, and other European wines.

Next door to Beringer is the most prodigious structure in the valley, the Greystone cellar of the Christian Brothers. Until 1984, when it was closed for structural strengthening to resist earthquakes, millions toured its tunnels, which once held 2 million gallons of aging wine. Upstairs, the Brothers long made their Charmat-process champagnes. When the repairs are completed, the Brothers are expected to start making bottle-fermented champagnes.

When the colossal building was erected in 1889, it was the largest stone winery in the world. During the 1880s, small Napa winegrowers could not afford to age their wines and had to sell them in bulk at ruinously low prices to San Francisco wine merchants, for no bank would accept wine as collateral for loans. William Bourn, the wealthy young owner of two Napa vineyards, of San Francisco's water company, and of sundry mines, conceived of an altruistic scheme. He offered to build this winery to make wine of the growers' grapes, to age the wine, and to lend them 10 cents a gallon until it could be sold. When Greystone was opened, however, the phylloxera vine plague had caused a wine shortage, and the building became a white elephant. It had a procession of owners during the next half century: Charles Carpy, the California Wine Association, Bisceglia Brothers, Central California Wineries, Roma, and Cresta Blanca. The low point was in the Depression year of 1931, when Bisceglia bought it at auction for $10,000. By 1945, The Christian Brothers needed extra space, rented part of Greystone, and five years later bought it from Roma. When in 1955 they decided to make Charmat-process champagne (which may erelong change to the *méthode champenoise*), that department was installed on the third floor. In the building's cornerstone, according to an early issue of the St. Helena *Star*, there repose bottles of Charles Krug and Bourn & Wise wines of the 1877 to 1884 vintages, and a bottle of 1883 Beringer brandy.

· 18 ·

In the competition to be called the oldest, the Charles Krug winery, across the road from Greystone, cites the date of 1861, when the Prussian emigré for whom it is named built his first winery there. However, only one stone wall of that winery remains, and credit for the many good and fine wines now made there belongs not to Krug, but to the Italian family named Mondavi, who have owned the site since 1943.

Krug was one of the pioneer winegrowers in the valley, but he was not the first. George Yount and several others preceded him by as much as twenty years. Charles (née Karl) Krug came to the United States in 1847, taught for a year in a freethinkers' school in Philadelphia, returned to Germany, and was imprisoned for participating in a revolt against the reactionary parliament, returned to the United States and became editor of the first German newspaper on the Pacific Coast, published in Oakland.

In 1854, he tried farming near "Count" Haraszthy's failing vine-yard in San Mateo County, next worked briefly in the San Francisco Mint, then followed Haraszthy to Sonoma, learned wine-making from General Vallejo, and planted a vineyard there. In 1860, the year Abraham Lincoln was elected President, Krug sold his Sonoma vineyard, moved to St. Helena, and married Vallejo's grandniece Caroline, the daughter of Dr. Edward T. Bale. Her dowry was the land on which he planted vines and erected the original winery in the following year.

During the next two decades, Krug became "the wine king of Napa Valley" and a prominent member of the first State Viti-cultural Commission. His wines and brandy were sold in the East, in Mexico, Germany, and England. Then phylloxera de-stroyed most of his vineyard, and Krug's estate was in debt when he died in 1892. A nephew ran the winery until Prohibition, when the then-owners, the Moffitt family of bankers and paper merchants, closed it down.

At Repeal, the cellar was leased to Louis Stralla's Napa Wine Company, until Stralla moved to the old Brun & Chaix place at Oakville in 1940. The Moffitts meanwhile declined to sell the estate, hoping to find a buyer who could reestablish the earlier prestige of its wines. In Lodi, one day in 1935, when Robert and Peter Mondavi were home from their studies at Stan-ford, their father asked them what kind of careers, if any, they had in mind after college. Cesare Mondavi, who had come to America from Italy twenty-seven years before, had a grape-shipping business in Lodi and Fresno and had begun making bulk wine at the Acampo Winery at Repeal. When the boys replied that they would like to get into the wine business, Cesare advised them that the future lay in table wines and that the Napa Valley was the place to go. After graduation, both sons were taught enology by University of California scientists. To start them off, Cesare bought the Sunny St. Helena Winery in 1937. When the chance came six years later to buy the Krug estate for $75,000, the Sunny St. Helena and Acampo wineries were sold.

When C. Mondavi & Sons took over at Krug, bulk wine shipped in tank cars to regional bottlers was the mainstay of their business. The Mondavis bottled their best wines under the Krug name, and within five years were winning medals at the state fair. They opened a tasting room, invited visitors to hold picnics and tastings on the estate, and published a newsletter named *Bottles and Bins* which has been circulating for almost thirty years.

In 1965, disagreements between the two brothers, brewing

since their father's death six years earlier, exploded into a family schism. Their mother and sisters joined Peter, the younger winemaker brother, in telling Robert his son Michael could not be employed by the winery. Robert responded by building his own winery six miles down the road. A bitter court fight ensued, and after the mother's death in 1976, ended in victory for Robert. Peter and Helen bought Bob's interest, ending the family feud. Charles Krug is now run by Peter, his UC Davis–trained son Marc, and Peter, Jr. The Charles Krug (or C. Mondavi & Sons) winery has grown to 6 million gallons and its vineyards between St. Helena and the Carneros district to 1000 acres. Only its best wines, thirteen under varietal labels and ten generically labeled, plus a "vintage select" Cabernet, are sold under the Charles Krug name. The rest are jug-quality "CK" Mondavi wines, available in sizes up to four liters, which include some from the San Joaquin Valley.

• 19 •

Continuing north on the Wine Road past Krug, the venerable stone cellar at your right, newly paired with an attractive tasting room labeled "Markham," is the rejuvenation of the million-gallon St. Helena growers' co-op winery, which was the Laurent Winery when it was built in 1876. Former advertising man H. Bruce Markham performed this rejuvenation in 1978, to provide a proper home for the 300 acres of premium grapes he had acquired three years earlier at Yountville, Oak Knoll, and Calistoga. Markham Winery is managed by UC Davis–trained enologist Bryan del Bondio, whose father makes Inglenook wines at Oakville. With new and modern equipment, the old cellar now turns out vintage-dated, vineyard-designated Markham "varietals," including Cabernet, Riesling and Muscat de Frontignan, and Vin-Mark Merlot and Gamay Beaujolais Blanc. If you wonder about the illustrations of the antique cannon on the Markham labels, they represent Bruce Markham's four years as a gunnery officer during the Korean War.

Beyond the Markham Winery, the century-old Victorian house at your left, with the terraced vines in front, is where Michael Robbins started the Spring Mountain Vineyards winery, selling it after he moved to the Tiburcio Parrott estate. The buyers in 1976 were ophthalmologist William J. Casey and his wife Alexandra, wine enthusiasts who had planned for years to own a winery. They renamed it St. Clement Vineyard for the doctor's ancestral home, St. Clement's Manor in Maryland, a seventeenth-century grant from the English crown, where the doctor had helped plant a vineyard. When their first St. Clement Vineyard wines were well received, the Caseys had a new 25,000-gallon stone winery, harmonizing with the house, built at the base of Spring Mountain in 1979. They commute three days a week from San Francisco, where the doctor has his practice.

On Lodi Lane, the next road to the right, is a pre-Prohibition stone cellar renamed by owner Charles Abela in 1977 as the Round Hill Vineyards winery. The various wines it makes are named for the round hill west of St. Helena, where Ernest Van Asperen, of Ernie's Wine Shops, lives and grows grapes, some of which reach the market in Round Hill wines. Ernie owns four Napa vineyards but produces no wine commercially.

Next on the right is Freemark Abbey, the moss-covered stone cellar with the gourmet shops and Abbey Restaurant upstairs, around the corner from Wine Country Inn. The "Abbey" dates from 1895 and was never a monastery; it was named by former owners who combined syllables from their names. It was reactivated as a modern winery in 1967. No tasting is offered, but there are cellar tours twice a day. Seven partners, three of them grape growers, own the winery, which has first choice from their six hundred acres of vineyards. Special wines are made from other vineyards, such as John Bosche's Cabernet. Bradford Webb, who made the first Hanzell wines, is one of the grower-partners. The chief partner is Charles Carpy, whose Bordeaux-born grandfather owned the Uncle Sam Cellars in Napa city in 1887, and was the largest shareholder in the California Wine Association when it was formed in 1894. In 1976, the Freemark group and more investors acquired the Rutherford Hill winery, described later. Some Freemark wines have set new high standards for California. The 1973 Edelwein, a botrytized Riesling, might have been labeled Beerenauslese if it had been grown in the Rheingau. In the following nine years, four more Edelweins were made. The 1976 and 1982, from partner Frank Woods's vineyard on Rutherford Cross Road, had Trockenbeerenauslese quality and were named Edelwein Gold.

The yellow farmhouse with surrounding wine equipment, a short walk beyond the Abbey and candle factory, is the 10,000-gallon Folie à Deux winery, whose name in French literally means "craziness for two." When St. Helena Hospital's psychiatrist Larry Dizmang and psychologist Gary Mills bonded the cottage cellar in 1981, to make wine from the Chenin Blanc and Chardonnay grapes Dr. Mills grows near Yountville, they chose the name given in psychiatry textbooks for odd behavior by two. A Rorschach inkblot adorns the labels of Folie à Deux wines.

On Ehlers Lane, a mile north of Freemark Abbey, is a venerable stone cellar with arched windows and a carving above the door that reads: "B. Ehlers, 1886." It is named in Frona Eunice Wait's 1889 book of California wines, and though idle during the Prohibition era, again has produced wine since Repeal. Owners of the Conn Creek and Vichon wineries used this cellar during the 1970s while preparing to build their own. In 1984, it was occupied by a new wine company, which renamed the cellar "Ehlers Lane Winery," indicating it expects to stay. Among its principals is Michael J. Casey, who owns the century-old building and the surrounding vineyard.

A half-mile farther on the right, scarcely visible behind a fence, are the four-acre Frog's Leap vineyard and tiny winery, bonded in 1981. The owners are physician Larry Turley, his wife Jeannine, winemaker John T. Williams, and his wife Julie. They named it when they discovered in an old ledger that the farm had raised frogs around the turn of the century for sale to San Francisco gourmets at 33 cents a dozen. Their Sauvignon Blanc and Chardonnay labels picture a frog at the height of its leap. Williams, trained at Cornell and UC Davis, made award-winning wines at the Glenora Wine Cellars in New York State before becoming the winemaker at Spring Mountain Vineyards, which is still his full-time job.

On Big Tree Road, a half mile ahead on your right, veteran farmer Arnold Tudal and his wife Alma planted Cabernet on their ten-acre farm in 1974, and five years later equipped their barn as the 10,000-gallon Tudal Winery to make estate-bottled wine, with weekend help from their son and two daughters, both flight attendants. They took samples of their young wine on a visit to relatives in France, who thought the wine was French but recognized that it came from young vines.

Across the road from the Tudals is the 40,000-gallon winery where, in 1978, former banker Charles F. Shaw began making *macération carbonique* (usually called *nouveau*) red wine of the forty-five acres of Napa Gamay grapes on the vineyard he had bought the year before. He was preparing to add estate-bottled Chardonnay and Fumé Blanc by 1984.

A short distance farther on the Wine Road, there is an unmarked private road on the left. If you have made an appointment, you may climb almost two miles up the dirt road and visit Stony Hill Vineyard. The vines rise almost a thousand feet above the valley and cover some thirty-five acres of rocky soil, which explains the name. The four wines made here—Chardonnay, Gewürztraminer, Riesling, and in some years a Sémillon de Soleil (sweet, made from sun-dried grapes)—are so prized by connoisseurs that most of the supply is sold before it is ready to be shipped. The story of Fred and Eleanor McCrea has inspired many others to embark on winegrowing careers. Eleanor has carried on since Fred, a San Francisco advertising executive, died in 1977. They bought their hillside in 1943 as a summer place, then wondered what to do with the extra land. Neighbors said it would be good for only goats or grapes, so they chose grapes. Knowing nothing about winegrowing, they asked experts what to plant, and were advised to try Chardonnay. Waiting for their vines to mature, the McCreas practiced winemaking in their home and threw the first batch away. Then, guided by friendly Napa vintners, they had their winery built and equipped by 1951. Nine years later, their Chardonnay was awarded the highest prize in the state, a gold medal at the state fair. Orders for the wine came in floods, but the McCreas kept their winery small—several dozen oak barrels holding 7000 gallons when full—and sold most of their grapes to neighboring wineries. Each September, when Stony Hill wines have a year or two of bottle age, a letter goes to a small mailing list stating which wines are ready for sale. If you place your order promptly it is likely to be filled, but it is wiser to order a year ahead.

• 20 •

On Larkmead Lane, a quarter mile off the Wine Road, are the champagne cellars of Hanns Kornell, where he makes his eight excellent "Third Generation" champagnes.

The Larkmead Vineyard has been famous since the 1880s, when it was owned by Mrs. Lillie Hitchcock Coit. She was known then as a sort of mascot to the San Francisco Fire Department because of her passion for running to fires, but she is remembered now as the donor of Coit Tower on that city's Telegraph Hill. Another owner before Prohibition was the Felix Salmina family from Switzerland, who after Repeal made some of the best Napa wines. A succession of proprietors followed, including National Distillers, Bruno Solari, and the Larkmead Co-operative, until Kornell took over in 1958.

Kornell is a stocky little man of incredible stamina and energy. He is more of a legend than his winery. In 1915, at the age of four, he picked grapes in his grandfather's vineyard at Lublinitz in Germany. At five, he was already cleaning bottles in the cellar. During his school years, his father taught him the art of tasting. At graduation he was sent to the Geisenheim enological institute, then worked in wineries in France, Italy, and England. When he was ready in 1939 to take over the family vineyard, the gathering war clouds warned him to go to America. With two dollars in his pocket, he hitchhiked from New York to California and worked first as a laborer, then at the Los Amigos and Fountain Grove Vineyard wineries. In 1942, he went to the Gibson winery at Covington, Kentucky, and made champagne out of California wine. Three years later, on a visit to the American Wine Company cellars in St. Louis, whom should I find three stories underground making Cook's Imperial Champagne, but Hanns Kornell? After that winery was sold to Schenley, Hanns returned to California, leased the rundown former Tribuno winery at Sonoma in 1952, and made his own champagne. Bottling and riddling by night and selling by day, he saved enough in six years to buy and move to Larkmead. In that year he married Marielouise Rossini, whose grandfather planted the first Souverain Vineyard seventy-two years before.

At the Kornell cellars you are shown every step in the making of bottle-fermented champagnes. Your amiable guide may be the indefatigable owner himself, or perhaps a member of the fourth generation, college-graduate son Peter Hanns or daughter Paula, who became the winery vice president in 1981. Both taste wine regularly with their parents. There are eight Kornell champagnes, blanc de blancs, brut, sec, extra dry, demi-sec, rouge, Muscat of Alexandria, and vintaged Sehr Trocken, extremely dry. The latter is aged five years or more on the yeast before it is disgorged. That many agree with Hanns Kornell's taste is evident from his steadily increasing business, including his exports to other countries, especially to Switzerland and Germany.

• 21 •

Past Larkmead Lane, a small sign at the left of the highway reads: "Schramsberg Champagne Cellars—Founded 1862." A narrow road from there winds nearly a mile up the southern slope of Mount Diamond through a thicket of redwoods, buckeyes, and madrones. You first pass an old stone winery partly hidden on your left, about which I'll tell you in a moment. In a wide clearing at the end is the scene that Robert Louis Stevenson described in *Silverado Squatters,* the same house with its broad verandas where Stevenson and his bride were entertained in 1880 by Jacob and Annie Schram, and the five underground cellars "dug deep in the hillside like a bandit's cave."

Schram (originally Schramm) arrived in America from the Rhineland in 1842, became an itinerant barber, and stopped in San Francisco long enough to get married. When he reached

Napa in 1862, Charles Krug had begun building his winery on the valley floor two years before. Schram had saved enough money to buy a mountainside of his own. While Annie supervised the planting of their vines, Schram continued tramping from farm to farm with his razor and shears. Eighteen years later, Stevenson found Schramsberg "the picture of prosperity." Schramsberger Hock, Golden Chasselas, and Burgundy of Refosco had already won a place on such wine lists as the Palace Hotel's in San Francisco and the Carlton Club's in London. When Jacob Schram died in 1904, his son Herman took over and made wine until Prohibition, when he sold the estate for a summer home. Following Repeal there were two brief revivals, the first by Joseph Gargano's California Champagne Company in 1940, the second in 1951 by the Douglas Pringles, who revived the Schramsberg label and made rather poor champagnes for a few years.

Meanwhile, San Francisco Wine and Food Society member Jack L. Davies had invested in a Cabernet-planting venture with Martin Ray in Santa Clara County, then sold his interest after a dispute with that controversial vintner. In 1965, Davies organized fourteen fellow wine lovers and bought Schramsberg from Pringle's former wife, Mrs. Louise de Laveaga Cebrian; he quit his job as a management consultant, moved with his wife Jamie Louise and their three children into the ninety-year-old Schram house, and set out to make the world's finest champagne. The cobwebbed, long-neglected tunnels were cleared, the earth floors paved, the old vineyard torn out and replanted with Chardonnay, Pinot Blanc, and Pinot Noir. During their first vintage of purchased grapes in 1966, the new crusher broke down. Jamie took off her shoes and finished the crushing the age-old way.

In February 1972, Schramsberg Champagne became world famous overnight. President Richard M. Nixon had flown an American champagne to Peking to serve at his historic, globally televised banquet for Premier Chou En-lai. A columnist identified the shipment as thirteen cases of Schramsberg, Nixon's favorite champagne.

Schramsberg and its vineyards were enlarged in subsequent years to 96,000 gallons and fifty acres. It now has five champagnes: Reserve Brut, aged four years or more before release, Blanc de Blancs Brut, Blanc de Noirs, Cuvée de Pinot, and semi-sparkling demi-sec Crémant made largely of the Flora grape. In 1982, in a joint venture named R and S Vineyards with Francois Heriard-Dubreuil of Remy-Martin Cognac, the Davies's began producing alembic brandy in Napa in stills imported from

France, and built the distillery on the site south of Napa mentioned earlier.

The old stone winery you passed on your way up the hill is on the site of the Alta Vineyard of master mariner Colin T. McEachran, from Greenock in Scotland, whom the Stevensons visited in 1880 on the day before they visited Schramsberg; the Schrams weren't home. In 1970, Stevenson-buff Benjamin Falk and his wife Rose bought and began replanting the forty-acre site of McEachran's vineyard and began restoring the old stone cellar. They have had their Alta Vineyard wines produced at other Napa wineries.

· 22 ·

As you approach the valley's upper end, a white, monastery-like structure comes into view atop the range of hills to the east. It is the Sterling Vineyards winery, the most spectacular in America and quite possibly in the world. To reach the winery, turn right on Dunaweal Lane, pass a smaller winery (of which more in a moment), and board an aerial tramway like those found at the costlier mountain ski resorts. For your fare (partly refunded if you buy wine), a yellow, four-person gondola lifts you 250 feet to the winery, which commands a dramatic view of the valley winescape and of towering Mount St. Helena. On disembarking, you take an instructive self-tour of the crushing and fermenting areas, then pass through stained-glass-illuminated cellars where some 600,000 gallons of wine age in oak barrels and casks. You then arrive in an area of mosaic-lined patios, fountains, and flowers overlooked by a carillon of European church bells that chime the hours. Here, selected wines are offered for tasting and for purchase to take home.

Sterling had its inception in 1964, when Peter Newton (whose new winery was described earlier) and former Navy fighter pilot Michael P. W. Stone, among the owners of San Francisco's Sterling paper products firm, invested in planting the 400-acre vineyard on the valley floor. They built a temporary cellar in 1968, and by the time the hilltop winery was built five years later, Sterling wines were already winning awards at the Los Angeles County Fair. In 1977, the Coca-Cola Company of Atlanta, which had bought the Taylor and Great Western wineries in New York State, bought Sterling and announced it would be the largest exclusively estate-bottling winery in the United States. A hundred acres were added on the slopes of Diamond Mountain, and four of the earlier Sterling wine types were discontinued;

thenceforth the winery would concentrate on Chardonnay, Sauvignon Blanc, Cabernet, and Merlot. When in 1983 Seagram bought Coca-Cola's wineries, Sterling began making champagne in association with world-famous Mumm's of Rheims.

Returning from Sterling to the Wine Road, you will find it interesting to visit the smaller (50,000-gallon) Stonegate Winery, on Dunaweal Lane. The owners of Stonegate are University of California journalism instructor James Spaulding and his wife Barbara. Their son David, trained in enology at Santa Rosa Junior College and in short courses at UC Davis, is the winemaker. The Spauldings came to California from Wisconsin in 1969 after a disappointing attempt to grow wine grapes at Mequon, a suburb of Milwaukee. Since starting this winery in 1973, they have produced mostly estate-bottled wines from their thirty acres of vineyard, half of which is at the winery and half on the upper slopes of Diamond Mountain to the west.

Diamond Mountain Road, a short distance north of Dunaweal Lane, climbs to extensive new vineyards, two new wineries, and to a pre-Prohibition stone cellar whose name nobody in the vicinity could remember until historian Irene Haynes identified the carved initials "RS" as those of Richard Schmidt, a San Francisco architect's son who owned 400 acres nearby and built the winery in 1888. One of the new wineries is former wholesale druggist Albert Brounstein's 20,000-gallon Diamond Creek Vineyards cellar, where he ages the three distinctly different Cabernet wines from the slopes of his vineyard that he calls Volcanic Hill, Gravelly Meadow, and Red Rock Terrace. A wine-appreciation course taught by Los Angeles *Times* writer Nathan Chroman in 1965, and a subsequent wine tour of France, inspired Brounstein to plant twenty acres on Mount Diamond and make his first wine in 1972. He aged his wines in the Schmidt winery until he built a new one in 1979.

A stone's throw from Brounstein's Diamond Creek winery is the much smaller Roddis Cellar, which produces estate-bottled, long-lived Cabernet Sauvignon and sells it to people on its growing mailing list. Bill Roddis was a helicopter crew chief-gunner in Vietnam, when a swimming accident while on leave in Florida made him a quadriplegic for life. He operated a wine store in Southern California, which taught him about wine, then came to the Napa Valley with his wife Patsy to cultivate the four-acre vineyard of old Cabernet vines that faces their home. Bill rides a wheelchair to run the winery, which was converted from a barn, and a golf cart to prune the vineyard, both with Patsy's help. The Roddises are members of Jehovah's Witnesses, who recognize Jesus' first miracle, the turning of water into wine.

• 23 •

A mile and a half farther north is Calistoga, the city that began in 1859 as the personal empire and obsession of the fabulous Sam Brannan, the wandering printer from the Ohio vineyard center of Painesville, who joined the original Mormons, brought two hundred of them to San Francisco by sea, founded that city's first newspaper, led the Vigilantes, quarreled with Brigham Young, and abandoned the Mormon faith. Brannan is said to have named Calistoga by a slip of his tongue, saying: "I'll make this place the Calistoga of Sarafornia." California's first millionaire, Brannan bought 2000 acres to found Calistoga around its natural mudpots and geysers, spent millions planting the 125,000 vines that he personally brought from Europe, and built a winery, brandy distillery, hotels, racetrack, and luxury baths. His Calistoga empire collapsed after his divorce in 1870. He soon lost his fortune, and in 1889 died penniless near Escondido in the arms of an Indian woman.

Two miles north of Calistoga, hidden in a grove a few hundred yards from Tubbs Lane, is an historic winery named Château Montelena. Its facade of many arches, pilasters, parapets, and towers is an architectural curio, reminiscent of some nineteenth-century Italian palace. It was built of native stone in 1882 by state senator and cordage manufacturer Alfred L. Tubbs, the patriarch of a noted San Francisco family, and has often been compared to Château Lafite. Tubbs, with Charles Krug and other winery owners, organized the Napa Valley Wine Company in 1883 to sell their wines and those of independent vineyardists to the retail trade. Eleven years later, the company was absorbed by the California Wine Association. A grandson, Chapin Tubbs, made wine sporadically here for a few years following Repeal. In 1947, a Chinese engineer bought the property, made the upper story of the empty cellar his home, and built the Oriental Water Gardens, five-acre Jade Lake with four islands, arched bridges, and an authentic five-ton Chinese junk in the center.

The winery had lain idle for some thirty years when in 1968 it was purchased by Lee and Helen Paschich, dedicated home winemakers who found it pleasant to live upstairs. Then the wine revolution exploded, and many investors became interested in old Napa wineries that might be revived to capitalize on the boom. Among those who saw the possibilities in Château Montelena were Southern California attorney James L. Barrett and Chicago supermarket developer Ernest Hahn. They became Paschich's partners, replanted the hundred-acre vineyard, installed modern equipment to hold some 170,000 gallons, and in 1972 brought in the great winemaker Miljenko (Mike) Grgich, whom we met earlier. Grgich made Château Montelena nationally famous with one of the wines of his second vintage—the 1973 Chardonnay—for this was the California white wine that those nine French experts, at that blind-tasting in Paris, chose as finer than four of the top white burgundies of France and five other California Chardonnays.

Château Montelena's vineyard is planted entirely to red varieties, mostly Cabernet Sauvignon and Zinfandel; its white wines are of purchased grapes. In 1982 the château's centennial observance included the release of its first (1978) estate-bottled Cabernet Sauvignon.

Bennett Lane extends a short way from Tubbs Lane to the modern 26,000-gallon Robert Pecota Winery and the forty-acre vineyard Robert and his wife Susan have been replanting with Cabernet and Sauvignon Blanc since they bought it in 1973. Before building the winery in 1978, Pecota was a buyer of grapes and bulk wine for the Beringer winery.

Four miles northwest of Calistoga, where the Wine Road becomes Highway 128, a gate at your left opens to the century-old Grimm Brothers Winery, and the three great hillside tunnels which have housed two new Napa valley wineries since 1979. Two of the tunnels are former Stanford history professor J. Bernard Seps' Storybook Mountain Vineyards winery, which is producing estate-bottled Zinfandel from the forty-acre Grimm Vineyard Dr. Seps and his wife Sigrid began replanting when they bought the property in 1976. The center tunnel is the Schug Cellars of Joseph Phelps Vineyards' winemaster Walter Schug, who with his wife Gertrude is producing Pinot Noir there from purchased Napa Valley grapes, and of whom more will be told later.

· 24 ·

From this point, it is time to turn back down the Napa Valley on Silverado Trail to the fourteen wineries along the Trail, and later to the dozen more along the crossroads and in the eastern hills.

Facing the Trail on your left, past the east end of Dunaweal

Lane, is the handsome Swiss-owned, Spanish-style, 120,000-gallon Cuvaison Winery with its graceful arches, stained-glass windows, and red-tiled roof. Built in 1974, it replaced a rustic structure erected four years earlier by engineers Drs. Thomas Parkhill and Thomas H. E. Cottrell. The latter contributed the name, a French word for the fermenting of red wines on the skins of grapes. The original small structure was transformed into a handsome tasting room with picnic tables outside, which welcomes visitors five days a week. When in 1979 Dr. Stefan Schmidheiny and his brother Alexander of Zurich bought Cuvaison, they also bought 392 acres along Duhig Road in the Carneros district, and as mentioned earlier, they are preparing to build a new Cuvaison Winery on the vineyard they have begun planting there. Since 1975, the winery has specialized in producing only three wines—Chardonnay, Cabernet, and Zinfandel; but since the new vineyard includes some Pinot Noir, the number may be expected to increase to four.

Next, hidden high in the forest on your right, is the new Rombauer Vineyards winery, which produced its first vintage in 1982. Koerner Rombauer, a great nephew of *Joy of Cooking* author Joy Rombauer, is a pilot for Pacific East Airline on the Los Angeles–Honolulu run. Adjoining Rombauer is the 6000-gallon Casa Nuestra winery of St. Helena attorney Eugene R. Kirkham and his wife Cody, bonded on their ten-acre vineyard in 1980. The lovely *petit château* across the road is Château Boswell, built in 1982 for retired Whittier dentist R. Thornton Boswell, but not yet in production when I last was there.

From Glass Mountain Road, next on your left, a private road leads left to a stately two-story stone cellar that bears the date "1881." As described in Irene Haynes' *Ghost Wineries of Napa Valley*, in the 1880s and 1890s this was the Villa Remi Winery of philanthropist Remi Chabot, for whom the college, observatory, and lake in Alameda County are named. In 1982, Richard W. Forman, the partner in the Newton Vineyards who earlier was the first winemaker at Sterling Vineyard, was making Forman wines in the Villa Remi cellar, until he could build his own winery at his new vineyard on Howell Mountain. Forman also is a consultant for several of the new north coast counties wineries.

At the intersection of Lodi Lane with Silverado Trail, on your right, is the Duckhorn Vineyards winery, opened in 1978 by former banker Daniel Duckhorn, his wife Margaret, and eight other families to make Cabernet and Merlot of the grapes grown by two of the families. Their first vintages were so well received that they expanded the winery to 50,000 gallons in 1983.

Three miles farther on your right is the 25,000-gallon Napa Creek Winery, bonded in 1980 by former Kentucky and Illinois wine marketer Jack Schulze, in a former meat-packing plant that he discovered was ideal for winemaking and for storage and aging of wines.

• 25 •

Taplin Road, at your left a half-mile farther south, takes you to a gateway curiously constructed of recycled lumber from century-old California railroad bridges. This is the entrance to the 300,000-gallon Joseph Phelps Vineyards winery, whose facade resembles the vineyard gate. In 1972 Phelps, conducting his construction business from Greeley, Colorado, was building the Souverain wineries in California when he bought land on Taplin Road and established his own 250-acre winegrowing estate. As his winemaster, he chose German-born, Geisenheim-trained Walter Schug, who had had experience with two California wineries since coming to this country in 1961. While Phelps built his winery, Schug planted 200 acres of noble varieties for him, including the German grape Scheurebe and Syrah, the red Rhone variety of Hermitage, which differs from California's Petite Sirah. Phelps Vineyards wines have been receiving lyric praises since the 1975 vintage, especially for its Rieslings, which in some years include late-harvest vintages equal to the best from Germany. Schug since has begun producing his own wines in Sonoma County, but still supervises the Phelps Vineyards. Touring and tasting are not offered at the Phelps winery, but you can buy wines by the case there on most weekdays, including its best buys, nonvintage Vin Blanc and Vin Rouge. Invitational tastings are held on occasion, when you may meet Walter Schug and, if he isn't away on some building project, perhaps Phelps himself.

Taplin Road continues past Phelps Vineyard to the winery and vineyard of Joseph and Alice Heitz, whose wines are among the most famous in Napa Valley. In 1944, after two years in a midwestern college, Airman Joe Heitz was chief of a night-fighter ground crew at the field near the then Italian Swiss Colony (originally La Paloma) winery outside Fresno. Dale Mills, the winemaker there, put Joe to work in the cellar by day, and discovering that he had an exceptionally keen palate, advised him to enroll at Davis and study enology. Heitz did so and won his master's degree in 1949. For ten years he worked at Beaulieu and other wineries, then taught enology at Fresno State College for four years. In 1961, married and with three children, he decided to start his own wine business. He bought Leon Brendel's "Only One" Grignolino vineyard on the Wine Road south of St. Helena, the site of the Heitz tasting room today. The orange-pink Grignolino wine he made there could not support his family, but Heitz has the rare ability to select lots from other wineries that will improve with blending and aging. Five-foot-tall Alice Heitz developed a mailing list and sent periodic letters to their customers, announcing each new Heitz selection. Soon a larger winery was needed, and in 1965 Heitz found the place in the small winery at the end of Taplin Road. On the property was an empty seventy-year-old winery building and an old house. He equipped the cellar with stainless-steel fermenters and European oak casks, some of them from the Hanzell Vineyard, and planted forty more acres of Grignolino, Chardonnay, and Pinot Noir. In 1972, when son David graduated from Fresno State and became his parents' winemaker, an additional winery was built, raising their capacity to 175,000 gallons. Most grapes for Heitz wines are produced by others, some of whose names appear on the labels. Most famous vineyard-labeled Heitz wine is the eucalyptus-mint-flavored Cabernet grown on Tom and Martha Mays' forty-acre vineyard near Oakville, the wines of which bring $50 a bottle or more when they are seven years old.

• 26 •

Two miles south of Taplin Road, a road curves a half-mile uphill to the attractive Rutherford Hill winery. This was named Souverain of Rutherford when it was built in 1972, while the Souverain of Alexander Valley cellar, visited in the preceding chapter, was being built near Geyserville in Sonoma County. In 1976, when Pillsbury Mills of Minneapolis sold both Souverain wineries, a group formed by vineyardist William Jaeger and other owners of Freemark Abbey bought this one and renamed it Rutherford Hill. Winemaker-partner Philip Baxter's aim is to make his eight vintage-dated "varietal" wines surpass those of Freemark Abbey, and he sometimes succeeds. There is daily tasting and a pleasant picnic area.

On your right, a minute's drive south, Highway 128 crosses Silverado Trail and takes you to two wineries in the direction of Rutherford. At the intersection with Conn Creek Road is veteran vineyardist Charles Wagner's Caymus Vineyard winery (named for the Caymus land grant). He built the 50,000-gallon cellar in 1971 to produce wines of the Cabernet, Pinot Noir, and Riesling grapes that grow on his seventy-acre vineyard. His wife Lorna and their son Charles J. (Chuck) work with him. Besides their estate-bottled wines, they make Zinfandel from purchased grapes, and sell it under a separate "Liberty School" label that pictures the nearby one-room school that Charles attended in his youth.

A short way farther, on your right, are the sixty-seven-acre HNW Vineyard and its 6000-gallon winery, built in 1982. The H in the name stands for partner State Superintendent of Public Instruction Louis "Bill" Honig, the W for partner Judge Daniel Weinstein of the San Francisco Superior Court, and the N for an earlier partner who sold his interest to HNW's manager and winemaker, UC Davis-trained Richard K. Tracy. The winery's Sauvignon Blanc is named for the late Louis Honig, Sr., Dr. Honig's father and Judge Weinstein's father-in-law.

If you return now to Silverado Trail, you will be facing two relatively new wineries just south of where Highway 128 crosses the Trail. First on your right is the 134,000-gallon French-style Conn Creek cellar. It was built in 1979, when the nineteenth-century Ehlers winery on Ehlers Lane, where the first five Conn Creek vintages were made, proved too small to accommodate all the grapes from Conn Creek Vineyards' 146 acres of vines. The vineyards and winery are owned by a partnership headed by Annapolis-trained former submarine officer William D. Collins and his wife Kathy, who were joined in 1981 by Francis Dewavrin and his wife Françoise Woltner, former co-proprietors of Château La Mission Haut-Brion in the Graves section of Bordeaux. The Dewavrins have bought the century-old Howell Mountain vineyard and winery in eastern Napa County and may reopen that winery someday. They have helped to develop European markets for Conn Creek wines, the best known of which are Cabernet, Chardonnay, and Zinfandel.

Immediately south of the Conn Creek cellar is the 80,000-gallon Shown & Sons Vineyards winery, also built in 1979. Estate-planner Richard Shown had been making wine as a hobby at home for twenty years when, on a Napa Valley visit in 1970, he noticed a vineyard for sale and realized he could make his hobby into a business. That is what he and his wife Sue did, developing seventy-six acres of vineyards with the help of their sons Steve and Chris, selling their grapes to wineries for several years, then building this one of their own. When I was last there, they were making estate-bottled Chenin Blanc, Riesling, and Cabernet, selling their output in fifteen states and to callers at the winery.

Another mile south you will see on your right the new ZD Winery, which former aerospace engineers Gino Zepponi and Norman de Leuze (whose surname initials supply the winery's name) started in the Sonoma Valley in 1969. A decade later, they moved to this new building in Napa Valley to continue making "varietal" wines from the few acres of grapes they grow and from those they buy in the coastal counties and in the Sierra foothills. Both are expert winemakers, but most of the wine is made by de Leuze, with the help of his son Robert. Zepponi oversees champagne production at Domaine Chandon.

In the grove of oaks facing Silverado Lane, a mile south of Skellinger Lane, is the 58,000-gallon Girard Winery, built in 1980 by the Stephen Girards, senior and junior, to make estate-bottled Chardonnay, Chenin Blanc, and Cabernet from the adjoining forty-acre vineyard that Girard Sr., board chairman of Kaiser Steel, purchased in 1974. Their second label besides "Girard" is "Stephens," for the wines they make of purchased grapes. In 1982 they began planting premium varieties on a second Girard vineyard, on a hillside near Domaine Chandon.

Oakville Cross Road leads to three more wineries and the site chosen for a fourth. From the stone pillar that reads "Mount Eden Ranch," a private road leads to the winegrowing estate of San Francisco financier James McWilliams and his wife Anne, the granddaughter of Bank of America founder A. P. Giannini. Since making this their country home in 1970, they have re-planted the eighty-acre vineyard, which dates from 1881, and have re-equipped and air-conditioned the 56,000-gallon winery, which turns out estate-bottled Cabernet, Pinot Noir, and Chardonnay.

Next door, to the west, construction was begun in 1983 for Atari computer executive Dennis Groth and his wife Judith's future Groth Vineyards Winery. The design calls for a three-level, 100,000-gallon cellar with a domed bell tower commanding a view of their 121 acres of vines. Their partner and manager is Nils Venge, who made the Villa Mount Eden wines during the nine preceding years. Across the road, a short distance away, is the three-story, 115,000-gallon Silver Oak Cellars, built in 1982 to replace the 20,000-gallon cellar Justin Meyer and Denver oilman Raymond Duncan started ten years earlier to produce Cabernets that are released only when they are five years old. Duncan and Meyer, who for fifteen years was the assistant cellarmaster of The Christian Brothers, were also the owners of the Franciscan Winery, which they sold to its present Swiss owners in 1979. They have vineyards here and in the Alexander Valley of Sonoma County. The fourth winery preparing to start is owned by Napa attorney R. Gregory Rodeno and his wife Mikhaela, who handles communications for Domaine Chandon. It is marked by an octagonal structure on the east side of Money Road.

Two miles farther is Yountville Cross Road, where Pasadena dentist Stanley B. Anderson and his wife Carol since 1979 have been producing champagne and table wines from their fifty acres of Chardonnay near State Lane.

Next, to the south, a two-level private road extends to the left from Silverado Trail to the Shafer Vineyards winery, bonded in 1979 by former publishing executive John Shafer and his wife Elizabeth on the sixty-five-acre vineyard they began replanting when they moved here from Chicago, seven years before. Their daughters Bett and Libby handle the marketing of their Cabernet, Zinfandel, and Chardonnay. The latter is married to Keenan Vineyards winemaker Joseph Cafaro.

Atop the hill across Silverado Trail is the 100,000-gallon, early-California-style Silverado Vineyards Winery, built in 1981 for Lillian (Mrs. Walter) Disney and her daughter, Diane Miller, on the 165-acre vineyard they have owned since 1976. Diane's husband is Donald Miller, the president of Walt Disney Productions. The winery's first vintage, managed by former Durney Vineyard winemaker John Stuart, was produced in 1981 of estate-grown Cabernet, Merlot, Chardonnay, and Sauvignon Blanc, with ten tons of purchased Gewürztraminer, which makes Lillian Disney's favorite wine.

• 27 •

A short distance south on your left, you come to two Stag's Leap wineries, a few hundred yards apart, whose owners have fought in the courts since 1972 over which is entitled to use the name.

Stag's Leap is a rocky promontory overlooking a vineyard valley east of Silverado Trail. Chicago financier Horace Chase is said to have named it after a legendary stag, when in 1888 he built the residence that later became the Stag's Leap Hotel. Warren and Barbara Winiarski left teaching jobs at the University of Chicago in 1964 to become winegrowers in the Napa Valley. They bought part of the Stag's Leap valley, planted vines, and in 1972 began building the 120,000-gallon Stag's Leap Wine Cellars. Two years earlier, while the Winiarskis were still planning their winery, Carl and Joanne Doumani, wine buffs from Los

Angeles, bought the old Stag's Leap Hotel, part of the original vineyard, and the ruins of Chase's winery. They make their home in the hotel's two lower floors and had the Rutherford Hill winery make wine for them, stored it in a cave bonded behind the ruined winery, and sold it labeled "Stags' Leap Vineyards," with the apostrophe after the final "s." Lawsuits ensued, the Winiarskis won, and the Doumanis appealed. Meanwhile, the Winiarskis' 1973 Cabernet made them world-famous, outscoring four first-growth chateau reds in the blind tasting by French experts in Paris in 1976. Both the Winiarskis and Doumanis sell wines with pictures of stags on their labels, receive one anothers' mail and phone calls, and await a final decision from the courts.

On the west side of the trail, a half-mile south of the Silverado Vineyard gate, is the 40,000-gallon Pine Ridge winery, established in 1979 by Colorado real estate developer Gary Andrus and a group of partners. They have three nearby vineyards of premium varieties, totaling seventy acres.

Next on your left, almost surrounded by the Chimney Rock Golf Course, is the Clos du Val 120-acre vineyard and 90,000-gallon winery, established in 1971 for John Goelet, a wealthy American who lives in New York and France and has vineyard properties in France, Australia, and South America. The manager and winemaker is Bernard Portet, a graduate of the French wine school at Montpellier, who worked in South Africa and at a chateau near Toulouse before coming here in 1968. Goelet also owns the Taltarni winery, managed by Portet's brother Dominique, in the Australian state of Victoria. They are the sons of André Portet, who was the long-time technical director of Château Lafite. Clos du Val's first wines were Cabernet and Zinfandel, to which Chardonnays called Gran Val were added in the 1980s. In 1983, Clos du Val introduced a red table wine blend priced lower than its Cabernet.

The handsome three-story stone cellar just north of Clos du Val was the Occidental Winery when it was built in 1878 by Terrill L. Grigsby, a pioneer who came west by oxcart and helped raise the Bear Flag over Sonoma Plaza to declare California's independence from Mexico in 1846. Portet leases the ancient cellar to store his aging Clos du Val wines.

A mile farther south, a right turn on Oak Knoll Avenue takes you to Big Ranch Road and the 82,000-gallon Monticello Vineyards winery, which in 1982 produced the first vintage of estate-bottled Gewürztraminer, Chardonnay, and Sauvignon Blanc from its 200 acres of vineyard planted since 1970. Principal owner

Jay Corley, proud of his Virginia heritage, named the winery for Thomas Jefferson's Virginia home.

Facing Silverado Trail, a mile south of Petra Drive on your right, is the 65,000-gallon Louis K. Mihaly Vineyard winery. Hungarian-born businessman Mihaly in 1982 took over the financially troubled Pannonia Winery, which had started three years earlier, and retained as its winemaker one of Pannonia's founders, Hungarian-trained Dr. John D. Nemeth, a graduate of the University of Budapest. Mihaly says the winery's future wines will all be estate-bottled from its thirty-four acres of Pinot Noir, Chardonnay, and Sauvignon Blanc.

Also on the right a quarter-mile south is the 25,000-gallon St. Andrews Vineyard winery, opened in 1980 on its all-Chardonnay vineyard planted several years before. The owner is Hungarian-born Napa businessman Imre Vizkelety.

Hardeman Avenue, to the east, leads to Atlas Peak Road and the Silverado Country Club, opposite which is the century-old onetime Hedgeside Distillery, where Elaine Wellesly, mentioned earlier, makes her Quail Ridge wines. Two miles north, on the left, is where agricultural economist William Hill plans to build a winery in 1984 to handle the crops of his Chardonnay and Cabernet vineyards here and on Mount Veeder.

• 28 •

In the hills to the east of Napa Valley are ten more wineries, old and new, reached by the roads that intersect Silverado Trail. Deer Park Road, opposite St. Helena, climbs past the onetime St. Helena Sanitarium, renamed Hospital and Health Center, to the pre-Prohibition Deer Park Winery and its seven-acre vineyard at the intersection with Sanitarium Road. Once owned by cousins of the legendary Captain John Sutter, inactive during Prohibition, reopened at Repeal and again closed for two decades, the venerable, two-story bulk-wine cellar was bought in 1979 by David and Kinta Clark from San Diego and two partners to make premium wines of home-grown and purchased grapes.

A quarter-mile farther, a small sign at your left points to Burgess Cellars. Former Air Force pilot Tom Burgess and his wife Linda bought this 27,000-gallon winery and its twenty-acre vineyard in 1972. Originally it was the Rossini vineyard, planted by Marielouise Kornell's grandfather in 1880. J. Leland Stewart built the winery in 1943 and called it Souverain Cellars, a name later applied, after Stewart retired in 1970, to two newer wineries in Napa and Sonoma counties. The Burgesses make a few wines from their own grapes but buy most of their needs from other vineyards. Their wines are highly praised, which they credit to enologist Bill Sorenson, a Fresno State University graduate who once operated the experimental winery at that institution.

Where Deer Park Road becomes Howell Mountain Road, it soon meets Las Posadas Road, which extends two miles east past a state forest to the handsome stone La Jota Vineyard winery, built in 1898. Closed since the beginning of Prohibition, it was reopened in 1982 by hobbyist winemaker and oil-lease specialist William H. Smith and his wife Joan. They have replanted the twenty-seven-acre vineyard and installed century-old oak oval casks from the original Cresta Blanca tunnels, near Livermore. This winery produced both the Liparita and La Jota wines that won gold and bronze medals in the Paris Exposition of 1900.

On White Cottage Road in the nearby town of Angwin, not far from the old Howell Mountain Winery, Randall Dunn and his wife Loralee bonded the cellar of their home as the 5000-gallon Dunn Vineyards winery, also in 1982. Their six-acre Cabernet vineyard adjoins their home. Dunn is the full-time winemaker of the Caymus Vineyard winery near Rutherford. He and the La Jota Vineyard owners have petitioned the government to recognize Howell Mountain as a distinct viticultural district.

Lower Howell Mountain Road climbs east from Silverado Trail at Pope Street to Conn Valley Road, from which Greenfield Road extends north to the Buehler Vineyard and its handsome winery, bonded in 1978. Winegrower John Page Buehler, Jr., and his wife Lisa live beside the cellar, which produces only estate-bottled Cabernet, Zinfandel, and Pinot Blanc Vrai. Retired Bechtel engineer John Sr. and his wife live above the sixty-acre vineyard, named Vista del Lago for the spectacular view it commands of Lake Hennessy to the south.

Highway 128, which extends east from Rutherford and is also called Sage Canyon Road, takes you to three wineries opposite Lake Hennessy. Three miles from Silverado Trail, there are two roads that climb steep Pritchard Hill. The first leads to the hundred-acre hilltop vineyard and spectacular pyramid-shaped winery of Donn Chappellet, who left the food-vending business in Los Angeles to found this winery in 1967. The second road climbs to the fifteen-acre vineyard on which Robert and Zelma Long opened the 5000-gallon Long Vineyards winery in 1978 to produce superb estate-bottled Riesling and Chardonnay from the fifteen acres of vines planted by Robert's father in 1966. Zelma is the winemaker at Simi Vineyards. Two miles farther, a private road on the right leads across a bridge to the 10,000-gallon Sage Canyon Winery, bonded in 1981 by retired biology teacher Gordon Millar and Eugenia, his lawyer-wife.

Three more miles of winding road take you to the hilltop winery of Jim Nichelini. It is an old-fashioned roadside cellar, built in 1890 by Jim's grandfather, Anton Nichelini, from Switzerland. Open to the public on weekends, it is a cheery place. Visitors are invited to sample the wines on the terrace, which Jim calls "the only outdoor tasting room in California." Several red and white wines are made, but the Nichelini specialties are Chenin Blanc and Sauvignon Vert. The wines are inexpensive and are stocked in a few Bay Area restaurants and stores, although a good part is sold to people passing the winery en route to and from Lake Berryessa, nearby. The fifty-acre Nichelini vineyard is a mile beyond the winery in Chiles Valley, where the Kentucky trapper, Colonel Joseph Chiles, was the first winegrower during the 1860s.

In a deep canyon on Chiles–Pope Valley Road is the fourteen-acre vineyard and 5000-gallon Green & Red Vineyard winery of former sculptor Jay Heminway, who grows only Zinfandel and named his winery in 1977 for the colors of his vines and the green serpentine and terra rossa soil.

When the Federal government in the late 1970s began determining the boundaries of viticultural areas that could be named in labeling and advertising of wine, most growers and vintners in Napa Valley favored a petition to limit the "Valley" name to the watershed of the Napa River. Owners of land in Pope, Wooden, and Gordon valleys beyond the hills east of the valley proper submitted historical evidence that grapes from their districts traditionally had been used in producing Napa Valley wines. The government decided in 1981 to include the eastern valleys and almost all of Napa County in the "Napa Valley" appellation. Petitions since have been filed to establish smaller districts as separate viticultural areas, such as the Carneros, Howell Mountain, and Stag's Leap districts. Still other Napa Valley districts such as Mount Veeder, Spring Mountain, Mount Diamond, Oakville, and Rutherford eventually may seek to be given viticultural area names of their own.

15

Alameda, Contra Costa, and Solano

C ALIFORNIA's new "green belt" laws, enacted to preserve farmlands from urbanization, have given a new lease on life to the vineyards that remain in Alameda, Contra Costa, and Solano counties, east of San Francisco Bay. Although forecasts of population growth envision the East Bay cities expanding into a megalopolis, some of the historic vineyards in their environs have been replanted in response to the table-wine revolution.

One can see this happening by visiting the Livermore Valley, which is reached by the MacArthur Freeway (Interstate 580) from the San Francisco–Oakland Bay Bridge, less than an hour's drive. It doesn't look like a valley, for it is an almost flat basin, fourteen miles long, between the low, grassy foothills of the Diablo and Hamilton mountain ranges. Beyond the Altamont Hills, only seventeen miles farther east, lies the hot San Joaquin Valley. But the climate of Livermore is Region III, like the upper Napa Valley and northern Sonoma County, because sunny days in Livermore are followed by evening breezes from the Bay. (The Federal government recognized Livermore Valley as a distinctive viticultural area in 1982.)

Most California wine literature describes Livermore as a white-wine district. Some writers state flatly that its climate and gravelly soil are unsuited for the growing of red-wine grapes. Though most of the Livermore wines that have attained national fame are white, the reason is neither climate nor soil, as we'll see presently, and you will find the red wines grown here quite as good as the whites.

Once primarily a vineyard and livestock center, the city of Livermore has multiplied ten times in size since the University of California built the Lawrence Radiation Laboratory nearby, in 1952. Electronic industries have followed the mile-square "Rad lab," and subdivisions to house new residents have crowded out many farms. One of the biggest vineyards has become a housing tract of 5000 people and five schools.

During the 1960s, mounting real estate values were threatening to tax out of existence Livermore's two principal vineyards—Wente and Concannon—which are two miles southeast of the city on Tesla Road. Members of the third generations of these two old winegrowing families, each with growing sons, pondered whether to sell out and move. In 1968, they decided to stay. By signing ten-year contracts with the county under the green-belting law, they dedicated their vineyards as agricultural preserves, which are taxable only on their highest value as farms. Now, as they begin their second hundred years of winegrowing, vineyard acreage in Livermore Valley is on the increase, reversing the decline that occurred in recent years.

• 2 •

The 250-acre Concannon Vineyard and half-million-gallon winery, which you reach on your left as you drive east from Livermore Avenue, is due for expansion since its purchase in 1983 by the Distillers Company, a subsidiary of Scotland's maker of Johnnie Walker Scotch, Gordon's Gin, and other famous spirits brands. In outward appearance, the Concannon winery has changed little in recent decades. The brick-fronted, old-fashioned winery still has no separate building for visitors; you are invited into the century-old cellar to taste the Concannon wines. Jim Concannon, who continues as president of the winery, likes it that way.

Founder of the winery was his grandfather, James Concannon, who emigrated from Ireland in 1865 at the age of eighteen. He landed in Maine and worked his way up from bellhop to management of a hotel, going to night school meanwhile. Ten years later he was traveling the west coast from San Francisco selling a new invention—rubber stamps—which were the rage before typewriters came into general use. His travels took him as far as Mexico City. There the resourceful Concannon got a franchise from dictator José Porfirio Díaz to set up the capital's first street-cleaning system, promptly selling it at a profit to a French syndicate. Back in San Francisco, he learned from Archbishop Joseph Alemany that money could also be made by producing altar wines for the Catholic Church. In 1883 Concannon bought a farm in the Livermore Valley and planted vines imported from

France, which others were beginning to plant there at that time. With his vineyard started, he needed capital to develop his winery. He returned to Mexico and got another concession from President Porfirio Díaz—to introduce French wine grapes to that country, where only the inferior Criolla or Mission grape had been grown until then. Between 1889 and 1904, Concannon shipped several million vine cuttings from Livermore to haciendas throughout the southern republic. (For what happened to the Mexican vineyards, see Chapter 23, "Wines of Mexico.") Concannon returned to Livermore and died there in 1911.

Altar wines were the Concannon winery's main products. Altar wines also kept the winery going through the thirteen years of Prohibition, when the founder's son, Captain Joseph Concannon, was in charge. Every five years for the rest of his life, "Captain Joe" expressed his appreciation by sending a barrel of his finest Muscat de Frontignan to the Pope in Rome.

Altar wines, sold mostly to the Catholic clergy, were still a twentieth of the Concannon Vineyard's business until the 1980s. This explains why most of its wines are white: A red wine would stain the purificator napkin with which the priest wipes the chalice during Mass. Even so, the best wine that Captain Concannon made was not white. His St. Julien, a wonderfully flavorful claret blend, was my favorite California dinner wine during the first few years after Repeal. But in 1936, the new Federal labeling regulations contained a provision specifically prohibiting use of the St. Julien name except on wines from that Bordeaux commune. This so angered "Captain Joe" that he withdrew his St. Julien from the market, and he never made that blend again.

Today, another red is the best-seller among the eight Concannon "varietal" wines, which are sold in some forty-four states. It is a dry, medium-bodied "varietal" of the Petite Sirah grape that grows beside the winery.

• 3 •

The Wente Brothers winery is at the right, a half-mile beyond Concannon, and is more than four times as big, because Wente table wines (the only types it made until it introduced a champagne in 1983) are sold in all fifty states. The winery and its separate tasting room are new and ultra-modern, having been built in the late 1960s, when the old facilities proved too small.

Carl Heinrich Wente came from Hanover to this country about 1870, learned winemaking from Charles Krug in the Napa Valley, then moved to Livermore and in 1883 acquired an interest in the fifty-acre vineyard planted four years earlier by Dr. George Bernard. Wente expanded his holdings and soon was cultivating a total of 300 acres.

He had three sons. The oldest, Carl F. Wente, was advised by his father to study bookkeeping, got a job as a bank messenger, and forty-five years later became president of the worldwide Bank of America. The second son, Ernest, preferred farming, was sent to the College of Agriculture at Davis, and on graduation took charge of the vineyards. The youngest son, Herman, studied enology at the University in Berkeley and became a winemaker, one of the greatest California has yet known.

Like the Concannons, the Wentes specialized in white wines, though for a different reason: In the old days bulk red wines, sold inter-winery, brought producers as little as 10 cents a gallon, while bulk whites seldom sold for less than 50 cents. The Wentes see no reason to change their specialties now.

Before Prohibition, the Wentes sold their entire output in bulk, much of it to the Napa & Sonoma Wine Company of San Francisco, of which they were part owners, and some to Oakland vintner Theodore Gier. During the Dry era they made altar wine in bulk for Georges de Latour of Beaulieu, but sold most of their grapes fresh.

In 1934, the year following Repeal, they bottled some wines for the first time, calling them "Valle de Oro"; the name of Wente wasn't yet known outside of Livermore. Then in 1939, Valle de Oro Sauvignon Blanc won the grand prize for white wines at San Francisco's Golden Gate International Exposition. This brought importer Frank Schoonmaker from New York, looking for California wines to introduce nationally with his import line. The first he chose were the Wentes' Sauvignon Blanc, Sémillon, Grey Riesling, Pinot Blanc, Ugni Blanc, and a light-bodied red named Mourastel. Though the labels called them "Schoonmaker Selections," the name of the Wentes was shown as the producer and became known in the East and Midwest.

By 1960—five years before the "greenbelting" law was passed—the Wentes could not afford to expand at Livermore, and a new 300-acre Wente vineyard was planted in the Salinas Valley near Greenfield in Monterey County. Their Arroyo Seco Vineyard has since spread to 800 acres, about half as much as the Wente acreage at Livermore. Since the Federal government has approved "Arroyo Seco" as a viticultural-area appellation, the Wentes have added a new term—"vintner grown"—to the labels of their Monterey County wines.

The Wentes always had made a red wine for their family

use, and had sold a burgundy after Repeal. During the 1960s they introduced annual vintages of Pinot Noir, Gamay Beaujolais, Petite Sirah, and Zinfandel. (The Mourastel was discontinued during the Second World War.) Ugni Blanc was never popular because of its hard-to-pronounce name and was withdrawn from the market, but reappeared in 1967 in a blend with Chenin Blanc under a new name: Wente Bros. Blanc de Blancs. But the best-selling Wente wine is their Grey Riesling, which may also be the single most popular "varietal" white wine sold under a single brand in the United States.

Wente wines come in bottle and half-bottle sizes and in magnums for some varieties, but also available at the winery tasting room are two Valle de Oro wines in 1.5-liter jugs. Priced a third to a sixth as much as other Wente wines, these are best buys. The jug white is so popular that people drive to the winery to load their cars with it in case lots. During the 1970s, the Wentes introduced a "California" bottle shape, similar to but shorter than the tall, traditional hock bottle, and have used it since for both their white and their red wines.

At Herman Wente's death in 1961, Ernest's son Karl became head of the firm. When Karl died in 1977 at the age of forty-nine, his sons Eric and Philip, with degrees lately earned at Stanford and at the UC Davis wine school, took charge of the winery, Eric as winemaker, Philip as the viticulturist. The name "Wente Bros." on Wente labels again became literally true. Their sister Carolyn is now the vice president; the treasurer is their mother Jean.

• 4 •

The most historic vineyard in the valley is Cresta Blanca. To get there from Livermore Avenue, take Wente Street (there is also a Concannon Boulevard), Marina Boulevard, and Arroyo Road. The million-gallon Cresta Blanca winery, with its great tunnels bored into the hillside, is inactive now, but even to see it from the exterior is worth the extra drive. In 1982, the Wentes bought the Cresta Blanca vineyard and began replanting it to produce more Wente Chardonnay.

Cresta Blanca was founded by journalist Charles Wetmore. A reporter for San Francisco newspapers, he became interested in wine and went to France in 1878 to report on the Paris Exposition for the California Vinicultural Society. He then wrote a series of sensational articles, declaring that 95 percent of French wine imported to the United States was adulterated *vin ordinaire.*

He denounced San Francisco restaurateurs for featuring European wines while selling the best California wines under counterfeit French labels or as their "house" wines with no labels at all. Wetmore's articles helped to get the State Board of Viticultural Commissioners established by an act of the legislature in 1880. Wetmore became the Board's executive officer and then decided to become a winegrower himself. He bought 480 acres of Livermore pasture land for $200 in gold coin, set out his vineyard, and named it Cresta Blanca for the white-crested cliff above. Wetmore then learned that the wife of Louis Mel, the French-born owner of the El Mocho Vineyard, was a friend of the Marquis de Lur-Saluces, the proprietor of world-famed Château d'Yquem near Bordeaux. Armed with a letter from Madame Mel, Wetmore went again to France and obtained from the Marquis cuttings of the three grape varieties that make the Yquem blend—Sémillon, Sauvignon Blanc, and Muscadelle Bordelais.

Wetmore divided the Yquem cuttings between his vineyard and that of Louis Mel, who later sold El Mocho to the Wentes. In Wetmore's vineyard, the vines from France produced wines that won two gold medals and a grand prix award for Cresta Blanca in the Paris Exposition of 1889.

During the 1940s, a successor to the Marquis de Lur-Saluces visited Livermore "to see how my children are doing." On tasting a sample of Herman Wente's Sauvignon Blanc, the marquis told Herman that no Bordeaux vintner had ever made a wine of such quality from that grape alone—that it was impossible in the Bordeaux climate. Perhaps the direct importation of vines from Yquem explains why, through the years, I have found Livermore Sauvignon Blancs richer and spicier in flavor than those made from this grape grown elsewhere in California. The Livermore producers, however, insist the reason is their climate and in particular their gravelly soil, which holds the heat after the summer sun goes down. I recall tasting a Sauvignon Blanc made by Herman Wente that was magnificent at the age of twenty years.

Cresta Blanca wines with such names as Sauterne Souvenir and Médoc Souvenir were nationally famous before Prohibition. They again were at the top rank of California wines after Repeal, when the vineyard was owned by Wetmore's younger brother, Clarence, and later by his chief salesman, Lucien B. Johnson.

In 1941, during the wartime liquor shortage, Schenley whiskey king Lewis Rosenstiel bought Cresta Blanca from Johnson. This enabled Rosenstiel to advertise on radio, from which his liquor brands were barred by the broadcasting industry code. In 1942 he produced the first advertising program for a wine brand to be aired on a national network. It introduced the first singing commercial for a California wine: "C-R-E-S-T-A" in rising notes and "B-L-A-N-C-A" going down the scale, then the two words repeated in the same notes and followed by the pop of a cork. Rosenstiel introduced the first California sherries to be priced higher than Spanish imports, Cresta Blanca Dry Watch and Triple Cream. But when wines came under wartime price controls, he used the Cresta Blanca label to sell enormous quantities of other wines—something wine merchants remembered when the war ended; his competitors wouldn't let them forget.

History was again made at Cresta Blanca in 1956, when winemaker Myron Nightingale produced there the first French-style sauterne ever made commercially outside of Bordeaux. He did it by spraying Sémillon and Sauvignon Blanc grapes in the winery with spores of *Botrytis cinerea*, the "noble mold" which grows naturally on late-harvested grapes in the Sauternes district of Bordeaux. Rosenstiel named the wine Premier Sémillon, priced it at $6 a bottle, and in 1961 unveiled it at a nationally publicized San Francisco tasting. In a speech later inserted in the *Congressional Record*, Senator Tom Kuchel hailed Premier Sémillon as "this product that has broken a European monopoly in one of the gourmet treasures of the world."

What made Premier Sémillon seem a historic breakthrough was a belief long expressed in textbooks, that not enough botrytis grows in California's dry climates to botrytize grapes naturally. In 1969 the Wentes found so much of the mold growing on Riesling grapes in their Monterey vineyard that they left the grapes to ripen for three extra weeks and produced California's first natural Spätlese Riesling. In 1973 they produced both a *Spätlese* and an *Auslese*, at which the German government protested to the United States government—which thenceforth pro-

Myron Nightingale, who made "Premier Sémillon," California's first botrytized wine, by spraying botrytis spores on grapes at Cresta Blanca in 1956. (*Beringer Brothers, St. Helena CA*)

hibited American wines from using these German terms. (But many "late harvest" California wines are described on back labels as meeting the German standards for both of the foregoing as well as *Beerenauslese* and *Trockenbeerenauslese,* the ultimate in degrees of sugar content produced by botrytis.) Now, so many botrytized wines are produced almost every year in California coast counties that the 1961 publicity about the artificially botrytized Livermore wine seems ludicrous in retrospect.

Premier Sémillon wasn't enough to restore Cresta Blanca to its prewar prestige. In 1965, the winery was closed to the public, and winemaker Nightingale and his wines were shipped to Schenley's big Roma winery at Fresno. When, six years later, Schenley sold the Cresta Blanca name to the Guild Wine Company of Lodi, Nightingale quit to join the Beringer winery in the Napa Valley. No more Premier Sémillon was made after the 1966 vintage. I have one bottle left in my cellar. Cresta Blanca wines have now come back on the market from Guild's winery in Mendocino County, and the famous Cresta commercial is often on the air again.

The Wentes in the 1980s bought the original Cresta Blanca vineyard and a total of several hundred more Livermore Valley acres and began replanting them all. Counting their 800 acres in Monterey County, the Wentes' total vineyards approached 2300 acres by 1983. A separate winery to make champagne, possibly in Monterey County, is included in their plans.

• 5 •

North of the Cresta Blanca vineyard, the name "Olivina" appears on the arch over an imposing stone gate at the intersection of Arroyo and Wetmore roads. Julius Paul Smith of "20-Mule-Team Borax" fame founded Olivina and planted vines there in 1881. The Olivina Vineyard was killed by phylloxera long ago, and except for the crumbling shell of the winery, the fields are bare. No trace remains of such other early Livermore wine-growing estates as Alexander Duval's Château Bellevue on Vallecitos Road, nor of the Chauché & Bon winery on Stanley Boulevard, nor of the vineyard Theodore Gier named Giersburg, four miles south of town.

But if you drive west along Vineyard Avenue toward Pleasanton, you still may see old vineyards, such as the Oakdale or Hagemann tract of 200 acres, which once was under lease to Almadén. Next is the equally large Ruby Hill Vineyard, planted by John Crellin in 1883 and named for the red knoll on which its handsome brick and stone winery stands. Ernest Ferrario bought the Crellin estate early in the Prohibition era, reopened the winery at Repeal, and produced excellent wines for three decades, including the best Malvasia Bianca then made in the state. With no sons to carry on his business, Ferrario quit making wine during the 1960s and stored wines made by other wineries until his death in 1974, when the land was sold to the Southern Pacific. A year later, a group of winemaker partners leased Ruby Hill, renamed it Stony Ridge, and produced several creditable estate-bottled table wines and champagnes. Then the Southern Pacific moved to replace the vineyard with a housing development. The city of Pleasanton and a "save the vineyards" movement blocked the housing project. Meanwhile, in 1983, Stony Ridge moved its winemaking equipment next door to the Hageman vineyard, and opened a tasting room on Ray Street in Pleasanton. Stony Ridge has changed the name of its Sémillon to "Chevrier," one of the other names of that white Bordeaux grape (and some other producers of Sémillon have begun doing the same).

One of the original Stony Ridge partners, chemistry teacher Lanny Replogle, has reopened the century-old George True winery a mile south on Vallecitos Road, and is producing his own "Fenestra" wines there. New owners of Ruby Hill have preserved that venerable winery, have begun replanting its vineyard, and say they will start a new winery there.

In Pleasanton City, a half block north of Main Street, is the million-gallon Villa Armando Winery, which has changed with the times. It was built in 1902 by Frank Garatti, and except during Prohibition, when it was closed, made mostly bulk wine until 1962. Then Brooklyn wine merchant Anthony Scotto bought it to produce the wines his Italian customers along the eastern seaboard preferred, the kinds they had made themselves during Prohibition. Included were a 16 percent earthy, semi-dry red called Vino Rustico, and another made of Muscat grapes from Delano, named Orobianco. By the 1970s, Scotto found that people's tastes were changing, and added vintage-dated California "varietals" as well as burgundy and chablis in bottles, jugs, and in the plastic "bag-in-the-box." A tasting room was built in front of the winery, a vineyard in Lodi was purchased, and another was planted in the Suñol Valley. Next door to the winery, Scotto's wife Theresa opened a restaurant she named La Villa Armando. In 1979, the Villa Banfi importing house at Farmingdale, New York, bought an interest in the winery, which Scotto runs with the help of his daughter and three sons. By

1983, Scotto needed more winemaking space, and he built another winery two miles south of Wente Bros. at the intersection of Tesla and Greenville roads, where he has acquired 200 more acres of potential vineyard land.

Six miles south of Pleasanton (via Suñol Boulevard and Interstate 680), there is an old Alameda County winegrowing district that has been partially replanted with premium wine grapes. This is the Suñol Valley, which can never become urbanized because it is part of San Francisco's municipal water system. In 1969, the city granted Almadén Vineyards a forty-year lease on almost a thousand acres there and in the nearby San Antonio Valley. Almadén later chose to plant in Monterey County instead. Other vintners began negotiating for the land. Anthony Scotto was the first to obtain a lease. In 1974, he planted there seventy acres of such varieties as Chardonnay, Pinot Blanc, Cabernet, and Merlot to supply his Villa Armando winery. At least 3000 more acres there are considered suitable for vineyards. The vineyards of Alameda County declined from 7000 acres in 1900 to less than 2000 acres in 1982, but can be more than doubled if the area around Suñol and the additional land owned by the Wentes are planted with vines. If all are planted, Alameda will produce more fine wine in the future than it ever did in the past.

• 6 •

Many other parts of the county, including Niles and the present cities of San Lorenzo, Hayward, and Alameda, were winegrowing districts a century ago. But the Mission San José district is older still.

Four miles south of Suñol, the Mission Boulevard exit from the freeway leads to the Mission San José de Guadalupe, founded in 1797. There the Franciscan Fathers planted the first vineyards in Alameda County, a quarter century before those at Sonoma. From the Mission, the padres at Mission Dolores in San Francisco obtained the grapes to make their wines for the Mass. And from there the English seaman Robert Livermore obtained the vines that he was the first to plant, during the 1840s, in the valley that bears his name. Among early-day wineries near the Mission were Joseph Palmer's Peak Vineyard, planted in 1852 with vines imported from Europe; the Los Amigos Vineyard of Grau & Werner, Conrad Weller's Willow Glen Vineyard, and Linda Vista, the vineyard and wine cellars of Charles McIver. Bigger than any of the Livermore vineyards was the 1000-acre tract which Juan Gallegos, a former Costa Rican coffee planter, owned around the Mission in the 1880s. The million-gallon Gallegos winery and distillery, two miles west at Irvington, was damaged by the earthquake of 1906 and had to be destroyed.

• 7 •

Four miles south of the Mission, a spring of hot water gushing from a hillside was visited by early Spanish California ladies who found it a convenient place to wash their linens. The place was named Rancho Agua Caliente, the Warm Springs Ranch. Clement Colombet from France built a stone winery there about 1850 and later built the Warm Springs Hotel around the springs. It was the most fashionable suburban spa around San Francisco until it was wrecked by the earthquake of 1868.

In the following year came Leland Stanford, the railroad builder, California governor, and United States senator, who bought a square mile around the springs. He cultivated a hundred acres of vines and made 50,000 gallons of wine per year. He later gave the place to his brother Josiah, who trebled its size and added a brandy distillery. Had the property not been occupied by his brother's prospering wine business, the senator might have built Stanford University there rather than at his Palo Alto horse farm. Josiah Stanford's son inherited the property and made 250,000 gallons of wine per year, until phylloxera destroyed the Warm Springs vineyard during the 1890s. Meanwhile, another earthquake shut off the springs.

In 1945, half a century later, Rudolf Weibel, the proprietor of the Weibel Champagne Cellar in San Francisco, went looking around the Bay Area for land on which to plant a vineyard of his own. Weibel had arrived nine years earlier from Switzerland with his son Fred, and had prospered making champagne under other vintners' brands. He bought the abandoned vineyard at Warm Springs, patched the old buildings, and replanted the vines. Weibel had never heard of Stanford or of the winery's history. He didn't learn it until a year later, when he came to consult me about his new labels, and I happened to tell him the Stanford story.

At Warm Springs, the Weibels continued making champagnes for other vintners, using the Charmat process, but fermented their best in bottles under their own name. They added table and dessert wines and a citrus-and-herb-flavored apéritif wine Rudolf had made in Switzerland, named Tangor.

When Rudolf Weibel died in 1971, a new city named Fremont

had grown up around Warm Springs, embracing the Mission and several surrounding towns. Fred Weibel then bought vineyards in Mendocino and Lake counties and built a new winery in Redwood Valley near Ukiah, where his son, Fred Jr., supervises production. Fred Sr. plans to stay in Warm Springs, keeping his vineyard of Chardonnay and Pinot Noir and making his champagnes there.

The Weibel winery on Stanford Avenue (Route 238), four miles south of the Mission, gets thousands of visitors per month because it is near both the 680 and 17 freeways. The visitors are received in an adobe-style "hacienda" tasting room, where both fermented-in-bottle and Charmat champagnes can be sampled. On weekdays, a girl from the winery office takes them on a tour of the old brick buildings, then around the sherry *soleras* and stainless-steel tanks the Weibels have added. Between the cellars and the vineyard is a pergola for picnics and a bandstand for concerts.

Among the three dozen wines labeled "Weibel," I have tasted some that were outstanding, but have found the Chardonnay Brut Champagne and the Dry Bin Sherry to be the best. In 1983, Weibel became the first winery to make a "Sparkling White Zinfandel" champagne, and followed it with a "Sparkling Chenin Blanc." It still makes champagnes for other vintners and uses so many hundreds of different labels that it has its own printing plant. To tell whether a champagne comes from Weibel, look for the address on the bottom of the label, which reads "Mission San José."

• 8 •

One winery inside another is Llords & Elwood, which has its main bonded winery in a corner of Weibel's property.

For two decades after Repeal, the late Julius Hugh (Mike) Elwood owned the Llords & Elwood pair of prestigious liquor stores in Los Angeles. He stocked the private wine cellars of such Hollywood luminaries as Charlie Chaplin, Ronald Reagan, and Gloria Swanson almost exclusively with European wines. American wines lacked age and glamour and were not expensive enough. Then, in 1953 Elwood and his wife took their first trip through the vineyards of Europe. He came back convinced that California wines could excel imports if someone would just give them enough aging and care. He decided that he was the one to do it, sold his stores, and became a vintner.

With his own ideas of how wines should taste, Elwood created his own blends. He bought grapes and wines and leased space in three wineries, two in San Jose for crushing and barrel-aging, and part of Weibel for bottling. He also gave his wines beguiling names, such as Castle Magic Riesling, Velvet Hill Pinot Noir, Ancient Proverb Port, and Dry Wit Sherry; and retained the name of a liquor store once named Llord's "because it sounds better than Elwood alone." His wines were introduced in 1961. Elwood's widow Irene and son Richard have carried on the business since Mike's death in 1974.

· 9 ·

Alameda County also has a dozen small wineries in its cities. The one that gets the most visitors is Wine and the People on University Avenue in Berkeley, west of the University of California campus. It began in 1970, when home winemaker Peter Brehm opened a store to sell supplies to fellow amateurs. As his business grew, he offered winemaking lessons, then added fresh and frozen grapes from California vineyards to his stock of merchandise. In 1977, he moved to a larger store across the street, added a crusher, press, tanks, and barrels, and sold his own vintage-dated wines in bottles and also in bulk to customers who bring their own barrels and jugs to be filled. Three members of the university administration at Berkeley are winery owners: public affairs officer Richard Hafner, journalism instructor James Spaulding (mentioned in earlier chapters), and vice president William B. Fretter, whose son Travis makes superb wines in a cellar near the campus from grapes they grow on a hillside above the Napa Valley. The new Montali winery is on Addison Street in Berkeley.

· 10 ·

Contra Costa County, despite its rapid housing and industrial growth since the Second World War, still has almost a thousand acres of vineyards. Few of its residents today are aware that this county had 6000 acres of vines and twenty-seven wineries and was one of California's finest winegrowing districts before Prohibition. Dr. John Marsh, the first physician in the county and its first winegrower, was producing wine as early as 1846 on his great ranch south of Brentwood. Another physician, Dr. John Strentzel from Poland, planted vines in the Alhambra Valley during the 1850s. He was succeeded by his son-in-law, the great naturalist John Muir. The Muir House, beside Highway 4 two miles south of Martinez, is now a national historic site, and includes a half-acre of Muir's Vineyard, replanted in 1969. Another Contra Costa winegrower was the educator John Swett. The wines from his Hill Girt Vineyard, which he planted during the 1880s, regularly won prizes at the state fair. His son Frank continued making wine there until Prohibition. Grapes still grow on the Hill Girt Farm on Alhambra Avenue, mainly Concords planted during Prohibition, but lately supplemented by Cabernet Sauvignon. In 1891, such major vintners as the Italian Swiss Colony and Theodore Gier had wineries in the Clayton Valley, and the Brookside Winery in the Ygnacio Valley was operated by the California Wine Association. In Martinez were the original novitiate and vineyard of The Christian Brothers, where they began making wine in 1882.

At Repeal, Joseph E. (Joe) Digardi reopened the winery in the Vine Hill district south of Martinez which his father had founded half a century before. Digardi sent two of his sons to Davis, and by the 1940s, the wines they helped him make were winning awards at the state fair. When his Diablo Valley Gamay won a gold medal in 1948, he sold most of it to Frank Schoonmaker for $6 a case. The Digardi vineyard is gone, ruined by smog from the oil refineries, but son Francis Digardi continues operating the winery with grapes from other coast counties.

Hidden beyond a hill, a half-mile west of Digardi, are the small Conrad Viano vineyard and winery on a patch of old-fashioned countryside surrounded by encroaching subdivisions. Connoisseurs who know its location, on Morello Avenue off the Highway 4 freeway, come to buy its wines by the case, especially the Zinfandel and Cabernet, which are aged three to six years in oak and binned for at least six months. Clement and Sharon Viano want to stay in the wine business. They have dedicated their vineyard as an agricultural preserve, expanded it to almost 125 acres, and have sent their sons John and David to the UC Davis wine school, from which Clement was graduated in 1958.

There are more vineyards in the far eastern corner of the county, where the climate is Region IV. Their grapes are usually shipped fresh to eastern markets.

• 11 •

The wine revolution has caused a revival of winegrowing in Solano County, which borders Napa on the west and Contra Costa on the south. Vineyards in the county increased from a low point of 700 acres in 1972 to 1271 acres, protected from urbanization by "green belt" and zoning laws, in 1982. In that year the Federal government granted petitions from grape growers to recognize Solano's Green Valley and Suisun Valley as viticultural areas that can be named in the labeling of their wines.

There is a new winery in Green Valley, the 40,000-gallon French Tudor–style Chateau de Leu, built with a tasting room in 1982 on Ben and Phyllis Volkhardt's eighty-acre vineyard off Green Valley Road, a mile south of the Green Valley Country Club. "De Leu" refers to a road near the winery, named for Volkhardt's uncle.

Within the Suisun Valley appellation are the 125-acre vineyard and 150,000-gallon Wooden Valley Winery of Mario and Richard Lanza (not related to the late singer, whose real name was Cocozza). The winery is busier than at any time since it opened in 1932; it is patronized by families from the huge Travis Air Force Base, a few miles away.

There also is new activity at Frank Cadenasso's 145-acre vineyard and 300,000-gallon Cadenasso Winery, just east of the Interstate 80 freeway, at Fairfield in the Suisun Valley. Frank's father planted his first vineyard in Green Valley in 1906, moved to Fairfield and planted another, sold it to the county as a hospital site, then planted the present vineyard, his third, across the road from the hospital, in 1926. Now that his Fresno State University–trained son John has taken charge of the vineyard, Cadenasso has begun to expand. His wines, especially his estate-grown Pinot Noir and Zinfandel, have been so reasonably priced that some of my friends have traveled from San Francisco to buy them by the case.

Although Solano County grape growers have won two viticultural-area appellations of their own—Green and Suisun valleys—they were also included in 1983, along with parts of Lake County, in the "North Coast" appellation, which its proponents wanted to limit to Mendocino, Napa, and Sonoma counties alone.

16

Santa Clara and Other Central Coast Counties

T HE COUNTIES north and east of the Golden Gate, described in the three preceding chapters, are publicized nowadays as "California's fine wine country." Yet there is fully as much to interest the visitor—famous wineries, great vineyards, and fine wines—in the coast counties situated south of the Bay. In fact, the visitor who travels south instead of north from San Francisco may get a clearer concept of the past, present, and future of premium California wines.

Viticulture is changing more dramatically in this central coast region than anywhere else in America. Exploding population around the Bay has caused the old vineyards in the upper Santa Clara Valley to be paved over for housing tracts and shopping centers. The historic showplace wineries remain, but the grape has retreated southward to less-populated areas, including some where vines were not grown commercially before. For example, a single new district, the Salinas Valley of Monterey County, already is larger than either Napa or Sonoma County in vineyard acreage, and someday may even surpass both in "fine wine country" importance.

Climatically, as the California map shows, the same ocean breezes and fogs which cool the sunny valleys of the northern Coast Range mountains perform the same beneficent function for the valleys of these mountain ranges extending south from San Francisco through San Mateo, Santa Clara, Santa Cruz, San Benito, San Luis Obispo, and Santa Barbara counties—a distance of more than two hundred miles. Summer temperatures in most of this area range from Region I to Region III, the best for growing grapes for superior table wines and champagnes. The new central

360

coast vineyards are therefore equal in climate to the old ones they replace, and they are already greater in size.

• 2 •

The best route south from San Francisco is the scenic Interstate 280 freeway. At your right, past San Bruno, you will see the series of Crystal Springs reservoirs, at the south end of which "Count" Haraszthy in 1854 planted his San Mateo County vineyard, which failed because of the locality's summer fogs. A few miles farther south, where the weather is warmer, you reach a part of this now-urbanized county that produced some of California's finest wines before Prohibition. Emmett Rixford's La Questa Vineyard at Woodside, planted in 1883, was especially noted for its Cabernets. His elegant winery was closed by the Dry law, was operated again by his sons for a few years after Repeal, and has since been converted into a residence. Another handsome cellar, at Menlo Park, once belonged to Governor Leland Stanford. It now houses a bank in the Stanford Shopping Center.

Avocational winegrowers now have three wineries around the wealthy town of Woodside. When home winemakers Robert and Polly Mullen built their new house on Kings Mountain Road in 1961, they did so primarily to provide a 4000-gallon winery downstairs. They have two acres of Pinot Noir and Chardonnay vines beside their house. They also care for and use the Cabernet grapes produced on the three remaining acres of La Questa Vineyard. The Mullens produce enough wines to supply themselves, the friends and neighbors who attend their spring wine tastings, and the Village Church, which uses their Woodside Vineyard wines for Communion. Another Woodside winery is computer expert Duane Cronin's 2000-gallon cellar on Old La Honda Road. He is president of the Santa Cruz Mountain Vintners Association, which in 1982 convinced the Federal government to establish a "Santa Cruz Mountains" viticultural-area appellation for parts of San Mateo, Santa Cruz, and Santa Clara counties. Electrical engineer Nathaniel Sherrill and his wife Jan, a former instructor at nearby Stanford University, have built a 15,000-gallon winery beside their home on Skyline Boulevard (Route 35), to replace the original Sherrill Cellar they started in the basement of the Woodside post office in 1973. They twice have planted a vineyard in front of the winery, each time to find the young vines eaten by deer that leaped their fence.

Three miles north of the Sherrills, overlooking Portola Valley and the nearby computerland called Silicon Valley, is the 15,000-gallon Thomas Fogarty Winery, built in 1982 by noted Palo Alto cardiovascular surgeon Thomas Fogarty and his wife Rosalie on the fifteen-acre vineyard of Chardonnay and Pinot Noir they planted three years before. Passing motorists are unaware that the redwood building east of the highway is a winery, because from the road it appears to be an unusually attractive two-story home. The upper story is where Dr. Fogarty's winemaker, Michael Martella, and his wife Suki live.

• 3 •

Santa Clara Valley is the oldest of the northern California wine districts. The Franciscan fathers planted grapes at Mission Santa Clara de Asis soon after its founding in 1777. This was almost half a century before Sonoma Mission (1823), from which winegrowing spread north of the Bay. Mission records show the Santa Clara padres producing twenty barrels of wine annually by 1827 and supplying some of it thereafter to Mission Dolores at San Francisco. They also gave vine cuttings to neighboring rancheros, who made their own wine. By midcentury there were half a dozen commercial winegrowers around Santa Clara and its satellite pueblo of San Jose. Many of them were French, and the Gallic influence was evident in the character of the top Santa Clara wines. By 1854, one of the French *vignerons,* Antoine Delmas, was already importing superior wine-grape varieties from his homeland and beginning to replace his Mission vines.

After the Civil War, winegrowing spread throughout the Santa Clara Valley, then east and west into the foothills of the Diablo and Santa Cruz mountain ranges, and became the main industry of the region. Names on San Jose maps recall such early vineyardists as Captain Elisha Stevens, Isaac Branham, and James Lick (the millionaire donor of Lick Observatory), whose winery was on the Santa Clara–Alviso Road. Another was retired Union Army General Henry M. Naglee (Naglee Street was named for him), who made fine wines but became most famous for his prize-winning brandy. Phylloxera attacked the Santa Clara vineyards during the 1880s and 1890s, but they were saved by grafting to resistant American roots brought back from France. By the turn of the century, Santa Clara County had more than a hundred wineries and 8500 acres of vines, more than in Napa County and almost as many as in Sonoma.

Prohibition failed to kill the vineyards. Grapes brought high prices when shipped east for basement winemaking, and a few local wineries continued making sacramental and tonic wines, so the farmers planted still more grapes. Prune growing meanwhile had become a rival industry, but there still were nearly 8000 acres of vines in 1933. When the Dry law was repealed in that year, sixty-four Santa Clara wineries reopened for business.

Then came the great westward migration, sparked by the Second World War. Millions of new California residents had to be housed. Chambers of commerce advertised the climatic advantages of the area south of the Bay, and subdivisions began invading the prime farmland on the valley floor. When land values soared, the vineyards were taxed more as real estate than their crops were worth, and one by one the grape growers were forced to sell. Of the 8000 acres that were producing grapes in this county in 1948, three-fourths had disappeared by 1970. In two decades of wild urban growth, the upper part of the valley, the onetime "garden of the world," was transformed into a sprawling Los Angeles of the North, and then came the smog. Why didn't Santa Clara preserve its vineyards, fresh air, and open space, as Napa has thus far? The chambers of commerce did their work too well.

Although urbanization destroyed most of the vineyards in the northern Santa Clara Valley, several new wineries opened, and a few planted small vineyards when the wine revolution of the 1970s reached its height. Santa Clara County still had 1500 acres of vines and thirty-one wineries, ten of them new, in 1982.

• 4 •

There are some lovely vineyards tucked away in the foothills of the Santa Cruz Mountains, above and west of residential Saratoga. The loveliest is Paul Masson's renowned 2000-foot-high "vineyard in the sky." On steep slopes, the old Pinot, Cabernet, and Riesling vines are still mostly cultivated by hand. The sparse crops of grapes they yield are no longer crushed in the venerable three-story stone mountain winery, which is State Historical Landmark no. 733. The oak casks inside store only ports and sherries that are made elsewhere and sent here for aging. The main Paul Masson producing wineries are now at Soledad in Monterey County and near Madera in the San Joaquin Valley. The vine-clad hillsides form a natural amphitheater in front of the stately mountain winery with its authentic twelfth-century Romanesque portal, brought around Cape Horn from

Spain. In this dramatic setting the famous Music at the Vineyards charitable-benefit concerts, with chilled champagne usually served at the intermissions, have been held on summer weekends since 1959. Except on the days of such events, the gates to the precipitous road up the mountain are kept closed.

On the valley floor in Saratoga are the Paul Masson Champagne Cellars, built in 1959, one of the most spectacular winery structures in the world. On a spiral ramp leading from the rotunda, a mosaic mural depicts the history of wine from ancient times. Almost 200,000 visitors climb the ramp each year. At the top, they watch a brief sound film and walk on an elevated gallery through the cellars, where each step in champagne making is viewed and explained by a recorded voice. The circuit ends in the tasting hall, where the company has samples of its more than forty different wines and five champagnes. A favorite white is the proprietary type, Emerald Dry, named for the Emerald Riesling grape, the principal variety used in its fresh-tasting blend. Among other Masson specialties are its Monterey estate-bottled "Pinnacles Selection" line of higher-priced, vintage-dated "varietal" table wines and its old dessert wine rarities, which come in heart-shaped, numbered bottles. An entirely new wine product bottled here in 1983 was "St. Regis Blanc," a dealcoholized wine.

The colorful story of Paul Masson Vineyards parallels that of Santa Clara wines. In 1852, two years after California became a state, Etienne Thée, a *vigneron* from Bordeaux, planted vines along Guadalupe Creek, five miles east of present-day Los Gatos. Thée was succeeded by his son-in-law, Charles Lefranc, and when son Henry Lefranc died in 1909, by Charles Lefranc's son-in-law, Paul Masson.

Born in 1859 near Beaune in Burgundy, Masson came to California at the age of nineteen. The phylloxera vine plague had devastated the vineyard on the Côte d'Or where his family had made wine for three centuries, and glowing descriptions of California's fabulous climate had already drawn many French wine-growers here. Young Masson first enrolled to study science at the University of the Pacific, which then was located in Santa Clara. While a student, he became acquainted with his compatriot Charles Lefranc, soon became the latter's employee, and in 1888 married Lefranc's daughter Louise. On their honeymoon trip to France, he bought French champagne-making equipment, brought French experts to Los Gatos to install it, and began making champagne in partnership with Henry Lefranc. In 1892, he bought Henry's interest in Lefranc & Masson and founded his own Paul Masson Champagne Company. His champagnes won numerous awards, including the grand prize at the Louisiana Purchase Exposition of 1904, but Masson was always proudest of the honorable mention an international jury gave them at the Paris Exposition of 1900. In 1896, he began planting the mountain vineyard, which he called La Cresta, and nine years later started building the mountain winery. When the 1906 earthquake destroyed St. Patrick's Church in San Jose, he bought its ancient portal and erected it as part of the winery facade.

Masson, the broad-shouldered, jovial Burgundian, was both a noted epicure and a flamboyant host. His lavish entertainments of San Francisco society and of such theatrical luminaries as singer Anna Held and Charlie Chaplin are legend. His most publicized exploit was the champagne bath he was said to have given Anna Held in 1917. (Historian Charles Sullivan has investigated this particular legend and questions whether the famous bath ever occurred.)

During the early Prohibition years, Masson held the first government permit to make medicinal champagne, sold by druggists on doctors' prescriptions. But one night in 1929, an armed hijack-

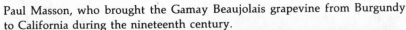

Paul Masson, who brought the Gamay Beaujolais grapevine from Burgundy to California during the nineteenth century.

ing gang raided his mountain winery and partially emptied it of wine. Masson thereafter made his champagne in a San Jose cellar, until he sold his business to former stockbroker Martin Ray in 1936. Four years later, Masson died at the age of eighty-one.

In the war year of 1942, when the big liquor distillers were buying up California wineries, the House of Seagram bought the Paul Masson vineyard and winery from Martin Ray. After the war, the late Seagram whiskey king Samuel Bronfman foresaw the future growth of wine consumption in America, and while his competitors in the liquor business got rid of their wineries, Bronfman kept a silent majority interest in Masson. European-trained experts Alfred Fromm and Otto Meyer managed the company from the 1940s, building Masson to a four-winery operation with 34 million gallons capacity and 4500 acres of vines. In 1960, Masson became the first American winegrower to establish an export department and to pioneer foreign markets for bottled California wines. Within a decade, Masson wines had established commercial distribution in some fifty countries around the world. "Our wines," Meyer explained, "had to go abroad to enhance their reputation in order to become fully appreciated at home."

In 1971, Seagram bought Fromm's and Meyer's minority interest in the company. A decade later it became part of a new Seagram Wine Company headed by London-born Michael P. H. Cliff, together with Gold Seal Vineyards of New York, which Seagram had owned since 1979.

When in 1983 Seagram bought the Coca-Cola Company's Wine Spectrum, which included three California wineries totaling 19 million gallons capacity (as well as Coke's two in New York State), Seagram became second only to the Gallo family of Modesto in production and sale of California wine. Then, to manage all of its worldwide wine properties, the company formed a Seagram Wine Group. To head the Group as chairman, Seagram brought to its New York headquarters Marc Henrion, the former president of its Barton & Guestier firm in Bordeaux. President of the Group is Richard L. Maher, the marketing genius who since 1972 had headed Nestlé's Wine World and Beringer winery in the Napa Valley.

Even before the Wine Spectrum purchase, Seagram was the world's biggest wine company, with wineries in five European countries, the United States and Canada, Latin America, Australia, and New Zealand. Two of its subsidiaries also market the products of many American and European estate wineries, both in this country and abroad.

• 5 •

Four more wineries are scattered through the rugged hills west and north of Saratoga. On your left, a half-mile up Pierce Road, which leads toward the Masson mountain winery, Kathryn Kennedy has made wine since 1979 in her onetime bomb shelter from the eight acres of Cabernet she planted on her estate six years before. A mile uphill, on Congress Springs Road (Highway 9) from Pierce Road, a steep dirt road on your left climbs a knoll to what is left of the pre-Prohibition winery of Pierre Pourroy. The Congress Springs Vineyards winery has expanded to 17,000 gallons since its founders, former Masson tour guide Daniel Gehrs and his wife Robin, moved into Pourroy's house and made their first vintage in 1976. A fifth winery is planned by former Stanford Research Institute scientist Dr. Thomas Mudd on the mountain vineyard he is planting south of Highway 9.

From Mount Eden Road northwest of Saratoga, a bumpy road winds up Table Mountain to five vineyards and two famous small wineries that controversial vintner Martin Ray established during three decades after he sold Masson to Seagram in 1942. Ray preached that his were the only fine American wines, priced them astronomically, and sold patches of land to investors, who waged court battles with him for years. When he died in 1976, a group of the investors owned his hilltop winery and the main Mount Eden Vineyard, and Ray had five acres left near his downhill home. Both Mount Eden and Martin Ray wines, the latter made under the supervision of Ray's adopted stepson, Stanford Professor Peter Martin Ray, still are rarities admired by connoisseurs.

Montebello Road, which starts at Stevens Creek Reservoir, climbs a ridge of towering Black Mountain and reaches an elevation of 2600 feet. Near the summit is the Ridge Vineyard winery, a 200,000-gallon winegrowing enterprise owned by eight families of wine enthusiasts. It began in 1960, when a talented home winemaker named David Bennion interested three of his fellow scientists at Stanford Research Institute in renovating an old vineyard and a ramshackle wooden cellar on the mountain, to make wine for themselves and for sale to their friends. With their wives and children, the partners climbed the mountain on weekends to tend the vineyard, to which a previous owner had added several acres of Cabernet and Chardonnay. Each autumn the families had great fun picking and crushing the grapes, and later everyone helped to bottle the wines.

Bennion soon found wine more exciting than electronics research, and quit his Stanford job in 1968. A year later came wine-lover Paul Draper, who had made wine in Chile and had traveled in France, and joined the partners, relieving Bennion as the winemaker. They then moved their equipment and wines uphill to the old stone Montebello Winery, which Osea Perrone had closed thirty years before. Then original partners Bennion, Hewitt Crane, and Charles Rosen were joined by four more, Stanford Professor Carl Djerassi, Los Angeles industrialist Richard Foster, and pharmaceutical manufacturers Alejandro Zaffaroni and George Rosenkranz.

Ridge Vineyard has fifty acres of vines; but most of its wines, nearly all red and predominantly Zinfandel, are made of grapes purchased from Sonoma, Napa, San Joaquin, and Amador counties' vineyards, whose locations are named on the Ridge labels. Some, named Monte Bello Ridge, come from opera singer James Schwabacher's nearby Jimsomare Vineyard. Ridge Vineyard wines are intense in flavor, from mostly old vines and extra days of fermentation on the skins and from aging in small oak casks. They seldom are fined or filtered; it usually is advisable to decant the reds.

Although Montebello is included in the newly established Santa Cruz Mountains viticultural area, its owners plan someday to ask for a "Montebello" appellation of their own.

• 6 •

High above the city of Los Gatos, on Highway 17, is the Sacred Heart Novitiate, established in 1888 to train young men, enrolled as novices, for membership in the Jesuit Order as priests or as brothers. Beside the imposing building is the Novitiate of Los Gatos winery, which during all those years has produced wines in accordance with the canon law of the Catholic Church, the sale of wine helping to support the order's educational work.

Until 1967, the novices helped to cultivate the order's vineyards above the Novitiate and around the old Jesuit Alma College on Bear Creek Road, but in that year the training of novices was moved to a new seminary at Montecito in Southern California. The Novitiate's Santa Clara County vineyards lately have supplied grapes to the Congress Springs and other nearby wineries. Most Novitiate wine is now made from the grapes it grows in San Benito and Stanislaus counties.

Brother Thomas Koller manages the half-million-gallon winery, and Brother Lee Williams supervises the winemaking. An earlier winemaker was Father Thomas Dutton Terry, who became president of the University of Santa Clara; he was the only winemaker–college president in this country, if not in the world. Brother Norbert Korte presides in the winery's moss-covered tunnel tasting room and offers daily cellar tours.

Until recent years, four-fifths of the Novitiate's output consisted of altar wines, with such names as L'Admirable, Villa Joseph, Guadalupe, and Vin Doré. The rest was sold commercially, labeled "Novitiate Jesuit Wines." Best known to connoisseurs is its Black Muscat dessert wine, made of the Muscat Hamburg grape it grows in San Benito County. There also is a rosé table wine named Black Rose, made of the same Muscat Hamburg grape, which in the Novitiate's Stanislaus County vineyard lacks sufficient color to make the Black Muscat dessert wine.

In the past, several church-owned wineries carried on the monastic tradition of winegrowing in the United States. Another Jesuit winery, the Villa Maria Vineyard on Stevens Creek Road southwest of Cupertino, was operated by the University of Santa Clara until 1938. The only church-owned wineries left are the Novitiate, The Christian Brothers, and the Saint Meinrad Archabbey and Theological Seminary in Indiana, where the wine is made only for use with the resident monks' meals.

• 7 •

Only one winery is left in the Guadalupe Creek district east of Los Gatos, where there were a dozen a few decades ago. This one, hemmed in by housing tracts, is the huge, sprawling home of Almadén Vineyards along Blossom Hill Road. It is where Almadén gets its founding date of 1852, for it was here in that year that Etienne Thée planted his vineyard, where he was succeeded by son-in-law Charles Lefranc and eventually by Lefranc's son-in-law, Paul Masson.

Only sixteen acres of the once-great home vineyard remain, serving mainly to separate the winery from the surrounding homes. The original, small adobe-and-brick cellar and the lovely Lefranc French gardens have been preserved. They are surrounded now by a new office building and by bustling modern cellars in which Almadén wines are finished and bottled and where the company's champagnes are made. Almadén's producing wineries are now two in San Benito County and one each in Fresno and Kern counties. There are almost 6000 acres of Almadén vineyards in the central coast counties of San Benito and Monterey. (Almadén's owners have also planted 1000 acres of vineyards in Brazil and have built a winery there.)

Almadén offers tasting and tours at its Los Gatos cellars, and tasting also at its visitor facility on Pacheco Pass Road, Highway 152. To taste all its wines would be an undertaking, for at last count there were more than fifty, ranging from moderately priced table wines in jugs and boxed plastic bags for everyday mealtime use, to top-quality, vintage-dated "varietal" wines under the Almadén and Lefranc Cellars brands. There also is a Caves Laurent-Perrier Chardonnay Blanc de Blancs, produced by Almadén in a joint venture with that famous French champagne house and introduced in 1982. It is a California equivalent of the *coteaux champenois* still wine sold in the Champagne district of France, and a hint that it might be followed by a joint-venture French-California sparkling wine.

The first wines named Almadén* were introduced by Charles Lefranc before he died in 1887. The Almadén name again appeared on labels at Repeal in 1933, when Charles Jones and his associates reopened the old winery and for a few years sold wines they called "Almadén Maison Blanc" and "Almadén Maison Rouge."

In 1941, the late San Francisco socialite, Louis Benoist, then president of the Lawrence Warehouse Company, bought the property as a place to entertain his weekend guests. He persuaded a great chef, Madame Louise Savin, to close her nearby restaurant and take charge of the kitchen at Almadén.

Benoist started looking for someone to tell him what to do with his idle winery. Learning that the importer and wine-writer Frank Schoonmaker was having success selling premium California wines in New York, Benoist placed a call for him there. That day Schoonmaker happened to be in San Francisco, where he had a wine shop on Maiden Lane. He became the wine advisor to Benoist, originated the style of Almadén labels, and wrote the company's "News from the Vineyards" until 1973. Schoonmaker also found a winemaker for Benoist; he knew that Oliver Goulet was no longer employed by Martin Ray. Goulet went to work for Almadén and made fine wines there until his death in 1962.

One day soon after the purchase, inspecting the old vineyard

*For the old quicksilver mine in the hills. *Almadén* means "mine" in Spanish.

with Benoist and Goulet, Schoonmaker noticed some Grenache grapes, which Goulet said were being used to make port wine. Schoonmaker asked him why they weren't used to make rosé, as in France's Rhone district of Tavel. Goulet's puzzled answer was: "What's rosé?" Six months later, Almadén started the pink-wine vogue in the United States by launching its first Grenache Rosé. With its fresh varietal aroma and intriguing puckery taste, Grenache Rosé is still one of the company's best-selling wines.

Benoist then bought and planted more vineyards in the Santa Clara Valley and in the Santa Cruz Mountains. During the Second World War, Almadén champagne and rosé became nationally known. But when the wine market crashed following the war, the firm began to lose money. Benoist then worked out a merger with the Madrone Vineyards of Eugene Selvage, boss of the Lucky Lager Brewery. They couldn't agree on what to name the merged firm, so it became "Almadén-Madrone." The merger lasted until 1950, when Selvage's Canadian backers suddenly ordered Madrone closed down. Almadén again became independent, with a new manager, Hans Peter Jurgens, who had headed Madrone.

Then suburban subdivisionitis began biting chunks out of Almadén's 900 Santa Clara and Santa Cruz acres, and Benoist saw his vineyards there were doomed. In 1954 the company began acquiring land in San Benito County and two years later started planting there. When the new vines came into bearing, all but a few dozen acres of the historic vineyard near Los Gatos had given way to a housing tract named "Almadén Estates."

In 1967, when Louis and Kay Benoist owned seven houses, two airplanes, and a 110-foot yacht named *Le Voyageur,* something went wrong between Benoist and his Lawrence Warehouse Company. The Benoists suddenly sold their yacht and their Aptos beach house, and Almadén was offered for sale. The wineries and vineyards were snapped up for $14 million by National Distillers, which had owned three California wineries during the Second World War but had sold them all when the conflict ended.

Under the new ownership, Almadén has enlarged its vineyards and wineries and has also become an importer of European wines. With its total storage capacity of 40 million gallons, it is now one of the six largest wine companies in the nation. It covers the entire spectrum of wine prices, quality, sizes, colors, and labels. On the one hand, it leads the industry in supplying table wines to restaurants for by-the-glass-and-carafe service, using both jugs and the 28-liter "bag-in-the-box." At the same time, it courts the buyers of luxury wines with new vintage "varietals," including a red of the rare Cabernet Pfeffer grape, a spicy Gewürztraminer, and a botrytized late-harvest Johannisberg Riesling that compares to the Beerenauslesen of Germany. These are the creations of German-born and -trained Klaus Mathes, who succeeded Alfred Huntsinger, Oliver Goulet's assistant, as Almadén's winemaster in 1974. To Almadén's assortment of ten bottle-fermented champagnes, which include both the inexpensive "Le Domaine" group and the top-rated "Blanc de Blancs" cuvée, Mathes has added a bone-dry vintage "Chardonnay Nature" and an "Eye of the Partridge" bronze sparkling wine produced from Pinot Noir, Pinot Blanc, and Chardonnay.

Paul Masson Vineyards has claimed to be California's oldest winegrower because the various figures in its history have produced wine continuously, including in the Prohibition period, from the time Etienne Thée's vineyard, planted in 1852, first bore grapes. Almadén Vineyards, on the other hand, says that it is "California's oldest producing winery" because it is headquartered at the probable site of Thée's vineyard, where Charles Lefranc was producing wine before he met Paul Masson. Meanwhile, Buena Vista at Sonoma says it is "California's oldest winery" because it was in 1857 that Agoston Haraszthy is reputed to have begun building the two original stone cellars at Buena Vista. We'll meet a fourth owner of an "oldest" title shortly.

• 8 •

There is one winery in the center of San Jose that ferments its own grapes and offers daily tasting and cellar tours. The 500,000-gallon Turgeon & Lohr Winery was built in 1974 on Lenzen Avenue, around the corner from the city's historic main artery, The Alameda, which is State Highway 82. Homebuilders Bernard Turgeon and Jerome Lohr of Saratoga had planted their 280-acre vineyard three years earlier in the Salinas Valley of Monterey County, and decided to build their winery in San Jose instead of eighty miles away. Turgeon & Lohr was too much of a mouthful, so they chose "J. Lohr" as the name for their wines, each of which bears a back label describing the grape variety from which it was produced and the oak casks in which it was aged. All are estate-grown, vintage-dated "varietals" except their proprietary, semi-dry Johannisberg Riesling blend, named Jade. Lohr manages the vineyard while Turgeon works in the winery with winemaker Barry Gnekow.

• 9 •

Across the Santa Clara Valley, in the Evergreen district on the slope of Mount Hamilton, Mirassou Vineyards invites visitors to tour its winery, to sample the wines in its hospitality room, to broaden their gastronomic knowledge at its food and wine education center, and to attend its frequent brunches and dinners. Since five generations of their family have grown grapes for wine continuously since 1854, the Mirassous are proud to call themselves the oldest winegrowing family in North America. Although their wines are among the best in California, only since the early 1970s have they been found in most restaurants and retail stores.

The Mirassous' ancestor, Pierre Pellier from La Rochelle in France, came to San Jose in 1853, bringing wine-grape cuttings ordered by his brother Louis, who had founded the City Gardens nursery there three years before. When the vines were planted, Pierre went back to France for more cuttings, returning in 1858. On the sailing ship, he carefully placed each twig in a sliced potato to protect it from drying out during the six-month trip around Cape Horn. In 1859, Pierre planted the present vineyard in the Evergreen district and built a cellar to age his wines. Pellier's son-in-law, Pierre Mirassou, succeeded him, followed by his son Peter, and then by Peter's sons Edmund and Norbert, the fourth generation since Pellier.

Edmund and Norbert, who own the winery, made only bulk wines for sale mainly to champagne producers until 1942, when they had labels printed in order to sell a few bottles to their neighbors. Then they entered a few wines in the state fair judgings, and when they received gold and silver medals, connoisseurs began coming to the winery to buy.

Meanwhile, boys of the family's fifth generation were growing up, getting experience in the vineyards and winery, and beginning to rear a sixth generation of Mirassous. In 1966, the fifth generation started taking over. Edmund's son Peter was already in charge of the Mirassou vineyards, which had spread to the Salinas Valley of Monterey County. His brother Dan now handles the marketing of Mirassou wines with his brother Jim. Winemaker Max Huebner, who had been with the Mirassous since 1941, has been succeeded by a group of UC-Davis-trained enologists. One of their chief consultants is Peter Stern.

At this writing, Mirassou vineyards and wineries totaled 1125 acres and 2.3 million gallons, including the Wehner vineyard and winery two miles to the southeast, established in the 1880s and taken over from the Cribari family in 1964. Mirassou wines are already sold in forty-six states and in five countries.

The wines currently total twenty, all vintage-dated and labeled with the counties where the grapes were grown, whether in Santa Clara or Monterey County, or in both. There are six reds, a Petite Sirah rosé whose name the fifth generation have abbreviated to Petite Rosé, seven whites, including a proprietary blend of Gewürztraminer, White Riesling, and Pinot Blanc, named Fleuri Blanc, and four bottle-fermented champagnes—a bone-dry "au Naturel," a brut, a late-disgorged brut called "LD" (aged four years before disgorging), and a Blanc de Noir. Six of the "varietal" table wines, called "Harvest Reserve," are priced 20 to 25 percent above the regular line.

• 10 •

Santa Cruz County, reached via Highway 17 from San Jose, was a famous fine-wine district before Prohibition, when thirty-nine wineries cultivated 1600 acres of vineyards between Ben Lomond, Boulder Creek, Corralitos, Felton, Glenwood, and Soquel. Less than 100 acres were left when I wrote the first edition of this book a decade ago, but a revival of Santa Cruz viniculture is in progress, lured by the challenge of growing superior wines in this cool, mountainous Region I climate. The number of wineries in the county has increased in the past decade from four to seventeen, and at least two more are preparing to start. There is talk of replanting many old vineyards in the next few years.

After Repeal, the best-known Santa Cruz wines came from lawyer Chaffee Hall's Hallcrest Vineyard on Felton-Empire Road at Felton. He closed the winery before he died in 1969, and his choice Riesling and Cabernet grapes went to the Concannon winery at Livermore. In 1976, Hall's daughter leased Hallcrest to Ridge Vineyard biochemist Leo McCloskey, Bonny Doon grape grower Jim Beauregard, and Western Airlines pilot John Pollard. They renamed it Felton-Empire Vineyard, installed new modern winery equipment, and within a year were producing finer wines than those that had made Hallcrest wines famous in the past. The most-praised current releases are its Rieslings and Gewürztraminers, which McCloskey makes each year in both dry and late-harvest styles. Since 1978 he has been producing "varietal" fresh grape juices of Gewürztraminer, Riesling, Zinfandel, and Gamay Beaujolais.

Also well known are the wines Dr. David Bruce produces at

his twenty-five-acre vineyard at 2000 feet elevation on Bear Creek Road, ten miles southwest of Los Gatos. Dr. Bruce, whose dermatology practice is in San Jose, pursues his three-day-a-week avocation of growing unique wines that he sells mostly to connoisseurs, who order them by mail. When he bought his hilltop site in 1961, there were a century-old farmhouse on the property and traces of a former vineyard. The doctor terraced the land and planted Chardonnay, Riesling, Pinot Noir, Cabernet, and Zinfandel. He studied viniculture texts, practiced making wine in small quantities, bonded a temporary winery in 1964, and three years later put David Bruce wines on sale in a few San Jose stores. He later built the present 50,000-gallon concrete-block cellar with modern equipment, some of it of his own design. During the first vintage in his temporary winery, he discovered he had more red grapes than his casks could hold, so he fermented the white juice of his Zinfandels without the skins, and made one of the first Zinfandel Blancs to become popular in California. Although he specializes in other varieties, Dr. Bruce hopes also someday to "bring the mountain-grown Zinfandel to the place it deserves in the world of fine wines." He holds tastings at the winery on Saturdays, but it is advisable to telephone ahead if you plan to attend. Available there, while the supplies last, are inexpensive nonvintage blends that he labels "Old Dog Vineyards." They are wines that don't fit into his "varietal" plans.

In 1977, Dick Smothers, of Smothers Brothers TV program fame, opened the small Vine Hill winery in his home on the pre-Prohibition Schermerhorn Vineyard, which extends east from Vine Hill Road to Highway 17. Six years later, I learned that the winery equipment was being prepared for a move to Sonoma County to use the grapes planted there by the other Smothers Brother, Tom. From Vine Hill Road south of the Smothers estate, Jarvis Road extends north to the fourteen-acre Santa Cruz Mountain Vineyard and 20,000-gallon winery of former Orange County restaurateur Kenneth Burnap and his wife Marie. An enthusiast about Pinot Noir, Burnap searched for an ideal place to grow this one wine, found it here, started building his winery in 1970, and made his first prize-winning vintage, unfined and unfiltered, in 1975. He also now makes a Cabernet from purchased mountain-grown grapes. Jarvis Road gets its name from John Jarvis, the co-founder of the Santa Cruz Mountain Wine Company, who is said to have planted the first vineyard in the Vine Hill district in 1858. Off Miller Hill Road, two miles east of Highway 17, is the 5,000-gallon Silver Mountain Vineyard winery that Air Force veteran Jerold O'Brien has built on the all-Chardonnay hilltop vineyard he began planting in 1981. A hand-hewn cave in the mountains above Nicasio Way near St. Clare's Retreat is electronic engineer Dan Wheeler's 5000-gallon Nicasio Vineyard winery, his hobby since 1952. He makes champagnes and table wines for sale to his mailing list of customers.

Still more wineries are scattered west of Highway 17. Atop a steep hill at the end of Hopkins Gulch Road, four miles northeast of Boulder Creek, is the six-acre vineyard of San Jose State University art professor Paul Staiger and his wife Marjorie. They bonded their tiny P. & M. Staiger winery beneath their home in 1973. Since their vines matured, they have made only estate-grown wines. On Bean Creek Road in Scotts Valley is the new Roudon-Smith Vineyards winery. It began in 1972 in the basement of Robert and Annamarie Roudon's home, beside their vineyard on Mountain View Road, but needing more space, it was moved in 1979 to this new 40,000-gallon cellar beside the vineyard of partners James and June Smith. Roudon and Smith are engineer emigrants from Los Angeles. Off Highway 9, near the intersection of Highway 236, is Dexter and Valerie Ahlgren's 5000-gallon winery, on their young Chardonnay vineyard of two and a half acres. Ahlgren is a consulting civil engineer at Boulder Creek.

The once-famous Bonny Doon district, north of the University of California's Santa Cruz campus, is showing signs of a renaissance. Felton-Empire winery partner Jim Beauregard plans to add 300 acres to his family's fourteen-acre vineyard on Pine Flat Road. He and his neighbors petitioned the Federal government in 1983 to establish Bonny Doon as a separate viticultural area. Beauregard is also preparing to replant the abandoned Locatelli vineyard, which adjoins the Lockheed plant near Eagle Rock. He plans to rebuild the onetime Locatelli winery and produce champagne there.

On Bonny Doon Road, west of the Beauregard home, is the first winery opened in Bonny Doon since pre-Prohibition days. It is the McHenry Vineyard winery, bonded in 1980. Dean E. McHenry, the retired founding chancellor of UC Santa Cruz in 1961, and his wife Jane have their home on the neat five-acre vineyard, and they tend the vines. Their son Henry, who teaches biological anthropology at UC Davis, comes on weekends with his wife Linda to make wine in the 4,000-gallon winery, which is built into the hill across the vineyard from the home. The first vintages of McHenry Chardonnay and Pinot Noir were released in 1983.

A half mile west of the McHenrys, UC Davis–trained wine-maker Randall Grahm has planted a vineyard of Burgundian, Bordeaux, and Provence varieties and has named his place the Bonny Doon Vineyard. He has built a winery to make wine of purchased grapes until his vines mature.

Until the Felton-Empire winery added a tasting room in 1983, the Bargetto Winery, founded fifty years earlier at Soquel, was the only one in Santa Cruz County with a public tasting room and daily cellar tours. Since the death of Lawrence Bargetto, his Davis-trained son Martin has helped his mother Beverly run the 150,000-gallon winery, and his brother John is also study-ing enology at Davis, to join the winery by 1985.

• 11 •

South of the Evergreen district, there are no more wineries until Morgan Hill, fifteen miles from San Jose. There were scores of vineyards and wineries before Prohibition from Morgan Hill south to beyond Gilroy. Now the vineyards are being invaded by housing tracts. A movement has been started by the Friends of the Winemakers to preserve the Joseph Malaguera winery, built in 1869 off Burnett Avenue in Morgan Hill, as a Santa Clara County Wine Museum. Before Prohibition, most of the small wineries here sold their product in bulk to the California Wine Association, which operated wineries at Evergreen, Los Gatos, and Gilroy. At Repeal, these winegrowers again sold in bulk to big wineries, but some of them developed a business of delivering wine in jugs each week to Italian stores and to the doorsteps of wine-drinking families, much as the dairies delivered milk.

One of the latter is the Emilio Guglielmo Winery, with its 150-acre vineyard on Main Avenue, two miles east of Morgan Hill. Before the Second World War, Emilio's Cavalcade Bur-gundy was one of the best wine buys in San Francisco. His son George took over after the war, expanded the winery with stainless-steel tanks to 400,000 gallons, opened a tasting room next door to his home, and since has been joined by his sons, George E. and Eugene. Cavalcade and Emile's burgundy, chablis, and Grignolino rosé, sold at the winery in inexpensive jugs, are still the Guglielmos' main wines, but they now also sell costlier bottle-numbered claret and vintage-dated "varietals" under their Mount Madonna brand.

Another that once specialized in doorstep delivery of jugs was John Pedrizetti's winery at his vineyard on San Pedro Avenue, a mile southeast of Guglielmo. Since John's son Edward and daughter-in-law Phyllis took over the winery in 1968, changes have been made. Phyllis has opened a tasting room on Highway 101, north of town, and has introduced a line of premium wines, including estate-bottled Petite Sirah and Zinfandel. Edward has installed stainless-steel tanks and doubled the winery capacity to 450,000 gallons. In 1977, he was joined by son Dan, an ordained Baptist minister who had been operating a farm for boys in Arkansas. The Pedrizettis have begun selling some of their wines in plastic bags together with attractive cabinets with spouts, from which restaurants dispense burgundy and chilled rosé and chablis to patrons by the glass or carafe.

For decades, billboards along Highway 101 have invited tourists to stop at a winery tasting room on Monterey Road in San Martin, four miles south of Morgan Hill. It is across the railroad tracks from the venerable 3-million-gallon brick San Martin Winery, built in 1908 and long operated by Bruno Filice, from Cosenza in southern Italy. During the 1960s, Filice family descendants were making every conceivable kind of wine there, ranging from Pinot Noir to apricot and strawberry champagnes.

In the early 1970s, new owners brought in winemaster Edmund Friedrich, who modernized the winery and transformed it into a producer of premium wines. Trained in the viticultural institute at Trier on the Moselle, where he was born, Friedrich had spent fourteen years at Paul Masson's Soledad winery and a season at the Wiederkehr cellars in Arkansas. On a study trip to Germany in 1975, it occurred to him that the softness of Germany's best white wines might be due to the low alcoholic content they reach in the cool German growing season, usually 9 percent or less, compared to the 11, 12, and higher percent strength usually reached in sunny California. Back at San Martin, Friedrich used cold fermentation and sterile filtration to produce California's first low-alcohol wines, which he called "soft" because they retain the delicious texture and taste of the grape. In order to sell his "soft" wines, Friedrich had to persuade California public health authorities to repeal a four-decade-old state regulation that prohibited the sale of California wines lower than 10 percent in strength. The regulation was repealed in 1979, reducing the minimum strength of California wine to the Federal minimum of 7 percent. This set off the "light wine" revolution, in which dozens of wineries in this country and abroad have begun making "light" and "soft" wines of 7 to 9.5 percent strength. In 1982, Friedrich became the president of the Chateau Elan vineyard and winery in Georgia. His successor at San Martin, UC Davis–trained Greg Bruni, continues making "soft" Riesling,

Chenin Blanc, and Gamay Beaujolais, ranging from 7 to 10 percent. Most of the other San Martin wines are vintage-dated premium "varietals," but also available at its tasting rooms are less costly nonvintage table wines, in four-liter jugs.

• 12 •

Gilroy is known as the nation's garlic capital, and it has celebrated the fact with an annual garlic festival since 1979. The pungent aroma from the dehydrators east of the city is sometimes quite pronounced. But traveling west of town on Highway 152, the road to Hecker Pass, you breathe a different aroma in autumn—the heady smell of fermenting wine. Clustered in two neighboring verdant, scenic valleys are eleven wineries, eight of them surrounded by vineyards of their own. In past decades only bulk wines were grown here for sale to larger wineries, or in jugs, demijohns, or barrels delivered to family homes, or sold to the roadside trade. Now, enthusiastic new proprietors have taken over some of the cellars, and since Americans discovered wine in recent years, have begun replanting the vineyards with the grape varieties that make premium wines. People from San Jose and the Bay cities come here looking for wine bargains, in such numbers that seven of the Gilroy vintners have opened public tasting rooms. Peter Scagliotti was the first to post billboards to attract tourists to his Live Oaks Winery, on Highway 152. Then Mario and Ernest Fortino, who come from Calabria, took over the old Cassa vineyard and winery, and operated it as the Fortino Winery, with such success that brother Mario started his own Hecker Pass Winery, also complete with tasting, next door.

In 1971, young ex-salesman Thomas Kruse from Chicago, having learned home winemaking from Gilroy vineyardist John Roffinella, bonded an old building near the Fortinos as a winery and started making a Grignolino rosé. Meanwhile, Tom started teaching a course in winemaking. Then, as an experiment, he bought grapes near Fresno and made the only wine I have ever seen labeled "Thompson Seedless"; it was neutral in flavor but quite drinkable, and Kruse has made and sold it every year since. His latest interest is in making bottle-fermented sparkling Zinfandel and Chardonnay.

Next door to Scagliotti, uphill from seven acres of Chardonnay vines planted in 1980, is the new 5000-gallon Sarah's Vineyard winery behind a ranch-style home. When asked "Who is Sarah?", winemaker Marilyn Otteman replies, "I dreamed her up to represent me." The wife of Whittier manufacturer John Otteman, Marilyn has been making wine since she worked in a home-winemaking supply shop in Los Angeles. Her first estate-bottled Sarah's Vineyard Chardonnay was the 1983.

Across the hill in the well-named Uvas Valley (*uvas* is Spanish for "grapes"), a transformation has occurred at the former Louis Bonesio Winery since it was purchased in 1976 by the family of Nikola Kirigin-Chargin, an enologist from Croatia, and was renamed the Kirigin Cellars. Stainless-steel tanks have been installed, and Malvasia Bianca, Cabernet, and Pinot Noir are now the featured wines, phasing out such old Gilroy favorite grapes as Malvasia Nera and Mataro. Chargin, a graduate of the University of Zagreb, came to the United States in 1960 and served as an enologist at such wineries as San Martin and Almadén before deciding to buy a winery of his own. Forty-eight acres of the former Bonesio vineyard at Day and Watsonville roads are now Chargin's. Householders to whom the Bonesios once delivered jug wines no longer enjoy that convenience, but jugs of some types are available at the winery and in stores. Tasting is offered at the winery, and there also is a picnic area with tables under the trees.

On Uvas Road, a mile northwest of Kirigin, former schoolteachers Walter and Mary Kaye Parks have modernized the old Marchetti winery and renamed it Sycamore Creek Vineyards, for the stream that runs through their fourteen acres of vines. Since 1977, they have introduced White Riesling and estate-bottled Carignane, Cabernet, Chardonnay, and Zinfandel. The latter is their specialty because it wins them the most medals in competitions.

Two of the oldest Gilroy wineries, Conrotto and Giretti, have taken down their "wine for sale" signs, but still supply their old and new customers with country-style wine by the barrel, demijohn, or jug.

• 13 •

From San Juan Bautista, a half-hour's drive south of Gilroy, the San Benito Valley extends southeastward between the Diablo and Gavilán (Hawk) mountain ranges for some sixty miles. To this valley outside the path of urban sprawl came Louis Benoist of Almadén in 1954, seeking land to replace his doomed vineyards in the Santa Clara Valley. The northern part of San Benito County is one of the oldest winegrowing districts in the state. The Franciscan friars who founded Mission San Juan Bautista in 1797 planted vines in the Mission garden to make wine for the Mass. A half century later, Théophile Vaché established the county's first commercial vineyard in the Cienega Valley, eight miles south of the Mission, and hauled his wine to market in a puncheon on wheels drawn by oxen. By the 1880s, there were 400 acres of vines in the county, and wines made at Cienega by William Palmtag, the mayor of Hollister, were winning medals in Europe. After Palmtag came Dr. Harold Ohrwall of San Francisco, who was joined in 1908 by Professor Frederic Bioletti of viticultural fame. During Prohibition, the San Benito wineries closed, but more vineyards were planted to supply grapes to the home-winemaking trade. There were 2000 acres of vines and eight bonded wineries in the county at Repeal in 1933. Edwin Valliant then owned the Palmtag winery, and during the late 1930s he made some of the best Rieslings in the state. He sold out to a subsidiary of the Hiram Walker distillers during the Second World War.

When Benoist came to San Benito County, he first leased and later purchased the Cienega winery and vineyard. In 1956 he began planting lands near Paicines, thirteen miles farther south, and soon afterward built a brandy distillery and a second winery there. By 1967, when he sold Almadén to National Distillers, his San Benito vineyards covered nearly 4500 acres, which then was the largest planting of premium-variety grapes under a single ownership in the world.

It is worth a trip through the valley to see these spectacular vineyards, almost five square miles of rolling hills carpeted with vines. They are watered by permanent overhead sprinklers, fed through hundreds of miles of underground plastic pipe. The sprinklers also protect the vines from frost; when temperatures drop to freezing, they switch on automatically to insulate the vines with a protective coating of ice. Almadén's Cienega Valley cellar is world-famous as "the walking winery." Palmtag unwittingly built the old cellar precisely astride the San Andreas fault, the most active earthquake belt in the United States; the halves of the winery move a half-inch farther apart each year. Seismologists come from many countries to observe the deep cleft in the cement floor because it keeps widening with each tremor of the earth. Although the winery is not open to visitors, you can stop and see the cleft in a concrete drain outside the building. In 1960, a comparatively mild temblor jolted a redwood tank off balance, and 8000 gallons of wine were lost through its loosened staves.

There is another famous sight across the road: A single roof covers four acres of barrels and tanks of aging wines. Almadén makes only red wines at Cienega. The whites are made at the Paicines winery; the company's sherry *soleras* are also there. Almadén brandy is distilled in the San Joaquin Valley and is blended and bottled by National Distillers at Cincinnati, Ohio.

Three new small wineries opened in San Benito County during the 1970s, and the government has recognized three San Benito viticultural areas—Paicines and the Cienega and Limekiln valleys. A mile south of Paicines is the 30,000-gallon Calera winery on the site of an old limekiln (*calera* is Spanish for "limekiln"). Two seasons working in the vineyards of Burgundy, after his student days at Yale and Oxford, convinced former San Francisco restaurant critic Josh Jensen that only limestone soil can produce great burgundies. That is what brought him and his wife Jeanne to this valley in 1975, to begin planting twenty-four acres of Pinot Noir on three limestone sites. Their first estate-bottled Pinot Noirs, made in 1978, have already won praise from connoisseurs. A short distance south of Calera is the 18,000-gallon Cygnet Cellars winery, whose name means a young swan. Bonded in 1977 by Jim and Paul Johnson and their partner Bob Lane, it has produced red and white wines from purchased grapes. On a former quarry at the end of Limekiln Road, which extends two miles west from Cienega Road, is the 25,000-gallon Enz Vineyards winery of civil engineer Robert Enz and his wife Susan, bonded in 1973. Their thirty-acre vineyard dates from the 1880s and contains the oldest known planting of Pinot St. George in the state.

· 14 ·

Across the Gavilán Mountains from the San Benito Valley is Monterey County, where a viticultural revolution has taken place since 1962. It began in the Salinas Valley, but now it is spreading west into the Carmel Valley, which begins at the outskirts of historic Monterey. By 1983, the vineyards of Monterey County totaled 35,000 acres, more than in any of the coast counties farther north. There already are twelve wineries in the county, a number expected to increase within a few years.

The eighty-mile-long Salinas Valley, long known as the "Salad Bowl of the World" for its vast plantings of iceberg lettuce and celery, has become the "wine bowl" instead. During the century when pioneer vintners were establishing the vineyards around San Francisco Bay, this valley was considered a poor place to grow grapes. It is mostly a level plain, ten to twenty miles wide, between the Gaviláns and the rugged Santa Lucia range, which rises abruptly from the Pacific shore, twenty-five miles away. Of 400 acres of vines in the valley during Prohibition, more than half were abandoned after Repeal. The chief reason was scant rainfall, only ten inches annually, half of the minimum required for adequate vineyard yields. Also, the strong wind that sweeps unimpeded up the valley from Monterey Bay each afternoon from May to November was regarded as injurious to vines.

Consequently, when Professors Winkler and Amerine at the university published their analyses of California climates, begun in 1935, their findings about the Salinas Valley went unnoticed. One of their findings was that growing-season temperatures in the valley's north-central part are the same as in the most-favored north coast districts, Region I and Region II. Twenty-five years later, as cities began closing in on the Santa Clara vineyards, the Mirassou brothers and their Paul Masson neighbors began an urgent search for other areas in which to plant vines. They first surveyed Sonoma County, and the Sierra foothills next, but neither offered sufficient flat open space. Then they noticed the old Winkler-Amerine figures, and decided to investigate for themselves. They discovered that the sparse Salinas rainfall was actually no problem, for through this remarkable valley flows the Salinas River, the greatest underground stream in America. Plentiful water, pumped from only a few hundred feet below the surface, already supplied artificial rain for the lettuce crops; it could do the same for grapevines. They saw that the afternoon gales could not damage the grapes if the vine rows were simply planted parallel to the wind. Vines planted on fertile benchlands above the valley floor would be virtually immune from damage by frost. And of perhaps greatest importance, being situated far from the fast-growing cities to the north and south, this area seemed safe for many years from urban sprawl.

In a multimillion-dollar gamble, these two vintners in 1957 bought 1300 acres in the valley between Soledad and Greenfield, and in 1962 began planting vines in what for grapes was virgin soil. The Mirassous set out 300 acres on the west side near the now-restored Soledad Mission, and Masson planted 1000 acres on the east side along Metz Road. A year later, the Wente Brothers of Livermore followed, choosing 300 acres near the Arroyo Seco southwest of the Mirassous. By the third year, the grapes showed such promise that Masson began building a winery on its vineyard near Soledad and started sending its grapes there from Santa Clara to be crushed. In the next few years, vineyard planting in the Salinas Valley multiplied no less than twelve times. Mirassou planted 600 more acres on its San Vicente Ranch. Masson added 4500 acres around Greenfield and Soledad and expanded its Soledad winery to 11 million gallons. Almadén followed in 1970, planting 2100 acres on grazing and vegetable land below King City and San Lucas. The conglomerate named Southdown planted the 6000-acre Viña Monterey west of King City, a vineyard so immense that special machines were built to pick the grapes from two rows of its vines at a time. International Vineyards, then related to the Gold Seal winery of New York State, planted vineyards between Chualar and Greenfield. Myron and Gerald McFarland, of the Kern County family for whom the town of McFarland is named, formed investor partnerships for whom they planted thousands of acres. But this was only the beginning, said Edmund Mirassou. "If there is enough demand for coast-counties table wine, vineyards in the Salinas Valley can reach a hundred thousand acres—more than all the vineyards of Napa, Sonoma, Mendocino, and the other coast counties combined."

During the late 1960s, the Mirassous and Wentes, with their Monterey vineyards almost a hundred miles distant from their wineries, faced the problem of keeping their grapes perfectly fresh during the long trip north. Peter Mirassou solved it in 1969 by adding to one of his family's mechanical-harvesting machines a grape-crusher-stemmer and a tank of carbon dioxide gas. The crushed grapes, protected from air by a blanket of carbon dioxide, then traveled in a cooled, pressurized tank truck to the Mirassou winery at San Jose. The resulting wine was later compared in blind tastings—and found superior—to wine made from the same grapes picked that day by hand.

• 15 •

Fifteen miles south of Salinas, the Monterey County seat, is the village of Gonzales, at the south end of which two large wineries stand side by side on a ninety-acre slab. One is the 4-million-gallon Monterey Vineyard cellar, with stained-glass windows and an observation tower and deck that offers a dramatic view across the valley to the Gavilán mountain range. It was built in 1974 by a group associated with the McFarlands to make premium wines of the McFarland partners' grapes, and was the first in Monterey County to offer daily tasting and cellar tours. During the 1970s it produced more wine under contracts for other growers and vintners than for sale under its own name.

Then in 1977, it was purchased by the giant Coca-Cola Company of Atlanta, which earlier that year had invaded the wine business by buying the Taylor and Pleasant Valley wineries of New York State and the Sterling Vineyard and winery of Calistoga.

The winery next door is almost four times as large, with more than 15 million gallons capacity on its seven-acre site. It was built in 1981 by Coca-Cola's Wine Spectrum to blend, age, store, bottle, package, and ship worldwide its moderately priced Taylor California Cellars wines, blends of San Joaquin Valley and coast-counties table wines, first bottled at the Franzia winery at Ripon and introduced in 1978. The Monterey Vineyard winery produced the coast-counties wines used in the TCC blends. There now are more than a dozen generically and varietally labeled TCC table and "light" wines and charmat-process champagnes, and four economy-priced valley-and-coast blends of table wines in jugs, called Vivante, introduced in 1983.

The new Taylor California Cellars winery was in the midst of its second vintage in 1983 when word came of its purchase, together with the rest of Coca-Cola's wine properties, by the worldwide Seagram wine empire. How Seagram's acquisition of the two wineries at Gonzales might influence Paul Masson operations at Saratoga, Soledad, and Madera, or whether TCC might continue as a Masson competitor, remained to be decided by the Seagram Wine Group.

Monterey Vineyard president and Wine Spectrum technical director Dr. Richard Peterson is the master blender who created the first TCC blends. After earning his Ph.D. at UC Berkeley in 1958, he served ten years as research director of the Gallo winery at Modesto, then six vintages as enologist at Beaulieu Vineyard with the great André Tchelistcheff, whom he succeeded when the latter retired to consult for other wineries. Dr. Peterson's daughters Heidi and Holly are both Davis-trained. Heidi is the winemaker at the Buehler estate in the Napa Valley. Holly teaches wine appreciation at the Academie du Vin and at a school of cuisine in Paris.

Dr. Peterson considers the northern Salinas Valley, from Chualar to Soledad, as Region I, the coolest winegrowing region in the United States, with the latest ripening dates. Examples are his Monterey Vineyard "December Harvest" wines and his 1978 wine of the Napa Gamay grape, which was not harvested until January 2, 1979. "Monterey wines have more intense varietal flavors than the same wines grown elsewhere," he says, thus explaining what some connoisseurs have described as the "vegetative" taste of northern Salinas Valley reds. Dr. Peterson ascribes it to the cool climate and to the fact that most of the vines were planted on their own roots in the sandy Salinas soil. (But in 1983, phylloxera was discovered killing vines in two vineyards north of Gonzales, and it appeared likely that much of the valley eventually would have to be replanted on phylloxera-resistant rootstocks.) Most of the red varieties originally planted north of Soledad have since been grafted over to whites. Exceptions are Pinot Noir, Gamay Beaujolais, and a few small red plantings, in warm locations of reds. You rarely hear any more complaints about "vegetative taste." Dr. Peterson adds that botrytis, "the noble mold," grows on grapes in northern Monterey vineyards every year. In 1974 he produced for the Monterey Vineyard a California approach to the sweet sauternes of Bordeaux, made from naturally botrytized Sauvignon Blanc and Sémillon and labeled "Botrytis Sauvignon Blanc." Four years later he produced a "Botrytis Pinot Noir," a fragrant red equivalent of sauternes but reminiscent of a low-alcohol tawny port. These, plus seven varietally labeled table wines and a 1979 bottle-fermented champagne, released in 1983, bear the Monterey Vineyard label and are distributed like Sterling Vineyard wines.

• 16 •

West of the town of Soledad is Mission Nuestra Señora de la Soledad, established by the Franciscan padres in 1791 and reconstructed since the 1960s. Each September at the Mission, the community celebrates Monterey County's arrival as one of the most important wine counties of the state. Soledad has become a wine community, with three wineries in its vicinity, the nearest and biggest of which is Paul Masson's Soledad cellars on Metz Road.

From Foothill Boulevard, opposite the old Mission school, a driveway climbs through a 250-acre hillside vineyard to the 100,000-gallon Smith & Hook winery, bonded in 1978 in a reconstructed barn on the onetime horse ranch for which it is named. Smith & Hook's Davis-trained winemaker, Duane de Boer, makes only estate-bottled Cabernet Sauvignon blended with Merlot and Cabernet Franc. Gerald McFarland says this is the first of a series of future chateaux to be built on McFarland partners' lands, each to produce a single estate-bottled wine, such as a burgundy-style or a champagne.

Nine steep miles east of Soledad and 2000 feet above the Salinas Valley are the 110-acre Chalone Vineyard and its 58,000-gallon winery, whose estate-bottled table wines are widely praised. It is ten miles from the nearest telephone line, and winemaker Peter Watson-Graff communicates by radio with the outside world. Moisture is so scarce at this elevation that in dry years water has been hauled up the mountain in tank trucks to water the vines. The Chalone bench in the Gavilán mountains was recognized as a distinct viticultural area by the Federal government in 1982. The vines first planted here by William Silvear in 1920 brought high prices from the Wente and Almadén wineries for three decades after Repeal. In 1965, Richard Graff, a Harvard music graduate who had studied for a year at UC Davis, bought Chalone from a group of hobbyists who had begun building the winery and had given up after a single season. Since then Graff has been joined by his younger brothers: John, from the University of Chicago, and Peter, a 1970 Davis graduate. Chalone is now owned by Gavilán Vineyards, a corporation headed by Richard, and has two sister wineries, Edna Valley Vineyards and the new Carmenet Vineyard in Sonoma Valley.

On Los Coches Road, six miles south of Soledad, is the 300-acre Ventana Vineyard, which former Navy jet pilot J. Douglas Meador and his wife Shirley began planting in 1972. Six years later, they converted a former dairy barn into the 50,000-gallon Ventana winery, began producing a dozen estate-bottled wines, and later made a brut champagne for release in 1984. Other wineries buy most of their grapes.

Just west of the town of Greenfield, on Walnut Avenue off US 101, is the Jekel Vineyard winery of William and August Jekel, identical twins who have a film studio in Southern California. They planted the 140-acre Jekel Vineyard in 1972, the same year as the Meadors, and also six years later, built their 200,000-gallon winery and tasting room. They produce superb estate-bottled Chardonnay, dry and late-harvest Rieslings, Pinot Blanc, Cabernet, and Pinot Noir. William's Davis-trained son Rick became the winemaker in 1983, when his predecessor, Dan Lee, also from Davis, joined his family in starting the new Morgan Winery near Salinas.

• 17 •

In western Monterey County, across a ridge of the Santa Lucia Mountains from the Salinas, is the lovely Carmel Valley, a tennis player's paradise that already has two wineries, is expected soon to have two more, and was granted its own viticultural-area appellation by the Federal government in 1982. On a hilltop above Cachagua Road is the valley's first winery, which began crushing its own grapes in 1977. It stands on the 140-acre "dream vineyard" planted since 1966 for Carnation Sea Foods president William Durney, of Los Angeles, and his screenwriter-wife, Dorothy. Their 1200-acre estate, where they raise rare Belted Galloway cattle, is named El Rancho del Sueño, Spanish for "dreamland." Uphill from the 30,000-gallon, adobe-brown winery are the Durneys' architectural gem of a summer house and its neighboring Ste. Genevieve Chapel, complete with an organ and nave for a choir; baptisms and weddings often take place here. The Durneys' son-in-law David Armanasco and their daughter Christine manage the winery and market their estate-bottled Riesling, Chenin Blanc, Gamay Beaujolais, and Cabernet. On Carmel Valley Road, five miles southeast of the intersection with Highway 1, is the valley's second winery, the 30,000-gallon Chateau Julien, built in 1983 for New Jersey petroleum executive Robert Brower and his wife Patricia, who have a home near Monterey. Also planting new vineyards in the valley are television personality Merv Griffin, Carmel tie manufacturer Robert Talbott, Casanova Restaurant owner Walter Georis, and San Francisco high-fashion apparel manufacturer Clement Galante, who, with his wife Jane, plans a winery on his vineyard, west of the Durneys. Jane Galante's grandfather founded the town of Carmel.

• 18 •

San Luis Obispo County, where the Salinas River begins, is an old winegrowing district that has become important again. Since the 1960s, when Americans began developing a taste for table wines, vineyard acreage in the county has exploded from 700 to 5000 acres. The number of wineries has jumped from three to twenty, and two European champagne companies have bought land to produce sparkling wines here.

The oldest vineyards are in the northern half of the county, where some Zinfandel vines date from the nineteenth century, but of fifteen wineries that participated in the annual wine festival that started at Paso Robles in 1983, all but three were new. The Federal government in 1983 recognized Paso Robles as a distinct viticultural district, a recognition already granted to the Edna Valley, south of San Luis Obispo, the year before.

Northernmost winery in the county is the 20,000-gallon Ranchita Oaks cellar, off Cross Canyons Road, in the foothills seven miles east of Mission San Miguel (founded 1797). It is on a forty-four-acre vineyard planted by Lodi grapestake manufacturer Ronald Bergstrom since 1972. Winemaker John Scott produced its first vintage of red wines in 1979. On San Marcos Road, four miles southwest of San Miguel, wine-buff property developer Dave Caparone and his wife Mary bonded a 10,000-gallon winery and made their first vintage of red wines in 1980. They have begun planting eight acres with such Italian grape varieties as Nebbiolo, intending to produce a California equivalent of the Italian Piedmont's great Barolo red.

The first new vineyard in the Paso Robles district was planted in 1964 by noted cardiologist and amateur winemaker Dr. Stanley Hoffman, on fifty-eight acres of his Hoffman Mountain Ranch, six miles west of town. Since 1982, when Dr. Hoffman returned to the full-time practice of cardiology at nearby Templeton, his vineyard and 100-gallon winery have been owned by a group of investors named HMR Limited. There is an HMR tasting room at the Black Oak corner in downtown Paso Robles.

Bordering the HMR vineyard on Adelaida Road is the San Ygnacio Ranch, where world-renowned musician-statesman Ignace Paderewski once grew Zinfandels that made medal-winning wines. Paderewski fell in love with the district when he went to Paso Robles in 1913 to take mud baths for his arthritis. He planted an orchard and vineyard on his ranch and considered starting a winery of his own, but gave up the idea at the approach of Prohibition. His vines were still producing grapes when he died in 1941, but they later became neglected and were removed.

Highway 46 extends east from Paso Robles to three wineries bonded since 1977. The first, on Buena Vista Road to your left, is the 20,000-gallon Martin Brothers winery, opened in 1981 in a converted dairy at the intersection of Buena Vista Road. The Martin brothers are young, UC Davis–trained winemaker Dominic, who four years earlier had made fine wines at the Lambert Bridge winery in Sonoma County, and his advertising executive brother, Tom. Their father, banker Edward T. Martin of Ojai, formed a corporation to establish the winery and begin planting seventy-five acres of wine grapes on the site to produce estate-bottled wines by 1984. Next, also on your left, is the 20,000-gallon Eberle Winery, an early-California-style stucco building with a tasting room, opened in 1983. The owners are Pittsburgh-born geneticist W. Gary Eberle and his wife Jeanie, who have forty acres of Cabernet and Chardonnay planted four years earlier along nearby Union Road. They decided to establish their own wine estate after Gary had devoted eleven years as the viticulturist and winemaster for his elder half-brother's, Los Angeles businessman Clifford Giacobine, half-million-gallon Estrella River Vineyards winery, three miles to the east. The Estrella

River winery, atop a hill facing Highway 46, is one of the most spectacular in California, with observation towers visible for miles. It crushed its first vintage in 1977 from the square mile of vineyards planted five years earlier, between the Estrella River and the highway. Five miles farther east is the 500-acre Tierra Rejada vineyard, planted since 1972 by a quartet of film and television luminaries headed by Wayne Rogers of former M-A-S-H television fame. Wines made of their grapes by various wineries have reached the market under their "Star Crest" brand.

Eight miles southeast of Tierra Rejada, south of the town of Shandon, is one of the main San Luis Obispo County winegrowing districts that was planted in recent years. The largest single planting is the 440-acre San Juan Vineyard, planted in 1972 for Tepusquet Vineyards, a group that includes retired business consultant Alfred Gagnon and the Lucas family, table-grape growers at Delano in Kern County.

The Templeton area, six miles south of Paso Robles, has long been noted for its Zinfandel grapes. The Las Tablas winery and its forty acres of vines on Vineyard Road, west of Highway 101, date from 1856, when French farmer Adolph Siot planted the first grapes in this locality. The place was owned successively by Joe, Clemente, and Mervin Rotta from 1905 to 1976, when it was purchased by San Jose mechanical engineer John Mertens and his wife Della. Their tasting room is housed in half of a giant old redwood wine tank. The nearby Pesenti Winery has only been in business since Repeal. On Highway 46, west of Templeton, former Los Angeles custom-furniture maker Pasquale ("Pat") Mastan and his wife Leona built a new Mastantuono winery and tasting room in 1983, to use the grapes of the fifteen-acre vineyard beside their original 18,000-gallon winery, opened six years earlier, on Willow Road. On Jensen Road, off Vineyard Road, electronics engineer Clifford Hight and nuclear physicist John Wyatt bonded the 18,000-gallon Rolling Ridge Winery in a converted barn in 1980, on their Old Casteel Vineyard of Zinfandel and Chardonnay, which Wyatt had purchased three years before. Wyatt's wife Barbara manages the vineyard, while Hight's wife Mary is in charge of selling their wines. On Willow Creek Road, near the Mastans' vineyard, psychology instructor George Mulder of California Polytechnic College and his wife Tahoma, who practices psychology at Atascadero State Hospital, bonded a converted barn in 1981 as the 1000-gallon El Paso de Robles Winery, and began making wine of their five acres of Zinfandel, planted three years before. Along Highway 46 at Jack Creek Road, five miles west of Templeton, is the sixty-acre tract, as yet unplanted, that Codorniu of Spain, one of the world's biggest champagne producers, purchased in 1982 to begin producing a Codorniu California sparkling wine.

Eight miles west of Templeton, off the road toward Cambria, is the 100,000-gallon York Mountain Winery, which became briefly famous, sixty years after its founding in 1882, by making medal-winning wine from Ignace Paderewski's Zinfandel grapes. Since 1970, the winery has had a new owner, veteran enologist Max Goldman, who after forty years of winemaking in California and New York, bought the place from the founder's grandson, Wilfred York. Goldman and his son Steve have built a tasting room onto the old cellar and have replanted some of the eighty-acre vineyard with premium varieties, including Zinfandel, with which to recapture York Mountain's onetime fame. They make a complete line of vintage-dated "varietal" table wines, a dry sherry, and a bottle-fermented champagne.

There is a new 159-acre wine estate in the foothill cattle-grazing country along Highway 58, twelve miles southeast of Creston and seventeen miles east of Highway 101. The 14,000-gallon Creston Manor Winery made its first vintage in 1982. The owners are a Southern California group that includes Christina Crawford Koontz, daughter of Joan Crawford; Christina's film producer–husband David Koontz; Beverly Hills business-man Lawrence Rosenbloom; and his wife Stephanie. The winery is between the 17- and 18-mile markers on Highway 68.

• 19 •

Another new winegrowing area in the county, with three new wineries, is the Edna Valley, south of San Luis Obispo, the county seat. It is only six miles from the Pacific Ocean, nearly on a direct line from Pismo Beach, and its climate is classed as Region II. The 700,000-gallon, Spanish mission–style Corbett Canyon Winery on Corbett Road was bonded in 1978 by a part-nership of Fresno State University–trained winemaker James S. Lawrence and two San Joaquin Valley grape growers. Three years later, the winery was sold to the Glenmore Distilleries Company. Onetime musician Norman Goss meanwhile had retired to the Edna Valley after selling his Stuft Shirt restaurants in Southern California, and with his son Tom had planted a seventy-acre vineyard on Orcutt Road, naming it Chamisal for a shrub that grows in the vicinity. In 1980, Goss built and bonded the 12,000-gallon Chamisal Vineyard winery with his son-in-law, Scott Boyd, as the winemaker, began producing estate-bottled Chardonnay, and by 1983 was also making champagne. In the same year, the 50,000-gallon Edna Valley Vineyard winery was built on Biddle Ranch Road, off Highway 227, by a partnership of Chalone Vineyard with former supermarket owner Jack Niven's Paragon Vineyard Company, which owns 600 acres of premium grapes planted there since 1973.

A century-old winegrowing district in the mountains ten miles east of Edna Valley came back to life in 1982, when farmers Bill and Nancy Greenough built and bonded their 5000-gallon Saucelito Canyon Winery on Hi Mountain Road, beyond Lopez Lake. The Greenoughs' vineyard includes three acres of Zinfandel, planted by Englishman A. B. Hasbrouck about 1880, when he started his St. Remy Vineyard winery and sold his Muscat, Riesling, Grenache, and Zinfandel wines "by the bottle, gallon, or barrel."

From San Luis Obispo, Highway 101 winds south past Arroyo Grande, three miles beyond which, along the east side of the highway, is a 150-acre vineyard of Pinot Noir, Pinot Blanc, Chardonnay, and Chenin Blanc, planted by viticulturist Dale Hampton in 1983 for the century-and-a-half-old Deutz & Geldermann Champagne firm of Ay in France. With traditional *méthode champenoise* equipment from France, construction of a spectacular, partly-underground champagnery and tasting room was begun in 1984 to make Deutz California champagne from purchased grapes. It is due on the market by 1986.

· 20 ·

In my first (1973) edition, this chapter on the central coast counties ended at the southern border of San Luis Obispo County, the Santa Maria River. But the latter-day vinicultural pioneers, who have planted nearly 9000 acres of new vineyards and opened seventeen wineries in the northern two-thirds of Santa Barbara County since the early 1970s, consider themselves part of the same "central coast" area as their San Luis Obispo neighbors. I am not the one to dispute them.

Santa Barbara County, and also nearby Ventura County, were important wine producers in the past century, as evidenced by the various "Vineyard Roads" you still see on their maps. Vineyards once flourished in the Santa Ynez Valley and east of the Sisquoc River. What is now downtown Santa Barbara was dotted with vineyards a century ago. Santa Cruz Island, thirty miles off the coast, was renowned before the Dry era for the prize-winning wines grown there by the late San Francisco importer and hardware merchant, Justinian Caire. His heirs made wine for a short time following Repeal, but the island winery was destroyed by fire and the vineyard was torn out. The city of Santa Barbara again has a producing winery, established on Anacapa Street in 1962 by architect and wine-buff Pierre Lafond. He since has established a vineyard in the Santa Ynez Valley.

The current revival is most extensive in a sparsely populated, twenty-mile-long belt of foothill land inland from Santa Maria, on the slopes of the Sierra and San Rafael mountain ranges. What is significant is the district's climate, cooled by ocean fog and by the Santa Maria wind. Its growing-season temperatures are Regions I and II, said by the university to be the best for top-rated table wine and champagne grapes. Beginning in 1964, 100 acres of such premium varieties as White Riesling, Cabernet, and Chardonnay were planted under sprinklers by San Joaquin Valley table-grape grower Uriel Nielsen, near the juncture of the Sisquoc River and Tepusquet Creek. His first Rieslings were made into wine three years later, at The Christian Brothers winery near Napa. During the 1970s, many more vineyards spread across Santa Maria's former broccoli and bean fields. The grapes were bought by north coast premium wineries and markedly improved some of their wines. I know of an instance in which Riesling grapes from Santa Maria made so fragrant a wine at a Napa winery that to sell it under its second label in jugs, the winery blended it down with a neutral grape variety to keep the jug wine from excelling the Riesling under its top brand.

The Santa Maria Valley won recognition by the Federal government as a viticultural area in 1982. I am told that the district has sufficient land and enough water to provide 10,000 vineyard acres, almost "another Napa Valley." (Santa Ynez Valley was so recognized in the following year.)

The Tepusquet Vineyards, 1500 acres managed by Louis Lucas, are the largest thus far in this new district. There are young vineyards on part of the 36,000-acre Rancho Sisquoc, owned by descendants of early California mining tycoon James Flood, and on the Newhall Land Company's even larger Suey Ranch. In 1977 the Floods bonded the first winery in the district, the 10,000-gallon Rancho Sisquoc cellar, off Foxen Canyon Road southeast of Santa Maria. Their ranch foreman, Harold Pfeiffer, has made several excellent wines. In 1980, eight grape growers, led by Bob Woods with his thirty-five acres, banded together to build the second winery, their own 100,000-gallon Los Viñeros (Spanish for "the winegrowers") cellar on Hanson Way in Santa

Maria city. Its first vintage of Sauvignon Blanc, made by Davis–trained enologist Kurt Lorenzi, won a gold medal at the Los Angeles County Fair.

Across the Solomon Hills to the west is another new vineyard district in the Los Alamos Valley, with several hundred acres of vines planted during the 1970s. Los Angeles attorney and avocational enologist Samuel D. Hale has made wine since 1974, in a 10,000-gallon winery on his 350-acre Los Alamos Vineyards, off Highway 135.

Most of the new Santa Barbara County wine estates are in the rich residential and tourist-oriented Santa Ynez Valley, some twenty miles south of Santa Maria. Old residents welcome the vineyards as barriers to the threat of urbanization. The first to revive grape-growing there was farmer Boyd Bettencourt, who with his neighbors owns the 30,000-gallon Santa Ynez Valley Winery, bonded in 1976. Bettencourt since has also become one of the partners in the Los Viñeros cellar.

The most impressive wine estate in this area is the showplace, 200,000-gallon winery, bonded in 1974, on the 300-acre Firestone Vineyard, five miles north of Los Olivos on Zaca Station Road. It is headed by Anthony Brooks Firestone of the tire and rubber family. The enologist is Davis-trained Alison Green, the daughter of Sonoma County vineyardist Russell Green. Winery visitors often meet Brook's charming wife Kate, the former ballerina with the London Royal Ballet, because with the title of bonded weighmaster, she helps in vintage season to weigh the grapes and also sometimes serves as a winery tour guide. Firestone Vineyard is a joint venture by Brooks and his father, the former U.S. ambassador to Belgium, Leonard K. Firestone, with Suntory Limited, which produces its own wines as well as its famous barley malt whiskey in Japan. Suntory, with a 31 percent interest, receives a third of the Firestone wine production.

Next largest winery in the valley is the 275,000-gallon Zaca Mesa cellar on Foxen Canyon Road, two miles east of Aliso Canyon Road. It is headed by former Atlantic-Richfield executive Louis M. Ream, and has 340 acres of vines, 120 of them at Santa Maria. Zaca Mesa wines, made by Fresno State–trained enologist Ken Brown, have been winning medals since the first vintage in 1975.

Two estate wineries, both bonded in 1978, are on roads leading north from the charming Danish village of Solvang. On Alamo Pintado Road is the 12,000-gallon J. Carey Cellars, whose owners include three physicians: retired obstetrician Dr. James Campbell Carey, who manages the forty-five-acre vineyard; Dr. James

Campbell Jr., who practices in Santa Barbara; and son Dr. Joseph S. Carey, a Los Angeles cardiac surgeon. Barbara, the daughter of James Jr., is the winery manager. On Ballard Canyon Road is a 15,000-gallon winery named for the road, owned by Santa Barbara dentist Dr. Gene Hallock and his wife Rosalie. They began planting the fifty-acre vineyard in 1974, first planning to build a complete winery, but later constructed it around an abandoned gasoline station they brought to the site. C. Frederic Brander, the winemaker at the Santa Ynez Valley Winery, also has his own forty-five-acre vineyard and 8000-gallon winery, bonded in 1980, on San Marcos Pass Road, east of Los Olivos. West of Solvang are two more wineries: Lompoc dentist Dr. William Mosby's 15,000-gallon Vega Vineyards cellar, off Highway 101 at Santa Rosa Road south of Buellton, opened in 1979 to use the twenty-six acres of grapes he began planting six years before. On Santa Rosa Road, nine miles west of Buellton, is the 35,000-gallon winery that onetime UC Santa Barbara classmates J. Richard Sanford and Michael Benedict opened in 1976 on the 110-acre vineyard they had begun planting a few years earlier. Sanford left the partnership five years later to start his own wine estate, halfway between the Benedict vineyard and Buellton.

Ventura County, Santa Barbara's southern neighbor, had hundreds of acres of vines in the Ojai Valley before and after Prohibition. There again are a half dozen small wineries in the county and eight acres of recently planted vines. On Creek Road at Oak View, five miles southwest of Ojai, schoolteachers Paul Belgum and Charles Branham and their wives reopened the former Antonio Riva Winery in 1981, in partnership with John and Carmel Maitland, who own the property, renamed it Old Creek Ranch, and began replanting Riva's vineyard. I have heard lately of other projects to revive the Ojai Valley wine industry, but its vineyards were replaced during the Dry era with citrus and avocado groves.

This chapter has covered 276 air miles through eight coast counties, almost 60,000 acres of vineyards, and 109 producing wineries, all south of the Golden Gate. As stated at the beginning, this area encompasses a great deal of the future, as well as the past and present, of California wines.

17

Southern California

THE WINEGROWING SCENE in Southern California, where the state's great vineyard industry was born two centuries ago, has undergone dramatic changes since the first edition of this book was published, in 1973. A few venerable wineries are still turning out the unique wines which the region has produced for generations, but their vineyards are steadily being decimated by smog and urban sprawl from nearby cities, where population is growing faster than anywhere else in the United States. Yet at the same time, some entirely new Southern California vineyards have sprung up on virgin lands outside the path of population growth, where the air is still clean. Some of the wines from these new vineyards are comparable to the best grown elsewhere in the state.

• 2 •

The Franciscan Fathers brought Vinifera vines to their Southern California missions from Mexico after the founding of San Diego Mission in 1769. Vineyards were set out at each of the missions. The padres made wine mainly for the Mass and for their own table use, but they also sold some of their wine and their *aguardiente* (brandy) to the early Spanish and American settlers. Their biggest wineries were at the San Gabriel and San Fernando missions, in present-day Los Angeles County. By 1821, San Gabriel, with three wine presses, was producing 400 barrels of wine and half that many of brandy each year. You can still see, behind that restored mission, the adobe building with its stone floor and sump where the Indians once crushed the grapes with their feet.

Within a few decades, vineyards were thriving where some

Anaheim Colony vineyards thrived from 1857 to 1884 on the present site of Disneyland. A mysterious disease (later called the Anaheim or Pierce's Disease) killed the vines. (*Anaheim Public Library*)

of today's great southern cities stand. Vignes Street in downtown Los Angeles commemorates California's first professional wine-grower, Jean Louis Vignes from Bordeaux. Aliso Street is where, by 1833, Vignes had imported European vines to his El Aliso Vineyard, which was entered through a grape arbor a quarter-mile long, and where, beginning in 1857, his nephews made the first California champagne. Boyle Heights recalls Andrew Boyle from County Galway, whose thirty-acre vineyard flourished in 1860 below the cliff on which his brick home stood. The first mayor of Los Angeles, Benjamin Davis Wilson, for whom Mount Wilson is named, won fame for the white wines from his Lake Vineyard, established near San Gabriel in 1854. Thirty-five years later, Wilson's son-in-law, J. de Barth Shorb, was boasting that his San Gabriel Winery, with a capacity of 15 million gallons, was the largest in the world. At Santa Anita Race Track, in nearby Arcadia, the fabulous Elias (Lucky) Baldwin produced medal-winning wines and brandies on his 1200-acre vineyard, which was described in the 1880s as "a second Garden of Eden, bewildering in its beauty." Baldwin's gingerbread mansion still stands as a historical monument. Anaheim in neighboring Orange County, the home today of Disneyland

The San Secondo d'Asti Church in the winery village at Guasti. (*Brookside Vineyard Co.*)

and baseball's Angels, began in 1857 as a utopian winegrowing colony of German immigrants. Anaheim was one of the leading wine districts of the state until 1884, when the vines suddenly died of a mysterious disease (the Anaheim or Pierce's Disease, whose bacterial cause has only lately been found). Other parts of Orange County had wineries and 600 acres of vineyards as late as 1910. In that year Los Angeles, San Bernardino, San Diego, and Ventura counties still had scores of wineries and 37,000 acres of vines.

There still were 5000 acres of vineyards and forty-nine wineries in Los Angeles County alone at the beginning of the Second World War. The last big vineyard, at John McClure's Burbank Winery above San Fernando Boulevard, was bulldozed to make room for a subdivision in 1947.

One Los Angeles winery survives because the city has saved it from razing for a development by naming it Cultural Historical Monument No. 42. The 100,000-gallon San Antonio Winery, with cellar tour, tasting, picnic garden, cafe, and delicatessen, is an oasis at the dead end of Lamar Street, two miles from downtown. No other American city has anything quite like it. Four members of the Riboli family make some forty different wines from Cucamonga, Lodi, and Sonoma grapes. Steve, Maddalena, Santo, and Cathy Riboli took over the winery from

Steve's uncle, Italian-born Santo Cambianica, who founded it in 1917.

• 3 •

Most of the wine grown in Southern California during the present century has come from the Cucamonga Valley, forty-five miles east of Los Angeles. The climate is classed as Region IV, like the northern San Joaquin Valley. Tiburcio Tapia planted the first vines on his Cucamonga Rancho in 1838. When the railroad arrived forty years later, others began growing grapes along the streams in the foothills north of Cucamonga, and between Redlands and Banning in southern San Bernardino and northwestern Riverside counties. But nobody thought of planting vines or anything else in the vast flat, sandy waste in between—the Cucamonga desert—until Secondo Guasti came. Guasti arrived in Los Angeles in 1878 from the Italian Piedmont via Mexico, an unschooled, penniless youth. He shoveled coal in the freight yards, cooked in a restaurant, married the owner's daughter, and saved enough to start a small Los Angeles winery in 1894 and to buy a vineyard in West Glendale. On occasional visits to the Cucamonga Valley, he noticed that the winter floods from the mountains flowed only as far as the desert and there disappeared. It occurred to Guasti that there might be water beneath the desert sand. One day he found a scraggly vine growing in the parched waste. Borrowing a shovel, he dug to find its root. Legend says that he discovered moisture after digging down twenty-four feet. In 1900, back in Los Angeles, Guasti organized the Italian Vineyard Company, selling shares to his countrymen. He bought eight square miles of the Cucamonga desert, built fences against rabbits, and planted a hundred varieties of grapes. He brought whole families from Italy to till the land and built an Italian town—which he named Guasti—with its own school, inn, general store, fire house, post office, and a church as lovely as those in the Italian countryside. Others planted in the desert, and more wineries were built. In 1911, Captain Paul Garrett acquired 2000 acres at Cucamonga to grow grapes for Virginia Dare wine. By 1917, Guasti was advertising the IVC vineyard as "four thousand acres, the largest in the world." San Bernardino County had 20,000 acres of vineyards, more than in Sonoma and twice as many as in Napa County, when Prohibition came in 1920.

During the early Dry years, instead of pulling out their vines, the Cucamonga growers reaped a bonanza by shipping their grapes fresh across the country to the eastern bootleg and home-winemaking trade. The Guasti winery switched to making the legal sacramental and kosher wines. Then Captain Garrett, at his Mission Vineyard and Winery in Cucamonga, created Virginia Dare Wine Tonic by adding beef extract, pepsin, and iron to port and sherry, which made the concoction salable under the Dry law. Guasti and the big Padre winery followed with their own wine tonic brands. When in 1929 Captain Garrett formed the Fruit Industries merger of old wineries to produce "Vine-Glo" grape concentrate, the Italian Vineyard Company was one of the first to join. By then, Secondo Guasti had died. Much of the nation's supply of "Vine-Glo" was made at Guasti during the latter Prohibition years.

At Repeal in 1933, the Cucamonga wineries had an opportunity to interest the connoisseur trade in at least three distinctive local wines. The great wine judge, Almond R. Morrow, rated Cucamonga port the best in the state. Cucamonga Zinfandel and Grignolino are unusually soft to the palate, yet possess flavors and aromas unlike any other red table wines. Home winemakers in the East long paid premium prices for Cucamonga Zinfandel grapes because of their distinctive, almost cheesy taste. Because of it, some Northern California winemakers refused to use Cucamonga wine in their blends. But the Cucamonga vintners, instead of capitalizing on the unique character of their grapes, ignored the connoisseur trade and tried to compete with the San Joaquin Valley wineries for the Los Angeles mass market in cheap dessert wines. There was one brief attempt before the Second World War to sell Cucamonga table wines as something different. Nicola Giulii, Guasti's brother-in-law, took the Italian Vineyard Company out of Fruit Industries in 1940 and advertised IVC wines as "better because they are made from nonirrigated grapes." Few people were impressed, however, because the IVC wines were low in price. Whatever the reason, Cucamonga wines have been sold at bargain prices during most of the years since Repeal.

When Henry Kaiser built his huge steel plant among the vines at Fontana in 1942, an industrial and housing boom began spreading eastward from Los Angeles. When the military flying field adjoining Guasti was expanded after the war to become Ontario International Airport, it displaced hundreds of acres of vines. Still more were bulldozed during the 1960s to make room for the adjoining Holiday Inn.

Meanwhile, smog, already withering the leaves of southern citrus groves and threatening to kill the Ponderosa pines in the

San Gabriel Mountains, began to affect the Cucamonga vines, too. What smog does to grapevines was strikingly shown by university experimenters, who in 1968 built plastic greenhouses around patches of vines at Cucamonga and filtered the air inside. The vines left exposed to smog yielded half as many grapes, with only four-fifths of the sugar content, as the grapes grown in filtered air.

• 4 •

When I revisited Southern California before writing the second edition of this guide in 1978, old Guasti, the wine town in the desert, appeared little changed by the passage of years. The massive stone buildings, the Louisa Guasti School, the post office, the store, and the lovely San Secondo d'Asti Church seemed much the same as I remembered them in earlier times. Secondo Guasti's baronial residence, with its luxuriant tropical gardens, was empty, as were the old distillery and the fermenting room. But there was bustling activity around two of the buildings. The main aging cellar, with its three-foot-thick walls, had been occupied by the Brookside Vineyard Company, organized by the French family Biane, who are Philo, his sons Michael and Pierre, and Philo's nephew, René. The adjoining cooper shop, converted into a Brookside tasting room, was crowded with visitors, who overflowed onto a picnic area under the trees. In a corner of the aging cellar, the Bianes had opened a Brookside wine museum which eventually will have a home in the San Bernardino County Museum. Some of the exhibits tell how things have changed at Guasti since the founder's time. During the wartime wine shortage, Horace Lanza of Delano bought the Italian Vineyard Company to get control of the huge Guasti grape crop. In 1945, the heirs of Captain Garrett bought Guasti from Lanza, transferred the Garrett winemaking operation there from New York, and changed Virginia Dare into a California wine. When the Garrett company was liquidated in 1961, its business was sold to Alta Vineyards of Fresno, but the Guasti vineyards were sold to Los Angeles oilman Edwin Pauley, who leased them back to the Alta interests. Then Alta was merged with Guild wines of Lodi, which licensed Canandaigua Industries of New York to revive Garrett's Virginia Dare as an eastern wine.

Other exhibits in the Brookside wine museum trace California wine history made by the forebears of the Bianes. Théophile Vaché from France started a wine business at Monterey in 1832, and pioneered winegrowing in the Cienega Valley of San Benito County about 1849. His nephews, Adolphe, Emile, and Théophile, moved to Southern California and established the Brookside winery near Redlands in 1883. The late Marius Biane came from Gascony in 1892, served the Vachés as their winemaker, and married Adolphe's daughter Marcelline. Marius Biane moved to Cucamonga in 1916 to make wine for Captain Garrett and acquired his own vineyards there. His sons, Philo and the late François, succeeded him, making wine for Fruit Industries, for Secondo Guasti, Captain Garrett, and the Cucamonga Growers Co-op Winery. In 1952, Philo Biane took the Cucamonga Co-op out of Fruit Industries and reestablished the Brookside Vineyard Company near Cucamonga. Five years later, he bought the Guasti cellar and moved Brookside headquarters there. Brookside wines were made at the Cucamonga Pioneer Winery until Brookside bought the 4-million-gallon Gallo (formerly Pio) bulk winery on Arrow Boulevard in 1972.

Brookside in 1973 had become a subsidiary of Chicago's Beatrice Foods conglomerate, which owns hundreds of companies that sell almost every kind of product from milk to mobile homes. Since taking over at Guasti, the Bianes had added some thirty-four winery branches in three states, to sell, in a unique winery-to-consumer operation, some eighty different Assumption Abbey, Brookside, Vaché, and Vins de Biane Frères wines.

In 1982, Beatrice Foods sold Brookside, its wineries totaling 6 million gallons, and its retail branches to a group of Northern California investors, who soon learned that the winery buildings at Guasti might be endangered after 1987 by further expansion of the Ontario Airport. Old Guasti, with its church, school, and Secondo Guasti's residence, would be safe, because a railroad line separates them from the planned air terminal site. All but five of the retail branches were closed.

When Brookside was sold, 5875 acres of vineyards were left in San Bernardino County, a little over a fourth of the 19,460 acres counted sixteen years before. Many of the vineyards now show signs of neglect, and some of them display "for sale" signs. During the years when vineyards elsewhere in the state had expanded at a record rate, the Cucamonga district had experienced the exact reverse.

A few wineries around Cucamonga still show signs of continuing life. Philo Biane has a charming 14,000-gallon Rancho de Philo winery of his own, opened in 1975 on the fourteen acres of vines around his home on Wilson Avenue, east of Archibald. He produces only cream sherry, one of his hobbies, in a *solera* (fractional blending) system using small oak casks. Rancho de Philo permits visitors to taste, but Philo's sherry may only be purchased in case lots. Liveliest winery in the area is Joseph Filippi's million-gallon cellar on his family's vineyard at Jurupa and Etiwanda avenues in Mira Loma (which originally was named Wineville when the big Charles Stern vineyard was established there). The Filippis make some three dozen wines and sell them in half a dozen Chateau Filippi tasting rooms around Southern California. The biggest Filippi branch is the former Thomas cellar in the center of Cucamonga, which some say is the oldest winery building in the state. Members of the Galleano family still make wine for sale at their 300,000-gallon cellar among the vineyards on Wineville Avenue. But Bonded Winery Number One on Eighth Street in Cucamonga, famous since 1934 for the Padre Sec champagne that Primo Scorsatto made for colorful James L. "Padre Jim" Vai, has made no wine since 1981. Its crushing equipment has been sold to a Livermore winery. The late John Ellena's Regina Winery at Etiwanda has been stripped of its champagne-making equipment and closed to the public. Heublein now owns the Regina Winery and makes wine for vinegar there. Only two walls remain of the once-great Garrett winery on Highway 66.

But while winegrowing in the Cucamonga Valley continues to decline, there is one new winery in another part of San Bernardino County, thirty-five miles to the east. In the Oak Glen hills that rise to 5000 feet beyond Yucaipa, former newspaper publisher and onetime Napa Valley winery proprietor Charles B. Colby established the Oak Glen Winery in 1977. His wines are made of apples and pears, but he says he plans to plant noble wine grape varieties among the apple orchards and develop a new vineyard district there.

• 5 •

New vineyards and wineries have sprung up since the late 1960s in Southern California districts closer to the Pacific Coast.

The Escondido district, north of San Diego, had 5000 acres of vines in the 1930s, when eight wineries opened at the repeal of Prohibition. Two of the old wineries are left: the Ferrara family's 45,000-gallon cellar on their two remaining acres west of the city, and Ross Rizzo's larger Bernardo winery, off Interstate 15. In 1973, Judge Charles Froelich and attorney Milton Fredman leased some San Diego city property along Highland Valley Road south of Escondido, planted 120 acres of premium wine grape varieties, and four years later began building the 112,000-gallon San Pasqual Vineyards winery on San Pasqual Road. Their Davis-trained winemaker, Kerry Damskey, has made several excellent red and white table wines. His best may be his Muscat Canelli, which President Reagan presented to the president of Mexico in 1982. The government has granted the vineyard a San Pasqual Valley viticultural district appellation of its own. The finest Muscat table wine in California in the 1930s was produced by one of the now-defunct Escondido district wineries, using the common Muscat of Alexandria grape.

There are two new vineyards twenty miles northwest of Escondido at Fallbrook, which had vineyards before Prohibition but now calls itself "the avocado capital of the world." Geologist John Culbertson and his wife Martha have replaced six acres of their avocado grove with Chardonnay vines and have bonded the 30,000-gallon Culbertson Winery, which introduced its first bottle-fermented champagne in 1983. The Culbertsons also make a still white table wine they have named "Cuvée Tranquille." Their winery is on Via Rancheros, off Winterhaven Road. Their neighbors, Tony and Sue Godfrey, have started planting a Riesling vineyard near their Olive Hill Greenhouses and plan to build a winery on Olive Hill Road when their vines mature. San Diego County now has 279 acres of vines.

In Orange County, an eight-acre drip-irrigated vineyard of Riesling, Chenin Blanc, Cabernet, and Petite Sirah was planted in 1973 on the O'Neill family's 42,000-acre Rancho Mission Viejo, twelve miles north of Mission San Juan Capistrano. When I last visited the vineyard, additional planting and construction of a winery were being planned.

· 6 ·

The most extensive new Southern California vineyards cover some 3000 acres in the southwestern corner of Riverside County, a smog-free area twenty-three miles from the Pacific Ocean. Most of them, and eight wineries east of Temecula bonded since 1974, are within Rancho California, the unique planned community of ranches built since 1965 by the mammoth Kaiser-Aetna land development combine. On sixty square miles of rolling land east of Temecula, there are country homes, a manmade lake, livestock and horse farms, avocado and citrus groves. Rancho California formerly was range land, too arid for grape growing, but 500-foot-deep wells now provide sufficient water for the farms. By the university system of measuring degree-days, the

Temecula district is Region III, much cooler than Cucamonga's Region IV.

First to plant a major vineyard in this new district was Philo Biane. He foresaw the decline of Cucamonga, searched as far as Arizona for a favorable new vineyard climate, and began planting the Brookside winery's present 425 acres east of Temecula in 1967.

The first to build a winery and to make Temecula wines famous was Ely Callaway, of the Georgia family best known for their public gift of Callaway Gardens, south of Atlanta. Callaway retired in 1973 from the presidency of Burlington Industries, the world's largest textile firm, at the age of fifty-four. Four years earlier, planning for retirement to farming and golfing,

Botrytis, the "noble mold," is starting to grow on these Chenin Blanc grapes in the Callaway Vineyard at Temecula. (*Ely Callaway, Jr.*)

he had planted 134 acres of premium grape varieties on a hilltop above Rancho California Road, five miles east of Temecula. On annual visits there from New York, he studied the effect of climates on grape quality. Convinced that breezes flowing from the Pacific through Rainbow Gap gave his vineyard a microclimate comparable to that of the north coastal counties, he decided to build a winery.

Visiting his vineyard in the autumn of 1973, I found Callaway ruefully surveying a gray mold that had formed on his first crop of Chenin Blanc grapes. The whole Chenin Blanc crop was about to be discarded. Curious, I examined the grapes and suggested that the mold might be botrytis. "What's botrytis?" Callaway asked. I explained that botrytis is the prized "noble rot," rare in dry California climates, that in Europe makes it possible to produce the greatest German Rieslings and French sauternes. The mold on his Chenin Blanc was indeed botrytis. Callaway sent the grapes to a Napa winery and had them made into California's first-ever botrytized Chenin Blanc. He named the wine "Sweet Nancy" for his then wife and sold the 1973 vintage for $15 a bottle. Morning mists that encourage botrytis are part of the local climate, which explains Temecula's Indian name, Temeku, which means "land where the sun shines through the white mist."

Callaway built his winery in the following year, having hired Karl Werner, the former winemaster of Germany's famed Schloss Vollrads. Werner stocked the winery with German-oak casks. The first Callaway wines were released in late 1975 and received rave reviews. His 1974 Riesling was chosen in 1976 by the Pilgrims Club for serving to England's Queen Elizabeth and Prince Philip, at their Bicentennial luncheon in New York. Callaway wines became the first from Southern California to win a place beside the world's premium vintages featured on wine lists and in stores.

Much of the credit for this belongs to Callaway's Cucamonga-trained viticulturist, John Moramarco, who personally finish-prunes and later cluster-thins each grapevine following these operations by his vineyard crew. In 1976, Werner was succeeded as winemaster by the late Stephen O'Donnell, who introduced botrytized wines of Riesling as well as of Chenin Blanc, naming them "Santana" for the region's summer winds. O'Donnell also made a Callaway port and began making a champagne.

Callaway made his winery the chief wine-touring attraction in Southern California, building a huge visitor center and offering daily tastings, wine appreciation classes, barbecues, and dinners.

From its original 50,000 gallons, it grew to 600,000 gallons in seven years. At the height of its success in 1981, Callaway sold the vineyard and winery to Hiram Walker distillers, retaining an adjacent young vineyard of his own. (Callaway has a new hobby, a Palm Springs factory that makes hickory golf clubs with steel cores, which he calls "Hickory Sticks.")

By 1983, there were seven more wine estates in the Temecula district, and still more vineyardists were preparing to build wine cellars of their own. Some Temecula grapes are sold to wineries in the north and to the dozen small wineries in nearby counties that have no vineyards of their own. Next door to Callaway, on Rancho California Road, is the 12,000-gallon Hart Winery, opened in 1980 by former Carlsbad junior high school teacher Joseph Hart and his wife Nancy, on the eleven-acre vineyard they had planted six years before. A mile farther east is Temecula's second oldest wine estate, former Los Angeles radio station owner John Poole's 150-acre vineyard and 90,000-gallon Mount Palomar Winery, bonded in 1975. West of the Mount Palomar estate are the 20-acre vineyard and 20,000-gallon Spanish-style winery bonded in 1981 by Fallbrook physician Dr. John Piconi and his wife Gloria. Across the road, a mile beyond Mount Palomar Winery, is the 5000-gallon Mesa Verde Vineyards winery of Keith and Lynne Kaarup, who have 140 acres of vines. On Calle Contento, near Rancho Vista Road, are the 14,000-gallon winery and ten-acre vineyard of Universal Studios lighting genius Vincenzo Cilurzo and his wife Audrey, who were pioneers in the district when they planted their vineyard in 1968. To the east, on De Portola Road, are the 22-acre vineyard and 12,000-gallon winery bonded in 1980 by pediatrician Dr. William Filsinger. His wife Kathy's family once were winegrowers in Germany. Two miles northwest of the Filsingers, also on De Portola Road, is the 4800-gallon Glenoak Hills Winery of Hugo Woerdemann, who once was a member of Werner von Braun's rocketry team.

Ely Callaway and his neighbors asked the Federal government in 1982 to recognize 33,000 acres that include the present Temecula vineyards as a viticultural area, but met resistance from owners of lands farther north, such as Murrieta, who wanted to be included in the "Temecula" appellation. By press time, the government had not been able to decide.

18

Lodi, Sacramento, the Foothills, and Davis

WHEN PEOPLE say "Lodi" (pronounced low-dye), they mean the fifty-square-mile expanse of flat, extremely fertile vineyards which completely encircle that city at the edge of the Sacramento–San Joaquin River Delta in northern San Joaquin County, California.

Off the six-mile stretch of Highway 99 that bisects the town of Lodi are thirteen bonded wineries which store some 50 million gallons of wine. Five of them have public tasting rooms and highway billboards inviting travelers to stop and sample their wines. The leading industry of Lodi is the production of grapes, wine, and brandy distilled from wine. The most elaborate vintage celebration in the United States is the Lodi Grape Festival and National Wine Show, held in mid-September, with grape exhibits, tastings, and a spectacular Sunday parade.

The Lodi district is viticulturally unique. Grapevines grow to enormous size in its deep, sandy-loam soil, washed down from the mountains for centuries. Many vines around Lodi are eight feet tall and have trunks as large around as trees. Summer days in San Joaquin County are less torrid than in the main Central Valley; the county's climate is Region IV. At Lodi, however, the vines are further cooled at night by moist westerly winds from the nearby Delta, with its thousand miles of tidewater rivers, bays, and sloughs. This is why the Flame Tokay table grape develops its flaming red color, which attracts buyers in the fresh fruit markets, only in the Lodi district. Lodi produces 98 percent of the Flame Tokays in the nation. Nineteen thousand acres are planted to Tokays and 14,000 to wine grapes. Many of the latter are Zinfandels and Carignanes, two wine varieties of which Lodi grows more than any other district in the state.

A tenth of California's wine output is made in Lodi. But you seldom can tell from labels which wines are Lodi-grown, because fleets of tank trucks bring millions of gallons from elsewhere to be bottled there, and other trucks take Lodi grapes and wines to wineries in other districts, which use them in their blends. In past decades, the Lodi wineries produced mostly sherry and port. The chamber of commerce in the 1950s publicized the district as "America's Sherryland," but since the late 1960s, the Lodi wineries have switched to making mostly table wines. The Federal government was asked in 1982 to recognize Lodi as one of the nation's unique viticultural districts.

• 2 •

Grape growing in San Joaquin County began in 1850 at Stockton, twelve miles south of Lodi, when Captain Charles Weber founded that city and planted Mission vines in his garden. Eight years later, a gold miner from Massachusetts, George West, planted vines he got from Captain Weber and began building his El Pinal Winery on West Lane, two miles north of Stockton. By the end of the Civil War, West had one of the greatest vineyards in California. In later years he and his son Frank owned vineyards and wineries in Fresno, Madera, and Kings counties, and shipped wines and brandy to their own sales depot in New York.

Lodi was watermelon and grain country during that time. Vineyards were already established in the Sierra foothills and in the rest of the Central Valley, but there were only scattered grape plantings at Lodi until Tokays were planted at the turn of the century. Then the eastern fruit auctions, supplied by trains of new refrigerator cars, made cross-country shipping of fresh grapes profitable. In two decades Lodi, with its brilliant red Tokays, became the most prosperous grape district in the United States. At Stockton, where Tokays ripened as elsewhere with only a dull buckskin color, the vineyards were attacked by phylloxera and died.

The first few wineries around Lodi were built after 1900, using the local wine grapes and providing a home for leftover Tokays. When Prohibition came in 1920, some of the wine grapes were shipped east for home winemaking, and the rest were used to make grape juice, concentrate, and sacramental and tonic wines. Huge tonnages of surplus Tokays were left to rot on the vines.

In 1933, as Repeal approached, the growers expected the new demand for wine to make them rich. But in that vintage season, only five Lodi wineries were ready to crush any grapes. When the wineries, flooded with grapes, offered the growers only $12 a ton, then $7, and in a subsequent rainy season only $5, the angry growers decided to build wineries of their own. Twelve farmer co-operative cellars were opened around Lodi during the next few years, and growers' groups built a dozen more co-op wineries in other parts of the state. The co-op wineries banded together in two Lodi-based marketing organizations to sell their wines.

One was Fruit Industries, the combine that had made "Vine-Glo" concentrate for home winemaking during Prohibition. The other, started in 1937 by the late Lawrence K. Marshall with a nucleus of two new Lodi co-ops, was California Wine Sales, which later became the Wine Growers Guild and the Guild Wineries & Distilleries of today.

Fruit Industries, managed by Walter E. Taylor of Lodi, became the post-Repeal giant of the wine industry, bigger than the California Wine Association of pre-Prohibition days. Fruit Industries, with eleven wineries throughout the state, changed its name to California Wine Association and adopted Eleven Cellars as its chief brand name. The choice of that name soon proved embarrassing, because one by one the member wineries dropped out of the group. The last to call itself "CWA" was the former Perelli-Minetti winery at Delano, which became part of the Sierra Wine Corporation.

The Guild in 1962 combined with a Fresno merger of old commercial wine firms (Alta Vineyards, A. Mattei, Cameo Vineyards, B. Cribari & Sons, Garrett). It then bought the wineries of its co-op members and became a single co-op, owned by its grower members throughout the state. In 1970, the Guild bought Schenley Distillers' Roma and Cresta Blanca wineries at Fresno, Kingsburg, and Delano and increased its membership to some 1000 growers. Already owning six wineries—three at Lodi, one at Ukiah, two at Fresno—the Guild thereby increased its total to nine. The Guild is both the nation's largest grower-owned wine firm and the third largest vintner in storage capacity (60 million gallons), and also the sixth in wine sales.

Most of the wine labeled with Lodi as the bottling address comes from the Guild's giant blending, bottling, and champagne-making winery at the northeast edge of town. There it makes Charmat (bulk) process and bottle-fermented (transfer) champagnes, the former labeled Guild Winemaster's and Cribari, and the latter with the Cresta Blanca and Cook's Imperial brands. It also bottles the Guild's brandies and its Silverado vodka, distilled at Fresno, the only American vodka made of grapes; the others made in this country are distillates of grain.

Adjoining the winery is the Guild's big Winemaster Hospitality House and restaurant, where hundreds of tourists stop daily to taste the wines and to be conducted on cellar tours, and where summer lawn concerts are held, accompanied by complimentary wines.

Of the Guild's more than 100 different wines, brandies, and champagnes, the most interesting and one of its best-sellers is a red table wine called Vino da Tavola, with a label that resembles a red-and-white-checkered tablecloth. One night in 1949, three Guild sales executives, dining in an Italian restaurant in Chicago, were discussing the wine industry's main post-Repeal problem—why most native Americans were rejecting dry red wines as "sour." Then they noticed that most of the people at tables around them were drinking dry red wine with Italian food. This gave them an idea: Why not sweeten dry red wine with a little port and sell it with a label like the restaurant's tablecloth, and with an Italian name? Then and there, they designed the label and chose the name, Vino da Tavola, which in Italian means "wine for the table." Back in Lodi, they challenged the Guild's then-winemaster, Lawrence Quaccia, to blend a wine to fit the name. He did it with Lodi Zinfandel, a touch of port, and a wood-aged Mendocino Carignane, a coast-counties wine, "to give it life," he said. Other wineries had made sweetened "vinos" before, but lively red Tavola with its tablecloth label quickly outstripped them all in sales. In the years since, it has taught millions of Americans to enjoy red wine with their meals. "What wine is served in the French Embassy in Washington, D.C.?" read a Guild magazine advertisement in 1969. It pictured General Charles de Gaulle holding a jug with a checkered label and saying, "I'll never tell." The French government protested indignantly to our State Department, but to no avail, for the French at the Embassy had indeed been consuming Tavola by the case.

Best of the Guild's many brandies is one distilled at its Bear Creek Winery near Lodi, entirely from Flame Tokay grapes. The first American brandy ever to bear a vintage date (1966), it was sold under the Cresta Blanca brand, which the Guild now owns.

A half-mile south of the Guild is the 7-million-gallon East-Side, Oak Ridge, or Royal Host winery, east of the town. This is the only local co-op that bottles much of its wine. Eighty Lodi families, led by Jacob Kurtz and his neighbors, the Mettlers, Preszlers, and Handels, joined in East-Side in 1934. Most of its members, and many in other Lodi co-ops, are descendants of German families who migrated to Russia in the time of Catherine the Great, then three generations later to the Dakotas, and finally to Lodi around the turn of this century. In front of the winery office stands "Das Weinhaus," a 50,000-gallon redwood wine tank converted into an attractive tasting room. On display inside are some of the hundreds of medals awarded to East-Side's Royal Host wines while Herman Ehlers was the wine-maker, a job from which he retired in 1970 after thirty-seven years. Ehlers and a few other East-Side members were among the first to plant in Lodi, during the 1950s, small acreages of superior grape varieties for table wines. Though East-Side still makes its popular Royal Host wines, it now also offers "select premium" varietally labeled table wines, under its Conti Royale brand. One of its other specialties has been a semi-dry white made of the university's new grape variety, named Gold.

Across the road from East-Side is the old Roma winery, a relic of Lodi wines of the past. It was here, when Prohibition ended, that the Cella brothers, Battista and Lorenzo, began ex-panding their Roma Wine Company into the biggest single com-mercial producer of California wines of the early post-Repeal years. On the roof of the winery, Roma wines were once "solar-ized"—an advertising gimmick that consisted of pumping them through glass tubing exposed to the sun—which did the wines harm instead of good. Roma's radio slogan was "Don't drink it, sip it," first broadcast by Art Linkletter from the Wine Temple at the San Francisco 1939 World's Fair. When the co-op wineries were built during the 1930s to crush most of the local grapes, the Cellas moved from Lodi to the Roma (now Cribari) winery in Fresno. For years the concrete tanks built by the Cellas have been rented by various wineries for temporary storage of bulk wines. In 1981, the massive brick building came back to life with a new wine product, a carbonated "California Cooler" of white wine and citrus juices. Former Lodi high school classmates Michael Crete and Stuart Bewley found this a place to start mixing the "Cooler" and to ship it, crown-capped in beer bottles, to markets throughout the West.

On Turner Road, across the highway from the old Roma, is a warehouse that once was the Shewan-Jones winery, which made the best Lodi table wines at the time of Repeal. There, a great winemaker named Elbert McSherry Brown and his then-assistant, Herman Ehlers, made Tokay and Burger juice into a sweet sauterne, which Shewan-Jones sold as "Château Yquem." When the Federal government in 1936 outlawed "Château Yquem" labels on American wines, owner Lee Jones created a French-sounding word out of his Welsh name, and made the wine nationally famous as "Château Lejon." In later years, "Le-jon" became the brand name of Heublein's (and more recently ISC Wines') Charmat-process champagnes.

In the village of Acampo, about two miles north of Lodi, is the lately modernized, 2-million-gallon Barengo or Lost Hills Vineyards winery, an example of how the local wineries have changed through the years. The main brick cellar and tasting room was originally a granary. At Repeal, a group of grape growers headed by Cesare Mondavi bought it and named it the Acampo Winery. As their winemaker, they hired Dino Barengo, who like Herman Ehlers had been trained in winemaking by Elbert Brown at Shewan-Jones. Barengo became the winery's owner when the Mondavis sold it to buy the Charles Krug cellar in the Napa Valley. He continued making bulk wine for the Mondavis, but developed specialties of his own, including the principal May wine (woodruff-flavored, white) produced in the United States. Then the winery was sold three more times: by Barengo in 1973 to a group of Monterey growers, by them three years later to an owner of Fresno vineyards, and in 1981 to Berrenda Mesa Farming Co., which has 1600 acres of vineyards near Lost Hills, in Kern County. Some two dozen Barengo and Lost Hills Vineyards wines are now sold across the nation, as are Dudenhoefer spiced wines. In California, they are also sold in Barengo and Lost Hills tasting rooms. One of the winery's specialties is wine in a 1½-liter, flexible plastic "bota bag" that is handy to take on picnics and that fits in the crisper section of home refrigerators.

Beside the Coloma tasting room, at the north end of Lodi, is the former Da Roza Winery, which still crushes grapes but doesn't ferment any into wine. Instead, it extracts the water by a vacuum process, and turns out Dennis Alexander's Sun Country canned grape concentrate syrups for the national home-winemaker trade. Strange to say, there are some vineyardists around Lodi who are Prohibitionists and refuse to sell their grapes to wineries. They are glad, however, to sell them to Alexander's California Concentrate Company, even though they know the product eventually will be made into wine. The syrup comes in two dozen varieties, ranging from "chablis" and "burgundy" to Chardonnay, Cabernet, and Pinot Noir. It is mainly sold in home-winemaking supply stores. Alexander uses grapes from the coastal premium districts of California as well as from his family's forty-acre vineyard on De Vries Road.

On Woodbridge Road, three miles northeast of Lodi, is Robert Mondavi's 6-million-gallon Woodbridge winery, more than treble the size of his cellar at Oakville in the Napa Valley. This once was the Cherokee grape growers' co-op cellar, built in 1936, when Cherokee was a member of Fruit Industries. In later years, it made wine under such names as Montcalm and Filice, and had been producing bulk wine for C. Mondavi & Sons when Robert bought and re-equipped it in 1979 to make his moderately priced white, red, and rosé. The "RM" insignia on their labels distinguishes them from his Napa wines.

Also on Woodbridge Road, west of Highway 99, is the 4-million-gallon former Lodi Vintners co-op winery, which in 1980 became the Turner Winery. John, James, and Ken Turner and their wives, who have 600 acres of vineyards in Lake County, bought and refurbished the 1935-vintage Lodi co-op plant rather than build a new cellar at their ranch. John Turner and his wife Sandra are in charge at the new tasting room. Their vintage-dated "varietal" wines are marketed at "affordable prices" in bottles, jugs, and in the plastic "bag-in-box."

Two small farm wineries opened in the Lodi district during the 1970s. David and Tamara Lucas, whose small vineyard and cellar are on North Davis Road, specialize in Zinfandel. On East Armstrong Road, south of town, Stephen and Beverly Borra have replanted part of Stephen's parents' old Zinfandel vineyard with Barbera, and that "varietal" has become their best-selling red. Both the Lucases and Borras sell all of the estate-bottled wines they can produce. A third such establishment, Dan and Hazel Borelli's Ciriaco Borelli Winery, opened in 1979 on Jack Tone Road, between Stockton and Linden. The other wineries in the Lodi district are Bear Creek and Del Rio, the two original grower–co-op members of the Guild; the independent Woodbridge co-op, the oldest in the state; the old Community co-op, which was the first of the CWA's "Eleven Cellars," then was one of the Heublein wineries, but now is part of the Allied Grape Growers–ISC Wines group; and the Liberty Winery, which has produced wine for Gallo in recent years.

Urbanization approached Lodi during the 1980s from the fast-growing cities of Sacramento on the north and Stockton on the south. Housing already has replaced some of the old Tokay vineyards and has caused some increased planting northeast of Lodi in the area around Clements, and to the west along Interstate 5.

• 3 •

The Flame Tokay is an oval, thick-skinned, fleshy grape with three seeds. It was introduced to this country a century ago from Algeria, where it is known as the Ahmeur bou Ahmeur. It has nothing to do with the medium-sweet, pinkish-red California dessert wine type called Tokay, which can be made from any grape and is usually a blend of sherry and port. I know of one "varietal" Tokay wine; the East-Side Winery makes it entirely of that grape and labels it Flame Tokay. Because the grape has a lower sugar content when ripe than most wine-grape varieties, large quantities were purchased in the early 1980s by wineries making the then-new, low-alcohol "light" wines. Neither the grape nor the wine is in any way related to the Tokay or Tokaj wines of Hungary, which are traditionally made of a grape called Furmint that is grown only experimentally in the United States.

When Jim Kissler, a graduate of the university's wine school at Davis, became San Joaquin County's farm advisor in 1957, he began trying to persuade Lodi growers to change from Tokays to the "varietal" grapes for table wines. "Why should we change," the Lodi growers responded to his pleas, "when our wineries have won all those medals at the fairs with wines made of Tokay?"

Kissler was more successful in getting "varietal" grapes planted outside the Tokay district. Some 1500 acres of recent plantings are on Mandeville, McDonald, Roberts, and Bacon islands, fifteen miles west of Lodi in the vast San Joaquin–Sacramento River Delta region. The islands are below sea level, protected by levees from flooding; they are the Netherlands of the West. Their soil is mostly inflammable peat; there used to be signs along the levee roads warning motorists "This land will burn!" But the soils at higher elevations on the islands are not peat. Kissler finds the Delta climate cooler than in the Lodi district proper, and the grapes of such quality that he foresees increased plantings on the islands for table wines, in future years.

• 4 •

The Sacramento Valley, which stretches northwest from Lodi and the Delta region for almost 200 miles, is older in winegrowing than the San Joaquin. Before Prohibition, there were scores of wineries and nearly 40,000 acres of vineyards in the nine Sacramento Valley counties. By 1970, only four wineries and less than 500 acres were left. But 7000 acres of new vineyards planted in the valley during the 1970s and early 1980s have made it important in winegrowing again.

In 1842, Captain John Augustus Sutter, the Swiss adventurer turned empire builder, began distilling brandy out of wild grapes in his fort at Sacramento, which he named New Helvetia. Ruined instead of enriched by the discovery of gold in 1848 at his Coloma sawmill, Sutter gave up his fort and moved to his 600-acre Hock

Farm on the Feather River in Sutter County, six miles south of Yuba City. There he planted a vineyard with cuttings he imported from Europe. Sutter's farm helped support him until he left California for Washington, D.C., where he died fourteen years later.

Sutter County is also where farmer William Thompson of Yuba City introduced the English hothouse grape he named Thompson's Seedless, which became the most widely planted variety in California.

Neighboring Butte County's wine industry was founded in 1847 by Captain Sutter's former aide-de-camp, General John Bidwell, on his ranch at Chico. Twenty-one years later, Bidwell married a fanatical Prohibitionist. Before the wedding, he emptied his winery, uprooted his wine grapes, planted table and raisin grapes instead, and in 1892 he became the Prohibition Party's candidate for President of the United States. At the turn of the century, Butte County still had five wineries and 1000 acres in grapes. By 1970 it had only 50 acres, which increased to 375 acres by 1982.

In Yuba County, which borders Sutter and Butte, winegrowing was begun in 1855 by Charles Covillaud from Cognac, who planted grapes at Simpson's Crossing, a mile north of Marysville, the city Covillaud named for his wife, the former Mary Murphy. Within five years the county had four more wineries and 800 acres of vines, which expanded by 1930 to 1000 acres, but then were gradually replaced by orchards of peaches and prunes.

Yuba County again has 461 acres of vines. Most of them are on the spectacularly contoured, drip-irrigated 360-acre Renaissance Vineyard, a winegrowing project begun in 1973 in the foothills gold country near Oregon House, thirty miles northeast of Marysville. It is a subsidiary of the Fellowship of Friends, an independent church colony devoted to esoteric Gurdjeff-Ouspensky philosophy. Founded in 1970 with its headquarters at Renaissance, it has centers in principal American cities and in several other countries. Leading the vineyard project is Fellowship member Karl Werner, the winemaster in the 1950s of Schloss Vollrads in the Rheingau and in the early 1970s of the Callaway Vineyards at Temecula. Construction of the 300,000-gallon Renaissance Winery was begun in 1979, when its first wines were made under an air-supported plastic dome. When completed, it will be a classic Greek temple with formal gardens, a pool, statuary, and two underground levels for wine aging and bottling. Werner says its first vintages of estate-bottled White Riesling and Sauvignon Blanc will reach the market by 1988, to be followed by an aged Cabernet and eventually by a champagne. Visiting Fellowship members contribute their labor to help the 200 resident members in the vineyard, the winery, and in the colony's quality-printing and furniture-restoration shops.

In Tehama County, Peter Lassen, the Danish pioneer for whom volcanic Mount Lassen is named, planted the upper Sacramento Valley's first acre of Mission vines in 1846. This was at Vina, on the east bank of the river twenty miles north of Chico. At Lassen's retirement, Henry Gerke from Germany enlarged the vineyard and built a 100,000-gallon winery. Gerke made brandy as well as wine and is said to have shipped some to Europe.

Then came wealthy California ex-Governor (and later Senator) Leland Stanford, who bought the Vina property from Gerke in 1881. Stanford expanded the vineyard to 5000 acres, making it then the largest in the world. He built there the costliest winery in the state, to hold 2 million gallons of wine, and brought expert winemakers from France. Stanford had two altruistic objectives in winegrowing: to prove that California could produce finer wines than those of Europe, and to combat drunkenness in America by mass-producing good table wines and promoting their temperate mealtime use. But though successful in his other careers as a lawyer, merchant, railroad builder, and breeder of champion racehorses, Stanford made a series of grievous winegrowing mistakes.

His first error was in turning over his original vineyard in Alameda County to his brother Josiah, because that coastal district would have been ideal for his purposes. His second was in choosing Vina and in planting there such varieties as Zinfandel, which in the hot Sacramento Valley in the days before refrigeration could make only poor table wines. When Stanford's first Vina vintage was ready in 1886, he realized his mistake; the wines had an objectionable earthy taste. He then switched to making only dessert wines and brandy, and Stanford became the largest distiller of brandy in the world. Barges brought his product in barrels down the then-navigable Sacramento River from Red Bluff, to be loaded on ships for New York. His brandy was excellent, if the one I tasted at a Wine and Food Society dinner at the time of Repeal was a fair example. Having learned his lesson about climate, Stanford succeeded in growing some fine table wines in a third vineyard, which he purchased in 1888 at Menlo Park, in San Mateo County. But he did not live to taste them; he died in 1893. All that remains of his third winegrowing venture is the winery building, which stands in the Stanford Shopping Center and has been converted into a bank.

At his death, the great Vina estate with its winery and distillery were bequeathed to Stanford University at Palo Alto, which he had founded eight years earlier in memory of his only son, who had died in Italy at the age of fifteen. The sale of wine and brandy helped support the university for a time. But Palo Alto was a wineless community, for Stanford had made still another mistake: The deed to land he had bought to expand the campus contained a proviso that no alcoholic beverage could ever be sold there. (Downtown Palo Alto remained Dry until 1970, when a court declared the eighty-year-old proviso void.) Also, Stanford's wife Jane was a teetotaler, violently opposed to wine except for medicinal use. She disrupted the university's management of its beverage business until she was mysteriously murdered by poisoning in 1905. Drys attacked the Stanford trustees for letting alcoholic drinks help to support the university. When a fire damaged the Vina winery in 1915, the trustees ordered the vineyards uprooted and sold the land in parcels for farms.

In 1955 the winery site and buildings were purchased by Trappist monks, who had decided to move there from Kentucky. For almost a century after emigrating from France in 1848, these Trappists had produced altar wine on the hillsides beside their monastery at Gethsemani in Nelson County, but had abandoned their vineyard in 1940 after a series of years in which their grapes often were found frozen in spring. At Vina, they named their new monastery Our Lady of New Clairvaux and gave consideration to planting vineyards again, but invested in fruit orchards instead. They have preserved Stanford's huge winery building beside the monastery, but they use it only to store and repair their orchard equipment.

In Stanford's time, Tehama County had two dozen wineries and 10,000 acres in grapes. After half a century, parts of his great vineyard near Vina again grow grapes for wine. Tehama County's 300 acres of new vineyards, planted since 1965, are mainly of high-acid varieties such as French Colombard, which if harvested early and properly handled can make good table wines. The grapes are trucked to wineries in cooler districts, such as the northern San Joaquin Valley and the coastal counties.

There also were vineyards as far up the valley as Redding in Shasta County, which counted 400 acres of grapes in 1890. Shasta County again had forty acres of vines by 1982.

The most extensive pre-Prohibition vineyards in the valley were in Sacramento County. Sacramento Sheriff Benjamin Bugbey grew wines at Folsom that won medals at the 1863 State Fair. A survey in 1889 listed twenty-four wineries between Sacramento, Mormon Island on the American River, Folsom, and Folsom Lake. The Natoma Vineyard south of Folsom covered nearly 2000 acres. The California Winery on R Street in Sacramento was four decades old when Prohibition in 1920 forced it to close. The vineyards then were concentrated around Florin, Galt, and Elk Grove. There still were 12,000 acres of vines in Sacramento County in 1933, when eight wineries reopened for business at Repeal. Then came urbanization, particularly after the Second World War, and the old vineyards were swallowed up by towns. Without grapes to crush, five of the wineries closed. The Frasinetti Winery, south of Florin, and the Mills Winery on Folsom Boulevard became retail outlets, the latter with numerous branches for a time. The 3-million-gallon Gibson Winery near Elk Grove continues producing, but it makes mostly berry, kiwi, other fruit wines, and hard apple cider, which can be sampled at the winery's tasting room, nearby on Highway 99. Gibson is now owned by the former Sanger growers' co-op of Fresno County and bottles the grape wines shipped from Sanger. Among the numerous Gibson products are retsina and kokinelli, the resin-flavored wines favored by consumers born in Greece; a "wassail" honey wine; Akadama burgundy, rosé, and chablis, and the grape-wine base of the Akadama plum wine that Suntory originally shipped unblended from Japan.

The oldest Sacramento County winery that produces only grape wines is City College English instructor Charles Myers' 11,000-gallon Harbor Winery, near the Port of Sacramento. Myers has been making prize-winning wines there since 1972, but exclusively from Napa Valley and Amador County grapes.

Grape growing in Sacramento County had virtually disappeared by 1960, when only 220 acres were left. Then came the table-wine boom of the early 1970s, and Sacramento vineyards had multiplied to 3891 acres by 1982. But the revival was mostly in a new area that had had few vineyards in the past—the Sacramento River Delta between Clarksburg and Courtland. Growers of grain and truck crops planted vineyards when they realized that high-quality wine grapes could be produced in their climate, which resembles that of Lodi and the San Joaquin County Delta islands; the nights are cooled by the winds from Suisun Bay. The first of these Delta vineyards were planted on the Sacramento County side of the river. The rest are on the Yolo side, where two wineries opened in 1979. Yolo County again had

934 acres of grapes in 1982. Most of the Delta grape crop is purchased by coast-counties wineries, and makes some of their fruitiest table wines.

Two miles southwest of the river village of Clarksburg is the 125,000-gallon R. & J. Cook Winery and tasting room on Netherlands Road. The "R. & J." stand for Roger, whose father Perry Cook began growing wine grapes in 1969 across Elk Slough from the winery site, and for Roger's wife Joanne. When Perry Cook started growing grapes, his corn- and wheat-grower neighbor, Warren V. Bogle, began doing the same along Road 144 on Merritt Island, across the river from the Sacramento County town of Hood. Warren and his wife Frances bonded the 34,000-gallon Bogle Vineyards winery on their 255-acre vineyard in 1979, the same year as the younger Cooks. The Federal government has granted a petition by the Cooks to recognize Clarksburg as a viticultural area, and another by the Bogles to name Merritt Island as a separate district.

A historical question that puzzled me for many years was: Why did 40,000 acres of vines disappear during Prohibition from the main Sacramento Valley, while almost 300,000 acres were being planted in the southern San Joaquin Valley counties of Fresno, Tulare, and Kern—since both of these districts have mainly Region V climates? The answer is related to autumn rainfall. When Prohibition shut down the wineries in the Sacramento Valley, the grapes that remained were mainly sun-dried for raisins, which can be ruined by early autumn rains. The raisin-growing industry then became concentrated around arid Fresno, where in most years grapes can be dried before the rain comes.

• 5 •

Scores of new vineyards and two dozen new wineries have sprung up in the historic Sierra foothills gold-mining country, popularly known as the Mother Lode, in response to the nation's increasing consumption of table wines. Acreage planted to grapes in Amador, Calaveras, El Dorado, and Nevada counties more than trebled, from 720 to 2201 acres, between 1965 and 1982.

The foothills counties have a winegrowing industry as old as the state. In Gold Rush days many miners, when the precious metal supply petered out, planted vines around their diggings and turned to making wine. El Dorado County alone had more vineyards in 1860 than either Sonoma or Napa. By 1890, more than a hundred wineries were operating at such locations as

Nevada City, Colfax, Lincoln, Penryn, Auburn, Placerville, Coloma, Shingle Springs, Ione, Fiddletown, Volcano, Jackson, San Andreas, Sonora, Columbia, and Jamestown. When Prohibition closed the foothills wineries, grape growing gradually moved to the hot Central Valley, where irrigated vineyards yield heavier crops.

In the mid-1960s, when urban sprawl compelled the coast-counties vintners to seek new places to plant vines, the foothill counties did not interest them because the available tracts in the rolling hills are too small for mass cultivation, and only those foothill locations with air drainage are safe from crop injury by frosts. There are more than enough such locations, however, with sufficient space for small winegrowing estates.

Test plots of premium wine grapes were planted about 1965 in foothill counties from Siskiyou to Mariposa, a stretch of 300 miles. Wine samples made at UC Davis of grapes from the test plots showed that wines of coast-counties quality could be grown in the Mother Lode.

At the same time, wine connoisseurs in the lowlands made a discovery about a grape grown in the foothills to which nobody had called their attention before. They discovered that Zinfandel grown in the Shenandoah Valley* and around Fiddletown in Amador County makes a wine of more intense flavor and greater alcoholic strength than wine from Zinfandel grown elsewhere in the state. The discovery is credited to Harbor Winery proprietor Charles Myers, of Sacramento. While still a home wine-maker in the 1960s, Myers vinified some Zinfandel from Ken Deaver's vineyard in the Shenandoah Valley. Sacramento importer Darrell Corti tasted Myers' Zinfandel, and was so impressed that he arranged for the Sutter Home Winery at St. Helena to make Deaver Vineyard Zinfandel for Corti to sell. The fame of Sutter Home Amador Zinfandel quickly spread. Within a few years, several premium Napa, Santa Clara, and Alameda County wineries were producing Zinfandels labeled "Amador," and selling them at premium prices.

---

*A cross-country controversy developed between California and Virginia in 1981, when Amador County winegrowers petitioned the Federal government to grant them a "Shenandoah Valley" viticultural appellation. Virginians promptly filed a rival petition to grant the appellation to their historic original Shenandoah Valley alone. The government resolved the issue in 1982 by establishing both appellations, requiring that "California" be added to labels of Amador's Shenandoah Valley wines.

Petitions for two more California foothill district appellations, "Fiddletown" and "El Dorado," were filed in 1982, and the former was approved in the following year.

There already was an old winery in the Shenandoah Valley that had been making Amador Zinfandel for three decades, but labeling it burgundy and selling it for 67 cents a bottle. The D'Agostini family's 185,000-gallon cellar, on Shenandoah Road eight miles northeast of Plymouth, dates from 1856, when Adam Uhlinger from Switzerland quarried rock from the 2000-foot-high hillside to build the cellar walls. Enrico D'Agostini bought the place from Uhlinger in 1911 and made wine until Prohibition. He was succeeded by his four sons, who enlarged the vineyard to 125 acres. After Repeal they made mostly old-fashioned sauterne, burgundy, and dry Muscat and sold them at the cellar door. But when Amador Zinfandel became recognized during the 1970s as something special, the D'Agostinis began labeling theirs "estate bottled" and selling it at four times the old price.

A dozen more wineries opened in the Shenandoah Valley when the fame of its Zinfandel spread. In 1973, Gilroy banker Walter Field financed construction of the 30,000-gallon Monteviña Winery, three miles from Plymouth on Shenandoah School Road. It since has grown to 195,000 gallons, and its 175 acres of vineyards include other varieties besides Zinfandel, such as Cabernet and Sauvignon Blanc. Also in 1973, Sacramento veterinarian and home winemaker Eugene Story built a 30,000-gallon brick winery on Bell Road, naming it Cosumnes River Vineyard because his thirty acres of vines adjoin the river; Amador's name was only beginning to become known to connoisseurs. After Story's death in 1981, his widow, Ann Story Ousley, renamed it the Story Vineyard winery. Near the Story winery are the new seventeen-acre Karly Vineyard and winery, named by former Air Force fighter pilot Lawrence Cobb for his wife, Karly Cobb. On Steiner Road, between the Monteviña and D'Agostini wineries, is the 30,000-gallon Shenandoah Vineyards winery, opened in 1977 by former ceramic missiles engineer Leon Sobon and his wife Shirley, who were home winemakers when they lived in Silicon Valley. Their six children help care for their ten acres of vines. Another former Silicon Valley home-winemaker scientist, Ben Zeitman, in 1980 opened the neighboring Amador Foothill Winery with his wife, Joan Sieber, who teaches psychology at California State University in Hayward. Also on Steiner Road is the Santino Winery, bonded in 1979 and owned by Nancy Schweitzer Santino, who employs German-trained enologist Scott Harvey, a part owner of the Beau Val winery, to make the Santino wines. On Plymouth-Shenandoah Road (E 16), also opened in 1979, is the 40,000-gallon Baldinelli Vineyard winery, where Kaiser engineering executive Edward Baldinelli makes estate-bottled Cabernet as well as red and white Zinfandels from a seventy-acre vineyard he owns in partnership with viticulturist John Miller. Newest winery in the valley is TKC Vineyards, owned by aerospace engineer Harold Nuffer and his wife Monica, who bonded the underground cellar on Valley Drive in 1981. It is named for their children: Tierre, Karina, and Courtnay. On Shenandoah Road are aeronautical engineer John Kenworthy's and his wife Pat's vineyard and their small winery, bonded in 1979 in a rebuilt century-old barn.

Other parts of Amador County have wineries, too. Near the famous gold-mining town of Sutter Creek is Gary and Loretta Porteous' 2000-gallon Stoneridge cellar, on Ridge Road two miles east of town. Porteous crushed his first vintage of Ruby Cabernet in 1975 from the three-acre vineyard he planted four years before, supplemented by the crops of pre-Prohibition Zinfandel vineyards that he cultivates nearby. Porteous works six days a week as a utility lineman and carves gravestones in his spare time. Off Willow Creek Road, between Ione and Plymouth, is the 10,000-gallon Argonaut Winery, which opened in time for Lodi winemaker Neal Overboe to crush the 1976 vintage of Shenandoah Valley grapes. Beside it are a vineyard of Barbera planted in 1972, and the home of one of the five Argonaut owners, Sacramento engineer James R. Payne. The Greenstone Winery, on Highway 88 off Jackson Valley Road, was named, when it opened in 1981, for the greenish mining-area soil nearby. Four Southern California teachers own the thirty-acre vineyard and the cellar: Dr. Stan van Spanje, who apprenticed at the Shenandoah Vineyard and now commutes weekly from a college in the South; his winemaker wife Karen; and the Fowlers, Durward and Jane. The Greenstone Winery partners want the Federal government to recognize Jackson Valley as a separate viticultural area.

El Dorado County, Amador's northern neighbor, began awakening in 1973 to its winegrowing past, when Gregory and Susan Boeger opened their 6000-gallon Boeger cellar on Carson Road north of Placerville, the county seat. Their site is that of the Lombardo Fossati winery, which operated from 1860 until Wartime Prohibition began in 1919. After making their first wines of purchased grapes, the Boegers replanted twenty of the Fossati acres and built a new 40,000-gallon winery, using their original cellar as their tasting room. Best-seller of their seven wines is a blend they label Hangtown Red. It is named for Placerville, which was called Hangtown when scores of bad men were strung up there during the lawless Gold Rush days. Boeger, a Davis-trained former grape statistician, thinks he was destined to become a winegrower because he is a grandson of Anton Nichelini, who founded the Nichelini winery in Napa County in 1890.

A year after the Boegers opened, home winemaker and electrical engineer John H. McCready and his wife Barbara began planting a fifteen-acre vineyard on a hilltop off Pleasant Valley Road, twelve miles southeast of Placerville. By 1977, they had bonded the 11,000-gallon Sierra Vista Winery, which is well-named; from it you can see the snowcapped peaks of the Sierra throughout the year. Besides caring for the vineyard and making wine, Dr. McCready teaches his original profession at the state university in Sacramento three days a week.

Four more El Dorado County wineries were bonded in the early 1980s: On Gatlin Road in Camino, not far from the Boegers, Placerville engineer Richard H. Bush and his Placerville-born wife Leslie built the 50,000-gallon modern Madroña Vineyards winery and developed a thirty-acre vineyard of premium vines. The other three are situated along Fairplay Road. Adjoining the Famine's End Nursery, two miles south of Somerset, is the 17,000-gallon FBF Winery, whose name stands for nursery owner Brian Fitzpatrick, who manages the fourteen-acre vineyard; winemaker partner William Bertram; and Brian's brother Michael, a banker. Fitzpatrick is the brand name of FBF wines. At Granite Springs Road, farther south, is Lester and Lynne Russell's 15,000-gallon Granite Springs Winery, bonded in 1981 on the twenty-acre vineyard they began planting on Lester's father's farm the year before. Lester, a young Air Force veteran, learned winemaking at the David Bruce Winery while working as a park ranger in Santa Clara County nearby. On Stoney Creek Road off Fairplay Road is the 6000-gallon winery, bonded in 1982 by county fair director Vernon Gerwer and his wife Marcia, both of whose families long have owned land in the Somerset area. Their first wines were made of grapes planted experimentally in the 1960s. A fourth winery on Grizzly Flat Road east of Somerset is planned by labor relations expert Frank Herbert and his wife Beverly, who have a twelve-acre vineyard, planted since 1974.

Calaveras County, Amador's neighbor on the south, retains its mining-days atmosphere with such names as Angels Camp, Murphys, and Dogtown Road. On San Domingo Road, off Sheep Ranch Road northwest of Murphys, is the 52,000-gallon Stevenot Vineyards cellar, bonded in 1979 by former naval officer Barden Stevenot, fifth-generation member of a pioneer California family, on a twenty-five-acre vineyard of premium wine grapes he began planting four years before.

Latest foothill district to have a winery is Nevada County. Orthopedic surgeon Dr. Richard Cobden, who has a five-acre vineyard beside his 3000-foot-high Nevada City home, joined in 1982 with attorney Allan S. Haley in building the 40,000-gallon Snow Mountain Winery on Spring Street, in the center of Nevada City. Deep beneath the winery is the Champion Mine, where histories of the Mother Lode say Senator George Hearst got his start. Dr. Cobden, Haley, and their talented winemaker, Tony Norskog, are fellow members of the Nevada City WCTU, which stands for Wine Connoisseurs and Tasters Union.

Another foothill district where new vineyards are reported springing up is Mariposa County, where farmers organized a county wine-grape growers association in 1982.

Those interested in Mother Lode history are fascinated by the meanings of the foothill counties' Spanish names, such as Amador ("lover"), El Dorado ("glistening one"), Calaveras ("skulls" or "daredevils"), Nevada ("snow-covered"), and Mariposa ("butterfly").

• 6 •

In pre-Prohibition times, western Yolo County, between Sacramento and Napa, had 2000 acres of vineyards and more than fifty wineries, scattered from Woodland to Winters, Madison, and Capay. The largest was the Orleans Vineyard of Arpad Haraszthy & Company, three miles west of Esparto, with its winery four stories high. Another was on a farm at Davisville, where Jerome Davis, a member of the Bear Flag rebellion, had settled about 1852. Yolo vineyards increased to 4000 acres during Prohibition, then dwindled after Repeal, when grape-growing in the Sacramento Valley declined.

Davisville, fourteen miles west of Sacramento, was renamed Davis when the University of California bought the Davis ranch in 1906 and opened a practical farming school with a beginning class of forty, including Ernest Wente of Livermore. Since then, the farm has become a university of 19,000 students in forty-five departments, including complete medical, law, and business schools. It now covers six square miles on both sides of Freeway 80, is by far the largest of the nine UC campuses, and even has its own airport, from which Davis experts fly to the university's experiment stations and the other campuses where agricultural courses are taught.

The Department of Viticulture and Enology at Davis has a winery and 140 acres of vineyard. More than 200 men and women, many of them from abroad, are enrolled in the dozen grape, wine, brandy, and brewing courses and in many research projects. More than 600 students in other fields take the introductory enology course each year. Short courses and seminars are also offered periodically for those professionally or avocationally engaged in growing grapes or making wine. There is a constant demand for Davis graduates to work in wineries in the United States and abroad.

In the two-semester general viticulture course, each student plants vines in a practice vineyard, cultivates, fertilizes, prunes, and thins them, and harvests the fruit for fresh use, for raisins, and for wine. Each three-term enology student makes red, white, pink, and sparkling wines, performing each step from crushing through fermentation, racking, aging, finishing, stabilization, and bottling to the analysis and tasting of the final product. Many also take the brandy-distilling course. What they make, however, cannot be drunk or taken from the department buildings. More than 100,000 research samples made since 1935 are stored in the temperature-controlled cellars under the Enology Building, where the winery and distillery are. The rest goes down the drain.

The university is still doing the same job the legislature assigned it in 1880, when Professor Hilgard began his work at Berkeley. Hilgard in 1889 hired as his cellar foreman Frederic Bioletti, an Englishman with an Italian name, who had worked in California and South African wineries, and who eventually succeeded Hilgard in charge of the work on wine. Among those trained by Bioletti were William Vere Cruess, who became the world's most renowned food scientist of his time, and Texas-born Albert Julius Winkler, who attained equal viticultural fame. Cruess in turn taught winemaking to several of his graduate students, especially one named Maynard Alexander Joslyn. At the repeal of Prohibition, this group around Bioletti, with French-born Professor Edmund H. Twight, trained many of the winemakers who after Repeal rebuilt the quality of the state's wines.

In 1933, Bioletti chose from among his graduates a tall, blond, green-thumbed young geneticist named Harold Paul Olmo and gave him a lifetime project—to breed better grapes for the unique climates of California. Olmo became the Burbank of the grape. He planted seedlings of old varieties to develop new ones and crossed old varieties to combine their best characteristics in new hybrid grapes. Then from thousands of vines, he chose the best producers, made wines from their grapes, aged and evaluated the wines. The few dozen best vines were replanted in different climates and soils, repeating the whole process until from among the dozens, a promising new variety was chosen. In 1946, Olmo introduced his first successful wine varieties, Ruby Cabernet and Emerald Riesling, followed twenty years later by Carnelian, Centurion, and Carmine, and in the late 1970s a Muscat-flavored white named Symphony, which makes a dry wine without the bitterness of dry Muscat types.*

Olmo also found time to travel to other grape-growing countries. He traced the routes through which the wine-bearing *Vitis vinifera* grape has been carried through the centuries, evolving its thousands of varieties in different soils and climates. He hoped someday to discover Vinifera's birthplace and the vine in its primitive state. In 1848, on a 7000-mile trek by plane, train, muleback, and on foot, his quest came to an end. In mud-walled villages at the border of ancient Persia and Afghanistan, Olmo found the original Vinifera vine growing wild. He brought seeds back to Davis, made them part of his breeding program, and began the ages-old evolution of the wine grape over again.

Beginning back in 1935, much of the university's wine research work was shifted gradually from Berkeley to the Davis campus, where the vineyards were. In that year Dr. Winkler, Bioletti's successor as chairman of viticulture, hired as his junior enologist at Davis a young graduate student named Maynard Andrew Amerine, who then was studying for his Ph.D. The only son of a California farming family, Amerine had grown up at Modesto, where his father raised grapes and other fruits. He had attended junior college there with Ernest and Julio Gallo, who lived a mile away. While the Gallo boys at their graduation went into the grape industry, Amerine continued his studies at Berkeley, where he received his plant-science degree. His first task under Winkler at Davis was to make experimental wines from grapes grown in each viticultural district of the state. Amerine later initiated scores of other research programs. By 1957, when he succeeded Winkler as department chairman, his bibliography totaled 122 separate publications. The first texts on winemaking after Repeal were published by Drs. Cruess, Joslyn, and their Berkeley colleagues in 1934. Six years later, Amerine teamed with Joslyn in writing a series of university bulletins and circulars on the commercial production of wines and brandies, Amerine

---

*Ruby Cabernet—Cabernet Sauvignon × Carignane—combines the quality of the noble Cabernet with the productivity and vigor of Carignane. Emerald Riesling is White Riesling × Muscadelle. Carnelian, Centurion, and Carmine are crosses of Carignane, Cabernet Sauvignon, and Grenache. Symphony is Alexandria Muscat × Grenache. Carmine was intended for cool coast-counties climates; the other reds make improved red table wines in the hot Central Valley.

presenting the viticultural aspects and Joslyn the enological side. The first Amerine-Joslyn bulletin on table wine summarized their scientific knowledge of that subject in 143 pages. By 1951, they had published a new 397-page text covering the same ground more fully. The same book appeared in 1970 in a second edition of 997 pages—a good index to how much has been learned by California investigators about this ancient art and science of table-wine production in a span of only thirty years.

At present the Department of Viticulture and Enology staff at Davis numbers fifty-two, including such noted research workers and professors as Chairman Cornelius Ough, James A. Cook, Mark M. Kliewer, Ralph E. Kunkee, Lloyd A. Lider, Klayton E. Nelson, Ann C. Noble, Vernon L. Singleton, Roger Boulton, and Robert J. Weaver, and newer members Carol Meredith, Lynn Williams, and Larry Williams. Drs. Olmo, Winkler, and A. Dinsmoor Webb are active in consulting; they are officially retired. Also at Davis are Dr. Austin Goheen, the Federal government's expert on grape virus diseases; professors in four other UC departments dealing with grapes or wine; and UC's extension enologist George M. Cooke and viticulturist Amand N. Kasimatis. The Davis wine school is now larger than such famous European stations as those at Geisenheim, Montpellier, and Conegliano, but the Russian vinicultural station at Yalta is twice as large.

19

The Main San Joaquin Valley

ALL OF THE vineyard districts covered in the last six chapters comprise only the top third of the California wine iceberg, so to speak. The other two-thirds of the state's wine production comes from the main San Joaquin Valley, a fabulous agricultural empire in which grapes are the chief income crop and the chief wineries are the biggest in the world.

From the Delta region west of Lodi, the valley of the San Joaquin River extends southeastward more than 200 miles. It is a trough, 30 to 50 miles wide and almost as flat as a table, between the snowcapped Sierra Nevada mountains on the east and the Coast Range on the west. A twentieth of its surface is covered by vineyards—some 550,000 acres, more than 800 square miles.

The summer climate is hot, mainly Region IV toward the northern end, and becomes still hotter—Region V—in the south. No rain falls there until autumn, and what falls thereafter is sparse, averaging only fourteen inches at Stockton and less than six inches at Bakersfield. Much of the land was a dry, barren waste until a century ago, when men began building dams in the Sierra to trap the melting snows and started to dig the irrigation canals that now crisscross most of the valley. Mountain water has transformed once-parched wasteland into lush farms more fabulously productive than the delta of the Nile.

In the sizzling heat and the rich valley soil, washed down from the mountains for eons, irrigated vines yield enormous grape crops, double the average in the coast counties. Here, eight to twelve tons per acre is considered a normal harvest of the common wine-grape varieties, and seventeen tons is not unusual from an acre of overcropped Thompson Seedless vines. From this valley come all of the raisins produced in the United States, two-thirds of the California table grapes that are eaten fresh or canned, nearly all of the port, sherry, muscatel, and brandy produced in the state, and more than half—a figure steadily rising—of California table wines and champagnes.

Much of the San Joaquin's agriculture is conducted by corporate farmers on a gigantic scale of mechanized agribusiness, a term coined here. Airplanes are used to spray the larger vineyards. Some of the big table-grape growers employ helicopters to dry their grapes on the vines after early rains. Vineyard managers and grape buyers travel such vast distances daily that they are required to fly company planes.

Fleets of wine-tank trucks, like those used to transport milk, ply the highways night and day through the year, exchanging their vinous cargoes between wineries in different parts of the state. Who owns or makes what and where in the California wine industry is increasingly difficult to figure out nowadays, but hints to some of the answers can be found in this chapter. Many of the largest valley vineyards and some of the big wineries are owned by farming corporations related to oil companies, by European-owned conglomerates, and by other unidentified foreign investors. Vineyards are scattered all the way from Manteca to the Tehachapi, vines even sprouting among the oil wells. Don't expect to find romantic, vine-draped little chateau wineries with aging-tunnels, such as are seen in the coast counties; the average valley winery is merely a processing plant among the farms.

• 2 •

The main valley is reached via Highway 99 from Stockton to the Manteca-Escalon district, in the southeastern corner of San Joaquin County. (We explored Lodi, with its Tokays that color red on cool nights, in the preceding chapter because Lodi differs climatically from the rest of the valley; it is a distinct viticultural district by itself.)

In the Manteca-Escalon area, chiefly wine-grape varieties are grown, especially the red Grenache, which retains some of its pronounced aroma when grown in Region IV. This district has supplied most of the Grenache grapes used by wineries in other parts of the state to make their Grenache rosés.

First on the route from Stockton is the attractive 24-million-gallon Delicato winery and tasting room, built in 1976, four miles above Manteca on the west frontage road beside Highway

99. The original small cellar was called the Sam-Jasper Winery when Gaspare (Jasper) Indelicato and his brother-in-law, Sebastiano (Sam) Luppino, built it in 1935. Jasper's sons and grandsons operate the winery now, but they call it Delicato Vineyards, an improvement over the family name. They sell a dozen wines in bottles, jugs, and in four-liter plastic pouches, but most of their production is in bulk for wineries in other parts of the state. During each vintage season, fresh grape juice is available for purchase by home-winemakers, a tradition Gaspare Indelicato established in 1935.

On Austin Road, off the freeway south of Manteca, is the 40,000-gallon Bella Napoli Winery, founded in 1934 by Tony R. Hat, who was born Anthony Cappello near Naples but translated his name to its English equivalent when he came to the United States in 1899. His four sons cultivate 500 acres of vineyards, which once grew mainly Carignane and Grenache, but to which they lately have added Chenin Blanc, Colombard, and Chardonnay. The eldest son, Lucas Hat, operates the winery, which has new stainless-steel tanks. Its table wines are sold to local restaurants and at the cellar door. The Cadlolo Winery in the town of Escalon has a tasting room, but most of its quarter-million-gallon capacity is used to produce bulk wine for other wineries.

Interesting to visit in this district is the 30-million-gallon Franzia winery on Highway 120, six miles east of Manteca. You can sample the prize-winning wines offered in the Franzia tasting room, and also this country's first almond-flavored champagne. The winery is an exemplar of mass wine production. Rows of shiny stainless- and epoxy-lined steel tanks stand outdoors on one of the Franzia vineyards, which total 4200 acres. The narrower ones are pressurized; they hold Charmat-process champagnes. The tanks are partly hidden from the highway by brick and concrete cellars, where each wine is processed, bottled, or packed in plastic bags and shipped—much of it in tank cars—across the United States. You can recognize the wines bottled here under any of the five different brands they bear, because all the labels give the address of Ripon, the town five miles to the south.

Giuseppe Franzia came to California from Genoa in 1893, worked for fifty cents an hour in truck gardens around San Francisco, saved enough to plant a vineyard, and started his winery in 1915. It was closed during Prohibition, but his five sons kept up the vineyard and reopened for business as Franzia Brothers at Repeal. At first they sold their output in bulk to eastern bottlers, then during the Second World War began concentrating on bottled wines, adopting the mass-production techniques introduced by the Gallos. (Ernest Gallo is the Franzia Brothers' brother-in-law.) The five brothers disagreed about the winery's future, and in 1971 they sold out to eastern investors. A subsequent owner, the Coca-Cola Bottling Company of New York, combined Franzia with the 6-million-gallon Mogen David winery at Westfield, New York, and with Tribuno vermouth of New Jersey. Tribuno vermouths are now made at Franzia, while Franzia wine, grape concentrate, and brandy are shipped in bulk to Westfield to become part of such Mogen David products as "MD 20-20" and "Golden Chablis." In 1981, Franzia and Mogen David were purchased from Coca-Cola of New York by The Wine Group, which is owned by onetime Gallo marketing executive Arthur Ciocca and his fellow members of the Franzia management team. What the sons of the Franzia Brothers did after their fathers and uncles sold the winery in 1971 is told on a later page.

• 3 •

Three miles toward Escalon from Franzia is a bulk winery almost as large. The sign outside the winery bears a new name, painted in 1983: ISC Wines, Inc. This once was the main Petri winery, from which in the 1950s grew the Petri–United Vintners complex of nine wineries with a tank ship, all of which in 1968 became part of the Heublein wine and liquor empire, which in 1982 became a subsidiary of R. J. Reynolds (tobacco) Industries. A year later, this winery at Escalon was sold—together with the Italian Swiss Colony at Asti, the Community winery at Lodi, and the onetime Wahtoke winery near Sanger—to the 1100-member Allied Grape Growers Co-operative, which had owned all of these wineries for several years before Heublein bought them in 1968. Allied Growers then formed a subsidiary, the new wine company named ISC Wines, to operate the four purchased wineries and to market their wines nationwide. It also bought from Heublein many old established wine brand names, including Italian Swiss Colony, Petri, Lejon, and Jacques Bonet for champagnes; Gambarelli & Davitto (G & D), Santa Fe, Parma, and Annie Green Springs for "pop" wines. ISC Wines, now headquartered at San Francisco, contracted at first for most of its wines to be bottled at Heublein's big winery at Madera, but was expected eventually to establish bottling facilities of its own.

Back in 1887, when California bulk wine was 8 cents a gallon, an immigrant from Tuscany named Raffaello Petri, who owned a hotel in the North Beach district of San Francisco, began selling wine as a sideline. When his son Angelo grew up, he joined his Uncle Amadeo's cigar factory, rolling fermented tobacco leaves into the twisted, double-ended, strong-tasting black Italian cheroots called Toscani. During the First World War, Marca Petri wine and Marca Petri cigars both became so popular among Italians across the country that Raffaello and a partner named Dante Foresti acquired their own vineyards and this winery at Escalon.

Foresti managed the vineyard during Prohibition and sold the grapes for home winemaking, while the Petris concentrated on their cigar factory in San Francisco and later on a boot-making venture in Tennessee. At Repeal, Angelo Petri returned the family to the wine business, leasing wineries in Napa and Escalon, all this in conjunction with the cigar company.

In 1933, Angelo's younger son, the late Louis Petri, was enrolled to study medicine at St. Louis University; his parents wanted him to become a physician. But Louis was in love with Flori, the younger daughter of Roma Winery president Battista Cella, and Flori's love letters from Lodi told him about exciting happenings in the reviving wine business. In his sophomore year, Louis quit medical school, came to San Francisco, married Flori, and went to work washing barrels at $75 a month in the cellar of the Petri cigar factory on Battery Street. In 1944, at the age of thirty-two, he became president of the Petri Wine Company.

Louis Petri, a restless young man who stuttered when excited, set out to dominate the wine industry. During the next eight years he bought the Tulare and Mission Bell wineries, and in a major coup, bought from National Distillers the Italian Swiss Colony wineries at Asti and Fresno, the Shewan-Jones winery at Lodi, and the Gambarelli & Davitto cellars at New York. Meanwhile, seeing more profit in selling wine than in making it, Petri organized the Allied Grape Growers co-op, then sold all his wineries to the co-op for $24 million, retaining their operation and the wine-marketing rights in United Vintners, which he headed as president. In 1957, he built the first wine tank ship ever to serve under the American flag, naming it the *Angelo Petri* for his father. He almost lost it one day three years later, when the ship became disabled outside the Golden Gate and drifted, rudderless, toward the beach. An SOS brought three tugs in time to tow the vessel back to port for repairs. Delivering 2.5-million-gallon cargoes of bulk wine from the Port of Stockton to Atlantic Coast ports through the Panama Canal seven times a year, and bottling the two dozen United Vintners wine brands in cellars in Newark, Chicago, and California, he was selling nearly a fourth of all the wine consumed in the United States. At forty-four, Louis Petri was the wine king of America.

Meanwhile, at Modesto in Stanislaus County, twelve miles south of Petri's Escalon winery, a rival—the E. & J. Gallo Winery—was beginning to challenge him for leadership in sales. The Gallo Brothers had negotiated in 1953 to buy the Italian Swiss Colony before Petri bought it for $16 million. The duel of Gallo versus Petri for dominance in the wine industry—billed in the trade press as "the battle of the giants"—lasted for more than a decade.

When, in 1957, Petri built the first American wine tanker for $7 million, his saving in freight costs enabled him to sell his wines for 10 cents less per bottle in eastern market centers than wines that were shipped east by rail. The Gallos parried by building at Modesto for $6 million the first glass factory ever owned by a winery. By making their own lightweight bottles, the Gallos could sell their wines in the East at the same price as Petri's and advertise that their wines were bottled in California.

Nine years later, Petri added the prestigious Inglenook Vineyard to his kingdom, but the Gallos stuck to their then policy of making and selling only inexpensive wines.

Gallo's sales crept up on Petri's during the sixties. By 1968, Gallo was well ahead. In that year, Heublein bought control of United Vintners for $33 million in Heublein stock. Three years later, the wine tanker *Angelo Petri* was sold. Meanwhile, Heublein joined a glass company in building a $16 million bottle factory, like Gallo's, beside its Mission Bell winery at Madera. Thereafter all of its enormous volume of California wines was bottled in California.

Louis Petri continued in the wine business as the largest single member of the Allied Grape Growers co-op, supplying grapes from his vineyards in Napa County to the complex of wineries he once controlled. He sold his last vineyard to Heublein in 1971 and, a multimillionaire, concentrated on his realty and hotel investments in Hawaii and San Francisco, until his death in 1980.

· 4 ·

In the Repeal year of 1933, young Ernest and Julio Gallo rented an old warehouse in Modesto, bought some new redwood tanks and a grape crusher on credit, and made their first wine. Ernest was twenty-four, Julio a year younger. While students at Modesto Junior College, they had planned to start a winery whenever Prohibition would end.

During boyhood, they had worked in their father's vineyard west of Modesto, and they remembered the small winery their grandfather, from Italy's Piedmont, had operated at Hanford before Prohibition. But all that the boys knew about winemaking was how their father had made wine in their basement for his own use. In the Modesto public library, they luckily found two of the university's pre-Prohibition pamphlets on winemaking, and the red wine they made in 1933 turned out sound. When it was ready, Ernest boarded a plane for New York with samples, called on the wine bottlers there, and sold them the 1933 vintage in bulk. Two years later, the brothers built a small concrete winery in the southern outskirts of Modesto, on the bank of Dry Creek.

I remember stopping there one day in the late 1930s. In a cramped office in front of the cellar, I found young Ernest Gallo. He told me that he and his brother were only making bulk wine to get started, but that someday the Gallo name with their family crest (the rooster, for which *gallo* is the Italian word) would appear on bottles that would be sold throughout the United States. His confidence impressed me, though his chances didn't.

Today, at that same location, the Gallos are bottling more than a fourth of the wine consumed in the United States. Their 93-million-gallon Modesto winery is almost a city by itself, with its hundreds of giant steel tanks, the biggest of which holds 1 million gallons, enormous bottling cellars, bottle and bottle-closure factories, research laboratories, and vast warehouses from which Gallo wines are shipped by the trainload to all fifty states. There is also, surrounded by parkland, an elegant new "contemporary-classical" administration building (pictured on some Gallo labels), where the brothers, their sons, and a son-in-law have their offices. Gallo wineries are not open to the public. There are no signs on or near any of the Gallo buildings; those who don't know the way through the maze of tanks and buildings don't belong. There are more Gallo wineries at Livingston, Fresno, and Healdsburg, which bring the total capacity to more than 300 million gallons. The 130-million-gallon winery at Livingston is the biggest in the world. A dozen other wineries around the state, some operating on long-term contracts, make all or most of their wines for Gallo. Altogether, more than 100,000 acres of California vineyards, including the 5000 owned by the family, produce the grapes for the company's more than four dozen different wines and champagnes.

A family-owned corporation, Gallo is firmly ruled by Ernest as chairman and brother Julio as president. The other directors are Ernest's sons David, who is involved with marketing, and Joseph, in charge of sales; Julio's son Robert, who manages all operations; and Julio's son-in-law, Jim Coleman, who supervises production, bottling, and shipping. Ernest himself concentrates on marketing, Julio on the vineyards and wineries, but important company decisions are made only by both brothers. Ernest, poker-faced behind his horn-rimmed glasses, is formidable in any business dealing, and he is cagey; those who seek interviews with him soon discover that he is interviewing them. For four decades he traveled each year through each market where his wines were on sale, often calling on fifty stores a day, watching how his bottles were displayed. Though now a multimillionaire, he still makes store calls wherever he goes. Winemaker Julio tastes wines every day. A farmer and hobbyist organic gardener, he resembles Ernest but is more easygoing, yet doesn't tell you what he is thinking, either.

When the Gallo name first appeared on bottles in 1940, the brothers' goal was to supply the nation with reliable mass-produced wines under a single name, priced for everyday use. But their wines were not yet reliably palatable; troublesome vineyard and winery problems had to be solved. During the early 1940s, many California table wines were unpleasant to drink. Those grown in the San Joaquin Valley often were flat-tasting and oxidized, and many of those in the coast counties were coarse, harsh, or puckery with excessive tannin. In the next fifteen years, the Gallos eliminated those defects. They brought good wines from Napa and Sonoma wineries to improve the taste of their valley table-wine blends. They planted better grape varieties in their vineyards, induced other growers to plant them by offering fifteen-year contracts at guaranteed minimum prices, and established a field staff to guide the growers in planting, cultivating, and harvesting their grapes. The Gallos were the first vintners to launch their own research program. Their staff of research enologists at Modesto is now the biggest at any winery anywhere.

To get rid of unpleasant wine flavors, the Gallos did some revolutionary things. They ripped out all of the wooden cooperage in their winery and replaced it with tanks of stainless steel and epoxy-lined. Some of the discarded redwood tank staves were salvaged in 1957 by their young brother, Livingston grape grower and dairyman Joe Gallo, who built a new house with them; for years afterward, the rooms of his house smelled of wine. To get rid of the mouth-puckering tannin in their press wines (red wines pressed from the pomace after fermentation), they began making Gallo wines entirely from the free-run (unpressed) juice. This inspired their radio-advertising jingle, nationally broadcast in the late 1950s: "Only the first / squeezing of the grapes / goes into Gallo wine." But Gallo Burgundy, when made from only free-run juice, lacked flavor; its taste was too bland. To remedy this, the Gallos then added some press wine—abandoning their "first squeezing" jingle—and in 1964 introduced the new blend as their "Hearty Burgundy," which since has been praised by wine authorities as one of the better California reds. To prevent the oxidized or sherrylike taste caused when wine is exposed to sunlight, the Gallo bottle factory introduced an amber-green "flavorguard" glass, which filters out the damaging ultraviolet rays.

In the 1950s, Gallo was the first American winery to introduce the then-new flavored wines, beginning with Thunderbird in 1957, then their lightly carbonated "pop" wines, starting with types called "Ripple" in 1960, and also wines of apples, strawberries, and pears. Their Boone's Farm apple wine was for a time the largest-selling single wine of any kind in the United States. This created a stir in the world market for that ancient fruit. The Gallos imported apple concentrate from several foreign countries, and in 1972 began planting their own 3000-acre apple orchard near Hopeton in Merced County.

The Gallos entered the champagne field in 1966 and started selling a Gallo brandy named "E & J" in 1968. Their first Charmat-process champagne was named Eden Roc for the fashionable beach club at Cap d'Antibes, but it soon was replaced by another called simply "Gallo Champagne" and then by the lower-priced "André," which now comes in four types and has become the largest-selling sparkling wine brand in the United States. When in the mid-1970s Michigan and New York wineries came out with "Cold Duck" sparkling wines made of Concord grapes, which do not grow well in California, the Gallos knew what to do. They went to the State of Washington for a supply and contracted for the entire output of the grape growers' co-operative at Grandview in the Yakima Valley, which ships them Concord juice in refrigerated tank cars.

Until the 1970s, connoisseurs of the Wine & Food Society rarely discussed or even mentioned Gallo wines because they

The Gallo winery, warehouses, and Gallo bottle factories at Modesto. (*by Ted Streshinsky*)

were all mass-produced, screwcapped rather than corked, and moderate in price. The Gallos were irritated and amused when they heard their connoisseur friends rhapsodize over high-priced imports, in which the Gallos usually could taste flavor defects. They once expressed these feelings rather snidely in a television commercial that said: "Gallo—for the man who doesn't care *what* it costs." Ernest Gallo has his own, original method of judging the quality of wines. He serves many bottles of different wines to a group of consumers, lets them pour for themselves, and keeps watch while the contents of the bottles disappear. He reasons that the wines in the bottles that are emptied soonest must be the best. As for the screwcaps on their bottles versus the corks that premium and foreign wineries used, the Gallos claimed that the screwcaps protected their wines better; that corks don't "breathe" as is generally believed, but only leak.

But, as the wine revolution approached its height in the 1970s, the Gallos saw millions of newly wine-educated Americans buying corked, varietally labeled wines at considerably higher prices than theirs. So in 1974 they introduced seven corked "varietals" of their own with an advertising campaign comparing them to the world's best. Their "varietals," however, included no oak-aged wines, and in particular no Chardonnay or Cabernet Sauvignon. In 1977, the Gallos went the rest of the way. They bought and modernized the century-old Frei Brothers winery west of Healdsburg, which had been making northern Sonoma wines for them; bought the crops of big new Central Coast counties vineyards, and began planting 1200 acres of new "varietal" vineyards on the Frei Brothers' former apple orchards. They had dug an enormous cave in the park beside their office building and bought enough Yugoslavian- and French-oak tanks to age 2.6 million gallons of wine. A new prestige label, "The Wine Cellars of Ernest & Julio Gallo," appeared on their first Johannisberg Riesling and Gewürztraminer in 1979, followed by oak-aged Chardonnay in 1981 and Cabernet Sauvignon, entirely of the 1978 vintage, in 1982. The Gallos had begun entering quality competitions in 1977, winning increasing numbers of awards, and they had always refused to label any of their wines with vintage dates. In 1983, the brothers finally added "1978 vintage" labels to a second batch of their Cabernet Sauvignon.

In the manner of General Motors, many Gallo products in recent years have borne separate company names. When their "varietal" wines put them for the first time into the premium field, the Gallos continued competing in the market for standard table wines with their Carlo Rossi brand, which sells for a fraction of their Cabernet's price. It comes in eight types in both bottles and the "bag-in-box." The label says the wine is "made and bottled by the Carlo Rossi Vineyards, Modesto." But Modesto means Gallo, and Carlo (Charles) Rossi is a Gallo cousin and sales executive. There now are five Boone's Farm low-alcohol "pop" wines, and Spañada and Tyrolia (a perry or pear wine) are still made, but the original "Ripple" is no more.

By 1983, when the fizzy, low-alcohol Lambruscos from Italy had become the largest-selling wines in the United States, the Gallos introduced California counterparts named "Polo Brindisi," the red at 9 percent and the white at 8. At the same time, they responded to the floods of wines imported from Europe by establishing an export subsidiary in England named E. & J. Gallo Winery Europe, Inc.

The former Frei Brothers winery near Healdsburg was renamed "Gallo Sonoma" in 1984, and with 7.6 million gallons capacity was already the largest in the North Coast area. A petition, supported by the Gallos, had been filed with the Federal government to establish "Northern Sonoma" as a viticultural-area appellation of origin.

These developments led to trade speculation that Gallo's premium table wines would soon begin to be estate-bottled at the

Gallo Sonoma winery, and that they eventually would be followed by a Gallo Sonoma *méthode champenoise* champagne.

• 5 •

Winegrowing in Stanislaus County dates from 1854, when George H. Krause from the Rhineland laid out his Red Mountain Vineyard near Knights Ferry, in the foothills some twenty miles east of Modesto. Krause and his successors made good wines before Prohibition, including a sherry in my cellar that is still in fair condition. Their cellar, a tunnel cut into the stone hillside, was again operated briefly after Repeal by Modesto restaurateur Emanuel Galas, who called it the Oakdale Winery. More than a century after Krause, the Gallos adopted "Red Mountain" as a name for their bargain-priced table wines, soon replacing it with their Carlo Rossi brand.

As in the neighboring Manteca-Escalon district of San Joaquin County, wine grapes predominate in the vineyards around Modesto, the Stanislaus County seat. Modesto, incidentally, means "modest." When the site of its railroad station was chosen in 1870, rail magnate Timothy Hopkins offered to name it for his associate, William Ralston, but Ralston declined the honor. Hearing this, a Mexican companion exclaimed, "¡El señor es muy modesto!" The sound of the Spanish word pleased Hopkins, who promptly marked it on the map.

But vineyardists around Modesto are not modest about the quality of their wine grapes, having planted some 6000 new acres of Chenin Blanc, Colombard, Barbera, Ruby Cabernet, Cabernet Sauvignon, Sauvignon Blanc, and Chardonnay since the prices of these "varietals" skyrocketed in the late 1960s. Led by Stanislaus County farm advisor Paul La Vine, the growers have organized a Grape Improvement Association to convince wineries that their grapes are as good as those grown in adjoining San Joaquin County. The argument, however, is more about climate than grapes. The growers' problem is that the university's classification in 1938 of California wine-district climates placed only three Stanislaus districts (Ceres, Hughson, and Vernalis) in Region IV. This seemed to leave Modesto, Salida, and the rest of the county in the hotter Region V. In consequence, they complained, wineries were paying growers $10 a ton less for grapes grown at Salida or Modesto than for those across the Stanislaus River in San Joaquin County, where the Escalon-Manteca district was recognized as in Region IV.

Growers in northern Merced County, Stanislaus's southern

neighbor, claim that they, too, get the cooling afternoon wind from the Delta that accounts for San Joaquin County's classification as Region IV.

In France and Italy, with their hundreds of district appellations of origin for wines, controversies have raged for generations over which vineyards are or are not entitled to label their wines with famous district names, which determine how much each bottle of wine is worth. Now that grape-district boundaries have become an issue in the United States, such questions have begun to be hotly argued here, too.

• 6 •

What did the sons of Joe and John Franzia do when the Franzia Winery was sold in 1971? Within two years, they had built their own JFJ Bronco Winery six miles south of Modesto, their uncle Ernest Gallo's home. The two Js stand for cousins John Junior and Joseph S., and the F stands for Fred T., Joe's younger brother, the president of their firm. Although "Bronco" in Italian means a trunk, stem, bough, or stump, they explain that it is also a colloquial Italian expression for "brothers and cousins," which these Franzias are.

Their Bronco Winery, at Bystrum and Keyes Roads three miles southwest of Ceres, held 38 million gallons in its stainless-steel tanks when I last checked, but it was designed for expansion to 60 million. It produces only table wines and Charmat-process champagnes.

A second 17-million-gallon Bronco Winery, built in 1977 ninety miles southeast in Fresno County, produces only bulk wine, in a joint venture with the $3 billion Getty Oil Company, on whose 9000-acre vineyard it stands. Its production is sold to other vintners, including Bronco at Ceres.

Bronco specializes in young, inexpensive "easy-to-drink" generically and varietally labeled table wines. It sells them under three brands, CC Vineyard, JFJ Winery, and Three Mountains, in bottles, carafes, jugs, and the plastic "bag-in-box." In 1982, the Bronco wineries' production capacity was listed by the *Wines & Vines Directory* as fourth in the United States, behind only Gallo, Heublein, and the Guild.

• 7 •

Merced County, with 1600 acres of vines, is in the upper half of the San Joaquin Valley. Although four-fifths of its vineyards are now planted to wine grapes, this county had no wineries for almost two decades, its few small ones having closed following the Second World War. But in 1970s, when the Gallos' Modesto plant reached its limit of expansion, they built a new 15-million-gallon winery on their vineyard along the south bank of the Merced River, west of Livingston. In the next few years, it was expanded to 100 million gallons, and all the grapes that formerly went to Modesto have since gone to Livingston to be crushed. The Gallos' Livingston vineyard covers 3500 acres.

Next to Merced is Madera County, and then Fresno, which marks the center of the valley vineyard area. Winegrowing began in this part of the valley about 1873, when Francis Eisen from Sweden planted the first commercial vineyard at Fresno and built his winery two years later. Half a dozen more wineries soon sprang up in the neighborhood, including the Eggers, Barton, Margherita, Mattei, and Henrietta estates. In 1880, George West & Son came south from Stockton to Minturn in Madera County and became partners with Thomas Minturn, in the big Sierra Vista vineyard and winery there. Before the turn of the century, the Wests were operating additional wineries at Fresno, Salma, and at Hanford. By 1900, the Italian Swiss Colony of Asti owned a winery at Madera and had built new wineries at Kingsburg and Lemoore.

The most colorful of the pioneer valley vintners was George H. Malter, whose St. George Winery was five miles east of Fresno on Fancher Creek. Malter, born in Germany, had already made a fortune as a mining engineer when he became a winegrower in 1879. He named his vineyard Maltermoro, issued his own scrip or currency, and advertised his wines and brandy as the best in the world. One of his products was a "bathing brandy," which he recommended as a feminine beauty aid.

The early wineries in this region made mostly sweet dessert wines and brandy; their table wines were poor. For this reason, Malter's St. George Winery bought the grapes for its table wines in the cooler coastal districts and fermented them in a northern St. George cellar at Antioch in Contra Costa County.

When Eisen laid out his vineyard at Fresno, one of the grapes he planted was the Muscat of Alexandria, which makes both wine and raisins. When the Thompson Seedless was introduced from Sutter County in the 1890s, Fresno became both the sweet wine and raisin capital of the nation. In 1900, with almost 70,000 acres of vineyards producing wine, raisins, and table grapes, Fresno was the leading vineyard county in the United States, the rank it still holds.

As Dry agitation reached its height in the early 1900s and Prohibition became a threat, the Fresno community preferred to publicize itself as the raisin capital. Its wine and brandy industry, under increasing attack, was not the basis of community pride. When the wineries, idle during the Dry era, reopened at Repeal in 1933, and the coast-counties wine towns revived their wine festivals, Fresno continued to celebrate its annual Raisin Day. This may explain why histories of Fresno County tell only of Eisen's part in founding the raisin industry, and omit mention of his winegrowing career. And descriptions of the county's Kearney Park, seven miles west of Fresno, refer to Kearney as a leader of the raisin industry, but ignore his role as a wine industry pioneer. M. Theo. Kearney was an eccentric man of mystery; his Fresno neighbors never learned his full name. He willed his 5000-acre estate, which he called Château Fresno, to the University of California, which exchanged it after his death for county land near Parlier and built its Kearney Horticultural Field Station there. At Kearney Park, which comprises the remaining 350 acres of Château Fresno, there is nothing to mark the site of the Kearney Winery, which stood near the eastern corner of the estate.

Such bits of local history also help explain why, during three decades following Repeal, wine in the valley was treated as the salvage by-product of the raisin and table grape industries, even when the by-product was using most of the valley grapes. Related facts were the flat, earthy taste of table wines then made in the valley, and that its people, including the vintners, seldom drank wine of any kind.

It was considered impossible to produce acceptable dry table wine in the hot valley climate, and with the coast counties producing more wine following Repeal than they could sell, there was no reason to try. Considerable quantities of "sauterne" and "burgundy" were nevertheless made in the valley, but were blended with table wines from the coast to make them palatable and were sold as "north coast and valley blends." Yet Almond R. Morrow, the great wine taster of the old California Wine Association, told me at the time of Repeal that "excellent dry wines can be made in the valley if you know how." Professor Hilgard, too, had known how, but had failed to convince the vintners that in sunny California, unlike Europe, grapes for good table wines must be harvested early, before their sugar content becomes too high and their acidity too low.

For thirty years after Repeal, the valley wineries continued paying the grape growers a premium for each extra degree of sugar content in their fruit. Grape prices per ton were based on "22 Balling, plus or minus $1 for each sugar point above or below 22." Moreover, the big wineries delayed buying grapes until after September 20, the last day it is considered safe for growers to lay their Thompsons on trays to make raisins without risking damage from early rains. The purpose was to keep the huge annual Thompson surplus out of the wineries by forcing them onto the trays. Table wines made in the valley from grapes harvested in late October or November, sometimes as late as December, did more than Prohibition to make Americans refuse to drink wine and turn to liquor or beer.

The abrupt, complete flip-flop that occurred in the San Joaquin Valley grape industry in less than a decade was partially described in Chapter 12. But not until the mid-1960s, when national consumption of table wines was about to exceed that of dessert wines, and the coast counties no longer could produce enough to supply the mounting demand, did the big vintners in the lower valley begin to realize that they were doing everything wrong. The demand for better table wines compelled them to learn the lesson of early harvesting that Hilgard had tried to teach eighty years before. Now, September instead of October has become the start of harvest season for wine in the valley, and some grapes for table wine are picked as early as the beginning of August. Now, farmers who previously grew only raisin and table grapes have planted the table-wine "varietals" that are newly in demand. For the first time in this century, people in the valley are beginning to realize that the main product of their vineyards is neither raisins nor table grapes, but wine and brandy, which now utilize three-fifths of the entire California grape crop.

Equally important is the revolution taking place in winemaking, for the valley wineries have adopted radically new production methods and installed refrigeration and other equipment needed to produce acceptable dry table wines. "Since I began making really good dry wine," the veteran winemaker at one of the major valley wineries confided to me in the early 1970s, "I've begun drinking it with my dinner every night."

• 8 •

The first fine table wines to be grown, bottled, and labeled as local products in Region V came in 1962 from the little Ficklin

Vineyard winery, on Avenue 7½, seven miles south of Madera.*
Fourteen years earlier, the late Walter Ficklin, a wealthy farmer
and wine buff, with his Davis-trained sons, Walter, Jr., and David, had built his 40,000-gallon cellar with the idea of making
one superior wine. Believing that the only fine wine that could
be grown in Region V would have to be either a port or a sherry,
they chose port. They obtained cuttings of Tinta Madeira, Tinta
Cão, Souzão, and other superior port varieties from the university, and made some of the finest ports thus far produced in
the United States. But, needing some table wine for their own
use, the Ficklins also planted an acre of Professor Harold Olmo's
then-new hybrid Vinifera grapes for hot climates, Emerald Riesling and Ruby Cabernet. They picked these grapes in mid-August
and fermented them at low temperatures. Soon their neighbors
and visiting connoisseurs, who came to buy their port, were
also buying all the table wine the Ficklins could produce. Introduced to San Franciscans at a gourmet banquet in the Hotel
St. Francis in 1965, Ficklin Emerald Riesling 1962 was chosen
by many of those present in preference to a château-bottled
white Bordeaux. Their Ruby Cabernet has since proved even
better than their white. The Ficklins still make only enough
table wine to sell at the winery, because they are too busy supplying the mounting demand for their ports, of which there are
two kinds. Their Tinta Port is a *solera* of all the vintages since
1948; the others are limited bottlings of vintage ports, obtainable
only direct from the winery. Both kinds in my cellar have developed greater bouquet with each passing year.

At the Avenue 9 exit from Highway 9, six miles south of
Madera, there is a 3-million-gallon winery that has shown even
more impressively than the Ficklins that Almond Morrow was
right when he said "excellent dry wines can be made in the
valley if you know how." Angelo Papagni has astonished the
wine world and contradicted the opinions of experts about Region V grapes, with the fine table wines he has produced in
his Papagni Vineyards winery since it was built in 1973.

In his temperature-controlled cellar, with the latest equipment
provided by modern technology, Papagni has made estate-bottled, vintage-dated but medium-priced table wines that are winning prizes in competitions and praises from many connoisseurs.
His Chenin Blancs, dry and medium-dry, his Zinfandels and

*From 1956 to 1968, Horace Lanza's Cal-Grape winery near Delano produced and bottled
small quantities of a creditable dry red table wine from the Italian Nebbiolo grape,
but the Nebbiolo label gave the company's San Francisco address.

Barbera, are being compared favorably to coast-counties wines. But Papagni's most surprising wine is a full-bodied, flavorful "varietal" of Alicante Bouschet, a grape hitherto scorned by everyone except those home winemakers who prize it only for its red juice. His three Charmat-process champagnes include a delicious equivalent of Italy's Asti Spumante that he calls Spumante d'Angelo, and its Muscat flavor is equally delicate in his nonsparkling Moscato d'Angelo and in a drier version named Muscat Alexandria.

Angelo credits the quality of his wines to the way his father, from Bari in southeastern Italy, taught him from boyhood to grow table and wine grapes for shipment across the United States. "As growers of 3000 acres of grapes mainly for sale fresh, we have to know how to manage the vines," he says. "We do it by the way and the times we irrigate; we balance nature with added moisture. We neither overcrop nor undercrop, and we don't rush the grapes; we know just when to pick." But there is still another explanation for the smooth tastes of his red wines: His winery is one of the few in the valley that age all their reds in 50-gallon oak barrels.

The Papagni winery offers tours by appointment, but at this writing had not yet added a tasting room. The winemaker is John Daddino, a veteran trained at three of the older valley wineries. Papagni's wife Blanche and their daughters Kathy and Dana help in the office. The winery also produces a white wine named Fu Jin for Chinese restaurants, several table wines sold in plastic bags, and *enocianina*, the grape dye that is used in perfumes, baby food, and to label meat.

Another ultramodern new Madera winery is the 10-million-gallon, Seagram-owned Paul Masson "sherry cellar" near Berenda, fifteen miles northwest of Papagni. Masson, headquartered at Saratoga in Santa Clara County, produces more table and "light" wines than sherry in this winery, built in 1974. It is designed to be doubled in capacity when wine sales require.

• 9 •

On Avenue 13, four miles southwest of Madera, is the Heublein 43-million-gallon Madera winery, once known as Mission Bell. Its 120-foot-high distillery tower dominates the landscape for miles around. With its lately added champagne cellar and bottle factory, this winery now is almost as big as Gallo's Modesto plant. It is not open to visitors, either, but is worth the side trip from Madera to see it from the outside.

This winery has had many owners. Before Prohibition, it belonged to the Italian Swiss Colony, until the Colony was absorbed by the California Wine Association. During the Dry years, the winery was purchased and named Mission Bell by Krikor Arakelian, the onetime melon king of California, who had become one of the biggest grape growers in the state. Arakelian, who came to America in 1895 from Armenia with five dollars in his pocket, made Mission Bell after Repeal the second-largest independent winery in the nation, then sold it in 1949 for $3.25 million to Louis Petri, who in turn sold it two years later to the Allied Grape Growers co-op. Then came Heublein, the Hartford, Connecticut, firm that John Martin had built from a small manufacturer of "A-1" meat sauce into one of the world's largest marketers of vodka, premixed cocktails, rum, tequila, cordials, beer, and European wines. And as mentioned earlier, Heublein in 1982 became a subsidiary of R. J. Reynolds (tobacco) industries.

Heublein, after buying United Vintners from Allied Grape Growers in 1968, made this its biggest winery. Made here are the much-advertised Inglenook Navalle wines (but not those called Inglenook Estate or Vintage), and such flavored wines as Jacaré and T. J. Swann. Also under the Inglenook name, Heublein sells table wines in beer kegs to restaurants, which dispense it, like beer, by the glass or carafe.

Two miles east of Heublein is the 6-million-gallon Bisceglia Brothers winery, since 1974 a subsidiary of the Sands family's group of wineries at Canandaigua, New York, Petersburg, Virginia, and Patrick, South Carolina. The Bisceglia family began producing wine at San Jose in 1888 and operated wineries at St. Helena and Fresno before taking over this, the former Yosemite Co-operative cellar. Besides shipping blending wines to the Sandses, it markets bottled California wines and champagnes under such brands as Bisceglia and Alfonse F. Bisceglia.

The newest and smallest Madera winery uses no Madera grapes. Andrew Quady, a Davis-trained former Lodi winemaker, who until 1981 worked as a process engineer at the Heublein winery, built this 35,000-gallon cellar in 1977 behind his home, a half-mile away, to pursue his spare-time hobby of producing vintage port from Zinfandel grapes he brings from Amador County. To arrest fermentation, he uses an aromatic brandy distilled for him at Lodi. In 1980, he added another dessert wine specialty, a 15 percent Orange Muscat he calls "Essensia," and followed it with a Black Muscat wine.

A seventh Madera County winery, to be named "Domaine

St. Jean-Marie," is planned during the 1980s by Mrs. Carolyn Peck, a daughter of the late valley farm leader Russell Giffen, on her young vineyard of premium wine-grape varieties on Highway 41, south of Route 145, in the foothills west of Millerton Lake.

Vineyards in Madera County increased from 35,000 to 86,000 acres during the 1970s rush to plant table-wine "varietals" in the San Joaquin Valley. Half are now wine-grape varieties.

• 10 •

Fresno County, with 210,000 acres of vineyards, four-fifths of them raisin and table grapes, has twenty-two wineries. They are a surprising assortment of sizes and kinds. Only a few bottle what they produce, and still fewer invite the public to visit their cellars.

Passengers on airliners approaching Fresno Airport can see three of the large wineries strung along Clovis Avenue, north and south of the field. The clump of enormous wine tanks a mile south is Gallo's Fresno winery, which now holds 92 million gallons, almost as much as in the Modesto plant. On its site in 1890, Benjamin Woodworth established his Las Palmas Vineyard, which he named for the line of palms that led to his estate. At Repeal, the Cribari family of San Jose bought the old wooden cellar and resumed making wine there until 1954, when Gallo bought and replaced it with tanks of steel. Each season now, this single winery crushes more than 300,000 tons of grapes.

Directly across McKinley Avenue from the airfield is the 4-million-gallon former Cameo winery, built by Harry Hitzl and associates in 1938. After the Second World War, it became part of the Alta Vineyards Company, which sued the city for damages when the airport was built next door, claiming that the vibrations of plane motors disturbed the aging wines (the suit was lost). When Alta merged with the Guild of Lodi in 1962, this winery became the principal Fresno cellar of the Guild.

Two miles north of the airfield stood the La Paloma Winery, with its handsome ivy-clad tower, built for vineyardist M. F. Tarpey by his son Arthur in 1910. During the Second World War, National Distillers bought La Paloma and added its output to that of the Italian Swiss Colony, then sold it, with the winery at Asti, to Petri's United Vintners, from which it was acquired by the Heublein conglomerate. In 1983, it was emptied of its wine tanks, and word spread that it was for sale. All that remains to recall the Tarpey family is the adjoining Tarpey Village housing tract.

To the wine tourist, the most interesting of the big Fresno cellars is the B. Cribari & Sons cellar—formerly the Roma Winery—at Church and East avenues in the city's industrial district. The huge casks in its great air-conditioned oak cellar are among the most spectacular in the state. When the Guild Company of Lodi bought Roma from Schenley Distillers in 1971, the bottling of Roma wines was moved to the Guild cellars at Lodi, where the Guild bottles Cribari and all (except Cresta Blanca) of the Guild's various wine and spirit brands. Since 1976 the big tasting room of the Fresno cellar, open daily, has featured mostly the twenty-eight Cribari table, dessert, and sparkling wines and some of those under the various other Guild brands.

Albert Cribari, the eldest grandson of Cribari founder Benjamin, is the Guild's vice president and winemaster, working with UC Berkeley–trained Elie Skofis, vice president for production, whose career with the Italian Swiss Colony, Schenley, Roma, and Guild dates from 1946. Before the Second World War, the House of Cribari, founded in 1904, owned thousands of acres in the Santa Clara Valley and operated wineries at Madrone, Fresno, and New York City.

The story of the Cella family, who owned this winery when it was called Roma, parallels that of the Petris. John Battista Cella and his brother Lorenzo came to the United States in 1898 from Bardi, in northern Italy. They worked as waiters in a New York restaurant, then went into the wholesale grocery business. They bought their cigars and wine from Raffaello Petri and Dante Foresti, whom Battista visited on trips to California. Three years before National Prohibition began, Battista bought the old Scatena wineries at Lodi, Manteca, and Healdsburg from Foresti, and made Roma sacramental wine through the Dry era, while Lorenzo stayed in New York to handle the sales. Then, when Lodi vineyardists began building their co-op wineries, Battista moved from Lodi to the then Santa Lucia winery at Fresno, renamed it Roma, and made his headquarters here. In 1942, the king of Schenley Distillers, Lewis Rosenstiel, bought Roma and Cresta Blanca. (These are events I especially remember because Rosenstiel then summoned me to his winter home at Tucson to give him a complete education in wine in three days. Rosenstiel thereupon tried unsuccessfully to convert the state's vintners to his liquor-selling ideas.) Cella soon resigned from Roma, and in 1944 bought the Rusconi vineyard and winery near Wahtoke, east of Sanger, which he renamed Cella Vineyards and expanded to 12 million gallons. It later was owned by United Vintners, then by Heublein, and now by Allied Grape Growers to make ISC Wines.

The oldest winery in Fresno County is the one at Lacjac, between Reedley and Parlier. Since 1945, it has been the Mount Tivy or Reedley winery of The Christian Brothers of Napa; the Brothers produce and bottle their dessert wines and brandy there. Originally this was the Sanford winery (named for Sanford Samuel), but nobody seems to know when it was built. In 1899, Lachman & Jacobi, the San Francisco wine merchants who then were fighting the California Wine Association's attempt to monopolize the state's wine supply, bought and enlarged the Sanford cellar to 1 million gallons and began to make their own wine. They later were absorbed by the CWA. At Repeal, Fresno Assemblyman Lucius Powers and associates reopened the old winery and changed its name from Lacjac to Mount Tivy, for a mountain named for an early settler of the county. During the Second World War, Seagram bought it from an intermediate owner and at the end of the conflict sold it to The Christian Brothers. Today the great cellars and the clusters of new outdoor stainless-steel tanks hold 4 million gallons of aging dessert wines, and the big distillery, with its continuous and pot stills, makes the Brothers' brandies, which long outsold all others in the United States. The Brothers own a thousand acres of vineyards in the vicinity, in which they grow three dozen wine-grape varieties. Included are Tinta Madeira for their port wines and the Muscat Canelli or Frontignan grape, which accounts in part for the delicacy of their Château La Salle sweet white table wine.

In the center of Sanger, twelve miles east of Fresno, is the 5-million-gallon Gibson winery, which also owns the Gibson winery at Elk Grove and ships the wines from Sanger for bottling there. Originally it was a co-op of 140 members, formed in 1945 as the Sanger Winery Association.

At Monmouth, a crossroads on the county map between Caruthers and Selma, are several acres of stainless-steel tanks and warehouses that resemble an army depot. This is the 19.6-million-gallon Vie-Del Company, headed by Massud Shahim Nury. It makes more than a dozen different winy products, but under the Vie-Del name sells only its trio of bottled "Wine Chef" dealcoholized concentrated wine flavors (sherry, sauterne, burgundy) for gourmet cookery. Another interesting product is blending-sherry, of which Vie-Del, partly owned by Seagram, is the nation's chief supplier. This is the heavy-bodied sherry that is blended with fine whiskeys, brandies, and rums, and accounts for their smooth taste. But the main product at Vie-Del is brandy. Its heady aroma can be breathed in the air at Monmouth, for almost 15 million gallons of it—the biggest concentration of brandy in the world—is aging in barrels in the warehouses for other producers, who have their brandy made or aged here.

On Central Avenue, between Cornelia and Chateau Fresno avenues, is the second Bronco Winery of the Franzia sons and cousins, mentioned earlier. It was built in 1977 on the 9000-acre vineyard planted five years earlier by the Getty Oil Company. Harvesting is done by machines that pick the grapes from two rows of vines at a time.

There are two wineries in the Kerman area of western Fresno County. The million-gallon former Morello cellar on Modoc Avenue in Kerman is now the Villa Bianchi or Bianchi Vineyards winery. Joseph Bianchi has modernized it to make six types of table wines, which he sells in cans, bottles, and jugs. Southeast of Kerman, adjoining the 3600 acres of "varietal" grapes planted in the late 1960s for the Noble Land & Cattle Company, is the 3-million-gallon Noble or Tuxpan winery, a stemmer-crusher and refrigerated tanks of stainless steel, which converts grapes, minutes after picking, into bulk table wines for shipment to a dozen wineries in other parts of the state.

In contrast to the giant valley wineries is the old-fashioned, 100,000-gallon cellar of the Nonini family, on their 200-acre vineyard on Dickenson Avenue in the Rolinda district, eight miles northwest of Fresno. When Antonio Nonini began making table wine in 1936, his principal customers were Basque sheepherders, who came down from the mountains each year to have their barrels filled with his dry burgundy, made from his Barbera grapes. Now that table wine has become a popular drink in the valley, numerous Fresno householders have begun emulating the Basque sheepherders, buying Nonini wines not only in bottles and jugs, but also in small barrels, which they bring back to be refilled at the bargain barrel-price.

Also unique is the 210,000-gallon cellar of the Nicholas G. Verry family, opposite the railroad tracks in the town of Parlier. The Verrys make retsina, the resin-flavored wine that is popular among the Greeks. Their other specialty is a light white wine they call Philery, which means "quick love" in Greek.

Between Selma and Kingsburg, the raisin-growing centers along Highway 99, is the onetime Italian Swiss Colony Kingsburg cellar, which became Schenley's after Louis Martini moved to the Napa Valley; it is now owned by Almadén of Los Gatos. The 7-million-gallon onetime Muscat Co-operative Winery, a mile north of there, is now operated by Vie-Del.

Worth a stop to take an instructive tour offered the public

on weekdays is the Sun-Maid Growers raisin-processing plant, on Bethel Avenue, two miles northwest of Kingsburg. It is the biggest of its kind in the world. Sun-Maid was organized in 1912, and during the First World War promoted its 5-cent package of raisins at candy counters with the slogan "Have you had your iron today?"—until it was stopped by the discovery that raisins contain very little iron. For many years, any mention that grapes also make wine was taboo in promoting the sale of Sun-Maid raisins. At Sun-Maid, you were told a legend of how the Fresno raisin industry began. In 1873, the story goes, an unprecedented hot spell dried Francis Eisen's grapes on his vines before he could pick them. (Omitted from the story was that Eisen's purpose in growing grapes was to make them into wine.) According to the legend, Eisen salvaged the heat-shriveled fruit by shipping it to a San Francisco grocer, who, inspired by the arrival that morning of a ship from Peru, put them on sale as "Peruvian delicacies." Soon the grocer was regularly sending Eisen orders for more. The taboo was finally lifted in 1978, when Sun-Maid entered the wine business, buying the 3-million-gallon one-time Del Rey co-op winery on Central Avenue, near Malaga. There Sun-Maid now makes bulk table and dessert wines, grape juice and concentrate, and highproof brandy.

· 11 ·

The Fresno area ranks next to Davis as a center of vinicultural teaching and research. There are two Federal experimental vineyards, one at Clovis, the other on Peach Avenue, in the southeastern outskirts of Fresno. On Manning Avenue near Parlier is the University of California's big Kearney Horticultural Field Station, where all kinds of vineyard problems are explored and where Dr. Harold Olmo first tested his new wine-grape hybrids for Region V. There is still another UC fruit-testing station at Five Points, on the west side of the valley.

Research is combined with the teaching of grape growing, winemaking, and raisin production at Fresno State University. Almost a third of the 600-acre campus on Shaw Avenue in northeastern Fresno is occupied by the university vineyard. Adjoining it is a 5000-gallon model winery, built in 1958 despite vehement protests by the local Drys. More than 150 students major in viticulture and in enology, and graduate students participate in research. Fresno State graduates manage vineyards and wineries throughout the United States and in two dozen other countries; the demand for them is greater than the school can fill.

Vincent Petrucci, an Escalon farm boy and onetime high school football coach, has headed the Fresno viticulture program since 1947, when he got his Master's degree at UC under Drs. Winkler and Olmo. Although Fresno lacks the scientific staff UC has at Davis, Petrucci has pioneered several research projects that have contributed to the improvement of valley wines. He believes the wine grapes now planted in the San Joaquin Valley can supply most of the nation's "better than average" table wines. The enology–food science course at Fresno is taught by UC Berkeley–trained Dr. Fred S. Nury and Davis-trained Dr. Carlos Muller, with the help of winemaker Kenneth Fugelsang. Each student is taught wine tasting and analysis and learns to make all of the principal still and sparkling wine types. What troubles Dr. Nury is having to destroy the wines his students make, a requirement of the Federal law that governs colleges' experimental wine cellars. "We at least ought to be allowed to sell our wines to the wineries instead of pouring it all down the drain," Dr. Nury says. The university does sell the grapes the students produce as part of their viticulture course. Each student is assigned five acres to farm, and shares in the profit when the fruit is sold. Some earn as much as several hundred dollars in a season.

• 12 •

Tulare County, with 85,718 acres of vines, almost four-fifths of them table-grape and raisin varieties, is second only to Fresno in the extent of its vineyards. Its wineries range from 17 million gallons down to 6000 gallons in size.

Largest is the Sierra winery on Highway 63, northeast of Tulare. It strikingly exemplifies the evolution of the valley wine industry during the present century. Back in 1904, Frank Giannini from the island of Elba owned a vineyard here and made wine for himself and his friends. His favorite was a dry wine of Aleatico, the red Muscat grape of Elba. Giannini had so many thirsty friends that he built a winery, which he named for Tulare, to sell them his wines. After his death in 1944, the winery had a series of owners until the Sierra Wine Corporation acquired it in 1963. By adding the onetime Cal-Grape winery at Trocha in 1970 and the Perelli-Minetti winery at Delano in 1981, Sierra became for a time the world's largest producer of bulk wine, also making grape concentrate, beverage, and highproof brandy, and (at Delano) champagne and vermouth, besides. At its Tulare plant the principal product is bulk table wine. An exception is one specialty of Sierra's production boss, Philip Posson. In the former Giannini home, which has been turned into a tasting room, you can sample "Philip Posson Dry Flor Sherry," a favorite of many California connoisseurs. When he began making it in 1964 by the submerged-culture *flor* process, Sierra became the first American winery to produce sherry on a commercial scale by this method, invented in Canada. Posson ages it in fifty-gallon barrels outdoors, where he says sherry flavor improves because it cools at night and warms during the day. He supplies it by tank truck to other California producers, who use it in their dry sherry blends. Also sold at the Tulare tasting room are Sierra's assortment of "Mission Valley" table wines and Charmat-process champagnes. The latter are made at the Bella Rosa Winery, where Sierra leases some of the space.

At Calgro, beside the tiny Armenian village of Yettem (Armenian for Garden of Paradise) on Highway 201, four miles south of Cutler, is the 10-million-gallon California Growers Winery, established in 1936 by the late raisin industry leader, Arpaxat (Sox) Setrakian. In 1972, his son Robert introduced bottled wines, champagne, and brandy under such brands as Growers, Bounty Vineyards, and L. Le Blanc.

Two other Tulare County wineries are hobby-size operations. On Avenue 306 near Exeter, fifteen miles northeast of Tulare, Newport Beach dentist Dr. Donald Anderson and his wife Catherine have been producing estate-bottled vintage-dated Chenin Blanc and Ruby Cabernet at their twenty-acre vineyard and 10,000-gallon Anderson Wine Cellars since 1980. Near Springville, fifteen miles southeast of the Andersons, financial consultant Glenn L. Wallace and his wife Marjorie bonded their 6000-gallon Arbor Knoll Winery in 1983, to make wine from a white grape that they alone grow on a four-acre vineyard and that they have named "Glennel." By arrangement with the University of California, Wallace has exclusive rights to this grape, a cross of Sémillon with Folle Blanche, bred by UC viticulturist Harold Olmo in collaboration with the late professor and brandy expert James Guymon.

• 13 •

Kern County, where the San Joaquin Valley ends in the foothills of the Tehachapi Mountains, had 90,000 acres of vineyards, almost half of it wine varieties, in 1982, centered between Delano and Wheeler Ridge. This is John Steinbeck country, the setting of his Pulitzer Prize–winning novel of 1940, *The Grapes of Wrath*. Thompsons and table grapes once comprised most of the county's

Antonio Perelli-Minetti, who was the oldest pre-Prohibition wine-grower when he died in 1976 at the age of ninety-five.

grape acreage, but almost half of it is now wine grapes planted since 1972. There are six big wineries in the county, but those across the Tulare County line at Trocha are regarded as within the Delano district, making a total of nine in the area. Around Trocha, five miles northeast of Delano, are the 5-million-gallon Delano Growers Co-op Winery, the 15-million-gallon former Cal-Grape Winery mentioned earlier, and the smaller onetime Del Vista cellar, which is now the L. K. Marshall Winery of the Guild.

Three miles south of Delano, at the Pond Road exit from Highway 99, is the 14-million-gallon former Perelli-Minetti Winery and tasting room, which was bought by the Sierra Wine Corporation in 1981 and resold two years later to a group of large valley grape growers, who renamed it the Bella Rosa Winery.

The colorful career of Antonio Perelli-Minetti had covered seven decades of California and Mexican wine history when he died in 1976 at the age of ninety-five, the oldest pre-Prohibition vintner then active in the state. He came to California in 1902 from Barletta, on the Adriatic coast of southern Italy, where his father owned two wineries, to make wine for the Italian Swiss Colony at Asti in Sonoma County. Later, he worked at Healdsburg and Livermore wineries, then went broke attempting in a partnership wine-selling venture at San Francisco to compete with the giant CWA. Told by a visiting Mexican vintner that he could recoup his fortunes quickly in Mexico, Perelli went there in 1910 and was hired to plant a vineyard near Torreón. In his sixth year below the border, the chaos of the Mexican Revolution compelled Perelli to return to California, where he settled at Ukiah. When Prohibition began in 1920, he made a grape syrup called Caligrapo, which bore an inviting label: "When diluted, do not store in a warm place because it will ferment, which is against the law." Repeal found him growing wine at Delano, where he built the present winery in 1936. His was one of the original members of Fruit Industries, which at the height of its power in 1950 resumed the name of the old California Wine Association. When the members of the CWA represented by its "Eleven Cellars" brand dropped out one by one, only the Perelli-Minetti winery remained. It then owned more than 200 famous wine and brandy brands of the past, some of which were licensed to another Kern County winery in 1982.

South of the Perelli–later–Sierra–now–Bella Rosa plant is the newest winery in Kern County, the 4-million-gallon establishment named ASV Wines, built in 1981. A mass of stainless-steel tanks, it makes bulk table wine and grape juice, which are shipped, refrigerated, in insulated tank trucks to wineries and other buyers in California, other states, and Canada. Its owner, grape grower Marko Zaninovich, whose cousin Vincent owns the Zaninovich brandy distillery at Orange Cove, says "ASV" refers to his Arroyo Seco Vineyard in Monterey County.

At Highway 99 and Whistler Road, south of McFarland, is the 9.4-million-gallon California Mission winery, built for rancher Hollis B. Roberts in 1974 and now owned by Almadén Vineyards of Los Gatos.

Six miles east of Bakersfield, facing Edison Highway at Edison Road, is the 12-million-gallon Giumarra Vineyards winery, which was built in 1946 to make bulk dessert wines and grape concentrate, but began producing vintage-dated "varietal" table wines in 1973. Giuseppe (Joe) Giumarra came to America from Sicily, sold bananas from a pushcart in Toronto, brought his family to Bakersfield, bought a ranch, and by the 1960s became the biggest shipper of fresh grapes in the United States. Joe continued rising at six each weekday morning to spend his day in the 8000-acre vineyard behind the winery. Meanwhile, his younger brother, John Giumarra, put them into the bottled-wine business, building a 3-million-gallon, air-conditioned addition to the bulk cellar and adding a tasting room. The Giumarras grow 1000 acres of "varietals" in their vineyards bordered by

Breckenridge Road. Their assortment of twenty "GV" wines, introduced in 1978, includes generics as well as "varietals" and also "mountain" wines in bottles, decanters, various-sized jugs, and plastic pouches for the restaurant trade.

Adjoining the post office named Di Giorgio, which maps show at Comanchee and Di Giorgio roads, ten miles southeast of Bakersfield, is the 36-million-gallon La Mont Winery. It has a tasting room. Since 1978, it has been owned by John Labatt, Ltd., the big Canadian brewing company, which also owns three wineries in Canada and ships them tank trucks of wines, brandy, and concentrate from here.

Grape growing at this end of the valley began in 1888, when the waters of the Kern River were diverted for irrigation. To Kern County in 1919 came the fabulous Giuseppe (Joseph) Di Giorgio, the Sicilian immigrant who rose from an eight-dollar-a-week clerk for a New York fruit jobber at the age of fourteen to become, at thirty-seven, the biggest grower and marketer of fresh fruits in the world. Di Giorgio began planting grapes around Delano, where predecessors were already cultivating 7000 acres of vines. Then he went exploring farther south in a virtual desert near Arvin, then known as "the weed patch." He found underground water, which eventually supplied 5600 acres. This is the vineyard district that is now Di Giorgio on the map. During Prohibition, Joe controlled the fruit auctions in eastern cities, where California grapes were bought by home winemakers and bootleggers. At Repeal he established his own wineries at Kerman in Fresno County and at Di Giorgio. When he died in 1951, he owned almost fourteen square miles of vineyards, more than anyone else in the world. Joe, who had no sons, sold the entire output of his wineries in bulk to bottlers and to other wineries. His nephews tried selling it in bottles, buying the old Santa Fe, Padre, and Vai Brothers brand names, acquiring bottling cellars in Los Angeles, and introducing "the Di Giorgio family of fine wines." After six years they gave that up, selling the brands to Petri's United Vintners, and resumed selling the wines in bulk. Then, because irrigation water reaching that part of the valley in Federal projects from the north was denied to single owners of more than 160 acres, they began disposing of the Di Giorgio vineyards. They sold the winery in 1966 to a new Bear Mountain grape growers' co-operative, named for a nearby peak in the Greenhorn Mountains. Bear Mountain in 1969 was the first Kern County winery to bottle its own line of wines. The bottle labels seldom mentioned the Di Giorgio address, but gave it as Lamont, which is four miles west of the winery.

In 1982, the LaMont Winery obtained from the Perelli-Minetti family a license to sell its wines and brandies under such old CWA brands as Guasti, Ambassador, A. R. Morrow, Aristocrat, and Victor Hugo, adding these to the Bear Mountain wine, champagne, and vermouth brands, which include M. LaMont, Mountain Gold, and Gold Peak. Added in 1982 were "Di Giorgio Vineyards FreshPak" table wines in the 4-liter "bag-in-box." Also in 1982, the giant Anheuser-Busch brewing firm of St. Louis entered the wine business by contracting for the LaMont Winery to supply "Master Cellars" table wines to the brewery's distributors in surplus stainless-steel draft-beer kegs. The kegged wines were sold to restaurants and bars for dispensing, chilled like draft beer, as "house wines."

The smallest Kern County winery is a 6000-gallon experimental cellar on Laval Road at Arvin, four miles south of Di Giorgio. It adjoins the 7000-acre Tejon Ranch vineyard, planted since 1973. Partly owned by the Los Angeles Times-Mirror Company, Tejon Ranch occupies 450 square miles in southeastern Kern County. It is the largest private landholding in the state.

20

_____

Wines of Other Western States

WHEN Dr. Konstantin Frank introduced his New York State Johannisberg Riesling and Chardonnay wines in 1965, writers of articles in national magazines heralded the news as a sensation, because to them this meant that California no longer was the only state that could grow the true Vinifera wine grapes of Europe.

What none of them seemed to notice was that Vinifera grapes had been growing during much of this century in Washington, Oregon, and Idaho. The reason these northwestern states were ignored was that they had not yet produced any fine wines of European types.

Beginning in the early 1970s, a virtual explosion of Vinifera-planting and winery-building has occurred in these states in response to "the wine revolution," in which table-wine consumption has quadrupled nationally and in the Northwest over the 1960s rate. Accompanying the explosion has been a radical improvement in the quality of northwestern wines. Vinifera "varietals" from these states are winning acceptance on the national market because they already rival California's and Europe's best.

· 2 ·

The State of Washington overtook New York State in grape production with a harvest of 159,000 tons in 1982, and became third after California and New York in wine production, with almost 4 million gallons made in that year. Eight thousand of the state's 28,000 acres of vineyards were Vinifera varieties planted since 1970, and more Vinifera were being planted at the rate of 1000 acres per year. The rest were Concords, mechanically harvested for fresh grape juice or jelly, or shipped as juice

459

to California wineries to make their Cold Ducks and "pop" wines. Washington wineries increased in number from three in 1968 to forty-seven by 1984, and still more were preparing to start. Washington-grown Vinifera grapes also were being shipped to other states and to British Columbia to be made into wines.

Grape growing in Washington began during the 1860s in the Walla Walla Valley and a decade later in the Puget Sound area, where Confederate Civil War veteran Lambert B. Evans planted vines on Stretch Island in 1872. The earliest record of Washington wine production is of a winery operated by Frank Orselli, from Lucca in Italy, near Walla Walla in 1876. Meanwhile, to Stretch Island on the Sound about 1890 came Adam Eckert from the Chautauqua Grape Belt of New York, who bred a black Labrusca grape variety he called Island Belle. Planting of Eckert's grape spread to neighboring islands and to the mainland, where a village was founded and named Grapeview.

Around 1906, irrigation water from the Cascade watershed began transforming the Yakima Valley in eastern Washington from an almost rainless desert into a lush fruit-growing region. The Island Belle grape then was brought there from the western part of the state. Grape-juice plants were built at Yakima, Grandview, and Prosser, and the Island Belle soon was displaced by the Concord grape of the East.

At the repeal of the Dry law in 1933, realtor Charles Somers started the St. Charles Winery on Stretch Island, the first in the state since 1876. Then almost overnight, everyone in Washington with so much as a berry patch wanted to build a winery; there were forty-two in operation, including three on Stretch Island, by 1937. Others started along the Columbia River, but the largest ones were at Seattle and in the Yakima Valley.

At Sunnyside, twenty miles down the valley from Yakima, lived a farmer, lawyer, and ex-schoolteacher named William B. Bridgman. Born on a farm beside Jordan Creek on the Niagara Peninsula of Ontario, where his father grew Labrusca grapes, Bridgman came to Sunnyside in 1902 aboard a horse-drawn stage when the valley's principal crop still was sagebrush. He promoted the local irrigation system, was elected mayor of Sunnyside, and became one of the area's principal grape growers. At Repeal, Bridgman built a winery, but he also took time to make a study of California and European vineyards. He concluded that the Yakima Valley climate is better for winegrowing than that of central France, having more and longer days of sunshine, and noted that its latitude (46° north) is midway between the lati-

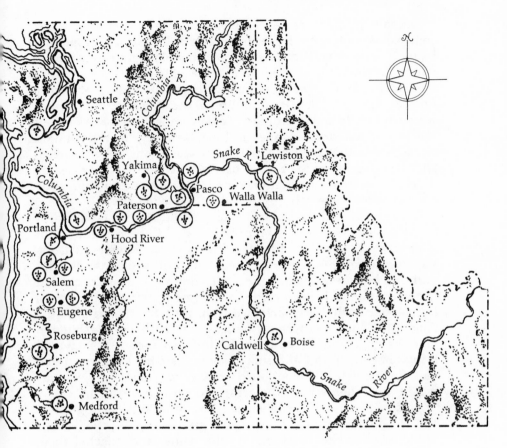

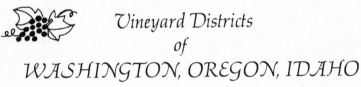

Vineyard Districts
of
WASHINGTON, OREGON, IDAHO

tudes of Burgundy and Bordeaux. This convinced Bridgman that Washington could grow finer European grapes than California could. He imported Vinifera varieties and supplied neighboring growers with cuttings from his vines. He hired a German wine-maker and produced such wines as Johannisberg Riesling and Cabernet. Unfortunately, however—and I recall this because I tasted an assortment that the late Herman Wente brought from Washington during the 1940s—Bridgman's wines were poorly made, and they soon were withdrawn from sale.

Another unfortunate development was the Washington liquor control law, adopted at Repeal, which established state monopoly liquor stores, thus discouraging most people from buying table wines. Washington wineries were allowed to sell directly to taverns, which gave them an advantage over out-of-state wineries. Prospering under their legal umbrella, the Washington vintners were content to make ordinary dessert wines, such as port and sherry, out of Labrusca grapes. In 1965, however, the Washington wineries saw that their protective law was about to be changed, and they persuaded the State University to start a wine research program at its Prosser Station. The law was changed four years later to allow wine sales by privately owned stores.

In 1966, I visited the Yakima Valley and saw several vineyards of such pedigreed wine-grape varieties as Cabernet and Pinot Noir. I was amazed to find the Washington wineries wasting these premium grapes, mixing them with Concord in nondescript port and burgundy blends. The only fine wine I tasted on that trip was a Grenache rosé made by a home winemaker in Seattle. I remarked to the late Victor Allison, then the manager of the American Wine Growers wineries, that perhaps Washington vintners might make some good Vinifera wines if they would bring someone from California to show them how. Allison asked me, "Such as who?" I mentioned a few good winemakers, including André Tchelistcheff, the great enologist of Beaulieu.

Allison persuaded Tchelistcheff to come to Washington in 1967 to discuss the state's winemaking potential. Tchelistcheff tasted most of the Washington table wines and rejected them all. But then a friend of the Seattle home winemaker whom I've mentioned let him sample a Gewürztraminer made from grapes grown in the Yakima Valley. Tchelistcheff was astounded; he pronounced it the finest Gewürztraminer yet produced in the United States. He accepted the challenge to show Washington vintners how to make fine wines.

Tchelistcheff first directed that the Vinifera vines in the American Wine Growers' vineyards be pruned to reduce the crop and to achieve proper sugar-acid balance in the grapes. He returned to Washington that September, selected perfect batches of Cabernet, Pinot Noir, Sémillon, and Grenache, and had them fermented at controlled temperatures. He had the Cabernet stored in American white oak barrels and the Pinot Noir in new Limousin oak from France.

In 1969, I accompanied Tchelistcheff to Seattle to sample his one- and two-year-old Washington wines. We tasted separately, scoring them as unfinished wines, and then compared our notes.

Tchelistcheff gave the 1967 Cabernet seventeen out of a possible twenty points, sixteen to the 1968 Sémillon, and fifteen and sixteen to the two Grenache rosés. The Pinot Noir wasn't yet ready to be tasted. I scored each Cabernet a point higher and my other scores were close to Tchelistcheff's.

A year later bottled samples of these wines, under the American Wine Growers' Ste. Michelle label, were sent to California. The San Francisco Wine Sampling Club rated them as "challenging the quality supremacy of California varietal wines." The new Washington wines were then introduced in a few eastern markets and were enthusiastically praised by connoisseurs.

American Wine Growers was purchased in 1973 by a group of Seattle investors, who resold it a year later to the United States Tobacco Company of Connecticut. Five hundred more acres of Vinifera vineyards were planted thirty miles east of Yakima. An elegant, new 2-million-gallon Ste. Michelle winery was built in 1975, fifteen miles east of Seattle. It is a Bordeaux-style château on an eighty-seven-acre park with trout ponds, footpaths, and picnic tables, off State Route 202 outside Woodinville. Opened in 1976, it offered cellar tours and tasting and received 2000 visitors a day. Grapes were trucked overnight to the winery at Woodinville from the vineyards across the Cascades in eastern Washington, 190 miles away. The company's first champagne, made at Woodinville and called "Blanc de Noir Sparkling Wine Méthode Champenoise," was introduced in the following year. Ste. Michelle continued producing its red wines (now mainly Cabernet and Merlot) at its older winery, on West Fifth Street in Grandview.

By 1978, the company was planting 2000 more acres of premium Vinifera at the junction of Routes 221 and 14 near Paterson, a crossroads inland from the Columbia River, thirty miles southeast of Grandview. The vines, planted in half-mile circles, are irrigated by the same center-pivot system used for wheat and corn in the Northwest.

There, in 1982 Ste. Michelle built a handsome 1½-million-gallon winery named River Ridge, with a spacious public tasting room, stone courtyards, and formal gardens. Half of it is underground, and it is designed eventually to be doubled in size. White grapes are vinified there, then taken to the Woodinville cellar for aging and bottling.

Tchelistcheff flies from California four times a year to taste the wines with Ste. Michelle's California-trained winemaster, Peter L. Bachman, and to visit the company's vineyards with its UC Davis–trained viticulturist, Dr. Wade H. Wolfe.

• 3 •

The home winemaker in Seattle who made the Grenache rosé that I tasted in 1966 was Dr. Lloyd Woodburne, a professor of psychology at the University of Washington in Seattle. In 1951, while at home recovering from a cold, Professor Woodburne happened to pick up a copy of Philip Wagner's first book on home winemaking. Intrigued, Woodburne telephoned his famous wine-buff colleague, Angelo Pellegrini, a professor of English, and asked, "Pelly, how difficult is this winemaking thing?" "Easy as boiling an egg," replied Pellegrini, who makes red wine from the Cabernet grapes he gets from his friends at the Louis Martini vineyards, in California.

Woodburne bought grapes and a barrel and made a batch of Zinfandel. He and his wife managed to drink it, liberally diluted with soda water. Three years later, he made some white wine from Delaware grapes he bought in the Yakima Valley, and invited some of his fellow professors over to sample it. They, too, bought grapes and became home winemakers. Soon, a total of eighteen families around the campus were doing the same. Someone in the group thought of buying a power crusher, which was installed in the Woodburnes' garage. But a lawyer-member, Professor of Law Cornelius Peck, warned against fermenting their grapes together, because the Federal law permits only individual householders to make tax-free wine in their homes.

Another member, Professor Philip Church, made a study of Washington's climates and found that the heat units in the lower Yakima Valley are the same as in Beaune, the center of Burgundy's Côte d'Or. In 1961, ten of the group formed a corporation, Professor Peck supplying the know-how, and bought five acres adjoining Bridgman's vineyard at Sunnyside. Each member was entitled to a tenth share of the grapes. When I tasted Woodburne's rosé in 1966 and found it outstanding, I had suggested that his group ought to start their own winery. A year later, with Tchelistcheff praising their Gewürztraminer (which came from Dr. Church's cellar), the professors took the plunge. They built a small winery in the Seattle suburb of Kirkland and moved the crusher from the Woodburnes' garage in time for the 1967 vintage. In the following May, as the "Associated Vintners," they introduced the 1967 Riesling and Gewürztraminer in a restaurant and in three Seattle gourmet shops. Word reached connoisseurs, who came from a hundred miles away to buy the wines. The 4000-gallon cellar soon became too small, and the professors since have moved twice, once to Redmond and then to Bellevue, another Seattle suburb, where their winery now holds 160,000 gallons. In 1979 they employed famous winemaker David Lake, a Canadian born in England and one of only two persons in the United States who have earned the British title "Master of Wine." They since have sold their vineyard, and now choose their grapes from the best vineyards in the Yakima and Columbia valleys.

• 4 •

Of the dozens of new wineries started in Washington since the mid-1970s, six are in the Yakima Valley, which was granted its own viticultural-area appellation by the Federal government in 1983. First to open there in this decade was the 24,000-gallon Hinzerling Vineyards winery, bonded in 1975 in a former garage on Sheridan Avenue in Prosser. Michael Wallace, an assistant to viticulturist Dr. Walter Clore at the Prosser research station, earned a master's degree in enology at UC Davis and teamed with his father Jerrell, a home winemaker, to start planting their twenty-five-acre vineyard on nearby Hinzerling Road. Michael makes Cabernet, Merlot, Riesling, champagne, a botrytized sweet Gewürztraminer named *der Sonne* (of the sun), and a blend of premium grapes the Wallace family call "Ashfall White." The

You can't see the vines in this December 1969 vineyard scene near Grandview in the Yakima Valley of eastern Washington. The cold-tender Muscat of Alexandria vines were buried with earth after Thanksgiving to protect them from injury during the freezing winter. They were uncovered and tied to the trellis wires in March, when the soil became warm again.

name commemorates the 1980 eruption of Mount St. Helens, 130 miles to the west. The blast coated Yakima Valley vineyards with a film of ash that had to be washed off the leaves.

On North River Road, across the river and west of Hinzerling, is the 14,000-gallon Yakima River Winery. It was started in 1978 by Hanford Nuclear Project welder John Rauner and his wife Louise, and already has won medals for its wines. On Ray Road, off US 12 in the outskirts of Sunnyside, farmers Dean and Rose Tucker have a large fruit stand, half of which they converted in 1981 to the Tucker Wine Cellars, to use the grapes from the twenty-acre Vinifera vineyard they had planted two years before. On Morris Road, five miles north of Zillah, is the handsome 125,000-gallon Quail Run Vintners winery and tasting room, which was rushed to completion in time to crush the 1982 vintage from its adjoining 100 acres of young Vinifera vines. Davis-trained Stan Clarke and winemaker Wayne Marcil run the vineyard and winery for a group of Yakima Valley orchardists. Also bonded that year was the small Hogue Cellars winery, in an industrial park on Meade Road, east of Prosser. Michael and Gary Hogue, who with their family cultivate 1200 acres of grapes, hops, spearmint, and asparagus, plan eventually to produce 150,000 gallons of wine per year. The 4000-gallon Kiona Vineyards winery, beneath the West Richland home of nuclear engineer Jim Holmes and his wife Patricia, was started in 1979. They plan to move it soon to neighboring Benton City, where their partners, nuclear engineer John Williams and his wife Ann, live on a thirty-acre vineyard planted in 1974. In 1982, the Kiona Vineyards winery became the nation's first to introduce a "varietal" wine of the spicy German red grape named Limberger. Viticulturist Dr. Clore recommends Limberger (which the Kiona winery spells "Lemberger") for planting in eastern Washington, but other vintners have been reluctant to use it because the name might remind people of that highly aromatic cheese.

· 5 ·

When the Federal government approved "Yakima Valley" as a viticultural-area appellation, it agreed to consider also approving an appellation for Walla Walla Valley, which is thirty-five miles to the east. Meanwhile, Chateau Ste. Michelle, with its River Ridge vineyard and winery at Paterson, proposed a "Columbia Valley" appellation, which would cover most of eastern Washington's other vineyard areas, including one where a major

West German wine company has built a winery, and the Snake River Valley, where the largest Concord vineyards are.

The West German project is the 500,000-gallon Franz Wilhelm Langguth Winery, built in 1982 on the Wahluke Slope a mile north of Highway 24, four miles north of the Columbia and six miles east of Mattawa, the *Weinbau*'s post office address. It is on a 230-acre, drip-irrigated vineyard, planted a year earlier in a joint venture with the Seattle investors who, a decade earlier, planted the 500 acres of spectacular Sagemoor, Bacchus, and Dionysus vineyards on the river shore, fifteen miles to the south. Langguth, with its home winery at Traren-Trarbach on the Mosel, is one of Germany's largest producers. To make Langguth Washington wines, it chose Swiss-born and -trained Max Zellweger, from the Château Benoit winery in Oregon. Its first, made from purchased grapes and released in 1983, were German-style Rieslings, an extra-dry at 11 percent and a late-harvest at 9.5. A third white and a red blend were to be sold under Langguth's "Erben" label in the following year.

Another Columbia Valley winery, the 20,000-gallon Champs de Brionne, which translates to "Bryan's Fields," was to be built in 1984 overlooking the river near Vantage, on Interstate 90. Seattle-area neurosurgeon Dr. Vincent Bryan and his wife Carol have planted 100 acres of premium Vinifera vines. To make their wines, they have employed Michael Hoffman, the young winemaker who produced the fine wines of Hoffman Mountain Ranch (HMR) in California until that winery was sold in 1982.

A Columbia Valley appellation would include the Preston Wine Cellars, between the Columbia and Snake rivers five miles north of Pasco, on US 395. This premium-wine estate has grown from fifty acres and 60,000 gallons to 200 acres and 160,000 gallons since it was established in 1976 by farmer and tractor-dealer S. W. (Bill) Preston and his wife Joann. Their Davis-trained winemaker, Robert Griffin, makes seventeen different wines. They are available for sampling daily in the spacious, second-story Preston tasting room.

• 6 •

The quiet city of Walla Walla, famous for "Walla Walla Sweet" onions, long grown in its locality, has become additionally famous for a Walla Walla wine that was described in 1982 as "the best Cabernet Sauvignon made in the United States." Young machinist Gary Figgins made the wine in his spare time, in the tiny (1500-gallon) winery behind the cottage on School Avenue that he and his wife Nancy bonded as the Leonetti Cellar in 1977. They named it for his grandfather and for his uncle Fred Leonetti, on whose truck farm in the suburbs Gary cultivates 1½ acres of Cabernet vines. His four-year-old Cabernet, which included Merlot from the Sagemoor Vineyard, won a gold medal in the annual eastern Washington competition at Pasco in 1982, and a month later was described by a California wine magazine, after a tasting of numerous samples, as the nation's best Cabernet. Gary since has planted an additional acre on Uncle Fred's farm, and his father has bought two dozen acres to plant beyond the Snake River, but the Leonetti Cellar has not yet been enlarged.

A second winery in the Walla Walla Valley was bonded in 1981 at Lowden, the wheat-growing center, on US 12 eleven miles west of the county seat. Richard (Rick) Small, who studied winegrowing while running his father's grain elevator, equipped the 7000-gallon winery in a shed across the road to use the grapes from their four-year-old Chardonnay vineyard in nearby Woodward Canyon, for which the winery is named. Rick's bride, land-use planner Darcey Fugman Small, helps run the winery and helped him document the petition to the government to establish Walla Walla Valley as a viticultural area.

Next door to the Smalls' cellar is the three-story Lowden Schoolhouse Winery. Walla Walla bank president Baker Ferguson and his wife Jean have equipped the lower floor with 4500 gallons of winery equipment, which Jean, who once taught chemistry, would use to make their 1984 vintage. The Fergusons live in the two beautifully furnished upper stories, the second of which they converted from the classrooms where Rick Small studied as a child. (It was banker Ferguson, a former professor at Whitman College, who researched and sent me the evidence that wine was being made commercially in Walla Walla Valley more than a century ago.)

• 7 •

As the great rivers of Europe flow through famous vineyard areas, giving scores of Old World wines their district names, so does the Columbia, which borders such vast new vineyard areas that some already describe it as America's vinous counterpart of the Rhine. If you drive some eighty miles west along the Columbia shore from Paterson, you will see a majestic sight, the deep, sixty-mile-long gash the river has carved in solid rock, called the Columbia Gorge. Its name may become an appellation for vineyards on both the Washington and Oregon shores.

Farmers Charles V. and Della Henderson, who since 1975 have operated their 14,000-gallon winery and tasting room in a refrigerated, former fruit storage building in the Washington town of Bingen, across the gorge from Hood River, Oregon, already have that idea. They have printed "Columbia Gorge" on their letterhead and are asking the government to establish it as their appellation. They also have changed their winery's name from "Bingen Wine Cellars" to "Mont Elise Vineyards," for their daughter Elise, a student. (It's just as well, because residents pronounce Bingen as "binge-in," although the town was named for the great German wine city Bingen-am-Rhein.) The best evidence for a separate appellation here is that while the eastern Washington vineyards would be drier than the Sahara if they were not irrigated, the Hendersons' thirty-five-acre vineyard, high above the river at nearby White Salmon, has had plenty of rain since it was planted in 1964. The Hendersons, veteran cherry growers, have sent their son Charles to study enology at UC Davis. They are proudest of their Gewürztraminer, but they also grow Pinot Noir and lately have planted some Riesling and Chardonnay.

Seventy miles farther west and three miles inland from the Columbia Gorge is the Salishan Vineyards winery, a mile north of La Center in Washington and only thirty miles from Portland, Oregon. Economist Lincoln Wolverton and his ex-journalist wife, Joan, planted their twelve-acre vineyard in 1971, naming it for the Salish Indians who once populated this area, and bonded their winery in 1982. Joan is the winemaker. The Wolvertons are proudest of their Pinot Noir, which wine critics have compared to that of Burgundy's Côte d'Or.

• 8 •

There are at least 50,000 acres that could grow grapes in the Columbia Basin; some say there is space for 200,000 acres more. Rainfall east of the Columbia Gorge ranges from only 6 to 7½ inches per year, but there is plenty of water for irrigation. William Bridgman was right about the area's sunshine, which provides 160 to 210 frost-free days per year. The total heat units vary from Region I to Region II. Days are longer in this northern latitude, adds horticulturist Walter Clore, who says "Washington is better for grape growing than New York State; we have milder winters, better soil, ample water, and more sun."

Eastern Washington's defect is low winter temperatures, which drop to seven degrees below zero in one year out of three, and to twelve to twenty below in one year out of six. Cold-tender Vinifera vines such as Muscats formerly were buried with earth each Thanksgiving to protect them during the winter, then were uncovered in March, when the soil became warm again. This is no longer done except for the youngest vines. Vinifera here are grown on their own roots instead of grafting them to phylloxera-resistant rootstocks, as is done in most of California and Europe.

Two wineries have opened in the Spokane Valley of far eastern Washington, only twenty miles from the Idaho border. In 1979, Spokane residents Jack and Phyllis Worden started their 25,000-gallon Washington Winery and tasting room, off I-90 six miles east of Spokane. Third-generation orchardist David Mielke had begun growing grapes experimentally near the Spokane River a year before. Then his brother, San Francisco hematologist Dr. Harold F. Mielke, joined him in opening the 30,000-gallon Arbor Crest Winery on Buckeye Avenue in Spokane in 1982. But most of the grapes thus far used by the Spokane wineries have come from the Columbia Basin, where the Mielkes have begun planting more vines.

• 9 •

Sixteen wineries have opened in rainy western Washington since the mid-1970s, and still more are planning to start. All of them are described, with their visiting hours, in Glenda and William Holden's 1983 Washington wine-touring book, with which every oenothusiast visitor to the Evergreen State should be armed.

In Seattle is former home winemaker Frank Daquila's 6000-gallon cellar in a store area on Western Avenue. To the south, not far from Boeing Field, is the 12,000-gallon winery that Boeing engineer Eugene Foote and his family have run since 1978. Near the Associated Vintners cellar, in Bellevue, is the 28,000-gallon winery and tasting room of former sociology teacher Paul Thomas, who makes excellent grape and fruit wines. In the suburb of Lynnwood is the 11,000-gallon Haviland Vintners winery of former CPA George de Jarnatt, who with his family and partners owns a fifteen-acre Cabernet vineyard in the Yakima Valley. To the east, in their tiny Quilceda Creek cellar near Snohomish, French-born chemical engineer Alex Golitzin and his wife Jeannette make Cabernets of eastern Washington grapes.

A ferry ride across Puget Sound from Seattle is the 4000-gallon

Bainbridge Island Winery, which made its first estate-bottled wine in 1981. Park Service planner Gerard Bentryn and his wife Joan have been growing Müller-Thurgau and other German grape varieties in their two-acre vineyard on the island since 1977. Also planting Müller-Thurgau and other test varieties are retired army surgeon Dr. Albert Stratton and his son and daughter-in-law, who opened the 12,000-gallon Mt. Baker Vineyards winery near Everson, in the far northwestern corner of Washington, in 1982.

Near Sequim on the Olympic Peninsula is the 8000-gallon winery of retired Lodi, California, grape grower Eugene Neuharth and his wife Maria. To the west of Sequim is the 1000-gallon Lost Mountain winery of research chemist Dr. Romeo J. Conca.

On a hill facing Highway 410 near Sumner, east of Tacoma, is the 50,000-gallon Manfred Vierthaler winery, a five-story Bavarian chalet and restaurant opened in 1976 by German-born restaurateur Vierthaler and his wife Ingeborg. They make ten different wines from Washington and California grapes.

The original St. Charles Vineyard on Stretch Island is still maintained by Charles Somer's son Bill, but he now sells the Island Belle crop on a "U-pick" basis to people who drive up from Tacoma, thirty miles away. He has transformed the winery into a maritime museum, displaying his hobby collection of old steamboat days, an exhibit well worth crossing the bridge from Grapeview on the mainland to see.

• 10 •

Oregon has a longer history of winegrowing than Washington State but has less than one-tenth as much vineyard acreage, 2200 acres in 1982. While the planting of new Oregon vineyards increased rapidly during the 1980s, some Oregon wines were being made of Washington grapes.

Among the settlers who traveled west over the Oregon Trail in the middle of the last century were some who brought vine cuttings and began producing wine in the Willamette Valley, south of Portland. Farmers at Ashland, in southwestern Oregon, were shipping Flame Tokays to market before the Tokay industry developed at Lodi, California, about 1900. When the national census of winegrowing was taken in 1880, Oregon's Jackson County was listed as producing 15,000 gallons of wine, and two Willamette Valley counties, Clackamas and Marion, reported producing 1900 gallons. Concord grapes were grown as far northeast as Umatilla County, in the Columbia Basin.

Around the turn of the century, Professor Frederic Bioletti, the California expert on viticulture, suggested that several Oregon localities seemed climatically suited for Vinifera wine grapes, but with the Prohibitionist crusade then at fever pitch, Oregon agricultural authorities recommended grape growing only for home gardens, not as a commercial enterprise. As late as 1965, when a new vineyard at Roseburg in Oregon's Umpqua River Valley had already produced its second crop of White Riesling, a circular published by Oregon State University concluded that "the American grapes, *Vitis labrusca,* are more suited [than Vinifera] to Oregon climates."

There were dozens of farmers' wineries in Oregon when Prohibition began in 1920, and the Dry law did not put them completely out of business. At Repeal in 1933, the state legislature made them legal by establishing a farmer's winery license of $25 per year for anyone making only light wine from fruit of his own production. From twenty-eight such small producers selling their wines at retail in 1937, the number dwindled, because few of their children were interested in winemaking, until only one was left in 1983.

The wine revolution in Oregon started at that Vinifera vineyard near Roseburg, mentioned two paragraphs earlier. The man who planted it is the father of today's Oregon fine-wine industry, the fame of which is spreading across the nation and abroad. When Richard Sommer was studying agronomy at UC Davis in the 1950s, he took an introductory course in viticulture taught by Professor Maynard Amerine. For six years after leaving college, Sommer worked at odd jobs, served a hitch in the army in Korea, then spent another year at the university, uncertain of what he wanted to do. Finally, he made up his mind to grow grapes. Remembering what Dr. Amerine had taught, that the finest wine grapes in California are grown in the cooler vineyard districts, Sommer went where it is still cooler, to Oregon. An uncle of his lived in the Rogue River Valley and grew Vinifera table grapes, but Sommer found that locality still too warm. He went farther north, testing the grapes in each locality. At Roseburg, in the Umpqua Valley, he found some Zinfandels in the eighty-year-old Doerner's Winery vineyard that tested right. In 1961, he bought a hillside farm on Elgarose Road ten miles west of Roseburg, planted vines from the Napa Valley, and bonded his winery two years later. His wines at first were not very good because his cellar equipment was faulty, but one of his Rieslings was well-balanced and fragrant, evidence that the Umpqua Valley can produce fine white wine. Within a few years, his Riesling was being featured in Portland restaurants and gourmet shops. Sommer has since built his present 60,000-gallon Hillcrest Vineyard winery and tasting room. His thirty-acre vineyard now also grows Chardonnay, Gewürztraminer, Sémillon, Sauvignon Blanc, Zinfandel, and Pinot Noir.

On a rainy January day in 1962, David Lett, a new graduate of the University of Utah, was in San Francisco waiting to start training for a career in dentistry. Having nothing else to do, he visited wineries in the Napa Valley and discovered that wine-growing appealed to him more than dentistry. He enrolled for a two-year viticulture course at UC Davis, earned his Bachelor of Science degree, then spent nine months visiting the wine countries of Europe, and decided to grow Pinot Noir in Oregon. The locality he chose was the red hills of Dundee in Yamhill County, overlooking the Willamette Valley. In 1965 he planted the valley's first Vinifera vineyard to be started in five decades. His bride Diana saw a red-tailed hawk soaring to its nest in a nearby tree and named the vineyard The Eyrie. In 1970, the Letts bonded the Eyrie Vineyard winery in a refrigerated former poultry processing plant in nearby McMinnville and a year later introduced their first "Oregon Spring Wine." Ten years later, in a blind tasting by French experts at Beaune in Burgundy, a 1975 Eyrie Vineyards Pinot Noir scored second, by 0.2 points, to a 1959 Chambolle Musigny. The Letts since have specialized in Limousin-oak-aged Pinot Noir and Chardonnay, although their twenty-acre vineyard and 15,000-gallon winery also produce Pinot Gris, Pinot Meunier, White Riesling, and Muscat Ottonel.

A third pioneer in Oregon's winegrowing revival was a home winemaker from California, electrical engineer Richard Erath. On a vacation trip through Oregon in 1967, he bought some grapes from Richard Sommer, took them home and made them into wine. A year later, Erath moved with his wife Kina and their children to Beaverton, Oregon, and bought fifty acres in the nearby hills. In 1972, when their vineyard was three years old, they bonded the Erath Vineyards Winery, beside Crabtree Park on Worden Hill Road, two miles west of Dundee. A few years later, wine-buff Seattle lumber executive Calvert Knudsen dropped by, tasted Erath's first vintage, hired him to plant a Knudsen vineyard, and became a partner in the winery. The Knudsen-Erath cellar since has grown to 100,000 gallons, and the two vineyards to 100 acres in all. Some of the wines are labeled Erath, some Knudsen, still others Knudsen-Erath, depending on which vineyard produced the grapes. Since I was last there, Erath has introduced a bottle-fermented Willamette Valley champagne.

At Oregon City, fourteen miles south of Portland, is the last of Oregon's pre-Prohibition wineries. Henry Endres, Jr., still makes wines from his father's four acres of Labrusca Concord, Worden, and Campbell's Early grapes, but also makes apple, berry, and rhubarb wines and "Henry's Lowball," a loganberry type. This part of the Willamette Valley, Endres says, is better for berries and apples than for grapes.

Sixteen wineries that have opened since 1970 are scattered through the Willamette and Tualatin valleys between Banks, west of Portland, and the state capital at Salem. Wine-touring has become a diversion for Portlanders, who head west and south on weekends to the Oregon wine country served by Highways 8, 47, and 99. On Seavy Road, northwest of Forest Grove, is the Tualatin Vineyards winery, bonded in 1973 in a onetime strawberry shed by UC Davis–trained William Lee Fuller, who left his job at the Louis Martini winery in the Napa Valley to move with his wife Virginia and their four children to the 160 acres they had bought in partnership with William Malkmus of San Francisco. Their winery and tasting room now hold 65,000 gallons, and their wines are sold in a dozen states. On Graham Road, two miles west of Banks, is the 7000-gallon Côte des Colombes winery, bonded in 1977 by Joseph Coulombe and his wife Betty, on a six-acre vineyard they had begun planting eight years before. Joe sold winemaking supplies and taught home winemaking at Portland Community College before starting to make his own for sale. Off Highway 8, west of Forest Grove, is the 10,000-gallon winery and tasting room that farmer-builder Harvey Shafer and his wife Linda opened in 1981, on their twenty acres of vines.

Three miles south of Gaston, on Olson Road, is the 30,000-gallon Elk Cove Vineyards cellar, bonded in 1977 by family physician Dr. Joe Campbell and his wife Patricia, on the twenty-acre vineyard they had begun planting five years before. Pinot Noir is their favorite wine. A herd of elk in the neighborhood inspired the winery's name.

Four miles south of Hillsboro, on Burkhalter Road off Highway 219, is the 70,000-gallon Oak Knoll Winery, a onetime dairy barn. Electronic engineer Ronald Vuylsteke and his wife Marjorie began making rhubarb and berry wines there in 1970. Marjorie taught home-winemaking classes and kept the winery going until Ron left his job to give their wine business his full time. They later planted a vineyard and now also make grape wines, with the help of their daughter and five sons.

Vandermost Road, five miles south of Beaverton, leads to the

18,000-gallon Ponzi Vineyard winery and tasting room, bonded in 1974 on the ten-acre vineyard Richard and Nancy Ponzi, from California's Santa Clara Valley, began planting four years before. Richard taught mechanical engineering at Portland Community College while waiting for their vineyard to bear grapes. The Ponzis were the first in the Northwest to produce a white wine of Pinot Noir.

On a hill facing Jacquith Road, which extends west from Highway 219 north of Newberg, is the 8000-gallon Chehalem Mountain Winery, bonded in 1979 by former Portland contractor Zane Mulhausen and his wife Pat, on the fifteen-acre vineyard they had begun planting six years before. Off Chehalem Drive, also north of Newberg, is the 12,000-gallon winery opened by David and Ginny Adelsheim in 1978, on the eighteen-acre vineyard they had begun planting when David was the sommelier at Portland's L'Omelette Restaurant.

Two miles south of Dundee, on Blanchard Lane, are the 125,000-gallon Sokol Blosser Winery, the largest in the district, and its tasting room, opened in 1977. Portland land-use planner William Blosser and his history-professor wife, the former Susan Sokol, began planting their forty-acre vineyard in 1971. Their winemaker is Dr. Robert McRitchie, who taught physiology at three eastern colleges before becoming the chemist at a Napa Valley winery, where he met the Blossers.

Off Mineral Springs Road, a mile north of Lafayette on Highway 99W, is the 24,000-gallon Château Benoit winery, opened by Eugene physician Fred Benoit and his wife Mary in 1979. They grow forty acres of Pinot Noir, Riesling, Müller-Thurgau, and Chardonnay.

In the same McMinnville building occupied by the Eyrie Vineyards winery, UC Davis–trained Fred Arterberry in 1981 made Oregon's first champagne, which he calls Sparkling Chardonnay. Arterberry's main product, however, is carbonated apple cider.

Off Rice Lane, two miles northeast of Amity, is the 15,000-gallon Amity Vineyards winery, opened in 1976 by population-researcher Myron Redford, his mother Ione, and partner Janis Checchia on the fifteen-acre vineyard they had begun planting six years before. On Eola Hills Road, southeast of Amity, is the 10,000-gallon Hidden Springs Winery, converted from a prune dehydrator in 1981 by former city planner Don Byard, his wife Caroline, attorney Alvin Alexanderson and his wife Jo to use the grapes from the families' twenty-five acres of vines.

On Orchard Heights Road, northwest of Salem, are the Glen

Creek winery and nine-acre vineyard started in 1982 by Thomas and Sylvia Dumm, who came to Oregon after running their own retail wine shop for four years in Long Beach. On Reuben Boise Road, west of the Dumms and a year older, are the 15,000-gallon Ellendale Vineyards winery and thirteen-acre farm of landscape artist Robert Hudson and his wife Ella Mae. On Dunn Forest Road, south of Salem, fellow librarians Glen and Cheryl Longshore in 1981 bonded a 3000-gallon winery beneath their home and named it Serendipity Cellars, because the fun of winemaking came to them as an unexpected surprise (which is what the name means).

Oregon's largest winery is the 160,000-gallon Honeywood Cellar in Salem, a mile east of the state capitol. It was built in 1934 to make wine of berries and currants. Paul and Marlene Gallick, formerly of Minneapolis, bought the winery and its tasting room in 1971. Of the forty-three wineries operating in Oregon in 1983, four produce mainly berry wines.

On the western edge of the Willamette Valley, near Alpine, is the Alpine Vineyards estate of Europe-traveled Dr. Daniel C. Jepsen, staff physician of the University of Oregon Student Health Center in Eugene, and his wife Christine. Their 8000-gallon winery on Green Peak Road produces estate-bottled Riesling, Chardonnay, Gewürztraminer, and Pinot Noir of the grapes from the twenty acres of vines they planted in 1976.

On Sheffield Road, northwest of Elmira and west of Eugene, is a wine estate named Forgeron, French for smith. George Leland Smith and his wife Linda learned French while spending four years in the diplomatic service in France. They bonded their winery in 1977, on the seventeen-acre vineyard they had planted seven years before. They since have built a new 20,000-gallon cellar and tasting room that features their estate-bottled wines. Southwest of Eugene, on Briggs Hill Road, is the attractive, 14,000-gallon red-brick Hinman Vineyards winery and tasting room, opened in 1979 by former high school teacher Doyle Hinman in partnership with wine-buff businessman David Smith and their wives. Hinman studied enology at Geisenheim in Germany and at UC Davis before starting to plant their nineteen-acre vineyard in 1972.

Sixty miles south of Eugene is Roseburg in the Umpqua Valley, where since Richard Sommer launched the Oregon wine revolution in 1963, the number of wineries in the locality has increased to four. On Reston-Tenmile Road, twelve miles south of Sommer's Hillcrest Vineyard, former schoolteacher Paul Bjelland and his wife Mary have had a 10,000-gallon winery since 1969, and since 1973 young viticulturist Jon Marker and his wife Laurie, a wildlife guide, have operated the 4000-gallon Jonicole Vineyards cellar on a four-acre vineyard off Highway 99–42, five miles south of town. In the early 1970s, design engineer Calvin Scott Henry, whose family have farmed in the Umpqua Valley for a century, started a test vineyard of Gewürztraminer, Pinot Noir, and Chardonnay on his 5000-acre livestock, prune, and wheat farm. By 1978, Scott and his wife Sylvia had expanded their vineyard to forty acres and built the 3000-gallon Scott Henry Estate winery on County Highway 6 in Umpqua, near the intersection of Route 9. When I last heard from the Henrys, they had expanded to 17,000 gallons and were considering a start at producing champagne. Their consulting winemaker is engineer friend Gino Zepponi, who comes each month from the Napa Valley, where he is a partner in the ZD Winery and manages production at Domaine Chandon.

Winegrowing has also returned to Oregon's Rogue River Valley, where vineyards and wineries prospered more than a century ago. In 1977, in the Applegate Valley, a tributary of the Rogue, Medford engineer-contractor Frank Wisnovsky and his wife Ann opened the 10,000-gallon Valley View winery on their twenty-three-acre vineyard, planted eight years before. They named it for the Valley View Vineyard winery Peter Britt from Switzerland had established nearby in 1854. Ann Wisnovsky has run the winery since her husband was accidentally drowned in 1980. It is on Applegate Road, a mile west of the village of Ruch, eight miles west of Jacksonville, and thirty miles southeast of Grants Pass. Its wines include Chardonnay, Gewürztraminer, Cabernet, Merlot, and Pinot Noir.

The second new winery in southern Oregon is the new, 20,000-gallon, chalet-style Siskiyou Vineyards cellar, started in 1978 on twelve acres of four-year-old vines, six miles from Cave Junction on the highway toward the Oregon Caves. The owner is Carol (Suzi) David, whose husband Charles died in 1982.

During the early 1980s, winegrowing spread to the northern border of Oregon, an area offering several times the acreage thus far planted in the western valleys of the state. At Hood River on the Columbia Gorge, businessman Cliff Blanchette and his wife Eileen in 1981 bonded the 6000-gallon Hood River Vineyards winery, on a ten-acre vineyard they had begun planting three years earlier behind their pear orchard, west of the town. More extensive wine-grape plantings meanwhile were starting as far as eighty miles to the east, in desert lands along the Columbia River's Oregon shore. In 1983, at Boardman, across the river from Chateau Ste. Michelle's principal vineyard at Paterson, wine-buff lawyer Ed Glenn and his wife Frances bonded the first unit of their future 20,000-gallon La Casa de Vin winery, on a twelve-acre vineyard planted three years earlier beside their home off East Wilson Road. Also being planted nearby were the 153-acre Boardman Farms vineyard, the largest thus far started in the state. At least still larger vineyard projects were being planned or started between Boardman and Irrigon, and as far as Umatilla and Hermiston, still farther east. Lawyer Ed Glenn, in touch with these projects, agrees with Chateau Ste. Michelle's owners that the Federal government should establish a "Columbia Valley" viticultural area, but only provided that it includes the Columbia's Oregon shore.

• 11 •

Oregon winegrowers, aiming to establish a high-quality image for their wines, persuaded their state liquor commission in 1977 to adopt the strictest wine-labeling regulation in the nation for their Vinifera table wines. The regulation set 90 percent as the minimum content of any grape variety used as a wine name, except 75 percent for Cabernet Sauvignon if blended with other red Bordeaux varieties. It prohibits Oregon Vinifera wines from being labeled with such "generic" names as chablis, rhine, sauterne, claret, chianti, or burgundy. The labels must bear appellations of origin, such as Oregon, American, county names, or Willamette, Umpqua, or Rogue Valley, and each wine must be made entirely of grapes grown in the appellation area. The regulation also sets a 2 percent limit on the addition of sugar to the wines, but the limit can be exceeded if the liquor commission permits.

Vinicultural research is being pursued by Oregon State University, guided by an Oregon Wine Advisory Board. In 1983, a $10 per ton assessment on grapes was raised by the legislature to $25, and 2 cents was added to the state's 65-cent-per-gallon table wine tax, one-third of the increased revenue to be used for research and one-third to develop the market for Oregon wines.

• 12 •

Idaho, like Oregon, had vineyards and wineries long before Prohibition, and since the "wine revolution" of the 1960s, Idaho has become a winegrowing state again.

At the 1898 Chicago World's Fair, a prize was awarded to the wine of Robert Schleisler, whose vineyard was in the Clearwater River Valley near Lewiston. J. E. Moore operated the Shaeffer Vineyards winery near Ahsahka in the early 1900s. After Repeal, Gregory Eaves had his winery near Juliaetta for several years.

Grape planting began to spread from neighboring Washington and Oregon to Idaho in the late 1960s, when it appeared that table wine might soon be freed from the Idaho state liquor monopoly and allowed to be sold in grocery stores. The legislature voted the change in 1969, and wine use in the state more than quintupled in the following ten years. A small winery making wine of French hybrid grapes opened at Troy, east of Moscow, in 1971, but proved a losing proposition and soon was closed.

In 1976, apple grower and home-winemaker Bill Broich at Emmett began making wine of the Riesling, Pinot Noir, and Chardonnay grapes planted five years earlier on the 1300-acre Symms Fruit Ranch, in the Sunny Slope district of southwestern Idaho. Broich's wife Penny named their winery Sainte Chapelle for the Gothic chapel in Paris she had admired on a trip to France. Wines of their first vintage won three awards in a northwestern competition. Two years later, they were joined by the Symms family in building the 120,000-gallon Ste. Chapelle Vineyards winery, octagonal in design like the chapel in Paris, in the Sunny Slope district. The winery is on a hilltop facing Lowell Road, off Highway 55 between Caldwell and Marsing, thirty-five miles west of Boise and only twenty from the Oregon border. Ste. Chapelle wines are already sold in forty states and include a bottle-fermented Pinot Noir *blanc de noir* champagne introduced in 1983. President of the winery is Dick Symms, whose brother Steve is the junior U.S. senator from Idaho.

Four more wineries have since opened in Idaho. In 1981, former restaurateur and musician Louis M. Facelli II and his wife Sandy bonded a 4000-gallon cellar near Wilder and began making grape, berry, and fruit wines. A year later, they moved to a new 15,000-gallon winery on US 95 in Wilder, built in partnership with a farm family who grow 165 acres of grapes nearby.

In 1982 former film maker Cheyne Weston opened the 5000-gallon Weston Winery a mile northwest of Ste. Chapelle, on a fifteen-acre vineyard he had begun planting in 1979. Open in 1982 was the small cellar of Spokane building inspector Eugene Pucci, on Garfield Road at Sandpoint, in the northwestern corner of the state. His first wines were made of California grapes.

Vineyard acreage in Idaho was estimated at 1400 acres in 1982. Planting has been limited because winter temperatures in much of the state sometimes drop to twenty below zero, and also because some of Idaho's big wheat growers have used the herbicide 2,4-D, to which grapevines are especially sensitive.

• 13 •

Arizona, which had wineries from the 1880s until Prohibition but for four decades thereafter grew only table grapes, has begun producing wine again. Four wineries have opened in as many Arizona localities since 1980—the first since the state went Dry in 1915—and more are in the planning stage.

New vineyards of "varietal" wine grapes have been planted in the mountains of eastern Arizona, where microclimates at 4000 to 5000-foot elevations approximate Regions I, II, and III. I have already tasted wines from these Arizona mountain vineyards that would impress any connoisseur.

At the same time, plantings of wine-grape varieties have been added to some of the large table-grape vineyards in Arizona's Salt River Valley, an irrigated desert where grapes ripen early in the blazing heat and reach eastern fresh-fruit markets ahead of those from California's San Joaquin Valley.

When the Arizona legislature in 1982 adopted a farm winery law, it envisioned development of both a premium mountain-wine industry and an everyday-wine industry, comparable to California's coastal premium-wine regions and to its main San Joaquin Valley, where mostly moderately priced wines are grown. Because grapes use less than half the amount of water required by such crops as alfalfa and cotton, vineyards are expected to help relieve the Grand Canyon State's problems of water shortage and shrinking farmland, caused by its swelling population.

The 20,000-gallon Soñoita Vineyard winery was built in 1983 on a corner of the 34,000-acre, 5000-foot-high Babocomari Ranch, in southwestern Arizona. It is off Route 83 south of Elgin, in Santa Cruz County. Partners in the winery and co-owners of the hundred acres of "varietals" planted there since 1977 are the Babocomari Ranch Company, University of Arizona Professor of Agriculture Dr. Gordon R. Dutt, past chairman Dr. Adrian Bosman of the Arizona Winegrowers Association, and members of the Dutt and Bosman families. Blake Brophy, of the family who own Babocomari Ranch, has already petitioned the government to establish a "Soñoita" viticultural-area appellation.

When the 15,000-gallon R. W. Webb Winery was bonded in 1980 by former winemaking-supplies dealer Robert Webb in an industrial area of Tucson, it was the first to open in Arizona since 1915. Webb has begun planting an eighty-acre vineyard of wine-grape "varietals" high in the mountains of Cochise County. Off Cherry Road, eight miles southeast of Camp Verde in Yavapai County, is the 5000-gallon San Dominique winery, opened in 1981 by Scottsdale insuranceman William Staltari on a six-acre hillside vineyard he began planting four years before. A fourth winery of 11,000 gallons was started in 1983 at the 4000-foot-high town of Patagonia, south of Soñoita, by former California architect and civil engineer Peter Beope and his wife Gwenn. They have built an attractive adobe Peter Beope Vineyard winery to use the grapes from the twenty-acre Vinifera vineyard they planted in 1982, but they made their 1983 vintage from grapes brought from Tecate in Baja California.

Seven years' research by Dr. Dutt and research scientist Dr. Eugene J. Mielke for the Four Corners Regional Commission led to the planting of the Soñoita Vineyard. Grapes grown experimentally in five states were brought to a research winery on the university campus at Tucson and were vinified by Dr. Wade Wolfe, who since has become the chief viticulturist for Chateau Ste. Michelle, in Washington State.

Arizona, with some 4000 acres growing table grapes, already was the twelfth state in the nation in annual grape production before the present plantings of wine grapes began. If soil problems such as root rot can be overcome—"and progress is being made," says Dr. Dutt—"as many as a half-million acres of wine-grape vineyards can be developed in Arizona in years to come."

• 14 •

In New Mexico, winegrowing thrived from the seventeenth century until it was interrupted by Prohibition, then revived briefly but soon languished after Repeal, and now is experiencing a spectacular rebirth.

When the Rio Grande Valley and neighboring western Texas were colonized by the Spaniards, grapes were cultivated at the Franciscan missions to make wines for the Mass. General Stephen Kearny reported finding viniculture already well established in the Rio Grande Valley when in 1846 he proclaimed New Mexico a territory of the United States. In his book *El Gringo,* published in 1857, W. H. Davis described the claret of Bernalillo as "better than that imported from France." The 1880 census of winegrowing listed New Mexico as fifth in the nation in wine production, making 908,500 gallons from 3150 acres of vineyards, almost double the figures shown in that year for New York State. Although those figures now seem incredible, scores of vineyards and wineries thrived in the Rio Grande and Pecos valleys during the nineteenth century and in the early twentieth, until in 1920 Prohibition forced the wineries to close. A dozen reopened at Repeal along the roadsides at Algodones, Bernalillo, Corrales, Albuquerque, Belen, Sandoval, Doña Ana, Mesilla, and Las Cruces. Then, unable to compete with the bulk wines from California, the New Mexico wineries dwindled in number, until by 1977 only three, at Corrales, Albuquerque, and Mesilla, remained. Some of them were making their wines of California grapes.

A rush to plant large vineyards of wine grapes in New Mexico, led by four separate groups of European investors, began in the 1980s. They were attracted by the expanding, still undeveloped market for wine in the United States and by New Mexico's low-cost land. Vineyards totaling 1200 acres but planned to cover tens of thousands of acres to supply huge projected wineries, were planted in five different areas north and west of Las Cruces during 1982 and 1983. A consortium of Swiss and French winegrowers planted 550 acres of Vinifera "varietals" around Engle in Sierra County, the beginning of a 21,000-acre project, relying on a pipeline to bring irrigation water from the Elephant Butte reservoir on the Rio Grande. Hundreds more acres, mostly of Vinifera, were planted in Luna County near Deming and in Hidalgo County south of Lordsburg, two areas separated by the continental divide. New Mexico ranchers also joined the planting stampede. Farmer John Sichler of Bosque in Socorro County put in 300 acres, mostly of French hybrids, near Belen.

Meanwhile, four new farm wineries were opening in other parts of New Mexico, increasing the total of wineries in the state to eight. Already operating was the 40,000-gallon Viña Madre winery, opened in 1978 in the Pecos River Valley by James and John Hinkle, grandsons of a former New Mexico governor, and James' artist wife, Elaine. It is a two-story brick structure in the style of a Spanish hacienda, on the Dexter Highway (state Route 2), thirteen miles south of Roswell. Their forty-acre vineyard of "noble" Vinifera varieties was planted in 1972.

The oldest winery in New Mexico is the 2000-gallon Joe P.

Estrada cellar on the outskirts of Mesilla, southwest of Las Cruces. Dan Estrada, the foreman at a chili dehydrating plant, lives there and cultivates three acres of vineyard, mostly of Mission grapes, planted by his grandfather about 1875. In Doña Ana County, about halfway from Las Cruces toward the Texas border, is the modern, 8000-gallon La Viña Winery, built on a seven-acre Vinifera vineyard as a hobby in 1977 by Dr. Clarence Cooper, a professor of physics at the University of Texas in El Paso. It is six miles west of Anthony, off Farm Road 28.

In 1976, young Anthony Claiborne, trained in enology at UC Davis and in three California wineries, took over and partly modernized the 4000-gallon Rico's Winery in Albuquerque, which was about to close. On a 6000-foot-high mountainside near Placitas, Claiborne found a flourishing three-acre Vinifera vineyard. From its black grapes he made a *blanc de noir* wine that he named Ojo de Perdiz (eye of partridge). It was as fine as most premium California wines. In 1983, Claiborne joined Albuquerque contractor Jim Winchell in building the 80,000-gallon Westwind Winery on Highway 44, a mile west of Bernalillo. He has closed the Rico's cellar, which the late Enrico Gradi had founded in 1947.

On Highway 85, a mile south of Belen, air-traffic controller Richard Chiavario in 1982 opened the stucco-fronted, 5000-gallon Chiavario Vineyards winery, on the nine-acre vineyard of French hybrids he had begun planting three years earlier. His wines are Paloma Blanca, a white blend of Seyval and Villard Blanc, and Mi Amigo Red, a blend of Chancellor and Villard Noir. In 1982, on Highway 75 in downtown Dixon, north of Santa Fe, former high school teacher Michael Johnson and his brother Patrick, a professional potter, with their wives Ellen and Michele opened their 5000-gallon winery. Its name, La Chiripada, is a Mexican idiom for "a stroke of luck," and was the name of the farm on which they have planted five acres of French hybrid vines. Near Las Cruces, on Highway 70 a mile west of the Rio Grande, is the 10,000-gallon Binns Vineyard winery, also opened in 1982, of Las Cruces contractor Eddie Binns and his engineer brother Glenn. They make Vinifera, berry, and apple wines from the fruit they grow on their family's twenty-five-acre farm across the river.

In arid New Mexico, with annual rainfall ranging from eight inches at Albuquerque to ten inches at Roswell, most of the vineyards since the seventeenth century were irrigated by ditches from the rivers. In the northern Rio Grande Valley, vines on river-bottom land, exposed to winter freezes, were covered with earth each autumn in order to survive. Although the vineyards lately planted in the state appear assured of water for irrigation, how they will withstand seasonal low temperatures remains to be seen.

Grapes from test vineyards in New Mexico made many fine wines during the 1970s while the Four Corners Regional Commission research program was under way. If equally fine wines are produced by the extensive winegrowing projects newly begun in the state, the time may not be far distant when Land of Enchantment wines (New Mexico's official nickname) will be admired by the nation's connoisseurs.

• 15 •

Utah, land of the Prohibitionist Mormons, has vineyards of Vinifera and Labrusca grapes, a winegrowing history that is unknown to most members of that church, and one small winery operated by a religious cult in Salt Lake City, the capital of Mormonland.

Many farmers in northern Utah grow Concords for home use and for sale. But in the Virgin River Valley of southwestern Utah, called "Dixie" for its warm summers and mild winters, there are vineyards of Thompson Seedless, a Vinifera variety, and an old three-story stone winery at Toquerville in Washington County in which the Mormons once produced wine.

J. Walter Fleming of Lodi found the winery by chance while touring the valley some years ago. Inside he found casks and an ancient wine press that showed evidence of generations of use. Local residents told him that wine for Communion had been made there from the 1860s until about 1910. On a later visit, Fleming found the building converted to a granary; all the traces of winemaking were gone.

Knowing that devout Latter-day Saints are teetotalers and are forbidden even coffee and tea, I wrote to the Mormon church historian in Salt Lake City for further information. By return mail came explanatory excerpts from *The Doctrine and Covenants*, which contains the revelations given to Prophet Joseph Smith, the founder of Mormonism; and a mass of historical details about past winemaking in southern Utah. The Saints there made wine not only for the Holy Sacrament, but for medicine, celebrations, and for sale to the Gentiles.

The original Mormons regularly used wine—"yea, pure wine of the grape"—at their services when the Church was organized in 1830 at Fayette, New York, for the Book of Mormon is winier than the Bible. The Saints then became persecuted for their polygamous ways, and were driven from New York to Ohio, then to Missouri and Illinois. One day in Pennsylvania, Prophet Smith was on his way to buy some wine for a religious service, when he was met by a heavenly messenger. "It mattereth not what ye shall eat or what ye shall drink when ye partake of the Sacrament," the messenger told him, according to *The Doctrine and Covenants*. On this revelation, the Mormons now base their use of water instead of wine for Communion. But in so doing, they ignore the rest of the revelation, for the heavenly messenger continued: "A commandment I give unto you, that you shall not purchase wine neither strong drink of your enemies; wherefore, you shall partake of none except it is made new among you." This clearly permits Mormons to use homemade wine, provided it is new. Their Church, however, construes "new" as permitting only unfermented juice.

This was not the view of President Brigham Young, the genius who led the Mormons to Utah in 1847 following the murder of Smith and his brother Hyrum in Missouri. Brigham Young during the 1850s sent Mormon colonies from Salt Lake to southern Utah expressly to plant cotton fields, sugar-cane plantations, and vineyards. He directed them to build wine cellars and to make as much wine as they could. He named an experienced winemaker from Germany, John Naegle, to take charge of the wine industry. Mission grape cuttings, a wine press, and a brandy distillery were brought from California. Brigham Young gave specific instructions for winemaking: "First, by lightly pressing, make white wine. Then give a heavier pressing and make colored wine." He ordered that the wine be "properly graded in quality . . . then stored in oak barrels as far as possible."

He permitted the wine to be drunk for Communion, but he guarded the Saints' sobriety. This he did by ordering special drinking vessels to be made for the Sacrament—"tumblers that will hold a swallow and no more."

"If my counsel is taken," Brigham Young added, "this wine will not be drunk here but will be exported." His counsel wasn't taken. The Dixie Mormons drank the wine at their social functions and used it as an article of trade. They also paid their tithes to the Church in wine, though not of their best, which they reserved for themselves. The Tithing Office at St. George finally decreed that tithes must be paid in other produce or in cash.

Winegrowing in southern Utah reached its peak at the turn of the century, then declined because by then the Church frowned on the Mormons' drinking and because their wines couldn't compete with the better article coming from California.

Because grapes grow well in "Dixie," there have been efforts to revive the local winegrowing industry, but thus far without success. Utah State University made test plantings of Vinifera during the 1960s, which led a few farmers in "Dixie" and around Moab to plant vineyards, mainly of Thompson Seedless grapes. Their crops are sold to teetotaling Mormons to make grape juice and to supermarkets as table grapes.

There is a three-acre vineyard of French hybrid wine grapes around the La Caille Restaurant at Sandy, nine miles south of Salt Lake City. Restaurateur David Martin plans to build a winery there to make wine for his patrons. Wine sale in Utah is restricted to the state's monopoly liquor stores and agencies, so Martin will have to sell his product to the monopoly. His patrons will buy it from the state agency in the corner of his restaurant in order to enjoy it with their meals.

The 5000-gallon Summum winery in Salt Lake City, federally licensed as a bonded winery in 1981, is unique in the world of wine. Summum, a religious cult founded by Salt Lake builder-contractor Claude R. "Corky" Nowell, practices meditation and attributes supernatural powers to things made in pyramids. In his three-story-high wooden pyramid on Genessee Avenue, Nowell ferments California grape juice into "Summum Nectar Rosé." To avoid selling it to the state monopoly, Nowell says he will distribute his "nectar" through bookstores for $5–$10 per bottle donations to his church.

• 16 •

In Colorado, orchardists and hobbyists planted about twenty acres of "noble" Vinifera varieties during the early 1970s, in the fruit-growing area around Palisade in the Grand Valley east of Grand Junction, where the winters are relatively mild. They expected to sell the grapes to a Denver winery, but it was closed in 1974. The Colorado Mountain Vineyards winery then was opened at Golden by former winemaking-supplies dealer James E. Sewald and his wife Ann; in 1981, they moved it to a new 8800-gallon cellar on Road E in Palisade. They make several Mesa County wines, such as Riesling and Cabernet, but most of their production is from grapes they bring from California and Washington State. The Sewalds have planted two acres of Riesling, cared for by their son Douglas. To encourage winegrowing in Colorado, the state legislature in 1977 passed a farm-winery law modeled after Pennsylvania's.

There also is a young wine-grape vineyard in Montana, and construction of a winery—the first ever in the Treasure State—is planned when the grapes mature. Missoula wine-buff and gynecologist Dr. Thomas J. Campbell and his son, Tom Jr., trained at UC Davis and in both California and Washington wineries, in 1980 planted twenty acres of Pinot Noir, Chardonnay, and Riesling on their Mission Mountains Vineyard at Dayton, on the west side of Flathead Lake. Grapes may be brought from Washington State to supplement their estate-grown Montana wines.

• 17 •

The westernmost American winegrowing estate is 2000 feet high, near Ulupalakua on Maui, second largest of the Hawaiian Islands, 2000 miles across the Pacific from California. The Tedeschi Vineyard winery, doubled to 9000 gallons since it was bonded in 1977, makes a *blanc de noir* bottle-fermented champagne, and in dry years an excellent red wine from its thirteen-acre vineyard of Carnelian, the grape bred by Dr. Harold Olmo of UC Davis for warm Central Valley climates. It also makes, "for cash flow," a dry pineapple wine called Maui Blanc and a pineapple champagne named Maui Brut.

Winegrowing is not new to the Hawaiian Islands, where in the semitropical climate grapevines yield two crops per year. King Kamehameha the Great, who united all the islands under his rule, granted land near Honolulu to Spanish horticulturist Francisco de Paula Marin in 1814 to grow wine for the royal household. Portuguese immigrants from Madeira later had vineyards and wineries on the islands of Hawaii and Maui.

Emil Tedeschi, who had worked in wineries near his home in the Napa Valley, on a vacation trip to the islands with his wife Joanne, became acquainted with C. Pardee Erdman and his wife Betsy, who raise cattle at Ulupalakua on the less-rainy side of the dormant volcano, Haleakala. They arranged with the Erdmans to plant an experimental drip-irrigated vineyard there in 1974. Experience since has shown Tedeschi that by reducing irrigation in late summer, he can limit his grape production to a single crop per year. Travelers on Highway 37 on Maui are welcomed to the Tedeschi winery tasting room, which once served as the cattle ranch's jail.

21

The Kosher Winemakers

For many decades after Repeal, the single best-known American wine, sold halfway around the world and never duplicated elsewhere, was the syrupy-sweet, red Concord-grape type with the Hebrew word kosher on its label.

Nine-tenths of its consumers had no clear idea of what kosher means, not being members of the Jewish faith. To most Americans, kosher—the Hebrew word for religiously proper, fit, or clean—suggests that a wine or food has a pronounced flavor, as in pickles, sausages, and in the "especially sweetened" purplish-red wine with the piquant, grapy Concord taste. Though nowadays there are dozens of wines of different flavors and colors labeled kosher, the one you could find in stores throughout the United States and in hotels as distant as Japan and Australia was Manischewitz Concord Grape, in the square bottle with the six-pointed Star of David on its label. It was the one that made kosher a part of the flavor-language of wine.

As table wines became increasingly popular during the 1970s, the buyers of heavy, sweet red Concord began to prefer drier wines. Producers in France, Italy, Spain, and Israel—countries that grow no Concords—began shipping dry red and white kosher wines to America. The makers of kosher red Concord in New York State responded with less-sweet white Concord, picking the grapes before *véraison*, the stage of ripening at which a grape begins to develop the color it will have when fully mature. They also introduced kosher champagnes. But the square bottle, found nationwide as the Passover season approaches, still contains only the sweet red Concord type.

Dozens of wineries in this country and Canada produce non-Concord wines called kosher, but to call a wine kosher they must make it under the strict supervision of an Orthodox rabbi, from the picking of the grapes to the bottling of the wine. Each such winery must use separate crushers, tanks, and bottling machinery for the wine in order for the label to bear the rabbi's *hechsher* seal. In California's Napa Valley, vintage-dated dry "varietals" such as Johannisberg Riesling, Chardonnay, and Cabernet are produced at a well-known winery by a group of UC Davis graduates under the name Hagafen, Hebrew for "the vine." The principal New York kosher producers are Monarch in Brooklyn, Royal (Kedem) at Milton on the Hudson, The Wine Group cellars at Westfield in the Chautauqua Grape Belt, and Schapiro's in New York City.

Oddly enough, the sweet red Concord kosher type became the best-known American wine purely by happenstance. At Repeal, young Leo Star, the son of a cantor from Russian Poland, bought a few wine tanks, rented a store with a double cellar at Wooster Street in New York City, ambitiously named it the Monarch Wine Company, and began bottling bulk port and sherry from California. Leo Star had bottled kosher port and sherry during the Dry years, when anybody could buy it legally by merely joining a Hebrew congregation; but that business had died together with the Eighteenth Amendment.

As a sideline after Repeal, Star also bottled a small quantity of a kosher New York State extra-sweet Concord wine called Mount Zebo, which he also had sold during Prohibition. Its only buyers, when the Dry era ended, were New York Orthodox Jewish families, who were accustomed to using it once a year as an essential part of their Passover feast, or Seder, in the spring.

When the Passover season of 1934 came to an end, those New York store proprietors who had stocked Mount Zebo for their customers found they had quantities of it left unsold. They told Star to take it all back because they could not sell it again until the following spring. Star took it back, and most of it spoiled. Before the 1935 Passover season, Star notified the store owners that they should order only as much Mount Zebo as they could sell—that he would accept no more returns. Again, after Passover, they had leftover stock and wanted Star to take it back. He refused and waited for complaints. To Star's amazement, instead of complaints, the stores sent him rush reorders. Their non-Jewish customers were trying the kosher wine, finding they liked the sweet Concord taste, and were coming back for more.

Star had launched the kosher wine industry, but he did not know it yet. When more reorders came, he thought the wine sold because it was kosher, so he contracted with the old firm of Manischewitz, famed for its kosher food products such as matzos, to let him use the Manischewitz name on his wine. When his "Man Oh Manischewitz What a Wine" radio commercials went on the air in 1945, he knew that the kosher wine type ("that Massachusetts wine" to many of its buyers) was here to stay.

It was also a happenstance that gave Star's biggest competitor its start. In Chicago on September 23, 1947, at 5:17 p.m., Max Cohen and Henry Marcus, owners of the Wine Corporation of America, sadly opened the drain cocks of their wine tanks and let all 40,000 gallons of their Barloma California port and sherry flow down the drain because something had gone wrong with the wine. The only stock they had left was a small quantity of their kosher sweet red Concord wine called Mogen David (Shield of David), left over from the preceding Passover season. Until more port and sherry could arrive from California, they began promoting the sale of Mogen David to the non-Jewish trade as "the wine like Grandma used to make." It soon so far outsold their Barloma wines that the company became the Mogen David Wine Corporation, which is now part of The Wine Group.

Other vintners saw the sensational sales successes of Manischewitz and Mogen David and rushed into production with their own sweet Concord wines. Gallo in California introduced one called Galloette, backed by a huge billboard advertising campaign. The big Welch Company jumped into the market with its Concord Refreshment Wine. But Gallo and Welch both had ignored a key element in the semantics of thirst, that a wine's label influences its taste. Without Hebrew names and characters and the word kosher, their sweet Concord wines didn't taste the same, and they failed to sell. Other wineries in California, New York, New Jersey, Michigan, the State of Washington, and in Canada saw the light, employed local Orthodox rabbis to make their Concord wines kosher, and designed labels liberally adorned with Hebrew characters and stars. Kosher wines with such names as Mazel Tov, Sholom, Mizpah, Maccabee, and Hadassim became a part of their trade.

However, there seems to be a limit on how much specially sweetened red kosher Concord people can drink. Sales in the United States rose to 10 million gallons in the 1960s, but have grown relatively little since. Manischewitz and Mogen David realized that their customers' tastes were turning from sweet toward dry. They began turning out semi-dry and dry white and pink kosher wines, and started making kosher burgundies, rosés, and champagnes. The biggest kosher producer still is Monarch (Manischewitz), which has grown to 3.5 million gallons at the Bush Terminal in Brooklyn, where it has been located since 1938.

Because kosher wines are the only sacramental wines normally sold to the public in this country, they are often used in Christian churches. I once asked the rector of the Episcopal Church in Sausalito which wine he was using for Communion. He couldn't remember the name, except that it was a sacramental wine, but he soon found the bottle for me. It was Manischewitz kosher Concord Grape.

22

Wines of Canada

MANY GOOD WINES are produced in Canada, including some that are excellent by other countries' standards. There also are some unorthodox Canadian wines that are not made anywhere else. Some of the best eastern Canadian wines regularly win awards in U.S. competitions, but they are still little-known elsewhere because most have only appeared since the wine revolution reached its peak during the 1970s.

Canada, too, had Prohibition during most of the years while the United States were legally Dry, and its provincial monopoly-liquor-store system, set up afterward, has long discouraged the use of wine. But Canadians returned from the Second World War and from travel abroad with a taste for table wine, and postwar immigration brought millions of people from the wine countries of Europe. Wine consumption in Canada has almost quintupled since 1964, from 12 million gallons, less than 5 pints per capita, to 57 million gallons, more than 2.3 gallons per capita (slightly above the U.S. 2.2-gallon rate) in 1982.* Almost nine-tenths are low-alcohol types.

So rapid has been the growth of wine use in Canada that it requires more good grapes than Canadian vineyards grow. Almost half of the wines sold by the Dominion's wineries, except those in Ontario province, contain grapes or bulk wine imported from California or Washington State, or bulk wine from Europe. (An Ontario winery's production must consist of at least 85 percent Ontario-grown grapes, but it may use up to 30 percent of material from elsewhere in its blends. Some Ontario wineries' labels read: "A blend of Ontario and California wine.")

---

*U.S. gallons, not British imperial gallons, which are approximately a fifth larger.

492

A relic of Prohibition is that Canadian restaurants have to buy their wines from the provincial monopoly stores and must pay the full retail price plus a service charge (except in Ontario, where they get a small discount). Exceptions are when they buy directly from local estate (farm) wineries, whose prices are marked up by the provincial governments. Because purveyors add further markups, wine in Canadian restaurants costs considerably more than in comparable establishments in the United States.

Québec province in 1978 allowed wine sale in its grocery stores, and consumption there has since increased almost 49 percent. Grower and consumer groups have organized campaigns to allow foodstore wine sale in Ontario and British Columbia, but thus far without success. Ontario wineries meanwhile have opened mini-stores to sell their wines near the food sections in department stores.

• 2 •

Since 1977, Canadian wineries have been allowed for the first time to open tasting rooms, to offer the public tours of their cellars, and to sell their wines to visitors as wineries do elsewhere. Thirteen estate wineries, like those below the border, have opened in the Dominion's two main grape-growing provinces—Ontario and British Columbia. Another opened in 1980 in Nova Scotia and will be described later.

The once predominantly Labrusca vineyards in Ontario and British Columbia are gradually being replanted with hybrid and Vinifera grape varieties. Spurring this improvement is the fact that since 1977, wines imported from other countries have outsold Canadian wines, which previously had dominated the market. The Canadian wineries, still bottling nearly half of the wine consumed in the nation, are determined to make their wines better than the imports in order to regain their former lead.

• 3 •

The eastern Canadian grape-growing district—the western district is 2000 miles away, beyond the Rocky Mountains—is mostly on the slender arm of the Niagara Peninsula that connects southwestern Ontario to Niagara County, New York. Some 26,000 acres, about nine-tenths of the vineyards of Canada, are on that narrow strip, which extends westward from Niagara-on-the-Lake some thirty-five miles beyond the city of Hamilton. A

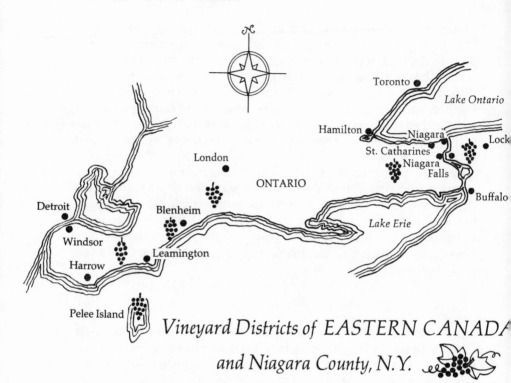

Vineyard Districts of EASTERN CANADA
and Niagara County, N.Y.

hundred miles southwest are additional vineyards, reaching almost to Windsor, opposite Detroit. The waters of Lake Erie,
and of Lake Ontario at the eastern end, moderate the climates
of these districts and protect the vines from winter damage and
spring frost. When, during the 1970s, subdivisions and industries
began competing with farms on the eastern end, vineyards expanded far southwest into Kent and Essex counties, where there
were vineyards before Prohibition.

Six of Canada's thirty large commercial wineries are located
between Niagara Falls and Hamilton, and produce about one-
fourth of all Canadian wine. On Martindale Road outside St.
Catharines, near the original Welland Canal built to carry ocean
ships around the Falls, is the 1.5-million-gallon Barnes winery,
the oldest in Canada. It was owned until 1973 by the sons and
great-grandsons of George and Thomas Barnes, who founded
it a hundred years before. The modern winery is built around
the stone-walled underground vaults. Later owners have replanted the twenty-acre vineyard with French hybrids, replacing
the Labrusca varieties—Agawam, Catawba, Concord, and Diana—from which Barnes wines previously were made. Barnes'

"Ontario Red" wine is made wholly of Ontario grapes, but its "Weinfest" white is a blend with Riesling grapes from California. Barnes also sells a "Grand Celebration" Canadian champagne.

Facing Dorchester Road, just outside the city of Niagara Falls, is Canada's biggest and second oldest winery, by a year— T. G. Bright & Company, with 11 million gallons and 1200 acres of vineyards. Lumberman Thomas Bright founded the company at Toronto in 1874. He moved it sixteen years later and changed its name to Niagara Falls Wine Company, but after his death his family changed it back to Brights. In 1933, Harry Hatch, boss of the Hiram Walker distillery, purchased Brights and hired Dr. John Eoff from Fruit Industries in California to modernize the winery. Eoff had as his assistant a talented young French chemist named Adhemar de Chaunac.

When de Chaunac started work, Brights was producing only ports and sherries. The young Frenchman searched the company's vineyards, which then consisted mainly of Concords, found some Delaware and Catawba grapes, filled two boxes with them, and took them home. He fermented them into a dry table wine and took it to the winery for Eoff and Hatch to taste. Hatch was so impressed that he started Brights making its first table wine.

With the end of the war in Europe, de Chaunac in 1946 brought several dozen French hybrid varieties to Brights from France, and with them a hundred Vinifera vines, including Chardonnay and Pinot Noir. (The company's chief viticulturist, George W. B. Hostetter, points out that this was before Dr. Konstantin Frank, who introduced Vinifera to the eastern United States, had left Germany for New York.)

Brights' first champagne, de Chaunac's blend of hybrids and Labrusca varieties, was introduced in 1949, and in the following year it won a bronze medal at the California State Fair. A decade later, Brights brought out Canada's first Chardonnay and a Pinot champagne made entirely of Chardonnay and Pinot Noir, followed by a Gewürztraminer that tasted as though it had been grown in Alsace. Brights now produces sixty-eight different wines. A tenth of the medals awarded at a recent eastern U.S. wine competition went to Brights' Baco Noir, Du Barry Rosé, and President port. "President," incidentally, is the name of a rare Munson grape variety from Texas, from which the port is principally made.

De Chaunac retired in 1966 and was honored by Ontario wine-growers in 1972, when they gave his name to Seibel 9549, at that time a widely planted red French-hybrid grape. Brights'

president, W. Douglas Hatch, recalls when his father, who preferred fine wines to whiskeys, asked de Chaunac to teach Douglas
how to make wine: "De Chaunac started me on a ladder taking
samples of wine out of the tanks and wouldn't even let me
handle a saccharometer at first."

Douglas, whose brother Clifford heads Hiram Walker, is noted
for his stable of thoroughbred horses and has given some of
them names like Cresta Roja and Cresta Blanca, which are among
Brights' many Canadian wine brands. Brights' newest product
is a citrus-flavored blend of sparkling white wine and spring
water, 5 percent alcohol, called "Club Spritz."

Also on the outskirts of Niagara Falls is the 5-million-gallon
Château-Gai winery, which dates from 1890. It is now owned
by John Labatt breweries. Château-Gai has two historic distinc-
tions. In 1928, it was the first in North America to make champagne by the Charmat or bulk process, which was perfected
in 1907 by Eugene Charmat in France. It also introduced the
process to the United States when it opened the Château Gay
winery (since closed) across the river at Lewiston, New York.
Its other historic contribution was in becoming the first Canadian
winery to export some of its wines to Great Britain, starting
in 1965. The British connoisseurs who sampled them at a tasting
in London's Ontario House were astonished at their quality,
and even more so to learn that any wines were grown in Canada
at all.

Off Niagara Parkway, a mile north of Queenston, is Ontario's
first estate winery. It is named Inniskillin, for the two-century-
old farm on which young nurseryman Donald Ziraldo began
planting wine grapes when he graduated in horticultural science
from the University of Guelph, in 1971. Karl Kaiser, an economics teacher and home winemaker from Austria, bought some
vines from Ziraldo, became his partner and winemaker, and then
took advanced studies in biochemistry and bacteriology at Brock
University. The partners made their first vintage in 1974 in a
converted packing shed. A year later they were granted the first
new Ontario winery license issued since 1929. They since have
built a modern 180,000-gallon winery and expanded their vineyard to sixty-eight acres. Inniskillin wines include Maréchal
Foch, Merlot, Chambourcin, dry Riesling, Gewürztraminer, and
blends called "Brae Blanc" and "Brae Rouge." Release of a bottle-
fermented champagne celebrates their tenth anniversary in 1984.

Another Ontario estate winery gaining fame is the 125,000-
gallon Château des Charmes, between Virgil and St. David's

on Four Mile Creek Road. For fifteen years after arriving in Canada from his native Algeria in 1963, University of Dijon-trained enologist Paul Bosc was the head winemaker at Château-Gai. By 1978 he had planted a fifty-acre, all-Vinifera vineyard that he owns with two partners, and had realized his lifelong dream—a winery with his name on every bottle it sells. His best wines thus far are estate-bottled Chardonnay, Aligoté, Riesling, Cabernet, Merlot, and a Gamay Beaujolais of the true Burgundian Gamay *noir á jus blanc* grape. He also makes champagne and nonsparkling hybrid-Vinifera blends called "Cour Blanc," "Cour Rouge," and "Primeur Rouge."

Two more estate wineries started in the next three years. In 1979, civil engineer Joseph Pohorly and his wife Betty opened the 20,000-gallon Newark Winery on their thirty-acre vineyard, but since have renamed it "Hillebrand Estates Winery" after forming a partnership with a wine firm in West Germany. Newest is the small Reif Winery, started on Niagara Parkway in 1983 by Ewald Reif, who had emigrated from Germany six years before.

On Ridley Road, at St. Catharines, is the 10-million-gallon Jordan & St. Michelle Cellars, owned by the Carling O'Keefe breweries since 1974 (in no way connected with Chateau Ste. Michelle in Washington State). "Jordan" refers to the former Jordan winery, founded in 1921, and to the nearby Jordan Historical Museum of the Twenty, which preserves the lifestyle and relics of the Empire Loyalists who fought on the British side during the American Revolution. The museum's name comes from Twenty Mile Creek, named by the early settlers for the creek mouth's distance from the Niagara frontier.

On Ontario Street in Beamsville, west of Jordan, is the 200,000-gallon, mainly Italian-owned, Montravin Cellars. It began in 1975 as the Podamer winery, when Karl Podamer from Hungary began making bottle-fermented Canadian champagne there.

Also west of Jordan, via roads lined with vineyards, is the 4-million-gallon Andrés winery at Winona. The stacks of sherry-aging barrels in front of the cellar are a landmark on Queen Elizabeth Way. The first Andrés winery was started in British Columbia in 1961 by Andrew Peller, a Hungarian brewmaster who had sold his brewery at Hamilton, Ontario, several years before. His son, physician Joseph Peller, took over Andrés management in 1971 and bought the Winona winery, which was called Beau Chatel when the Imperial Tobacco Company built it in 1967. Andrés, Château-Gai, Jordan & Ste. Michelle, and Brights each operate additional wineries in other Canadian provinces and are the Dominion's largest producers of wine.

At Grimsby, east of Winona, is the Rieder Distillery, which since 1973 has been distilling surplus Concord and de Chaunac grapes into Canadian brandies called "Bordulac," "Ontario Small Cask," and "Trillium." Ninety miles farther west is the 3.5-million-gallon London Winery, still operating in a locality where there are few vineyards, but where there were many when it was founded in 1925.

A young Ontario winery that is becoming famous for good wines is on Highway 3, near Blenheim in Kent County, more than 100 miles west of the big cellars clustered between Hamilton and Niagara Falls. It is the Charal Winery & Vineyards, named for its owners in 1968, when twenty-three-year-old Allan Eastman and his wife Charlotte planted three acres of vines and made 1000 gallons of wine beside their fruit and vegetable store. They had expanded to 70,000 gallons and 100 acres when I visited them in 1982, and I hear they since have planted 100 acres more. Charal produces eleven wines from French hybrids and Vinifera, including a sparkling sweet "Light White Spumante" that sells well at the winery and in the Ontario monopoly stores. The latest variety planted in their vineyard is Siegfriedrebe, one of the Riesling crosses developed in Germany. Charal Chardonnay has won gold medals in wine competitions in the eastern United States.

A century ago one of the principal wineries in Ontario was the Vin Villa Vineyard cellar on Pelee Island, just across the international boundary from the Lake Erie Islands of Ohio. Old residents tell how, when the Pelee Island winery was moved to the mainland, its huge casks—too unwieldy to be brought to the mainland on lake boats—were emptied, floated in the lake, hitched to a tugboat, and towed ashore. During Canadian Prohibition, the vineyards on the island were replaced by more profitable plantings of tobacco and vegetables. During the 1970s, with table-wine consumption soaring in Canada, vineyard-planting on Pelee Island began again. When I visited Pelee in 1982, the young White Riesling, Kerner, and Scheurebe vines appeared to be growing well. A group of investors, headed by viticulturist Walter Strehn from Austria, had announced plans to build a winery on the island, but I now hear they have changed their minds and are building it on the Erie shore near Leamington instead.

On Queen Street in Harrow, eighteen miles west of Leamington, is a 260,000-gallon winery, built in 1980, named Colio Wines of Canada. Partly owned in Italy, it is the first European investment in winemaking in the Dominion. Winemaster Carlo Negri, from Udine in the Grave del Friuli district of northeastern Italy, makes quite palatable semi-dry and dry table wines, blends of French hybrids and Vinifera, called Rosso, Bianco, Rosso Secco, Bianco Secco, and Rosato. The latter is a crackling (semi-sparkling) wine.

Ontario wineries are selling more of their table wines in 4-liter plastic "bag-in-box" packages than wineries in the United States do. They also have introduced wines in liter and quarter-liter pouches, made of foil-lined plastic, that are sold in brick-shaped cartons.

• 4 •

If your interests are in grapes or in wine research, the place to visit in Ontario is the Horticultural Experiment Station at Vineland, off the highway a mile east of Jordan village. It was the leading wine-research laboratory in eastern North America during the 1950s and 1960s, when Ralph Crowther first showed me around and introduced me to grape breeder Oliver (Ollie) Bradt, whose Canadian hybrids have changed the character of many Canadian wines and of some New York and midwestern wines as well.

Crowther is most noted for his invention of the Crowther-Truscott submerged-culture *flor* sherry-making process, which has revolutionized the production of dry sherries in Canada and the United States and has even been studied by enologists in the sherry country of Spain. Others have claimed to have invented the process, including a Spanish researcher who even got a patent on it in Spain in 1968. I can testify, however, that Crowther was making his *flor* (Spanish fino-type) sherry at Vineland as far back as 1955, because I was there in that year and tasted his then unrevealed "seven-day wonder," the simple, quick way to give sherry the pungent *flor* character which old-time winemakers describe as "the bedbug taste." It takes years to develop by the method used for centuries in Spain. There, the *flor* yeast (*Saccharomyces beticus*) grows naturally as a film on the surface of the wine, but it often fails to do its job, which is how a Spanish sherry becomes an amontillado instead of a fino. Crowther started his work with *flor* yeast in 1952 because the Canadian Wine Institute asked him to try growing it on the surface of wines made from Ontario grapes. At first,

Crowther used the Spanish film-yeast method, but the yeast failed to grow on some of his wines. Then he discovered that by agitation—by circulating the *S. beticus* culture through the wine—he could make the yeast work harder and produce the *flor* taste reliably in days instead of years. The Ontario wineries were the first to use his process, and I have tasted some excellent fino-style sherries in their cellars. Now wineries in the United States have begun adding *flor* wines, made Crowther's way, to many of their sherry blends.

More important than sherry is Vineland's grape-breeding program. Hundreds of new, non-Labrusca wine-grape varieties have been bred at Vineland since Ollie Bradt went to work there in 1938. Some of his hybrids, such as Veeport and Vincent, have been widely planted, and have been introduced in some U.S. vineyards as well.

Vineyard improvement has become the theme of the Niagara Grape and Wine Festival, which is held at St. Catharines during the third week of each September. The festival was started in 1952 to aid tourism with its parade and other events, but its main event now is the crowning of the Grape King, who is chosen from among Ontario growers for the quality of his grape crop. When the king is selected, his vineyard gets an official visit from the premier of the province.

Proposals in recent years to establish government quality standards for Ontario wines have made little progress, except that wines made wholly of Ontario-grown Vinifera or hybrid grapes may now be labeled "Ontario Superior." To earn that designation, a wine must be approved by a government-and-wine-industry tasting panel which meets regularly at Vineland.

• 5 •

An entirely new, though small, Canadian winegrowing district is the temperate southwestern side of Nova Scotia that faces the Bay of Fundy. Some sixty acres of wine grapes have been planted in the Annapolis Valley there since 1977. By 1983, the 10,000-gallon Grand Pré winery, beneath the owner's three-story home near Kentville, was bottling its fourth commercial vintage of Maréchal Foch, Pinot Noir, Cabernet, Chardonnay, and of two winter-hardy Russian black-grape varieties, Severnyi and Michurnitz. Proprietor of the winery is California-born wine lover Roger Dial, who helped manage a California winery before he came to Nova Scotia to teach political science at Dalhousie University, in Halifax.

Dr. Dial says this area, at the forty-fifth parallel of latitude, has a climate like the Mosel valley of Germany and the Champagne district of France. His main vineyard is at Grand Pré, the village from which the British in 1757 expelled the French Acadians from Nova Scotia, as described in Longfellow's tragic poem about Evangeline and her lover Gabriel. The first estate-grown Grand Pré wine, made of a white grape bred at Vineland, was named L'Acadie Blanc.

· 6 ·

Winemaking began earlier in eastern Canada than in most of the United States. In the year 1636, Jesuit missionaries at Québec were making sacramental wine from the wild grapes that thrive along the St. Lawrence River.

The first commercial winery in Canada was Clair House, established in 1811 by a German ex-soldier, Corporal Johann Schiller, near the shore of Lake Ontario at Cooksville, now a suburb of Toronto. The Toronto *Leader* for July 8, 1867, records that Clair House wines were shipped to France for judging at the Paris Exposition and that the wine jury found them "pure and of excellent quality," comparing them to French *vin ordinaire.*

By the 1890s there were 5000 acres of vines and thirteen flourishing wineries in Ontario, but meanwhile the Dry crusade in the United States had spread northward into Canada, and towns were voting themselves Dry.

Then in 1916 and 1917, while Canadian soldiers were away fighting in Europe, all but one of the Canadian provinces adopted Prohibition laws. Québec, with its French heritage, held out until 1919 and then forbade the sale of liquor, but allowed its people to continue buying wine and beer.

Ontario, then Canada's only wine-producing province, prohibited liquor and beer, but to protect its grape growers, permitted its wineries to continue making wine for local sale. Buyers had to go to the wineries to make a purchase, and by law they could buy no less than a five-gallon keg or a case at a time. The export of wine to foreign countries was also permitted, and when the United States went Dry in 1920, several new Ontario wineries opened for business. Canadian wine "exports" rose to levels never reached before or since. Shipments destined ostensibly for faraway countries found their way into the United States despite the American border, lake, and river patrols. Sailors along the Canadian shore of Lake Erie still chuckle over recollections of "those one-hour trips to Cuba." When United States Prohibition was repealed, the "exports" of Canadian wines abruptly ceased.

By 1927, Ontario and the neighboring provinces had had enough of Prohibition, and they legalized the sale of liquor. Prohibition had come earlier and had ended sooner in Canada than in the United States. But it left the country's wine industry more handicapped than the industry in the United States was at Repeal, because in place of Prohibition, all of the Canadian provinces established government monopoly liquor stores. Until the 1960s, each consumer had to buy a $2 annual permit in order to purchase any alcoholic beverage. Ontario, however, allowed its wineries to continue selling their wines to consumers. It became easier to buy wine in Ontario than anywhere else in Canada, for besides the government liquor stores, there were fifty-one special wine stores owned by the Ontario wineries. That was the number of wineries in Ontario during Prohibition. The big wineries promptly bought out the small ones and closed them down, because all they wanted was the store licenses. Since 1976, the wineries have been allowed to open as many stores as they wish. The store assortments are limited, however, because a winery may sell only wines of its own production.

• 7 •

Canada's other winegrowing district is beyond the Rocky Mountains, in the far western province of British Columbia. The story of its wines is a curious one, as the following incident will illustrate.

In March 1967, the San Francisco Wine and Food Society and the Medical Friends of Wine were planning to hold a champagne tasting. Having just returned from a research trip to the eastern states and Canada, I suggested that we invite champagne producers outside of California to participate. The committee agreed, and the invitations went out. Acceptances came from nine California wineries, from three located in Canada, three in New York State, and from one each in New Jersey, Ohio, Michigan, and Illinois. When our several hundred members and guests gathered for the event in the Rose Room of San Francisco's Palace Hotel, we faced an array of sixty-seven white, pink, and red sparkling wines—thirty-four from California and thirty-three from outside the state.

As is usual among such tasting audiences in winy San Francisco, those accustomed to California champagnes preferred them to those from the eastern states and Canada, most of which had in varying degrees the Labrusca taste of native American grapes.

But of particular interest to the members of our group were the Canadian champagnes. Typical of the tasters' responses was what "Winemaster" Henry Rubin wrote in his wine column in the San Francisco *Chronicle:* "I was pleased to note some acceptable Canadian wine." He noted that some had "strange" Labrusca flavors, and ended with: "The best one seemed to me the Richelieu De Luxe Champagne Brut of British Columbia."

Because I had visited the British Columbia wineries a few weeks before, I was able to explain to Henry Rubin why he had preferred that particular champagne. It had been made, I told him, entirely from California grapes.

In fact, British Columbia wines have been made partly, and in some years wholly, from California grapes since 1934. The labels say "Canadian champagne," "Canadian sherry," "Canadian burgundy," and so forth, but some of the grapes have come in refrigerated trucks from California or from the new vineyards in Washington State.

Wine consumption in British Columbia is the highest in Canada, 3.57 gallons per capita in 1982, compared to the 2.22 gallons in Ontario and 2.32 gallons for the nation as a whole.

• 8 •

The grape-growing district of British Columbia is the Okanagan Valley, a 120-mile-long, narrow, steep-walled stretch of farmland, lakes, and resorts between the Trepanier Plateau and the Monashee Mountains. It extends from the head of Okanagan Lake, above Vernon on Highway 97, southward across the United States border. When speaking of the Okanagan, you usually include the lower Similkameen River Valley from Keremeos and Cawston to the Washington State line near Osoyoos.

That part of British Columbia was inhabited only by Indians, fur traders, and missionaries until the introduction of placer mining brought gold prospectors after 1860. The Oblate Fathers built a mission about 1864 at a point seven miles south of the present city of Kelowna. The Fathers planted a few vines, but when farmers settled in the valley during the next few decades, they grew apples, peaches, and apricots; nobody thought of planting vineyards.

During the 1920s, the first two British Columbia wineries started operating on Vancouver Island, more than 200 miles west of the Okanagan. The wine they made was not from grapes,

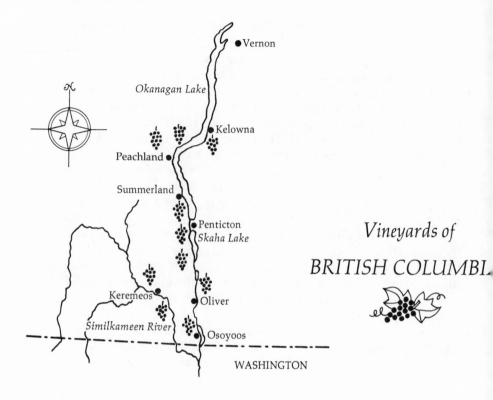

Vineyards of

BRITISH COLUMBL

but from the loganberries grown north of Victoria on the island's Saanich Peninsula.

About that time a Hungarian winemaker, Dr. Eugene Rittich, visited the Okanagan Valley and thought its climate might be suitable for wine grapes. Most of the valley lies between the forty-ninth and fiftieth parallels of latitude, which are regarded as the northernmost limits of viticulture; Germany's Rheingau is at latitude 50° and the Champagne district of France is at latitude 49°. But the deep waters of Okanagan, Skaha, and the other lakes, dug out by prehistoric glaciers, prevent the temperature from going to extremes and give parts of the Okanagan a growing season as long as 185 days. Farming is on the bench lands above the lake level, and this normally protects the plants from frost. Rainfall is only eight to twelve inches per year, but water for irrigation is plentiful in the lakes and upland streams.

Dr. Rittich made some experimental plantings that proved him right, and he interested farmer Jesse Willard Hughes in planting a vineyard near the old Oblate Fathers Mission in 1926. Four years later, the first commercial grape wine in British Columbia was made from Hughes' grapes in the Growers' Winery at Victoria.

In 1932, the depth of the Great Depression, Okanagan Valley apples were unsalable at a penny a pound and were rotting on the ground. A Kelowna hardware-store owner named William Andrew Cecil Bennett talked about it with the Italian grocer next door, Pasquale "Cap" Capozzi, and they decided the way to salvage the apples was to turn them into wine. Though both were teetotalers, they became partners and started a winery, Calona Wines Limited, in Kelowna, with Bennett as its president. Their apple wine couldn't compete with the Growers' Winery's genuine wine made of Hughes' grapes, so in 1934 Calona started buying grapes from California. The wineries on Vancouver Island began doing the same.

For the next twenty-six years, the British Columbia wineries prospered by making "Canadian wines" almost entirely from California grapes. As wine consumption in the province grew, more wineries were built.

This was the situation when Bennett, Capozzi's former partner in the Calona winery, became Premier of British Columbia in 1952. He had sold his shares in the winery eleven years earlier when he was first elected to the parliament of British Columbia.

As Premier, teetotaler Bennett turned his attention to the wineries. He decided that if they were to continue selling their wine in the British Columbia government stores, they ought to be required to make it out of local grapes. In 1960, he ordered his Liquor Board to establish quotas, minimum percentages of British Columbia grapes which wines made in the province must contain in order to be sold. There then were only 585 acres of vineyards in the Okanagan Valley, so the quota for 1961 was set at 25 percent; but the Board announced it would go up to 50 percent in another year and to 65 percent by 1965.

A stampede to plant more vineyards began. Vines were put into the ground without waiting for grape stakes. In four years, the Okanagan Valley vineyards were quadrupled, to 2400 acres. But in December of 1964, a spell of sixteen-below-zero temperatures and forty-mile winds hit the Okanagan, freezing most of the vines to the ground. Only 334 tons of grapes were picked in the following autumn, and the Liquor Board rescinded the quota for that vintage. This explains the all-California flavor of the British Columbia champagne that we tasted at San Francisco in 1966. A decade later, the Okanagan vineyards totaled more than 3500 acres, and the quota on the proportion of local grapes that British Columbia wines must contain had risen to

This vineyard facing Okanagan Lake in British Columbia has been thriving since the 1920s, when it was planted by farmer Jesse Willard Hughes.

80 percent. It was relaxed again, however, after the freezing winter of 1978.

• 9 •

The Calona winery was sold by the Capozzi family in 1971 to Standard Brands of Montreal, a subsidiary of Standard Brands in the United States, and its capacity was quadrupled to 4 million gallons. You still could find rotund, cheery "Cap" Capozzi there on occasion when the winery was headed by his second son, Tom. "Cap" always enjoyed telling how he arrived nearly penniless from Naples in 1905 and worked his way up from a railroad section hand to become the owner of Kelowna's biggest businesses. Calona produces a complete assortment of table, dessert, and sparkling wines. Included are proprietary blends called Schloss Laderheim, Haut Villages, Sommet Blanc, and Sommet Rouge.

South of Kelowna, on a knoll overlooking Okanagan Lake, stands one of the most attractive winery buildings in Canada, a mission-style structure with a bell tower and containers for 900,000 gallons of wine inside. It was named the Mission Hill winery when orchardist R. P. (Tiny) Walrod formed a company to build it in the 1960s, but Walrod died before construction began, and the place was sold. Then came the new regulation allowing British Columbia wineries to have tasting rooms and cellar tours and to sell visitors their wines. The new owner let the place decline, but it was bought in 1981 by a Canadian wine-importing firm, which has restored the beauty of the place and the palatability of its wines.

At Penticton, between Okanagan and Skaha Lakes, thirty-nine miles south of Kelowna, is the 2.6-million-gallon Casabello winery, built in 1966 by a group of local businessmen headed by former hotel-owner Evans Lougheed. They made the building architecturally attractive, anticipating that British Columbia wineries might someday be permitted to receive visitors. When the permission came in 1976, Casabello was the first to open a tasting room. The winery features an "estate selection" of Vinifera varieties in addition to wines with such proprietary names as Alpenweiss, Osoyoos Select White and Red, Fleur de Blanc, and Burgon Rouge. Lougheed's son-in-law, Walter Davidson, has a twenty-acre vineyard near Osoyoos, planted in 1972 with French hybrids and such Vinifera varieties as Riesling, Chardonnay, Chenin Blanc, Gewürztraminer, and Pinot Noir. It supplies the grapes for Casabello's "estate selection" line. The winery was purchased by Labatt breweries in 1978.

In 1980, the big Brights winery of Ontario built an attractive 800,000-gallon winery and tasting room on Highway 97 three miles north of Oliver and named it Brights Wines of B.C. The manager is British Columbia–born John Bremmer, and the winemaker is his wife Lynn. Brights has contracted for the planting of 300 new acres of British Columbia vineyards and is buying the rest of its grapes.

Three more British Columbia commercial wineries are in the Vancouver area, 200 miles west of the Okanagan. In Surrey, twenty-five miles southeast of Vancouver, is the 4-million-gallon Ste. Michelle winery, built in 1977 with a partly underground aging cellar and a visitors' reception room. Ste. Michelle is the new name of the Growers' winery, which operated at Victoria on Vancouver Island for fifty-two years until it was purchased by the Carling O'Keefe breweries and moved to this mainland site. It is just off Highway 10, at Johnson and Colebrook roads. Josef Zimmerman, trained at the Geisenheim Institute in Germany, is the winemaster of the Jordan & St. Michelle wineries in both Ontario and British Columbia. The wines made here include Chardonnay, Grey Riesling, Ruby Cabernet, and proprietary types with such names as Château Blanc, Château Rouge, and Rougelais.

On Vintner Street at Port Moody, ten miles east of Vancouver, is the original Andrés winery. It has grown to 3 million gallons since Andrew Peller had it built in 1961. Visitors are invited to tour its cellars and taste its British Columbia wines, which number more than three dozen, including a pleasant white of Verdelet and an excellent red of British Columbia–grown de Chaunac named Similkameen Superior Rouge.

The first Andrés winemaker, Wallace Pohle from California, disliked the Labrusca grapes then grown almost exclusively in the Okanagan. Pohle talked Peller into planting French hybrids and a few Vinifera on forty acres near Cawston, in the Similkameen. His successor was another Californian, Davis-trained Guy Baldwin (more recently director of enology for Paul Masson in California and for Seagram-owned wineries on three continents). It was Baldwin who made the champagne that was praised at our San Francisco tasting.

For three decades, scientists at the Summerland Research Station in the Okanagan had advised the British Columbia farmers to plant hybrids and Labrusca grapes, not Vinifera, because Okanagan winters were too cold. Californians Pohle and Baldwin disagreed with the Summerland scientists, who since have begun breeding new, non-Labrusca hybrids for wine. Cold-resistant Vinifera varieties should suffer no worse in Okanagan winters than the hybrids, said Baldwin, pointing out that Vinifera were grown successfully in eastern Washington, only 200 miles south. "If the Okanagan growers would produce three tons per acre instead of six to sixteen tons," he added, "this part of British Columbia could grow some of the best Vinifera wines in the world."

In 1977, the Inkameep Indian Band planted a hundred acres of Vinifera on their reservation in the Okanagan, the first large-scale test of whether the Californians might be right. The Inkameep tribe are the first organized North American Indian growers of grapes. "If this test succeeds," commented *Vancouver Magazine* writer Malcolm Parry, "we shall see one of the niftiest role-reversals ever between immigrant settler and aboriginal population; the Indian will have brought good wine to the white man." Among the plantings are cold-resistant German crosses of Riesling and Sylvaner, named Ehrenfelser and Scheurebe. The best wine I tasted on my last visit to the Okanagan was Andrés winemaker Ron Taylor's experimental batch of Ehrenfelser, grown at the Inkameep Vineyard.

• 10 •

During the 1970s, the British Columbia government began licensing estate wineries like those in Ontario. In British Columbia, they may sell up to 30,000 gallons each per year directly to consumers and restaurants, but must use only grapes grown in the province and make not over 150 gallons per ton of grapes, compared to the 250 gallons per ton the Ontario commercial wineries are allowed.

Oldest of the five thus far licensed is the Claremont Estate, with a 70,000-gallon winery on its twenty-acre vineyard facing Trepanier Bench Road north of Peachland, overlooking Okanagan Lake. Former Calona winemaker Robert Claremont and his wife Lee opened the winery in 1979. Their wines include Johannisberg Riesling, Gewürztraminer, and a red of the French hybrid called Rougeon.

In a golf clubhouse off Highway 97, north of Summerland, former grape grower Lloyd Smith and wine marketer Harry McWatters in 1980 installed winemaking equipment and opened the 50,000-gallon Sumac Ridge Estate Winery. They realigned fairways of the nine-hole course to accommodate some of their twenty acres of vines. The clubhouse also holds their tasting room and wine shop, besides the golf club's dining room. Gewürztraminer, Chardonnay, Verdelet, and Chancellor are the principal Sumac Ridge wines.

On Camp Road in Okanagan Center, former apple grower George Heiss and his wife Trudy have opened the 6000-gallon Gray Monk Estate winery, their translation of one of the grapes, Grauer Mönch, in their twenty-acre vineyard. Their wines include "varietals" of Foch and German varieties called Bacchus, Kerner, and Auxerrois. The latter is listed in some ampelographies as a synonym for Chardonnay, but in others as a synonym for Melon or Muscadet.

Mining geologist David Mitchell and his wife Susan have opened the Uniacke (which means unique) Estate winery on Lakeshore Road, east of Kelowna. They produce Chelois, Merlot, Pinot Noir, Johannisberg Riesling, and the Riesling cross named Müller-Thurgau.

Youngest British Columbia estate winery is Joseph Busnardo's Divino Estate cellar on Road 8, south of Oliver.

• 11 •

Not to be confused with the Ontario and British Columbia wineries are a dozen others, all big, in such places as Truro,

Nova Scotia; Moncton, New Brunswick; Moose Jaw, Saskatche-
wan; Calgary, Alberta; Selkirk, Morris, and Winnipeg, Manitoba;
and Dorval, St-Hyacinthe, Lachine, and Laval, Québec. It may
seem strange that wine is made in these places because no grapes
are grown commercially in any of them. These wineries without
vineyards make and sell wines and champagnes of all types,
but rarely from Canadian grapes. Their raw materials are mostly
California fresh or frozen grapes or juice or grape concentrate
(condensed juice) imported from California or such European
countries as France, Spain, Cyprus, and Greece. A few also make
wines from locally grown apples and berries. One of the wineries
using concentrate has advertised its products as "produced from
the finest European grapes, fermented and bottled in Canada."

Concentrate wine fits the legal definition of wine in most countries, including the United States, but in grape-growing countries,
concentrate is used only to sweeten wines or to increase the
sugar content of juice. Concentrate has been one of the materials
for homemade wines since Prohibition days. There also are concentrate wineries in Latin American countries, such as Guate-
mala, where few grapes are grown.

The original reason such wineries were built in Canada during
the 1960s was that by operating a plant and employing local
people in a given province, the owners automatically got their
products listed in the province's monopoly liquor stores. Concentrate wines usually have a slightly raisiny taste, but those of
the Seagram-owned Maison Secrestat at Dorval near Montréal
are blended with wines from France or South America and are
difficult to distinguish from wines of fresh grapes.

· 12 ·

Half of Canadian wine is not made in its wineries, but is
fermented in the basements and kitchens of Canadian homes.
Rather than buy from the government liquor stores, which
among other things charge a high price for wine, many people
prefer to ferment their own from locally grown or California
grapes or from concentrate. While this is especially true of consumers of European-immigrant backgrounds, large numbers of
other Canadians who are not particularly interested in saving
money have taken up winemaking as a fascinating hobby. Stanley Anderson of Vancouver, who started the business called
Wine-Art, estimates that one of every five families in British
Columbia makes its own wine. There is a B.C. Amateur Winemakers Association, which outdoes such avocational groups in

the United States. Eight of its members even have their own vineyard, six acres on Highway 3A in the Similkameen Valley, between Keremeos and Osoyoos.

• 13 •

Canadian wine laws differ from those of the United States, which explains some of the unorthodox Canadian wines. Crackling (semi-sparkling) wines are nationally popular in Canada because they are much less expensive than crackling wines in the United States. The Canadian types mostly get their sparkle from artificial carbonation like American "pop" wines, and pay the same tax rate as still wines if they contain no more than an extra atmosphere of carbon dioxide. In the United States and much of Europe, wines labeled crackling (or *pétillant* or *frizzante*) are costly because they must be fermented in closed containers like champagne, and they pay the same tax rate as champagne.

More important is a group of Canadian carbonated wines fully as effervescent as champagne, with such names as Baby Duck, Canada Duck, Fuddle Duck, Daddy Duck, Cold Duckling, Baby Deer, Cold Turkey, Lonesome Charlie, and Golden Goose. They usually have Labrusca flavors and are sweet. These are less expensive than the crackling type because they contain no more than 7 percent alcohol and therefore are taxed only half as much as wines over 7 percent. They are permitted under a section of the Canadian law originally intended to encourage the sale of sparkling apple cider. Brights was selling such a wine, called Winette, in beer bottles in 1953. Some years later, Andrés in British Columbia used champagne bottles for one it called Chanté. Sales of the type exploded in 1971 when Andrés named the wine Baby Duck. The company claims it now outsells all other wines in Canada, regardless of source.

In 1964, the French government sued the Château-Gai winery to stop it from calling its sparkling wines "champagne," and the French won the suit in 1967. But the verdict was handed down in the fiercely French province of Québec by a judge of French descent. In 1980, Canada removed the ground for the lawsuit by canceling the 1933 trade agreement which had stipulated that "champagne" in Canada had to come from France. Incidentally, bulk-process champagnes in Canada are not required to state that fact, which is mandatory in the United States.

The Canadian monopoly liquor store system does one thing of which many visiting Americans approve. It answers, without being asked, one of the questions most frequently posed by shoppers for wines: Is this wine dry or sweet, and if it is sweet, just how sweet? The Canadians have devised a numbering system that ignores such deliciously confusing label terms as dry, semi-dry, medium dry, extra dry, sec, and brut. Each wine for sale in the Canadian stores has now been given a number between zero for very dry and 15 or 25 for very sweet. The system works very well, although an American kosher wine and an English ginger wine have already broken through the top of the scale with sugar contents of 26.

Canadian wines are seldom given more than passing mention in most wine books, and British author Hugh Johnson omitted them entirely from his *World Atlas of Wine*. When asked to explain, Johnson replied that the one Canadian wine he had tried was the worst he had ever tasted. The Canadian growers' indignant replies to this slur received nationwide publicity and brought many patriotic drinkers to the defense of their country's wines. In 1976, Toronto wine writer Michael Vaughan carried an assortment of fourteen "Ontario Superior" wines to England and invited a dozen London connoisseurs, including Johnson, to sample them in a "blind" tasting at Ontario House. The British author and the others were all favorably impressed. Johnson gave high praise to three of the samples, and conceded that none of the assortment resembled the Canadian wine he had tasted before.

23

Wines of Mexico

GUIDEBOOKS to Mexico list, among the attractions that lure millions of us across our southern border each year, its archaeological wonders, its colorful native customs, its fabulous scenery, resorts, and excellent fishing—but usually omit any mention of Mexican wines. Partly because of this, few Americans are aware that the land of the conquistadores has extensive vineyards and imposing wineries, some of them centuries older than ours, and that many Mexican wines are good and are getting steadily better.

The chief reason the wines of Mexico are little known is that the nation's wine industry, despite its ancient beginnings, is really new. Its oldest winegrowing estates have just lately been revived, replanted, and rebuilt. Most of the approximately sixty wineries in the Republic have only started operating since the 1950s. A new generation of enologists, technically trained in European and California wine schools, has taken charge of the modern cellars and is producing wines of types and qualities not made in Mexico before. A few are even being exported to the United States.

Why is this happening only now in an industry that began more than 450 years ago? The answers are in Mexico's turbulent history and in its relatively recent emergence as a nation of the modern world.

• 2 •

Wine was first made in Mexico in the time of the conqueror, Hernando Cortez. As the governor of New Spain from 1521 to 1527, Cortez established mines and farms. He insisted that all ships coming from Spain to Vera Cruz should bring with them

Principal Vineyard Districts of MEXICO

supplies of plants and seeds. In 1524, Cortez made it a rule that every Spaniard holding a *repartimiento* (a grant of land and of Indians to till the soil) must plant, annually for five years, 1000 grapevines for each 100 Indians. Wine was an essential part of the Spaniards' diet and was indispensable for their priests to celebrate the Mass. Ships brought the wine in casks from Spain and the Canary Islands, but space in the ships was limited. The conquistadores first made their wine from wild grapes, then from cultivated grapes when their vineyards bore fruit. By 1554 winegrowing was well established at haciendas as far west as the present state of Michoacán. The first two commercial wineries or *bodegas vinícolas* in Mexico were established in 1593 and 1626 at Parras in Coahuila, 500 miles north of Mexico City. One again is producing wines today.

But Spain was jealous of the New World's blossoming viniculture. The vintners of Cadiz were complaining as their shipments shrank. Philip II acted in 1595 to keep the wine trade as a Spanish monopoly; he issued an edict forbidding new plantings or replacements of vineyards in New Spain. The viceroys repeated

Philip's edict during the next two centuries, and some went so far as to order that all existing vineyards be uprooted. But wine-making continued despite the edict, though without any records of the quantities made. It was from Mexico—not from Europe—that winegrowing spread during the sixteenth century to Peru, Chile, and Argentina, and during the seventeenth and eighteenth centuries to what is now the western United States.

Padre Miguel Hidalgo, the revered Father of Mexican Independence, was the only one who dared openly to defy the Spanish law. At his village of Dolores, the rebel priest taught the natives to raise grapes, which he himself pressed into wine, and the civil authorities came repeatedly to Dolores to tear up his vines. One of Father Hidalgo's aims in launching the revolution against Spain in 1810 was to end the Spanish prohibition against wine-growing in Mexico. Although the revolution finally succeeded eleven years later, Hidalgo meanwhile had been captured and shot.

Viniculture languished during the half-century of disorder that followed. Only two new wineries of any importance were established during the first seven decades of Mexican independence—the Bodegas Ferriño at Cuatro Ciénegas in Coahuila in 1860 and the Bodegas de Santo Tomás in Baja California in 1888. Most of the country's vineyards still grew the same grape variety originally introduced by the conquistadores. It was the Criolla or Mission, which is a member of the Vinifera wine-grape family, but not a very good one, because it is deficient in acidity and color. It is now thought to have grown from a seed brought from Spain in the time of Cortez.

The first step toward better Mexican wines came during the dictatorship of President Porfirio Díaz, who came to power in 1876. Díaz, the *mestizo* "strong man of Mexico," surrounded himself with young men called *científicos* and welcomed foreign capital and modern industry. In 1889, the Irish-American winegrower from Livermore, James Concannon, seeking more capital to develop his own vineyard in California, went to Mexico and convinced Díaz that viticulture in the Republic could be developed on a commercial quality basis and that he, Concannon, was the man to do it. The dictator granted him a concession to introduce better wine grapes to the country, and even assigned him a cavalry escort to impress the *hacendados* whom he would visit. From Livermore, where the better French varieties were just then being planted, Concannon shipped several million cuttings to haciendas throughout Mexico, with pamphlets in Spanish on grape cultural methods, and sent his brother Thomas along to superintend the deliveries. The biggest plantings were made at Hacienda Roque near Celaya, which was owned by the father of Díaz's daughter-in-law. By 1904, the project was completed and Concannon returned to Livermore. Díaz meanwhile assigned a young Hungarian viticulturist, the son of the Hungarian ambassador, to see to it that every state in the Republic would have at least one vineyard. With the better grape varieties from California, the Mexican wine industry started to boom.

In 1910, the boom attracted to Mexico the Italian-American winemaker Antonio Perelli-Minetti from California, seeking an opportunity to recoup the fortune he had lost in a wine venture at San Francisco. On his arrival in Mexico, Perelli was taken to Chapultepec Palace to meet the dictator, who told him about the grape plantings. Díaz encouraged Perelli to join the Mexican industry—"The sky is the limit here"—but warned him to stay out of politics, saying, "Don't let the fever of commanding get hold of you." Perelli went to work for Felipe Cárdenas of Ocampo, a brother of the former governor of Coahuila. His assignment was to plant vines on Cárdenas' Rancho El Fresno near Torreón. Perelli brought from California cuttings of Zinfandel, Petite Sirah, Malaga, and Flame Tokay and planted almost 900 acres, the largest vineyard in Mexico at that time.

Then came the Revolution of 1910, led by Francisco I. Madero, and the bloody civil war that lasted for ten years and cost a million lives. During the chaos, most of the vineyards fell into neglect and many were destroyed. Perelli stayed on at the Cárdenas rancho, guarding his young vines. To Torreón in 1913, the year President Madero was murdered, came Pancho Villa, the former bandit chieftain who had become a general of the Revolution. Perelli promptly presented Villa with a basket of grapes and pleaded for protection for the vineyard. Villa consented and assigned him a guard of three soldiers. But a year later Villa left Torreón to join General Alvaro Obregón in Sonora. Conditions then became so chaotic that Perelli quit his job in 1916 and returned to California, where he went on to make his fortune in the San Joaquin Valley.

Perelli often returned to Mexico after the Revolution, and later it was he who helped to establish some of the new wineries that are making good Mexican wines today.

After the years of conflict, the tragic remnants of Mexico's vineyards continued to shrink. Wineries that started in Baja California imported grapes from San Diego and Cucamonga to make some of their wines. This was a period when grapes were scarce and sugar cheaper. Mexican wines were often "baptized" (watered), and they earned a poor reputation, something the present industry would prefer to end and forget. The vintners' trade association, the Asociación Nacional de Vitivinicultores, takes the position that though their industry is actually the oldest in the Americas, it is also the youngest. Its director, Rafael Almada N., says, "It was not until 1939 that the Mexican wine industry began its true development with characteristics that augur its future."

• 3 •

One summer morning in 1929, a thirty-six-year-old grocery merchant of Saltillo, the capital of Coahuila, went for a drive through the nearby countryside. It was election day, and because Nazario Ortiz Garza was a candidate for governor, he had decided to spend it outside the city. Passing an old hacienda, he noticed a few abandoned grapevines that had grown to enormous size and saw that they bore a crop of luscious-looking grapes. It occurred to him that it might be worthwhile to buy the hacienda, plant more vines, and make the place his country home—which he proceeded to do after winning the election. That day's drive in the country started don Nazario's second career, which made him Mexico's *capitan de la vitivinicultura,* the largest producer of wine and brandy in the Republic at that time.

The vineyard that he planted grew well. When he began making wine, he sent his second son, Mario, to the University of California at Davis to study viticulture and enology. A few years later he won another election which made him a member of the Mexican Senate. Then in 1946 President Miguel Alemán appointed him Mexico's secretary of agriculture. In that post— already owning wineries at both Saltillo and Mexico City—don Nazario traveled on government business throughout the Republic for the next six years. Wherever he went, he distributed grapevine cuttings to everyone who would agree to start a vineyard. He also bought, for his own account, 700 acres of wasteland in the State of Aguascalientes, planted most of it in vines, and there built his third winery in 1952. He went on establishing new vineyards in Coahuila, Durango, and Chihuahua, and at Torreón built a brandy distillery in 1966. By then he was using, in his four plants, one-fourth of the grapes grown in the nation.

• 4 •

Following the Second World War, the Mexican government stimulated the planting of vineyards by quadrupling the tariffs on European wines and by putting quota restrictions on wine imports. The result was that French, Spanish, and American wines cost five times as much as Mexican wines. When the supply of grapes increased, European and American companies began establishing their own plants in Mexico—such firms as Pedro Domecq, Martell Cognac, Seagram, and Osborne—though primarily to make brandy rather than wine. In three decades, the area planted to vineyards in Mexico multiplied more than forty times, from 4000 acres in 1939 to 173,000 acres in 1983.

Don Nazario says that is only the beginning, that Mexico has enough unused land to multiply its grape crop many more times. The country's wine consumption is estimated by the Asociación as about 1 million gallons a year or as a little over 1 pint per capita, less than one-fifteenth of the rate in the United States. If the Mexican government would help to remove obstacles to wine use, don Nazario declares, it could be increased ten times within a few years.

One of the obstacles is that wine is still a new product to most of the Mexican people, though table wines should go well with the highly seasoned native cuisine. Wine has three formidable competitors in Mexico: pulque, beer, and soft drinks. Pulque, the ancient Aztec drink fermented from the sap of the maguey cactus or century plant, is a whitish, cloudy liquid of about 4 to 6 percent alcohol. Millions of gallons are sold annually at farms and in the pulquerías in the cities, and a pasteurized version of it now is even sold in cans. From special types of pulque the Mexican liquors called tequila and mezcal are distilled.

Another obstacle to wine use is that, selling so little, restaurateurs and storekeepers have not yet learned to store it properly. Consequently, some of the table wine becomes partially spoiled before it is used. On my last six visits to Mexico, I tasted—at the wineries—some 1400 wines, and all but seven ranged from palatable to very good. But of the table wines served to me in restaurants and hotels, more than a few had the objectionable oxidized or sherrylike taste that comes from storage in warm rooms or sunlight or with corked bottles stood upright instead of laid horizontal. This kind of partial spoilage occurs in other countries, too, especially in South America, and in some parts of the United States. The best place to judge Mexican wines, therefore, is at the wineries, where they have not yet had an opportunity to spoil.

A greater barrier to wine is that the Mexican government misunderstands the role of table wine as the temperate mealtime beverage, lumps it with distilled spirits, and favors beer as "*la bebida de moderación*." Licenses to sell wine are costly and difficult to obtain, and table wine is taxed beyond the reach of Mexican households, at an average of 11 cents per liter, more than 40 cents per gallon. A law prevents vineyard ownership by wineries, an obstacle the vintners circumvent, however, by dividing vineyard ownership among members of their families.

The final obstacle to Mexican wines is the lack of an appreciative audience. Wine is bought mostly by wealthy and upper-middle-class people to serve on special occasions, for which many choose the expensive brands imported from Spain and France. Mexican wines thus suffer from snobbery—but of a kind more deeply rooted than that which long hindered American wines in the United States. The Mexican kind even has a name—*malinchismo.** It is the attitude prevalent among the wealthy in Mexico for four and a half centuries, that no native product or custom can equal its counterpart in Europe, from which civilization came to the New World.

A blow against *malinchismo* was struck by the Mexican Congress in 1965 with a pronouncement that all restaurants and night clubs in the Republic should offer Mexican-made wines and Mexican cheese on their menus. Since the restrictions on imports, some of the Spanish and French wine shippers have licensed Mexican wineries to bottle their best wines under the old European brand names the *malinchistas* have favored in the past. These Mexican wines bring higher prices than the rest and cope with snobbery to some extent.

• 5 •

Mexico has nine main vineyard districts: northern Baja California, the Laguna district at the border of Coahuila and Durango, Parras and Saltillo in Coahuila, Aguascalientes, the San Juan del Rio–Tequisquiapan region in Querétaro, the area between Ojo Caliente and Fresnillo in Zacatecas, Delicias in Chihuahua, and the Hermosillo-Caborca district in Sonora. Some grapes also are grown in San Luis Potosí, Puebla, Guanajuato, and Hidalgo. There are wineries around Mexico City that are supplied with grapes or wines grown farther north.

Some viticultural authorities consider Mexican climates too

*From Malinche, the Indian girl who, as the interpreter, mistress, and slave of Cortez, guided him up from Vera Cruz to his conquest of Montezuma's Aztec empire between 1519 and 1521. For betraying her race, according to legend, she was condemned to wander forever in tears and agony beneath the waters of Lake Texcoco by day and through the surrounding country by night. *Malinchista* became the term applied to people who show a preference for customs other than Mexican, and their snobbery became *malinchismo.*

warm for grapes because almost half of the country lies south of the Tropic of Cancer. But the central vineyards are situated on Mexico's mile-high Central Plateau, where elevation is as important as latitude. For each thousand feet of elevation, the average annual temperature decreases about three degrees, and there is a further factor: Summer days are shorter than in the higher latitudes. A trouble in the high plateau region is the extreme fluctuation of day and night temperatures. On warm days in the fall, the vines continue to grow under cloudless skies, making them vulnerable to freezes that sometimes follow during the nights. But the main flaw is too little moisture or too much. Dry districts depend on severely limited supplies of water for irrigation. Others have too much rain during the grape-growing season.

· 6 ·

Six fertile, irrigated valleys in the temperate northern tip of mostly arid Baja California produce some of Mexico's best table wines. This is "the Napa Valley of Mexico," cooled like the coast counties of Alta California by ocean breezes and fogs from the Pacific, which here is only twelve to thirty miles away. Much of the wine produced in these valleys travels in tank trucks to aging and bottling cellars around Mexico City, a three-day trip because it is some 1500 miles away.

New plantings of wine grapes during the 1970s are estimated to have increased the vineyards from 3000 to approximately 24,000 acres in these valleys—Santo Tomás, thirty miles south of Ensenada; Santa Isabel, twenty-five miles farther south past San Vicente; Guadalupe, thirty miles below the California border; and the Valle Redondo, Tanama, and Rancho Viejo districts around Tecate, across the border from San Diego County. Rainfall ranges from five to eighteen inches per year, but is supplemented by underground water supplies.

Only one of the seven wineries in the district is open to visitors. If Pedro Domecq, which in 1972 built the spectacularly attractive, ultramodern million-gallon Vides de Guadalupe winery in its Calafia Valley, fifteen miles northeast of Ensenada, would begin bottling here some of its nationally popular Calafia, Los Reyes, and Padre Kino table wines—and open a tasting room—"the Baja wine country" could attract thousands of American visitors per year. It is only a two-hour drive from San Diego via the Tijuana-Ensenada toll freeway to Domecq's winery on Highway 3. What prevents this is that a tasting room couldn't pay its expenses in wine sales. The U.S. law allows "Baja" visitors to bring in only one bottle of wine per adult when they recross the border from Mexico.

Visitors are welcome for tours and tasting at the oldest and biggest Baja California winery, the Bodegas de Santo Tomás, whose cellars, with 1.8 million gallons' capacity, span Avenida Miramar in Ensenada. It was founded in 1888 by Francisco Andonegui, an Italian gold miner who built an adobe winery near the ruins of Santo Tomás Mission. In the late 1920s, when Andonegui was dying, he sold his property to the then governor, General Abelardo Luis Rodríguez, who owned it for forty years. Rodríguez, the revolutionary general who later became president of Mexico, was prodigiously wealthy, owning fleets of tuna and shrimp boats, canneries, factories, and some eighty other businesses, including the Caliente racetrack, which he sold in 1932. After his term as president ended in 1934, General Rodríguez moved the winery from Santo Tomás Valley to the port city of Ensenada. He later planted more vineyards at Rancho Guadalupe to supplement those near the mission.

In 1962 the general hired Dimitri Tchelistcheff, son of the famous André, as the technical director of Santo Tomás. Dimitri, born in Paris in 1930, learned winemaking from his father at Beaulieu, earned his degree in viticulture and enology at UC Davis, and had worked at Napa's Schramsberg Vineyard and at the Gallo winery in Modesto. Dimitri replanted some of the general's vineyards with Cabernet, Pinot Noir, Riesling, Chenin Blanc, and Chardonnay, and installed new equipment in the winery for the cold fermentation of white wines. He produced excellent wines, notably his aged Barbera and San Emilion, which have been imported to the United States, and the first two Baja California *vinos espumosos* (champagnes),* a Charmat-process extra-dry called Cordon Azul and a bottle-fermented brut named Calviñe. An ammunition tunnel dug uphill from the winery during the Second World War became the champagne cellar of Santo Tomás. After fifteen years, Dimitri left Santo Tomás in 1977 to become a freelance vineyard and winery consultant, and now makes his home on the Island of Maui. His successor is his former assistant, Octavio Jiménez, a chemical graduate from the University of Mexico, who has kept up the quality of the wines.

General Rodríguez died at his Ensenada home in 1967, at the age of seventy-eight. The vineyards and winery passed to his

---

*During the 1960s, the government of France persuaded Mexico to prohibit its vintners from calling their sparkling wines champagne.

widow, the former Aida Sullivan of San Diego, and to his three sons, but were sold a year later to the Elias Pando wine-importing firm of Mexico City.

The Guadalupe Valley, the upper portion of which Domecq has named "Calafia Valley," was settled early in this century by a religious colony of immigrants from Russia. They are said to have lived in poverty, even robbing beehives for food, until General Rodríguez advised them to plant vineyards and sell him their grapes. There now are three wineries in the valley. Oldest is the Formex-Ybarra winery, built in 1957, which sends its Terrasola wines and brandy in bulk to its plant in Mexico City, as Domecq does. Three miles farther north is Domecq's handsome Vides de Guadalupe, built in 1972, with an equally handsome aging cellar named Bodegas de las Misiones, added six years later.

Across the road is a still larger winery named Vinícola la Cetto, built during the 1970s by Luis Angel Cetto, who manages Domecq's winery and two other Baja California wineries that he owns. Cetto also manages the Fiesta de la Vendímia sponsored by Domecq, held with much dancing at Colonia de Guadalupe during the vintage in September.

Another Domecq property is the Vinícola de Ensenada on Avenida Cipres, between Ensenada and Estero Beach. It was built to make wine and is still managed by Estaban Ferro, who once managed the Santo Tomás winery for General Rodríguez, but now produces only the part of Domecq brandy that is made from British Columbia grapes.

The original Cetto winery is the Productos de Uva cellar in Tijuana. Angelo Cetto came from Italy to Guadalupe in 1923, worked as a laborer, then went north to Tijuana and began making bulk wine. He sent his sons to college in Mexico City, and when his eldest, Luis Angel, joined his business, it began to grow. The Tijuana cellar began bottling wine under the F. Chauvenet brand of France. Luis now owns vineyards at both Guadalupe and Valle Redondo, and also the winery at Tecate that was established during the 1950s by José Vasquez. His brother, Ferruccio Cetto, owns the independent Productos de Uva winery and distillery at Aguascalientes.

At Valle Redondo, between Tecate and Tijuana, the principal vineyard is the 125 acres owned by Humberto Pérez. In 1940, when his father Conrado began making El Mirador wines and Casa Blanca brandy in his Vinícola Regional winery in Tijuana, it was out in the country, but booming Tijuana now surrounds the site. Humberto was trained in viticulture and enology at UC Davis, where one of his classmates was Dimitri Tchelistcheff.

It was Humberto who told Tchelistcheff that General Rodríguez wanted to hire a California-trained enologist, and suggested that Dimitri apply for the job. Humberto now teaches biochemistry at the University of Baja California, besides running his vineyards and winery.

The remaining Baja California district, Rancho Viejo, is a small valley between brush-covered hills eight miles off the Ensenada-Tecate highway. The vineyard and winery there were established about 1940, but production has been limited by the scarcity of water.

• 7 •

Hacienda Alamo at Saltillo, where Nazario Ortiz Garza planted his first vines, is now the headquarters of all his *viñedos* (vineyards) in four Mexican states. Though situated directly on Federal Highway 54, only three miles from the modern city, the hacienda cannot have changed much since colonial times. It is a self-contained village, with its own ancient adobe church and primary school, and the homes of vineyard workers cluster around the baronial residence of Mario, don Nazario's son. Its vineyard, however, has shrunk lately to half of its original 450-acre size. Lack of water is the reason: The fast-growing city of Saltillo has first call on the supply that is pumped from local wells, which now range in depth from 600 feet to a half-mile.

On Xicotencatl Street in Saltillo, near the railway station, is don Nazario's oldest winery, where he now makes only brandies. His own are called Club 45, Señorial, and Saviñon, and he also makes the Mexican brandy of Gonzalez-Byass of Spain. Remy H. Remy, a graduate of Montpellier and the University of Caen, is in charge.

In the State of Aguascalientes, nine miles north of Aguascalientes city, is don Nazario's principal winery. If you travel on the Carretera Internacional (CN 45) between El Paso and Mexico City, you cannot miss it, because his property spans the highway. On one side, a mammoth wine bottle perched atop his winery dominates the valley skyline and can be seen for miles. Across the road, a rococo portal announces the entrance to his Viñedos San Marcos. San Marcos and Alamo are the brands of his principal wines and brandies. Behind the winery is a hacienda even greater than that of Alamo, again with its own church and primary school. Fifty families live there, and the hacienda has its own school bus that takes the children to the Aguascalientes high school.

This winery has the most impressive visitor and tasting facility in Mexico, a project of Mario Ortiz—a semi-underground reception building, called Sala de Recepcion des Visitantes, connected by a 300-yard-long tunnel with the winery, where guides show you around. Mario plans to add a railroad in the tunnel.

Aguascalientes wines achieved premium quality in 1970, when don Nazario employed as his enologist José Romagosa from Chile, who was born in Spain and trained at the Vilafranca del Panadés enological station and the Codorniu champagne cellars nearby. Since Romagosa began modernizing the winery equipment, San Marcos has produced Cabernets of Bordeaux character and bottle-fermented champagnes called Champ d'Or Naturel and Brut.

The oldest Aguascalientes winery is Bodegas Brandevin, established by Filemon Alonso in an old woolen mill in 1948. Francisco Hill operates it now, making grape concentrate and sangría.

The Fería de la Uva y el Vino in Aguascalientes has been celebrated in mid-August since 1954.

• 8 •

At Paila, on the Saltillo-Torreón highway (CN 40) through southern Coahuila, you turn off on state Route 35 through a valley of pecan groves and vineyards to reach Parras de la Fuente, sixteen miles to the south. Most guidebooks neglect Parras, merely mentioning it as the birthplace of the martyred president of Mexico, Francisco I. Madero. It is a lovely, unspoiled colonial town that still has horse cabs, but no tourist guides. For the wine tourist, a visit to the valley is interesting because the oldest wineries in Mexico are there.

The first was the Vinícola del Marqués Aguayo, founded in 1593 by a Spanish captain, Francisco de Urdiñola. Urdiñola found wild grapes growing in the valley, and named it Santa María de las Parras ("of the grapevines"), which was changed after the French invasion of 1862–1867 to honor Antonio de la Fuente, a hero of that conflict. If local historians are correct, the Parras valley was the cradle of viniculture in the Americas. They say that from here, Urdiñola sent his wines and vines to Peru, Chile, and Argentina before any vineyards existed in South America, and that he continued doing so until the Spanish authorities enforced the royal order that wine in the New World must come only from Spain. Urdiñola's great-granddaughter married a Spaniard, who through the captain's influence was given a title, and when the marqués inherited the property, he gave it his new name.

Although this is the oldest winery on the American continent, all that remains of the original structure is a single adobe wall, and under its present owners, the Almacénes Guajuardo merchants of Monterrey, its main product is brandy, distilled for another firm.

Second oldest, and with its 10-million-gallon capacity one of the most important in Mexico, is the Bodegas de San Lorenzo of Casa Madero. Founded in 1626 (perhaps as early as 1597) by Lorenzo Garcia, it is now owned by members of the Madero family, cousins of the late president. There are ruins of many more wineries around Parras. Despite the Spanish law, every early hacienda had its own vineyard and made wine.

The Maderos have owned the bodegas since 1870. In that year, Evaristo Madero Elizondo, a young merchant from northern Coahuila across the border from the United States, bought Hacienda San Lorenzo and Captain Urdiñola's original property, Hacienda Rosario. Don Evaristo traveled to Europe and brought back superior grape varieties from Italy, Switzerland, Spain, Portugal, and France. In Cognac he bought a brandy still, and brought French experts to install it at Parras. By the turn of the century, don Evaristo's wines and brandies were winning medals at the Paris, Buffalo, and St. Louis expositions. After his death in 1911, the property passed to his sons by his second wife, although he had the foresight to incorporate his Parras holdings. To his sons and grandsons by his first wife he willed lands in the Laguna district. One of these grandsons was Francisco, the idealistic cotton planter and intellectual who started the Revolution of 1910 and became President Madero of Mexico.

In don Evaristo's time, vineyards covered 3000 acres in the Parras Valley, but most of them were destroyed by the phylloxera and the rest by neglect during the Revolution. The thousand acres replanted since, of which the Madero descendants own half, are all on phylloxera-resistant roots.

Rebuilt since 1962, with its beautiful church beside the cellars, Casa Madero is one of Mexico's handsomest wineries. It is also hospitable; signs on the road from Paila invite you to visit the bodegas. After you tour the cellars and the distillery, with its quaint French-type pot stills, you are served wines beside the three-century-old Casa Grande. But one time *not* to visit Parras, unless you have reserved accommodations months in advance, is during its Fiesta de Uva in mid-August, the annual grape festival which the Madero family revived in 1946.

Casa Madero's main products are pot-still brandies; wines have been less than one-tenth of its output in recent years. When

José Milmo became the manager in 1973, a small modern winery was built within the big winery especially to make table wines. Milmo, trained in enology at Montpellier in France, views wine as the drink of the future in Mexico. The improvement in Casa Madero wines was evident in my last three visits. The best recent wines, made by enologist Francisco Rodriguez, who spent two years of study at Montpellier, were of Pinot Blanc, Cabernet, Ruby Cabernet, Merlot, and Zinfandel. Madero also makes a *mistela* called Panache, an unfermented juice plus brandy, resembling the Pineau des Charentes of Cognac.

Eduardo Madero's son Joaquin studied plant propagation in France and has continued his studies at a Zacatecas center for vine research. Eduardo's brother Benjamin, who was educated in Michigan and played guitar in the university orchestra there, says Mexican wines will continue to improve as better grape varieties are planted. He has kept temperature records at Parras since 1953 and concludes that Parras, 5000 feet above sea level, has a Region IV climate, comparable to Lodi in California and Florence in Italy.

· 9 ·

Two hours' drive west of Parras, clustered at the border of Durango and Coahuila, are the charming old triplet cities of Gómez Palacio, Lerdo, and Torreón, only minutes apart. Torreón, the largest, is on the Coahuila side. Around the cities, in the reclaimed Laguna district, hundreds of former cotton fields have been replanted with vineyards since Mexico's grape industry came back to life in the early 1940s. At Torreón in 1966, the Mexican government established its first mother vineyard with stocks from Davis to propagate and supply the grape growers with virus-free vines.

The two newest wineries in La Laguna, those of Nazario Ortiz Garza and Pedro Domecq near Torreón, were designed to make brandy, into which go more than nine-tenths of the grapes grown in Mexico.* Eight times more brandy is now made than wine.

---

*This came about partly through a quirk in the semantics of drink. The Spanish word for spirits is *aguardiente,* literally burning water. New, water-white grape brandy is *aguardiente de uva,* and aged beverage brandy is *coñac* in Spanish. But after the Second World War, the Mexican government prohibited all *coñac* labels except on those from the Cognac district of France. The Mexican *coñac* distillers, suddenly left without a label for their products, adopted its English name, though there is no such word as brandy in the Spanish language. It turned out to have such snob appeal to Mexicans that brandy has since passed rum and tequila as the chief distilled liquor drunk in Mexico.

Oldest winery in the district, the Vinícola del Vergel near Gómez Palacio, also makes brandy, but devotes some of its production to wine. It invites visitors to tour its cellars and to taste its assortment of table and dessert wine types.

Vergel (Spanish for flower garden) was built in 1943 by one of the district's leading cotton planters, the late Luis Garza (not related to don Nazario). The founder's son, Santiago A. Garza, is now in charge. With its outdoor batteries of temperature-controlled tanks of Mexican-made stainless steel, Vergel resembles the modern wineries of California. But beneath the main building is one of the most spectacular Old World underground cellars in North America. Its vaulted roof and supporting pillars are made entirely of rough marble quarried in the nearby mountains. Each of the large casks in the cellar bears the name of a saint.

Santiago Garza says Mexico's vintners have been too busy in recent years trying to keep up with their expanding brandy business to pay enough attention to wine, but that he has created a new division in Vergel to specialize in producing only table wines. Vergel has planted new vineyards of premium wine-grape varieties at high elevations in Zacatecas, where the climates are cooler than La Laguna's Region V. Vergel plans to build a winery there, but meanwhile is having its grapes from Zacatecas vinified at its Industrias de la Fermentacion brandy plant in Aguascalientes.

• 10 •

At Hermosillo, in the semitropical west coast state of Sonora, vineyards were planted among the orchards and cotton fields beginning about 1961. The grapes, however, were mostly the early-ripening table varieties, intended for shipment to the United States in competition with the early Coachella Valley crop from California. A winery was built at Hermosillo in 1965, but its principal product was brandy, not wine. In the early 1970s, the plantings spread 150 miles north to Caborca, only 50 miles below the Arizona border, again with vines such as Thompson Seedless and Perlettes. Some growers at Caborca also planted wine varieties because of the heavy yields. There now are five plants crushing grapes mainly for brandy in Sonora, which has become Mexico's chief grape-growing state with more than half of the vineyards in the nation. A Fiesta Vendímia is held in Hermosillo five days after the first grapes are picked in mid-July.

In Chihuahua, table grapes and brandy are also the chief products of the vineyards. Farmers found it more profitable to raise grapes than cotton after the Second World War. There are two wineries at Ciudad Delicias, one making brandy, the other table wine.

· 11 ·

The southernmost vineyard district of Mexico is the valley of the Río de San Juan, 100 miles north of Mexico City in the state of Querétaro. It is also one of the highest, 6100 feet above sea level. Though situated two degrees within the Torrid Zone, the valley successfully grows the delicate grape varieties that make superior table wines.

A mile east of the old colonial town of San Juan del Río is a handsome stone winery named Cavas de San Juan, which produces Hidalgo wines. Francisco Domenech, born in Catalonia, where his family produced vermouth, built the winery in 1958 to make both wine and brandy, but primarily table wines. As his enologist he employed Carlos Reulet, a graduate of the vinicultural school of Onde near Bordeaux and a former pilot in the Free French Air Force. Meanwhile, Domenech sent his son, Francisco Domenech T., to the wine school at UC Davis to be trained. When young Francisco came home, he began replanting the vineyard with such varieties as Cabernet Sauvignon, Pinot Noir, Gamay, Pinot Gris, Chenin Blanc, and Chardonnay. The winery then supplemented its Blanco Seco, Blanco Amabile, Rosado Seco, Clarete, and Tinto with a vintage-dated (as many Mexican wines are now) Cepa Cabernet Sauvignon, a Cepa Pinot Noir, a Blanc de Blancs of Chenin and Ugni Blanc, and an assortment of Charmat-process *vinos espumosos* (champagnes).

At Calle 9 on the road toward Tequisquiapan is the Cruz Blanca (white cross) winery, established in 1968 by Eugenio Nicolau and his son Eugenio Jr. Cruz Blanca is their very acceptable standard table wine, sold in liters and jugs. They have older wines for sale in restaurants under their Montebello brand. Eugenio Jr. was trained in enology at the Agrario Institute at Trento in Italy. The Nicolaus have a hundred acres of vines, but most of their grapes come from the vineyards of José Fernando Muñoz Castillo, young Nicolau's brother-in-law.

Down the road from Cruz Blanca is the Madrileña winery, which resembles a fort. It was built in 1969 for the Velasco Brothers, Mexico City wine merchants whose father Pedro came from Castile in 1908. Madrileña's enologist, Edgardo Ruggeri, is from Argentina, where he was trained in the Mendoza wine school. He makes a pleasant red wine called "Viñalta Malbec & Cabernet" and a "Tres Coronas" sherry. Half of the sherry is aged two years in oak barrels in the sun, then is blended with the other half in stainless steel.

Twelve miles north of San Juan del Río, near the picturesque village of Tequisquiapan, are a vineyard, winery, and distillery that produce table wines and brandy for Martell of Mexico, an affiliate of Martell Cognac of France. I was amazed when I tasted its first red wine, called Clos San José Tinto, for although it was only six months old and came from a stainless-steel tank, it was pleasant to drink and had the balance of body, acid, and tannin of a young Bordeaux. Enologist Georges Mondié, from Montpellier via North Africa, said it was Cabernet with a blend of Merlot. Another of his *tintos* is called Chatillon. Miguel d'Orcasberro makes Martell's Mexican brandies, which are called Cheverny and Tradición. The 800 acres of Martell vineyards planted since 1965 are principally of Ugni Blanc for the brandy, and of Cabernet, Merlot, Sauvignon Blanc, and Grenache for table wines. Mondié was experimenting with producing *espumosos* when I paid him a return visit in 1982.

Wine grapes also grow in the neighboring state of Guanajuato, but only one small winery operates there. It is Hugo Gamba's Bodegas San Luis Rey on Plaza Morelos in the small town of San Luis de la Paz. Founded in 1870, it is worth a visit to see the maze of wine-aging tunnels beneath the cellar, dug centuries ago by Jesuit priests as places to hide from warring native tribes. The tunnels store wines and brandies dating from the Revolution, including a sacramental Muscat of 1912 vintage that is still good to drink.

· 12 ·

At altitudes of nearly 7000 feet, even higher than San Juan del Río, are the vineyards of Mexico's newest winegrowing district, the area between Ojo Caliente and Fresnillo in the state of Zacatecas. Thousands of irrigated acres have been planted there since 1970 because the climate is mainly Region III, land is plentiful, and there is minimal damage from summer rains.

The largest vineyard, at Ojo Caliente, is the Viñedos don Luis, planted to grow grapes for Vergel table wines and named for Santiago Garza's father. Nearby is the first Zacatecas winery, Bodegas de Altiplano, started in 1981 by Francisco Javier Gonzales after he spent two years studying winemaking at Montpel-

lier. The handsomest brandy distillery in Mexico is Victor Caste-
lazo's Vides de Zacatecas at Luis Moya. Daniel Carrera Salcedo's
Rancho el Saucito, south of Fresnillo, produces mainly wine for
brandy.

Since 1979 Zacatecas has celebrated the vintage each September with a Fería de la Uva y de la Tuna at Ojo Caliente. *Tuna*
is the edible prickly pear.

• 13 •

Around Mexico City, there are many wine and brandy establishments, and some of them can be visited by appointment,
but be sure to telephone for a specific time and to get driving
directions before you start out.

In the suburb of Los Reyes, an eleven-mile drive on the road
toward Puebla, is the impressive brandy and wine blending, aging, and bottling plant of Pedro Domecq of Mexico, related to
the great sherry-making family of Spain. It is worth the trip
to see Domecq's great brandy *soleras,* the lovely "La Sacristía"
with its display of glass-fronted barrels showing the year-by-
year benefits of aging brandy in oak, the murals depicting the

The late Pedro F. Domecq of the Domecq sherry family of Spain headed Domecq wine and brandy production throughout Mexico from his headquarters
at Los Reyes, near Mexico City, from 1951 until his death in 1983.

history of Mexican beverages starting with pulque in pre-Columbian times, and also the dozen ornamental but genuine *tinajas,* the giant earthenware vessels in which wines in Spain were aged for centuries before the eras of wooden, then concrete, and now stainless-steel tanks.

Domecq produces several Mexican table wines in its Calafia winery in Baja California, but no sherries, because Domecq sherries come only from Spain. Its "Los Reyes" Tinto, Blanco, and Rosado are among the best table wines in Mexico and are exported to the United States. Equally good are its "Calafia" Blanco and Tinto wines. The newest Domecq products are the pleasant light red and white (only 8.8 percent alcohol) "Padre Kino" wines, named for Father Francisco Esebio Kino, the Italian Jesuit priest who founded the missions in Arizona before he came to Mexico in 1681 and colonized its northern regions. There also is "Val de Reyes," a tinto supplied in two-liter jugs to restaurants and stores. Since 1982, Domecq has begun adding the year of vintage to the labels of some of its table wines.

From 1951 until his death in 1983, Domecq operations in Mexico were headed by onetime mining engineer Pedro F. Domecq, a great-great-grandnephew of the original Pedro. The technical director, supervising the eleven bodegas and vinicolas that produce Domecq's Mexican brandies and wines, is Marcial Ibarra, who learned enology from Professor Cruess at the University of California and later taught it at the University of Mexico.

At ancient Tlalnepantla, several miles north of the capital, off the road to Querétaro, are the old Bodegas Santa María. Ricardo Fernandez, whose father once owned the winery, now makes brandy and wine there for Bobadilla, the producer of sherries at Jerez in Spain. Around Mexico City, too, are the modern plants of such world-famous companies as Seagram, Cinzano, and Martini & Rossi. The latter two make their vermouths from Mexican wines. Also at Tlanepantla are the Cavas Bach cellars, founded in Mexico in 1972 by the owners of the Bach vineyards and winery at Vilafranca del Penedés near Barcelona. Its chief products are brandy and a pleasant champagne called Champbrule, but it also has table wines from Baja California and Aguascalientes with such varietal labels as Nebbiolo. Cavas Bach also makes a sparkling red wine labeled Cold Duck, whose name printed in English, and translated from a German pun, may be difficult to explain to the company's Mexican customers.

The busiest winery in Mexico City is Nazario Ortiz Garza's cellar on Avenida Mixcoac. There he bottles a six-year-old red under the brand name of Federico Paternina of Haro, in the

Rioja district of Spain, and also a medium-sweet brown sherry, sun-baked in the rear of the cellar, called Jerez Solera Alamo.

• 14 •

To visit all of the Mexican vineyard districts in a single trip is impractical except by car, or preferably by private plane. Tor-reón, Aguascalientes, and Chihuahua are served by scheduled airlines, but at this writing Ensenada, San Juan del Río, and Saltillo are not. For private planes, arrangements can be made to use the airstrip at Parras adjoining the Casa Madero vineyards.

Wine-touring in Mexico will become increasingly interesting in the future, as the better grape varieties lately planted come into bearing and as the quality of Mexican wines, vastly better than they were in the past, continues to improve.

24

Hobbyists and Small Wineries

WHILE BIG WINERIES have been getting bigger in order to slake America's growing thirst for wine, production by little winemakers has been increasing at an even more rapid rate.

Small wineries that sell their own products have nearly trebled in numbers since 1965, and as more states reduce their exorbitant minimum license fees for wineries, they will continue to multiply in years to come. Almost as important, in terms of millions of gallons, is the fast-growing trend toward home winemaking. Both kinds of small-scale winemaking are doing as much as the commercial wineries to change viniculture in America.

• 2 •

Home winemakers, who ferment juice only for their own use, fall into several categories, which sometimes overlap. During Prohibition, more than 30 million gallons were made annually in home basements in this country, especially by immigrant European families, to whom wine was a mealtime necessity. Most of their immediate descendants, however, have given up the fermenting of grapes as too much trouble. Today's noncommercial winemakers are a new breed.

They usually start with the simple kitchen experiment of adding yeast to a crock of crushed grapes, juice, or reconstituted concentrate. Some try it once and give it up when they find they have made inferior vinegar instead. But many go on to spend hundreds and often thousands of dollars on crushers, presses, chemicals, and testing instruments, and many even to making their own champagnes.

While some who make wine regularly are merely saving

533

money, another and more numerous category is primarily hobbyists, motivated not by economy but by their fascination with the mystique and romance of wine. They are mostly talented white-collar people bitten by the wine bug, who have found in this scientific kind of handicraft a hobby of continuing interest, more aesthetically satisfying than collecting coins, stamps, or books. Wine, because it keeps changing and takes months and years to mature, gives the winemaker a sense of the future that no other hobby does. The oenothusiast knows that better wine than he makes can usually be bought for little more or even less at the store.

Most devoted of the avocational winemakers are professional people, particularly physicians, engineers, chemists, college professors, accountants, artists, and writers. The doctors are the most avid of them all. Far more M.D.s than people of any other occupation are counted among the customers of the winemaking supply firms. Why wine especially fascinates physicians is explained in a book called *Vine and Scalpel* by Dr. Max Lake, who owns a vineyard in Australia. "The doctor," he writes, "has a comfortable amount of winemaking science as part of his medical training. He must also learn to evaluate sensory impressions and cultivate mental discipline, two attributes that tend to make him a wine connoisseur."

Hundreds of home winemakers' societies have been formed across the United States because amateur enologists want others to taste and compare their wines. Their national organization, the American Wine Society, lists 2200 members and eighty chapters in three dozen states, and publishes its own quarterly journal.

Since 1979, when a new Federal law removed most of the decades-old restrictions on home winemaking and brewing, amateur enologists have become more numerous than ever before. They no longer have to register in advance with a Federal office, nor is the right to make wine at home limited to heads of households, as it was since the repeal of Prohibition in 1933. Anyone of legal age now can make 100 gallons of wine or beer each year—200 gallons in homes with more than one resident—for personal use and not for sale.

When the old prohibition against transporting homemade wine from one's dwelling was also repealed, scores of annual judgings of homemade wines immediately were established, by clubs and by county and state fairs. The lure of possibly winning prizes for their best vintages was added as a motive for making wine at home. Amateur winemakers are as proud of their achievements as flower growers, dog breeders, artists, and others who hold quality contests; perhaps even prouder, for winemaking is both an art and a science. (The first public judging of homemade wines in this country was held in August 1972 at Mason City, Iowa, as part of the North Iowa Fair. The first national judging was held, with advance Federal permission, at San Francisco in February 1973.)

A conservative estimate, based on annual interstate carlot shipments of grapes, is that at least 7 million gallons of wine are now being made noncommercially in the United States each year. But if wines made from grape concentrate (condensed juice) are counted, the quantity may be closer to 10 million gallons, enough to supply a half-million amateurs with 40 gallons each. And this does not include the production by those householders who ferment only dandelions, rhubarb, elderberries, blueberries, or honey (to make mead), as their grandmothers and great-grandmothers did.

A multimillion-dollar accessory industry has come into existence to supply amateur enologists with home-winemaking materials, equipment, corks, and even with labels printed with their names, such as "Chateau Smith Vin Blanc" or "Maison Jones Private Stock." Some firms offer free classes in winemaking and distribute bumper strips with such messages as MAKE WINE NOT WAR.

Purists, of course, prefer to make their wines out of fresh grapes or juice, which can only be bought at vintage time. Frozen grapes and grape concentrate, available year-round, are more convenient for winemaking at home. The revived use of concentrate recalls the Prohibition era a half-century ago, when millions of gallons of "Vine-Glo," "Caligrapo," and "Forbidden Fruit" concentrates were fermented to wine in American homes.

Concentrate wines generally lack aroma; they are not Sunday wines. Experiments in progress have attempted to extract the aromatic essences of wine grapes before the juice is concentrated. The idea is to supply home winemakers with the bottled essence, to be added after the wine is made.

A beginner's winemaking kit, which can be bought for only a few dollars, contains a quart of concentrate, small envelopes of yeast and chemicals, fermentation locks, siphon hose, a collapsible plastic jug, and a recipe to make a single gallon (about five bottles) of table wine. Bigger kits at higher prices are sold in states where exorbitant taxes make commercial wines expensive or where wines can be bought only in state monopoly stores. Some colleges now offer classes in winemaking, wine chemistry, and expert tasting, and scores of books are published for those who make wine at home.

• 3 •

The truest of all wine lovers are those who grow their own grapes. Their appreciation of the final product is multiplied by the years of back-breaking labor, suffering the depredations of weather and of grape-eating birds, and waiting for their first crops. How patient they must be is evident from the three to five years it takes from the planting of a vine until it bears a usable crop. If you add four years for a fine red wine to mature, you see that the new winegrower is investing a decade of his life. Yet there are many who consider the rewards infinitely greater than those from the raising of other crops that one cannot drink.

Philip Wagner, whose books have encouraged thousands of amateurs to plant wine grapes, spells out the attractions. A hundred healthy vines in the lower end of a back yard, he says, will yield a vintage of sixty gallons, which supplies the grower with three hundred bottles, or almost a bottle of table wine per day throughout the year. (In sunny California, Dr. Albert Winkler calculates that a hundred vines can produce three times as much as Wagner's figure.)

• 4 •

Most of the small winegrowers who have bonded their cellars hope to make a profit by selling their wines. Whether they profit or lose depends on many factors, including their talent, industrial habits, business sense, and particularly on whether the law of the state where the small winery is situated sets a reasonable minimum annual license fee, such as $20 a year, for a farm winery. The law must permit the winegrower to offer complimentary tasting, to sell his product at both retail and wholesale, and to stay open on Sunday because that is the day most people like to go on wine tours. More than two dozen states have adopted farm winery laws in recent years.

In winegrowing, as in most other industries, it costs multiple millions to start out in competition with the leaders. But wine is one of the few products an individual can start producing on a small acreage and make something in his home basement that he can sell. Better yet, of course, is to start out wealthy, with no thought of early profits, as many have done. For some there is sufficient reward in merely achieving the admired status of winegrower and enjoying the praise usually lavished on one's estate-grown wines.

Decades ago, Herman Wente gave me some advice to pass on to the many would-be winegrowers who have come to me for guidance. The small winegrower can succeed, Herman said, only if he remains small and sells his wine at retail. Thereby he makes not only the profits (if any) of the grape grower and of the wine producer, but the profits of the wholesaler and of the retailer in addition. To my knowledge, those who have followed Herman's advice have prospered thus far.

Small winegrowers also have an advantage that Herman didn't mention. Because their output is limited, their wines become rarities, which lends them extra charm. Connoisseurs nowadays gladly pay extra prices for good wines if they are especially scarce and hard to find. I know some small winegrowers who sell all they can make, at prices considerably above those of the well-known premium brands, by merely sending announcements to the customers on their mailing lists that their latest vintages are ready to be shipped.

A quandary facing small winegrowers is to decide how they would like themselves to be described. They resent being called "boutique wineries," a term that came into use in the 1970s, because they consider it a slur. Yet "boutique" does suggest to many a small place where things of quality can be found. Some consider "small winery" a sufficiently descriptive term. In France, small wineries call themselves châteaux, though few of them resemble castles. I prefer to call them "farm wineries" or "estate wineries" because these terms and these wineries' very existence help to educate the public and legislatures about what wine is. Seeing a small winery on a vineyard teaches people the key fact that distinguishes wine from manufactured beverages, that wine is a natural product grown on a farm like other foods. It tells the story of wine better than any book can.

There is no truth, of course, in the belief held by many connoisseurs, that fine wines can only be made in small quantities. The American wines that are now winning high praise around the world come from sizable wineries that have modern equipment and staffs of expert enologists.

Yet commercial wines need to be filtered, fined, made brilliantly clear and sufficiently stable to survive transportation for great distances and storage in excessive heat and cold while awaiting sale. The small winegrower can let his wines clarify themselves, can bottle them while they still contain grape solids that will precipitate in the bottles, and he can explain this to his customers.

In particular, commercial grape growers have found it economically necessary to abandon their old hillside vineyards, which once produced their finest wines. Their tractors and mechanical harvesters cannot operate on steep terrain, and labor costs have made hand-cultivation prohibitively expensive. (This is also happening in Europe.) Only the avocational winegrower can afford to till the hillsides.

The small winegrower may not make wines that are finer than others, but what he makes will at least be excitingly different. Only he can afford to experiment in places where grapes have not been grown before, planting new grape varieties and developing wines with new regional characters.

I was discussing the future of fine American wines recently with André Tchelistcheff. He pointed out that as the production of the leading vintners in Europe and America continues to grow in volume, their wines become more uniform; they have less opportunity to engage in pioneering experiments. "The apostolic mission of the future," said Tchelistcheff, "belongs to the small winegrower."

25

"Varietal Grapes" and Their Wines

W HEN AMERICAN VINTNERS, during the half-
century following Repeal, introduced al-
most a hundred wines newly named for grape varieties, they
multiplied the delicious confusion that surrounds the subject
of wine. Most of the varietal names on bottle labels and restaurant wine lists present a viticultural puzzle to most buyers of
wine.

But in adopting varietal labeling, the vintners also contributed
vastly to the improved quality of American wines. For by renaming their best and costliest vintages for the grapes from which
they are made, the wineries gave vineyardists a profit motive
to plant superior wine-grape varieties in place of the more prolific
fresh-juice, raisin, and table grapes that long had been used to
make American wines.

If, for example, the vintners had not taught wine merchants
that Chardonnay, White (Johannisberg) Riesling, Cabernet Sauvignon, and Pinot Noir make the world's finest table wines, the
grape growers would not have planted the more than 60,000
acres of these noble varieties that have been added to American
vineyards since the mid-1960s. Buyers who have learned to recognize these varietal labels now gladly pay dollars more per
bottle for these wines than for their old generically named equiv-
alents—chablis, rhine wine, claret, and burgundy. And once sta-
tus-conscious Americans master the pronunciation of such
tongue-twisting names as Cabernet Sauvignon and Pinot Noir,
they proudly order them in stores and restaurants to display
their knowledge of fine wines.

How this motivates vineyard-planting is evident from the
prices wineries pay growers for "varietal grapes," from double

539

up to several times the per-ton prices for the old varieties that make ordinary wines.

Grapes whose names appear on labels of premium-priced wines are commonly miscalled "varietal grapes," but this is a redundancy, because every grape, including those that make poor wines, is a member of some variety, no matter what its botanical lineage may be. Another foggy popular term is "varietal wines," which doesn't describe the wines, but only means that their labels tell you the grape varieties from which they are principally made.

Wines sold under grape names are usually better than those labeled with the old generic names of European geographic origin. But not always; some wineries' blended clarets, burgundies, chablis, and rhine wines are better than their Cabernets, Chardonnays, and Pinot Noirs, because quality depends on all the care a wine is given, from the planting of the vine to the time it is aged and released for sale.

Adding to the varietal confusion is that most Old World grapes have several different names, by any of which wines made from them have been called. Many grapes are misnamed, and European vintners, now imitating the American varietal labels, are adding to the tangle with their own versions of grape-variety names. The result is that one needs an ampelography, which can't be found in the average library, to be even partially guided through the wine-nomenclature maze.

• 2 •

A start at unraveling some of the varietal names was made in a grape-certification program founded by the University of California in 1952. Vinifera vines certified as correctly named, and also as free of virus diseases, have since been supplied to growers by cooperating nurseries. The program's purpose was not to untangle grape nomenclature, but to supply the wine industry with disease-free vines. It was prompted by advances in plant pathology after the Second World War, which showed that most of the world's vineyards are hosts to a previously unidentified disease called leafroll virus, which reduces vine vigor and productivity without killing the plants. Were it not for this virus, plant pathologists say, the vineyards of Europe would have more frequent vintage years than they do. One of their surprising discoveries was that the much-admired autumn coloring of vineyards is mostly caused by the leafroll virus—that the leaves of healthy vines seldom develop those spectacularly lovely shades of red.

Unfortunately, when the vineyard-planting spree of the late 1960s began, supplies of certified-healthy vines were not sufficient to meet the demand. Thousands of acres were recklessly planted with cuttings from diseased vines, purchased from infected vineyards and from nurseries with uncertified stocks. When this was realized, quarantines against virus-infected vines were hurriedly established in some states. The shortage of virus-free stock was relieved by exposing vines to controlled heat for several weeks, after which cuttings could be taken from them that were free of disease. An assembly-line method of growing grapes in moisture-controlled greenhouses, called "mist propagation," has since made it possible to produce a million cuttings per year from a single parent vine.

• 3 •

In California, for almost a century, except during Prohibition, university viticulturists tested wine grapes, growing more than a hundred different varieties in various parts of the state, making experimental wines of each variety and evaluating the wines. As the main result of this research, the university listed some two-score varieties as acceptable or recommended for planting in specific climatic regions to make wines of high quality and to earn the growers a profit. The university recommended that the four *cépages nobles* (Chardonnay, Riesling, Cabernet, Pinot Noir) be grown only in the cool coast counties, Regions I, II, and III. For Regions IV and V, the varieties mainly recommended were Ruby Cabernet and Barbera for red table wines and "French" Colombard and Chenin Blanc (in Region IV) for whites. For port wines in warm climates, the university favored such Portuguese grapes as Tinta Madeira, Touriga, and Souzão.

Most of the university's planting recommendations were followed, but not all. The high prices vintners paid during the 1970s for the four noble varieties in the coast counties led farmers in the hot Central Valley to plant them in their Region IV and V climates, where they yielded more tons per acre. This alarmed the university savants. "It would seem wise," warned Professor Maynard Amerine, "that these labels not be debased by using wines of varieties grown in regions that do not meet present expectations of quality." He added that if the top varietal names were thus "debased" by the valley growers, the coast-counties vintners might be compelled to start labeling all their products as "Coast Wines." Many vintners now prominently label their wines with the names of coast-counties viticultural areas, the boundaries of which were defined by the Federal government during the early 1980s.

• 4 •

The Federal labeling regulations first adopted in 1936 allowed any wine to bear a varietal name if it contained as little as 51 percent of the grape named. This said nothing about the other 49 percent, which might have had an entirely different taste. Forty-six years later, in 1983, the varietal minimum was raised to 75 percent, except for wines of Concord and other Labrusca, and of Muscadine varieties, which at 75 percent could produce wines too flavorful to drink.

Since any minimum over 51 percent seemed an improvement, why wasn't it made 100 percent? That would have been a mistake, because many wines need blending with wines of different grapes to be at their best. No single grape variety can be relied on, year after year, to produce wines of ideal balance in every respect. Blending of wines for maximum palate-appeal is one of the highest of vintners' arts. Moreover, complexity of wine flavor, an elusive quality that many American wines formerly lacked, often requires blending with different grapes. The best wines of the French Champagne region are traditionally blends of Pinot Noir and Chardonnay, and the French appellation control permits them to contain as many as four additional grapes (Pinot Blanc, Pinot Gris, Arbanne, Petit Meslier). The best clarets of the Médoc district of Bordeaux have always been blends: Cabernet Sauvignon there is blended with such varieties as Merlot, Cabernet Franc, Petit Verdot, and Malbec. French sauternes are always blends of Sémillon and Sauvignon Blanc, sometimes with the addition of Muscadelle. While the famous Côte d'Or red burgundies owe their greatness to Pinot Noir and the famous whites to Chardonnay, the Côte d'Or vineyards also contain appreciable acreages of Gamay Noir, Aligoté, Pinot Blanc, Pinot Gris, and Melon (which in the Loire Valley is called Muscadet). The French appellation control permits as many as fifteen different grapes to be blended in Châteauneuf-du-Pape, the most renowned of Rhone Valley reds.

Although most wine books call Cabernet Sauvignon the chief French claret grape, that variety represents only a fraction of the red-grape acreage of Bordeaux. In the great châteaux of Saint-

Emilion, for example, if you ask a *maître du chai* what percentage of Cabernet Sauvignon his wine contains, he is likely to reply, *"Pas du Sauvignon."* Jacquelin and Poulain, in their *Wines and Vineyards of France,* state that nine-tenths of the Château Margaux vineyard is planted to Cabernet Sauvignon but that Château Lafite-Rothschild is five-eights Cabernet Sauvignon and three-eights Cabernet Franc and Merlot. Few Bordeaux château proprietors claim that their wines contain more than a third of Cabernet Sauvignon. In fact, if you wish a wine made 100 percent of that noblest of Bordeaux grapes, you are likely to find it only in the United States.

In years past, more Cabernet Sauvignon was grown in the Médoc than now, but because its wines required many years to mature, it gradually was replaced by the other grapes. Now that Bordeaux winegrowers have learned—as American winemakers also have—to speed the aging of their red wines by removing them from the skins before fermentation is complete, they are reported to be planting Cabernet Sauvignon again. Meanwhile, American Cabernet producers have begun emulating the French; since 1973, California growers have planted 2161 acres of Merlot and 265 acres of Cabernet Franc, which were rarities in America before. Both of these grapes now also are being made into excellent "varietal" wines.

Some vintners still say the 75 percent minimum varietal-content regulation is too high, and in particular that 65 percent would be high enough for Cabernet, which blending with the other Bordeaux varieties could improve. Meanwhile, some wineries are naming on their labels two or three grape varieties contained in their blends, stating the percentage of each different grape.

• 5 •

How do you describe the varietal taste of a wine? The grapy or foxy flavor of Labrusca wines is familiar to anyone who has ever tasted grape jelly or Welch's grape juice. Also recognizable, with some practice, are wines made from the scented, aromatic, or "spicy" grapes—the Muscats, Gewürztraminer, Sauvignon Blanc, and sometimes Grenache. Zinfandel wines are often recognizable, too, because they have an aroma subtly reminiscent of raspberry, which, however, may not be perceptible when the wines are old.

Cabernet Sauvignon wine has a powerful, astringent flavor, as distinctive, when the wine is new, as that of a stale cigar.

Professor Amerine says that even when the noble Cabernet is blended down to 51 percent, unless with Zinfandel or another grape of high flavor, the Cabernet will still dominate the blend. Its great virtue is that when its wine is properly aged in cask and in bottle, it gradually loses its astringent taste and develops a fine bouquet. California vintners used to say that Cabernet was undrinkable until it had been aged at least four years in wood and had undergone a malolactic fermentation. Lately, however, I have tasted some samples, fermented only briefly on the skins, that were fruity and delicious at less than a year of age.

Most other Vinifera wines have only winy or vinous tastes, developed during vinification, that are not readily identifiable when the wines are new. Chardonnay is the best example. The juice of this tiny, thin-skinned, translucent grape, which makes the greatest white burgundies and champagnes, ferments to a young wine that has no outstanding flavor. But Chardonnay is one of the few white wines that are capable of improving greatly after a year in wood and further aging in bottles. Because of its ideal combination of body, delicacy, acidity, and alcoholic strength, it develops an enchanting winy bouquet. The new winegrowers who are planting Vinifera vines in the East and Midwest choose Chardonnay above other varieties because of its high quality and the high prices its wine commands, and also because (like White Riesling) it survives freezing winters better than many other Old World grapes. Other whites that are likely to improve with age, but only after bottling, include Riesling and Sauvignon Blanc.

Dr. Amerine and Dr. Vernon Singleton, in *Wine—An Introduction for Americans,* offer some terms descriptive of the principal varietal flavors in Vinifera wines. They describe the taste and aroma of Cabernet Sauvignon as "green olive, herbaceous," Ruby Cabernet as "green olive, weedy, tannic," and Malbec as "krautish, soft." They say Pinot Noir is "pepperminty" and that Gamay Beaujolais is "fruity, tart." Nebbiolo they describe as "fruity, licorice," and Tinta Madeira as "prunish, cheddar, rich." Their descriptions of Vinifera white wines mainly use such terms as "fruity," "tart," "spicy," and sometimes "floral," but the character of Chardonnay is described as "applish" and that of Sémillon as "figs, faintly cigar-like." Omitted from their descriptions is the flavor of European-oak barrels, which is perceptible in most French clarets and white burgundies and nowadays in many American wines. The University of California at Davis has not encouraged the use of European cooperage because the oak obscures the delicate flavors contributed by superior grapes.

• 6 •

Muscat grapes, of which there are scores of different varieties, all of them "spicy," are a study by themselves. The one commonly grown in California is Muscat of Alexandria, which is primarily a raisin and table grape but nevertheless makes most of this country's muscatel. Its wines lack the delicacy of the smaller Muscat Blanc, which is called Moscato Canelli in Italy and Muscat Frontignan in France. Canadian and New York State wineries have made good muscatels from the Canada Muscat, a hybrid developed at the Geneva station in upstate New York.

The name of Muscat seems to lack appeal, however, to many buyers of wine. For example, when The Christian Brothers in the 1940s introduced a delectable table wine called Light Sweet Muscat, few people would buy it; but when they changed its name to Château La Salle, it became one of their best-selling wines. Muscat wines are most delicious when they are made sweet and low in alcohol, as are Louis Martini's Moscato Amabile at 10 percent and the Muscat champagne of Italy called Asti Spumante, at 9. Muscat wines are usually harsh or bitter when fermented completely dry. Dr. Harold Olmo has bred a Muscat × Grenache cross named Symphony, the wine of which has spicy flavor but is neither harsh nor bitter when fermented dry. Recently planted in some parts of California, its wines are expected to reach the market by 1985.

There also are dark-colored Muscats, such as Aleatico, which makes wines that are popular in Italy, and Black Hamburgh, from which the Novitiate of Los Gatos makes its famous Black Muscat dessert wine. A French ampelography tells an intriguing story about the Black Hamburgh grape. It once was widely grown in France, but when the phylloxera vine louse devastated the French vineyards, the Black Hamburgh disappeared. Many years later, a Frenchman visiting a hothouse in England noticed a beautiful black grape named Venn's Seedling and brought it to France, where it was identified as the long-lost grape. The only thing wrong with the story is that the Black Hamburgh was never lost; it has been grown continuously under its own name for more than a century in graperies in the eastern United States.

• 7 •

A somewhat similar story is told of the plump, oval-shaped Thompson Seedless, the most widely planted grape in California. Its origin is something of a mystery. Some say it is the Sultanina or Sultanieh of Persia. Others identify it with the Oval Kishmish or Chekirdeksiz of Turkey, the Ak-Kishmish of Russia, or the Sultana of Australia. Sultana in California, however, is a different grape, also seedless, but smaller than the Thompson.

Back in 1872, an Englishman named William Thompson brought to his farm at Yuba City in California's Sacramento Valley a hothouse grape named Lady de Coverly. Some say he had known it in England, but that he bought it from a grapery in Connecticut; others say he found it at Rochester, New York. Who Lady de Coverly was remains a mystery, too. The Yuba City farmer became known as Seedless Thompson, although he fathered seventeen children. When the raisin industry became important around Fresno in the 1890s, vineyardists there began planting Thompson's seedless grape. It became the three-way grape of the valley, salable for fresh use or dried as a raisin, and after Repeal to make neutral-flavored dessert wines and brandy. When the table-wine revolution began in the 1960s, the valley wineries learned that if harvested early, the Thompson makes a clean though bland-tasting table wine, called by some cynics "Fresno Chardonnay." It also is useful in making inexpensive champagnes, and because of its neutral flavor has become many vintners' favorite grape to make both brandy and the flavored, sweet "pop" wines.

• 8 •

The other famous mystery grape is Zinfandel, the most widely planted red variety of California, where during the 1980s its acreage finally exceeded Carignane. Except for scattered transplants from California to Oregon and Mexico, Zinfandel is said to be found nowhere else in the world.

Zinfandel is a round, thin-skinned, very sweet and juicy grape, and if eaten fresh in any quantity it has a cathartic effect. Depending on where and how it is grown and vinified, it makes many different wines. In cool coast-counties climates, it usually makes a fresh, bright-ruby wine which while young has the famous raspberrylike or "bramble" aroma. It long was California's favorite young red wine, as Beaujolais *primeur* or *nouveau* is in Paris. Grown in Region IV climates, Zinfandel also makes fruity but fuller-bodied wines and is useful, blended with other grapes, in making rosés and red ports. When, during the 1970s, Amador and other Sierra-foothill counties began producing superior wines, they won fame mostly for their Zinfandels. In Region

V, however, Zinfandel is subject to bunch rot (unless sprayed with the plant hormone giberellin, which makes the berries larger and loosens the bunch), and if harvested late, makes only an ordinary port or an alcoholic, flat-tasting table wine. If a well-made Zinfandel is aged in wood and in bottle for several years, it develops a bouquet as fine as the noble Cabernet. But few vintners age their Zinfandels more than a year or two, because long aging is costly and unprofitable except for Cabernet and Pinot Noir, the prices of which rise steeply as their wines increase in age.

During the 1970s, wineries discovered they could make delicious other types of wine from Zinfandel—not only rosés, but especially white Zinfandels, and from late-harvested grapes, very sweet, deliciously portlike wines called Zinfandel Essence. By the 1980s, there were too many different kinds and styles of Zinfandel wines on the market, and its popularity began to decline; a consumer would go to a store to buy Zinfandel and be frustrated in searching for the particular kind he liked. Growers and wineries now have formed a "Zinfandel Guild" to develop terms on labels to help buyers distinguish among the too-numerous kinds.

Hundreds of articles have been written about the mystery of Zinfandel. Who brought it from Europe, when, from where, and what was its original name? The sons of "Count" Agoston Haraszthy claimed that he introduced the grape to California from his native Hungary between 1851 and 1862. But Zinfandel was never listed among his importations, and no such red grape has been found in Hungary—only a white grape named Zierfahndler or Zierfandel (which are among the many names of Sylvaner). However, a red European grape named Zinfandel was grown under glass by William Robert Prince on Long Island, New York, as early as 1830, ten years before Haraszthy emigrated to the United States. Prince wrote in his *Treatise on the Vine,* published in that year, that the Zinfandel came from Hungary. During the 1840s, noted hybridizer John Fisk Allen also grew a "Zinfindal" at Salem, Massachusetts, and his description of it, published in 1848, exactly matches California's adopted foundling, Zinfandel. Los Gatos historian Charles L. Sullivan has also found evidence that a grape called Black St. Peter's, brought from New England to the Santa Clara Valley in 1852, was actually the Zinfandel. Since many of the Vinifera grapes brought to California during the nineteenth century came from eastern nurseries rather than directly from Europe—and it was William

Prince who first mistakenly called Zinfandel a Hungarian variety—it may well have come first from a hothouse in his nursery at Flushing, New York.

If Dr. Austin Goheen, who doesn't claim to be an ampelographer, knows Zinfandel when he sees it on the vine, the mystery of its origin may already have been solved. In the autumn of 1967 Goheen, the U.S. Department of Agriculture plant pathologist who originated "mist propagation," was returning from a meeting in Germany and stopped at Bari, in the southeastern Italian province of Puglia, to visit his colleague, Giovanni Martelli. On his arrival in Bari, Goheen was served a red wine at dinner that tasted to him like Zinfandel. "When did you start importing wine from California?" he asked. Martelli replied that of course the wine was local, of a grape widely grown in Puglia. The next day, Goheen visited the vineyards between Bari, Gioia del Colle, and Taranto, and saw grapes and vines that looked exactly like Zinfandel. Farmers called the grapes "Primitivo di Gioia." Goheen arranged with Martelli to send him cuttings of Primitivo, which after a quarantine period were planted at Davis in 1971 beside a row of Zinfandel. Nobody has yet been able to tell the Primitivo vines or their grapes, seeds, juice, or wine from those of Zinfandel. In 1976, Dr. Wade Wolfe made electronic comparisons at Davis of the enzyme patterns of Zinfandel and Primitivo and found them identical. Goheen then learned that a grape resembling Zinfandel and Primitivo—called "Plavac Mali"—grows on the Dalmatian coast of Yugoslavia, across the Adriatic from Puglia. When I visited Dalmatia at harvest time in 1983, I compared color photographs of Zinfandel leaves with those from many Plavac vines and found the leaves identical; and the many Plavac wines I tasted could easily have been accepted as Zinfandel. At least one Italian exporter is already supplying the United States with "imported Zinfandel."

Dr. Goheen hasn't published his findings, but he is willing to bet that when Harold Olmo makes enough additional trips to Europe to visit the vineyards of Puglia and Dalmatia, he will confirm that Goheen has discovered the origins of Zinfandel.

• 9 •

The many French hybrid wines I have tasted in the eastern, midcontinent, and Canadian wineries have been mostly winy, not grapy, in flavor. Many of the whites and some of the reds could easily be taken for fine Vinifera wines. Both reds and whites generally have tended to be soft and especially pleasant to drink young. A red that often has developed a fine bouquet with cask- and bottle-age is the Maréchal Foch. Another hybrid red has had an outstanding varietal character, easily recognized when tasted "blind." The name of the grape is Baco Noir; the flavor of its wine is as powerful as that of Cabernet Sauvignon. The most popular hybrid white wine thus far seems to be Seyval Blanc, which some call "the Chardonnay of the East," but my present favorite among the whites is Vidal Blanc.

Great as has been the impact of the French hybrids on the wine industry east of the Rockies, the change these varieties have made in the vineyards and wines of France is far greater. A fact never mentioned in French wine publicity, and therefore not yet realized in the wine trade, is that fully one-fifth of French wine production comes from the hybrids. Every French vineyard district, including Bordeaux, Burgundy, and Champagne, grows them extensively, and although the hybrids legally are not permitted to be used in making any of the *appellation contrôlée* wines, many hybrid grapes are specifically recommended by the French government to be grown for *vins du pays*. (The French, by the way, call them "the American hybrids.")

How and when did this revolutionary change in French viniculture come about? It will be remembered that the phylloxera aphid, accidentally introduced to France on botanical specimens brought from America, spread like a plague, and that between 1860 and 1910 it devastated the vineyards of Europe. About 1869, French viticulturists discovered (as had already been learned in this country) that the tough roots of native American vines resist the deadly phylloxera. The French then sent to America for rootstocks and replanted their vineyards with American vines, onto which they grafted their Vinifera. It was thus that American roots saved the vineyards of Europe. But the French winegrowers were not satisfied. They wanted *producteurs directs* (direct producers)—phylloxera-resistant vines that would produce grapes without the labor and expense of grafting. This started their viticulturists in hybridizing (crossing) the robust American wine varieties with the delicate Vinifera. The first resulting hybrid vines did resist the phylloxera, but the grapes they produced tasted like their wild American parents. Hybridizers in the United States had already made such crosses, with the same disappointing results. The French, however, kept trying, because their motive was more compelling; winegrowing is their nation's chief agricultural industry and supports much of the French population. By 1900, they had succeeded in producing a number of hybrids which made wines resembling Vinifera types. These first nonfoxy hybrids were widely planted in France. Much better hybrids were developed in the few following decades, and still better ones have kept coming from France, and also from grape breeders in the United States and Canada, during the past several years.

The vines Philip Wagner first imported to Baltimore during the 1930s were the early creations of two French hybridizers, Maurice Baco and Albert Seibel. The Baco No. 1 variety was the most successful of the early reds. Most of the French hybrid grapes were named for their originators, such as Georges Couderc, Seibel, Baco, Galibert, Landot, Ravat, Seyve-Villard, and Vidal, and were distinguished by the hybridizers' seedling numbers. Later, however, those that make the best wines have been given names, which have now begun to appear on the varietal labels of the wines. For example, Baco No. 1 became Baco Noir; Seyve-Villard 5276 is now Seyval Blanc, and the black Seibel 10878 became Chelois.*

Bitter controversy surrounds the French hybrids in Europe. Some countries have restricted them or even have prohibited them from being planted, lest they replace the Vinifera varieties that made their wines famous in the past. Germany prohibits them by law; Italy permits some hybrid varieties in the cool Alpine foothill regions. Some small plantings made in southern Germany before the restrictions became effective were allowed to remain. In this country, Dr. Konstantin Frank opposes the planting of the hybrids, claiming that Vinifera can survive eastern climates as well as the hybrids can. Philip Wagner recommends the hybrids over Vinifera for the East as more likely to produce annual crops. He says the care of Vinifera vines in eastern climates requires a high order of expertise. Many eastern and midwestern farmers have developed such expertise. They warn, however, that Vinifera succeed in such climates only when planted on ideal sites and when given twice the care the hybrids require. One especially knowledgeable vineyardist comments: "Perhaps they first should grow the hybrids in order to learn how to grow the Vinifera."

---

*Other red-wine hybrids include Bellandais (Seibel 14596), Cascade (S. 13053), Chambourcin (Joannes-Seyve 26205), Chancellor (S. 7053), Colobel (S. 8357), Couderc (Couderc 7120), De Chaunac (S. 9549), Florental (Burdin 7705), Garonnet (S-V 18283), Landal (Landot 244), Landot Noir (Landot 4511), Leon Millot (Kuhlmann 194–2), Maréchal Foch (Kuhlmann 188–2), Plantet (S. 5455), Ravat Noir (Ravat 262), Rosette (S. 1000), Rougeon (S. 5898), and Villard Noir (Seyve-Villard 18315). Among white-wine hybrids with new names are Ambros (Seibel 10713), Aurore or Aurora (S. 5279), Baco Blanc (Baco 22A), Rayon d'Or (S. 4986), Ravat Blanc (Ravat 6), Roucaneuf (S-V 12309), Verdelet (S. 9110), Vignoles (Ravat 51), and Villard Blanc (S-V 12375).

It is unfortunate that the demeaning word "hybrid" was attached to the French-American varieties when they were first introduced in the United States. Were it not for this term, the wines made from these grapes would be judged impartially for whatever qualities they possess. After all, many commercially grown Vinifera wine grapes are also hybrids—crosses made with other varieties either artificially or by chance.

• 10 •

Since varietal labeling reached its present height of popularity, vineyardists have discovered that some of the grapes they have been growing for generations may be misnamed. Australian winegrowers have recently learned that the grape they have long called "Riesling" is really the Sémillon of Bordeaux.

Each year, from 1949 to 1953, wine juries at the California State Fair awarded the gold medal for Traminer to the Charles Krug Winery of St. Helena, until the vineyard was inspected and it turned out the grapes were not Traminer, but Veltliner, an Austrian variety. In a similar case, the Inglenook Vineyard was winning medals regularly for its Barbera wine until Dr. Albert Winkler studied the vines and identified them as a similar variety, called Charbono or Charbonneau. For Inglenook, the mistake turned out lucky, for its then-owners enjoyed a monopoly on the hearty red wine relabeled Charbono, until other vintners began growing the same wine.

The Traminer grape. One of its clones makes the spicy Gewürztraminer wine.

Krug meanwhile is back on the market with a wine of the true Gewürztraminer grape. There are several Traminers, but the one called Gewürztraminer has a distinctly "spicy" flavor; Gewürz means "spicy" in German. Incidentally, Gewürztraminer now has a California relative named Flora. UC viticulturist Harold Olmo developed the Flora by crossing the Gewürz variety with Sémillon. Flora has some Gewürz aroma, yields more tons per acre than its flavorful parent, and shows promise of becoming a popular California "varietal" in years to come.

The viticulturists at Davis say the grape called Petite Sirah, which makes flavorful, sometimes "peppery" red wines (as well as rosés and ports) in California, is probably misnamed. It differs from the Syrah (Sirah or Shiraz) grape of Persia, which contributes a piquant flavor to the best red wines of Tain l'Hermitage in the Rhone Valley of France, but more closely resembles another Rhone variety the French call Durif. Dr. Wade Wolfe has found that the enzyme patterns of California's Petite Sirah closely resemble those of Durif and differ from those of Syrah and Shiraz. Dr. Olmo has imported the French Syrah, and a few California vineyards now grow it, labeling the wines Syrah. He says the red-wine variety named Refosco in Italy and California is also the Mondeuse of France. The grape called Early Burgundy in California may be the variety the French call Portugais Bleu. Folle Blanche, which means "crazy white" and which makes tart wines that somewhat resemble chablis, is called Picpoule or Piquepoul Blanc in France.

A particularly knotty example is the story of the Gamays, the principal grapes of southern Burgundy. The late Paul Masson, on visits to his native France, brought home to his California vineyards many Burgundian grape varieties, including a red grape named Gamay Beaujolais. His successors labeled its rich, flavorful red wine with the name of the grape. They believed it to be the variety from which the famous red wines of the Beaujolais region south of Mâcon are made, attributing its richer flavor to the differences in climate and soil.

In 1946, when I still was secretary of the Wine Institute, France formally demanded of the United States government that the Masson Vineyard be stopped from selling its red wine as Gamay Beaujolais, on the ground that only a French wine should be allowed to use the name of Beaujolais. I prepared the reply for our government, pointing out that the varietal label was true, because ampelographies had long recognized Gamay Beaujolais as the name of the grape. The French, on consulting their own ampelographies, were astounded when they found I was right.

Meanwhile, a more productive red grape called Gamay had been planted extensively by California growers, mainly in Napa and Sonoma counties. Its wine has a distinct flavor quite different from Gamay Beaujolais. The grape became known as "Napa Gamay."

Then Professor Olmo, on one of his periodic trips to Europe, found that the principal grape grown there was not Masson's variety, but another called Gamay Noir *à jus blanc,* "black Gamay with white juice." (There are both red and white Gamays in France, and some red Gamays whose juice is red instead of white. The French call the latter Gamays *teinturiers,* literally "dyers," and use them to darken their burgundies, which often lack color.) Further research soon convinced Olmo that Masson's Gamay Beaujolais is actually a clone of Pinot Noir. Olmo then tried to persuade California vintners to change their Gamay Beaujolais wine labels to "Pinot Noir." Most of them refused, saying that this clone makes wines distinctly different from those of other Pinot Noirs. Besides, their wines were selling too well as Gamay Beaujolais. What the true name of Napa Gamay may be will be told a few pages hence.

If you find this confusing, you are not alone. Most wine merchants and even most grape growers do not understand it yet. Nor do the French, who use "Gamay Beaujolais" as one of their synonyms for Gamay Noir.

Like other plants and animals, including people, each Old World grape variety has changed through the centuries, by crossbreeding and by natural selection to fit particular environments, into different strains or clones. The only grapes that have not yet changed and developed clones are the new hybrids, which when planted as cuttings, produce grapes with the same flavors as the original vines. There are said to be at least 200 clones of Pinot Noir. Wines made from its different clones, even when grown in the same vineyard, may differ markedly in aroma and taste. There are dozens of strains of Cabernet Sauvignon in California and many more in France. Clones of both old and new varieties are now being chosen for ease of picking by the new harvesting machines. Nurserymen who sell the new heat-treated, virus-free Vinifera vines now call them "super-clones."

• 11 •

Because the Old World wine grapes have many interchangeable names, vintners naturally choose those which best sell their wines. Before Prohibition, California vineyardists grew a luscious white grape they called "White Zinfandel." After Repeal, when varietal labels were first becoming popular, they learned that one of the names of the grape in France is Pineau Blanc de la Loire, so they began selling its dry wine as "White Pinot." In 1955, the Mondavi brothers of the Charles Krug winery made a semi-dry version of the wine and introduced it under the grape's other French name, Chenin Blanc. Though their customers couldn't pronounce it, they liked both the name and the wine, which is fresh and delicious when drunk young, like the wines this grape makes in the Vouvray district of the Loire. Other wineries soon emulated Krug, and semi-dry Chenin Blanc (although some wines under this name are dry) has since become the second most plentiful of all California "varietal" white wines. The Christian Brothers made two different wines of the same grape: the younger one called Chenin Blanc, the finer one labeled Pineau de la Loire. Krug kept selling its dry version as White Pinot.

A century ago, West & Sons of Stockton brought to their El Pinal Vineyard from France a vigorous-growing white grape and named it "West's White Prolific." The late L. K. Marshall of Lodi rediscovered the variety after Repeal and named it Winkler, for the famous viticulturist. Dr. Winkler, however, declined the honor. Meanwhile, Dr. Olmo identified the grape as the French Colombard. Because it is prolific, and its high-acid juice is useful in making white wines and champagnes, it has become the principal white-wine variety grown in California, chiefly planted now in Regions IV and V. Its correct name is simply "Colombard."

Sauvignon Blanc, the grape that contributes the spicy taste to fine French sauternes, makes spicy white wines in California, but its varietal name on wines once lacked appeal to many American buyers. Robert Mondavi remembered that Sauvignon Blanc is also the grape that produces the Loire Valley wine named Pouilly-Fumé, and that its name there is Blanc Fumé.* He conceived of the bright idea of renaming his dry Sauvignon Blanc "Fumé Blanc." His wine became so popular that other wineries began also using the name as an alternate label for their Sauvignon Blanc.

Wines of Sémillon, the principal white grape of the Bordeaux region, lacked popularity in the United States during the 1970s, perhaps because its name was often mispronounced. Then some California vintners who study ampelographies noticed that

---

*The French say the Sauvignon Blanc grown around Pouilly-sur-Loire has both a smoky and a spicy taste; hence *fumé* (smoked).

among its several synonyms is a more glamorous-looking name: Chevrier. At this writing I have already tasted two newly popular wines with that name.

Wente Brothers of Livermore during the 1940s sold a dry white wine named for their Ugni Blanc grape, but withdrew it from the market when their customers insisted on calling it "Ugly Blank." The Wentes knew that Ugni Blanc is called Trebbiano in Italy, where it is one of the four varieties used to make the classic red chianti. Actually, the grape has a third and more salable name, St. Emilion, by which it is called in the Cognac region of France. At least one California winery has introduced a wine called St. Emilion, but the Wentes now identify their Ugni Blanc as part of the blend with Chenin Blanc that they call "Blanc de Blancs."

"Blanc de Blancs" means "white of whites," and is used in France to tell you that champagnes so labeled are *not* made of the principal grape of the French Champagne region—Pinot Noir—but entirely of white grapes, particularly Chardonnay. Most American champagnes were made of white grapes, but were never called "Blanc de Blancs" until Almadén and Schramsberg adopted the term for their special champagnes made mostly of Chardonnay. Then California producers began also using Pinot Noir to make some of their sparkling wines, as French champagne producers do, and many California champagnes are now labeled "Blanc de Noirs."

American winemakers used to wonder why the French use Pinot Noir, the black grape with white juice, to make most of their fine champagnes. The answer is in Amerine and Joslyn's 1970 edition of *Table Wines:* "The cool climate [of the French Champagne region]," they say, "necessitates growing the early-ripening Pinot Noir in order to have adequate sugar for a balanced wine." In California climates, white grapes ripen with plenty of sugar every year, and black grapes are not needed to make champagne. Some of the "Blanc de Noirs" of California have faint salmon tints.

Because varietal names project glamour and attract buyers who search for new flavors in wines, some vintners sell "varietals" that don't deserve varietal names. Green Hungarian, for example, is a flavorless grape that is valuable only to make white blending-wines, but its name has an intriguing winy sound. Semi-dry wines called Green Hungarian, pleasant but with no outstanding flavor, first appeared in 1945 and became popular throughout the United States. Royalty, Rubired, and Salvador are grapes with red juice, extensively grown in the San Joaquin Valley because they are useful to darken wines that lack color. You can write a letter with their juice in your fountain pen. There now are dry red table wines named Royalty, although that grape has a harsh, unpleasant taste. Palomino, a hardy, tough-skinned grape, is the principal variety grown in the sherry-producing districts of Spain. Its only virtue in making sherry is that its juice rapidly becomes oxidized, a grave fault in making any other type of wine. In California, Palomino is sometimes miscalled Golden Chasselas, and a few wineries have used it to make a white table wine under that name. It is not related to the true Chasselas grapes, from which the Germans make their excellent Gutedel and the Swiss make their Fendant.

Carignane, which was the principal red-wine grape grown in California until it was overtaken by Zinfandel, is principally noted for the vigor and high productivity of the vine. However, when it is grown on ideal sites and pruned to keep it from overcropping, it sometimes produces an excellent, highly flavorful table wine. On the other hand, the historic Mission grape usually makes poor red table wines, yet is useful in making some dessert-wine types.

• 12 •

In the eastern and midcontinent states, there are many varietally named table-wine types made not of the French hybrids, but of native American grapes, principally those of *Vitis labrusca* and *riparia* parentage. They are tame descendants of the many species of wild grapes that abound in North America. (There are few wild grapes south of the Equator.) The Labrusca varieties, often called "foxy," are also called "slipskin" grapes because their skins do not adhere to the pulp. (They are not related to the Lambrusco wines of Italy.) Another term for them is "American hybrids." Some are thought to be chance hybrids with the Vinifera grapes that were brought to this country from Europe during the eighteenth century. Others are crosses by early grape breeders between the various native species, and in some cases with Vinifera varieties. Concord is the principal native grape grown in North America, but far better Labrusca "varietals" are the Delaware, Dutchess, and Catawba. The foxy aroma, even of Concord, is said to disappear as the wines age.

Longworth, the early Ohio winegrower, always maintained that Catawba improved with age. He had trouble convincing his contemporaries, the Dufour brothers, of this. The Dufours preferred the Alexander grape, with which they pioneered winegrowing in Indiana. To win his point, Longworth gave one of the Dufours three bottles of Catawba. Dufour drank one after six months, another at the end of a year, and buried the third in his vineyard. Many years later, when Dufour lay on his death-bed, he made a last request to his doctor, that the bottle be dug up and brought to him for a final taste. Dufour was propped up in his bed, the cork was drawn, a glass was held up to the light, and he tasted the wine. "Ah, doctor," he said, "Longworth was right. Catawba improves with age."

Labrusca-type grapes such as Concord are said to be unsuited to the warm climates of California, and California wineries rely on the State of Washington to supply them with the Concord juice used in their Labrusca-flavored wines. Three Labrusca varieties have been grown experimentally in the Gallo vineyard at Livingston, in Merced County. One is Golden Muscat, the "secret magical grape" which the Gallos once advertised as the mysterious ingredient in their Eden Roc Champagne. The others are Iona and Ives.

The best of all native American red-wine grapes has no Labrusca flavor. It is the Norton, which makes excellent nonfoxy red wines in Missouri. Also grown in Missouri and in Arkansas is a possibly identical grape called Cynthiana. Their parentage is unknown. Another name for both is "Virginia Seedling," which recalls that Dr. D. N. Norton first found the Norton growing at Richmond, Virginia.

The principal other "varietal" native American grapes are the cherrylike Muscadines (*Vitis rotundifolia*), including the Scuppernong, about which you read in Chapter 3. Labrusca and Vinifera bunch grapes have often been planted in the lowlands of the southeastern states, but the vines have died after producing fruit for a short time. Phylloxera, which does not attack the Muscadines, was long blamed. During the 1950s, however, plant pathologists discovered that what killed the bunch grapes was not phylloxera, but the deadly plant pathogen called Pierce's Disease, which thrives in humid climates, and to which the Muscadines and other indigenous grapes of the Southeast are resistant. Pierce's Disease (lately identified as bacterial) clogs the phloem, tissue channels through which vines get moisture and nutrition from their roots.

Since 1945, Professors Loren Stover and John Mortensen of the University of Florida experiment station at Leesburg have developed several new bunch grape varieties that are resistant to Pierce's Disease. The best for winemaking, named Stover, makes good white wine and champagne without any trace of

Muscadine flavor. Grape-breeding continues in the southeastern states, and there already are some new vines of Muscadine parentage but without any Muscadine taste. This makes them usable for the production of Old World–type wines.

• 13 •

A visit to the United States in 1980 by Dr. Pierre Galet, viticulture chairman of the Ecole Nationale Supérieure Agronomique at Montpellier in France, has opened new questions about the correct names of several "varietal" grapes long grown in California. Studying the collection of wine-grape varieties in the experimental vineyard at UC Davis, Galet concluded that four of them were misnamed, and on his return home published his findings in *La France Viticole*. He wrote that "Napa Gamay" is the Valdiguié variety of southwestern France; that the principal grape called "Pinot Blanc" in California is really the Melon of Burgundy, which in the Loire Valley is called Muscadet; that California's "Grey Riesling" is actually the Trousseau variety of the Jura, and that the grape Californians call Pinot Saint-George is not a Pinot, but the Négrette variety of France's Côtes du Frontonnais.

The UC Department of Viticulture and Enology has appointed a faculty committee to examine Dr. Galet's conclusions. Meanwhile, the Federal agency which approves wine labels has appointed a committee to review the varietal names of wines sold in the United States and to determine whether the list of those thus far approved can be reduced.

The number of "varietal" wines continues to grow, not only as breeders develop new wine-grape varieties, but also with recent plantings in Canada and the United States of new varieties being planted in Germany. They are mainly productive, winter-hardy crosses of White Riesling with other Vinifera grapes, with such names as Scheurebe, Ehrenfelser, Kerner, Ortega, Rieslaner, Optima, and Bacchus. There already are "varietal" wines called Scheurebe in California, and some of the other German varieties have been planted experimentally in both Canada and the United States.

• 14 •

The identification of grapes is a science by itself. When varieties closely resemble one another, only an expert can tell them apart. One must study the canes, shoots, leaves, the sizes and shapes of the clusters, and single berries selected from the center, not the outside of the bunch. Many vineyardists are not certain of which varieties they grow. Those in English-speaking countries were supplied for the first time with a means of identifying the grapes in their vineyards, when Cornell University Press in 1979 published Virginia viticulturist Lucie T. Morton's *A Practical Ampelography—Identification of Grapes,* a translation of Dr. Galet's *Précis d'Ampelographie pratique,* adapted to the principal grapes grown in North America. As Galet's first American graduate student, she accompanied him on most of his trip through the United States and since has written a second volume, *Winegrowing in Eastern America,* to be published by Cornell in 1985.

The truly dedicated student of wine must also be a student of grapes. The only sources of precise data on individual grape varieties are the colorfully illustrated books about vines, called ampelographies. Hundreds of ampelographies have been published in Europe, and they often disagree. The greatest is the seven-volume *Traité Géneral de Viticulture* by Professors Pierre Viala and Victor Vermorel, the French viticulturists who with some sixty collaborators labored from 1890 to 1910 compiling 24,000 names and synonyms of grapes and gathering paintings of the principal varieties. The first American ampelography to picture grapes in full colors was published by the California Vinicultural Association in 1877, with water-color paintings, made in the vineyards, of ten varieties. In 1908, the Geneva, New York, experiment station published *Grapes of New York,* the monumental work of Professor Ulysses Prentiss Hedrick, in which he described almost 1500 native American grapes.

Dr. Olmo has been compiling a new California ampelography since 1936. After thirty-five years of research, half a lifetime, he published in 1971 his work on a single variety, Chardonnay. It is a four-page folio containing a color photo of Chardonnay and its foliage, a diagram of its leaf, a history and description of the variety and its many clones and mutations, and a bibliography. Olmo plans to follow with similar folios of forty-nine more varieties. The Chardonnay folio was priced at $5. If the rest cost that much, Olmo's planned work covering fifty varieties would cost $250, which would make it the most expensive new wine book in the world.

But there can never be a complete book of grapes, for there are almost 10,000 different grape varieties from which wines of some sort can be made, including many not yet tried in America. As still more wines appear on the market named for their grapes, the mystery of wine becomes increasingly fascinating, because we can never know the full story of any grape.

26

Meanings of Some Wine Terms

AMERICAN WINE NOMENCLATURE, once much simpler than that of Europe, has become increasingly complex in recent years, and some terms have acquired obscure meanings that need explaining.

What is the meaning of appellations of origin on American wines? "American" as an appellation of origin usually means that the wine is a blend of wines from two or more states. A state or county appellation means that at least 75 percent of the wine was produced from grapes grown within the state (or states) or counties named. But if the appellation is one of the nearly 100 delimited viticultural areas the Federal government began establishing during the early 1980s, at least 85 percent of the grapes must have been grown in the delimited area. The wine may have been produced outside the appellation area, but only within the same state (or states) in which the viticultural area is located. If the appellation is "California" or any part of California, the wine must have been made and finished within the state and only of California grapes, but it could have been bottled outside the state.

What do "Estate Bottled" and "Vintner Grown" mean? Originally, "Estate Bottled" was the rare designation permitted only for use by small winegrowing estates, equivalent to the French *mise en bouteille au château*. It now means that the named winery grew all the grapes on land it owns or controls within the same Federally delimited viticultural area, and that the wine never left the winery until after it was bottled. Grapes grown by members of a co-operative are eligible to be considered vintner-grown. The large size of some delimited viticultural areas enables wineries to include vineyards many miles apart in their "estates." "Vintner-grown" is a term estate wineries use when some of the vineyards they own are in a viticultural area outside that of the estate.

Are wines whose labels say "Produced and Bottled by," preceding the vintner's name, more reliable than others using the words "Made" or "Vinted" or "Cellared," rather than "Produced"? Federal regulations define "produced" as meaning that the vintner either fermented and finished at least 75 percent of the wine in the bottle, or that he changed its class, as when a winery makes champagne of wine produced by someone else. To the buyer of wine, "Produced" is intended to mean that the vintner did not just buy the finished wine from someone else. However, the name following the word "Produced" sometimes is not that of the producing winery, but of someone who has contracted with the winery to produce or bottle the wine for the person or company named. The foregoing meanings may soon be changed by proposed new Federal regulations under discussion at press time. "Made" once meant that the winery "produced" at least 10 percent of the wine, but this detail has been eroded by time. "Vinted" means only that the winery cellar-treated the wine; or at least blended or changed it in some way. Some vintners, however, prefer to say "Made" or "Vinted" on all of their labels, rather than try to keep separate those they actually produce or have other wineries make for them.

Are there any legal definitions of "dry," "brut," "natural," "extra dry," "medium dry," and "sweet"? "Dry," which simply means the opposite of sweet, is the most abused single term in the language of alcoholic beverages. Vintners long ago learned that most American and British buyers prefer wines that are labeled "dry" but that taste at least slightly sweet. Champagnes labeled "brut" are almost dry, but "extra dry" means semi-sweet, and only "natural" on a champagne label means it is really dry. There are only two legal regulations of dryness or sweetness in North America. One is the definition of "dry" in Ontario, Canada, as meaning sugar content not over 1 percent. The other is a California regulation that defines the permissible range of sweetness in sherry, dry sherry, sweet or cream sherry, California tokay, and other dessert-wine types. Dryness is not a measure of quality, because all musts (unfermented wines) are sweet until their sugar is fermented to the degree of dryness the vintner desires.

Why are some champagnes labeled "bulk process" or "Charmat process," others "fermented in the bottle," still others "fermented in this bottle," and what is meant by "méthode champenoise"? For two centuries after champagnization was discovered in France, reputedly by the monk Dom Pérignon, all champagnes were given their secondary fermentation in the bottles in which they were sold. In 1907, Eugene Charmat in France developed his method of fermenting them in large tanks, virtually giant bottles, and bottling them under pressure. Because this is a less costly procedure, the Federal regulation requires such wines to be labeled with such words as "bulk process" to show the method used. If the original wines were of identical quality and the champagnes are given no additional aging, the Charmat process should produce sparkling wine equally good as that fermented in the bottle. However, leading producers who use the bottle-fermentation method also age their best champagnes in the bottles before disgorging (removing the sediment caused by secondary fermentation). Prolonged contact with the sediment gives these champagnes a flavor and bouquet different from those not so aged.

Since the 1950s, many producers of bottle-fermented champagnes have adopted the "transfer method," developed in Germany, of removing the sediment without the necessity of disgorging each bottle. Instead, the bottles are emptied under pressure, the champagne is filtered to remove the sediment, and then is rebottled. Producers who use the old disgorging process label their champagnes "fermented in *this* bottle" and with still other terms, such as *méthode champenoise*. Some producers in this country only call their champagnes "sparkling wine," thereby agreeing with the French claim that no wine should be called "champagne" unless it comes from France.

What are crackling wines? Until 1972, the Federal regulation defined crackling, *pétillant,* or *frizzante* wines as those made naturally effervescent—but less so than champagne—by a secondary fermentation in the bottle, like champagne. An amendment in 1972 permitted crackling wines also to be made by the Charmat process, but if so, their labels were required to say "bulk process."

Since many of the proprietary-named "pop" wines are made effervescent by artificial carbonation, why don't their labels say so? "Pop" wines first appeared in the United States when the Federal law was amended in 1958 to allow table wines to contain up to 0.5 atmosphere (about 7 pounds of pressure per square inch) of added carbon dioxide without paying the higher ($2.40 per gallon) Federal tax rate on carbonated wines.* The law has since been amended, doubling the permissible pressure to 1 atmosphere, about 14.7 pounds, compared to 60 to 90 pounds in champagnes. These wines may not be labeled or represented as effervescent, because if they were so represented, the higher tax rate would apply.

---

*The rate is $3.40 on *naturally* sparkling wines such as champagnes and crackling wines.

At such low carbonation, they give a slight "pop" when opened, but you seldom see any bubbles; they only cause a prickly sensation on the tongue.

Does "mountain" on a wine label mean that the grapes were mountain-grown? It once did, but it doesn't anymore. In ancient times it was already known that the finest wines are those grown in mountainous regions. Virgil wrote that "Bacchus loves the hillsides." In the United States, Frank Schoonmaker first used "mountain" in 1939 on labels of two wines from the Paul Masson Mountain Vineyard, when he also used "lake" to designate his "varietal" selections from the Widmer Cellars of New York State. Later, "mountain" having never been defined in terms of how high or steep a vineyard should be, the word began to appear on labels of wines made from grapes grown in any of the hilly California counties. Then, through the years, "mountain" gradually became the designation of wines sold by some wineries at lower prices and lesser quality than their best.

Why do many labels omit the year of the vintage? Vintage labels on American wines do not serve the purpose for which they are needed on certain European wines, to differentiate the bad-weather years from the good. Vintage labeling on American wines is useful mainly in identifying batches or casks that vary from others in character, and especially in telling you the age of a wine that you lay down for aging in your cellar. Some wineries refuse to use vintage labels because with reserve stocks they can blend together wines of different ages, adding the freshness and aroma of the young to the mellowness and bouquet of the old. Such blending also enables them to maintain year-to-year uniformity in the flavor of each type of wine they sell. A further objection to vintage labeling was that the original Federal regulation required 100 percent of the wine in the bottle to be of the year stated. But some wine evaporates while stored in barrels before bottling, and the barrels need to be "topped" (replenished) frequently to keep the wine from being injured by exposure to air. Vintners seldom had enough additional wine of the same age and type with which to do the topping. In 1972, the U.S. regulation was amended to permit wines to be topped with up to 5 percent of wines of other years without losing the right to be labeled with the year of vintage. No European government has such a strict regulation.

What does "solera" on wine labels mean? Solera is the Spanish name of the fractional-blending system used in the sherry bodegas of Spain. Traditionally, a *solera* consists of tiers of barrels containing sherries of different ages. Wine for sale is taken from the oldest barrel at the bottom, which is left at least half full. The quantity withdrawn is replaced from the next oldest, and so on. New wine goes always into the top tier, thus gradually blending the new with the old. This is why sherries rarely are labeled with the year of vintage. Many American wineries maintain fractional-blending systems for both sherries and ports, equivalent to the Spanish *soleras*.

What do alcoholic content statements mean on wine labels in this country? * Table wines sold in the United States, if labeled with a specific statement of alcoholic content, may vary within a three-degree range. If the label says "12% by volume," it means the wine is between 10.5 and 13.5 percent. Appetizer and dessert wines are permitted a two-degree range; a label that reads "18%" means 17 to 19 percent.

Wines up to 14 percent, the maximum normally reached by fermentation, pay a Federal excise tax of 17 cents per gallon. Between 14 and 21 percent, levels usually reached by adding brandy, the Federal tax is 67 cents.

Labels may omit the alcoholic content if they read "table wine," which means they are not over 14 percent; but some states' laws or regulations require a numerical statement of alcoholic strength.

The original purpose of requiring alcoholic content statements on labels was to deal with the ancient practice, still common in some countries, of watering wine before sale. In Europe, alcoholic strength is regarded as a measure of wine quality. The French legal minimum standard for Beaujolais wine, for example, is 9 percent; if it reaches 10, it becomes Beaujolais *supérieure*. *Vin ordinaire* in France is sold in three quality grades, 9, 10, and 11 percent; the higher the alcohol, the higher the price. European families value the stronger wines because they can dilute them with water at the table for drinking with meals. A certain California winery sells a special 14 percent wine for its Italian trade.

One reason Europeans associate alcoholic content with quality is that grapes develop more natural sugar—which ferments to more alcohol—in their intermittent years of good weather, the so-called vintage years. By this measure, hot countries should make the best wines, but the opposite is true.

Advanced technology, such as the use of pure yeast cultures, sterile filtration, and aseptic bottling, now makes it possible to

---

*Alcoholic strength of wines is stated as percentage by volume, not by weight as it is for beers, and not as "proof" as it is for distilled spirits. ("Proof" is simply double the percentage of alcohol by volume.)

produce wines that keep sound at much lower alcohol levels than in the past. It is unfortunate that the old association of alcoholic strength with quality still prevails among Europeans, because many of the most delicious and most healthful wines are as low as 8, 9, and 10 percent.

What do such terms as "Private Stock," "Reserve," "De Luxe," and "Special Selection" on wine labels mean? They usually are an individual vintner's way of distinguishing his higher-priced from his lower-priced wines of the same types. If a winery sells only one price class of wine, such terms have no meaning.

27

A Brief Chronology of Wine in North America

1524   Cortez, conqueror of Mexico, ordered vineyards planted in the New World with grapes brought from Spain.

c. 1564   The first American wine was made in Florida, probably from wild Scuppernong grapes.

1595   Philip II, to suppress competition with Spanish wine exports, prohibited further planting of vines in New Spain.

1609–1716   Franciscans brought the Mission (Criolla) grape from Mexico to their missions in New Mexico and made wine for the Mass.

1619–1773   Unsuccessful attempts to grow European grapes by Lord Delaware in Virginia, Lord Baltimore in Maryland, William Penn near Philadelphia, Thomas Jefferson at Monticello, and by others in Alabama, Georgia, Massachusetts, New Hampshire, New York, Rhode Island, South Carolina.

1636   Jesuit missionaries at Québec in Canada made sacramental wine from wild grapes.

c. 1732–1741   The first domesticated native (Labrusca) grape was planted by James Alexander in Pennsylvania. The Alexander grape was introduced throughout the East and wine was made from it with varying success.

1769   Father Junipero Serra founded Mission San Diego, then brought Mission grapes from Baja California. Wine was being grown at most of the 21 Alta California missions by 1824.

1793   The first commercial winegrowing venture in the United States, the Pennsylvania Vine Company, was formed. It established a vineyard and winery at Spring Mill on the Susquehanna River, northwest of Philadelphia.

1801   Jean Jacques Dufour organized the Kentucky Vineyard Society, failed to grow Swiss grapes in Kentucky, then planted the Alexander grape at Vevay, Indiana, in 1904, and a wine industry continued there for many years.

1810   Scuppernong wine was being made and sold at many North Carolina farms.

1811   The first commercial vineyard and winery in Canada was established by Johann Schiller at Cooksville, Ontario.

1818   Deacon Elijah Fay cultivated wild grapes at Brocton in the Chautauqua Grape Belt of New York.

1823   Nicholas Longworth planted his first vineyard at Cincinnati, Ohio. In 1842 he made the first American champagne.

1823   Major John Adlum introduced the Catawba grape at Washington, D.C.

1823   The Florissant vineyard was established near St. Louis, Missouri.

1824   The Harmonists established vineyards and wine vaults at Economy on the Ohio River near Pittsburgh, Pennsylvania. Wine was produced in the Pittsburgh area until 1900.

1824   Joseph Chapman founded California's first commercial vineyard at Los Angeles.

1827   Dr. Richard Underhill planted the first large vineyard in the Hudson River Valley; he later established a winery and sold "Croton Point Wines."

1829   Reverend William Bostwick began cultivating grapes at Hammondsport in the Finger Lakes district of New York, but no wine was made there commercially until after 1860.

1833   Jean Louis Vignes imported French vines to California and planted them in his El Aliso Vineyard at Los Angeles.

1840   German immigrants planted vineyards on the Lake Erie Islands and around Sandusky in northern Ohio.

1850–1860   Grape planting boomed in California during and after the Gold Rush.

1854   The Concord grape was introduced by Ephraim Wales Bull of Massachusetts.

1856   Kohler & Frohling, the San Francisco vintners, began exporting California wines to England, Germany, Russia, China, and Australia.

1859   Southern Ohio vineyards were attacked by black rot and mildew. Winegrowing then expanded in northern Ohio, Arkansas, the Carolinas, Illinois, Indiana, Missouri, and Tennessee.

c. 1860   The phylloxera vine pest attacked vines in France and during the next half-century destroyed most of the vineyards of Europe. Phylloxera was controlled, beginning about 1880, by grafting Vinifera vines to American wild-grape roots.

1861   Mrs. Abraham Lincoln began serving American wines in the White House.

1861   "Count" Agoston Haraszthy, assigned to study wine-growing in Europe, sent 100,000 vines of 300 varieties to California.

1862   French viticultural experts, sent to survey American vineyards, reported they found California "capable of entering serious competition with the wines of Europe."

1864   The U.S. established tariff protection for American wines against imports. California, New York, and Ohio growers fought off French attempts to get the tariff reduced.

1867   Overplanting of vineyards created a grape surplus in California. Cycles of boom and bust occurred repeatedly in California during the next hundred years.

1869   On completion of the transcontinental railroad, California wines invaded eastern and midwestern markets, competing with Ohio, Missouri, and New York wines.

1870   California became the leading winegrowing state, surpassing Missouri and Ohio.

1870   Drs. Thomas and Charles Welch founded the fresh grape juice industry, introducing "Dr. Welch's Unfermented Wine" at Vineland, New Jersey. The Welch Company moved in 1896 to New York State and later established plants in Pennsylvania, Michigan, Arkansas, and Washington.

1872   William Thompson planted an English hothouse grape on his farm at Yuba City, California, and named it "Thompson's Seedless."

1873   Phylloxera attacked vines at Sonoma. Before it was controlled in about 1900, it destroyed many vineyards in the Napa, Sonoma, Livermore, and Sacramento valleys.

1876   American wines won two awards at the Paris Exposition.

1880   The University of California began research and instruction in viticulture and winemaking by order of the state legislature.

1880   Wineries were reported thriving in Alabama, Arkansas, California, Georgia, Illinois, Indiana, Iowa, Kansas, Kentucky, Mississippi, New Jersey, New Mexico, New York, North Carolina, western Oregon, Pennsylvania, Tennessee, southern Utah, and Virginia.

1880   Kansas became the first state to enforce statewide Prohibition. By the First World War, 33 of the 48 states were legally Dry.

1887   A California law prohibited the use of sugar in wine-making within the state, but an act of Congress in 1894 allowed its limited use in other states.

1900   American wines won three dozen medals at the Paris Exposition.

1904   The first grapes were planted at Outlook in the Yakima Valley of Washington.

1910   During the Mexican Revolution, most of the vineyards of Mexico were abandoned or destroyed. They were revived beginning in the early 1940s.

1916   Eight Canadian provinces adopted Prohibition laws, but Ontario wineries prospered, being permitted to make wine for local sale. Seven of the provinces repealed their Prohibition laws in 1927.

1920   National Prohibition began in the United States. More than 100 wineries continued limited production under government permits, making sacramental, medicinal, and salted cooking wines.

1921–1931   Grape growers prospered by supplying home winemakers and bootleggers during the early Prohibition years, but the grape market crashed in 1925. The Federal government loaned millions to convert surplus grapes into "Vine-Glo" concentrate for home winemaking, but called a halt when the Drys objected.

c. 1930   The first commercial grape wine in British Columbia was made at Victoria from Okanagan Valley grapes.

1932   Congress legalized 3.2 percent beer and 3.2 percent "McAdoo wine."

1933   National Prohibition ended in the United States, but many states and localities remained legally Dry. Oklahoma finally repealed its Dry law in 1959, Mississippi in 1966.

1934   Wine consumption in the U.S. was less than 29 million gallons in the first Repeal year.

1934   The Wine Institute was incorporated and California adopted state wine quality standards. Federal wine quality and labeling standards became effective in 1936.

1935   Philip Wagner of Baltimore began importing French hybrid wine grapes, which later spread through the East and Midwest.

1939   Varietally labeled American wines introduced by Frank Schoonmaker began their rise to popularity.

1940   Wine consumption in the U.S. reached 86 million gallons, but less than a third was table wine.

1941–1946   War caused a wine shortage. Whiskey distillers bought many wineries, but sold most of them after the war.

1945   The kosher wine type was first advertised to the general public at New York and soon became the best-known North American wine.

1946   The University of California released the first new wine-grape varieties bred at Davis—Emerald Riesling and Ruby Cabernet.

1950   "The wine awakening of America" began after the Second World War, and the consumption of table wine began a steady rise. The U.S. started trading away import-tariff protection for American wines.

1950   The American Society of Enologists was organized at Davis.

1950   Research begun after the war produced greater advances in the sciences of viticulture and enology than had been made in the preceding 2000 years. During the next two decades, the new California technology revolutionized grape growing and winemaking in other winegrowing countries worldwide.

1951   A Federal move to tax wine on its alcoholic content was defeated, and Congress voted tax rates of 17¢ per gallon on table wines, 67¢ on dessert wines.

1956   James Zellerbach brought Burgundian barrels to his hobbyist winery at Sonoma, and California vintners discovered the "complex" bouquet of wines aged in European instead of American oak.

1956   California premium producers began nationwide "blind" tastings to prove their wines equal to Europe's best.

1957   After three centuries of repeated failures to grow Vinifera grapes in the East, the first New York State Johannisberg Riesling and Chardonnay grapes were produced by Dr. Konstantin Frank in the Gold Seal Vineyard at Hammondsport.

1959   Congress authorized wines to contain 7 pounds (later raised to 14 pounds) of carbon dioxide pressure without additional Federal tax. Low-alcohol flavored "pop" wines became nationally popular a decade later, competing with beer.

1965   Mechanical harvesting machines began picking grapes in New York State and later in Pennsylvania, Ohio, Washington, California, and Ontario.

1968   Table wine had become reliably palatable for the first time in history. This set off the wine revolution. In 1968, for the first time since before Prohibition, consumption of table wine exceeded dessert wine in the U.S. and then quadrupled during the next 14 years.

1968 Pennsylvania passed the first farm winery law, which when followed during the next 14 years by 22 other states, increased the number of winegrowing states from 19 to 38.

1973–1984 Giant corporations in other fields and French, Italian, Spanish, Swiss, German, and Canadian wine and champagne firms entered the American wine industry. The boundaries of almost 100 American viticultural areas were legally defined as designations for premium wines. During the mid-1970s came the white wine boom; served cold, before as with meals, whites displaced reds and rosés as the leading table-wine types. In 1980, wine consumption outstripped that of distilled spirits for the first time in history, and almost nine-tenths was table wine. Imports from Europe increased, supplying more than one-fourth of U.S. total wine consumption by 1983, and the U.S. developed an oversupply of grapes. The American Grape Growers Alliance pleaded in vain with the International Trade Commission to impose countervailing duties on subsidized European wines. Americans drank more than 500 million gallons of wine at a rate of 2.25 gallons per capita in 1983, a record expected to double within 10 more years.

Acknowledgments and Notes

I<small>N DOING</small> the research for this book, I have had generous help from hundreds of individuals and institutions, only a small number of whom are named in the text. In expressing my appreciation, I should make it clear that none of them is responsible for the errors and omissions that are unavoidable when one volume attempts to encompass the whole complex subject of North American wines. I also should mention, because the sections on individual wineries often differ from the romantic versions in their advertising, that no vintner has read what I have written about him or his wines before it appeared.

My most valuable single American sources of historical material have been the writings of the great professors of viticulture, George Husmann and Ulysses Prentiss Hedrick; of San Francisco's wine-loving journalist of the 1880s, Frona Eunice Wait Colburn; of Herbert B. Leggett, who in 1941 was the first to attempt a history of the early California wine industry; and of Vincent P. Carosso, who in 1951 published the most complete study of the industry's formative years. Dr. Carosso in turn gives well-deserved credit to the research of Dr. Irving McKee, whom I persuaded in 1943 to undertake his dozen research papers on the histories of California wine counties and their pioneer winegrowers.

Recent research by Dr. John R. McGrew, the plant pathologist and grape breeder at the U.S. Department of Agriculture Fruit Laboratory in Beltsville, Maryland, required revisions of my first-edition versions of early winegrowing in Maryland and of the origin of the Alexander or Cape Grape. Another revision, thanks to avocational winegrower J. Edward Schmidt of Schwenksville, Pennsylvania, credits the Pennsylvania Vine Company, formed in 1793 at Spring Mill near Philadelphia, as this country's first commercial winegrowing venture, rather than the circa 1818 winery of Thomas Eichelberger at York.

Early viticultural and wine journals, such as *The Grape Culturist, Cozzens Wine Press,* and the *American Wine Press and Mineral Water News,* have provided details of many pioneer winegrowers' histories. For California,

572

I have found the best sources to be the three books privately published since 1954 by Ernest Peninou and Sidney Greenleaf. Ernest Peninou still has an unpublished treasure trove of early California wineries' histories, which he has compiled during three decades of persevering research at their sites.

The winegrowing histories of several states and localities have been amplified by such new books as Clarence Gohdes' *Scuppernong, North Carolina's Grape and Its Wines;* Charles L. Sullivan's *Like Modern Edens,* about winegrowing in Santa Clara, Santa Cruz, and San Mateo Counties; Ruth Teiser's *Winemaking in California;* and Michael Holland's *Late Harvest,* about the Santa Cruz Mountains district; and by John Marshall's recently completed history of winegrowing in Minnesota. Other valuable new historical compilations are by veteran wine editor Roy Brady of Northridge on early California wineries; by Baker Ferguson on nineteenth-century winegrowing at Walla Walla, Washington; by University of Indiana Professor Ledford C. Carter on Jean Jacques Dufour's vineyards in Kentucky and Indiana; by Kenneth Coleman of the University of Georgia on winegrowing in Colonial times; by Francisco Watlington-Linares on the native grapes and early wines of Florida and South Carolina; and by Dr. McGrew's research into the life of Dr. Daniel N. Norton, the physician and grape-hybridizer of Virginia.

It would have been impossible to cover all of the interesting small vineyards and wineries of North America without the excellent annual directory of the wine industry published by the industry's leading trade publication, *Wines & Vines,* ably edited by my fellow vineyard explorers and tasters, Philip and Philip E. Hiaring. Nor can anyone keep up to date on significant developments in the industry without studying every issue of this monthly magazine, which has been published at San Francisco (originally as *The California Grape Grower*) continuously since 1920. Also greatly helpful have been Phyllis van Kriedt's *California Wineletter,* J. William Moffett's and Hope Merletti's *Eastern Grape Grower and Winery News,* Bob Morrisey's (now Marvin Shanken's) *The Wine Spectator,* Hudson Cattell's and Linda Jones McKee's *Wine East,* Mildred Howie's *Wine West,* and Shanken's *Impact;* also the *Wine Investor, Vintage, Wine World,* Ed Everett's and John Gay's *Wine Merchants Gazette,* and such regional books as the illustrated *Wine East of the Rockies,* by Cattell and Lee Miller; the Oregon and Washington wine tour books by Ronald and Glenda Holden; *Northwest Wine* by Ted Meredith; *Wines of the Midwest* by Ruth Ellen Church; and the regional California wine books by Richard Paul Hinkle and Patricia Latimer.

For their invaluable and continuing help I wish particularly to thank:
The University of California Departments of Viticulture and Enology and Food Science, and especially Drs. Albert J. Winkler, Maynard A. Amerine, Curtis J. Alley, Roger Boulton, Maynard A. Joslyn, Harold P. Olmo, Lloyd Lider, Vernon Singleton, James Cook, Dinsmoor Webb, Mark Kliewer, Ralph Kunkee, Ann Noble, Professor Harold Berg, and Extension Specialist Amand Kasimatis. Also the great plant pathologist Dr. William B. Hewitt, and Dr. Kirby Moulton, the agricultural econo-

mist at UC Berkeley. Equally generous with assistance have been Dr. Austin C. Goheen, the U.S. Department of Agriculture plant pathologist at UC Davis; Professor Vincent Petrucci and Dr. Fred Nury, the respective heads of viticulture and enology at Fresno State University; and the dedicated farm advisors, especially Pete Christiansen, Fresno; Bruce Bearden, Mendocino; Keith Bowers, Napa; and his predecessor, James Lider; James Kissler, San Joaquin; Edio Delfino, El Dorado; Donald Luvisi, Kern; Paul La Vine, Stanislaus; Rudy Neja, Monterey–Santa Clara; James Foott, San Luis Obispo; and Robert Sisson, Sonoma.

The Wine Institute staff, especially the former head of its legal department, James M. Seff, who recently joined the national wine law firm of Buchman, Buchman, & O'Brien; the present legal staff, Wendell Lee and Julie Rubinstein; James Crawford and Wade Stevenson of the Economic Research Department, Arthur Silverman, librarian Joan Ingalls, and publicist Brian St. Pierre.

University and government horticulturists, food scientists, agricultural economists, and statisticians who have supplied much essential data, including Drs. Gordon Dutt and Eugene F. Mielke of the University of Arizona at Tucson; the staff of the Summerland, B.C., research station and John Vielvoye, the British Columbia Ministry of Agriculture grape specialist at Kelowna; Dr. Robert P. Bates of the University of Florida Food Science Department at Gainesville; Loren H. Stover and Dr. John A. Mortensen at the University's Research Center at Leesburg; Dr. Mohammed Ahmedullah of the Research Station at Prosser, Washington; Extension Agent Anton S. Horn of Boise, his collaborator Robert Wing of Lewiston, and R. Bruce Higgins at the University of Idaho at Moscow; Drs. Raymond Folwell and Charles P. Nagel of Washington State University at Pullman; Dr. Walter Clore, the retired horticulturist in Washington; horticulturist Thomas Schueneman of Kansas State University; Drs. Roy Mitchell and Clinton McPherson of Texas Tech University; Drs. George Ray McEachern, Sammy Helmers, and Ronald Perry of Texas A&M University; Drs. Dan Hanna and William Lipe at the El Paso and Lubbock research stations, and Extension food technologist Al B. Wagner; Dr. Charles O. McKinney and Gene Drennan of the University of Texas; Michigan State University pomologist Dr. Gordon S. Howell; Drs. Burton Wise, Walter Porter, Clinton P. Hegwood, Boris Stojanovic, and Jean Overcash of Mississippi State University; Dr. Alex P. Mathers of Matherville; Bruce Zoecklein and Larry Lockshin of the University of Missouri; Drs. Esteban Herrera and Darrel T. Sullivan and Colonel John Carroll of New Mexico State University; John Lilley, Dr. Louis Gattoni, F. Baron Brumley, and Anthony Claiborne of the New Mexico Wine and Vine Society; Drs. Tom Cottrell, Terry Acree, Robert Pool, Willard Robinson, and Nelson Shaulis, and Professor Elmer S. Phillips of Cornell University; extension agents Trenholm D. Jordan for the Chautauqua Grape Belt, William Sanock at Riverhead, and Tom Jabadal; Drs. Joe F. Brooks, William B. Nesbitt, Dan Carroll, and John Earp of North Carolina State University; Dr. Justin Morris of the University of Arkansas; Drs. J. M. Beattie, Garth

Cahoon, and James Gallander of Ohio's Agricultural Research and Development Center; Ralph Crowther and Oliver Bradt of the Ontario Research Station at Vineland; the staff of the Summerland, B.C., research station and John Vielvoye, the Ministry of Agriculture grape specialist at Kelowna; Drs. Carl W. Haeseler and G. L. Jubb of Pennsylvania State University; Dr. Harold Sefick, now retired from Clemson University; Dr. J. LaMar Anderson of Utah State University; extension specialist Don A. Huber, and W. Grant Lee of the Utah statistical reporting service; John K. Couillard of the Ontario Liquor Control Board; viticulturist Dr. Wade Wolfe of Château Ste. Michelle in Washington State; Dr. Jesus Moncada of the Centro de Investigaciones at Torreón, Mexico; Barney T. Watson and Drs. Ralph Garren and Porter Lombard of Oregon State University; Harold C. Abney of the Maison Secrestat winery at Dorval, Québec, and Dennis O'Dowd of Les Vins Andrés de Québec; Director Rafael Almada N. of the Asociación Nacional de Vitivinicultores of Mexico.

Historians, librarians, and others who performed special research on historical questions include Franklin (Busty) Aulls of Hammondsport, N.Y.; Aycock Brown of Manteo, N.C.; Julia L. Crawford of the Philadelphia Library; Elizabeth L. Crocker, historian of Chautuaqua County, N.Y.; Christopher B. Devan, director of the New Castle Library at Wilmington, Del.; Thomas E. Harman of the Distilled Spirits Council of the United States; Mrs. Renno J. Hawkins, North Carolina Department of Conservation; Grace Hodge of Camp Hill, Pa., for her investigation of early winegrowing at York; Mrs. Cornelia K. Lane of Grapevine Cottage, Concord, Mass.; Mrs. Maurine Madinger of Wathena, Kans.; Carl Oehl of Amana, Iowa; Eleanora M. Lynn, head of the Maryland Department of the Enoch Pratt Library, Baltimore; John Matthews, assistant historian of Ulster County, N.Y.; Allan R. Ottley, California Section, California State Library; Research Supervisor Lauritz G. Petersen of the Church of Jesus Christ of the Latter Day Saints; Marie C. Preston, historian of Livingston County, N.Y.; Reverend Arthur D. Spearman, archivist of the University of Santa Clara's Orradre Library; Edwin S. Underhill III of the Corning (N.Y.) *Leader;* Wilson B. Tillery of Stevensville, Md.; Margot Timson of the Boston Library; Rosalie F. Wilson of the Westchester County (N.Y.) Parks Department, and Mrs. Prudence H. Work, editor of the Brocton (N.Y.) *Beacon.*

Additional historical facts of importance were contributed by Allen A. Arthur of Los Angeles, the late Burke H. Critchfield and Andrew G. Frericks, and Louis Stralla of St. Helena; Robert Eaton, Lester Bricca, Henry Bugatto, of San Francisco; Julius H. Fessler of Berkeley, Guy Baldwin of Los Gatos, Evins Naman of Fresno, and Wallace H. Pohle of Stockton.

I am deeply indebted to the following friends who traveled great distances to investigate particular facets of winegrowing for the book: Dr. Paul Scholten, who explored the vineyards of New Mexico; Dr. Thomas N. Poore, who took the trouble to find grapevines in Hawaii; J. Walter Fleming, who found and revisited the old Mormon winery in Utah; Dr. Klaus Dehlinger, who investigated the present vineyards in southern Utah; twins Bob and Bill Damoth of Detroit; Martha and Dr. Keith Witte, who explored the wineries of Wisconsin in my behalf; Thomas R. Hill of Los Alamos, N.M.; and food editor Jane Moulton of the Cleveland *Plain Dealer.*

Warm personal thanks are due those who so kindly guided me through their respective wine districts, especially viticulturist Lucie T. Morton Garrett of Virginia; John Bremmer of Brights winery at Oliver, B.C.; George W. B. Hostetter of Brights at Niagara Falls; Mario Ortiz Rodriguez of Saltillo, Coahuila, Mexico; Octavio Jiménez of Ensenada, Baja California; Marcial and Eustaquio Ibarra of Pedro Domecq, Mexico; Bill Konnerth of North East, Pa.; Beth Schwartz, the originator of the Cayuga Wine Trail in the Finger Lakes; winegrowers Jim and Carol Doolittle of Frontenac Point Vineyard on Cayuga Lake; Marilyn Webb of Bethel Heights Vineyard in Oregon; Edward Schmidt III of Iowa City, Iowa, and Herman J. B. Wiederkehr of Altus, Ark.

Professionals and oenothusiasts who supplied invaluable help in many areas include Raymond F. Baldwin, vice president of Seagram Vintners International, who since 1956 has pioneered the postwar export of American wines to international markets; Clay Easterly, Edward Irwin, John Watkins, Judge William O. Beach, Norman Gailar, and their colleagues of the Tennessee Viticultural and Oenological Society; Winifred Appleby of Sun City, Ariz.; Dr. Helmut Becker, leader of the Grape Breeding and Propagation Institute at the Geisenheim Institute in West Germany, who has brought German viticultural wisdom and planting stocks to the eastern United States and Canada; Kay Jones of Chateau Kay-Armand Vineyard at Lipan, Texas; Andrew Beckstoffer, whose Vinifera vineyards are among the most important in Napa, Sonoma, and Mendocino counties; Dr. Henry C. McDonald, who had me view from his balloon his Chateau Montgolfier Vineyard near Fort Worth, Tex.; John Berezansky, Jr., of Fairport, N.Y.; nurseryman and avocational winemaker Alfonso Boffa of Clairsville, Ohio; Brooks G. Tish of Boise, Idaho; Florida historian Joseph Pizzo of Tampa; Thomas R. Clarke of Connecticut; Russel Raney of West Germany; William Archer of the Michigan Liquor Control Board; Jack Daniels of Salt Lake City, director of the Society of Wine Educators; importer Peter M. F. Sichel of New York; Bryan and Helen Doble, who grow fine Vinifera wines on their Oak Knoll Vineyard in Tryon, N.C.; Timothy Thielke, the viticulturist of Chateau Biltmore at Asheville; Dr. Wilfred W. Enders, who grows wine grapes near Moline, Ill.; Fred Galle, the director of horticulture at Callaway Gardens in Georgia; Edward Gogel, the Tampa enologist who has made major contributions to vinicultural progress in the eastern, midwestern, and southern states; avocational champagne maker Dr. Arvin T. Henderson of Palo Alto; veteran enologist Ed R. Haynes, who has produced some of the best wines of Ontario and upstate New York; wine consultant Dr. Philip Jackisch of Baton Rouge and his wife Margo, who for many years was the guiding light of the American Wine Society; novelist Marion F. Sullivan of Yuba City, who directed me to Captain John Sutter's Hock Farm; talented vineyardist Louis Lucas, who planted the principal vineyards of the Santa Maria and Shandon districts in California, and his counterpart, Dale Hampton of Coastal Farming; Dr. Tom and Mary Quilter of Shamrock Vineyard at Marion, Ohio; soil expert Dr. David A. Mays of the Tennessee Valley Authority at Muscle Shoals, who is responsible for the test vineyards on reclaimed strip-mined coal land in Alabama and Tennessee; Judy Lyons Wolf, editor of the *Maryland Grapevine;* George Riseling of Lucust Grove, Va., my correspondent on winegrowing there and in nearby states; Sarah Ryan of Peace Dale, R.I., and her son, William T. Ryan of Beringer and Crosse & Blackwell Cellars, who keep me informed about vineyards in the Ocean State; enologist–wine consultant Howard Somers, who supplied material on the first post-Repeal Washington wineries and now lives at San Anselmo; Ben and Leora Sparks of Possum Trot vineyard and winery in Indiana, who are also the leaders of that state's Winegrowers Guild; Gary, Page, Robert, and Martha Woodbury, who introduced fine winegrowing to Dunkirk, N.Y.; Dr. Robert Adamson and his wife Dorothy, whose vineyards are in the Napa Valley.

Finally, I wish to express thanks to my wine-knowledgeable friends who have read some of the chapters for accuracy and clarity and who have made many valuable suggestions: Eleanor Adams, *Bon Appétit* magazine wine editor Henry Rubin, Lee and Jack Pollexfen, and James Field.

Index

Under the more comprehensive subjects, the page numbers of the principal references are in *italics*.